The Parables of Jesus the Galilean

MATRIX
The Bible in Mediterranean Context

PREVIOUSLY PUBLISHED VOLUMES

Richard L. Rohrbaugh
The New Testament and Social-Science Criticism

Markus Cromhout
Jesus and Identity

Pieter F. Craffert
The Life of a Galilean Shaman

Douglas E. Oakman
Jesus and the Peasants

Stuart L. Love
Jesus and the Marginal Women

Eric C. Stewart
Gathered around Jesus

Dennis C. Duling
A Marginal Scribe

Jason Lamoreaux
Ritual, Women, and Philippi

The Parables
of Jesus the Galilean

Stories of a Social Prophet

ERNEST VAN ECK

FOREWORD BY

JOHN S. KLOPPENBORG

CASCADE *Books* • Eugene, Oregon

THE PARABLES OF JESUS THE GALILEAN
Stories of a Social Prophet 9

Cascade Books
An Imprint of Wipf and Stock Publishers
199 W. 8th Ave., Suite 3
Eugene, OR 97401

www.wipfandstock.com

PAPERBACK ISBN: 978-1-4982-3370-5
HARDCOVER ISBN: 978-1-4982-3372-9
EBOOK ISBN: 978-1-4982-3371-2

Cataloguing-in-Publication data:

Names: Van Eck, Ernest.
Title: The parables of Jesus the Galilean : stories of a social prophet / Ernest van Eck; foreword by John S. Kloppenborg.
Description: Eugene, OR: Cascade Books, 2016 | Series: Matrix | Includes bibliographical references.
Identifiers: ISBN 978-1-4982-3370-5 (paperback) | ISBN 978-1-4982-3372-9 (hardcover) | ISBN 978-1-4982-3371-2 (ebook)
Subjects: LCSH: Jesus Christ—Parables. | Bible—Gospels—Social scientific criticism. | Bible—Gospels—Criticism, interpretation, etc. | Kloppenborg, John S., 1951–. | Title. | Series.
Classification: BT375.2 V36 2016 (print) | BT375.2 (ebook)

Manufactured in the U.S.A.   AUGUST 8, 2016

Dedicated to my greatest supporter
and
the members of the Context Group,
patrons who have practiced generalized reciprocity without end

Contents

Foreword

John S. Kloppenborg

THE PARABLES ASCRIBED TO Jesus have, at least since the birth of critical scholarship, enjoyed a privileged place in canon of materials that are routinely employed to think about the historical Jesus. The beginning of critical work on the parables is usually located with the major commentary by Adolf Jülicher, *Die Gleichnisreden Jesu*, whose first edition appeared in 1886. As is well known, Jülicher rejected the allegorizing exegesis that had been popular up to that time, distinguishing sharply between "simile" (*Vergleichung*) and "metaphor" (*Metapher*). In a simile the point of comparison is made clear by the comparative particles "like" or "as"; but a metaphor always says one thing but means another. Therefore the metaphor requires some form of interpretation. But Jülicher insisted that the parable was not a metaphor but an expanded simile containing two parts, a "picture" (*Bild*) and an 'object' (*Sache*) joined by a comparative particle. This required the auditor or reader to find the point of comparison (*tertium comparationis*). Jülicher thought this to be a relatively simple matter and, as a scholar embedded in the dominant hermeneutical matrix of post-Enlightenment conceptions of religion, sought this point of comparison in morality.

Jülicher was able in almost all instances to find a moralizing meaning. The parable of the Faithful and Unfaithful Steward (Matt 24:45–51 and *par.*) was meant to stir the disciples "to the most earnest fulfillment of their duty toward God." The message of the Entrusted Money (Matt 25:14–30 and *par.*) is that "reward comes only with effort; only the one who uses God's gift to the best of their abilities can expect the highest and ultimate reward; nonperformance excludes one from the kingdom of heaven, regardless of excuses.[1] It was only in rare cases that he was unable to derive a moralizing

---

1. Jülicher, *Gleichnisreden Jesu*, 161, 495.

meaning—the parable of the Tenants (Mark 12:1–12) was a case in point—and thus judged that in these cases what we were reading was not a parable from Jesus but a construction of his followers.

There were really two fundamental parts of Jülicher's project: first, he sought in the parables of Jesus realistic stories in place of the rather fantastic allegorizing narratives that these stories had generated in patristic and mediaeval exegesis. And second, in the realistic stories of a slave owner and his steward, or a departing master commissioning slaves to care for his property Jülicher sought a moral lesson. The first part of Jülicher's project was continued in varying forms by a number of exegetes of the parables, from Dodd to Jeremias, to Cadoux and Derrett, to Via, Funk, and Crossan. At some level the parables traded in realism even if there were twists in the plot and sometimes unexpected outcomes. But none of these was committed to Jülicher's moralizing approach to the message of the parables, and various other hermeneutical frames were applied, from eschatology to existential analysis.

Van Eck is clearly an heir to much of this thinking on the parables but goes beyond both the first part of Jülicher's project and the second, hermeneutical one. In arriving at a "realistic" story, scholars had not made many attempts to decide what was "realistic" in first-century Palestine. In many cases, what seemed realistic to the twentieth-century scholar was supposed to be realistic to the Palestinian peasant of the first century. It was only a very few who were prepared to engage in a serious and sustained examination of the agricultural and economic sectors featured in the parables and to ask whether vineyards, the fishing industry, and the management of slave households operated the way *we* might assume they did. This would involve looking not only at literary sources, including elite Greek and Roman writers and the often-cryptic remarks found in the Mishnah and Talmuds, but documentary sources that directly described vineyards, fishing, and the problems of slave households. Classically, Martin Hengel's analysis of the parable of the Tenants paid attention to what could be learned from Graeco-Egyptian papyri about conflict in vineyards and produced a revolutionary reading of the parable that began to take seriously what the ancient auditor might hear from the parable.[2]

Thus one of the critical dimensions of the description of the parables as realistic narratives involves a good measure of rather thankless sifting through papyri, much of it untranslated and fragmentary, to construct a social and economic world in which to read the parables. If it were to turn out that a given story was entirely unintelligible given what we know of the

---

2. Hengel, "Den Bösen Weingärtnern," 1–39.

workings of ancient society and its social relations, then, like Jülicher, we would probably have to conclude that the story in question was a piece of fantasy created for other purposes. Although the large task of reconstructing a social and economic would for the parables has only just begun (and Van Eck's work is part of that), so far the results have not required this expedient.

The second, hermeneutical part of the project has now turned from looking for solid nineteenth-century bourgeois German values in the parables and endeavored to see the social dynamics that were part of ancient society, but which are far more remote from contemporary north Atlantic cultures: *patonalia* and *clientalia*, the promise of honor and the threat of dishonor as motivators of behavior, the opprobrium that was attached to newfound wealth and the newly rich, the strongly positive values attached to primary agriculture and especially to the ownership of farms, and concerns about purity and defilement. The list could go on, but point is that the parables were not composed for *us*, but for persons who inhabited a premodern world that played by very different values and told stories in which their values, not ours, were embedded.

Thus, the exegetical part of parables research, if it is to bring us back to something approximating the historical Jesus, must be informed by the values of first-century Mediterranean culture and by cultural anthropology and its accounts of the logics of behavior. Van Eck's *The Parables of Jesus the Galilean* thus engages those values and the methods of cultural anthropology to produce a reading of the parables that brings us closer to the strange and perhaps counterintuitive world of the first century.

Acknowledgments

The following chapters are revised versions of previous published articles or book contributions and are reprinted with permission of the publishers. The author and publisher gracefully acknowledge the cooperation of these publishers.

Chapter 1, "Interpreting the Parables of the Galilean Jesus," was first published as "Interpreting the Parables of the Galilean Jesus: A Social-Scientific Approach" in *Hervormde Teologiese Studies/Theological Studies* 65 (2009) 1–12.

Chapter 2, "The Sower (Mark 4:3b–8): In the Kingdom Everybody Can Have Enough" was first published as "The Harvest and the Kingdom: An Interpretation of the Sower (Mk 4:3b–8) as a Parable of Jesus the Galilean" in *Hervormde Teologiese Studies/Theological Studies* 70 (2014) 1–10.

Chapter 3, "The Mustard Seed (Q 13:18–19): A Wild and Chaotic Kingdom Taking Over," was first published as "When Kingdoms are Kingdoms No More: A Social-Scientific Reading of the Mustard Seed (Lk 13:18–19)" in *Acta Theologica* 33 (2013) 226–54.

Chapter 4, "The Feast (Luke 14:16b–23): A Kingdom Patron," was first published as "When Patrons Are Patrons: A Social-Scientific and Realistic Reading of the Parable of the Feast (Lk 14:16b–23)" in *Hervormde Teologiese Studies/Theological Studies* 69 (2013) 1–14.

Chapter 5, "The Lost Sheep (Luke 15:4–6): A Surprising Shepherd," was first published as "In the Kingdom Everybody Has Enough—A Social-Scientific and Realistic Reading of the Parable of the Lost Sheep (Lk 15:4–6)" in *Hervormde Teologiese Studies/Theological Studies* 67 (2011) 1–10.

Introduction

THE HISTORY OF THE interpretation of the parables can broadly be divided into three periods. In the *premodern* period—starting with the
time of the writing of the gospels up to and including the Reformation—the
parables were interpreted as *allegorical moralisms*. The allegorization of the
parables, which most probably started in the period during which the parables of Jesus were transmitted orally, is first evidenced in the gospels,[1] and
continued throughout the patristic period (Irenaeus, Tertullian, Augustine,
Clement of Alexandria, Chrysostom, Origen,), the Middle Ages (Gregory
the Great, Bede, Thomas Aquinas), and the Reformation (Maldonatus,
Luther, Calvin).[2] The result of this approach was a *social one-sidedness*; the
parables only had something to say to the believer(s) and the church.

The second period of parable interpretation, the *modern* period, without question was inaugurated by the work of Adolf Jülicher. Jülicher's contribution to the interpretation of the parables will be discussed in chapter
1 in more detail. Here it suffices to remark that Jülicher's interpretation of
the parables brought an end to the allegorization of the parables as the main
approach to interpretation, and opened the way for several new approaches,
all of which had to reckon with Jülicher's conclusions. In this period, ending more or less in the 1970s, the study of the parables has gone through
several phases guided by different methodologies and emphases. Bugge[3]
and Fiebig,[4] for example, studied the relationship between Jewish parables

1. Mark 4:14–20; Matt 19:30—20:16 (esp. Matt 19:30, 20:8c and 20:16); Matt
18:21–35.

2. Luther, Calvin, and Maldonatus had a distrust in the allegorical interpretation of
the parables and argued that each parable wants to make a central point. The central
point of the parables, for Luther, was Christ, and for Calvin it was either a theological
truth or ethical rule. Therefore, Luther and Calvin simply replaced the allegorization of
the parables with a theological (allegorical) interpretation.

3. Bugge, *Haupt Parabeln Jesu.*

4. Fiebig, *Altjüdische Gleichnisse.*

and the parables of Jesus; Bultmann and Cadoux, using form criticism, attempted to trace the forms in which the parables were transmitted;[5] Smith and Manson focused on the parabolic nature of the parables in the Synoptic Gospels;[6] Hunter's purpose was to show ordinary readers how modern scholars understand the parables;[7] Jeremias, like Bultmann and Cadoux, used the form-critical approach to identify the "original forms" of the parables (i.e., as they were told by the historical Jesus);[8] Wilder also focused on the poetics of parabolic speech;[9] Via pioneered the existential approach;[10] Fuchs, Jüngel, and Linnemann saw the parables as language events;[11] and Funk's interest was the metaphorisity of the parables.[12]

One specific focus of this period was the question of understanding the term "kingdom of God," often referred to by Jesus in his parables. Was the kingdom of God referred to in the parables an eschatological (futuristic) or a present reality? Weiss and Schweitzer viewed the parables as presenting an imminent eschatological kingdom;[13] Dodd argued for a "realized" eschatology in the parables,[14] and Perrin was of the opinion that the parables describe a nontemporal, symbolic kingdom of God.[15] The focus on the kingdom of God as an eschatological expression at times dominated parables research during this period, and in many cases the parables were interpreted as *apocalyptic symbols*. This interpretation of the parables resulted in a *metaphysical one-sidedness*; the kingdom of God was seen as something "out there."

John Dominick Crossan's initial work on the parables can be viewed as the beginning of a new approach to the parables,[16] described by Kloppenborg as a "material turn" in parables research: a reading of the parables

---

5. Bultmann, *Synoptic Tradition*; Cadoux, *Art and Use*.

6. Smith, *Parables of the Synoptic Gospels*; Manson, *The Teaching of Jesus*.

7. Hunter, *Interpreting the Parables*; Hunter, *Then and Now*. Hunter's interpretation of the parables is based on the work Dodd and Jeremias. He also follows the work of Via, in that the parables speak to the modern reader in "an existential rather than a merely moralizing way." Kissinger, *History of Interpretation*, 144.

8. Jeremias, *Parables of Jesus*.

9. Wilder, *Language of the Gospel*.

10. Via, *Parables*. See also Jones, *Art and Truth*.

11. Fuchs, *Hermeneutischen Problem*; Fuchs, *Frage*; Jüngel, *Paulus und Jesus*; Linnemann, *Parables of Jesus*.

12. Funk, *Language*.

13. Weiss, *Die Predicht Jesu*; Schweitzer, *The Quest of the Historical Jesus*.

14. Dodd, *Parables of the Kingdom*.

15. Perrin, *Kingdom of God*.

16. Crossan, *In Parables*.

that pays special attention to Mediterranean anthropology, stressing the key first-century Mediterranean values of honor and shame, limited good, personality and purity and pollution, and institutions of exchange such as patronage, euergetism, and clientism.[17] Although the work of Bernard B. Scott was the first study of the parables that took this approach,[18] Crossan's initial study of the parables was the first attempt to understand the parables inside their own world (historical context) as stories that proclaimed a new world and time that challenged and reversed the world of the hearers, empowering them to life and action (response).[19] The parables of Jesus, according to Crossan, proclaimed a "permanent eschatology, the permanent presence of God as the one who challenges the world and shatters its complacency repeatedly."[20]

Bernard B. Scott, in his reading of the parables, follows Crossan by paying attention to the literary aspects of the parables, their originating structure, and historical context. Scott situates the first performance (historical context) of the parables in the Galilean village in the time of Jesus, thus drawing their repertoire from peasant experience.[21] Historical context, for Scott, is more than a mere sociohistorical description of the Galilean village in the time of Jesus:

> The text belongs to a specific world. . . . That world is first-century Palestine, and it forms part of the nexus in which the narrative operates and which is taken up into the text and transformed into the narrative. It informs the repertoire, the conventions, world view, ideologies, and stereotypes active in the text.[22]

For Scott, the meaning of a parable is to be found in the nexus between the conventions, worldview, ideologies, and stereotypes implied in the text (the peasant repertoire or known network of associations), and how these aspects are represented diaphorically[23] in the parable. To identify this nexus,

17. Kloppenborg, "Commentary," 1. The benefit of using these models (reading scenarios) developed from cross-cultural anthropology is that they provide modern readers with insights into the contrasting attitudes and values of first-century Palestinian societies from those of contemporary readers. Bidnell, "Cultural-Literal Reading," 19. It is, as put by Oakman, to use the "known to illuminate the unknown." Oakman, *Jesus and the Peasants*, 11.

18. Scott, *Hear Then the Parable*.

19. Crossan, *In Parables*, 36.

20. Ibid., 26.

21. Scott, *Hear Then the Parable*, 79.

22. Ibid., 76.

23. Ibid., 61. "Most common metaphors are epiphoric: the associations are the bearers of the implied symbolic meaning. But in the Jesus tradition, the relation is

Scott focus on what John Kloppenborg has called the "material turn" in parable research: First-century personality, social relations within the family, the in-group and the out-group, status, limited good, and patronage and clientism. Scott thus employs an approach that has now become known as social-scientific criticism, although he does not explicitly describe it as such. Interpreted from this perspective, the parables are "handles on the symbol of the kingdom of God,"[24] stories that challenge and subvert conventional wisdom. As performative acts, the parables bring the kingdom of God into existence, a kingdom that is a present reality.

Since the publication of Scott's *Hear Then the Parable*, several scholars have turned to social-scientific criticism as an approach to interpret the implied first-century Mediterranean cultural scripts (social realia) embedded in the parables. William R. Herzog, for example, places the parables in the social and economic world of agrarian societies and in the political world of aristocratic empires in an attempt to indicate how the parables performed by the historical Jesus communicated in that setting.[25] The parables of Jesus, according to his reading, exhibited "a form of social analysis," exploring "how human beings could respond to break the spiral of violence and cycle of poverty created by exploitation and oppression."[26] In his reading of the parables Herzog makes use of several social-scientific models (reading scenarios) like honor and shame, status, patronage, the role of retainers, hospitality, and the perception of limited good.[27] As in the case of Scott, Herzog does not explicitly state that he is using social-scientific criticism to interpret the parables.[28] From his analysis of the parables, however, it is clear that he uses social-scientific criticism as an exegetical approach.

The best examples of a "material turn" in parables research comes through in the work of Oakman and Rohrbaugh.[29] In his work on Jesus and the peasants, Oakman studies Jesus in relation to the political-economic situation of first-century Palestine, and uses cross-culturally informed models and theories (i.e., social-scientific criticism) "in mitigating the

---

frequently diaphoric: Jesus' discourse changes or challenges the implied structural network of associations."

24. Ibid.

25. Herzog, *Parables as Subversive Speech*, 52.

26. Ibid., 3.

27. Also see Herzog, *Prophet and Teacher*.

28. Also Bailey, *Jesus through Middle Eastern Eyes*; Crossan, *Power of Parable*; Schottroff, *Parables of Jesus*; Funk, *Honest to Jesus*.

29. These two scholars are part of the Context Group: A Project on the Bible in Its sociocultural context, a working group of international scholars committed to the use of the social sciences in biblical interpretation. See http://www.contextgroup.org/.

ethnocentric and anachronistic problems of modern urban-industrial consciousness."[30] Oakman's study does not focus on the parables per se, but in his study of Jesus and his relationship to the peasantry of his time several parables are interpreted from a social-scientific perspective. In his analysis of the parables social-scientific models are used to study first-century Mediterranean cultural scripts such as reciprocity, the moral economy of the peasantry, purity and pollution, and patronage.[31]

The work of Rohrbaugh on the parables is probably the best example of the "material turn" in parables research. Rohrbaugh, in several contributions, uses the social-scientific approach to analyze the cultural scripts and social networks implicitly evoked by the parables. In his analysis of the parable of the Feast (Luke 14:15–24) he uses the following social-scientific models as reading scenarios for understanding the parable: he studies first-century personality, in-groups and out-groups, the social interaction between the elite and nonelite people, honor and shame, ceremonies, reciprocity, purity and pollution, social stratification, and demography and spatial organization in the preindustrial urban system.[32] In his interpretation of the parable of the Minas (Luke 19:12–27), Rohrbaugh uses the first-century peasant's perception of limited good and the important difference between use value and exchange value in agrarian worlds as reading scenarios. In this interpretation, the third servant—who is not willing to shamelessly put his master's money out for gain and rather honorably preserves the money—is the hero of the story. This reading questions the traditional anachronistic Western capitalist reading of the parable and underscores the importance of culturally sensitive readings of ancient texts.[33] In a later article Rohrbaugh returns to the parable of the Feast, and uses a social-scientific model on gossip in oral cultures (such as the first-century Mediterranean world) as a reading scenario to interpret the invitations and excuses in the parable. Finally, in his interpretation of the Prodigal (Luke 15:11–32), Rohrbaugh uses first-century personality (dyadism), the importance of honor, and the social dynamics of peasant family life as reading scenarios to argue that the parable most probably focuses on family reconciliation rather than on repentance and forgiveness.[34]

30. Oakman, *Jesus and the Peasants*, 2.

31. For example, see ibid., 34–37, 94–95, 112–17, 174–80, 270–71.

32. Malina, "Reading Theory Perspective," 151–80.

33. Rohrbaugh, "Text of Terror," 32–39.

34. Rohrbaugh, *Cross-Cultural Perspective*, 89–108. For a collection of reading scenarios or conceptual schemes that describe first-century Mediterranean norms and values over against which the parables can appropriately be read in terms of the social system and cultural context shared by the original first-century hearers of the

Recently the study of papyri from early Roman Egypt has become part of the "material turn" in the study of the parables attributed to Jesus. Kloppenborg, in several studies, has indicated that these papyri, where applicable, provide detailed information on social realities and practices evoked by the parables of Jesus;[35] practices and realia that should be taken into consideration to avoid running the risk of serious anachronism when interpreting the parables.[36] These documentary papyri are sometimes the only resource available to assemble solid ancient *comparanda* on the practices and social realities the parables presuppose.[37] Kloppenborg, for example, has made use of these papyri in his volume on the parable of the Tenants (Mark 12:1–12 and *par.*).[38] As this volume indicates, the papyri relevant to the interpretation of the parable enabled Kloppenborg to identify ancient *comparanda* on the practices and social realities implied by the Talents, and to critically assess the verisimilitude of the available extant versions of the parable.

This volume builds on the "material turn" in the study of the parables attributed to Jesus. From a methodological point of view, the analyses of the parables in this volume have as their premise three specific points of departure. First, the parables are not interpreted within their literary contexts in the Synoptics and Gospel of Thomas but within the political, economic, religious, and sociocultural context of the historical Jesus (27–30 CE). The focus is thus the historical context in which the parables were performed by Jesus, not the literary contexts in which the parables have been transmitted. Second, in an effort to avoid anachronistic interpretations of identified social realia, social-scientific criticism—which has developed several models (reading scenarios) to interpret specific identified social realia in biblical texts—is used to facilitate a culturally sensitive readings of the parables. Third, where applicable, available documented papyri are used to identify the possible social realities and practices (cultural scripts) evoked by each parable.

The different aspects of this methodology (which will be described in chapter 1) clearly build on the work of Crossan, Scott and Herzog (who focus on the parables of the historical Jesus), of Rohrbaugh (who consistently

parables, see Malina and Rohrbaugh, *Social-Science Commentary on the Synoptic Gospels*, 325–425.

35. Kloppenborg, *Tenants in the Vineyard*; Kloppenborg, *Synoptic Problems*, 491–511, 556–76, 600–30; Kloppenborg, "Burglar in Q"; Kloppenborg and Callon, "Parable of the Shepherd." Also see Bazzana, "*Basileia* and Debt Relief."

36. Kloppenborg, *Synoptic Problems*, 2.

37. Ibid., 1–2, 490–91; Kloppenborg, "Burglar in Q," 288.

38. Kloppenborg, *Tenants in the Vineyard*.

uses social-scientific criticism), and Kloppenborg (who gives realistic readings of the parables).

The specific contribution of this volume to parables research is that it is the first volume that explicitly focuses on the parables as sayings of the historical Jesus, interpreted from a social-scientific and realistic perspective. Building in this way on the material turn in the study of the parables of the historical Jesus, this volume proposes that the parables of Jesus can be seen as *symbols of social transformation*.

Organization of This Volume

In chapter 1 the method that will be used to read a selection of the parables of the historical Jesus is discussed. In chapters 2–12 eleven parables are analyzed, using the methodology as set out in chapter 1. The parables that are analyzed are the Sower (Mark 4:3b–8), the Mustard Seed (Q 13:18–19), the Feast (Luke 14:16b–23), the Lost Sheep (Luke 15:4–6), the Vineyard Laborers (Matt 20:1–15), the Unmerciful Servant (Matt 18:23–33), the Tenants (Gos. Thom. 65), the Merchant (Matt 13:45–46), the Friend at Midnight (Luke 11:5–8), the Rich Man and Lazarus (Luke 16:19–26), and the Minas (Luke 19:12b–24, 27). In the analysis of each parable the same structure is followed. Attention is first given to the specific parable's history of interpretation. After the presentation of each parable's history of interpretation, which will be presented as briefly as possible, each parable's integrity and authenticity is discussed. In these sections, the version of the parable that can get us the closest to the earliest layer of the Jesus tradition is identified, and provisional remarks are offered about the parable's authenticity. Thereafter, the reading scenarios (cultural scripts) that can help modern readers to read the parable in its social context are identified and explained. In the following section, the parable is interpreted using the proposed reading scenarios. Finally, in each case, the question is asked if the particular parable can be considered as a parable of the historical Jesus or not. The volume concludes with a final chapter in which it is proposed that the parables, as symbols of social transformation, depict Jesus as a social prophet.

The order in which the parables are discussed was not haphazardly chosen. The Sower is discussed first, as it is argued that with this parable Jesus draw the broad outlines of what he meant when he spoke about the kingdom of God. The next two parables—the Mustard Seed, and the Feast— have as focus the porous boundaries of the kingdom; the so-called impure are included in a polluted kingdom. The next five parables (the Lost Sheep, Vineyard Laborers, Unmerciful Servant, Tenants, and the Merchant) are discussed in this order since in all these parables the kingdom of God is likened to the actions of a negatively marked (dubious) characters—persons not normally associated with the kingdom. In all these parables, Jesus specifies these as persons whose actions exemplify kingdom values. In chapters 10 and 11, the Friend at Midnight and the Rich Man and Lazarus are analyzed, two parables in which Jesus criticized behavior that does not exemplify kingdom values. The final parable, the Minas, in a certain sense stands on its own. In this parable, Jesus indicated how the exploited could protests against those who created a world in which the peasantry almost always received the short end of the stick, a world in which survival was a daily struggle.

Abbreviations

1 Bar	*1 Baruch*
1 En	*1 Enoch*
1 Esd	*1 Esdras*
1 Macc	*1 Maccabees*
ABD	*Anchor Bible Dictionary.* Edited by D. N. Freedman. 6 vols. New York, 1992
Aen.	Virgil, *Aeneid*
Anab.	Arrian, *Anabasis*
Anic. Fal. Prob.	Augustine, Letter to the widow of Sextus Petronius Probus
Ant.	Josephus, *Jewish Antiquities* (*Antiquitates judaicae*)
Ant. rom.	Dionysius of Halicarnassus, *Antiquitates romanae*
Aristocr.	Demosthenes, *In Aristocratem* (*Against Aristocrates*)
b.	Babylonian Talmud (*Babli*)
BAGD	Bauer, W., W. F. Arndt, F. W. Gingrich, and F. W. Danker. *Greek-English Lexicon of the New Testament and Other Early Christian Literature.* 2d ed. Chicago, 1979
Ben.	Seneca, *De beneficiis*
Ber.	*Berakot* (Mishna or Talmud)

BGU	Aegyptische Urkunden aus den Königlichen (later Staatlichen) Museen zu Berlin, Griechische Urkunden
Bibl. Hist.	Diodorus Siculus, *Biblical History*
BTB	*Biblical Theology Bulletin*
B. Qam.	*Baba Qamma* (Mishna or Talmud)
CBQ	*Catholic Biblical Quarterly*
Cher.	Philo, *De cherubim* (*On the Cherubim*)
Comm. in Matt.	Origen, *Commentarium in evangelium Matthaei*
Congr.	Philo, *De congressueru ditionis gratia*
Diat.	Tatian, *Diatessaron*
Did.	*Didache*
El.	Sophocles, *Elektra*
Epist.	Jerome, *Epistulae*
Eth. nic.	Aristotle, *Ethica nichomachea* (*Nichomachean Ethics*)
EvT	*Evangelische Theologie*
FF	Foundations and Facets
Fr.	Aristophanes. *Fragments*
Frag.	Menander Comicus, *Fragments*
Geogr.	Strabo, *Geography* (*Geographica*)
Gos. Thom.	Gospel of Thomas
Haer.	Irenaeus, *Adversus haereses* (*Against Heresies*)
Hag.	*Hagiga*
Hdn. Gr.	Herodianus, *Herodiani Technici reliquiae*, ed. A. Lentz, Leipzig 1867–70.
Herm. Vis.	Shepherd Hermas, *Vision*
Hist.	Herodotus, *Historiae* (*Histories*)
Hom. Matt.	John Chrysostom, *Homiliae in Matthaeum*
Hom. Matth	Jerome, *Commentariorum in Matthaeum libri IV*

Hom. Heb.	John Chrysostom, *Homiliae in epistulam ad Hebraeos*
HvTSt	*Hervormde Teologiese Studies*
Ios.	Philo, *De Iosepho* (*On the Life of Joseph*)
Is. Os.	Plutarch, *De Iside et Osiride*
Kil.	*Kiľayim* (Mishna or Talmud)
JRS	*Journal of Roman Studies*
JSNT	*Journal for the Study of the New Testament*
JSOT	*Journal for the Study of the Old Testament*
JTS	*Journal of Theological Studies*
L	Lukan *Sondergut*
Life	Josephus, *The Life* (*Vita*)
LXX	Septuagint (the Greek Old Testament)
Lacr.	Demosthenes, *Contra Lacritum* (*Against Lacritus*)
Leg.	Plato, *Leges* (*Laws*)
Lev. Rab.	*Leviticus Rabbah*
m.	Mishna
m. B. Quam	*Bava Qamma*, Mishnah
m. Qidd.	*Mishnah Qiddušin*
M	Matthean *Sondergut*
Marc.	Tertullian, *Adversus Marcionem* (*Against Marcion*)
Metam.	Apuleius, *Metamorphoses* (*The Golden Ass*)
Mid.	Demosthenes, *In Midiam* (*Against Meidias*)
Mid.	*Middot* (Mishna or Talmud)
Migr.	Philo, *De migratione Abrahami* (*On the Migration of Abraham*)
Mor.	Plutarch, *Moralia*
Nat.	Pliny, *Naturalis historia* (*Natural History*)
NovT	*Novum Testamentum*
NTS	*New Testament Studies*

Od.	Homer, *Odyssea* (*Odyssey*)
De Off.	Cicero, *De officiis*
Off.	Ambrose, *De officiis ministrorum*
Opfic.	Philo, *De opificio mundi* (*On the Creation of the World*)
Opif.	Lactantius, *De opificio Dei* (*The Workmanship of God*)
Oratio 21	Demosthenes, *Orationes* 21
Or. Bas.	Gregory of Nazianzus, *Oratio in laudem Basil*
P.Amst.	Die Amsterdamer Papyri I
P.Batav.	Textes grecs, démotiques et bilingues
P.Berl. Möller	Griechische Papyri aus dem Berliner Museum
P.Cair. Masp.	Papyrus grecs d'époque byzantine, Catalogue général des antiquités égyptiennes du Musée du Caire
P.Cair. Isid.	The Archive of Aurelius Isidorus in the Egyptian Museum, Cairo, and the University of Michigan
P.Cair. Zen.	Zenon Papyri, Catalogue général des antiquités égyptiennes du Musée du Caire
P.Col. Zen.	Zenon Papyri: Business Papers of the Third Century B.C.E. dealing with Palestine and Egypt I
P.Flor.	Papiri greco-egizii, Papiri Fiorentini (Supplementi Filologico-Storici ai Monumenti Antichi)
Phaed.	*Plato, Phaedo*
P.Harr.	The Rendel Harris Papyri of Woodbrooke College, Birmingham
P.Heid.	Veröffentlichungen aus der Heidelberger Papyrussammlung
P.Hib.	The Hibeh Papyri
P.IFAO	Papyrus grecs de l'Institut Français d'Archéologie Orientale

P.Köln	Kölner Papyri
P.Lond.	Greek Papyri in the British Museum
P.Mich.	Michigan Papyri
P.Mil. Vogl.	Papiri della R. Università di Milano
P.Münch.	Die Papyri der Bayerischen Staatsbibliothek München
P.Mur.	Les grottes de Murabba'ât
P.NYU	Greek Papyri in the Collection of New York University
P.Oxy.	The Oxyrhynchus Papyri
P.Phil.	Papyrus de Philadelphie
P.Princ.	Papyri in the Princeton University Collections
Prob.	Philo, Quod omnis probus liber sit (That Every Good Person Is Free)
Pro Phorm.	Demosthenes, *Pro Phormione* (*For Phormio*)
P.Ross. Georg	Papyri russischer und georgischer Sammlungen
P.Ryl.	Catalogue of the Greek and Latin Papyri in the John Rylands Library, Manchester
PSI	Papiri greci e latini
P.Tebt.	The Tebtunis Papyri
P.Tor. Choach.	Il Processo di Hermias e altri documenti dell'archivio dei choachiti, papiri greci e demotici conservati a Torino e in altre collezioni d'Italia
P.Zen. Pestm.	Greek and Demotic Texts from the Zenon Archive
Q	A reconstructed Synoptic Gospel source (German *Quelle*, "source")
Qidd.	*Qiddushin* (Mishna or Talmud)
Rom. Hist.	Dio Cassius, *Roman History*
Rust.	Varro, *De re rustica*
Sanh.	*Sanhedrin*

SB	Sammelbuch griechischer Urkunden aus Aegypten
Sib. Or.	Sibylline Oracles
Sifre Deut.	*Midrash on Numbers and Deuteronomy*
Sir	Sirach
Spec.	Philo, *De specialibus legibus*
Str-B.	Strack, H. L., and P. Billerbeck. *Kommentar zum Neuen Testament aus Talmud und Midrasch*. 6 vols. Munich, 1922–1961
t.	Tosefta
T. 12 Patr.	*The Testament of the Twelve Patriarchs*
Theocr.	Demosthenes, *In Theocrinem* (*Against Theocrines*)
Timocr.	Demosthenes, *In Theocrinem* (*Against Timocrates*)
Top.	Aristotle, *Topica* (*Topics*)
UPZ	Urkunden der Ptolemäerzeit (ältere Funde)
War	Josephus, *Jewish War* (*Bellum judaicum*)
W.Chr.	Grundzüge und Chrestomathie der Papyruskunde
WUNT	Wissenschaftliche Untersuchungen Zum Neuen Testament
y.	Jerusalem Talmud (*Yerushalmi*)
Zenoth.	Demosthenes, *Contra Zenothemin* (*Against Zenothemis*)

CHAPTER 1

Interpreting the Parables
of the Galilean Jesus

Introduction: The Important Contribution of Adolf Jülicher

MODERN (CRITICAL) PARABLES INTERPRETATION and the name Adolf
Jülicher are synonymous. In his *Die Gleichnisreden Jesu* (1888)
Jülicher questioned the allegorical interpretation of the parables that had
reigned supreme for the first eighteen centuries of parable interpretation.
Jülicher suggested, on the model of Aristotle, that the two basic units in parabolic speech are the simile (*Vergleichung*) and the metaphor.[1] According to
Jülicher, the parables of Jesus fall into the former category—they are similes
(not metaphors or allegories—that is, successions of metaphors); they need
no interpretation; and in their purpose of teaching, their meaning or intention is clear.[2]

Jülicher identified three categories of parables: the similitude (*Gleichnis*), the fable (*Parabel*) and the example story (*Beispielerzählung*). The
similitude is an expanded simile consisting of two parts: an object from real
life (*Sache*) and a picture (*Bild*), with only one (moral) point of comparison (*tertium comparationis*) between the object and the picture. Therefore,
the intention of the similitude is to prove.[3] The fable is also a similitude

1. Jülicher, *Gleichnisreden Jesu*, 52–57. Jülicher understood the difference between
the simile and the metaphor as absolute: the simile is a literal or direct form of speech
(*eigentliche Rede*) while the metaphor is a nonliteral or indirect form of speech (*un-
eigentliche Rede*). The metaphor says one thing but means something else; it needs to
be interpreted and remains incomprehensible. The simile needs no interpretation; it is
clear and self-explanatory.

2. Jülicher, *Gleichnisreden Jesu*, 58.

3. Ibid., 58–80.

1

but refers to an imaginative story in the past with the intention of putting forward a general truth.[4] The example story is in itself an illustration of the truth it means to demonstrate (e.g., the parable of the Samaritan) and has the intention of providing guidelines for correct behavior.[5]

Apart from his classifying the parables, Jülicher also argued that the authenticity of the parables as presented in the Synoptics cannot simply be assumed. Jesus most probably did not utter the parables as we have them in the Synoptics and the Gospel of Thomas. The parables in the Synoptics have been translated, transposed, and transformed. This, Jülicher argued, is clear from the fact that the reports of the same parable by two or three evangelists never fully agree. They vary in terms of viewpoint, arrangement, occasion, and interpretation. One thus can speak of a Lukan accent of a specific parable in contrast to its Matthean version. The parables thus existed prior to their incorporation into the gospels, and the voice of Jesus can only be identified in the voices of the evangelists through the use of critical and careful analysis.[6]

Jülicher's definition of the parables as similes that make only one point, his classification of the parables into different categories, and his conviction that the evangelists retold the parables of Jesus in a way that served their own interests has had a huge impact on the critical interpretation of the parables since the beginning of the nineteenth century. Almost all subsequent interpreters have, in general, rejected the allegorical interpretation of the parables and are in agreement with Jülicher that the parables make a single point.[7] Jülicher's understanding of the language of the parables as simile has led to the view that the parables are open-ended language events (extended metaphors),[8] and much attention has been given to the classification of the

4. Ibid., 92–111.

5. Ibid., 112–15.

6. Ibid., 11.

7. Jülicher interpreted the single point of the parable in moral terms. Although subsequent interpreters agreed with Jülicher that the parables only make one point, they replaced Jülicher's general moral point with a specific point related to the historical circumstances of the ministry of Jesus. Dodd, *Parables of the Kingdom*, 34–35; and Jeremias, *Parables*, 21, for example, defined the one point of the parables in terms of Jesus' proclamation of the imminent arrival of God's reign. McGaughy, "The Fiction of the Kingdom," 8; and Cadoux, *Art and Use* relate the specific point of the parables to Jesus' relationship with the Jews.

8. The understanding of the parables as extended metaphors can be traced back via the work of especially Dodd, *Parables of the Kingdom*, 61; Wilder, *Language of the Gospel*, 134–51; Funk, *Collected Essays*, 29–51; and Funk, "Jesus of Nazareth," 89–93. Dodd's definition of a parable, *Parables of the Kingdom*, 5, is well known: "At its simplest the parable is a metaphor *or* simile, drawn from nature or common life, arresting the listener by its vividness or strangenes—and leaving the mind in sufficient doubt about

parables.[9] Finally, and maybe most important Jülicher's demonstration of

its precise application to tease it into active thought." Italics added. Wilder, *Language of the Gospel*; Wilder, "Naiveté and Method," combining the exegetical approaches of New Testament scholarship with literary criticism, defined the parables as narrative metaphors; stories through which the world of God's kingdom might come to life in the imagination of the listener. Funk, building on the work of Jülicher, Dodd, Jeremias, and Wilder, understands the parables as extended metaphors that disclose new meaning or a new reality. As metaphors, the parables frustrate the inherited expectations of their listeners and invite them to re-envision the actual world in unaccustomed ways. See Beutner, "Haunt of Parable." Or, in the words of Funk, "Jesus of Nazareth," 89. "A parable is a short, short story that confronts the hearer with a dilemma and then invites the hearer to make a choice."

9. Jülicher's classification of the parables as similitudes, fables or example stories gave rise to an array of classifications of the parables. Here I name a few: According to Dibelius, *Tradition to Gospel*, 254–55, there are four types of parables (parables that have as content that which is commonplace, typical, extraordinary or imaginary); Bultmann, *Synoptic Tradition*, 166–79, uses the categories of *Bildworte*, metaphors; *Gleichnisse*, parables that do not picture a typical recurrent event; and *Beispielerzählungen* to classify the parables. Trench, *Notes*, 1–10; Lockyer, *All the Parables*, 14–17, uses the categories similitude (parable), fable, mythus, proverb and allegory; and Bruce, *Parabolic Teaching*, v–vi, 1–9, classifies the parables as didactic, evangelic, or prophetic. Bugge, *Haupt Parabeln Jesu*, 59–66, uses the categories of argumentative, illustrative, paradoxical and didactic; Smith, *Parables of the Synoptic Gospels*, 3–15. Smith classifies the parables as similitudes, parables, example-stories, arguments, and allegories; Manson, *Teaching of Jesus*, 56–81, divides the parables into two groups (ethical parables and parables that exhibit some aspect of God's rule); and Hunter, *Interpreting the Parables*, 42–91 groups the parables under the topics of the coming of the kingdom, the grace of God, the men of the kingdom, and the crisis of the kingdom. Jones, *Art and Truth*, 135–66, uses the categories of contextual, didactic and existential; and Linnemann, *Parables of Jesus*, 3–12, in following the classification of Jülicher, uses the categories of similitude, parable proper, illustration and allegory. For a detailed discussion of these classifications, see Kissinger, *History of Interpretation*, 69–193. The trend to classify the parables into different categories is also present in some of the most recent publications on the interpretation of the parables: Kistemaker, *Stories Jesus Told*, 9–11, categorizes the parables as either true parables, story parables, or illustrations; Stein, *Introduction to the Parables*, 18–21, identifies proverbs, metaphors, similitudes, example stories and allegories in the parables of Jesus; Osborne, *Hermeneutical Spiral*, 236; Stiller, *Preaching Parables*, 10–11, follows Stein and add figurative sayings to Stein's list of categories; Boice, *Parables of Jesus*, 10, categorizes the parables as parables of the kingdom, salvation, wisdom, and folly, Christian life, and judgment; and Hultgren, *Parables of Jesus*, 3, 6, identifies two types of parables, namely, narrative parables and the similitude. The categories of Blomberg, *Preaching the Parables*, 15–17, consist of one-point, two-point, and triadic parables; Hedrick, *Many Things in Parables*, 6–8, uses the categories of simile, similitude, metaphor, symbol, and allegory; and Zimmermann, "Leseanleitung," 25–28, typifies the parables as *narrativ, fiktional, realistisch, metaphorisch, appellativ*, or *kontexbezogen*. Snodgrass, *Stories with Intent*, 9–16 suggests the following classification of the parables: aphoristic sayings, similitudes (double indirect extended analogy which lacks plot development), interrogative parables (parables presented entirely as questions), double indirect narrative parables (metaphoric analogies with plots), juridical parables (parables that elicit a self-condemnation from the hearer through the aid of

the "often ill and awkward fit of the parable to its gospel context" (to use the apt description of Scott[10]) has steered modern parable scholarship into two opposing directions: those who interpret the parables in the Synoptics as if they are the very words of Jesus (the obvious differences between the extant versions of a specific parable notwithstanding) and those who argue that the authenticity of the parables in the Synoptics cannot simply be assumed.[11] These scholars argue that Jesus did not utter the parables as we have them in the Synoptics, are aware of the peril of "gospelizing Jesus,"[12] and focus on establishing the authenticity of the parables using the extant version(s) of the parables as we have them in the Synoptics (and other noncanonical or sayings gospels like Q and Gospel of Thomas).

A Social-Scientific and Realistic Approach: Points of Departure

Interpreting the parables of Jesus entails a few simple yet far-reaching choices. Are we interested in the parables of Jesus, the Galilean peasant; or the synoptic versions that have redactionally been used by the gospel writers? Here again one is reminded of Jülicher's taunting observation. How do we go about finding the "original" parables (the original voice) of Jesus? On what grounds can one make a decision that a specific parable (or a part thereof) is authentic or not? Is it possible to make such a decision? Is it important to take into account that Jesus told his parables in a (cultural) world totally different from ours? If the world of Jesus and his hearers was that of an advanced agrarian society, what are the implications for the interpretation

---

an image), single indirect parables (example stories), and "how much more" parables (parables that say that God's actions by far exceed or are not like the person's depicted in the parable). Dodd, *Parables of the Kingdom*, 5. Crossan, finally, distinguishes between riddle, example, and challenge parables. Crossan, *Power of Parable*, 47.

10. Scott, *Re-Imagine the World*, 5.

11. Scholars who take as point of departure Jülicher's conviction that the authenticity of the parables in the Synoptics cannot simply be assumed, and thus focus their attention on the "original" parables of Jesus (the parables as uttered by Jesus, the Galilean Jewish peasant) are inter alia: Cadoux, *Art and Use*; Bultmann, *Synoptic Tradition*; Jeremias, *Parables*; Perrin, *Rediscovering the Teaching*; Crossan, *In Parables*; Crossan, *The Power of Parable*; Wilder, "Naïveté and Method"; Scott, *Hear Then the Parable*; Scott, *Re-Imagine the World*; Scott, "Reappearance"; Kloppenborg, *Excavating Q*; Kloppenborg, *Tenants in the Vineyard*; Funk, *Honest to Jesus*; Funk, *Collected Essays*; Funk, "Jesus of Nazareth," 2007; Miller, "The Pearl"; Borg, *Jesus*; McGaughy, "The Fiction of the Kingdom"; Beutner, "Mercy Unextended"; Beutner, "Dishonest Manager"; Beutner, "Gist from the Liturgist"; Beutner, "Haunt of Parable"; Oakman, *Jesus and the Peasants*; Funk et al., *Five Gospels*.

12. Van Eck, "Jesus and Violence," 1764.

of Jesus' parables? Do we have to take the values and culture of the first-century Mediterranean world into consideration when trying to interpret the parables of Jesus? Methodologically speaking, what exegetical approach can help the interpreter to take serious cognizance of the social world of the parables? Is it important to at least try not to read the parables of Jesus from an ethnocentric or anachronistic point of view? How important are the internal structures of the parables in the process of interpretation? Can one identify a central idea or symbol in Jesus' parables that can guide their interpretation? How important is the classification of the parables (e.g., as metaphor, similitude or example story) when one takes the first hearers of the parables into consideration? Is a definition of the term *parable* essential to an understanding of this particular understanding?

This volume deems the following questions (linked to the previous methodological ones) as also important. What, most probably, was Jesus' aim in telling parables? Are Jesus' parables theocentric (i.e., telling us something about the character of God)? In other words, are the parables of Jesus about religion or theology, or even about politics and economics? Can the parables help us to understand something of who the historical Jesus was? Do Jesus' parables make ethical points? More specifically, can we identify certain values in the parables of Jesus that can be applied morally in a post-modern society?[13] And finally, what picture of Jesus the Galilean can be drawn from the parables he told?

In suggesting an approach to interpret the parables of Jesus, these questions must be addressed, and specific choices will have to be made. One should be clear on the method used to address these questions and make these choices. The method of interpretation put forward to be used in this volume has as a starting point three convictions: First, Jülicher's distinction between the context of Jesus and the gospels is to be taken seriously. The interest here is the parables of Jesus the Galilean. Second, an effort has to be made to consciously try to avoid the fallacies of ethnocentrism and anachronism. In an effort to achieve this goal one must gain an understanding of the cultural values and social dynamics of the social world of Jesus and his hearers. To help us as moderns gain some understanding of the social world of Jesus, social-scientific criticism presents itself as the obvious approach. Finally, where applicable, available documented papyri should be used to identify the possible social realities and practices (cultural scripts) evoked by each parable.

---

13. This question is of special importance for the current South African context in which corruption, nepotism, bribery, the falsification of academic qualifications to get appointed, and the plundering of the treasury for personal gain are the order of the day.

Method Explained

The Authenticity of the Parables in the Synoptics and Gospel of Thomas

Jülicher was the first scholar to suggest that the authenticity of the parables in the Synoptics cannot simply be assumed. The extant versions of the parables in the Synoptics are redactional versions (allegories or interpretations) of the "original" versions of the parables, and at times the parables used by the gospel writers fit poorly into their gospel contexts. The first scholar who took up these suggestions was the German Joachim Jeremias.[14] Using the insights of form critics (Dibelius and Bultmann), who studied the development of the oral tradition of Jesus' sayings, Jeremias developed laws of transmission for the parables in order to reconstruct the original words of Jesus. For Jeremias, the interpretation of the parables was determined by their life situation (*Sitz im Leben*), their original context. Jeremias also saw the parables in Gospel of Thomas as independent witnesses to the parables of Jesus—the first parable scholar to do so. Jeremias' insights were taken up by Amos Wilder and Norman Perrin, who also questioned the authenticity of the synoptic parables. Wilder attributed the allegorizations of the parables to the evangelists and saw the kingdom parables in Matthew 13 and Mark 4 as the bedrock teaching of Jesus of Nazareth.[15] Perrin focused on reconstructing the earliest forms (primary stratum) of the parables.[16] In an effort to distinguish between the synoptic and the earlier "authentic" versions of the parables, Perrin developed the now well-known criteria of dissimilarity, multiple attestation and coherence. His conclusion was that only a few parables in the Synoptics approximate their original forms, and this is so only because the point of the parable as originally intended by the historical Jesus served the interests of the early church. The bulk of the parables, however, has been modified in the tradition, transformed into allegories, supplied with conclusions, or reinterpreted to serve the need of an early church that was constantly changing.

Not many interpreters of the parables have followed in the footsteps of Jülicher, Wilder, and Perrin. This impasse is the result of at least three points of view among the majority of parable scholars. The first view is that the versions of the parables in the Synoptics concurs with the parables as Jesus told them—notwithstanding the obvious differences that can be indicated in the

---

14. Jeremias, *Parables of Jesus.*
15. Wilder, *Language of the Gospel.*
16. Perrin, *Kingdom of God*; Perrin, *Rediscovering the Teaching.*

case where two or more of the Synoptics have different versions of the same parable,[17] the fact that the contextual fit of at least some of Jesus' parables in the Synoptics predetermine their "meaning,"[18] or the fact that some of Jesus' parables have been given a different contextual fit (and therefore a different meaning) in the Synoptics.[19] Scholars who fall into this category include, for example, Kistemaker, Boice, Blomberg, Stiller, and Snodgrass.[20] A second view argues that although the versions of the parables in the Synoptics most probably are not the same as Jesus told them, they do agree with the teaching of Jesus in general. Thus, although we sometimes have more than one version of a specific parable in two or three of the Synoptics, the different versions of the same parable do not distort that which Jesus wanted to teach when he told the parable.[21] The third view, given the evolutionary character of the gospels, dismisses the possibility of constructing the parables as Jesus told them. Such constructions are either hypothetical[22] or impossible.[23] These scholars argue that what we do have are the versions of Jesus' parables in the Synoptics, and to interpret these versions is less hypothetical and more sure-footed than working with hypothetical alternatives.

North American parable scholars, however, have taken a different route. Taking seriously Jülicher's cue on the different contexts of the parables, they have opted for an approach to the parables of Jesus that is aptly described by Hedrick as follows:

> What is at issue . . . is where . . . the reading of a parable begin(s) . . . If one is interested in the evangelist's understanding of the parable, reading begins with the literary context, but if one is

17. See, for example, the parable of the Mustard Seed (Matt 13:31–32; Mark 4:30–32; Luke 13:18–19) or the parable of the Wedding Banquet or the Feast (Matt 22:1–14; Luke 14:15–24).

18. See, for example, the parable of the Samaritan (Luke 10:25–37) or the parable of the Friend at Midnight (Luke 11:5–8).

19. See, for example, the parable of the Talents or Minas (Matt 25:14–30; Luke 19:11–27).

20. Kistemaker, *Stories Jesus Told*; Boice, *Parables of Jesus*; Blomberg, *Preaching the Parables*; Stiller, *Preaching Parables*; Snodgrass, *Stories with Intent*. Snodgrass, *Stories with Intent*, 31, for example, states that "the parables [in the Synoptics] are indeed the surest place where we have access to Jesus' teaching"; and Blomberg, *Preaching the Parables*, 23 defends this position as follows: "The parables are authentic in the forms and contexts in which they appear in the canonical Gospels. One does not have to pit original meaning against the evangelist's use of the parables in some new setting."

21. Stein, *Introduction to the Parables*; Schottroff, *Parables of Jesus*.

22. Hultgren, *Parables of Jesus*, 16.

23. Schottroff "Die suche nach dem authentischen Jesusgleichnis ist im Ansatz verfehlt"; Schottroff, "Das Große Abendmahl," 4.

interested in the parable in the context of Jesus' public career some forty years or so earlier than the gospels, reading begins with the parable and ignores the literary setting. Those who begin with the literary setting proceed on the assumption that the *literary* context of the parable in the gospels (usually around and after 70 C.E.) accurately reflects the *social* context in the public career of Jesus (around 30 C.E.) . . . Jesus' invention of the parable in the social context of first-century life preceded the writing of the gospels.[24]

For these scholars[25] the most important issue is to ascertain the parables of the historical Jesus within his social context around approximately 30 CE, as constructed by the tools of historical criticism. Herzog gives the following description of this approach:

This approach to the parables requires that their canonical form(s) be scrutinized with care. As they stand in their present narrative settings, the parables serve the theological and ethical concerns of the evangelists. However, if the purpose they served in Jesus' ministry was quite different from the purposes of the evangelists, then they have to be analyzed with a concern for making this distinction clear. Consequently . . . [this approach] utilizes the tools growing out of the historical-critical method, including form criticism and redaction criticism. Conversely, this approach devotes little attention to the narrative contexts of the parables and uses literary-criticism approaches more sparingly.[26]

24. Hedrick, *Many Things in Parables*, xvi. Italics in the original. See also Levine, *Short Stories by Jesus*, 16. "The evangelists are our first known interpreters of the parables. By adapting the language and providing a setting they have already foreclosed some meanings; by providing explications the foreclose others."

25. See, for example, Funk, *Language*; Funk, *Honest to Jesus*, 113–20; Funk, *Collected Essays*, 89–93; Scott, *Hear Then the Parable*; Scott, *Re–Imagine the World*; Scott, "Reappearance"; Herzog, *Parables as Subversive Speech*; Herzog, *Prophet and Teacher*; Crossan, *Power of Parable*. To these names can be added scholars like Kloppenborg, *Tenants in the Vineyard*; Borg, *Jesus*; McGaughy, "Fiction of the Kingdom"; Beutner, "Mercy Unextended"; Beutner, "Dishonest Manager"; Beutner, "Gist from the Liturgist"; Beutner, "The Haunt of Parable"; Oakman, *Jesus and the Peasants*; Funk et al., *Five Gospels*. In a South African context my work on the parables follows the same approach. See Van Eck, "Rich Man and Lazarus"; Van Eck, "Minas"; Van Eck, "Lost Sheep"; Van Eck, "Friend at Midnight"; Van Eck, "Mustard Seed"; Van Eck, "Feast"; Van Eck, "Sower"; Van Eck, "Unmerciful Servant"; Van Eck, "Merchant."

26. Herzog, *Parables as Subversive Speech*, 3–4. So Crossan, *Power of Parable*, 57, 88: "First, I remove the story . . . from the later literary context of Luke and . . . return . . . the separate story to its earlier social context . . . We will have to imagine their original *oral* context as distinct from their present *written* condition." Italics original.

The most thorough application of this approach to the parables has been done by the Jesus Seminar. In using a specific set of criteria[27] the fellows of the Seminar concluded that twenty-two authentic parables of Jesus have been recorded in the gospel traditions.[28] Many parables scholars have complained that this enterprise is too hypothetical, and they are correct. The fact of the matter is that all interpretation is hypothetical. Trying to discern from the parables transmitted in the Synoptics and in the Gospel of Thomas those of the historical Jesus is to be reminded that we work with hypothetical texts, since "the very Greek New Testament we work with is a hypothetical construct, since we do not possess the original manuscripts. It is a scholarly construction."[29]

The methodology to be followed in this volume to identify the "authentic" forms of the parables most probably the closest to the layer of the historical Jesus will take the method of the Jesus Seminar as its cue. First of all, with a few exceptions only parables that pass the criteria of early, multiple, and independent attestation will be considered authentic. Mark, Q and the parables in Gospel of Thomas will be used as independent sources. Second, the contexts of the parables in the Synoptics will be considered as secondary (e.g., Luke 11:5–8).[30] Special attention will be given to introduc-

---

The following remark of Oakman, *Jesus and the Peasants*, 75, should also be noted: "The parables represent [the historical] Jesus' attempt to publicly express critical truths in . . . a repressive [socioeconomic] political context. For this reason, they can always with probability be made to mean something else [within the textual world]. This was the way Jesus protected himself. However, the basic meaning of the parables must always be assessed vis-à-vis their original audience and sociopolitical [and economic] context."

27. The set of criteria used by the Seminar includes the following: The parables of Jesus are metaphors taken from everyday life that surprise and tease the reader with its possible application. The genuine parables of Jesus thus have no conclusions, and always exhibit characteristic plot structures that have the marks of oral composition. Parables recorded in two or more independent and early written sources (Mark, Q, Gos. Thom., M, and L) are more likely to preserve the oral tradition and most probably can be attributed to the historical Jesus (the criteria of early, independent and multiple attestation). Only parables that can be traced to the oral period (30–50 CE) most probably go back to Jesus. The narrative contexts in which the evangelist placed the parables, interpretive conclusions added by the evangelists, as well as the grouping of parables in clusters are considered to be secondary. Evidence of the social location of the early Christian community and common wisdom on the lips of Jesus also fall into this category. See Funk et al., *Red Letter Edition*, 16–19; Funk et al., *The Five Gospels*, 16–33.

28. Funk, *Honest to Jesus*, 165–66.

29. Scott, *Re-Imagine the World*, 1–2.

30. In its narrative context the parable of the Friend at Midnight (Luke 11:5–8) is used by Luke as an example of boldness in prayer. If you keep on praying, knocking and asking (like the friend outside the door), God will answer your prayers (the door will be opened). Therefore the parable gives expression to the vertical relationship between

tions of the parables added by the evangelists to fit the narrative contexts of their respective gospels, as well as to interpretative conclusions added by the evangelists.[31] A third criterion will be to look for strains of the ideologies of the respective evangelists that might have been deposited into the parables. For this an ideological-critical reading of the parables, where necessary, will be applied.[32] Finally, the criterion of coherence will play a major role in the decision-making process. By applying the criteria of early, multiple, and independent attestation certain values that Jesus stood for can be identified. When some of these values are identified in a specific parable, even if the parable does not pass the criteria of early, multiple, and independent attestation, the possibility exists that at least the gist of that specific parable does go back to Jesus. Although this is a general rule, each and every parable will have to be judged on its own merit.

The idea of the above set of criteria is *not* to construct the "original" parables of Jesus. This is simply not possible. It is, however, possible to make an informed judgment whether a specific parable represents what Funk has called the "voice print" of Jesus.[33] Put differently: the above set of criteria

---

God and man. If the parable is taken out of this secondary context provided by Luke, the possibility is opened up to read the parable as focusing on horizontal relationships between man and man, on what honorable actions are as well as on the principle of generalized reciprocity between two peasants vis-à-vis the principles of balanced or negative reciprocity. For a description of these terms, see Malina, *Christian Origins and Cultural Anthropology*, 98–106.

31. A classic example is the parable of the Samaritan (Luke 10:30–35). In its Lukan context the Samaritan has been provided with an introduction (Luke 10:29) and conclusion (Luke 10:36–37) that are linked by means of the parable. When the parable is stripped of its Lukan introduction and conclusion, the question is if the parable is still all about identifying one's neighbor. See also Tolbert, *Perspectives on the Parables*, 115, who also argues that the gospel settings themselves often violated the integrity of the parable stories.

32. The parable of the Tenants or Leased Vineyard in Mark 12:1–12 and *par.* can serve here as a good example. Kloppenborg has indicated that Mark 12:1–2, when compared with Gos. Thom. 65 (that is most probably closer to the tradition of the historical Jesus), has turned the tenants into a story "of salvation history in allegorical dress." Kloppenborg, *Tenants in the Vineyard*, 111. Using this insight of Kloppenborg, Van Eck—in an ideological-critical reading of the Tenants—has indicated that, because of Mark's allegorical interpretation of the tenants, Jesus is pictured as condoning violence. In Gos. Thom. 65, however, the direct opposite point of view can be attributed to Jesus. Mark thus employed the tenants in his gospel to serve his ideology. This example iterates the necessity for ideological-critical readings of the parables. See Van Eck, "Tenants"; also Oakman, *Jesus and the Peasants*, 246.

33. Funk, *Collected Essays*, 171–76. Funk uses the concept "voice print" to describe the way Jesus told his parables (his strategy), as well as for the content of his vision. In terms of Jesus' strategy, he offered his hearers a different way of looking at everyday life. With his parables Jesus regularly frustrated the expectations of his hearers by offering

will be used to identify what was typical of the Galilean's message. Starting with the content of those sayings and parables of Jesus that pass the criteria of early, multiple, and independent attestation, a picture of Jesus' message will be built as we read his parables. In the end, we hope, it will be possible to paint a coherent picture of the message of Jesus as represented by his parables.

Social-Scientific Criticism

When the focus of interpretation is the parables of the Galilean Jesus, the social location of the parables is not the different sociohistorical contexts of the Synoptics (*c.* 72–96 CE) but the sociohistorical context of the historical Jesus (*c.* 27–30 CE). The social location of Jesus most probably was that of the Galilean peasantry; this means that the interpreter of the parables should ask the question what message the parables carried in this rural context, and how the parables were heard by their rural audience.[34]

Almost all of Jesus' parables are native to Palestine and have a rural context.[35] The stories he told were about a farmer sowing his field (with all the hazards the small farmer faced, Mark 4:3–8; *par.* Matt 13:3–8, Gos. Thom. 9:1–5, and Luke 8:5–8), planting a mustard seed (Mark 4:30–32; *par.* Gos. Thom. 20:2–4, Luke 13:18–19, and Matt 13:31–32) or reaping a harvest (Mark 4:26–29); a woman who is looking for a lost coin (Luke 15:8–9) and a shepherd for a lost sheep (Luke 15:4–6; *par.* Matt 18:12–13 and Gos. Thom. 107:1–3); a man finding a treasure in a field (Matt 13:44; *par.* Gos. Thom. 109:1–3) and a merchant a costly pearl (Matt 13:45–46; *par.* Gos. Thom. 76:1–2); a woman that works leaven into flour (Luke 13:20–21; *par.* Matt 13:33 and Gos. Thom. 96:1–2) or loses her flour on the way home (Gos. Thom. 97:1–3); a slave storing money by burying it in the ground or

---

them a different way of looking at life, "a fleeting glimpse of what lies behind the boundaries of the everyday." Jesus talked about God's domain in everyday, mundane terms; made use of typifications; did not cite Scripture; made no personal confessions; did not have ordinary reality in mind; reversed the anticipations of his hearers; made free use of parody; and never answered questions directly (see ibid., 172–75). The content of his vision was the kingdom of God, or God's domain; that region or sphere where God's dominion was immediate and absolute (see Funk, "Jesus of Nazareth," 89).

34. In his categorization of the parables, Crossan typifies some of Jesus' parables as challenge parables because these parables "challenge us to think." Crossan, *Power of Parable*, 47. This approach to the interpretation of the parables is ethnocentric. The parables were not told to modern readers in the first instance, but to the rural audience of Jesus.

35. Except maybe for the parable of the Pearl (Matt 13:44–45). See Miller, "Pearl," 65.

wrapping it in a cloth (Matt 25:14–28; *par.* Luke 19:13–24); tenants working a vineyard (Mark 12:1–12; *par.* Matt 21:33–44, Luke 20:9–19, and Gos.
Thom. 65); a friend borrowing bread from a neighbor in a peasant village
(Luke 11:5–8); and peasants being hired as day laborers to work in the vineyard of an elite owner (Matt 20:1–15).

In cases where the social setting of the parable is most probably that
of the preindustrial city, Jesus used images well known to the first-century
peasant—a peasant who had most probably lost his land because of unpaid
taxes and outstanding loans and rent, who has become a beggar (Luke
16:19–26); or an elite trying to collect a debt (Matt 18:23–33), and an elite
person inviting other elite persons to a meal (Luke 14:16b–23).[36]

These are all mundane stories of day-to-day peasant life and experience, stories that contained meaning for people close to the soil; these images indicate that the village was the predominant context for the ministry
of Jesus. It thus seems natural to assume that Jesus shared many of the same
values and expectations as his peasant audiences.[37] The interpretation of
Jesus' parables thus should start with what is known typically about peasant values and expectations.[38] Jesus, however, also told parables that give
evidence of elements common in advanced agrarian (aristocratic) societies:
debt (Matt 18:23–34; *par.* Luke 16:1–8a); patrons (Luke 16:19–26); elite using their status to coerce tenants (Gos. Thom. 65:1–7; *par.* Matt 21:33–39,
Mark 12:1–8, and Luke 20:9–15); the existence of large estates and tenants
working on large estates most probably because they had lost their land
through excessive taxes or debt[39] (Gos. Thom. 65:1–7; *par.* Luke 20:9–15,

36. Hedrick, *Many Things in Parables*, 39: "Most of the parables portray common
folk engaged in average, down-to-earth activities. And even those parables featuring
characters not of the peasant class portray them in actions true to their status in society."

37. Malina, *New Testament World*, 73; Fiensy, *Jesus the Galilean*, 45; Oakman, *Jesus
and the Peasants*, 172–73.

38. Oakman, *Jesus and the Peasants*, 172–73: "Jesus was a rural artisan working often within typical peasant contexts. His parables reflect these contexts. This means that
while Jesus could and did move beyond village during his life, his fundamental world of
values and his fundamental interests and loyalties were shaped within and oriented to
the village. The interpretation of Jesus' parables must start with what is known typically
about peasant values and expectations. Indeed, many of the parables themselves urge
this starting point, assuming as they do knowledge of the Palestinian countryside under
the early Roman Empire."

39. "During the republic and the early years of the empire, most of these taxes were
collected by tax farmers . . . They contracted with the government to raise the taxes of a
particular area and to collect a fee for this service. The fee, however, was only part of the
profit. Since many agricultural taxes were collected in kind, publicans made large profits by reselling the goods collected or by hoarding them until the price rose . . . When
a farmer could not pay his taxes, publicans would offer to lend him money at 12 to 48

Matt 21:33–39, Mark 12:1–8, Gos. Thom. 63:1–5 and Luke 12:16–20); elite persons loaning money at most probably very high rates and so amassing wealth, which was seen as theft in a limited-goods society (Matt 25:14–28; *par.* Luke 19:13–24); the elite playing the social game of challenge and riposte to gain honor and status *(Gos. Thom.* 64:1–11; *par.* Luke 14:16–23 and Matt 22:2–13); day laborers waiting to be hired (Matt 20:1–15); and the poor not being looked after (Luke 16:19–26). These stories are not mundane. They not only assume knowledge of the Palestinian countryside under the early Roman Empire, but also show the ugly face of the exploitation of the peasantry by the elite common to advanced agrarian (aristocratic) societies. They are stories about the kingdoms of Caesar and the temple elite. By telling these parables, Jesus most probably acknowledged the needs and frustrations of the peasants in his first-century rural context.⁴⁰ The way he did this was to tell stories of the kingdom of God, stories that addressed the social world of the peasants and expendables in villages and their surroundings.⁴¹ As Oakman puts it, "One must assume a rural context for Jesus parables. The question always should be: How would a rural audience have heard it? The more it looks like the views of urban culture and literati, the less likely it will be the view of Jesus."⁴²

It must be clear that by referring to "context" in this volume the reference is not the specific context in which the parables were told, that is, "the living contexts in which Jesus spoke and people listened."⁴³ These original (situational) contexts are lost to us. Moreover, since Jesus most probably retold some of his parables, the parables had more than one original context. What is meant by context is what Miller calls the "emergent context" of the parables.⁴⁴ Emergent context refers to, for example, observations Jesus made that lead to the creation of a parable (e.g., a patron mistreating a client or an elite practicing negative reciprocity), or even a direct response to some event or confrontation. The cue taken here is that the exploitative situation

---

percent. Such loans grew rapidly as interest and new tax liabilities accumulated, and eventually the land was confiscated by the publicans" (Gonzales, *Faith and Wealth*, 38).

40. Oakman, *Jesus and the Peasants*, 118–19.

41. Bessler-Northcutt, "Learning to See God," 55.

42. Oakman, *Jesus and the Peasants*, 117. See also the following important remark by Elliott, *Social-Scientific Criticism*, 11: "The acid test to be applied to all the conclusions of literary and historical critics of the Bible is to ask the questions, Did people really think and act that way and, if so, why? Do these exegetical conclusions square with ancient patterns of believe and behavior? Are the statements of the texts as suggested by exegetes in fact coherent with the actual perceptions, values, worldviews, and social scripts of the communities in which these texts originated?"

43. Miller, "Pearl," 75.

44. Ibid., 75–76.

of the peasantry in first-century Palestine, as result of the ideologies of the kingdom of the *pax Romana* and the kingdom of the temple elite, served as emergent context for the parables of Jesus. "The basic meaning of the parables must always be assessed *vis-à-vis* their original audience and sociopolitical context."[45]

To avoid ethnocentric readings of the parables of Jesus the interpreter must take cognizance of the dominant cultural values and norms of the first-century Mediterranean world. The parables of Jesus describe the interaction between Jesus and his first-century hearers, who lived nineteen centuries ago in the eastern part of the Mediterranean basin. The social and cultural context of the parables of Jesus (the world of the New Testament) is therefore different from ours, "a world that, were we to be transported into it, would puzzle us and send us into a profound culture shock."[46] We should therefore be cautious when we read the New Testament. If we really want to understand the parables of Jesus, we will have to take the social and cultural values of Jesus and his hearers seriously (the culture of the first-century Mediterranean). Above all, the texts we have of the parables are products of a high-context society.

> The New Testament . . . consists of documents written in what anthropologists call a "high context" society where the communicators presume a broadly shared acquaintance with and knowledge of the social context of matters referred to in conversation or writing. Accordingly, it is presumed in such societies that contemporary readers will be able to "fill in the gaps" and "read between the lines."[47]

---

45. Oakman, *Jesus and the Peasants*, 25. See also the following remark of ibid., 118–19: "It seems natural to assume that Jesus shared many of the same values and expectations of his peasant audiences. His ministry addressed in significant ways the needs and frustrations of his first-century rural context. Somewhere along the line . . . literate followers of Jesus arranged and recorded his words. For these followers . . . the meaning of the traditions shifted. Speaking from a different 'place,' these early traditors perceived the meaning of Jesus' appearance and words in more abstract and general terms . . . Sacred written traditions and the somewhat artificial arrangement of Jesus' words began to overshadow the concrete context of first-century Palestinian villages for assessing the meaning of Jesus." See also Levine, *Short Stories by Jesus*, 8–9.

46. Fiensy, *Jesus the Galilean*, 1. "Another maxim that frequently holds for biblical studies is that the world of the people who wrote and first heard the texts is different from our world. We cannot map onto their cultures and contexts our own values or expectations. What seems odd to us might be perfectly normal to them." Levine, *Short Stories by Jesus*, 10.

47. Elliott, *Social-Scientific Criticism*, 11. In this regard Snodgrass, *Stories with Intent*, 167, is correct in stating that the parables "do not give unnecessary details." Snodgrass, however, is not correct that this aspect of the parables is typical of the general

Without knowledge of the historical and cultural world of Jesus, the interpreter will not be able to make evident what *social realia* are evoked by a specific parable, that is, cultural scripts that would have been known and therefore assumed by Jesus and his hearers.[48]

> A reader must engage the cultural world in which the parable was invented in order to hear it as the earliest audience might have hear it. The social facets and dynamics of that world may be strange, even foreign, to modern readers, but a first-century auditor would have understood subliminally aspects of the story escaping the modern reader. Such subliminal awareness operates in every culture. Persons who are strangers to the culture need to have explained to them what natives instinctively know without explanation.[49]

But is there really such a big difference? The following examples speak for themselves: the most dominant value in the world of Jesus was honor and shame[50] (in our society it is most probably money), and any contact between two males was seen as a challenge of one's honor that most of the times ended up in the social game of challenge-riposte (we are not agonistic in nature, or are we?); the first-century personality was dyadic or group oriented (we are individuals); all goods were perceived as limited, and their accumulation was perceived as immoral (for us the accumulation of wealth is a status symbol); patron-client relationships were the order of the day—between equals it meant general reciprocity, and between nonequals clients got access to goods and services that otherwise would not have been accessible (in our society access to goods is based on financial ability);

---

rhetorical structure of the parables. This is an ethnocentric interpretation. The parables do not give "unnecessary details" because of their high-context character; for the first hearers of the parables, as "insiders" of the cultural world in which the parables were told, the details were enough.

48. Scott, *Re-Imagine the World*, 141: "A substantial bar to making the parables applicable today is the great distance between them and us. Jesus was a first century, Jewish, Galilean peasant and his concerns, speech, and idioms belong to that culture. We belong to a very different world. The transition is difficult."

49. Hedrick, "Good News about the Historical Jesus," 42–43.

50. "If then the great-souled man claims and is worthy of great things and most of all the greatest things, Greatness of Soul must be concerned with some one object especially 'Worthy' is a term of relation: it denotes having a claim to goods external to oneself. Now the greatest external good we should assume to be the thing which we offer as a tribute to the gods, and which is most coveted by men of high station, and is the prize awarded for the noblest deeds; and such a thing is honor, for honor is clearly the greatest of external goods. Therefore the great-souled man is he who has the right disposition in relation to honours and disgraces . . . since it is honor above all else that great men claim and deserve." Aristotle, *Eth. nic.* 4.3.9–12.

kinship (family) was the most important social institution, family life was patriarchal, and women and children had no social status (think of our bill of children's rights); people, places, and times were divided into pure or impure based on the divisions made by God at creation (we do not believe that a person with leprosy is a sinner, that having sexual relations makes one impure; or that certain foods can make you unclean); meals were seen as the redrawing of existing boundaries—likes only ate with likes, and different kinds of foods were served depending on someone's honor and status (we make sure that everybody gets enough of everything); first-century persons believed in the evil eye (we have never believed this); people called other people names to discredit and ostracize them socially (this we try to do, but it does not necessarily work); first-century cities had areas where only the elite were allowed to live, the nonelite lived at the edges of the cities, and those who were socially unclean had to sleep outside the city (we also have this, except for the fact that our bank balance determines where we stay); and sickness was seen as the result of misfortune (we understand sickness as a biological deficiency).

From these few examples it becomes clear that we enter a totally different world when we read the parables of Jesus. To simply dismiss this distance and to look at them through the lens of our culture (as if "our" culture and "their" culture are simply the same thing) is to misrepresent and misunderstand the parables; it can only lead to anachronism and ethnocentrism.[51] A study of the New Testament's social background or the culture of the New Testament is, therefore, "not the icing on the cake of New Testament studies; it is the flour from which the cake is made. This enterprise is not a hobby one pursues in addition to the serious stuff of exegesis; it is the way the serious stuff is done."[52]

It is clear that the understanding of the parables of Jesus necessitates a cross-cultural approach (culturally sensitive reading). To understand the parables in their first-century Mediterranean context the reader must have clarity on the social system presupposed in Jesus' parables. For this we need reading scenarios,[53] and social-scientific criticism offers those. Social-scientific criticism, in short, is a way of

---

51. Elliott, *Social-Scientific Criticism*, 11: An anachronistic or ethnocentric reading of the parables entails a reading that reads "into the text information from some present social context rather than comprehending the text in accord with its own contemporary social and cultural scripts."

52. Fiensy, *Jesus the Galilean*, 2.

53. Malina, "Reading Theory Perspective," 14–17.

envisioning, investigating, and understanding the interrelation of texts and social contexts, ideas and communal behavior, social realities and their religious symbolization, belief systems and cultural systems and ideologies as a whole, and the relation of such cultural systems to the natural and social environment, economic organization, social structures, and political power.[54]

Social-scientific criticism approaches texts from the premise that the historical contexts of texts have more social dimensions than only "what was going on when and where." From a social-scientific point of view, the contexts of texts also refer to social behavior involving two or more persons, social groups, social institutions, social systems, and patterns and codes of sociality. Texts are likewise shaped in their language, content, and perspectives by the social systems in which they were produced. Texts also serve as a vehicle for social interaction. The contexts of texts are social contexts, contexts shaped by societal conditions, structures, and processes. In their content, structure, strategies, and meaning, texts presuppose and communicate information about the social systems of which they are a product. Social-scientific criticism thus moves beyond the mere collection of independent social and historical data to the study of the interrelationship of ideas and communal behavior, of belief systems and cultural systems and ideologies as a whole, and of the relationship of such cultural systems to the natural and social environment, to the economic organization, social structures, and political power. Social-scientific criticism also takes as a premise the dynamic that all ideas and concepts are—that all knowledge is—socially determined.[55]

In order to (re)construct the social and cultural context of the New Testament texts (e.g., the parables of Jesus) social-science criticism draws on modern anthropological studies of Mediterranean and Near Eastern (advanced) agrarian communities. On the premise of cultural continuity, social-scientific criticism uses these studies to construct models which can in turn be used to gain insight into texts like the parables of Jesus. Social-scientific criticism employs models scripts (reading scenarios) as interpretative tools to facilitate understanding. A model is a conceptual vehicle for articulating, applying, testing, and possibly reconstructing theories used in the analysis and interpretation of specific social data. In short, models are tools for transforming theories into research operations. Models are always perceptual in nature and heuristic in function and have to be constructed.

54. Elliott, *Social-Scientific Criticism*, 13.

55. This summarized description of the salient aspects of social-scientific criticism is from ibid., 9–16.

In short, models are theories in operation. Some of the models (reading scenarios) applied in social-scientific criticism pertain to aspects such as honor and shame, patronage and clientism, dyadic personality, ceremonies and rituals, labeling and deviance, sickness and healing, purity and pollution, kinship and the social stratification of society.[56]

A social-scientific analysis of the parables therefore has two foci: First, social sciences are used to construct theories and models for collecting and analyzing data that illuminate salient features of, for example, ancient Mediterranean and early Christian society and culture. Second, it aims to elucidate the structure, content strategy, and intended rhetorical effect of the text within its social context. The text is analyzed as a vehicle of communication whose genre, structure and content, theme, and aim are shaped by the cultural and social dynamics of the social system and the specific historical setting in which it is produced and to which it constitutes a specific response.[57] In this regard, the parables of Jesus are a good example.

The Parables and Realism

An anachronistic interpretation of the parables entails an interpretation that reads "into the text information from some present social context rather than comprehending the text in accord with its own contemporary social and cultural scripts."[58] Cultural awareness of the "other," however is only half of the problem when it comes to cross-cultural communication. Cultural self-awareness is also necessary to understand why we frequently project ourselves onto the language and thinking of others.[59] This, of course, holds true for our theological awareness as well.[60]

56. Again, see ibid., 37–59.

57. "Social-scientific criticism . . . studies the text as both a reflection of and a response to the social and cultural settings in which the text was produced" to determine "the meaning(s) explicit and implicit in the text, meanings made possible and shaped by the social and cultural systems inhabited by both authors and intended audiences" (ibid., 8). Social-scientific criticism approaches texts as units of meaningful discourse that express (because of their ideological dimension) certain ideas and beliefs (cultural perceptions, values, and worldviews), that describe social relations, behavior and institutions, and that serve to motivate and direct social behavior. Therefore texts either legitimate social institutions or serve as vehicles of social change. Ibid., 49–50.

58. Elliott, *Social-Scientific Criticism*, 11.

59. Rohrbaugh, "Hermeneutics as Cross-Cultural Encounter," 563.

60. The dominant interpretation of the parable of the Unmerciful Servant (Matt 18:23–33) can serve as an example. Because sin, from a theological perspective, is seen by many as a debt to God or fellow humans, this understanding of debt is projected onto the parable; the king is seen as God, and the interpretation can only go in one

The parables, as Dodd puts it, are realistic narratives about everyday events in first-century Palestine.[61] The parables of Jesus are stories about dinner parties, prodigal sons, seed being sown, laborers in a vineyard and persons accruing debt. As suggested by Kloppenborg, in some cases "a vineyard or a shepherd in a parable of Jesus is just a vineyard or a shepherd."[62] This is also the point of view of Herzog: The narrative repertoires (social scenarios) depicted in the parables are not incidental, irrelevant or unrelated to social reality, but "are grounded in the story-tellers social, political, and cultural milieu." Hence, the social settings of the parables are windows to their meanings.[63]

Recent studies have shown that papyri from early Roman Egypt provide "solid ancient *comparanda* on the practices and social realities which the sayings of Jesus and the parables presuppose."[64] The Graeco-Egyptian papyri, and a few papyri preserved from the 'Arava, are contemporary with first-century Palestine and reflect similar nonelite social strata and processes. With "due allowance made for legal and cultural differences between Egypt and Palestine" these papyri "can provide useful comparative

---

direction. To read the parable from this perspective is to depict a Jesus that made theological statements. Jesus, on the contrary, had no doctrine of God, made no theological statements, and never used abstract language. See in this regard Funk, "Jesus of Nazareth," 90, who states that the parables of Jesus "are not stories of God—they are stories about God's estate." See also Herzog, *Parables as Subversive Speech*, 3. "The parables were not earthly stories with heavenly meanings, but earthly stories with heavy meanings." The following quote from Kloppenborg, *Synoptic Problems*, 490, should also be taken note of: "Few nowadays would defend the preposition that Jesus was an allegorist, speaking in one discursive realm but in fact intending to evoke other discursive realms, for example, salvation history or the care of the soul." Also see Hedrick, *Many Things in Parables*, 39. "In the stories Jesus told, realism trumps theology. In the interpretations of the evangelists and the contemporary church, theology trumps realism—and has the final word."

61. Dodd, *Parables of the Kingdom*, 10. See also Zimmermann, "Leseanleitung," 25: A parable is "a short narrative text that refers in its narrated world to a known reality, but which by means of implicit or explicit signals makes it clear that the significance of what is narrated is to be distinguished from the wording of the text. In its appeal it requires a reader to accomplish a metaphoric transfer of meaning, guided by contextual information." Translation from Kloppenborg, "Burglar in Q," 287.

62. Kloppenborg, *Synoptic Problems*, 490. See also Levine, *Short Stories by Jesus*, 16–17.

63. Herzog, *Parables as Subversive Speech*, 135–36; see also Scott, *Hear Then the Parable*, 270.

64. Kloppenborg, *Synoptic Problems*, 2. See also Bazzana, "*Basileia* and Debt Relief"; Bazzana, "Violence and Human Prayer"; Van Eck and Kloppenborg, "Unexpected Patron"; Van Eck, "Unmerciful Servant."

data for understanding the realia which the parables presuppose"[65] These documentary papyri are important because they are nearly contemporary with Jesus' parables, and because they reflect the actual economic and social practices presupposed by the parables but often ignored as more elite writers. Moreover, the practices evidenced in early Roman Egypt cohere with practices that are later mentioned (albeit in much more lapidary and fragmentary way) in Rabbinic writings from Palestine in the third and following centuries.

Several studies on the parables by Kloppenborg have indicated that papyri from early Roman Egypt provide detailed information on social realities in the parables.[66] In the interpretation of the parables, Kloppenborg argues, the social *realia* invoked in the parables cannot be neglected, "and we ought to get clear on the most basic meanings of the images in question before moving to abstract, symbolic or allegorical meanings."[67]

> We have to assemble solid ancient *comparanda* on the practices and social realities which the sayings of Jesus and the parables presuppose. For such a project, documentary papyri are usually our most plentiful, and sometimes only, resource.[68]

In interpreting the parables one should assume that the first audiences of Jesus' parables, most probably the peasantry in Galilee, already had cultural competence in these ancient practices, and had native (emic) knowledge of the social realia referred to in the parables. It is therefore "hardly a surprise that the Synoptics do not bother to explain or elaborate on any of these matters."[69] When interpreting the parables, we thus run the

---

65. Kloppenborg, "Burglar in Q," 289.

66. Kloppenborg, *Tenants in the Vineyard*; Kloppenborg, "Violence in Synoptic Parables," 323–51; Kloppenborg, "Burglar in Q," 287–306; Kloppenborg, *Synoptic Problems*, 491–511, 556–76, 577–99.

67. Kloppenborg, *Synoptic Problems*, 490.

68. Kloppenborg, "Burglar in Q," 2. See also see also Bazzana, "*Basileia* and Debt Relief," 511, 517.

69. Kloppenborg, *Synoptic Problems*, 2. The reason for this "lack" of explanation is that, as was referred to earlier, the texts we have of the parables are products of a high-context society According to Rohrbaugh, the main problem for modern readers of the parables is "that we do not know what we do not know." Rohrbaugh continues: "The current consensus view of parables is that they are something like open-ended, extended metaphors that force the reader to arrive at conclusions of his/her own. That may or may not be accurate, but of course the missing piece is knowledge of the context. If we knew all about the setting in which these stories were first told perhaps we would get the point in the fashion a high-context person would expect. But lacking it . . . we arrive at conclusions that often bear no relation to an ancient context whatsoever." See Rohrbaugh, "Hermeneutics as Cross-Cultural Encounter," 567.

risk of serious anachronism if these practices and realia are not taken into consideration.[70]

Related Points of Departure

The Context of Jesus' Parables: The Sociocultural, Political, Economic, and Religious Realities of First-Century Palestine

First-century Palestine, the world in which Jesus told his parables, was an advanced agrarian society[71] under the control of the Roman Empire. Advanced agrarian societies had two main characteristics: It was aristocratic in nature, and the main "economic" activity was the working of the land (agriculture). Society was divided into the *haves* (rulers) and the *have-nots* (the ruled). The ruling class (elite) comprised of more or less 2 percent of the population and lived in the cities, while the rest of the population, the peasants (the ruled or non–elite), lived in rural areas. No middle class existed.

Although comprising only 2 percent of the population, the elite controlled most of the wealth (up to 65 percent) by controlling and exploiting the land and sea; its produce and its cultivators (the peasantry and fishermen) whose labor created the produce. The elite had contempt for manual labor,[72] and thus exploited cheap labor with slaves and tenant farmers. Local, regional and imperial elites imposed tributes, taxes, and rents; extracting wealth from non-elites by taxing the production, distribution and consumption of goods. The elite themselves were known for their conspicuous consumption and displayed their wealth in housing, clothing, jewelry, food and ownership of land and slaves. The elite thus lived at the expense of the non–elite.

The elite did not rule as a result of democratic elections, but rather through the use and abuse of power and hereditary control of land. The rulers treated controlled (conquered) land as their personal estate to confiscate, distribute, redistribute and disperse as they deemed fit. All matters of importance were in the hands of the elite, and no legitimate channel for political participation by the peasantry existed. The elite ruled through coercion, using the Roman army, and any kind of rebellion was met with

70. Kloppenborg, *Synoptic Problems*, 2.

71. For a short summary of the salient attributes of an advanced agrarian society, see Hanson and Oakman, *Palestine in the Time of Jesus*, 94–100. The difference between a (simple) agrarian and an advanced agrarian society is that the latter is more advanced in certain aspects of technology and production, for example in the use of iron tools.

72. Sirach 38:25–34; Cicero, *De Officiis* 1.150.

immediate and ruthless military retaliation. The legal system exercised bias towards the elite by employing punishment appropriated not to the crime, but to the social status of the accused.

Patron-client relationships were part and parcel of advanced agrarian societies. The elite stood in patron-client relationships with other elites by dispensing patronage in the form of land and political positions, expecting personal loyalty and support for political programs in return. Elites also entered into patron-client relationships with the poor and the peasantry to enhance honor and status, to display wealth and power, to build dependency, and to secure loyalty, dependence and submission from the nonelite. From the side of the peasantry these patron-client relationships at times enabled them to secure something more than just subsistence living.[73]

Since rulers in advanced agrarian societies usually came to power through the use of force, they used different kinds of legitimization to justify their rule and declare their divine right to rule. This was done, first and foremost, by claiming the favor of the gods. Rome's imperial theology claimed that Rome was chosen by the gods, especially Jupiter, to rule an "empire without end."[74] This imperial theology was bolstered and legitimized by especially the imperial cult (temples, images, rituals and personnel that honored the emperor). To legitimize their power even further, the elite controlled various forms of communication (political propaganda: e.g., the designs on coins), rhetoric (speeches at civic occasions), various forms of writings (e.g., history, philosophy), and the building of monuments. Development—in the form of the building of cities, roads and aqueducts—was another form of legitimization, since it gave the impression of prosperity (although these projects were built with forced labor). The elite also favored traditional forms of rule (indirect rule) and allowed the use of local temples or cults/religions. All this persuaded the nonelite to be compliant.

The building of cities that displayed Rome's elite power, wealth, and status ensured maximum control over the surrounding territories, and served as the basic unit for the collection of tribute and taxes—thus codifying, conserving, and construing "normal" society and producing an image of peace and an ordered state (*pax Romana*), and disseminating the ideology and values of the ruling class.

Therefore the elite shaped the social experience of the empire's inhabitants, determined their quality of life, exercised power, controlled wealth,

---

73. "A patron-client relationship is a vertical dyadic alliance i.e. an alliance between two persons of unequal status, power or resources each of whom finds it useful to have as an ally someone superior or inferior to himself." Landé, "Dyadic Basis of Clientelism," 20.

74. Virgil, *Aeneid* 1.278–79; Cicero, *De Officiis* 2.26–27.

and enjoyed high status. Social control was built on fear, and the relationship between the ruling elite and the ruled nonelite was one of power and exploitation.[75]

Focusing more specifically on Galilee and Judea, what did the political, economic, and religious landscape in which Jesus told his parables look like? Note, in brief, the following:[76] In 63 BCE, after Rome's initial conquest of Judea, Galilee,[77] and other parts of Palestine, the Romans laid the Judeans and Galileans under tribute. According to Josephus (*Ant.* 14.202–203), Rome required a quarter of the harvest every second year (roughly 12.5 percent per year). In 47 BCE, when Herod the Great (born as an Edomite in Idumea), was appointed by his father Antipater as military governor of Galilee, he very soon extorted a hundred-talent allotment from the Galileans.[78] For the Galileans these were difficult times: periodic warfare, enslavement, lean years,[79] the extra economic burden placed on them by the Roman tribute, and special levies of taxes over and above the dues already paid to the Hasmoneans made survival difficult. In 37 BCE Herod the Great was appointed as the client king of Rome as the sole ruler in Judea ("the king of

75. The above description of the salient features of advanced agrarian societies makes use of the insights of the following scholars: on economy see Polanyi, *Great Transformation*; Carney, *Shape of the Past*; Finley, *Ancient Economy*; Oakman, *Jesus and the Economic Questions*; Oakman, *Jesus and the Peasants*; on social stratification see Lenski, *Power and Privilege*; on patron-client relationships see Eisenstadt and Roniger, "Patron-Client Relations"; Saller, *Personal Patronage*; Elliott, "Patronage and Clientism"; on the exploitative relationship between elite and nonelite see Fiensy, *Land Is Mine*; Fiensy, *Jesus the Galilean*; Freyne, "Urban-Rural Relations"; Hanson and Oakman, *Palestine in the Time of Jesus*; Rohrbaugh, "Agrarian Society"; Stegemann and Stegemann, *Jesus Movement*; Herzog, *Prophet and Teacher*; Carter, *Roman Empire*; Carter, "Matthew's Gospel"; on conflict and peasant resistance see Lintott, *Violence in Republican Rome*; Horsley, *Spiral of Violence*; Horsley, *Jesus and Empire*; Scott, *Weapons of the Weak*; Malina, *Social Gospel of Jesus*.

76. The framework of the following description of the political, social, and economic realities that can be considered as the backdrop of the parables of Jesus is based on the work of Horsley, *Social Context of Jesus*, 29–36; Horsley, *Covenant Economics*, 81–91.

77. The Romans appreciated the exploitable resources of the Galilee, which included the agricultural potential of the land to produce wheat, olives, olive oil and wine, wool, flax and textiles, as well as the potential of the Sea of Galilee to produce fish and fish sauces. Sawicki, *Crossing Galilee*, 27.

78. Horsley, *Social Context of Jesus*, 29. The tribute and taxes extracted from the peasantry came from the so-called surplus of the harvest, a "euphemism for goods and labor that previously had been tied up the village level." See Sawicki, *Crossing Galilee*, 115.

79. Josephus has a number of references to instances when bad harvests created physical hardship and economic disaster for the peasantry. See Josephus, *Ant.* 14.28; 15:299–303, 365; 16:64; 18:8; 20:101.

the Judeans"), and soon became famous for his tight economic control and administration skills.[80] From Sepphoris, one of his lavish building projects situated in the heart of lower Galilee's agricultural activity, Herod, in collaboration with the Herodians (the new elite and retainer classes, replacing the old Hasmoneans), ruled and taxed Galilee.[81] He increased demands for royal taxes,[82] and improved the efficiency of tax collection.[83] After the death of Herod the Great in 4 BCE, Herod Antipas was appointed by Augustus as a client king (tetrarch) of Galilee at the age of merely seventeen: the first Roman client ruler who resided in Galilee. Antipas implemented a "policy of urbanization, establishing cities as a way of controlling and exploiting the countryside."[84] Antipas immediately rebuilt Sepphoris (known as the "ornament of Galilee") from where the peasant farmers and Galilee were taxed, and in 17 CE built Tiberias (in honor of the new emperor Tiberius) to administer the taxation of the fishing industry around the Sea of Galilee.[85]

80. Freyne, *Galilee from Alexander the Great to Hadrian*, 190. "Despite his self-centered ruthlessness Herod was also a shrewd administrator and businessman. His treatment of the people during the famine of 25 BCE—provision of grain, clothing, and the like—is indicative of his control of the overall financial situation, and his recognition that a prosperous kingdom called for skillful exploitation of its resources."

81. Applebaum, "Judaea as a Roman Province," 373, gives the following description of the taxation of the peasantry under Herod the Great: "It is to be assumed, accordingly, that Herod's subjects had both to pay tribute to Rome and to cover the King's enormous expenditure on his ambitious programme of urbanization and building, as well as the cost of his elaborate administration and the numerous grants that he made to his friends and to Greek cities outside Judaea. This burden, moreover, came after twenty years of destructive warfare, and a series of arbitrary and oppressive monetary exactions imposed by a succession of Roman potentates, including Antony himself."

82. Apart from the 900 talents Herod the Great had to pay to Caesar, the *laographia* (or *tributum capitis*) was also levied, at a rate of one denarius per head per year, as well as taxes on houses (Josephus, *Ant.* 19.229), sales (Josephus, *Ant.* 18.90), internal tolls and customs. See Applebaum, "Judaea as a Roman Province," 373–74; Sawicki, *Crossing Galilee*, 114. These taxes, according to those who opposed Archelaus before Augustus to become king after the death of Herod the Great, "filled the nation full of poverty." See Josephus, *War* 2.86.

83. According to Josephus (*War* 2.386), the total annual revenue paid by Judea was the equivalent of the revenue obtained from Egypt in a month. According to Strabo, (*Geography* XVII.798, Ptolemy Auletes' income was 13,500 talents, which would mean an annual Judean revenue of some one thousand talents. See Applebaum, "Judaea as a Roman Province," 375. This number compares well with Josephus (*Ant.* 17.318–320), who states that Herod's yearly income, just before his death, amounted to somewhat over 900 talents.

84. Horsley, *Covenant Economics*, 87.

85. The elites, especially Herodians, legitimated their taxing of the of the peasantry through the claim that the ownership and use of land, the flow of goods, and the demands for any surplus that might accrue "corresponded to the natural order of

Although Antipas' estimated private income from his territories was less than a quarter of that of Herod the Great (200 talents; see Josephus, *Ant.* 17.318; *War* 2.95), most peasants were exploited to such a degree that they barely lived at a level of subsistence. This amount of money was raised in part through land taxes both from Antipas' private leased estates and from private holdings, and in part from tolls, rents, and customs taxes. "In all probability there was the Roman tribute[86] too, which would have equaled the amount of private revenue, though we have no direct information on the matter."[87]

When Antipas was appointed in 4 BCE, Augustus declared Judea and Samaria a Roman province (administered by Syria) and appointed the priestly aristocracy (centered in the temple in Jerusalem)—under the control of a Roman military governor or prefect (Pilate in the time of Jesus)—to maintain order and collect the Roman tribute (indirect rule). This political situation was new to the Galileans, and the priestly rulers in Jerusalem who now no longer had direct jurisdiction over Galilee. The priestly aristocracy in Judea—who was responsible for charging and delivering the royal tribute—and Antipas now competed for influence and revenues from the Galilean peasantry. To keep their base of power (the temple system) intact, the temple elite added to the Roman tribute tithes, offerings and contributions during the festivals. Even the peasants of Galilee were subject to this demand, although they lived outside the jurisdiction of Judea. Peasants that could not pay were labeled unclean. Although the land (ideologically speaking) belonged to peasant smallholders who inherited their ancestral plots, the priestly elite also added peasant's land to their estates by investing in loans.

The Galilean peasantry thus was burdened by at least three levels of taxation: the Roman tribute, taxes to Herod (and the local elite), and the

things: the annual tribute to the emperor and the agricultural and other offerings for the temple ensured that the highest authority's claims were clearly established, and as the immediate representatives of this twin authority, client rulers and Jerusalem priests, were entitled to their share by association." Freyne, *A Jewish Galilean*, 18–19. The cities, according to Sawicki, *Crossing Galilee*, 115, enabled the Romans to "interrupt the traditional local cycles of production and consumption."

86. The Roman tribute consisted of two basic forms: the *tributum soli* (land tax) and the *tributum capitis* (poll tax), and nonpayment of these taxes were seen as rebellion against Rome.

87. Freyne, *Galilee from Alexander the Great to Hadrian*, 191–92.

tithes[88] and offerings[89] demanded by the high priesthood situated at the temple in Jerusalem, the centralized economic institution that dominated the economy of Judea. Because of the impact of lean years and the different layers of taxation, peasant farmers and village communities began to disintegrate.[90] If one adds to these religious dues the different levels of Roman taxation and the provision of seeds for the following season, at best mere subsistence farming was possible.[91] Peasant farmers fell into debt, "often to Herodian officials who controlled stores of food."[92] The Roman and Herodian elite, as well as the temple aristocracy, used this dire situation of the peasantry to enhance their income by exploiting the peasant's need to pay the expected tribute, taxes, tithes, and curtail their debt.[93] The Herodian elite and temple aristocracy—using the surplus funds created by resources coming from diaspora communities (the temple tax) and from local revenues—made loans[94] (with and interest rate up to 20 percent) to peasants in debt who struggled to survive and feed their families after meeting their obligations for tribute, tithes, offerings and sacrifices. The income accumulated from these loans not only increased the wealth of the elite, but also enabled them to foreclose on loans that could not be paid.[95] Normally, this meant that peasants lost their land, and in a downward spiral became tenants, day laborers and beggars.

88. Priestly caste status carried the right to agricultural tithes. This was a steady income for the priestly elite "sheltered from Roman taxation and protected from erosion by inflation of the coinage." Sawicki, *Crossing Galilee*, 125.

89. The offerings that was due to the temple inter alia included the *terumah* (a heave offering), a specific portion of the harvest (one–fortieth to one eightieth) which had to be given to the priests (Freyne, *Galilee from Alexander the Great to Hadrian*, 278).

90. This changing economic situation of the peasantry also brought about a change of values among the ever-increasing group of deprived and exploited small landowners. The system of tithes and other agricultural offerings, devised to underline Yahweh's ultimate ownership of the land and a mode of production based on trust in Yahweh's seasonal blessings to Israel, was replaced by "one driven by greed, opulence and exploitation, inevitably fractured the tenuous connection between land, people and religious concerns. Elites, on the other hand, had no particular attachment to the land other than to exploit its resources to the maximum, literally and metaphorically draining it" (Freyne, *A Jewish Galilean*, 46).

91. Freyne, *Galilee from Alexander the Great to Hadrian*, 186.

92. Horsley, *Covenant Economics*, 89.

93. Applebaum, "Judaea as a Roman Province," 370.

94. The mention of the *trapezai* ("money changers") and *archeai* ("moneylenders") at Sepphoris is evidence of the harsh realities of peasant economics in Galilee. Freyne, *Galilee from Alexander the Great to Hadrian*, 181.

95. Goodman, *Ruling Class of Judaea*.

Archeological evidence and passages in Josephus indicate that during Antipas's reign more and more of the land in the Judean hill country was transformed into large estates owned by absentee landlords and worked by tenants—who most probably worked the land they previously owned[96]— and day laborers (who most probably had also lost their land). When it is taken into consideration that the great plain just south of Galilee had long ago become royal land (owned by the Herodian elite or retired Roman soldiers), it is clear that less and less land in Judea belonged to the peasantry. [97]

In Galilee the situation was the same. While most of the peasantry still lived on their ancestral inherited land, spiraling debt was only a step away from lad loss.[98] It also seems that most of the cultivatable land in Galilee was owned by the elite, as recent research on the Parables of Enoch (1 En. 37–71)—written in Galilee[99] in the time of Herod the Great or in the

96. Many tenants, who originally may have been owners of their own plots, in a bad year bartered their land in order to pay tribute, taxes and tithes; in order to feed their families or buy grain for the following season. "Once that had happened there was never any possibility of their retrieving the situation, and they were fortunate indeed if they could survive as tenants on what was formerly their own land." Freyne, *Galilee from Alexander the Great to Hadrian*, 195.

97. According to Applebaum, several factors contributed to a considerable increase of the tenant class in Judea in the Herodian period. The displacement of Jewish population from the coastal plain and Transjordan under Pompey converted large numbers of Jewish cultivators into landless laborers. In addition to this, Herod's numerous confiscations of the property of his political opponents (e.g., the Hasmoneans) must have increased the areas of royal-owned land. Applebaum, "Judaea as a Roman Province," 373–74. See Josephus, *Ant* 16.155; 17.147, 305–307. The owners of these large rural properties most probably were "the councilors and upper religious hierarchy in Jerusalem," and elites residing in other urban centers. Ibid., 372. Herod Antipas owned private estates in the region where he built his new city Tiberias. See Josephus, *Ant*. 18:37. Herod Antipas most probably also owned estates in the region of Sepphoris. Freyne, *Galilee from Alexander the Great to Hadrian*, 165. No direct information is available on Herod the Great's handling of the land situation in Galilee, but it can be presumed that the pattern was similar to other parts of the country; "the best lands became part of the royal possessions, either through confiscation or because their owners could not meet the heavy taxes which Herod exacted from the country people." (Ibid., 164.

98. Horsley, *Covenant Economics*, 91.

99. This provenance for 1 Enoch 37–71 is based on the Jewish character of the Book of the Parables, the description of the elite owning the land, and the peasantry (previous landlords) demoted to tenant farmers. As Charlesworth put it, "Most scholars will have little difficulty in perceiving that the *Parables of Enoch* is an anti-Herodian polemic." Charlesworth, "Date and Provenience," 53. Aviam is very specific in postulating a provenance for the Book of the Parables. Based on the geographical references in 1 Enoch 6.6 and 13.7, the botanical references in 1 Enoch 19.19; 24.1; 31.2; and 32.4, and the historical reference in 1 Enoch 56.5 that connects with the geographical references in 1 Enoch 46.8, Aviam suggests Migdal in Lower Galilee as place of writing 1 Enoch 37–71. Aviam, "Galilean Archeology and Landscape," 159–69.

early decades of the first century[100]—indicates.[101] In the Parables of Enoch there are several references to the future judgment and punishment of the "sinners," the "chosen ones," the "strong," the "kings of the earth," and the "mighty" who possess the "dry land" or "the earth."[102] Based on the cursing of kings in texts such as 1 Kgs 21:10 and 13, Isa 8:21 and Qoh 10:20, and rulers in Exod 22:28, Lev 4:22 and Prov 28:15, the "kings of the earth" referred to in 1 Enoch most probably denote the Roman emperors.[103] The "dry land," Charlesworth argues, refers to the cultivatable land near wet areas of swamps, which was situated in vast areas west of the Kinneret, the low country near the coast, and in the Hulah Valley.[104] "The author of the *Parables of Enoch* laments that he and other Jews labor on such land, while the strong, the sinners, 'eat of the produce of such land.'"[105] According to 1 Enoch 62, these sinners are "the kings, the governors, the high officials, and the landlords,"[106] those who "eat all the produce of crime,"[107] and whose deeds are criminal and oppressive.[108] The oppressed, on the other hand, long to rise, eat and rest.[109] In the end, however, the governors, the high officials, and the landlords will not be saved by their gold and silver.[110] Clearly, this picture depicts the situation in Galilee in the time of the Herods.

From this it is clear that, also in Galilee, vast amounts of cultivatable land was owned by the elite and worked by the peasantry for the benefit of kings, governors, high officials and landlords; a picture that fits the description of the political, social and economic situation in Galilee in first-century

100. Charlesworth bases this dating of the Parables of Enoch on five arguments: the insignificance of the fact that no fragment of 1 Enoch has been identified among the fragments found in the Qumran caves, the late composition of the Parables of Enoch within 1 Enoch in Galilee, the fact that it was not composed in Qumran, the curse on the landowners in 1 Enoch 62, and the reference to the Parthian invasion in 1 Enoch 56. This invasion, described by Josephus in *Ant.* 14.333–344, ended in 40 BCE, the same year when Herod was declared by the Roman senate as "king of the Jews." Charlesworth, "Date and Provenience," 43–49.

101. Charlesworth and Bock, *Parables of Enoch.*

102. 1 Enoch 38.1, 3–5; 40.8; 41.2, 8; 45.2, 5; 46.4–6; 48.8; 53.2; 54.1–2; 55.4; 62.1–6, 9; 63.1–10; 63.12; 67.8.

103. Charlesworth, "Date and Provenience," 48.

104. Ibid., 49.

105. Ibid.

106. 1 Enoch 62.1, 3, 6. Translations in this come from Knibb, *Ethiopic Book of Enoch*, vol. 2.

107. 1 Enoch 53.2.

108. 1 Enoch 53.2; 54.62.

109. 1 Enoch 62:14.

110. 1 Enoch 53.28.

Palestine. Galilee thus did not escape the advancing aggrandizement of the Herodian dynasty as more and more of the best land of Palestine fell into the hands of the ruling elite. [111]

The many silos containing grain for the Roman tribute found in upper Galilee (in Gischala),[112] in the south at Beth Shearim,[113] as well as the vaults in the lower city of Sepphoris, are evidence of the economic structure in which Rome demanded and the peasant farmers rendered up tribute and taxes.[114] Roads were needed to transport these goods. Very soon after being appointed as client king of Rome in Judea, Herod the Great built a port, Caesarea-Maritima, and roads to support trade and the transport of goods (e.g., wheat) to Rome. According to Sawicki, roads had networked Galilee from time immemorial, but the Romans resurfaced and graded existing roads to better accommodate wagons to transport goods and tribute more efficiently.[115] Where necessary, new roads were built to connect Galilee to world markets. The covert function of these roads was to siphon wealth out of the land. As such, roads symbolized Roman occupation, imperial economic pressure and the exploitation of the peasantry who produced the goods that were transported on Roman roads.[116]

This then, was the situation of the peasantry in Palestine in the time of Jesus. Taxation was exploitative—an act of domination that subordinated the peasants against their will. Rome assessed its tribute and then left Antipas and the temple elite free to exploit the land to whatever degree they saw fit.[117] Food and debt were a constant problem. Rising indebtedness led to the loss of land (which had been the base of the peasant's subsistence), as well as the loss of the peasant's place in the traditional social structure. By using unconventional means, the elite in Galilee and Judea became the controlling force of most private land. Small peasant farmers were increas-

---

111. Applebaum summarizes the situation of the peasantry at the beginning of the first century as follows: "The Jewish peasant at the end of the last century BC was suffering the effects of expropriation from the coastal plain, Samaria and Transjordan; he had been afflicted by a succession of wars and arbitrary impositions, was desperately short of land and reserve capital, and continued to experience grueling taxation coupled, where a considerable section of his class was concerned, with an oppressive and humiliating tenurial regime exacerbated by debt and the non–Jewish or pro–Roman attitude of its administrators and landlords." Applebaum, "Judaea as a Roman Province," 378.

112. Josephus, *Life* 71.

113. Josephus, *Life* 118–119.

114. The parable of the Rich Fool (Luke 12:16–20) depicts such storage capacity.

115. Sawicki, *Crossing Galilee*, 31, 112.

116. Ibid., 117–18, 132, 178.

117. For a detailed breakdown of these three levels of taxation, see Hanson and Oakman, *Palestine in the Time of Jesus*, 106–10.

ingly replaced by large estates owned by the powerful and exploiting elite. In Galilee, especially, agriculture was commercialized; which in turn lead to a monetization of the economy. All this left the peasantry "on the edge of destitution, and often over the edge."[118]

The Central Theme of Jesus' Parables: The Nonapocalyptic Kingdom of God

There is consensus in parable scholarship that the kingdom of God was at the center of Jesus' message.[119] What Jesus meant by the kingdom of God, however, is not a point of consensus. Based on the paradigm created by Weiss and Schweitzer (and Dodd) at the turn of the twentieth century, most parable scholars in the twentieth century held the position that Jesus, when he used this term, proclaimed an apocalyptic eschatology (imminent eschatology).[120] Jesus thus had the expectation that the kingdom would

118. Borg, *Jesus*, 227. Chancey gives the following summary of the economic pressures on the peasantry in first-century Palestine that is worth noting: "These economic pressures are, in turn, often associated with the actions of Herod Antipas, particularly his rebuilding of Sepphoris and his foundation of Tiberias . . . Antipas' creation of new cities placed new strains on the peasant majority of Galilee. The cities required a reorientation of the distribution of agricultural products; whereas farmers had once focused on growing crops for their own subsistence, they now had to produce surplus crops to feed the cities. Taxes and rents imposed by the parasitic cities and their elites combined to facilitate this transfer of foodstuffs. But taxes served not only to feed the cities; tax increases would have been necessary just to build them. The cities served as focal points for the collection of taxes not only for Antipas but also for Rome. To pay their taxes, peasants had to sell off their surplus for coins, and Antipas minted bronze coinage for just this purpose, to facilitate payment of taxes. These intertwining policies of taxation and monetization pushed family farmers beyond what they were able to produce, causing them to seek loans from city-based lenders and to sell their lands to city-dwelling estate owners. Some farmers became tenants on what had been their own lands, others were forced to become day laborers, others became artisans and craftsmen, others resorted to begging, and still others turned to social banditry. It is within this context of a debilitating economic crisis that we must place the historical Jesus, with his call for a different type of kingdom." Chancey, "Disputed Issues," 1–2.

119. Borg, *Jesus*, 165: "God and God's kingdom were at the center of Jesus' life and mission." Hoover, "Gaining and Losing," 18: "The central idea or symbol of Jesus' teaching was the kingdom of God . . . The kingdom is what Jesus' teaching is and is also the goal he was aiming for."

120. This volume follows Crossan's definition of *eschatology*. According to Crossan, Jesus was eschatological but not apocalyptic. This "odd" statement is clarified by Crossan's understanding of eschatology either being apocalyptic or ethical in character: ethical eschatology can be defined as transformative, social, active and durative; while apocalyptic eschatology refers to an eschatology that is destructive, material, passive and instantive. See Crossan, *Birth of Christianity*, 257–92; Borg et al., "Jesus Was Not an

come in the near future by means of a cataclysmic or dramatic intervention by God; this position was recently defended by Allison.[121]

Many scholars no longer support the apocalyptic hypothesis of Weiss and Schweitzer. The undermining of this hypothesis started with the work of Käsemann, who argued that Jesus did not share with John the Baptist a future-oriented, apocalyptic expectation. Jesus rather associated the kingdom of God with his person and preaching. A next beacon on the road was the work of Kloppenborg on Q.[122] Kloppenborg identified in Q a layer of wisdom sayings of Jesus (which he calls Q1) that has an absence of apocalypticism. Koester[123] and Kloppenborg, Meyer, Patterson and Steinhauser[124] came to the same conclusion in their work on the Gospel of Thomas and Q by indicating that in Gospel of Thomas an early stage in its development can be identified that also has no apocalyptic references. The interpretation of the parables also added to the demise of the apocalyptic hypothesis. Many parable scholars, following Jülicher, have indicated that the apocalyptic understanding of the parables is bound up with their secondary allegorization. All this has led to the idea that Jesus, when he spoke of the kingdom, did not speak of a future, apocalyptic event "but of the immediate reign of God that is now present in the potential of the human imagination to see the world differently and to act accordingly."[125]

Apocalyptic Prophet," 69.

121. Allison, *Jesus of Nazareth*. Allison bases his understanding of Jesus as an apocalyptic eschatological prophet on five arguments: 1) Many early followers of Jesus thought the eschatological climax to be near (Acts 3:19–21; Rom 13:11; 1 Cor 16:22; Heb 10:37; Jas 5:8; 1 Pet 4:17; Rev 22:20), and Jesus' vision of the future was continuous with his most prominent predecessor (the Baptist) and his most prominent successor (Paul); (2) the resurrection language used in the New Testament is apocalyptic language); (3) the language used in the New Testament to describe the death of Jesus is eschatological language; (4) apocalyptic eschatology was widespread in the first century CE; and (5) several New Testament texts compare Jesus to eschatological figures like John the Baptist, Theudas, and Judas the Galilean. It is clear that Allison locates the apocalyptic expectation of early Christianity in the pre-Easter message of Jesus, while many historical Jesus scholars locate the apocalyptic expectation of early Christianity in the post-Easter community.

122. Kloppenborg, *Formation of Q*.

123. Koester, *Ancient Christian Gospels*.

124. Kloppenborg et al., *Q-Thomas Reader*.

125. Borg et al., "Jesus Was Not an Apocalyptic Prophet," 71. Several scholars define the kingdom in the same manner: "Jesus' Kingdom had been ethical and this-worldly. It was about committing oneself ethically to life and to one's neighbour here and now, in this world, and in the present." Cupitt, "Reforming Christianity," 55. "The kingdom was for the earth, political and religious and involved a transformed world." Borg, *Jesus*, 168. "The kingdom of God was a kingdom of this world. Jesus always talked about God's reign in everyday, mundane terms: he talked about dinner parties, travelers being

A recent study of the term βασιλεία in documented papyri by Bazzana confirms the nonapocalyptic character of the kingdom Jesus proclaimed.[126] Bazzana argues convincingly that Jesus was not the first to use this term. The term is present in four papyri from the Ptolemaic era dated third to first century BCE. In two of these papyri[127] the term βασιλεία is linked to the welfare of subjects; the term "gestures towards a complex theological and political construct, in which the sovereign plays a determinant role as broker of divine benefits to his or her human subjects and as guarantor of natural, as well as social order."[128] This relationship between care and kingship is also evidenced in papyri from the Roman period, beginning at the end of the second century CE.[129] In analyzing passages in Q that refer to the βασιλεία, Bazzana identifies two groups of sayings. The first links with the Hellenistic ideology of care as conveyed by the term, depicting the βασιλεία as satisfying the very basic needs of hunger, poverty, indebtedness, and illness,[130] while the second group of sayings depicts the βασιλεία as a spatial entity.[131] From this analysis, Bazzana concludes, "the figure of Jesus . . . seems to acquire those characters . . . the Hellenistic royal ideology used to attribute to sovereigns in their role as brokers of divine benefits and benefactors of humankind."[132] This conclusion of Bazzana links Jesus' use of the term to the Hellenistic and Ptolemaic use of the term: to the welfare of others and care for the hungry, poor, and indebted. This, clearly, relates to a present βασιλεία, the immediate reign of God that is now present.

Miller is thus correct when he states that the question as to whether Jesus was an apocalyptic prophet "may well be the single most important one about him because it goes directly to the essential nature of his message and mission."[133] If the kingdom of God is apocalyptic, the parables of the mustard seed and the leaven, for example, are growth stories. If not,

---

mugged, truant sons, laborers in a vineyard, the hungry and tearful." Funk, "Jesus of Nazareth." "All the signs are that he [Jesus] regarded his own work not simply as pointing forward to this kingdom but actually as inaugurating it: his actions only makes sense if he believed that through them the kingdom was in some sense present, not simply future. These two cannot be played off against each other." Borg and Wright, *Meaning of Jesus*, 48.

126. Bazzana, "Q Concept of Kingship," 151–68.

127. UPZ I.113 (156 BCE); P.Tor. Choach. 12 (117 BCE).

128. Bazzana, "Q Concept of Kingship," 155.

129. SB XVI 13034; SB XIV 11648. Ibid., 156–59.

130. Q 6:20; 10:9; 11:2; 12:31; 13:18–20.

131. Q 7:28; 11:17–20; 11:52; 13:28; 22:30.

132. Bazzana, "Q Concept of Kingship," 166.

133. Miller, "Introduction," 1.

these parables are "wickedly clever satires of imperial values and religious respectability."[134] Miller's interpretation clearly relates to a nonapocalyptic kingdom here and now, a transformed world, a kingdom "that challenged the kingdoms of this world."[135]

Crossan also understands the phrase "kingdom of God" in terms of the other "kingdoms" present in the time of Jesus.

> To speak of God's "kingdom" is to use a word that is both archaic and patriarchal. What the word focuses on in its original language is best translated as "style of rule" or "ruling style." It ponders how this world would be if God were actually seated down here ruling—as it were—from a human throne. How would the "ruling style" of God differ from that of a human emperor? That is what is at stake in the phrase "kingdom of God."[136]

In comparing John the Baptist's understanding of the kingdom of God (as apocalyptic eschatological) with that of Jesus (as ethical eschatological), Crossan characterizes Jesus' proclamation of the kingdom as present (rather than imminent), collaborative (rather than interventionist), and nonviolent (rather than violent).[137] For Crossan the phrase "kingdom of God" is not about heaven but about earth; it is "always about God's earth itself."[138] Every part of the kingdom proclaimed by Jesus did not point to "the *future soon*, but the *present now* of the kingdom of God."[139] Moreover, Jesus was not just

134. Miller, "Is the Apocalyptic Jesus History," 113.

135. Borg, *Jesus*, 186.

136. Crossan, *The Power of Parable*, 119. Scott prefers the phrase "Empire of God," arguing that the word "kingdom" in English is too vague and ethereal. "The more exact term is 'empire' because of the dominant political reality of the ancient world was the empire. So I prefer to translate this phrase 'the Empire of God.' Empire suggests a stronger, more dominant reality and has the virtue of implying its opposite. The opposite of the Empire of God is the Roman Empire." Scott, "Reappearance of Parables," 99. Scott is correct in arguing that the kingdom proclaimed by Jesus was an alternative to the empire of Rome. It was also, however, an implicit alternative to the "kingdom" of the temple elite. For this reason the phrase "kingdom of God" is preferred in this volume. See also Boucher, *The Parables*, 63–64., who prefers the phrase "reign of God," because the word kingdom suggests a territory or a community. "But the idea is rather that God reigning in our lives as individual and as a society; it is *God's saving act in history.*" Emphasis in the original. Boucher's understanding of the term kingdom is not only theological (the saving acts of God); it also misses the point that Jesus' use of the term indeed was territorial and aimed at a new community.

137. Crossan, *Power of Parable*, 120.

138. Ibid., 124.

139. Ibid., 126; italics original. Crossan bases this interpretation on his interpretation of Luke 17:20–21, Luke 16:16 and *par.*, Luke 11:20 and *par.*, Luke 10:23b–24 and *par.*, Mark 2:19–20 and *par.*, and Mark 1:14b–15 and *par.* Ibid., 125–26.

announcing that God's kingdom was present; he announced that it is "*only present if* and *when* it is accepted, entered into, and taken upon oneself."[140] It is from this perspective that the phrase "kingdom of God" in the parables of Jesus the Galilean will be interpreted in this volume.

If it is indeed the case that central theme of Jesus' parables was the nonapocalyptic kingdom of God, this implies that the parables of Jesus are *not stories about God (theocentric) but stories about God's kingdom.*[141] A general tendency among parable scholars is to identify the actors or characters in the parables with God (or Jesus himself).[142] Here are a few examples: In the parable of the Unforgiving Servant (Matt 18:23–34) the king who shows compassion towards a hugely indebted slave is seen as a symbol for God;[143] in the parable of the Prodigal (Luke 15:11–32) the father symbolizes a compassionate God;[144] in the parable of the Tenants (Matt 21:33–39; Mark 12:1–8; Luke 20:9–15 Gos. Thom. 65:1–7) the owner is seen as God and his son as Jesus;[145] and in the parable of the Workers in the Vineyard (Matt 20:1–15) the owner is also interpreted as a symbol for God, and the steward as a symbol for Jesus.[146]

To read the parables from this perspective is to depict a Jesus that made theological statements and told stories about heaven. Jesus had no doctrine of God, made no theological statements, and never used abstract language. "His parables are not stories of God—they are stories about God's estate."[147] Or, as Herzog puts it, "The parables were not earthly stories with heavenly meanings, but earthly stories with heavy meanings."[148] They are stories about "the gory details of how oppression served the interests of a ruling class," exploring how human beings could break the spiral of violence

140. Crossan, *Power of Parable*, 134; italics original.

141. Hultgren, *Parables of Jesus*, 10. The parables are not "thoroughly theological," as Hultgren argues. In the stories Jesus told, realism trumps theology; it is the allegorical interpretations of the evangelists that imported theology into the parables of Jesus. See again Hedrick, *Many Things in Parables*, 39.

142. See, for example, Snodgrass, *Stories with Intent*, 20: "Many parables are 'monarchic'; i.e., they are dominated by the figure of a father, master, or king, who is generally an archetype for God. Some deny that these monarchic figures reference God . . . and render Jesus' parables lame and ineffective."

143. Hultgren, *Parables of Jesus*, 27; Borg, *Jesus*, 177.

144. Hultgren, *Parables of Jesus*, 86; Borg, *Jesus*, 17; Snodgrass, *Stories with Intent*, 128.

145. Bailey, *Jesus through Middle Eastern Eyes*, 425; Wright, *Victory of God*, 178.

146. Hultgren, *Parables of Jesus*, 36; Bailey, *Jesus through Middle Eastern Eyes*, 364; Snodgrass, *Stories with Intent*, 20, 377.

147. Funk, "Jesus of Nazareth," 90.

148. Herzog, *Parables as Subversive Speech*, 3.

and cycle of poverty of an oppressed society created by the power and privilege of the elite (including the temple authorities).[149]

From this perspective, the father in the parable of the Prodigal is a father who subverts the patriarchal system of his day; the story tells how a father—who is part of the kingdom—should treat his prodigal son; it is a story that pictures a totally new understanding of what family entails. The owner in the parable of the Tenants is not God but a patron who treats his clients in a totally different way than was normally the case in the kingdom of Rome. In the parable of the Workers in the Vineyard the owner again is not God but rather a patron who acts in an unexpected manner. In the parable of the Sower, the sower is not God or Jesus but a peasant farmer sowing tilled land. And in the parable of the Unforgiving Servant the king is not God the "heavy," but a king who exercises authority by releasing debt in a way befitting the kingdom of God.[150]

The characters in the parables do not point to God, and the parables do not refer to a heavenly world.[151] The parables point to the kingdom of God; "there is something about the parable as a whole that is like the kingdom of God."[152]

149. Ibid.

150. In this parable God is never "heavy." The moment God is cast outside the parable "we are in a fresh position to understand the irony of Jesus when he speaks of God's domain in terms of a kingdom." If Jesus speaks "ironically of the activity of God as kingdom, he may well mean 'whatever else you think of, do not think of kingdom; think instead of its exact opposite.'" When this happens, the king in the parable of the Unforgiving Servant no longer has divine attributes; he is a mere mortal like the hearers, and we and the hearers no longer feel compelled to automatically "defend his every action as wise, reliable and irreversible." Think then of this king as an elite that usurped their land, much despised by the peasantry. Think then what Jesus wants to say about the way authority should be exercised in the kingdom of God. Beutner, "Mercy Unextended," 36–37. See also Verhoefen, "First Will Be First," 49, on the parable of the Workers in the Vineyard (Matt 20:1–15): "Through many centuries scholars have identified the owner as a God figure . . . the parable is about God's kingdom, not about God. The parable is clearly a response to a question Jesus' audience might have asked regularly: what is the kingdom of God like? Not: what is God like!" According to Verhoefen this is also the case in the parables of the Prodigal and the Samaritan; the figures of the father and the Samaritan are all human beings whose behavior is an example of human behavior in God's kingdom. As such, the parables is about the "breaking down of conventional wisdom, the tearing apart of social barriers, the display of unconditional love for the righteous and sinners alike . . . the breaking-in of God's kingdom." Ibid.

151. Galston, *Embracing the Human Jesus*, 64.

152. McGaughy, "Fiction of the Kingdom," 11.

Jesus' Parables Are Atypical Stories (Comparisons)

Since Jülicher's classification of the parables as similitudes, fables, or example stories the interpretation of the parables based on their classification seems to be a sine qua non for most parable scholars. How the parables should be classified, however, is a matter of considerable disagreement amongparable scholars.[153] This is even the case when parable scholars steer away from classifying the parables and use a broad category like metaphor to describe the parables.[154] The classifying of the parables is a modern construct and is to be considered obsolete. How would a rural audience have heard Jesus' parables? As similitudes, example stories, double indirect extended analogies, double indirect narratives, or single indirect parables? Most probably as none of the above. But, then, how did they hear the parables?

One can start answering this question by looking at the content of Jesus' parables. First of all, Jesus' parables were drawn from the common life experiences of his listeners.[155] The question whether these stories were fictional or not does not really matter.[156] What matters is the question whether the stories Jesus told described behavior that would have been considered by his hearers as typical or not. When one reads the parables of Jesus, it becomes clear that the stories he told described the atypical and unexpected: a man plants a weed-like mustard seed in his garden (thus making it impure) that becomes a bush in which all the birds in the sky nest (instead of nesting in the mighty cedars of Lebanon); a Samaritan becomes the hero when somebody is in dire straits; a patron pays day laborers the same wage in spite of the fact that some worked a full day and some only a few hours; a father atypically does not chastise his prodigal son but welcomes him back; a king (a patron) atypically does not throw one of his servants in jail because he did not want to write of a small debt of one of his other servants (after the king has written of a huge debt of his unforgiving servant); a member of the elite invites the "wrong" people to his feast; an owner does not take up his "right" to kill his tenants because of their violent actions; corruption (leaven) is used as a description for God; and a shepherd leaves ninety-nine

153. See again note 47.

154. Liebenberg, *Language of the Kingdom and Jesus*, 48–166.

155. Dodd, *Parables of the Kingdom*, 5.

156. See Borg, *Jesus*, 151; Crossan, *Power of Parable*, 142. Both these scholars see the parables of Jesus as fictional narratives involving fictional characters. That most of Jesus' indeed were fictional narratives involving fictional characters is most probably the case, but not in all cases. The parable of the Minas (Luke 19:12–27), for example, refers to a historical event in 4 BCE when Archelaus journeyed to Rome to have his kingship over Judea confirmed (see ch. 12).

of his sheep unprotected to go and look for one that is lost instead of turning to violence to make up his loss.

Stories work in one of two ways—"they can either support the world as defined and perceived by the dominant culture, or they subvert that world."[157] Jesus' parables fall in the latter category. His parables cut against the social and religious grain of his day, they went against the expected and acceptable; they directly opposed the way "we do things here." His parables were not "business as usual," but rather surprised and shocked, questioned the status quo, characteristically called for a reversal of roles, and frustrated common expectations.[158] His parables told the story of a different world, of the way things ought to be, of "life as ruled by God's generosity and goodness."[159] They reenvisioned the actual world in wholly unaccustomed ways,[160] and offered hearers an alternative world to the world created by aristocratic society (Rome), privilege and power, tradition and custom, religious authorities, temple ritual and sacred texts.[161] Therefore Jesus' parables can be seen as analyses of the social, political, and economic experiential world of his hearers—analyses that expose the hidden social injustices that were the result of the way rulers of the day wielded their power and privilege.

Not many parable scholars will agree with this characterization of the parables. Hedrick, for example, argues that the parables of Jesus were not designed to lead to a social analysis geared to expose the unjust conditions of the peasant class.[162] *Contra* the point of view of Hedrick, this volume heeds to the call of Jameson[163] not to follow the conventional habit of distinguishing between texts that are social and political and those that are not (e.g., "religious texts" like the parables).[164] This volume takes seriously

157. Scott, *Re-Imagine the World*, 13–14.

158. Laughlin, *Remedial Christianity*, 91; Hoover, "Incredible Creed, Credible Faith," 92, 94; Beutner, "Haunt of Parable, 2"; Scott, "Reappearance of Parables," 15–16, 118.

159. Hoover, "Incredible Creed, Credible Faith," 92.

160. Scott, "Reappearance of Parables," 15–16.

161. Hoover, "Incredible Creed"; Ibid., 98; Borg, *Jesus*, 167.

162. *Contra* Hedrick, *Many Things in Parables*, 75.

163. Jameson, *Political Unconscious*, 19–20.

164. Social systems inter alia consist of social institutions. According to Parsons, *Structure and Process*, the dominant social institutions in almost all societies is (at least) kinship, politics, economics and religion. Of these four institutions, religion "forms the meaning system of a society and, as such, feeds back and forward onto kinship, economic, and political systems, unifying the whole by means of some explicit or implicit ideology." Malina, *Social Gospel of Jesus*, 16. Since the documents of the New Testament antedate the Enlightenment, the authors of these documents did not deal with religion and economics as areas separable from kinship and economics. Instead, in the

"the reality of empire" as "an omnipresent, inescapable, and overwhelming sociopolitical reality"[165] with its concomitant parasitic economic system,[166] which depends on a coercive, fear-inspiring dominion achieved through military conquest and enslavement.[167] By reading the parables "against the grain,"[168] the position is held that the parables of the Galilean Jesus proclaim the kingdom God vis-à-vis the suppressing kingdoms of Rome and the temple elite. Jesus' parables, however, were not only revolutionary; they were doubly revolutionary.[169] Jesus' parables also questioned his hearers' "own cultural assumptions that belittled them, their own participation therein, and their own enforcement of those oppressive mores against their neighbours."[170]

The reenvisioned world depicted in the parables Jesus called the kingdom of God. And because it was called a kingdom, it challenged all other kingdoms, especially the kingdom of Rome (the *pax Romana*)[171] and the kingdom of the temple.[172] In a certain sense, therefore, the parables can be described as "comparisons"[173]—they compare one world with another: that

first-century Mediterranean world kinship and politics determined economics and religion, in the sense that one can only speak of domestic (kinship) religion and political religion, and domestic economy and political economy. This means that in first-century Palestine a "religious" statement in essence also was a "political" statement; to proclaim "the kingdom of God with God's rule imminent is clearly a political statement in which religion is embedded." Malina, *Social Gospel of Jesus*, 94. The parables of Jesus, therefore, are not a mere "religious" texts, simply because "religious" language and "political" language in first-century Palestine were inseparable. Ibid., 16.

165. Segovia, "Biblical Criticism and Postcolonial Studies," 56.

166. De Ste Croix, *Class Struggle in the Ancient Greek World*, 382–83.

167. Parenti, *Assassination of Julius Caesar*, 36.

168. Elliott, *Arrogance of Nations*, 22.

169. The parables did not only challenge the injustice and oppression that Jesus saw as endemic within his own society as result of the power and policies of the Roman and temple elite; the parables also challenged "the militant aspirations of the revolutionaries themselves . . . These things hung together: a society that insisted angrily on its own purity towards outsiders would also maintain sharp social distinctions, and perpetuate economic and other injustices, within itself." Borg and Wright, *Meaning of Jesus*, 36.

170. Bessler-Northcutt, "Learning to See God," 56.

171. See also Borg, *Jesus*, 47: "Jesus' parables were provocative, disturbing and subversive. His parables flowed from, inter alia, his observations of the conditions of peasant life. As an alternative he proclaimed the kingdom of God, a kingdom that was a radical critique of the domination system of his day, it embodied a social vision of how the world would look if God was king, and not Caesar."

172. Scott, *Re-Imagine the World*, 131; Beutner, "Gist from the Liturgist," 17.

173. The word "parable" (*parabole*) is simply a transliteration of the Greek word, which means to "cast (*bole*) alongside (*para*) something else." Hedrick, *Many Things in Parables*, 1. Therefore the parables "employ contrasts." Galston, *Embracing the Human*

is, one kingdom with another kingdom, the kingdom of the *pax Romana* and the kingdom of the temple with the kingdom of God.[174] Therefore, the parables were atypical stories, stories that did not describe what was typical, but what was possible.[175]

The Parables of Jesus and Ethics

Jesus had no ethical system. He did not design a theory of proper behavior, nor did he develop criteria for a moral way of life.[176] The parables of Jesus, however, do make ethical points, albeit they have to be constructed first.[177]

> Jesus thinks in in parables and aphorisms. To discuss Jesus' ethical system is to discuss something that we must first construct. He himself does not discuss ethics. Jesus' ethical system is implied, not stated. It was never conscious with him.[178]

Jesus' "ethics," for example, condemned the use of violence (including the taking part in systemic violence), questioned the so-called importance of status and honor and the labeling of certain peoples as impure,

Jesus, 46.

174. McGaughy, "Fiction of the Kingdom," 7; Scott, *Re-Imagine the World*, 17; Carter, "Matthew's Gospel," 190.

175. Borg and Wright, *Meaning of Jesus*, 40. Jesus announced God's kingdom, "believing that the kingdom was breaking in through his own presence and work, and *summoning other Jews to abandon alternative kingdom visions and join him in his.*" Italics original.

176. Scott, "From Parable to Ethics," 119; Stegemann, "Contextual Ethics of Jesus," 45–60.

177. Galston, *Embracing the Human Jesus*, 64 argues the opposite. Galston, however, contradicts himself. If one looks at his description of what he calls the "five gospels of Jesus" (the gospel of the anonymous self, equilibrium, comedy, nonviolent resistance, and joy), it is clear that he does see specific ethical behavior as part of the message of the parables of Jesus. See ibid., 119–39.

178. Scott, "From Parable to Ethics," 119. Three scholars recently studied the ethics of the historical Jesus from this perspective. Crossan, *Historical Jesus*, 421–22 defines the ministry of Jesus as consisting of free healing and common eating, at once advocating religious and economic egalitarianism and negating hierarchy and exploitative patronal structures. Borg, *New Vision*, 83–92, 128–42, in distinguishing between what he calls a politics of holiness (the temple's exclusion of the so-called impure) and a politics of compassion (Jesus' inclusion of the so-called impure and marginalized), has indicated that ideology has a direct effect on ethical behavior. Wink, *When the Powers Fall*, 7 has studied the ethics of the New Testament through a lens he calls the "Domination System," and typifies Jesus as an egalitarian prophet who repudiated the so-called right of some to lord over other by means of privilege, power, titles, status, honor, and wealth. See Scott, "From Parable to Ethics," 117–18.

and criticized ignorance in those cases where the poor were involved. His parables also advocated the sharing of resources, the practice of general reciprocity, and the release of debt. Therefore, his parables addressed behaviors and attitudes that should either be enacted or avoided.[179]

Where do we have to look for these behaviors and attitudes that Jesus advocated or condemned? In the parables of Jesus as interpreted and applied by the Synoptics (i.e., the parables in their literary context in the Synoptics), or in the parables as Jesus uttered them in a 27–30-CE context in first-century Palestine?[180] This is an important question. The parable of the Friend at Midnight (Luke 11:5–8) can here serve as an example. Does this parable exhort believers to keep on praying, knocking and asking until God answers? Or is it a critique on balanced or negative reciprocity (the accumulation of debt)? And does, or does not, the parable say something about honorable behavior between neighbors? These questions only come into play if the parable is interpreted in its social context of first-century Palestine in 30 CE.[181]

This volume argues that modern readers, when interested in social justice, should consider the possibility that the parables of Jesus do have something to say about personal and social ethics.[182] In his parables Jesus imagined a different world and spoke of a different reality.[183] Jesus' parables unmasked "the pretense of the bogus civility of an oppressive world" and revealed "the fault lines shivering beneath the surface of its moral posing."[184] The kingdom, for Jesus, was this-worldly: it was about the here and now,

---

179. "A good bit of Jesus' 'ethics' recommend behaviors and attitudes aberrant to the business-as-usual of his society." Miller, "Is the Apocalyptic Jesus History?," 107.

180. Linked to the important difference between the literary and social-historical contexts as interpretive framework for the parables of Jesus is another opposing interpretive framework: that of an apocalyptic or nonapocalyptic reading of the parables. The latter framework has serious consequences for the possible ethics that can be inferred from Jesus' parables. When the parables of the Leaven and the Mustard Seed are interpreted as spoken by Jesus as an apocalyptic prophet, these two parables are growth stories. From a nonapocalyptic framework, these two parables question religious respectability and imperial values, indirectly advocating ethical behavior. See Miller, "Is the Apocalyptic Jesus History?," 112–16.

181. See again Hedrick, *Many Things in Parables*, xvi.

182. See also Hoover, "Gaining and Losing," 21.

183. Scott, *Re-Imagine the World*; McGaughy, "Fiction of the Kingdom," 14. See also Levine, *Short Stories by Jesus*, 4.

184. Beutner, "Mercy Unextended," 35.

about his world, about *his* present.[185] His ethics were ad hoc and an integral part of the symbolic moral system of *his* culture.[186]

Ethical behavior, values, or norms inferred from the parables for application in the present should be constructed on the values or norms that arose from Jesus' sociohistorical location, and not the sociohistorical contexts of the evangelists. From the example given above it is clear that when this approach is not taken, we no longer have the values of Jesus in focus, but the values of Jesus as interpreted, applied, or distorted by the theological or ideological interests of the evangelists.[187]

Indeterminacy of the Meaning of the Parables

The meanings of the parables are polyvalent, as can be seen from the allegorization of the parables in the Synoptics, from the different interpretations of the same parable by the different gospel writers, as well as from the differences in interpretation within parable scholarship. Several reasons for the polyvalency of the parables can be given: the inherent structure of the parables, their (fictional) narrative contexts in the gospels, and the problem of constructing the original contexts of the parables.[188]

Parable scholars can more or less be divided into three groups regarding the polyvalency of the parables. For some, the rule of thumb is that anything goes. The parables, they argue, are polyvalent to such an extent that it is impossible to delimit all the possible meanings of one parable to just one possibility. Jesus' parables were essentially open-ended, which means that not even Jesus thought of his parables as having only one specific meaning (as attested to by the allegorical interpretations of the parables in the Synoptics). A second group of scholars argues that the meanings of the parables

185. Cupitt, "Reforming Christianity," 55.

186. Stegemann, "Contextual Ethics of Jesus," 51.

187. According to Snodgrass, *Stories with Intent*, 32, the "original" parables of Jesus "never have sufficient breadth to become the basis of ethical thinking or the authority to instruct the church or those seeking to understand Jesus." The reason for this, he argues, is that any constructed original parable of Jesus is a rewriting thereof. Snodgrass surely misses the point here. It is the parables in the gospels that are rewritings of the earlier uttered parables of Jesus. To use his own words: the parables were placed in "narrative contexts for theological and rhetorical effect," and the words of the parables have been nuanced "to assist the reader in understanding the intent of Jesus, or to emphasize the significance of his teaching." Ibid., 31–32.

188. "We today are in much the same position in commenting on Jesus' parables. We can certainly use anthropology, sociology, history, and archeology to *imagine* how first-century Jewish audiences *might* have responded. But we can never tell how they did in a specific case." Crossan, *Power of Parable*, 133; italics original.

are to be found in their narrative contexts. Although fictional, they are all we have. And since the gospel writers were closer to Jesus than we are, the gospel writers should be trusted and their interpretations accepted as the original intentions of Jesus. These scholars are particularly negative towards any attempt to construct a historical and social context for the parables (e.g., the context of first-century Palestine peasantry). This context, they argue, will never be rich enough to curb the polyvalency of the parables of Jesus.[189]

A third group of parable scholars is of the opinion that a construction of the historical, social, political, and economic circumstances of first-century Palestine does provide a rich enough background to curb at least some of the polyvalency of the parables. Such a construction, combined with a social-scientific approach to reading the parables, seems to be a responsible approach to the parables since it takes into consideration the specific historical and social world (cultural norms) in which the parables originated.[190] This construction, of course, must go hand in hand with a "de-contextualization" of the parables from their narrative contexts in the gospels, as well as a consistent "de-apocalyptization."[191]

Of course, no interpretation of a parable of Jesus "can ever be established with absolute certainty, due to the ambiguous nature of the parables and to the recontextualization nature of the tradition."[192] The above proposed approach, however, at least limits the polyvalency of the parables to a certain extent.

Summary

The focus of this volume will be the parables of the historical Jesus, uttered in his 27–30-CE, first-century Palestinian, social, economic, political, and religious context. We enter a totally different cultural world when reading the parables of Jesus in this context; to dismiss this cultural (and historical) distance can only lead to anachronism and ethnocentrism. To bridge this cultural divide, a culturally sensitive readings of the parables are essential.

189. See, for example Liebenberg, *Language of the Kingdom and Jesus*, 59, 69.

190. "Retrojecting the understanding of the parables into the setting of first-century Roman Palestine, and employing social-scientific perspectives seems to be a responsible hermeneutical cue." Oakman, *Jesus and the Peasants*, 180.

191. Above it was argued that the apocalyptic understanding of the parables went hand in hand with their secondary allegorization. See Borg et al., "Jesus Was Not an Apocalyptic Prophet," 75. This logically implies that the apocalyptic interpretations of the parables of Jesus as found in the Synoptics are later interpretations the parables as uttered by Jesus.

192. Oakman, *Jesus and the Peasants*, 180.

This volume suggests that social-scientific criticism in combination with realistic reading offer the relevant reading scenarios to interpret the social realia evoked by the narrative worlds of the parables. Retrojecting the parables into the setting of first-century Roman Palestine and employing social-scientific perspectives seems to be the responsible hermeneutical approach when interpreting the parables of Jesus. Such an approach at least limits the polyvalency of the parables to a certain extent.

The social context in which Jesus told his parables—first-century Palestine—was that of an advanced agrarian (aristocratic) society. In first-century Palestine power and privilege belonged to two "kingdoms": the kingdom of Rome and the kingdom of the temple. These two "kingdoms" exploited the peasantry to such an extent that they lived at the edge of destitution. Jesus' parables should be understood against this social (cultural, economic, religious, and political) background. In his parables, Jesus offered his hearers a different world than that created by the privilege and power of Rome and by the ruling religious elite. This world Jesus called the kingdom of God: a kingdom that challenged all other kingdoms. Therefore, Jesus' parables can be described as comparisons: atypical stories that envisioned a nonapocalyptical kingdom that reenvisioned the actual (present) world in wholly unaccustomed ways.

The content and rural context of the parables place Jesus among the peasantry. His parables were religious, and therefore political; in essence, the parables were social critiques. Jesus' parables, therefore, were not stories about God, but stories about God's kingdom. His parables, put differently, are the kingdom. Therefore, the parables do make ethical points and can be used as a criterion for personal and social ethics in a postmodern world.

CHAPTER 2

The Sower (Mark 4:3b–8): In the Kingdom Everybody Can Have Enough

T HE INTERPRETATION OF THE parable of the Sower (Mark 4:3b–8) has been approached in the past mostly from an allegorical or theological perspective. In these readings certain specifics of the parable are deemed important to unravel the parable's meaning. Based on this presupposition, the seed is interpreted as a reference to the gospel, the act of sowing presents the proclamation of Jesus, and the different kinds of soil refer to the different kind of hearers of the gospel (seed).

The most prominent interpretation of the parable focuses on the abundant outcome of the harvest (cf. Mark 4:8b). In these readings known agricultural practices in first-century Palestine are used to depict the outcome of the harvest as either realistic or unrealistic. These interpretations are mostly eschatological in character, reading the parable as a parable of growth.

The interpretation of the Sower that follows does not focus on the assumed realistic agricultural practices in first-century Palestine. The focus here are the political, social, and economic realities of the world in which Jesus told the parable. The reading suggests that the parable encouraged its first hearers to align themselves with the kingdom of God and describes what the results of such an alignment will be. In a world of little choice, the parable created a vision of how to cope in an exploitative world.

History of Interpretation

The earliest interpretations of the parable of the Sower, apart from the Synoptics' allegorical interpretation of the parable,[1] are the allegorical

1. See Crossan, *Power of Parable*, 25.

interpretations[2] of the church fathers,[3] the interpretations from the medieval period,[4] and the historical and literal (theological) interpretations of Calvin, Maldonatus, and von Harnack.[5] Interestingly, the main foci of the interpretations of Maldonatus (e.g., the different kinds of soil as response or lack of response to hearing the word), Calvin (the sowing of seed as preaching and the fertility of the soil compared to different kinds of hearing), and von Harnack (the steady growth of the harvest as symbol for the kingdom) are also the focus of almost all later and recent interpretations of the Sower. Apart from a few interpretations that focus on the parable as a whole—either allegorically (i.e., drawing unintended meanings from the parable)[6] or theologically (i.e., reading the parable in terms of later doctrinal

2. For the sake of clarity, Levine's understanding of the difference between parable and allegory will be used in this volume as definition for *allegory*: "A parable requires no external key to explain what its elements mean; an allegory does." Levine, *Short Stories by Jesus*, 7. Based on this definition, allegory would include for example the drawing of unintended meanings from a parable, or the reading of a parable in terms of theological points of view or doctrinal beliefs.

3. In the interpretation of Irenaeus (*Haer.* IV.xxvi.1), the field is a reference to the world and the seed hidden in the field a reference to Christ. Augustine in his *Sermones XXIII* equates the wayside, stony ground and thorny places with the "bad Christians" in the church; and for Chrysostom (*Hom. Matt.* XLIV.1) the focus of the parable is the decision to accept Christ or not. See Kissinger, *History of Interpretation*, 20, 29.

4. Thomas Aquinas sees the parable as a picture of the spiritual life representing a threefold perfection: The seed that yields thirtyfold is the usual or average attainment of perfection, the seed that yield sixtyfold represents the believer who has gone beyond average attainment, and the hundredfold yield symbolizes the believer who has progressed to a stage where a foretaste of ultimate salvation can be experienced. For Bede the seed that do not germinate and bear no or little fruit symbolize the believer who hears a sermon, but because of evil thoughts, evil spirits remove the message from the memory. See Bugge, *Haupt Parabeln Jesu*, 37, 74.

5. For Maldonatus, *A Commentary*, 430–35, the parable focuses on the response or lack of response when hearing God's word. Calvin's interpretation also focuses on the preaching and hearing of the gospel; the preaching of the gospel is like a seed planted and not fruitful everywhere because of the fertility of the soil. See Calvin, *Harmony of the Gospels*, 3:79–80. Von Harnack follows more or less the same interpretation: the parable explains how the kingdom steadily grows when the message of Christ comes to the individual and enters the soul by laying hold of it. Harnack, *What Is Christianity?*, 75.

6. See, for example, the interpretations of Morgan, *Parables and Metaphors*, 40–41; Pentecost, *Parables of Jesus*, 46–48. In Morgan's interpretation the field is the world, the seed is the people invited to become part of the kingdom (the hearers), the sowing is the proclamation of the kingdom, and the soil represents the tribulations, persecutions and temptations people (hearers of the parable) endure. For Pentecost Jesus is the sower, the seed is the Word that will be sown throughout the ages, and the different kinds of soil the varying responses to the sowing of the sower, depending on the preparedness of the hearer. See also Boice, *Parables of Jesus*, 15, who also reads the parable as an allegory: the different soils represent the hardened heart, the shallow heart, the strangled heart,

beliefs)[7]—most scholars focus in their interpretations of the parable on one of the specifics in the parable, namely, the seed (as the gospel), the sowing (as the proclamation of Jesus), the different kinds of soil (the hearing), or the abundant outcome of the harvest.

Scholars who focus on the parable's depiction of the outcome of the harvest read the parable as evidence that Jesus' proclamation and understanding of the kingdom was eschatological in character. Taking eschatology as his cue, Dodd labels the Sower story as a parable of growth: the parable illustrates the coming of the kingdom in the ministry of Jesus under the figure of harvest.[8] In the same vein, Schweitzer understands the parable as an illustration of the constant and gradual unfolding of the kingdom,[9] and Weiss identifies the message of the Sower as the hope of the coming of the kingdom of God, whose fulfilment was at hand in the ministry of Jesus.[10] Jeremias' well-known interpretation also takes as its cue the supposed eschatological content of Jesus' proclamation of the kingdom. In the parable, Jeremias argues, the dawn of the kingdom is compared with a harvest that yields of thirty-, sixty- and one hundredfold that "symbolizes the eschatological overflowing of the divine fullness."[11] Therefore, the parable is an exhortation to converts to examine themselves and test the sincerity of their conversion, and assures Jesus' disciples that what God has begun in his ministry, despite apparent failure, will have ultimate success.[12] Several scholars have taken up Jeremias' interpretation of the Sower as the standard for its interpretation. According to Schippers, Jesus tells the parable to give assurance that the kingdom in future will bear fruit,[13] for Drury the parable is a window looking towards the future consummation of the kingdom,[14] Kistemaker identifies the point of the parable as the assurance of an abundant

---

and the heart open to accept the gospel.

7. Lockyer, *All the Parables*, 174–81, for example, interprets the parable, as Calvin does, from a theological perspective. According to Lockyer, the parable is Trinitarian: God, Jesus and the Holy Spirit are the sower of the Word (seed), and the soil refers respectively to believers as wayside hearers, stony-soil or emotional hearers, thorny-soil hearers, and good-soil hearers. From this perspective, the parable depicts the blessed advantages of receiving, understanding and obeying the Word.

8. Dodd, *Parables of the Kingdom*, 145–47. See also Westermann, *Parables of Jesus*, 186.

9. Schweitzer, *Kingdom of God*, 36.

10. Weiss, *Die Predicht Jesu*, 69.

11. Jeremias, *Parables of Jesus*, 150.

12. Ibid., 79.

13. Schippers, *Gelijkenissen van Jezus*, 20.

14. Drury, *Parables in the Gospels*, 51–52.

(eschatological) harvest despite the farmer's ups and downs,[15] and Lohfink reads the meaning of the parable as "the reign of God which is coming."[16] Crossan, like Dodd, understands the Sower as a parable of growth.[17] With regard to the meaning of the parable, he follows Jeremias' interpretation: the surprise of of the bountiful harvest suggests the future advent of the kingdom. Finally some scholars, although not following Jeremias' interpretation, also come to the same conclusion about the Sower's meaning: Gladden, an adherent of the Social Gospel movement, sees the parable as a description of the orderly development of the kingdom of righteousness in the hearts of people and in the life of society, and Fuchs—who understands the parables as *Sprachereignisse*—reads the parable as a reference to the future harvest or the final reckoning.[18]

Scholars who focus on the seed or the act of sowing in the parable link the act of sowing with Jesus' preaching activity through the allegorical interpretation of the Sower in Mark 4:14–20. For these scholars, the sower in the parable refers to Jesus and the seed to the word (Jesus' message) or the Word (the gospel).[19] Some of these interpretations understand Jesus' preaching within the "standard" eschatological framework of Jeremias,[20] while others emphasize the failure or success of Jesus' ministry of preaching.[21]

When the different kinds of soil are seen as the interpretative key to unlock the meaning of the parable, scholars see the act of hearing and understanding, or the hearing of specific groups, as the focus of the parable. Liebenberg, for example, reads the parable as a metaphor; in the parable sowing is preaching which exhorts that listening is understanding.[22] Several other scholars interpret the parable in the same vein: For Snodgrass the parable, in a nutshell, is a parable about hearing the message of the kingdom,[23]

15. Kistemaker, *Stories Jesus Told*, 37.

16. Lohfink, *Jesus of Nazareth*, 108.

17. Crossan, *In Parables*, 50.

18. Gladden, *Things New and Old*, 4; Fuchs, *Frage nach dem Historischen Jesus*, 428–30.

19. Boucher, *Parables*, 80; Tolbert, *Sowing the Gospel*, 121–22; Marcus, *Mystery of the Kingdom*; Timmer, *Kingdom Equation*, 24; Reid, *Parables for Preachers*, 81.

20. Guelich, *Mark 1–8*, 197.

21. Donahue, *Gospel in Parable*, 34; Boucher, *Parables*, 80; Timmer, *Kingdom Equation*, 24; Reid, *Parables for Preachers*, 82; Luz, *Mt 8–17*, 2:310.

22. Liebenberg, *Language of the Kingdom and Jesus*, 362–363, 370, 375. See also Weder, *Die Gleichnisse Jesu als Metaphern*, 110; Dronsch, "Vom Fruchtbringen," 304; Painter, *Mark's Gospel*, 78–81; Flusser, *Die Rabbinische Gleichnisse*, 385.

23. Snodgrass, *Stories with Intent*, 152.

while others highlight the aspect of hearing and not hearing.[24] Some argue that the "hearing or not hearing" aspect of the parable is directly addressed to the disciples to encourage them to comprehend the teaching of Jesus,[25] to encourage them in spite of their failures,[26] or to assure them that the kingdom is indeed coming.[27]

A few scholars interpret the parable as a parable of the historical Jesus told by Jesus in his sociohistorical context (i.e., not in the literary context of Mark). Cadoux understands the parable as a "parable of vindication" in which Jesus explains his conduct to his disciples and the multitude, and Galston sees the parable as a satirical look at horticulture.[28] The sower is a failure, and his failure is a prelude to an average harvest. From this perspective, the point of the parable is to regard the sower with sympathy. Lambrecht reads the parable as parable of "contrast and confidence"; in the parable Jesus speaks of himself and his messianic work and gives, notwithstanding many failures and hopeless situations, the assurance of an abundant eschatological harvest.[29]

A few minority interpretations of the parable can be noted. Scott reads the parable as representing the miracle of God's activity—the presence of kingdom lies in failure and everydayness.[30] For Garland, the parable explains why Israel rejected Jesus as the Messiah, Wright and Garnet interpret the seed as the remnant of the true Israel that Jesus is sowing in Israel's own land, and Bowker and Evans see the parable as a midrash on Isa 6:9–10.[31]

---

24. Peters, "Vulnerable Promise," 79, 81; Baarslag, *Gelijkenissen des Heeren*, 328; Schottroff, *Parables of Jesus*, 67–68; Kistemaker, *Stories Jesus Told*; Blomberg, *Interpreting the Parables*, 289, 293; Stiller, *Preaching Parables*, 36.

25. Kilgallen, *Twenty Parables*, 22–23.

26. Jones, *Studying the Parables of Jesus*, 195; Edwards, *Gospel according to Mark*, 138.

27. Barclay, *Parables of Jesus*, 23; Hunter, *Interpreting the Parables*, 47, 101–2. Some scholars identify the intended hearers of the parable as the early church or even the Christian believer. According to Hultgren, the parable exhorts the church to be faithful in the proclamation of the word that will have surprising and abundant results. Hultgren, *Parables of Jesus*, 191. Groenewald sees the parable as directed at the modern believer who must sow, independent of the reactions of the different kinds of soil (believers and nonbelievers), while Jones is of the opinion that the parable warns against all that debilitates Christian presence and mission. See Groenewald, *In Gelykenisse Het Hy Geleer*, 28–30; Jones, *Matthean Parables*, 299.

28. Cadoux, *Art and Use*, 138; Galston, *Embracing the Human Jesus*, 80–81.

29. Lambrecht, *Once More Astonished*, 104.

30. Scott, *Hear Then the Parable*, 361–62.

31. Garland, *Reading Matthew*, 144; Wright, *Victory of God*, 230–39; Garnet, "Parable of the Sower," 39–54; Bowker, "Mystery and Parable," 115; Evans, *To See and Not Perceive*, 103.

Bultmann and Linnemann find no original intent in the parable; the original meaning of the parable has been lost, and the allegorical interpretation in Mark 4:13–20 is that of the early church.[32]

From this concise history of the interpretation of the Sower it is clear that most of the interpretations interpret the parable through the lens of realistic agricultural practices in first-century Palestine, focus on some or other individual aspect of the parable, and tend to be allegorical. In this interpretation of the parable a different approach is taken, guided by the following question: what if the parable is interpreted against the political, social, and economic world in which Jesus told the parable? And more specifically, what possible meaning can be inferred from the parable when it is read in terms of power relations, land ownership, and taxes and tithes expected from those who worked the land (extracting the so-called surplus of the land) in the Galilee of Jesus?

Versions and Authenticity

We have four extant versions of the Sower,[33] namely, Mark 4:3–9, Matt 13:3–9; Luke 8:4–8; and Gos. Thom. 9:1–5. A nearly unanimous consensus exists among interpreters of the Sower that Matthew and Luke made use of Mark for their respective versions of the parable.[34] That Matthew and Luke

32. Bultmann, *Synoptic Tradition*, 202; Linnemann, *Parables of Jesus*, 117.

33. Dronsch also list *Agraphon* 220, handed down by Abu Hamid al-Ghazali (a Muslim theologian, jurist, philosopher, and mystic of Persian descent [450–505 AH/1058–1111 CE]) as a possible parallel of the Sower. Dronsch, "Vom Fruchtbringen," 310–11. Except for the obvious differences between *Agraphon* 220 and the extant versions of the Sower, the mere date of the text disqualifies it as a possible parallel for the Sower.

34. The few exceptions to this scholarly consensus are the points of view of Wenham, Nolland, Luz, Funk, Hoover and the Jesus Seminar, and Scott. Wenham argues for a pre-Markan version used by all three Synoptics (thus explaining the differences between the three versions), Nolland is of the opinion that Luke made use of a second source besides Mark (that explains the differences between Mark and Luke), and according to Luz the Matthean and Lukan version used a deutero-Markan reworking (explaining the agreements of Matthew and Luke against Mark). Concerning the latter, only two agreements can be noted, namely "καὶ ἐγένετο ἐν τῷ σπείρειν" (Mark 4:4) and "καὶ ἐν τῷ σπείρειν αὐτὸν" (Matt 13:4; Luke 8:5), and "ὃς ἔχει ὦτα" (Mark 4:9) and "ὁ ἔχων ὦτα" (Matt 13:9; Luke 8:8). These two agreements between Matthew and Luke against Mark hardly make Luz's proposal viable. Funk et al. poses the possibility that Luke's version is based on an independent version of the parable, and Scott supports the possibility that Luke's version is based on Mark and an independent version. See Wenham, "Parable of the Sower," 305; Nolland, *Luke 1—9:20*, 377, 382; Luz, *Mt 8–17*, 2:237; Funk et al., *Five Gospels*, 54; Scott, *Hear Then the Parable*, 350.

are dependent on the Markan version of the parable is clear from the verbal similarities between the three versions, the verbal similarities between Mark and Matthew, the verbal similarities between Mark and Luke, and the minor verbal similarities between Matthew and Luke (against Mark). These verbal agreements can be tabulated as follows:[35]

Mark 4:3–9	Matthew 13:3–9	Luke 8:4–8
[3] ἐξῆλθεν ὁ σπείρων	[3] ἐξῆλθεν ὁ σπείρων	[5] ἐξῆλθεν ὁ σπείρων
[4] καὶ . . . ἐν τῷ σπείρειν	[4] καὶ ἐν τῷ σπείρειν αὐτὸν	καὶ ἐν τῷ σπείρειν αὐτὸν
μὲν ἔπεσεν παρὰ τὴν ὁδόν, καὶ . . . τὰ πετεινά . . . κατέφαγεν	μὲν ἔπεσεν παρὰ τὴν ὁδόν, καὶ . . . τὰ πετεινά κατέφαγεν	μὲν ἔπεσεν παρὰ τὴν ὁδὸν καὶ . . . τὰ πετεινά . . . κατέφαγεν
[5] ἔπεσεν ἐπὶ . . . ὅπου οὐκ εἶχεν γῆν πολλήν, καὶ εὐθὺς ἐξανέτειλεν διὰ τὸ μὴ ἔχειν βάθος γῆς [6] ἐκαυματίσθη καὶ διὰ τὸ μὴ ἔχειν ῥίζαν ἐξηράνθη	[5] ἔπεσεν ἐπὶ . . . ὅπου οὐκ εἶχεν γῆν πολλήν, καὶ εὐθέως ἐξανέτειλεν διὰ τὸ μὴ ἔχειν βάθος γῆς· [6] καυματίσθη καὶ διὰ τὸ μὴ ἔχειν ῥίζαν ἐξηράνθη	
[7] ἔπεσεν τὰς ἀκάνθας, καὶ ἀνέβησαν αἱ ἄκανθαι καὶ αὐτό	[7] ἔπεσεν τὰς ἀκάνθας, καὶ ἀνέβησαν αἱ ἄκανθαι καὶ	[7] ἔπεσεν αἱ ἄκανθαι αὐτό
[8] ἄλλα ἔπεσεν εἰς τὴν γῆν τὴν καλὴν καὶ ἐδίδου καρπὸν	[8] ἄλλα ἔπεσεν εἰς τὴν γῆν τὴν καλὴν καὶ ἐδίδου καρπόν [9] ὁ ἔχων	[8] ἔπεσεν εἰς τὴν γῆν τὴν ὁ ἔχων
[9] ὦτα ἀκούειν ἀκουέτω	ὦτα ἀκουέτω	ὦτα ἀκούειν ἀκουέτω

There are also differences between the three synoptic versions. Mark, for example, refers to the first two seeds planted in the singular (ἐν τῷ σπείρειν in Mark 4:4 and ἄλλο in Mark 4:7); to the seeds that fall in the good soil (here Mark uses the plural ἄλλα; Mark 8:8) he adds "ἀναβαίνοντα καὶ αὐξανόμενα καὶ ἔφερεν" (Mark 8:8), and the seeds that fall in the good soil

35. In the above table the agreements between all three versions are given in the normal font, the agreements between Mark and Matthew are underlined, the agreements between Mark and Luke are italicized in bold, and those between Matthew and Luke are italicized.

produce a yield of thirty-, sixty- and one hundredfold. In Matthew all the seeds planted are referred to in the plural (see ἃ μὲν ἔπεσεν in Matt 13:4, and ἄλλα in Matt 13:4 and 7), and the yield of the seed that falls in the good soil is reported in a reversed order to Mark (a hundred-, sixty- and thirtyfold). Luke has the seed sown on the road trampled on, the second and third seed sown are described as ἕτερον (another; Luke 8:6, 7), and the seed that fell in the good soil produced a yield of a hundredfold (Luke 8:8).[36]

In spite of these differences, the verbal similarities between the three synoptic versions indicate that Matthew and Luke made use of Mark's version.[37] Mark, therefore, can be considered as the earliest version of the three Synoptics. Also, if one considers the possibility that Mark 4:9 was redactionally added by Mark (see below), and then taken over in Matt 13:8 and Luke 8:8, it strengthens the possibility that Matthew and Luke used the Markan version as basis for their respective versions.

But what about the Thomasine version?[38] Most scholars dismiss the Thomasine version of the Sower as the possible earliest or original version of the parable. Marcus, Henaut, and Hultgren see Gos. Thom. 9:1–5 as a reworking of Mark,[39] while others dismiss the Thomasine version as the earliest form of the parable because of its "gnostic" features.[40]

---

36. For a detailed description of the differences between the three synoptic versions of the parable, see Hultgren, *Parables of Jesus*, 183–85; Snodgrass, *Stories with Intent*, 150–51.

37. Also see Marshall, *Gospel of Luke*, 318; Fitzmyer, *Gospel according to Luke*, 2:700; Hultgren, *Parables of Jesus*, 183, who hold the same view.

38. Funk et al., *Five Gospels*, 478, offer the following Greek translation of the Gos. Thom. 9:1–5 from the Coptic: "Jesus said, Look the sower went out, took a handful (of seeds), and scattered (them). Some fell on the road; the birds came and gathered them. Others fell on rock, and they didn't take root in the soil and didn't produce heads of grain. Others fell on thorns and they choked the seeds and worms ate them. And others fell on good soil, and it produced a good crop: it yielded sixty per measure and one hundred twenty per measure."

39. Marcus, *Mystery of the Kingdom*, 33; Henaut, *Oral Tradition and the Gospels*, 226–232; Hultgren, *Parables of Jesus*, 184.

40. According to Crossan, the Thomasine version "read and understood [the parable] as depicting the failures and successes of true gnosis." Crossan, *In Parables*, 42–44. Kistemaker sees the "Gnostic mold" of the parable in the Gospel of Thomas 9 in the one hundred twenty-fold that is yielded by the seed sown in good soil; the number 120 was seen by gnostics as the number of perfection. Kistemaker, *Stories Jesus Told*, 237 n. 20. Blomberg, in following Schrage, depicts Gos. Thom. 9:1–5 as a free gnostic interpretation of Mark. Blomberg, *Interpreting the Parables*, 288. Peters interprets the expression "up to heaven" in the Gos. Thom. 9:3 and 9:5 as reflecting the "gnostic conceptual framework of the document." Peters, "Vulnerable Promise," 70–71. This interpretation of Peters is based on the translation of Thomas from the Coptic by Messrs. Brill of Leiden, which reads as follows: "Jesus said: Behold, the sower went forth, he

Mark's version of the parable is most probably the extant version that is the closest to the layer of the historical Jesus tradition. The original structure of the parable most probably was triadic (three instances of sowing and failure—consisting of three phrases each—contrasted with three successful yields), and is the best preserved by Mark. Mark also left the probable original conclusion of the parable unaltered.[41] The repeated Semitism in Mark 4:7 (καὶ ἀνέβησαν αἱ ἄκανθαι καὶ συνέπνιξαν αὐτό, καὶ καρπὸν οὐκ ἔδωκεν) and Mark 4:8 (καὶ ἐδίδου καρπὸν ἀναβαίνοντα καὶ αὐξανόμενα) also seems to point to Mark as most probably being the earliest extant version of the parable.[42]

Most scholars, when interpreting the parable, simply assume that the Sower is an authentic parable of the historical Jesus, while others explicitly state its authenticity, albeit for different reasons. For Scott, "Mark's thirty, sixty and hundredfold lack both symmetry and logical closure," indicating authenticity.[43] Crossan emphasizes the paratactic nature of the parable and the folkloric contrast between three varying degrees of wasted seed (road, rocks, and thorns) and three varying degrees of fruitful seed (thirty, sixty, and a hundred), which, he argues, indicates authenticity.[44] Boucher sees the realism of the parable (e.g., the method of sowing, and sowing that precedes plowing), as well as the language of the parable that shows traces of an Aramaic original, as signs of authenticity.[45] Hultgren interprets the abundance of Semitisms as mark of authenticity, and for Marcus the agricultural mo-

---

filled his hand, he cast. Some fell upon the road; the birds came and gathered them. Others fell on the rock, and sent no root down to the earth nor did they sprout any ear up to heaven. And others fell on the thorns; they choked the seed, and the worm ate them. And others fell on the good earth, and brought forth good fruit unto heaven, some sixty-fold and some a hundred and twenty-fold" (http://www.goodnewsinc.net/othbooks/thomas.html/). Recently Patterson et al. have argued convincingly that the Gospel of Thomas is not gnostic. Patterson et al. date the Gospel of Thomas in the last decades of the first century, and place the sayings collection in the gospel within the well-used genre of ancient literature known as *logoi sophon* (sayings of the wise). Rather than being gnostic, Thomas is one of the earlier attempts to read the Jesus tradition through the lens of Middle Platonism. Patterson et al., *Fifth Gospel*, 33–38, 41, 47.

41. Funk et al., *Five Gospels*, 54. Interestingly, this position of Funk et al. is contradicted in their discussion of the Gos. Thom. 9, where they state that "Thomas has preserved . . . the form of the parable of the sower that is closest to the original." Also confusing is the following statement in the same paragraph: "Originally, the yields were probably thirty, sixty, one hundred, as Mark records them, although the doubling of sixty to one hundred and twenty may have been original." Ibid., 478.

42. See also Crossan, *In Parables*, 43.

43. Scott, *Hear Then the Parable*, 350.

44. Crossan, *In Parables*, 43.

45. Boucher, *Parables*, 80. See also Lambrecht, *Once More Astonished*, 98.

tive and obscurity point to authenticity.[46] Finally, scholars like Klauck and Brouwer, who read the parable through an eschatological lens, also deem the parable to be authentic.[47] According to Klauck, the eschatological slant in the parable fits only with Jesus, and Brouwer argues that in the parable Jesus, by proclaiming God's rule, is also establishing it; this is an aspect of Jesus' ministry that is typical. Only a few scholars see the parable as not coming from Jesus. Drury, because of the parable's interpretation in Mark 4:13–20, reads it as a Markan creation, and Carlston renders the parable as not authentic because "Jesus was not concerned with people's hearts."[48]

Integrity

The structure of Mark 4:1–34, that includes the parable of the Sower, is a Markan construct. The redactional hand of Mark in constructing this narrative unit is well documented by several scholars.[49] In delimiting the Sower, as a smaller narrative within Mark 4:1–34, the following are important. First, it is clear that Mark 4:1–2 serve as introduction and geographical setting beside the sea for the teaching in the larger narrative,[50] with Mark 4:33–34 as its conclusion. Second, Mark 4:10 and Mark 4:33–34 link with Mark 4:2 as structural markers in the larger narrative; in Mark 4:2 Jesus begins to teach in parables, in Mark 4:10 those around him ask him about the parables, and in Mark 4:33–34 it is stated that Jesus taught only in parables as those present were able to hear it (which links with Mark 4:11–12).[51] Mark 4:10–34 most probably is redactionally inserted between Mark 4:9 and Mark 4:35.[52] On the basis of these structural markers and the structure of Mark 4:1–34, the Sower can be delimited as a narrative unit consisting of Mark 4:3–9.

46. Hultgren, *Parables of Jesus*, 189; Marcus, *Mystery of the Kingdom*, 294.

47. Klauck, *Allegorie und Allegorese*, 78; Brouwer, *De Gelijkenissen*, 140.

48. Drury, *Parables in the Gospels*, 55; Carlston, *Parables of the Triple Tradition*, 148.

49. Lambrecht and Dewey identify a five-part chiasmus in Mark 4:1–34, namely A (4:1–2a), B (4:2b–20), C (4:21–25), B' (4:26–32) and A' (4:33–34). Lambrecht, *Once More Astonished*, 86–87; Dewey, *Markan Public Debate*, 150. Snodgrass and Donahue identify a seven-part chiasmus, demarcated as A (4:1–2), B (4:3–9), C (4:10–12), D (4:13–20), C' (4:21–25), B' (4:26–32) and A' (4:33–34). Snodgrass, *Stories with Intent*, 157; Donahue, *Gospel in Parable*, 29. For a discussion of the possible pre-Markan traditions used by Mark to construct Mark 4:1–34, see Jeremias, *Parables of Jesus*, 13–18.

50. See Lambrecht, *Once More Astonished*, 90, for a discussion of Mark 4:1–2 as a Markan addition.

51. Jeremias considers Mark 4:11–12 as pre-Markan ("a very early tradition"), stemming from a Palestinian tradition. Jeremias, *Parables of Jesus*, 15.

52. Snodgrass, *Stories with Intent*, 152.

Mark starts the parable of the Sower in Mark 4:3a (as a second introduction to the parable) with Ἀκούετε; (Listen!), the only time a parable of
Jesus is introduced in this manner.[53] Mark 4:3a is thus most probably redactional. This possibility is confirmed with Mark 4:9, which serves as conclusion to the parable, when hearing again is the focus. Hearing is also referred
to in Mark 4:12, this time as conclusion to the logion in Mark 4:11–12. The
parable proper thus can be delimited to Mark 4:3b–8.

With regards to the integrity of Mark 4:3b–8, Peters is correct that
since the exact content of the pre-Markan version of the parable is not
known to us, "it is unproductive to speculate on possible Markan modifications to the tradition."[54] Important is that Mark 4:3a–8 has a triadic
structure (three sections in which the seed fails, each section consisting of
three phrases, contrasted with three levels of success); this triadic structure
is characteristic of oral discourse.[55] Following Peters, we can conclude that
"the pre–Markan tradition, utilized by Mark and inherited by Matthew and
Luke, was very similar to what we have in Mark 4:3b–8."[56] Therefore, Mark
4:3b–8 should be considered the version of the parable closest to the layer
of the historical Jesus tradition.

First-Century Agriculture and Realism

In finding a possible meaning of the parable, it is commonplace for interpreters to make use of agricultural arguments to render the parable as a
realistic representation of agricultural practices in first-century Palestine.
When realism is the topic, two aspects of the Sower are normally discussed,
namely the sowing of the sower, and the size of the yield.

The sowing of the sower, as described in the parable, is seen by the
majority of interpreters as a realistic portrayal of ancient farming practice in
first-century Palestine.[57] These scholars' understanding of the realism of the
parable is based on the opinion of Jeremias that in first-century Palestine
sowing preceded plowing.[58] If this indeed was the case, it means that the

53. Hultgren, *Parables of Jesus*, 190.

54. Peters, "Vulnerable Promise," 72.

55. Funk et al., *Five Gospels*, 54.

56. Peters, "Vulnerable Promise," 72.

57. Hunter, *Interpreting the Parables*, 17; Kistemaker, *Stories Jesus Told*, 31; Linnemann, *Parables of Jesus*, 115; Boucher, *Parables*, 80; Stein, *Introduction to the Parables*,
36–37; Scott, *Hear Then the Parable*, 352–53; Blomberg, *Preaching the Parables*, 106;
Snodgrass, *Stories with Intent*, 166–67; Pentecost, *Parables of Jesus*, 46.

58. Jeremias, *Parables of Jesus*, 11, in following Dalman. See also Jeremias,

sower was not careless, reckless or clumsy; he sowed in a way that was normal practice. Jeremias' viewpoint has sparked a meaningless debate about the realism and possible meaning of the parable. White, Drury, and Hultgren question this sequence (arguing for first plowing and then sowing),[59] while Payne argues for both sequences, depending on the season in which the sowing takes place.[60]

The yield described in Mark 4:8 also has attracted too much attention in the history of the interpretation of the parable. Is the size of the yield (thirty-, sixty- and hundredfold) realistic or not? In addition, is Mark describing the yield of individual seeds or the yield of the harvest? Different points of view exist among scholars on these two questions. Those who understand the yield as referring to individual seeds see the yield as normal (indeed prosperous but not exaggerated).[61] Others deem the yield extraordinary and impossible.[62] For some it is a typical example of parabolic hyperbole,[63] and for others an exaggerated figure to emphasize the contrast between the first three soils and the last one.[64]

The reading below argues that the parable indeed is realistic; the realism of the parable, however, should not be sought *in* the parable but *behind* the parable. Assumed first-century Palestinian agricultural aspects and practices should not be the focus when interpreting the parable. The focus, rather, should fall on the realism of the world in which the parable was told.

"Palästinakundliches," 48–53.

59. White, "Parable of the Sower," 300–307; Drury, *Parables in the Gospels*, 56–57; Hultgren, *Parables of Jesus*, 187.

60. Payne, "Order of Sowing and Ploughing," 123–29.

61. Linnemann, *Parables of Jesus*, 117; Oakman, *Jesus and the Economic Questions*, 63–64; Scott, *Hear Then the Parable*, 357; McIver, "One Hundred–Fold Yield," 606–608; Hedrick, *Many Things in Parables*, 43; Schottroff, *Parables of Jesus*, 73; Snodgrass, *Stories with Intent*, 155. Lohfink interprets the thirty-, sixty- and hundredfold yield of the seed that fell in good soil also as realistic, but from a different perspective. According to him, what is involved here is what is called "stocking"; when grain germinates, it first produces only one shoot. At an early stage of the germinating process, the lowermost nodes also push outside shoots that cause the main stem to branch out beneath the earth. Since the normal number of grains per ear is more or less thirty, the thirty-, sixty- and hundredfold simply means that in the first case there was no stocking, in the second case a stocking of two stems took place, and for the hundredfold yield there was a stocking of three stems. The yield described in the parable is thus realistic. Lohfink, *Jesus of Nazareth*, 106–107.

62. Hultgren, *Parables of Jesus*, 187.

63. Malina and Rohrbaugh, *Social-Science Commentary on the Synoptic Gospels*, 160; Stiller, *Preaching Parables*, 39.

64. Blomberg, *Preaching the Parables*, 106; Blomberg, *Interpreting the Parables*, 289.

The Political, Social, and Economic Realities behind the Parable of the Sower[65]

The political, social, and economic realities in which Jesus told his parables, including the parable of the Sower, have been described in chapter 1. With specific reference to the Sower, where a peasant farmer is sowing his land, the following aspects of the political, social, and economic realities of the first-century peasant farmer described in chapter 1 can be reiterated.

Within first-century Palestine, an advanced agrarian society, the elite controlled most of the wealth by controlling and exploiting the land and sea. Local, regional, and imperial elites extracted wealth from the peasantry by taxing the production, distribution, and consumption of goods. The peasantry in first-century Palestine was burdened by at least three levels of taxation: the Roman tribute, taxes to Herod and the local elite, and the tithes and offerings demanded by the temple elite. The Roman tribute consisted of two basic forms: the *tributum soli* (land tax) and the *tributum capitis* (poll tax). The local elite extracted tolls, rents, and customs taxes. To this tribute and taxes the temple elite added tithes, offerings (agricultural and others), sacrifices, and contributions during religious festivals. The tribute, taxes, and tithes extracted from the peasantry came from the so-called surplus of the harvest: goods and labor that previously had been used in villages.

For the peasant farmer it was nearly impossible to meet the obligations for tribute, taxes, and tithes. Above all, the provision of seeds for the following season was also a burden, and bad harvests and lean years were always a possibility. All these factors put the peasant farmer in a situation where, at best, mere subsistence farming was possible. Peasant farmers often fell into debt, took loans to survive, bartered their land in an effort to pay outstanding debts, and normally lost their land as a result of foreclosing. When this happened, peasant farmers became tenants, and in a downward spiral, became day laborers and beggars.[66] The elite, on the other hand, transformed foreclosed land into large estates that focused on commercial farming, and enriched themselves by using former peasant landowners as tenants or day laborers to work their land."

---

65. The framework of the following discussion of the political, social, and economic realities that can be considered as the backdrop of the Sower is based on the work of Horsley. See Horsley, *Social Context of Jesus*, 29–36; Horsley, *Covenant Economics*, 81–91.

66. As example of this downward spiral, see the parables of the Tenants (Gos. Thom. 65), the Vineyard Laborers (Matt 20:1–15), and the Rich Man and Lazarus (Luke 16:19–26).

Reading the Parable

The peasants who owned small plots in Judea and Galilee believed that Yahweh had driven the nations out of Canaan in order to provide Israel with a promised land. The land belonged to Yahweh,[67] and he alone was responsible for deciding who would dwell there. The land thus was given to them by Yahweh,[68] and they had the privilege to work the land as tenants.[69] Yahweh promised that the land will yield its fruit and that there would be no hunger,[70] and as long as they obeyed his commandments, the land would stay in their and their offspring's possession;[71] a land in which they would eat bread without scarcity and would lack nothing.[72] With this belief, the peasant smallholders worked the land—the main crops being wheat, maize, olives, figs and grapes—and were able to support a relatively comfortable lifestyle. Since the "system of tithes and other agricultural offerings had been devised to underline Yahweh's ultimate ownership of the land," the peasantry had no problem with the tithes and offerings dedicated to the temple.[73] Outsiders, however, were now enjoying the fruit of this land. The largest part of the best agricultural land was owned by Romans, Herod Antipas, the veterans of Herod the Great's armies, the Herodians, and the temple elite. The peasantry, on the other hand, who still owned land in most cases, had to be content with a shortage of good cultivatable land, minimal land size, thorns and roads at the edge of small fields, and rocky patches because of shortage of plowland.[74]

Above all, numismatic evidence (read Roman propaganda), especially from the period of Augustus (the so-called *aurea aetas* or golden age), communicated that the land belonged to Caesar, and not to God.[75] On one coin minted by Augustus, the emperor is depicted as a single ear of corn or a grain bundle with three, four, or even six ears of corn.[76] The propaganda of this coin is made clear by the inscription of ΚΑΙΣΑ[ΡΟΣ] located to the right and left of the image; it is the emperor who is identified with the har-

67. See Gen 35:12 and Lev 25:23.

68. See Exod 6:3, 8; Num 33:53; Lev 1:21; and Deut 17:14.

69. See Lev 25:23.

70. See Lev 25:19.

71. See Gen 48:4 and Deut 1:8 and 8:1.

72. See Deut 8:9–10, and Ps 85:12.

73. See Deut 26:2–3. References from Freyne, *Jesus, a Jewish Galilean*, 46.

74. Schottroff, *Parables of Jesus*, 72–73.

75. Weissenrieder, "Didaktik der Bilder," 501.

76. Ibid., 504.

vest, and it is the emperor who feeds his subjects.[77] Another coin, minted by Tiberius (dated 29 CE), depicts an altar from the imperial cult with grain and wine, which indicates that, according to Roman propaganda, the fruit of the land belongs to the rulers of the country.[78]

According to Sawicki, any environment "expresses the terms in which its residents value their world and negotiate their identity. The landscape is also a mindscape."[79] Also, if land is like a text,[80] and embodies certain social realities,[81] what would have been the "mindscape" of the first hearers of the Sower, and what social realities did it communicate? What is the implication in the Sower when, for the peasantry, wheat was the staple diet, as well as the main taxable item? Exactly what we find in the parable of the Sower when not read as a realistic story about farming and harvest in first-century Galilee, but as a realistic depiction of the political, social, and economic situation in the time of Jesus.

When Jesus starts the parable with the phrase "a sower went out to sow," what will happen with the harvest to follow is all too clear in the "mindscape" of the hearers of the parable. Because the elite believe that the harvest belonged to them, tribute will be involved, taxes and rents will have to be paid, and the temple elite will also take their share.[82] Little will be left for the one who is working the land. These, after all, were the social realities of Galilee around 27–30 CE.

As the sower sows, one part of the seed falls on the road (ὃ μὲν ἔπεσεν παρὰ τὴν ὁδόν; Mark 4:4a). Is the sower sowing recklessly? Will he plow after sowing? Has he plowed already? This traditional way of interpreting the parable most probably was not part of the mindscape of the first hearers of the parable. As Jones indicated, using agricultural arguments to define the meaning of the parable told by Jesus is missing the point.[83] The seed that falls on the road symbolizes that part of the harvest where tax, tribute and rents were paid in kind, or where taxes or rents were exacted in money, and

77. Ibid., 504, 506.

78. Ibid., 508.

79. Sawicki, Crossing Galilee, 14.

80. Ibid., 84.

81. Ibid., 86. See in this regard also Brueggemann. "'Land' continually moves back and forth between literal and symbolic intentions . . . A symbolic sense of the term affirms that land is never simply physical dirt but is always physical dirt freighted with social meanings derived from historical experience." Brueggemann, Land, 2.

82. The rate of rents that had to be paid, in Rohrbaugh's estimation, could range from one fourth to one half and even two thirds of the crop. Rohrbaugh, Cross-Cultural Perspective, 27.

83. Jones, Matthean Parables, 289.

where peasants had to make use of roads to transport their goods to local markets to sell to wholesale merchants.[84] Roads, for the peasant farmer, symbolized pressure and exploitation, silos and vaults, trade and markets—aspects that were not part of the mindset of peasants working their land to provide for family and village. Roads, in short, assisted the elite siphoning wealth out of the hands of peasant farmers.[85]

This metaphorical understanding of the part of the harvest that will go to the elite is strengthened by Mark 4:4b, ἦλθεν τὰ πετεινὰ καὶ κατέφαγεν αὐτό (the birds that come and devour the seed). Birds not only were seen as pesky intruders of cultivated lands and the natural enemies of the sown[86] but also served (especially the eagle) as the primary symbol of Roman divine favor and election, Roman military might, and concomitantly Roman imperial ideology.[87] Thus, just as in 1 Kgs 16:3–4 birds are seen as harbingers of evil,[88] so birds spelled evil for the sower. A part of the harvest will be devoured by the elite.[89]

As the sower sows, another part (ἄλλο; Mark 4:5) falls on rocky places. Why? Because in some places in the Galilee the soil merely provided a shallow covering for the rocks underneath that the sower did not know and could not see?[90] Or because a farmer is working the land where the abundance of rocks is the result of the exploitation of the peasantry by the

84. Hopkins, "Rents, Taxes and Trade," 209.

85. Paved Roman imperial roads mostly date from the second century CE. Archeological research done in *The Survey of Western Palestine*, however, indicates that a dense network of tracks, ways and roads covered Roman-period Galilee. "The network was the imprint of everyday travel in the Galilee for trade, some of it from cities like Sepphoris or Tiberias and some from villages like Nazareth or Shikhin. Part of the network is international, but the majority is formed of local trails." Strange, "Galilean Road System," 268–69. If one takes into consideration that Antipas rebuilt Sepphoris from where the peasant farmers and Galilee were taxed and in 17 CE built Tiberias to administer the taxation of the fishing industry around the Sea of Galilee, then the existence of a network of roads between these two cities and villages is noteworthy. If one adds the archeological evidence of vaults in the lower city of Sepphoris, it is indeed possible that for the peasants these roads symbolized the exploitation of the so-called surplus of the harvest. These roads symbolized taxes, and taxes spelled exploitation.

86. Oakman, *Jesus and the Peasants*, 116.

87. Peppard, "Eagle and the Dove," 445–47. See also the parable of the Mustard Seed (Luke 13:18–19), where the birds that come to nest is ironically used as a contra-Roman symbol, plundering the base of Roman taxation. Van Eck, "Mustard Seed," 245.

88. Blomberg, *Preaching the Parables*, 107.

89. This is also the point of view of Herzog, who interprets the predators (birds) in Mark 4:4 (and the weeds in Mark 4:7) as coded symbols for the Herodian aristocrats who exploit the peasantry through taxes. Herzog, *Parables as Subversive Speech*, 193–95.

90. Snodgrass, *Stories with Intent*, 155.

elite who expropriated most of the best land? The latter is most probably the case. In Galilee, vast amounts of cultivatable land was owned by the elite and worked by the peasantry to the benefit of the elite. The peasantry, on the other hand, had to be content with a shortage of good cultivatable land. As Schottroff puts it, "The parable thus documents not an uneconomical method of planting, but the critical economic situation of the people in Palestine at this time, who had to cultivate the tiniest bits of ground, even if they contained rocky areas."[91] Thus, according to the parable, a second part of the harvest is also lost, even before sowing starts. This was life for the peasant in first-century Galilee, looked at from below. Some parts of the harvest that is toiled for will reap no gain; it already belongs to elite.

Yet, another part of the harvest will also have to be given up. When the sower sows, Jesus tells his hearers, a third part (ἄλλο; Mark 4:7) falls among the thorns; The thorns will grow up and choke the seed, it will yield no grain, at least not for the peasant farmer working the land. What is a possible metaphoric reference for the thorns in Mark 4:7? In the Old Testament, thorns commonly describe the wicked.[92] In Num 33:55, for example, the enemies of God's chosen people are described as thorns,[93] in 2 Sam 23:6 thorns are used to describe the godless, and in 4 Esdras 16:77 the wicked—because of their sins and iniquities—are also metaphorically described as thorns. For the hearers of the parable, who were these thorns? Most probably the temple elite who also, in terms of tithes and offerings, claimed their part of the harvest. The fact that a part of the seed falls among thorns thus reveals its inevitable fate: a part of the harvest will grow but will be choked by the temple elite.

But all is not lost. The Sower is not only about what *happens* with the harvest, but also about what *can happen* with the harvest. Many seeds (ἄλλα; Mark 4:8) fall on good soil, grow and produce a crop that yields a harvest of thirty-, sixty- and a hundredfold; a part of the harvest that belongs to the peasant farmer. Why does this part of the seed sown yield such an abundant crop? Because this is what can happen when the harvest is shared with those who also barely live above a level of subsistence. Large parts of the harvest go to Rome, the Herodian and temple elite, but a part is left that has the potential to make the kingdom visible. How can this be done? Oakman suggests one possibility: that the point of the Sower "may have to do less with the harvest than with the untaxed . . . seed available for gleaning."[94] What

91. Schottroff, *Parables of Jesus*, 73.

92. Scott, *Hear Then the Parable*, 354.

93. See also Ps 118:12, and Ezek 2:6.

94. Oakman, *Political Aims of Jesus*, 140.

Oakman implies, if interpreted correctly, is the sharing of that part of the harvest that in the end does belong to the peasant who sowed the land. What is left can be used to support others in need by sharing, by giving to everyone who begs from you (Q 6:30), by not asking for goods taken from you (Q 6:30), by doing to others as you would have them do to you (Q 6:31), and by lending expecting nothing in return (Q 6:35)—in short, by being merciful just as the Father is merciful (Q 6:36). When the leftover yield of the harvest is shared by supporting others in need, the kingdom becomes visible. Therefore, the kingdom is good news to the poor (Luke 4:18), the place where the hungry will have a feast (Q 6:21), where those who weep will laugh (Q 6:21), where bread is provided day by day (Q 11:3), where everyone who asks receives (Q 11:10)—a place where one does not have to worry about what one is going to eat (Q 12:22).

This interpretation of Mark 4:8 resonates with Jesus' saying in Mark 10:29–30: "Truly, I say to you, there is no one who has left house or brothers or sisters or mother or father or children or lands, for my sake and for the gospel, who will not receive a *hundredfold* now in this time, houses and brothers and sisters and mothers and children and lands."[95] This saying promises abundance to those who repented and aligned themselves with the good news of Jesus (Mark 1:15). When this happens, the kingdom of God has arrived.

Concluding Remarks

The parable of the Sower, as a parable of Jesus the Galilean, is neither a parable about the obstacles of farming in first-century Palestine nor a parable about good and bad soils and hearers of the "word." The Sower is a story about life, suffering, power, taxes, tithes and choices; it depicts the everyday life of the peasantry in first-century Galilee. It describes the political, social, and economic situation of its first hearers; invites its hearers to align themselves with the kingdom of God; and describes what the results of the acceptance of this invitation can be. The parable describes the kingdoms of Rome and the temple elite, but also the kingdom of God. In a world with little choice, the parable gives a vision on how to cope in an exploitative world.

95. Italics added. Funk et al. consider this saying, without the additions of "for my sake and for the sake of the good news" (Mark 10:29) and "with persecutions—and in the age to come eternal life" (Mark 10:30)—which are considered as later redactional additions to the text—as an authentic saying of the historical Jesus. Funk et al., *Five Gospels*, 93.

Jesus' first followers knew that there was no escape, no place
to go to get away from the civil and personal evils confronting
them. They had to figure out how to live in a landscape compro-
mised by colonial oppressions. They would seek and find God's
kingdom precisely in the midst of that.[96]

In the Sower, Jesus tells his hearers how to find and live the kingdom in
a world where imperial coins depict those in power as the ones who own the
harvest and feed their subjects. In the end, the harvest belongs to God; God
is in control of the harvest when it is shared with others. When it is shared,
everyone will have enough and receive "a hundredfold."

Therefore, the Sower envisions a different, and possible, reality for its
hearers. This is typical of all the parables of Jesus. "Unlike an allegory, a
parable asks the reader or hearer to imagine a differently organized world
with different set values. The aim of the parable is to awaken the hearer in
this present world to an altered experience of reality."[97]

Bernard B. Scott argues that the distinctive voice of Jesus can be heard
in the parables of the Leaven (Q 13:20–21; *par.* Gos. Thom. 96), the Empty
Jar (Gos. Thom. 97), and the Samaritan (Luke 10:30–35). The Leaven is a
vehicle and metaphor for the kingdom[98] and redefines the divine; the divine is identified with the unclean, with a kingdom where the unclean and
marginalized are welcome (e.g., note Jesus' association with outcasts, lepers
and sinners). Like the Leaven, the Empty Jar identifies the kingdom with the
marginalized, the female, and the unclean, and implies that the kingdom is
present in absence. The parable of the Samaritan, Scott argues, indicates that
in the kingdom the basis for human relationships in an otherwise agonistic
world, is cooperation and sharing, not competition.[99]

In this volume the parable of the Sower is proposed as basis for understanding Jesus' proclamation of the kingdom of God. To understand this
parable is to understand what Jesus meant when he told stories about God's
kingdom—to take one from Jesus' book (Mark 4:13).[100] The kingdom is a
different kingdom than the kingdoms of Rome and the temple elite; it is a
kingdom (a world) in which everybody has enough. In order for everybody

96. Sawicki, *Crossing Galilee*, 155.

97. Galston, *Embracing the Human Jesus*, 80.

98. Scott prefers the term "empire."

99. Scott, *Re-Imagine the World*, 119–34.

100. See also Crossan. "Mark is emphasizing that this single example of the Sower is
a *paradigm* for parables, a model for others. If you understand this one parable, he says,
you will understand all parables. If not, you will not understand any of them." Crossan,
Power of Parable, 19.

to have enough, the kingdom is differently organized and has a different set of values than its two competing kingdoms.

It is a world in which the unclean are invited to share and be filled, in which violence is never an option, in which honor and status have no importance, in which patrons act in surprising and unexpected ways, in which honor lies in the act of releasing debt, in which neighbors should act in terms of general reciprocity: it is a world in which one does not participate in the exploitative actions of the elite. It is a world in which everybody has enough; it is a new way of being in a world riddled with social injustice and the exploitation of the weak.

CHAPTER 3

The Mustard Seed (Q 13:18–19):
A Wild and Chaotic Kingdom Taking Over

T HE HISTORY OF THE interpretation of the Mustard Seed shows that the parable is dominantly interpreted as a parable of growth or contrast, with possible allusions to imagery from the Old Testament. Because of these interpretational lenses, the parable depicts the kingdom of God as an (apocalyptic) eschatological entity: the kingdom starts as something insignificant but becomes something large. In this chapter this "stock" interpretation of the Mustard Seed is questioned. The parable is not a parable of growth or contrast and does not allude to the Old Testament. The parable rather questions religious respectability as understood by the kingdom of the temple, and undermines the imperial interests of the kingdom of Rome. Just like the parable of the Feast (Luke 14:16a–23), the parable Mustard Seed depicts the kingdom subverting or inverting the exploitative social systems of the kingdom of Rome and the temple.

History of Interpretation

The earliest interpretations of the Mustard Seed are the allegorical interpretations of the church fathers. In these interpretations the mustard seed represents the word (the gospel)[1] or Jesus,[2] the land (or garden) represents the

---

1. See Clement of Alexandria (150–215 CE) in *The Paedagogus*, I, Tertullian (*c.* 160–225 CE) in *Adversus Marcionem*, IV, and John Chrysostom (347–407 CE) in his *Homiliae in epistulam ad Hebraeos*, 21. See also *Apostolic Constitutions*, III (written in Syria about 380 CE), in which the mustard seed is described as "the word with a fiery nature." Minority opinions are those of Basil the Great (329–379 CE) and Jerome (347–420 CE). Basil, in his *De Spiritu Sancto*, compares the insignificant mustard seed with the testimony of the martyrs, and Jerome sees in the mustard seed an analogy for the church (*Comm. Matt.* IV.66).

2. Irenaeus (*c.* 115–202 CE), in *Fragments from the Lost Writings of Irenaeus*,

world,[3] the tree the church or heaven, [4] and the birds represent divine angels and lofty souls.[5] The theological interpretations of Luther and Calvin—who, with John Chrysostom, Thomas Aquinas, and John Maldonatus attempted to break away from the allegorical interpretations of the parables—did not succeed in deconstructing the dominant (allegorical) interpretation of the parable. In Luther's interpretation the mustard seed is equated with Christ and the believers with the branches that spread from the mustard bush,[6] and for Calvin the parable serves as an encouragement to those who would shrink back in offense at the lowly beginnings of the gospel.[7]

Since Jülicher's groundbreaking contribution to parable interpretation in the early twentieth century, most parable scholars have moved away from an allegorical interpretation of the parables, focusing on the meaning of the parables in their literary contexts. The more recent history of interpretation of the Mustard Seed is indicative of this shift in focus. Except for a few allegorical interpretations,[8] most focus on the meaning of the Mustard Seed in its literary contexts in the Synoptics (Mark 4:30–32 and *par.*), and are unanimous about the meaning of the parable: the Mustard Seed is a "parable of growth" or a "parable of contrast." Snodgrass' interpretation can be seen as representative of this "received view" of the supposed meaning of the Mustard Seed; the parable depicts the presence of the kingdom in Jesus' ministry and Jesus' expectation of the certain full revelation of the

---

equates the mustard seed with Jesus Christ, who, after his resurrection, sprang up like a big tree that became the shelter for the nations, while Augustine of Hippo (354–430 CE) in his *Contra Faustum Manichaeum*, XII, describes the seed as Christ that takes over the whole world.

3. See Tertullian (*Marc.* IV) and John Chrysostom (*Hom. Heb.* 21; *Hom. Matt.* 46).

4. This is inter alia the interpretation of Clement of Alexandria (*Fragments from the Hypotyposes*, V) and Gregory of Nazianzus (*c.* 329–389/390 CE) in his *Or. Bas.* 42.

5. See Clement of Alexandria, in his *Fragments from the Hypotyposes*, V.

6. Luther, *Luther's Works*, 54:88.

7. Calvin, *Harmony of the Gospels*, 3:79–80.

8. According to Marcus, the birds in the trees refer to the Gentiles; for Bugge the birds represent the nations of the world, and Scharlemann sees in the birds the devil's messengers as part of Satan's tactics referred to in Matt 13:19. Marcus, *Mystery of the Kingdom*, 214; Bugge, *Haupt Parabeln Jesu*, 34–35; Scharlemann, "Leaven and the Mustard Seed," 346. Heil, Keach, Marcus, and Scharlemann equate the sowing of the seed with the proclamation (sowing) of Jesus or God to the people (land), and for Morgan the smallness of the seed refers to the small beginnings of the church. Heil, "Reader-Response," 283–85; Keach, *Exposition of the Parables*, 244; Marcus, *Mystery of the Kingdom*, 213–16; Marcus, *Mark 1–8*, 329, 331; Scharlemann, "Leaven and the Mustard Seed," 346; Morgan, *Parables and Metaphors*, 48–49.

kingdom to come—"like a mustard seed God's kingdom starts as something insignificant but becomes something quite large."[9]

This emphasis on growth or contrast was introduced by Arnot in 1872[10] and since has become part of the dominant interpretation of the Mustard Seed. With these two features of the parable as interpretive lenses, interpreters focus on some or other aspect of growth or contrast in search of the meaning of the parable: Some emphasize the *growth aspect* of the parable,[11] while others emphasize the *contrast* between small beginning and large end.[12] As a subset of these two interpretations, some scholars—when emphasizing the growth aspect of the parable—focus on the *significance of the coming of the kingdom* in due course (the parable's end)[13] or the kingdom's *orderly development*,[14] while others—who emphasize the contrast aspect— see as focus of the parable its *small beginnings*.[15] Because of the dominance of this emphasis, readings of the parable that do not focus on growth or contrast are exceptional, and can be considered minority readings.[16]

9. Snodgrass, *Stories with Intent*, 223. See also, for example, Zimmermann, *Puzzling the Parables of Jesus*, 252.

10. Lockyer, *All the Parables*, 185–86.

11. See Brouwer, *De Gelijkenissen*, 148; Buttrick, *Speaking in Parables*, 75; Dahl, *The Parables of Growth*, 147; Münch, "Gewinnen Oder Verlieren," 333; Perkins, *Hearing the Parables*, 85–88; Westermann, *The Parables of Jesus*, 186.

12. See the interpretations of Carter, "Matthew's Gospel," 181–201; Donahue, *The Gospel in Parable*, 37; France, *The Gospel of Mark*, 216; Jones, *The Matthean Parables*, 327; Kümmel, *Promise and Fulfillment*, 128–131; Lang, *Pictures and Parables*, 78; Mussner, "Das Gleichnis Vom Senfkorn," 128–30; Reid, *Parables for Preachers*, 103; Schippers, *Gelijkenissen van Jezus*, 87–93; Snodgrass, *Stories with Intent*, 221; Stein, *Introduction to the Parables*, 94–95.

13. See, for example, Beasley-Murray, *Jesus and the Kingdom of God*, 123–25; Blomberg, *Preaching the Parables*, 122–24; Capon, *Parables of the Kingdom*, 117; Davies and Allison, *Matthew*, 417; Dodd, *Parables of the Kingdom*, 190–91; Fuchs, *Frage nach dem Historischen Jesus*, 291–92; Gundry, *Matthew*, 230; Hultgren, *Parables of Jesus*, 395, 401; Jüngel, *Paulus und Jesus*, 139–74; [AQ]Kendall, *Complete Guide to the Parables*, 34–41; Kistemaker, *Stories Jesus Told*, 51; Marcus, *Mystery of the Kingdom*, 113; Schweitzer, *The Kingdom of God*, 34; Smith, *Parables of the Synoptic Gospels*, 120; Weiss, *Die Predicht Jesu*, 69; Wierzbicka, *What Did Jesus Mean?*, 278–87.

14. See Baarslag, *Gelijkenissen des Heeren*, 429; Boucher, *Parables*, 67–69; Bruce, *Parabolic Teaching*, 77; Gladden, *Things New and Old*, 3–4; Groenewald, *In Gelykenisse Het Hy Geleer*, 32–38; Hunter, *Interpreting the Parables*, 57; Hunter, *Then and Now*, 45–46; Rauschenbusch, *Gospel for the Social Awakening*, 51–52; Zimmermann, *Puzzling the Parables of Jesus*, 254.

15. For this emphasis in the interpretation of the parable, see especially Brouwer, *De Gelijkenissen*, 148; Dibelius, *Tradition to Gospel*, 255–58; Wills, "The Gospel according to Mark," 68.

16. See, for example, Crossan, *Historical Jesus*, 50; Oakman, *Jesus and the Peasants*, 111–17; Scott, *Hear Then the Parable*, 387; Lambrecht, *Once More Astonished*, 101. A

The second approach that also dominates the interpretation of the Mustard Seed was introduced by Funk in 1973, nearly a hundred years later than Arnot's emphasis on growth and contrast.[17] Funk argues that Jesus in the original version of the parable employed the surprising figure of the mustard seed as a figure of speech for the kingdom. His audience would probably have expected the kingdom to be compared to something great, not something small. As the original parable was passed on in the oral tradition, it came under the influence of two symbols from the Old Testament: the mighty cedar of Lebanon—in the prophetic tradition—as a metaphor for a towering empire (that of Israel under Saul, David, and Solomon; see Ezek 17:22–23) and that of the apocalyptic tree in Dan 4:12 and 20–22. This is the reason, Funk argues, why the synoptic writers changed the image from a plant to a tree. From this perspective, the mustard seed is a parody (satire or burlesque) of the cedar of Lebanon in Ezekiel and the apocalyptic image of Daniel. Funk was not the first scholar who identified possible Old Testament imagery in the Mustard Seed,[18] but he was the first to propose that the "tree" in the Matthean and Lukan versions, as a later addition to the original parable, is a "burlesque" on the two named Old Testament images (*contra* Jeremias and Dodd). Since Funk's reading of the parable, several scholars have followed suit in their interpretations of the Mustard Seed.[19] There are, however, scholars who argue against the Old Testament imagery

---

reading that clearly is a minority reading is that of Cottor, who argues that the smallness of the seed symbolically refers to the secrecy of the mission of the Q-community. See Cottor, "Mustard Seed and Leaven," 45–48.

17. See Funk, "Looking-Glass Tree," 3–9; Funk et al., *Five Gospels*, 59–60.

18. Baarslag, Dodd, Bultmann, and Jeremias, for example, have seen in the birds' dwelling in the tree or plant some Old Testament imaginary present in Isa 10:33—11:1 and 14:4–20; Zech 11:1–2; Judg 9:15; Ezek 17:23; 31:6; Dan 4:12, 21 [LXX]; Pss 37:35–36; and 104:12. See Baarslag, *Gelijkenissen des Heeren*, 425; Bultmann, *Synoptic Tradition*, 179–205; Dodd, *Parables of the Kingdom*, 191; Jeremias, *Parables of Jesus*, 149.

19. Blomberg, *Preaching the Parables*, 122–24; Buttrick, *Speaking in Parables*, 77; Perkins, *Hearing the Parables*, 85–88; Scott, *Re–Imagine the World*, 35–46; Wenham, *The Parables of Jesus*, 53. Taking Funk's interpretation as point of departure, Reid interprets the image of the tree in the parable as follows: Rather than thinking of the coming reign of God as a majestic cedar tree that is imported from Lebanon, Jesus uses the image of a lowly garden herb. God's realm is not a dominating empire, but its power erupts out of its weakness. The mustard plant cannot be eradicated once it infests a field. The parable thus states that God's realm will always overcome antagonistic forces. Reid, *Parables for Preachers*, 104–6. Funk's interpretation of the parable can also clearly be seen in Wills' interpretation when he states: The parable is "satirical and humorous, and highly suggestive: the kingdom is like a scrubby invasive bush!" Funk, "The Gospel according to Mark," 68.

as a later addition to the parable,[20] while others deny any allusion to the Old Testament in the parable.[21]

The history of the interpretation of the Mustard Seed indicates that the parable in almost all cases is interpreted through an eschatological lens. The parable's history of interpretation indicates that it does not really matter if the parable is about growth and not contrast (or vice versa), or if it does refer to the Old Testament or not; in essence all these readings suggest that the Mustard Seed is about the delay of the parousia, about a kingdom still to come, a kingdom only to be consummated in future.[22] Dodd, for example, argues that the parable has nothing to do with growth or contrast, but the capacity of the shrub to afford shelter to the birds of the heavens. Therefore the parable announces that the time has come when the multitudes of Israel, perhaps even of the Gentiles, will flock to the shelter of the tree.[23] Jeremias is also clear on the so-called eschatological intent of the parable: Just as a tall shrub can grow from a small seed, the few followers of Jesus will swell into a mighty host of the people of God in the messianic age, embracing Gentiles.[24] As can be seen from the history of the parable's interpretation,

20. Davies and Allison, *Matthew*, 3:420; Hultgren, *Parables of Jesus*, 396; Marcus, *Mystery of the Kingdom*, 204.

21. These scholars argue that the wording of the parable is not close enough to any text in the Old Testament to identify one text to which allusion is made. See Crossan, *In Parables*, 47; Liebenberg, *Language of the Kingdom and Jesus*, 289–90; Snodgrass, *Stories with Intent*, 224. Crossan, for example, sees these allusions as not explicit or appropriate; if it refers to a tree, it can only refer to Ps 104:12, which refers only to God's loving providence. Crossan, *In Parables*, 46; see also Donahue, *Gospel in Parable*, 37.

22. The focus on growth and Old Testament imagery in the history of the interpretation of the Mustard Seed is most probably the reason why the Thomasine version of the parable has not really received attention by parable scholars. Even in the cases where the Thomasine version is deemed to be the most original, the focus quickly shifts to the synoptic versions. See, for example, Crossan, *In Parables*, 47; Donahue, *Gospel in Parable*, 36; Funk et al., *Five Gospels*, 194. When the Thomasine version, Gos. Thom. 20:1–4, does receive attention it is rendered as a gnosticized version of the parable in the Synoptics. Crossan, for example, sees Thomas' "tilled earth" (Gos. Thom. 20:4) as a "gnostic admonition," while Hultgren argues that the mustard seed represents "the spark of light, the enlightenment that comes to the Gnostic," while the tilled ground refers to "the readiness of the Gnostic to receive it." Crossan, *In Parables*, 49; Hultgren, *Parables of Jesus*, 395. Recent studies, however, have shown that Thomas is not "gnostic" but rather one of the earliest attempts to read the Jesus tradition through the lens of Middle Platonism. Patterson, *Fifth Gospel*, 47.

23. Dodd, *Parables of the Kingdom*, 191.

24. Jeremias, *Parables of Jesus*, 149. According to Jeremias, the eschatological character of the parable is established by the use of κατασκηνοῦν in Mark 4:32, "an eschatological technical term for the incorporation of the Gentiles into the people of God." Ibid., 147. Jeremias bases this interpretation on the occurrence and meaning of κατασκηνοῦν in Joseph and Aseneth 15:7. There is little evidence for this interpretation.

Jeremias' and Dodd's eschatological emphasis is representative of the lens through which the parable is read: The coming of the birds to make their nests in the shade of the large plant is interpreted as an eschatological image of the incorporation of the non-Jews (Gentiles) into the people of God, an image that is sometimes, but not always, based on references to the Old Testament.[25]

Snodgrass is thus correct when he states:

> Despite disagreement over details and over whether the focus is contrast or growth, there is a surprising agreement about the intent of the parable. Here, virtually unquestioned, we hear the voice of Jesus asserting a vital and central element of his eschatology, his understanding of what God was doing to the kingdom in Jesus' own ministry, even if others do not recognize it, and Jesus' expectation of the certain full revelation of the kingdom to come.[26]

The above quote from Snodgrass begs a question about the "surprising agreement about the intent of the parable." Does the supposed eschatological emphasis in the parable represent the voice of Jesus speaking in 27–30 CE among the peasantry somewhere in rural Galilee or at the shores of the Sea of Galilee? Or does the focus on eschatology reflect the Jesus of the Synoptics or, for that matter, the voices of the (modern) interpreters of the parable?

Interestingly, the few scholars who interpret the parable as coming from the historical Jesus, and who try to construct a historical context for the parable, do not refer to an eschatological kingdom. In the Mustard Seed, according to Lambrecht, Jesus reveals the nature of the present kingdom of God,[27] or, as Manson puts it, God's present rule.[28] Scott, in his reading

---

As indicated by Snodgrass, the verb κατασκηνοῦν "is often translated as 'nest' but merely means 'dwell.'" Snodgrass, *Stories with Intent*, 224. See also Louw and Nida, who translate κατασκηνοῦν as "to make a nest (or possibly to find shelter)." Louw and Nida, *Greek–English Lexicon*, 1:71.

25. See Drury, for example, who sees the point of the parable as a reference to the eschatological arrival of the kingdom, and Wenham, who states that the parable looks forward to the time when God's kingdom, inaugurated in Jesus' ministry, will appear. Drury, *Parables in the Gospels*, 86; Wenham, *Parables of Jesus*, 53. See also Kilgallen, Boucher, Fleddermann, and Grässer as representative of the eschatological reading of the parable. Kilgallen, *Twenty Parables*, 72; Boucher, *Parables*, 69; Fleddermann, "Mustard Seed and the Leaven," 233–34; Grässer, *Das Problem der Parusieverzögerung*, 141–43.

26. Snodgrass, *Stories with Intent*, 222.

27. Lambrecht, *Once More Astonished*, 101.

28. Manson, *Sayings of Jesus*, 73.

of the parable, focuses inter alia on the planting of the mustard seed in a garden, which associates Jesus and a present kingdom with uncleanness, which I will show.[29] In the most extensive reading of the Mustard Seed thus far as a parable of the historical Jesus, Oakman also presents a noneschatological reading.[30] In this reading, the mustard seed is accidentally sown in a cultivated field with another crop. (It is so small, it cannot be seen.) The mustard seed grows fast and wild, and quickly overwhelms and takes over the cultivated field.[31] In this reading, the seed and birds are negative symbols in the parable: "As a metaphor for the reign of God, this 'weed' stands over against the basic arrangements of civilization. It threatens the foundation of the edifice in its threat to the cultivated field."[32] Jesus thus likens the kingdom to a harvest-time weed. The presence of the weed makes it possible for the birds to roost and to meet their need for food. For the cultivated field (the exploitative arrangements of Jesus' world as the basic arrangements of civilization), the weed (the kingdom) is not good; it simply takes over. Crossan, in his book on the historical Jesus, follows Oakman's interpretation. The point of the parable is not the contrast between small beginnings and large endings, but that the seed tends to take over, tends to get out of control and to attract unwanted birds; the kingdom is thus like a pungent shrub with dangerous takeover properties.[33]

These interpretations of the Mustard Seed indicate that, *contra* Snodgrass, no "surprising agreement" exists in the interpretation of the parable. This is especially the case when one is interested in the meaning of the parable on the level of the historical Jesus, insofar as it is possible to determine. One persistent problem in parable research that is yet again clear from the history of the interpretation of the Mustard Seed is the indiscriminate way versions of the parables in the Synoptics (and Gospel of Thomas) are frequently ascribed to "Jesus," and not, for example, specifically to the Jesus of Matthew or Luke. Moreover, certain "meanings" of Jesus' parables are sometimes uncritically assumed as *the* meanings, while they suggest certain values and convictions directly opposed to values and convictions of Jesus that can be linked to the earliest layer of the Jesus–tradition.

The latter remark touches the nerve of the history of the interpretation of the Mustard Seed. If one takes as a point of departure that Jesus was (apocalyptic) eschatological in orientation, the parable can be seen as

29. Scott, *Hear Then the Parable*, 387.
30. Oakman, *Jesus and the Peasants*, 111–17.
31. See Oakman, *Political Aims of Jesus*, 140.
32. Oakman, *Jesus and the Peasants*, 116.
33. Crossan, *Historical Jesus*, 278–79.

a parable of growth or even contrast, and the birds that flock to the bush or tree can be understood as the future universal character of a kingdom to come. From this perspective, the parable begs for an eschatological interpretation. However, if one takes as a point of departure the possibility that Jesus in his parables depicted the kingdom as a present reality, then the Mustard Seed cannot be about growth or about the contrast between "beginning" and "end." Then, as Miller has indicated, the Mustard Seed rather leans toward a story that is a clever satire of "religious respectability,"[34] and, added to this, a story that undermines some of the exploitative measures of the Roman occupation of first-century Palestine. From this perspective, the Mustard Seed is a story about the way in which the kingdom of God subverts the kingdom of Caesar and the kingdom of the temple.

Versions and Integrity

We have four extant versions of the Mustard Seed, namely, in the Gos. Thom. 20:1–4; Mark 4:30–32; Matt 13:31–32; and Luke 13:18–19. The Matthean and Lukan versions of the parable most probably stem from Q (Q 13:18–9).[35] Some scholars argue that Mark has the earliest version of the parable,[36] others believe Gos. Thom. 20 is the earliest,[37] while a third group sees Q as representing the earliest version, best preserved by Luke.[38] A fourth point of view is that all the extant versions are 'original', since Jesus

34. Miller, "Is the Apocalyptic Jesus History?," 113.

35. The verbal similarities shared by Matthew and Luke that are not paralleled in Mark indicate that these two versions most probably stem from Q. These similarities include ὁμοία ἐστὶν ἡ βασιλεία (the reign is like) in Matt 13:31 and Luke 13:18, ὃν λαβὼν ἄνθρωπος (a man took) in Matt 13:31 and Luke 13:19 (not in Mark), the mustard seed that becomes a tree (δένδρον) in Matthew 13:32 and Luke 13:19 (omitted from Mark), and the identical wording of ἐν τοῖς κλάδοις αὐτοῦ (in its branches) against Mark. Based on these similarities against Mark, several scholars is of the opinion that the Matthean and Lukan versions stem from Q. See Bultmann, *Synoptic Tradition*, 172; Donahue, *Gospel in Parable*, 36; Hultgren, *Parables of Jesus*, 393; Kloppenborg, *Excavating Q*, 148–51; Lambrecht, *Once More Astonished*, 99; Polag, *Fragmenta Q*, 66; Manson, *Sayings of Jesus*, 123; Streeter, *Four Gospels*, 291.

36. See, for example, Dupont, "Le Couple Parabolique," 340–45; Jones, *Studying the Parables of Jesus*, 84; Klauck, *Allegorie und Allegorese*, 210.

37. See Crossan, *Historical Jesus*, 47; Donahue, *Gospel in Parable*, 37; Funk et al., *Five Gospels*, 194.

38. Dodd, *Parables of the Kingdom*, 191; Fleddermann, "Mustard Seed and the Leaven," 226; Hultgren, *Parables of Jesus*, 400–401; Jülicher, *Gleichnisreden Jesu*, 421; Luz, *Mt 8–17*, 2:231; Scott, *Hear Then the Parable*, 377. Some scholars also attempted to reconstruct the "original parable," but without convincing results. See Fleddermann, "Mustard Seed and the Leaven," 214–217; Hultgren, *Parables of Jesus*, 397–98.

told the parables more than once, especially parables of the kingdom like the Mustard Seed.[39]

A close reading of the four extant versions indicates that the only similarities between the four versions are the kingdom that is compared to a mustard seed (implied in Gospel of Thomas) and the birds (τὰ πετεινὰ) that dwell in what the planted mustard seed turns out to be. Otherwise the four versions differ on almost every detail. In Mark, Matthew and the Gospel of Thomas the mustard seed is the smallest of all seeds. In Mark and Matthew the mustard seed turns into the largest of all garden plants. For Mark, the mustard seed is the smallest seed "on the earth" (not for Matthew), and in Matthew the largest of all garden plants is called a tree (not so in Mark). In the Gospel of Thomas, the mustard seed simply grows into a large plant. Mark and Matthew thus have the "smallest-largest" comparison, and Gospel of Thomas has only the mention of smallness (without largeness). Luke, interestingly, does not have the smallest-largest comparison. The four versions also differ with regards to where, how, and by whom the mustard seed is planted. In the Gospel of Thomas it simply falls (takes root?) on prepared soil, in Mark it is planted in the earth (ἐπὶ τῆς γῆς), in Matthew it is planted by a man in his field (ἐν τῷ ἀγρῷ αὐτοῦ; Gos. Thom., prepared soil?), and in Luke it is, as in Matthew, planted by a man, but in his garden (εἰς κῆπον ἑαυτοῦ). The final outcome of the parable also differs in the four versions. In Mark the mustard seed turns into the largest of all garden plants (μεῖζον πάντων τῶν λαχάνων), with the emphasis on its big branches and their shade in which the birds can dwell or perch (κατασκηνοῦν). Matthew's mustard seed turns into tree (δένδρον), the largest garden plant (μεῖζον πάντων τῶν λαχάνων), with branches in which the birds dwell. In Luke the mustard seed simply turns into a tree (δένδρον), also with branches in which the birds dwell. In the Gospel of Thomas, finally, the mustard seed turns into a large plant (not a garden plant); no reference is made to its branches (as in the three other versions); neither is its shade emphasized (as in Mark), but the large plant is used by the birds for shelter.

According to Snodgrass, these differences between the four versions are

> interesting, but they—apart from the possible significance of the "tree"—do not constitute a difference in meaning. The smallness of the seed is mentioned in Mark and Matthew *and assumed in Luke*, and whether it is sown *in a field, the earth or a garden*

---

39. Snodgrass, *Stories with Intent*, 222. This point of view, which in essence negates *Redaktionsgeschichte* in principle, surely should be considered as a minority opinion.

changes nothing in terms of the parable's intent. In the end there
is not much significance to the variation in wording.⁴⁰

This remark of Snodgrass is surprisingly uncritical. Nowhere in Luke
is the smallness of the seed assumed; it is simply not there. The interpreter
might make a deduction because the interpreter has three other versions.
More important is the question whether the smallness of the seed was part
of the earliest version of the parable or not, especially if one is interested
in the intent of the parable in a 27–30 CE context. Moreover, as will be
indicated below, whether a mustard seed is sown in a field, in the earth, or in
a garden makes a serious difference in terms of the parable's possible meaning. The fact of the matter is that the redactional activity of the evangelists
is evident in the differences between the extant versions. Therefore, if one
is interested in postulating—as far as it is possible—the earliest version of
the parable, it is necessary to sift through the redactional activity that can be
indicated in the extant versions. Only then can one postulate a version that
is most probably the closest to the "original" parable Jesus told. The details
of this version then can be used to postulate the possible intent Jesus had
with the parable.

Let us start with the version in Mark 4:30–32. Mark's introduction to
the parable (καὶ ἔλεγεν αὐτοῖς) is also found in Mark 4:2, 11, 21, and 24,
and is thus typically Markan. Mark's mustard seed is sown in the earth (ἐπὶ
τῆς γῆς), which is also typically Markan.⁴¹ Mark's description of the mustard seed as "the smallest of all seeds on the earth" (μικρότερον ὂν πάντων
τῶν σπερμάτων τῶν ἐπὶ τῆς γῆς), importantly, is also a Markan redaction.
Mark's description of the mustard seed as the smallest of all seeds is part
of a literary construction that Donahue has coined as a "Markan insertion
technique," whereby Mark makes an insertion into the (oral or pre-Markan)
tradition he used, and then repeats after the insertion the phrase which preceded it.⁴² This insight of Donahue is important for the interpretation of the
parable; the reference to the mustard seed as the smallest of all seeds most
probably was not part of the earliest version of the parable.⁴³ By implication,

---

40. Ibid.; italics added. See also Lang, *Pictures and Parables*, 186.

41. See Mark 4:1, 5, 8, 20, 26, 28, 32.

42. See Crossan, *The Historical Jesus*, 46. Mark 4:31–32a, "ὡς κόκκῳ σινάπεως, ὃς
ὅταν σπαρῇ ἐπὶ τῆς γῆς, μικρότερον ὂν πάντων τῶν σπερμάτων τῶν ἐπὶ τῆς γῆς, καὶ
ὅταν σπαρῇ," thus read "ὡς κόκκῳ σινάπεως, ὃς ὅταν σπαρῇ ἐπὶ τῆς γῆς" in the tradition Mark used. Some examples of this Markan technique are Mark 2:9b–11 and Mark
10:47b–48b. Perrin noted that Donahue identified forty seven instances of the "Markan
insertion technique" in Mark. Perrin, "The Christology of Mark," 173–87. See Crossan,
The Historical Jesus, 46 n. 6.

43. Also Dodd, *Parables of the Kingdom*, 191; Hultgren, *Parables of Jesus*, 397.

Mark's reference to the mustard seed turning into the largest of all plants thus also was not part of the original parable. In short, Mark changed the parable of Jesus into a growth parable.

Some scholars view the Thomasine version as independent of the synoptic versions,[44] because it does not have the problem with the "smallest and largest" of Mark, and the shrub of Mark that turns into a tree in Q. Others believe that the Thomasine version is a dependent and edited version of the Mustard Seed in the Synoptics.[45] The latter argument seems to be the case, especially when the Thomasine and Markan versions of the parable are compared. From a structural point of view, Gos. Thom. 20:1–4 has the same structure as Mark 4:30–32, except for the parenthesis in Mark 4:31–32a. Other similarities are the seed as the smallest seed (Mark 4:31 and Gos. Thom. 20:3), the use of "when" (ὅταν) in Mark 4:32 and Gos. Thom. 20:4, and the correspondence between "on prepared soil" (Gos. Thom. 20:4) and "on the ground" (Mark 4:32).[46] Interestingly, in the Gospel of Thomas the "smallest seed" (as in Mark) does not turn into the largest plant, but simply into a large plant. These differences and similarities between the Gospel of Thomas and Mark most probably indicate that Gos. Thom. 20:1–4 is a reworked version of Mark's version.

Turning to Q 13:18–19, Matt 13:31–32 has conflated his source (Q) and Mark. Except for the typically Matthean introduction to the parable (Ἄλλην παραβολὴν),[47] Matthew has taken over the smallest-largest (μικρότερον and μεῖζον) comparison of Mark, as well as Mark's reference to the largest plant as a garden plant (τῶν λαχάνων). Distinctive to Matthew is that the seed is sown in a cultivated field (ἐν τῷ ἀγρῷ), but it has the tree of Q.[48]

The Lukan version of Q 13:18–19 (Luke 13:18–19) is seen by most scholars as closest to the original parable of Jesus. The main reason for this point of view is that Luke is the only version that does not have any element of Mark's redactional "smallest and largest." The Q version, it seems, had no element of growth as part of the parable. As Matthew did, so Luke kept Q's seed that turns into a tree. Distinctive to Luke is that the seed is planted in a garden (κῆπον). The coming of the birds to the bush, tree, or large plant for shelter or to perch in its shade—in Luke a tree in which the birds perch in its branches—should also be considered as part of the original parable. As

44. See, for example, Hedrick, *Parables as Poetic Fictions?*, 250; Patterson, *Gospel of Thomas and Jesus*, 27–28.

45. For proponents of this view, see Hultgren, *Parables of Jesus*, 394, n. 8.

46. Ibid., 394–95.

47. Also Matt 13:24; 13:33; and 21:33.

48. For other features of the Matthean redaction of the parable, see Hultgren, *Parables of Jesus*, 399–400; Jones, *Matthean Parables*, 323.

referred to above, some scholars argue that that this image in Mark 4:32 and *par.* is a later addition to the original parable to facilitate the apocalyptic, eschatological imagery, based on the Old Testament, of the incorporation of the Gentiles into the people of God.[49] Hultgren makes a strong case that this imagery was not added later and should be seen as integral to the original parable; the imagery belongs to the basic structure and content of the parable, it is part of all four extant versions, and no actual Old Testament text is quoted, "but only a rather elusive symbol derived from a number of texts is alluded to."[50]

To summarize, the Markan version of the parable, used in the Gospel of Thomas, redactionally added the growth aspect to the Mustard Seed, and Matthew conflated the Markan version with the Q parable. The Lukan version of Q seems to be the closest to the original parable of Jesus. The Lukan version of the Mustard Seed (= Q), without the growth metaphor (smallest-largest), and with the seed being planted in a garden, which turns into a tree to which the birds flock, most probably goes back to the earliest layer of the Jesus tradition we have. Luke's version constitutes a definite difference in the meaning of the parable, a meaning that has to do with the essence of what Jesus wanted to convey when he compared the kingdom of God with a mustard seed.

Reading Scenarios

The first hearers of the Mustard Seed were first-century peasants from Galilee who, in an advanced agrarian society, worked the land in an effort to make a living. These first hearers of the parable can be described as "emic listeners," that is, listeners of the parable from a native's point of view. By this is meant that the parable contained certain background information not known by modern readers, and also evoked certain cultural norms or scripts (social values) of the first-century Mediterranean world that are implicitly embedded in the story Jesus told, social values also not readily available to modern readers. These social values were part of the repertoire of the teller and audience of the parable; a shared cultural world of references.[51] Social-scientific critics (inter alia) focuses on this aspect of ancient texts; texts are seen as products of social systems, and therefore no text can responsibly be interpreted if the social system that produced the text is not taken seriously.

49. Funk, "The Looking–Glass Tree," 3–9; Crossan, *The Historical Jesus*, 48–49.

50. Hultgren, *Parables of Jesus*, 396; so also Crossan, *The Historical Jesus*, 48; Oakman, *Jesus and the Peasants*, 114.

51. Scott, *Re-Imagine the World*, 109–17.

Regarding the social values embedded in the Mustard Seed that play a role in the dynamics of the parable, the following seems to be important: What kind of mustard seed is referred to in the parable, and what were its characteristics that may be important to understanding the intent of the parable? Can a mustard seed become a tree? Were birds that flock to trees perceived by peasants in an advanced agrarian society as positive or negative? Was it normal or acceptable to plant mustard seed in a garden? Bernard Scott, from a social-scientific perspective, has attended to this important question in his interpretation of the parable.[52]

The mustard seed was proverbially known for its smallness[53] and used as a familiar term to mean the tiniest thing possible[54] but was not the smallest seed, as Mark has it.[55] The seeds of the orchid and cypress, for example, were known to be smaller.[56] The seed of the mustard plant is approximately 1 millimeter in diameter, germinates within 5 days and grows quickly to about 2–3 meters in height. The mustard plant is "an annual herb with large leaves clustered mainly at the base of the plant. Its central stem branches abundantly in its upper part and produces an enormous number of yellow flowers and small, many-seeded linear fruits."[57] The mustard plant thus is a shrub, and not a tree;[58] its branches are not sturdy enough to support the nests of birds.[59] The plant has a very pungent taste, and oil derived from the plant was used as seasoning in food and for medicinal purposes.[60] In

52. See Scott, *Hear Then the Parable*, 381; Scott, *Re-Imagine the World*, 35–46. For other contributions that applied this approach to certain aspects of the parable, see Crossan, *Historical Jesus*, 278–279; Oakman, *Jesus and the Peasants*, 111–17; Miller, "Is the Apocalyptic Jesus History?" 112–16.

53. See Matt 17:20 and par., *m. Niddah* 5.2, *b. Berakot* 31a, *m. Teharot* 8.8, *m. Nazir* 1.5, and *Lev. Rab.* 31. For Hellenistic sources, see Hultgren, *Parables of Jesus*, 395.

54. See *y. Pe'ah* 7.4, and *b. Ketubot* iiib.

55. Funk et al., *Five Gospels*, 194; Jones, *Matthean Parables*, 326; Scott, *Hear Then the Parable*, 377.

56. Snodgrass, *Stories with Intent*, 220.

57. Zohary, *Plants of the Bible*, 93.

58. In antiquity the term δένδρον was sometimes used to refer to tall plants, but that does not make the mustard plant a tree. Hultgren, *Parables of Jesus*, 396. *Y. Pe'ah* 7.4, and *b. Ketubot* iiib, indeed describe the mustard plant as a tree, but they are exaggerations in an attempt to describe the fertility of Israel prior to the destruction of the temple. Snodgrass, *Stories with Intent*, 220, n. 205. According to Baarslag, the mustard plant referred to in the parable is not the *sinapis alba* but the *salvadore persica* that one can find near the Dead Sea and the Sea of Galilee, of which its berries tastes like mustard and can reach a height of 7–8 meters. Baarslag, *Gelijkenissen des Heeren*, 426. See, however, the discussion below.

59. Reid, *Parables for Preachers*, 104.

60. Scott, *Hear Then the Parable*, 380. According to Pliny, *Natural History* 20.87,

spite of these properties, the mustard plant was not popular in Palestine. It grew very rapidly and aggressively and spread like a weed or invasive shrub. Because of its tendency to take over, it needed persistent control.[61]

Pliny (*Nat.* 19.171), as well as the Mishna, distinguishes three kinds of mustard plants. Of the three kinds in the Mishna one is wild (*laphsân*), and the other two domesticated (*hardâl* and *hardâl misri*). These three varieties most probably correlate with the three varieties of mustard that today grow in Palestine, namely, the *brassica nigra* (black mustard = *hardâl*), *sinapis nigra* (white mustard = *hardâl misri*), and the *sinapis arvensis* (charlock = *laphsân*).[62] According to Oakman, the mustard plant referred to in the parable most probably is the *brassica nigra*, one of the domesticated varieties that could be planted in a garden for its medicinal and herbal qualities. Oakman here is probably correct, since Mark 4:32 and Matt 13:32 describe the mustard plant in the parable as the "largest of all garden plants" (μεῖζον πάντων τῶν λαχάνων). But, as Crossan states, even when one deliberately cultivates the domesticated mustard seed for its medicinal or culinary properties "there is an ever present danger that it will destroy the garden . . . The mustard plant . . . is, as domesticated in the garden, dangerous and . . . deadly."[63]

Another aspect that is important for the understanding of the Mustard Seed is the way Jesus introduces the parable: ἡ βασιλεία τοῦ θεοῦ καὶ τίνι ὁμοιώσω αὐτήν; ("What is the kingdom of God like? And to what shall I compare it?" Q 13:18). Different from the other parables of Jesus in which

---

the mustard herb, when pounded with vinegar, can be used a liniment for the stings of serpents and scorpions, and it effectively neutralizes the poisonous properties of fungi. It can be used to cure an immoderate secretion of phlegm, and when mixed with hydromel, it can be used as a gargle. The mustard seed can also be chewed for toothache, and is very beneficial for all maladies of the stomach. Taken with the food, it facilitates expectoration from the lungs, and, in combination with cucumber seed, helps for asthma and epileptic fits. It has the effect of quickening the senses, effectually clears the head by sneezing, relaxes the stomach, and promotes menstrual discharge and urinary secretions. When beaten up with figs and cumin, it is used as an external application for dropsy. Mixed with vinegar, mustard resuscitates persons who have swooned in fits of epilepsy or lethargy, as well as females suffering from hysterical suffocations. It is also a cure for lethargy, inveterate pains of the chest, loins, hips, shoulders, and, in general, for all deep-seated pains in any part of the body, as well as blisters and indurations of the skin. Combined with red earth, it helps for alopecia, itchscabs, leprosy, phthiriasis, tetanus, and opisthotony.

61. "It [mustard] grows entirely wild, though it is improved by being transplanted: but on the other hand when it has once been sown it is scarcely possible to get the place free of it, as the seed when it falls germinates at once." Pliny, *Natural History*, 29.54.

62. Oakman, *Jesus and the Peasants*, 114.

63. Crossan, *Historical Jesus*, 278.

the kingdom is also likened to something (e.g., the actions of a vineyard owner, a patron-king, or a merchant), and similar to the parables of the Leaven (Luke 13:20) and the Sower (Mark 4:30), the Mustard Seed explicitly compares the kingdom to other kingdoms.[64] To use the Wright's metaphor, first-century Palestine was the place where three winds met to create the perfect storm. The first wind, blowing from the far west, was that of the superpower Rome, the new social, political, and economic reality of the day with its military superiority and exploitative economic program. The second wind, blowing from the temple in Jerusalem, was the indirect rule of Rome, the power-seeking priestly elite with an understanding of the God of Israel that added to the oppression and exploitation of ruled. The third wind, blowing from Galilee, was the message of a peasant who proclaimed that the kingdom of God has arrived, a kingdom directly opposed to that of Rome and the temple elite.[65]

The Mustard Seed, like the Sower, explicitly compares the kingdom of God with these two other kingdoms. What was the kingdom of the temple like? During the Second Temple period the priestly elite (and Pharisees) understood God in terms of holiness as expressed, for example, in Lev 19:2 ("Be holy because I, the LORD your God, am holy"). God's holiness was understood in the way he created. The way God created was to separate and create order. He separated day from night and the days of the week from the Sabbath; birds, animals, and fish were created different from one another, and only in "pure" forms (no hybrids); land was separated from the sea (the waters), and every living creature were allocated its proper place in creation (e.g., the fish in the water and the birds in the sky). God's creation, in a nutshell, meant order in terms of place, time, living beings, and status (hierarchy). There was a place for everything, and everything had its place. God's holiness meant order, and to be holy as God is holy meant that God's order—as set up at creation—had to be respected. In the time of Jesus, the temple (as the *axis mundi*), the central religious symbol of the Jewish *ethnos*, personified God's presence and holiness (order). To replicate God's holiness, purity laws were put into place. These rules inter alia determined which animals could be sacrificed (no hybrids or animals with defects), which persons were to preside over the sacrifices, which persons were allowed to take part in these sacrifices (only "pure" Israelites with no bodily defects), and when and where these sacrifices had to take place.

---

64. See again the interpretation of the Sower in chapter 2, where the kingdom is likened to the kingdoms of Rome and the temple.

65. Wright, *Simply Jesus*, 27–56.

Fundamental to the purity rules was that things that were not alike were not to be mixed. These rules covered areas such as gender (a woman shall not wear anything that pertains to a man, nor shall a man put on a woman's garment; Deut 22:5), agriculture (you shall not sow your vineyard with two kinds of seed; Deut 22:9), husbandry (you shall not plow with an ox and an ass together; Deut 22:10), and clothing (you shall not wear mingled stuff, wool and linen together; Deut 22:11). The prohibition against mixing things that were not alike is summarized in the purity code of Leviticus as follows: "You shall keep my statutes. You shall not let your cattle breed with a different kind; you shall not sow your field with two kinds of seed; nor shall there come upon you a garment of cloth made of two kinds of stuff" (Lev 19:19). Separation led to order and purity, while mixing things not alike meant chaos and pollution. One therefore was not allowed to plant in a garden whatever one liked. To summarize, the kingdom of the temple was pure, not polluted.

With regard to the kingdom of Rome, first-century Palestine, as part of the Roman Empire, was an advanced agrarian society. All agrarian societies were aristocratic in character (divided into the rulers and the ruled). The elite ruled by hereditary control of the empire's primary resources of land and labor, and controlled most of the wealth (from one-half up to two-thirds) by controlling the land, its produce, and the peasants, whose labor created the produce. Control over the land, its yield, its distribution, and its cultivators was exercised by extracting taxes, tribute, and rents: an act of domination that subordinated the peasants against their will. The peasantry was exposed to three levels of tribute taking: Roman tribute, tribute to Herod Antipas together with the Herodian aristocracy centered in Sepphoris and Tiberius, and tribute to the temple aristocracy in the form of tithes and offerings to support the temple as well as Roman rule. These forms of tribute taking followed "a pattern often found in aristocratic empires and colonial powers."[66] This tribute taking left the peasantry in a situation where their level of subsistence had a very narrow margin. For the kingdom of Rome, however, the land and its yield was life. No harvests or smaller harvests meant less income. For Rome, this meant a slow death. It was, after all, a kingdom of exploitative tribute taking.

Reading the Parable

The Mustard Seed is not a parable of growth or contrast that envisages an apocalyptical, eschatological kingdom. The tradition behind the Mustard

66. Herzog, *Prophet and Teacher*, 52.

Seed as a parable of growth and accordingly a parable about the eschatological kingdom of God is Mark; by redactionally introducing the smallest-
largest comparison into the parable, Mark opened the door to interpret the
Mustard Seed as depicting an eschatological kingdom, a kingdom that will
be realized somewhere in future. Q 13:18–19, the version of the parable that
is most probably the closest to earliest Jesus tradition, does not contain the
smallest-largest comparison. Also, a serious case can be made that Jesus in
his parables pictured the kingdom as a present reality.[67]

The Mustard Seed, as often argued, does not play into Old Testament
imagery by means of the symbols of the mighty cedar of Lebanon as a metaphor for a towering empire (Ezek 17:22–23) and the apocalyptic tree of Dan
4:12, and 20–21. Would first-century illiterate peasants, when they heard
a parable about the kingdom of God that is like a mustard seed that turns
into a tree, have connected the dots between the tree in the parable and
the imagery in the Old Testament about the cedar of Lebanon and Daniel's
apocalyptic tree? In the early Christian communities where Old Testament
texts were studied through the lens of the Jesus-event, this was possible; but
most probably it was not for peasants tilling the soil and trying to survive
exploitative circumstances and to rise above mere subsistence living. Even
in a scribal tradition this so-called imagery in the parable can be questioned.
In Ezek 17 and 31, and Dan 4, the mighty cedar represents the enemies
of Israel. "The metaphor is that God brings low the powerful empires of
Babylon and Egypt that once stood proudly like tall cedars."[68] Would one
compare the kingdom of God with other known despised kingdoms? As
Reid puts it, "When Israel is the small sprig become a lofty cedar . . . can it
be exempt from such humbling"?[69] Also, if the kingdom of God is like a lofty
cedar, in spite of its small beginning, is the kingdom of God not exactly like
the kingdom of Rome? Miller answers this in the positive: "In this respect
the kingdom of God embodies the same values as the kingdom of Rome,
which grew from a small town into a worldwide empire." The parable then
asserts that "God is on the side of the victor, exactly the lesson Rome wanted

67. See Van Eck, "Interpreting the Parables," 315–16. See also the following remark from Galston: "The parable on its own remains the inverse of apocalyptisism . . .
[T]he Mustard Seed parable masquerades a scrawny and troubling wild shrub as the
image of the kingdom of God. The Mustard Seed parable makes a mockery of a mighty
God and a powerful state. It is the dignified Cedars of Lebanon that are supposed to
stand for glorious Zion and the favor of God (Ezek 17:22–24), but the mustard plant
places the kingdom as a nuisance growing at our feet. The Mustard Seed parable is a
satire of apocalyptism, for a shrub spreading at our feet is hardly a natural location for
end-time vision." Galston, *Embracing the Human Jesus*, 83.

68. Reid, *Parables for Preachers*, 105.

69. Ibid.

to teach its subjects."[70] If this is what the parable intended to communicate, peasants would have heard it as, to borrow Rohrbaugh's words, a "text of terror." If the kingdom of God was as exploitative and domineering as the kingdoms of Rome and the temple, it was not something a peasant wanted to hear about.

What was most probably Jesus' intent with the Mustard Seed? In the parable Jesus does not use the mustard seed as a comparison for the kingdom because of its smallness;[71] the mustard seed is used because of its well-known characteristics among first-century Galilean peasants, the first hearers of the parable. The kingdom is like a mustard seed that when it becomes a plant, can be put to good use in terms of its culinary and medicinal properties. This is the kingdom of God, like a mustard plant that can be put to good use. So, nothing new or extraordinary thus far.

But watch out! Although it is an annual, it reseeds itself and keeps on reseeding. It comes up again and again. You cannot stop or eradicate it; it grows very rapidly and aggressively and spreads like a weed or invasive shrub. Because of its tendency to take over, it needs persistent control. As long as it grows in the wild, this is not really a problem. But then a twist in the parable; the kingdom of God is not only like a mustard seed, but like a mustard seed that is planted in a garden. Someone who planted mustard seed in a garden was looking for trouble. First, planting a mustard seed in a garden was prohibited according to the purity rules of the kingdom of the temple. In an ordered society, as in a garden, everything had its place, and there was a place for everything; things that were not alike (i.e., that were different) were not to be mixed (Lev 19:19). Separation led to order and purity, while mixing things not alike meant chaos and pollution. The elaboration in the Mishnah on this purity rule is clear: the mustard seed constitutes a mixed kind (*m. Kil.* 1.5),[72] and therefore it was strictly prohibited to plant a mustard seeds in a garden (*m. Kil.* 3.2).[73] By planting the

70. Miller, "Is the Apocalyptic Jesus History?" 113.

71. So Miller: "Other examples (than the mustard seed) could have served just as well. After all, every plant starts from a seed. The mustard is actually an uninspiring example for a lesson about growth. If the object is to contrast inconspicuous origins with impressive results, why single out a lowly mustard bush? Why not a tree: the rugged olive, or the stately palm? Better yet, why not the strong and lofty cedar of Lebanon, a tree that symbolizes world empires in Ezekiel and Daniel?" Ibid.

72. "Although the long radish and the round radish, mustard and wild mustard, the Greek gourd and the Egyptian or bitter gourd are like to each other, they are accounted Diverse Kinds." Danby, trans., *The Mishnah*, 29.

73. "Not every kind of seed may be sown in a garden-bed, but any kind of vegetable may be sown therein. Mustard and small beans are deemed a kind of seed and large beans a kind of vegetable." Ibid., 31.

mustard seed in the garden, one thus violates the law of diverse kinds and pollutes the garden.[74] The garden is unclean, a symbol of chaos. If mustard seed in a garden is a metaphor for the kingdom of God, then the kingdom of God is polluted and unclean. An ordered kingdom has been replaced by a chaotic and polluted kingdom. But it has not only been replaced; it has been taken over by a unclean "mixed kind" that grows wild, that is invasive and difficult—almost impossible—to control.[75] Therefore, if we follow the metaphor of the mustard seed, then the kingdom of God, like the plant, is dangerous and deadly. In time it will take over the ordered and unpolluted garden (ordered society) centered in the temple. Order is turned into chaos; the kingdom of God is taking over the kingdom of the temple.

The mustard seed, however, is also taking over the kingdom of Rome. In what sense? This is the surprise in the parable, a surprise typical of the parables of Jesus.[76] The mustard seed does not grow into a garden shrub whose branches would scarcely support a nest for birds much less offer any significant shade. No, it turns into a tree with branches strong enough for wild birds to roost and nest in, [77] a tree in which they can make a home. And what do these wild birds do? As pesky intruders onto cultivated lands, the natural enemies of what is sown, they feed of the land by plundering the cultivated fields.[78] From their safe haven they take from the kingdom of Rome by plundering its base of taxation. And this meant only one thing:

74. Scott, *Hear Then the Parable*, 381.

75. "Even when one deliberately cultivates the domesticated mustard seed for its medicinal or culinary properties there is an ever present danger that it will destroy the garden . . . The mustard plant . . . is, as domesticated in the garden, dangerous and . . . deadly." Crossan, *Historical Jesus*, 278.

76. According to Crossan, the seed turning into a tree is the question of the parable. Ibid., 48. This is only the case when one thinks of a mustard seed turning into a tree in terms of botanical or horticultural properties, or sees the tree as a "biological misfit." Scott, *Re-Imagine the World*, 35–46. The seed turning into a tree is part of the narrative artistry of the parable that leads to the parable's surprise, as we have surprises in almost all of Jesus' parables: A Samaritan becomes the hero when somebody is in dire straits (Luke 10:30–35), a patron does not exploit day laborers by paying them all the same wage (Matt 20:1–15), a father does not chastise his prodigal son but welcomes him back (Luke 15:11–32), a patron cancels the huge debt of one of his slaves (Matt 18:23–33), an elite invites the wrong people to a banquet (Luke 14:16–23), an owner does not take up his right to kill his tenants because of their violent actions (Gos. Thom. 65), and a shepherd leaves ninety-nine of his sheep unprotected to go and look for one that is lost instead of turning to violence (Luke 15:4–6).

77. See Louw and Nida, *Greek-English Lexicon*, 1:44. The expression "πετεινὰ τοῦ οὐρανοῦ" is an idiom for wild birds in contrast with domesticated birds, such as chickens.

78. Oakman, *Jesus and the Peasants*, 116.

The smaller the harvest and the "surplus of the land," the less tax went into the coffers of the kingdom of Rome.

Read from the above perspective, the Mustard Seed questions religious respectability as proposed by the kingdom of the temple[79] and undermines the imperial interests of the kingdom of Rome. The parable tells of a kingdom where God is associated with uncleanness, where boundaries are porous, and where separation cannot and should not be maintained. The kingdom of God spreads effortlessly, takes over and pollutes, bringing along its unwelcome wild and pesky intruders that subvert the kingdom of Rome (and the temple). With its expansive power, the kingdom of God is subverting or inverting the exploitative social system of its day.[80] The mustard seed thus indeed has medicinal properties; it can heal the causes of exclusive, exploitative, and domineering kingdoms.

A Parable of Jesus?

The parable as interpreted here has all the earmarks of a Jesus parable. Typical of Jesus' parables, it cuts against the grain of the exploitative world of first-century Palestine and most probably represents the earliest layer of the historical Jesus tradition. It resonates with Jesus' attitude toward the temple purity system (exclusivity) and toward the negative impact imperial Rome had on the lives of the peasantry.

In terms of the criteria of early, multiple, and independent attestation, and coherence, the parable displays typical values that Jesus supported. With regards to Jesus' critique of the temple's purity system, the parable parallels Jesus' sayings in Gos. Thom. 14:5 and Mark 7:14–15 and *par.* (it is not what goes in that defiles, but what goes out).[81] The values in the parable are also paralleled in other Jesus parables, either in a positive or negative way. In the parable of the Leaven (Q 13:20–21; Gos. Thom. 96:1–2) the kingdom is also described as being unclean or impure. Like the host in the parable of the Feast (Luke 14:16a–23), Jesus regularly associated with the so-called impure, and ate with the so-called sinners of his day. Like the Sower, the Mustard Seed subverts the values of both the kingdoms of the temple and Rome.

79. Miller, "Is the Apocalyptic Jesus History?" 113–14.

80. Kloppenborg, *Excavating Q*, 391–92.

81. This aphorism, according to Funk et al., "is a categorical challenge to the laws governing pollution and purity. Since the saying need not be taken entirely literally . . . it can also be made to apply to other forms of pollution . . . since it challenges the everyday, the inherited, the established, and erases social boundaries taken to be sacrosanct." Funk et al., *Five Gospels*, 69.

The Feast (Luke 14:16b–23): A Kingdom Patron

WHY, IN THE PARABLE of the Feast, are the guests invited twice? Who is the host, and who are the invitees? Why do only three of the invitees excuse themselves, but not one of the "many" invited (Luke 14:16b) shows up? And what does it mean when the slave is sent by the host to invite those in the wider streets, squares, narrow streets, and alleys (Luke 14:21), and those in the roads and country lanes or hedges (Luke 14:23)? To untangle the possible meaning of the parable, these are the important questions.

History of Interpretation

The history of the interpretation of the parable shows that scholars approach it in one of three ways. The parable is interpreted allegorically or theologically, or it is read in terms of its Lukan context, or it is included as an authentic saying of Jesus used by Luke. Interpreters who choose the third option sometimes discuss the redactional activity.

The earliest interpretations of the parable of the Feast are the allegorical interpretations of Augustine, Origen, Bede, and Aquinas,[1] and the

---

1. Augustine (*Sermon LXII*) equates the host with Jesus and the invitees with Israel. The first excuse refers to the "spirit of domination," the five oxen to the senses of the body that make people seek earthly things and things of the flesh, and the third excuse refers to the lust of the flesh. The parable calls on believers to do away with the vain and evil excuses of the flesh and come to the Eucharist. Schaff, *Nicene and Post-Nicene Fathers*. Contrary to Augustine, Origen identifies the banquet as the spiritual food of God's mysteries. Snodgrass, *Stories with Intent*, 308. In Bede and Aquinas' interpretation the streets and alleys of the town (Luke 14:21) and the roads and country lanes (Luke 14:23) represent the teaching and errors of the heathen that have to be brought (corrected) into the church (the dinner party). Kissinger, *History of Interpretation*, 40, 43.

historical and literal (theological) interpretations of Luther, Calvin, and Maldonatus.[2] Scholars who read the parable in its Lukan context focus on different aspects of the parable and come to a plethora of conclusions regarding the crux of the parable. Scholars who focus on the invitations in the parable see salvation history as key to unlock its meaning,[3] while others see the parable as representing one of Luke's main theological themes: the announcement of the kingdom to the poor.[4] Another interpretation that follows this approach focuses on the grace, mercy, and compassion of God symbolized by the action of the host;[5] some argue that the Lukan Jesus

2. Luther understands the dinner as symbolic of the feast God prepared through Christ (salvation), with the phrase "all things are ready" (Luke 14:17) referring to the price God has paid in Christ for all sins. Hunter, *Then and Now*, 32. For Calvin the focus of the parable is election; many are called and hear the word, but only a few are chosen because only a few prove their faith by newness of life. Calvin, *Harmony of the Gospels*, 3:105–10. Maldonatus interprets the parable in more or less the same vein as Calvin: many are called, but only few come—not all who come to the church when called will be saved. Maldonatus, *Commentary on the Holy Gospels*, 222–30.

3. In this interpretation the first invitees are the Jews, and the second and third the Gentiles. Because the Jews rejected the invitation, the parable is a judgement on Israel as nation. See Keach, *Exposition of the Parables*, 544; Lockyer, *All the Parables*, 276; Schippers, *Gelijkenissen van Jezus*, 41; Swartley, "Unexpected Banquet People," 177; Timmer, *Kingdom Equation*, 57. Hultgren differs marginally from these scholars in his interpretation of the invitations but comes to the same salvation-historical conclusion: the first invited are the Jewish aristocracy, the second the lower-class Jews, and those invited third the Gentiles. The parable thus teaches that salvation is not only for the Jews (sinners and tax collectors), but also are available to the Gentiles. Hultgren, *Parables of Jesus*, 336–37. See also Haenchen, in Swartley, "Unexpected Banquet People," 188.

4. Bruce and Knapp were the first scholars to read the parable from this perspective. Bruce, *Parabolic Teaching*, 32; Knapp, *Gelijkenissen des Heeren*, 97–112. This interpretation is supported by Schottroff, "Gleichnis vom Grossen Gastmahl," 211; Schottroff, *Parables of Jesus*, 55; Schottroff, "Das Große Abendmahl," 593; Perkins, *Hearing the Parables*, 98; Wenham, *Parables of Jesus*, 134; Young, *Jesus and His Jewish Parables*, 176. Read from this perspective, the parable spells out the Lukan Jesus' attitude towards the poor and teaches that the kingdom is for the hungry. Luke is using the parable to confront the rich of his own community who are avoiding association with poor Christians, and exhorts them, in their abundance, to aid the poor, the common people, and outcasts of society, whom nobody cares for. Rohrbaugh, "Pre-Industrial City," 142.

5. Boice, *Parables of Jesus*, 66; Braun, *Feasting and Social Rhetoric*, 131; Manson, *Teaching of Jesus*, 75; Swartley, "Unexpected Banquet People," 189; Trench, *Notes on the Parables*, 24–30. Linked to this interpretation, some focus on the decision of the hearer of the parable. God's grace implies that all are invited to the feast, an invitation that asks for a decision: the kingdom is present, but only those who come to the feast will partake in it. Hunter, *Then and Now*, 96; Kistemaker, *Stories Jesus Told*, 163; Linnemann, *Parables of Jesus*, 91–92; Sanders, "Ethic of Election," 260–64. Read from this perspective, the parable teaches that the nature of the kingdom is that it is a gift offered to humanity, an invitation to enter. Morgan, *Parables and Metaphors*, 181. Nobody is excluded from God's kingdom except by choice. The parable thus urges the hearer to discern the signs

used the parable of the Feast as a symbol to portray the future eschatological or messianic banquet,[6] and some see the parable as a challenge to the Pharisees to reconsider the exclusion of people from the cultic sphere they deem impure[7]—a parable that calls them into a mission to the impure and to Gentiles.[8]

Most scholars who read Luke's version of the parable as an authentic saying of the historical Jesus do not differ much in their interpretations from those who read the parable as redactionally used by Luke. In most cases the same themes are identified, namely, salvation,[9] Jesus' attitude toward the poor,[10] the need for decision and repentance,[11] the eschatological banquet,[12] the defense of the gospel's being extended to outcasts (the vindication of the good news),[13] and mission.[14] For these scholars, it seems, the message of the parable in its Lukan context (96 CE) concurs with what Jesus intended when he told the parable in a 27–30 CE context.

Three readings of the parable that do take the 27–30 CE social and contextual world of the parable seriously are those of Crossan; Funk, Hoover, and the Jesus Seminar; and Rohrbaugh.[15] For Crossan and Funk the startling element or surprising twist in the parable is the random and open commensality of its meal, and the socially marginal that fill the hall—an aspect of the parable that makes it a genuine Jesus story. Rohrbaugh's reading of the parable identifies the same startling element. The lens he uses to read the parable, however, differs from that of Crossan and Funk. Whereas the Crossan and Funk focus on the social dynamics of meals (as ceremonies) in the first-century Mediterranean world, Rohrbaugh reads the parable in terms of its implied preindustrial setting and the pivotal role honor and

---

of the times and repent before it is too late. Hunter, *Then and Now*, 85.

6. Hendrickx, *Parables of Jesus*, 113; Stein, *Introduction to the Parables*, 85–86. See also Groenewald, who argues that when read from this perspective, the parable implies that those who do not accept God's invitation to his dinner (salvation) will be judged (*In Gelykenisse Het Hy Geleer*, 198).

7. Arens, "Ein Tischgespräch," 452.

8. Dormeyer, in Swartley, "Unexpected Banquet People," 188.

9. Boucher, *Parables*, 103.

10. Jeremias, *Parables of Jesus*, 64; Kilgallen, *Twenty Parables*, 82.

11. Brouwer, *De Gelijkenissen*, 94.

12. Bailey, *Poet and Peasant*, 89, 92; Marshall, *Gospel of Luke*, 587; Scott, *Re-Imagine the World*, 109–117; Snodgrass, *Stories with Intent*, 311, 316; Stein, *Introduction*, 87.

13. Bailey, *Poet and Peasant*, 111; Jeremias, *Parables of Jesus*, 64.

14. Boucher, *Parables*, 103; Perkins, *Hearing the Parables*, 97.

15. Crossan, *Historical Jesus*, 261–264; Funk et al., *Five Gospels*, 351–53; Rohrbaugh, "Pre-Industrial City," 151–80.

shame played in the first-century Mediterranean world. These readings, as will be indicated below, are valuable pointers for reading the parable as a realistic narrative (verisimilitude) in a 27–30 CE setting.

Versions and Integrity

Extant Versions

The three extant versions of the parable, namely, Luke 14:16b–24; Gos. Thom. 64:1–12; and Matt 22:2–14, all have been redacted; the earliest form of the parable is thus not clear. The same can be said of the parable's origin. Some scholars argue that Matthew and Luke have drawn their respective parables from oral tradition (M and L),[16] others are of the opinion that both versions stem from Q,[17] and still others argue for Gospel of Thomas as the original parable used by Matthew and Luke.[18] Broadly speaking, the versions in the Gospel of Thomas and Luke are similar, while Matthew's version differs considerably from the other two. Do we have a common source behind all three extant versions, do the versions in Luke and Matthew stem from two independent oral versions or from Q, does the Thomasine version represent an independent tradition, or is Gos. Thom. 64:1–12 a redacted version of Luke, or even Q? To answer these questions, a closer look at the redactional activity that can be traced in the three versions is necessary.

Almost all scholars agree that the Matthean version of the parable is secondary.[19] Matthew's version of the parable is a conflation of two parables,

16. Davies and Allison, *Matthew,* 3:194; Dodd, *Parables of the Kingdom,* 95; Drury, *Parables in the Gospels,* 125; Gnilka, *Matthäusevangelium,* 2:235; Groenewald, *In Gelykenisse Het Hy Geleer,* 198; Hill, *Gospel of Matthew,* 301; Hultgren, *Parables of Jesus,* 335; Kistemaker, *Stories Jesus Told,* 164–65; Linnemann, *Parables of Jesus,* 160, n. 2; Luz, *Mt 18–25,* 3:233; Plummer, *St. Luke,* 359; Smith, *Parables of the Synoptic Gospels,* 203; Snodgrass, *Stories with Intent,* 310; Stein, *Introduction to the Parables,* 83; Streeter, *Four Gospels,* 244; Via, *Parables,* 129; Weiser, *Die Knechtgleichnisse,* 59–60.

17. Brouwer, *De Gelijkenissen,* 171; Conzelmann, *Theology of St. Luke,* 111; Donahue, *Gospel in Parable,* 140; Hagner, *Matthew 14–28,* 627; Hendrickx, *Parables of Jesus,* 131; Hunter, *Then and Now,* 56; Jones, *Matthean Parables,* 401; Klein, "Botschaft für Viele," 430–37; Manson, *Sayings of Jesus,* 129–30; Polag, *Fragmenta Q,* 70; Schippers, *Gelijkenissen van Jezus,* 41; Schulz, *Die Spruchquelle,* 391–98; Schottroff, *Parables of Jesus,* 53; Schottroff, "Das Große Abendmahl," 593; Scott, *Hear Then the Parable,* 167; Scott, *Re-Imagine the World,* 109–17; Trench, *Notes,* 24–30; Weder, *Die Gleichnisse Jesu als Metaphern,* 178.

18. Crossan, *In Parables,* 72; Fitzmyer, *Gospel according to Luke,* 2:1052; Jeremias, *Parables,* 63; Perrin, *Rediscovering the Teaching,* 35.

19. Boucher, *Parables,* 103; Brouwer, *De Gelijkenissen,* 70; Hunter, *Then and Now,* 56; Linnemann, *Parables of Jesus,* 93; Perkins, *Hearing the Parables,* 95; Scott, *Hear Then*

the parable of the Marriage Feast (Matt 22:2–10) and a parable that can be called the Visit and Judgment of the King, or the Wedding Garment (Matt 22:11–14).[20] Matthew uses the first parable as an introduction to the second[21] and has redacted both parables heavily.[22] The first parable (Matt 22:2–10) has Jerusalem as the setting and changes the great supper or feast (δεῖπνον) of Luke into a wedding feast (γάμους) that a king prepares for his son. This redactional change enables Matthew to turn the parable into an allegory of the history of salvation.[23] Also, when one compares Matt 22:2–10 with the parable of the Tenants (Matt 21:33–44)—which immediately precedes the Marriage Feast in the Matthean narrative—is it clear that Matthew has redactionally edited the parable of the Marriage Feast to parallel his version of the Tenants by taking up its theme and phrases.[24] The reference to good and evil (Matt 22:10) refers to the church, which Matthew consistently views as mixed, and parallels Matthew's interpretation of the parable of the Planted Weeds (Matt 13:24b–30).[25] Matt 22:2–10 also picks up themes from other parables in the gospel and is the climax of three parables in Matthew (Matt 21:28–32; 21:33–44; and 22:2–10) that all depict the church as the

---

the Parable, 162; Smith, Parables of the Synoptic Gospels, 16; Gundry, Matthew, 433.

20. Crossan, In Parables, 69.

21. Jeremias, The Parables of Jesus, 67–68.

22. In Matt 22:9–11 the king invites people without any preconditions, and then in Matt 22:11–13 expects all the gathered guests to have wedding garments. This expectation breaks the logical unity of the parable, indicating that Matt 22:11–13 was added to Matt 22:2–10. Crossan, In Parables, 69.

23. A king (God) prepares a feast for his son (Jesus) and invites (three times) his subjects (Israel) to the wedding. The invitees refuse the second invitation of the servants (the prophets), and when they are invited yet again by a greater number of servants (the apostles and missionaries), some pay no attention to the invitation while others kill the king's servants. The king is angered, and retaliates by destroying the invited guests and their city (Jerusalem). He then invites others (Gentiles) to the wedding who respond positively and fills the wedding hall. See ibid., 69–70; Funk et al., The Five Gospels, 352; Funk et al., Red Letter Edition, 43; Perkins, Hearing the Parables, 95; Scott, Re-Imagine the World, 109–117; Calvin, A Harmony, 3:105–110.

24. Matt 22:3–4 parallels Matt 21:34 and 36 (sending of the servants), the killing of the servants in Matt 22:6 is repeated in Matt 21:35, and the king's retaliation in Matt 22:7 (the burning of the city of those who declined the invitations—clearly a reference to the destruction of Jerusalem in 70 CE) parallels Matt 21:41 (the killing of the tenants of the vineyard—the chief priests and Pharisees). Without reading the parable of the Tenants the parable of the Marriage Feast is thus not intelligible. Drury, Parables in the Gospels, 97–98. Or, as Goulder puts it, "The Marriage Feast parable is nothing but a second version of the Wicked Husbandmen, with suitable Christian gloss, and in the Matthean manner." Goulder, Midrash and Lection, 415. See also Perkins, Hearing the Parables, 95.

25. Scott, Re-Imagine the World, 112.

true Israel,[26] and castigate the opponents of Jesus.[27] Finally, the expression ὡμοιώθη ἡ βασιλεία τῶν οὐρανῶν in Matt 22:2 is a typical Matthean feature (see also Matt 3:24; 18:23), as is Matthew's use of ὡμοιώθη (is like or compare; ὁμοιόω; see also Matt 7:24, 26).

To this allegory Matthew has added the parable of the Visit and Judgment of the King (Matt 22:11–14),[28] also heavily allegorized. The parable links with the reference to good and bad—Matthew's alternative for Luke's poor, maimed, blind and lame—in the previous parable (Matt 22:10), and serves as a warning to the good and bad that they will be judged.[29] Judgment depends on whether one is properly dressed or not (having a wedding garment).[30] The wedding garment serves as an allusion "to Christians who join the community but turn out not to fit and so expelled,"[31] to "those who do not produce proper fruit."[32] The reference to the outer darkness in Matt 22:13 is also a typical way of Matthew to end his parables (Matt 13:42, 50; 24:51; 25:30;[33] see also Matt 8:12; 24:13). Matthew 22:14, finally, is either a Matthean invention[34] or an independent logion,[35] a textual variant of Matt 20:16. By adding the second parable, Matthew has transformed the first parable into an outline of the history of salvation starting with the prophets, then Christian missionaries and the fall of Jerusalem, ending with the messianic banquet in the new age and the last judgment.[36]

The themes of the two parables (or one parable, the Marriage Feast) are the result of Matthew's redactional activity. In Matthew the parable

26. Dillon, "Tradition–History of the Parables," 1–42; Scott, *Hear Then the Parable*, 162–63.

27. Hultgren, *Parables of Jesus*, 343.

28. Boucher, *Parables*, 104; Perkins, *Hearing the Parables*, 98; Snodgrass, *Stories with Intent*, 300; Via, *Parables*, 128–32.

29. Funk et al., *Five Gospels*, 43; Funk et al., *Red Letter Edition*, 235; Snodgrass, *Stories with Intent*, 300.

30. The reference to not being properly dressed is a typical Matthean theme, namely that "the Christian community is a mixture of the good and the bad, the deserving and undeserving, who will be sorted out at the judgment (see the sabotage of the weeds—Matt 13:24–30; the allegory of the last judgment—Matt 25:31–46." Funk et al., *Five Gospels*, 235. See also Perkins, *Hearing the Parables*, 95.

31. Funk et al., *Red Letter Edition*, 43.

32. Scott, *Re-Imagine the World*, 112.

33. Respectively the parables of the Planted Weeds, Fishnet, Servants and the Entrusted Money.

34. Funk et al., *Five Gospels*, 235; Perkins, *Hearing the Parables*, 95.

35. Snodgrass, *Stories with Intent*, 300.

36. Boucher, *Parables*, 103; Drury, *Parables in the Gospels*, 72–73, 78; Jeremias, *Parables of Jesus*, 69.

of the Marriage Feast becomes an allegory of Jewish rejection, Christian acceptance, and final judgment.[37] Matthew's allegory is alien to Jesus; the parable looks back on the destruction of Jerusalem,[38] and the condoning of violence in Matt 22:7—as coming from Jesus—cannot be reconciled with Jesus' stance on violence seen from the parables of the Lost Sheep (Luke 15:4–6) and the Tenants (Gos. Thom. 65:1–8).[39] There is, to cite Funk, "very little left of the original parable in Matthew's version."[40] None of Matthew's themes are part of the Lukan version of the parable. Matthew's version of the parable, above all, destroys verisimilitude.[41] The parable lacks realism, and the parable has been turned into metaphorical theology.

Luke's version of the parable (Luke 14:16b–24) also had undergone some editorial modifications. In Luke the parable of the Feast is part of table talk in the house of a Pharisee (Luke 14:1) that consists of four short narratives that all are introduced either explicitly or implicitly by the giving of an invitation to a meal. In the first short narrative (Luke 14:1–6) Jesus is invited to a meal on the Sabbath where Pharisees and the impure—a man suffering from dropsy, falling into the category of the poor, the crippled, the lame, and the blind—are present. The focus of this short narrative is the question, should one heal (accept) or not heal (refuse) someone in need on the Sabbath? The themes in this short narrative (meals, guests, invitation, acceptance, and refusal) set the scene for the rest to follow in the larger narrative (Luke 14:1–24). In Luke 14:7–10 the focus is the acceptance or refusal of places of honor at a dinner table (seating arrangements), and Luke 14:12–14 focuses on who one should invite. The main thrust of the latter two short narratives is that one should refuse the place of honor at a table, and invite those without honor.

This contextual introduction to the parable (most probably a Lukan construction) has influenced the way Luke narrates the parable of the Feast. The parable is, as Bernard Scott argues, an example of the counterwisdom of Jesus explained in Luke 14:1–14.[42] The first invitation in Luke 14:21 parallels

37. Scott, *Re-Imagine the World*, 122.

38. Funk et al., *Red Letter Edition*, 43.

39. Van Eck, "The Lost Sheep"; Van Eck, "The Tenants."

40. Funk et al., *The Five Gospels*, 235. This conclusion is the direct opposite of that of Snodgrass. According to Snodgrass, the differences between the Matthean and Lukan version of the parable are the result of Jesus' telling of a given parable on more than one occasion in different contexts; both versions thus go back to the historical Jesus. In Matthew's version of the parable, as been indicated above, several redactional features clearly are those of Matthew. These redactional changes make it difficult to understand and support Snodgrass' argument. See Snodgrass, *Stories with Intent*, 310.

41. Scott, *Hear Then the Parable*, 162.

42. Ibid., 169.

Jesus' advice in Luke 14:13 (inviting the poor, crippled, blind, and lame), a favorite theme of Luke (see Luke 4:18–19; 7:22).[43] To this first invitation Luke adds a second to match his account of the advance of the gospel in his second book (Acts), first to the Judeans (who live, figuratively, in the town), then to the Gentiles (who live, figuratively, outside the town, in the countryside).[44] Luke also adds Luke 14:24 to reiterate the exclusion of the Pharisees, who exclude the lame, poor and blind from the (messianic) banquet (Luke 14:15).[45] Luke thus not only, like Matthew, allegorizes the parable into an image of the history of salvation, but also moralizes it by emphasizing the correct "how" (do not choose places of honor) and "who" (inviting the impure and outcasts) when it comes to taking part in or inviting people to a meal.

Scholars are divided on the question of whether the Thomasine version is dependent on one or both Synoptic versions, or based on an independent tradition.[46] A decision on the origin of the Thomasine version plays no role in what scholars see as redactional in Gos. Thom. 64:1–12. Whether being an independent tradition or dependent on one or both Synoptic versions—most scholars see a close parallel with Luke[47]—the redactional features identified in Gos. Thom. 64 by scholars from both positions are the same. Gos. Thom. 64 has four excuses, namely, merchants owing money (Gos. Thom. 64:3), the buying of a house (Gos. Thom. 64:5), a friend getting married (Gos. Thom. 64:7), and the buying of an estate (Gos. Thom. 64:9). Thomas' four excuses—when compared with the Synoptic versions—are either the result of Thomasine redaction,[48] or because Thomas' version is independent.[49] Scholars on both sides also agree that the Thomasine version fits the antiwealth and antibusiness stance of Gos. Thom. 63–65, emphasized by Thomas' addition of Gos. Thom. 64:12.[50] Whether independent or not,

43. Funk et al., *Five Gospels*, 352; Hultgren, *Parables of Jesus*, 336; Stein, *Introduction to the Parables*, 90.

44. Funk et al., *Five Gospels*, 352; Jeremias, *Parables of Jesus*, 64; Scott, *Re-Imagine the World*, 112.

45. Brouwer, *De Gelijkenissen*, 224; Funk et al., *Five Gospels*, 352; Hultgren, *Parables of Jesus*, 336.

46. See Hultgren, *Parables of Jesus*, 335, n. 8–9.

47. According to Scott, *Re-Imagine the World*, 112, the main difference between Luke's and Thomas' versions is that Luke modified the invitation to others, while Thomas reworked the excuses of those first invited.

48. Ibid., 167; Snodgrass, *Stories with Intent*, 310.

49. Crossan, *The Historical Jesus*, 261; Funk et al., *Five Gospels*, 352; Hultgren, *Parables of Jesus*, 335.

50. "Unlike Luke who has three excuses, Thomas has four. We should immediately be suspicious of four excuses, since oral storytelling prefers threes. Furthermore the

Gos. Thom. 64 lacks what is typically Jesus (the marginalized), and focuses on the gospels' antiwealth and antibusiness stance ("this-worldly" affairs).[51]

Which version of the parable represents the earliest layer of the Jesus tradition? As we have seen, most scholars agree that Matthew's version is secondary. Some scholars argue that both versions represent the earliest Jesus tradition,[52] some opt for the Thomas–version as the earliest,[53] while others argue for Luke as the "most original" version.[54]

Those who argue for Luke's priority point out that although his version as we have it fits his context,[55] when 14:15–16a and 24 are excluded, his version has no redactional or allegoristic features when taken out of its narrative context, Luke 14:1–24, and interpreted in terms of the characteristics of a preindustrial city in first-century Palestine: a lens that enables readers of the parable to identify its realistic features. The position taken here is that Luke's version of the parable is the closest we can get to the earliest layer of the Jesus tradition, and because Luke respected the authenticity of the parable, he did not edit the version of the parable he most probably borrowed from Q. This position is based on the following argument: Luke did not edit the parable to fit the context of Luke 14:1–24 but constructed Luke 14:1–15 to make it possible to add and use the parable of the Feast in the way he wanted to. This is not the only instance in the gospel where Luke uses this narrative technique. Another example is Luke's use of the parable of the Friend at Midnight (Luke 11:5–8). This parable, when Jesus told it, most probably criticized the practice of some peasants who in dire straits decided to practice balanced reciprocity by imitating the exploitative elite—thus

---

excuses given in Thomas all have to do with the management of business. Even the excuse dealing with a marriage, which finds a parallel in Luke, has to do with the management of the wedding feast. These excuses fit with Thomas' final warning, "Buyers and merchants will not enter the places of my Father.'" Scott, *Re-Imagine the World*, 112. See also Crossan, *Historical Jesus*, 261; Crossan, *In Parables*, 70–71; Funk et al., *Five Gospels*, 352; Funk et al., *Red Letter Edition*, 43; Perkins, *Hearing the Parables*, 95; Scott, *Hear Then the Parable*, 167; Snodgrass, *Stories with Intent*, 305.

51. Snodgrass, *Stories with Intent*, 310.

52. Funk et al., *Red Letter Edition*, 43.

53. Crossan, *In Parables*, 72; Crossan, *Historical Jesus*, 261; Fitzmyer, *The Gospel according to Luke*, 2:1052; Jeremias, *Parables*, 63; Perrin, *Rediscovering the Teaching*, 35.

54. Bailey, *Poet and Peasant*, 83; Hendrickx, *The Parables of Jesus*, 133; Hultgren, *Parables of Jesus*, 339; Linnemann, *Parables of Jesus*, 90–92; Manson, *The Sayings of Jesus*, 130; Marshall, *The Gospel of Luke*, 586–87; Perrin, *Rediscovering the Teaching*, 113; Smith, *Parables of the Synoptic Gospels*, 203; Weder, *Die Gleichnisse Jesu als Metaphern*, 185–90; Young, *Jesus and His Jewish Parables*, 169.

55. Scott, *Hear Then the Parable*, 163; Stein, *Introduction to the Parables*, 83; Young, *Jesus and His Jewish Parables*, 169.

dismissing the shared social value of hospitality and the practice of gener-alized reciprocity: that is, giving without expecting any return by treating neighbors and friends as kin (see chapter 10) Luke's version of the parable is sandwiched between his version of the Lord's Prayer (Luke 11:1–4) and three short "ask-receive" sayings (Luke 11:9–13)—with persistent prayer as the topic (a typical Lukan theme). Because of this narrative fit, the parable becomes an example of how one should be persistent in prayer. The context thus determines its meaning.

We have the same situation in Luke 14:1–24. By adding the parable of the Feast (Luke 14:16b–23) to a carefully constructed narrative in Luke 14:1–14, and providing it with an introduction (Luke 14:15) and a fitting conclusion (Luke 14:24), Luke determines the parable's meaning for his audience. The parable becomes either a symbol to portray the future mes-sianic banquet or a symbol of the history of salvation. Put differently, Luke's use of the parable makes possible an allegorical interpretation because he constructed a narrative "fit" for the parable. This is something else other than arranging a different version of the parable for a theological purpose, as Snodgrass argues Luke did.[56] The allegorical meaning of the parable in Luke 14:1–24 fits not because of Luke's so-called redactional changes of the parable, but because of Luke's narrative use of the parable. Luke's narrative technique in Luke 14:1–24—as I indicated—is first parable and then con-structed context, not first context and then constructed parable.

This argument finds support in a remark from Crossan.[57] Crossan, in his discussion of the possible editorial activity in the extant versions of the parable, refers to the odd discrepancy between Luke 14:12 and 14:16b–20. In Luke 14:12 Jesus explicitly states that when one invites people to a din-ner, one should not invite the rich. But this is exactly what happens in Luke 14:16b–20: the host first invites the rich, and only after their refusal, the poor, crippled, blind, and lame. It can be surmised that Luke, if he did re-dactionally edit the parable to follow Luke 1:1–14, would have redaction-ally addressed this discrepancy. Luke did not, most probably because he respected the version of the parable he borrowed from Q, and also because the discrepancy did not impact on the theological purpose he wanted to achieve.

The above line of argument begs the question about the opinion of several scholars that because of Luke's redactional activity in Luke 14:16–24, the first invitation in Luke 14:21 should be seen as paralleling Luke 14:13; because inviting the poor, crippled, blind, and lame is a favorite Lukan

56. Snodgrass, *Stories with Intent*, 306.
57. Crossan, *In Parables*, 70.

theme, the parable has been edited to include this motif. If the argument made above holds, the direct opposite should rather be assumed: because eating with the poor, crippled, blind, and lame was so important for Jesus, Luke included it in Luke 14:1–14. A decision on this point is important for the understanding of the parable in the 27–30-CE context, as will be indicated below. Did the "typically Lukan" became the "typically Jesus" in the parable, or did what was typical of Jesus influence the narrative context Luke created by using a Jesus parable? This is the important question.

Integrity

Luke 14:15, 23, and 24 are central when it comes to verifying the integrity of the parable. Although some accept Luke 14:15 as part of the original parable,[58] it is a Lukan creation linking the parable with Luke 14:1–14, especially with the macarism in Luke 14:14.[59] Luke 14:15 is Luke's introduction to the parable, through which he wants the hearer to understand an original Jesus parable: at the eschatological banquet, those who excluded the poor, crippled, lame, and blind (Luke 14:13; 21) will themselves be excluded. Since Jesus, in his parables at least, did not conceive of the kingdom as an eschatological entity, this verse cannot be traced to the earliest layer of the Jesus tradition.[60]

Arguments for the authenticity of Luke 14:24 differ, and at times the same arguments are used to include or exclude Luke 14:24. Hendrickx, for example, argues that Luke 14:24 was part of the pre-Lukan source to emphasize the great number of people the host wanted to fill his house,[61] and Groenewald is of the opinion that Luke 14:24 refers to Jesus' divine mission to the Gentiles at the earliest level of the parable's tradition.[62] Young also defends the originality of the second invitation, but for a different reason, namely, that Luke 14:24 stresses the urgency of Jesus' message.[63]

---

58. See, for example, Stein, *Introduction to the Parables*, 86.

59. Brouwer, *De Gelijkenissen*, 224; Hendrickx, *Parables of Jesus*, 113.

60. Van Eck, "Interpreting the Parables," 1–10, contra Manson, who argues that Luke 14:15, as an introductory statement to the parable, is "probably too good to be invented." Manson, *Sayings of Jesus*, 129. See also Bailey, *Poet and Peasant*, 89., for the same evaluation of Luke 14:15.

61. Hendrickx, *Parables of Jesus*, 120.

62. Groenewald, *In Gelykenisse Het Hy Geleer*, 200.

63. Young, *Jesus and His Jewish Parables*, 176.

According to Snodgrass, Luke 14:24 was not originally part of the parable of Jesus.[64] This view can be supported by the following arguments: Luke 14:24 forms an inclusio with Luke 14:15.[65] Since Luke 14:15 was not part of the original parable, Luke 14:24 should per se be excluded. Second, all three extant versions of the parable end with a conclusion fitting the specific version (Matt 22:14; *par.* Luke 14:24 and Gos. Thom. 64:12).[66] Third, the use of λέγω ὑμῖν (I tell you, pl.) in Luke 14:24 is odd. All through the parable the host addresses a single servant (Luke 14:17, 21, 23). One should therefore have expected λέγω σοί (I tell you, sing.).[67] Why this shift from singular to plural? In Luke (see, e.g., Luke 10:24; 11:8; 12:4, 27; 13:24; 15:7, 10; 16:9; 18:8, 14; 19:26) λέγω ὑμῖν is used by the Lukan Jesus as an introduction to the final judgment.[68] Because this use of λέγω ὑμῖν fits the eschatological slant of Luke's parable, Luke uses λέγω ὑμῖν, conforming to its use as a pronouncement formula in the gospel.[69] Luke 14:24 should thus be attributed to Luke's redactional activity.[70]

The point of view taken here is that Luke 14:24 most probably is a Lukan creation. In this final verse of the Lukan parable, the Lukan Jesus spells out who the people are who will be excluded from the messianic banquet. They are the Pharisees (Luke 14:1), who pick the places of honor at the table (Luke 14:7); only eat with friends, relatives, neighbors, and the rich; and refuse the invitations of the host (Luke 14:18–20): such people are epitomized by the Pharisee of Luke 14:15, who believes that one can constantly seek honor and exclude those without honor, and still be part of the final banquet. Luke 14:24 binds the narrative of Luke 14:1–24 neatly into a unit, and states the consequences for those who have rejected the invitation.[71] In the parable's narrative context Luke 14:24 indeed fits—without it, Luke's

---

64. Snodgrass, *Stories with Intent*, 691 n. 259. See also see also Bailey, *Poet and Peasant*, 109; Marshall, *Gospel of Luke*, 591.

65. Kilgallen, *Twenty Parables*, 82; Scott, *Hear Then the Parable*, 164; Swartley, "Unexpected Banquet People," 185.

66. Scott, *Hear Then the Parable*, 168.

67. Hultgren, *Parables of Jesus*, 338.

68. Jeremias, *Parables of Jesus*, 177.

69. Hultgren, *Parables of Jesus*, 338.

70. See also Funk et al., *Five Gospels*, 352; Schottroff, *Parables of Jesus*, 52.

71. Snodgrass, *Stories with Intent*, 691, n. 259; Weder, *Die Gleichnisse Jesu Als Metaphern*, 186. Derrett also argues that Luke 14:24 should be seen as the denouement of the parable, but for a different reason. According to him, Luke 14:24 does not spell out who will be excluded from the final messianic banquet; it is the refusal of an angered host to send portions of his meal to the absent guests. Derrett, *Law in the New Testament*, 141.

use of the parable has no "final nail in the coffin," metaphorically speaking. Without the context, the parable does not need Luke 14:24—in fact, without the context it does not "fit."

Some also consider Luke 14:23 a Lukan addition to the original parable, and for different reasons. Some argue that Luke added Luke 14:23 because of Luke 14:13;[72] those who read the parable as a history of salvation argue that Luke added 14:23 to also include the Gentiles,[73] while those who read the parable as a reference to the messianic banquet argue that Luke added the verse to emphasize the great number of people the host wanted to fill his house.[74].

In the reading of the parable that follows, Luke 14:16a–23 is seen as the parable closest to the earliest Jesus tradition. Luke 14:15 and 24 are excluded on the basis of the arguments above. Luke 14:23, however, is included. This inclusion is not based on the arguments normally put forward for inclusion. The basis for inclusion is verisimilitude. Luke's version of the parable is realistic when compared with the common features of the preindustrial city in advanced agrarian societies.[75] Luke's version of the parable, when taken out of its context in Luke 14:1–24 and interpreted inter alia through this perspectival lens, is not an allegory or a metaphor; it is a parable, an atypical story of what was typical and surprising in the world of Jesus and his hearers.

Reading Scenarios

Emic and Etic Reading[76]

The parable of the Feast is a story about a man (the host) who prepared a feast and invited many guests (Luke 14:16b). When the feast was ready, he

72. Scott, *Hear Then the Parable*, 165.

73. Bailey, *Poet and Peasant*, 101–6; Drury, *Parables in the Gospels*, 123; Fitzmyer, *The Gospel according to Luke*, 2:1053; Funk et al., *Five Gospels*, 352; Streeter, *Four Gospels*, 186; Vögtle, *Gott und Seine Gäste*, 78–79.

74. Hultgren, *Parables of Jesus*, 338; Jeremias, *Parables of Jesus*, 64. Jeremias is also of the opinion that in the extant versions of the parable only Luke has the second invitation and thus should be seen as secondary.

75. See Rohrbaugh, "Pre-Industrial City," 151–80.

76. The terms *emic* and *etic* were coined by Kenneth Pike in analogy to the concepts of phon*emic* and phon*etic*. *Emics* refers to "cultural explanations that draw their criteria from the consciousness of the people in the culture being explained," and *etics* refers to "cultural explanations whose criteria derive from a body of theory and method shared in a community of scientific observers." Gottwald, *Tribes of Yahweh*, 785. Or, as defined

sent his servant to tell those who had been invited to come (Luke 14:17). The invited guests all alike began to make excuses, giving reasons why they could not come: The first guest had bought a field and had to go to inspect it, the second guest had bought five yoke of oxen and was on his way to try them out, and the third guest had recently gotten married and therefore could not attend (Luke 14:18–20). When the servant informed the host about the turn of events, he became angry and sent his servant to the streets and alleys of the city to invite the poor, crippled, blind, and lame (Luke 14:21). The servant did what was ordered, and then reported back to his master that his house (the banquet hall) still had some places left (Luke 14:22). The master then sent his servant to invite the people who lived on the roads and country lanes to fill up the feast he prepared (Luke 14:23).

An emic reading of the parable (that is, a reading from the native's point of view) evokes several cultural norms (social values) of the first-century Mediterranean world that are implicitly embedded in the parable. These social values (cultural scripts) were part of the repertoire of the teller and audience of the parable—a shared cultural world of references that resonance in the parable.[77]

The social values embedded in the story that play a role in the dynamics of the parable are at least the following: The feast is a meal and thus a *ceremony* (boundary making) in which *purity* and *status* play a role, the invitations imply the pivotal role of *honor* as well as *patronage*, and accepting an invitation in the first-century Mediterranean world implied *reciprocity*. Also embedded in the parable, as Rohrbaugh has indicated, is the social function *gossip* played in the world of its audience.[78] Finally, the characteristics of the preindustrial city as a backdrop (social setting) of the parable,[79] the social dynamics implied by the inviting of guests in the first-century Mediterranean world, and the reason why guests excused themselves should also be taken into consideration if the modern interpreter of the parable wants to avoid the fallacies of ethnocentrism and anachronism.

---

by Elliott: "The term 'emic' identifies information provided by a native from a native's point of view as determined by his/her cultural setting, experience, and available knowledge. The term 'etic' identifies the perspective and categories of thought of the investigator or interpreter as determined by his/her different social, historical, and cultural location, experience, and available knowledge." Elliott, *Home for the Homeless*, 11. Therefore, an etic reading, in using specific reading scenarios, enables the interpreter to "see as the natives see[,] . . . value what they value[,] . . . and understand how and why they act the way they do." Neyrey, "Honor and Shame in the Passion Narrative," 115.

77. Scott, *Re-Imagine the World*, 109–117.

78. Rohrbaugh, "Gossip in the New Testament," 239–59.

79. Rohrbaugh, "Pre-Industrial City," 151–80.

Only a few scholars thus far have subjected the parable to a social-scientific reading, albeit with a limited scope. Scott focused on the social function of meals, the honor-shame culture of first-century Palestine, reciprocity and purity.[80] Snodgrass also refers to meals as a means of organizing Mediterranean society, and the pivotal role played by honor and shame in the world of Jesus. These social values, however, do not play any significant role in his analysis of the parable.[81] Donahue attends to purity and pollution as keys to understanding social and cultic boundaries in first-century Palestine, and the way the parable shatters these boundaries; boundaries that will only be shattered when the community celebrates the eschatological meal.[82]

An exception is Rohrbaugh's social-scientific reading of the parable. Rohrbaugh focuses on the social function of meals as ceremonies, on honor and shame, on reciprocity, on purity and pollution, on friendship and patronage. His contribution regarding the social function of gossip and the characteristics of the preindustrial city is especially noteworthy. Work done by Rohrbaugh on the parable does not only open up the social world of the parable, but importantly, enables a realistic reading of the parable. Several aspects of the reading of the parable below are indebted to his work.

The Backdrop of the Parable: The Preindustrial City

In preindustrial cities social status, honor, and where one lived went together, with walls clearly demarcating who belonged where, and gates controlling the interaction between the different social groups that inhabited the city. The elite occupied the walled-off center of the city, with the nonelite occupying the outlying area of the city, located between the inner and outer walls. Inside the city walls the elite and nonelite were physically and socially isolated from each other. The center of the city normally contained the palace, the temple and the residences of the political and religious elite—that is, those with honor, status, power, and privilege. The city center, apart from having its own internal walls, was clearly demarcated from the rest of the city (the outlying area) by an additional wall. Occupation of this outlying area (between the inner and outer wall) normally was organized in terms of particular families, income groups, guilds, ethnicities and lines of work. Living conditions in this area was not pleasant: The streets were unpaved, narrow, and badly crowded, with no passage for wheeled vehicles. Refuse

80. Scott, *Hear Then the Parable*, 161–74.
81. Snodgrass, *Stories with Intent*, 308.
82. Donahue, *Gospel in Parable*, 144–45.

and the presence of scavenging dogs, pigs, birds, and other animals made this area an unpleasant place to stay. The preindustrial city also "housed" a third group of people, the socially ostracized (prostitutes, beggars, tanners and other social outcasts such as lepers) People who were part of this group lived outside the outer walls of the city, and were only allowed to enter the city during the day, to (for example) look for work as day laborers.[83]

The preindustrial city thus was an example of what can be called "human territoriality,"[84] "the attempt by an individual or group to affect, influence or control people, phenomena, and relationships, by delimiting and asserting control over a geographical area."[85] What is important for the understanding of the parable is that social contact between the different groups, especially between the elite and nonelite, was nearly nonexistent.

> A member of the urban elite took significant steps to avoid contact with other groups except to obtain goods and services. Such a person would experience a serious loss of status if found to be socializing with groups other than his own. Thus social and geographical distancing, enforced and communicated by interior walls, characterized both internal city relations and those between city and country.[86]

Below it will be indicated that the characteristics of the preindustrial city is an important lens to understand the implications of the third and final invitation in the parable when the slave is ordered to go and invite those in the streets and alleys of the city (τὰς πλατείας καὶ ῥύμας τῆς πόλεως; Luke 14:21), and then those in the roads and country lanes (τὰς ὁδοὺς καὶ φραγμοὺς; Luke 14:23). These specific references not only place the story of the parable firmly in the social location of a preindustrial city, but also spell out the implications these invitations had for the host.

The Social Dynamics of Invitations in the First-century Mediterranean World

Greek papyri found in Egypt that has as content invitations to dinners indicate that the structure and form of these invitations likely were used

83. Rohrbaugh, "Pre-Industrial City," 133–46.
84. Ibid., 136.
85. Sack, cited by ibid.
86. Ibid.

to invite people to dinners like those mentioned in the New Testament.[87] Most of the invitations have the same form, including an invitation verb, the names of the invited guest and host, the purpose and occasion of the dinner, the date and time, and the venue where the dinner was to take place. Importantly, most of them either suggest that a double invite to a dinner was commonplace or included it.[88] This means that the two invitations in the parable can be considered realistic (verisimilitudes), drawn from the life and customs of first-century Palestinian Judaism.[89]

How do parable scholars interpret the invitations in the parable? According to Scott, the invitations referred to in the parable (Luke 14:16b and 17) normally were written by hosts and then orally conveyed (or read) by messengers to possible guests some time before a dinner. These messages were then followed with a courtesy reminder or second invitation with the messenger (most probably a slave) escorting the guests to the dinner.[90] Evidence of this practice is found in the Near Eastern custom of slaves arriving to announce that a banquet was ready.[91] The second invite also was a special sign of courtesy especially practiced by the wealthy elite in Jerusalem.[92]

What was the purpose of this double invitation? First, the initial invitation gave the invited guests ample notice of an occasion that was going to take place to which they had been invited, an invitation they had to respond to.[93] Second, as Bailey argues, a host had to prepare for the meal (e.g., proper meat), and for this the number of guests was needed.[94] The first invitation helped the host to know how many people would attend and how much food had to be prepared.[95] The first invitation was serious, and "acceptance

87. Kim, "The Papyrus Invitation," 391–402.

88. See, for example, Esth 5:8 and 6:14; Apuleius (*Metam.* 3.12); Gos. Thom. 64:1; *Midrash Rabbah Lamentations* 4.2; Sir 13:9; Plutarch (*Mor.* 511D–E); and Philo (*Opfic.* XXV.1.78). For examples from Greek papyri, see ibid., 393.

89. Stein, *Introduction to the Parables*, 84. *Contra* Crossan, *In Parables*, 73; Crossan, *The Historical Jesus*, 261., who argues that if the plot behind all three extant version of the parable is taken into consideration, there were no first invitations. The feast was unannounced, and because of the untimeliness of the invitation, the excuses offered are perfectly reasonable. See Rohrbaugh for a critique of Crossan's point of view, "a view that we suggests is a simple but obvious anachronism on the part of a modern interpreter with a busy schedule." Rohrbaugh, "Pre-Industrial City," 141.

90. Scott, *Hear Then the Parable*, 171.

91. Hultgren, *Parables of Jesus*, 333; Hunter, *Then and Now*, 93.

92. Jeremias, *The Parables of Jesus*, 176. See also Linnemann, *Parables of Jesus*, 87; Perkins, *Hearing the Parables*, 97; Scott, *Hear Then the Parable*, 169.

93. Crossan, *In Parables*, 73.

94. Bailey, *Poet and Peasant*, 94. See also Lockyer, *All the Parables*, 275.

95. Wenham, *Parables of Jesus*, 136.

of it a firm commitment, since the host prepared the amount of food on the basis of how many accepted the invitation";[96] guests who accepted the first invitation were duty bound to appear.[97] The second invitation was only extended if the first invitation was accepted, which happened at the hour of the banquet.[98] The second invitation thus was "a courtesy reminder, extended only to those guests who previously accepted the invitation."[99]

This "consensus-understanding" of the purpose of the double invitation is anachronistic, a nice fit to how things are done in a world to which modern interpreters of biblical texts belong. Much more is at stake here. The first invitation, from a social-scientific point of view, should rather be seen as an honor challenge. The purpose of the second invitation, also, can only be determined when gossip as a social game—that was part of the world of the parable—is taken into consideration.

Gossip[100]

In the majority of oral (nonliterate) cultures like that of the parable, gossip most of the time was the only way of obtaining information.[101] Gossip, in its cultural form, was understood as a "sort of game,"[102] a "catalyst of social process,"[103] a necessary and positive social activity of informal social bonding and formation, control and order.[104] In nonliterate societies gossip was an institutionalized means of informal communication, interwoven in the daily affairs and interactions between people, and everybody partook in it.[105]

96. Bailey, *Poet and Peasant*, 94.

97. Ibid. See also Timmer, *Kingdom Equation*, 56.

98. Kistemaker, *Stories Jesus Told*, 163.

99. Scott, *Hear Then the Parable*, 171.

100. For a more extensive description of gossip as a necessary social game in inter alia the first-century Mediterranean world, see Van Eck, "Invitations and Excuses," 2–9.

101. Paine, "What Is Gossip About?," 282; Malina and Rohrbaugh, *Social-Science Commentary on John*, 103.

102. Gluckman, "Gossip and Scandal," 307.

103. Paine, "What Is Gossip About?," 28–30.

104. Abrahams, "Performance-Centered Approach," 296; Gluckman, "Gossip and Scandal," 307; Paine, "What Is Gossip About?," 278.

105. Andreassen, "Gossip in Henningsvær," 41.

Gossip, as "a naturally recurring form of social organisation"[106] or "cultural form,"[107] can in short be defined as conversations or critical talk about absent third parties.[108] This definition implies the following as characteristics of gossip: 1) Gossip is "signed" or face-to-face–talk about people who are not present;[109] 2) for gossip to occur, it requires that participants know each other, understand the import of the situation, and share evaluative categories;[110] 3) gossip overlaps with simple word-of-mouth "news" about what is going on[111] and is often the principal means of information-exchange in nonliterate villages;[112] 4) gossip is evaluative talk and usually implies assessment of one kind or another;[113] 5) gossip normally serves the interests of individuals (self–interest) and the groups individuals belong to;[114] and 6) its main cause is often the intense competition for public reputation (honor)[115] and community status (personal power).[116]

These characteristics imply several social functions of gossip as a controlled cultural form. Rohrbaugh identifies the following four social functions of gossip: 1) Clarification (consensus building), maintenance (re-affirmation) and enforcement (sanction) of group value; 2) group formation and boundary maintenance; 3) the moral assessment of individuals; and 4) leadership identification and competition.[117]

106. Handelman, "Gossip in Encounters," 212.

107. Spacks, *Gossip*, 15.

108. Daniels defines gossip as follows: "Gossip is face-to-face communication involving at least two persons, two groups, or a single group, engaged in transacting information, either positive or negative in character, about a third-party subject who is either actually absent or rendered absent to the conversation. A gossip encounter occurs as a response to a generative event, or reports such an event, that undercuts or challenges the established social-cultural expectations of persons, in an attempt to (re) assert or (re)construct reality." Daniels, "Gossip's Role in Constituting Jesus," 38–39. This definition of Daniels is noteworthy since it incorporates the characteristics, social function, reason, and aim of gossip as a social game. See also Gilmore, "Varieties of Gossip," 92; Haviland, *Gossip, Reputation, and Knowledge*, 28; Hunter, "Gossip and the Politics of Reputation," 300.

109. Rohrbaugh, "Gossip in the New Testament," 241.

110. Yerkovich, "Gossiping," 192.

111. Rohrbaugh, "Gossip in the New Testament," 241.

112. Arno, "Fijian Gossip as Adjudication"; Paine, "What Is Gossip About?," 282.

113. Rohrbaugh, "Gossip in the New Testament," 241.

114. Ibid.

115. Ibid., 245.

116. Abrahams, "Performance-Centered Approach," 292.

117. Rohrbaugh, "Gossip in the New Testament," 251–56. See also Malina and Rohrbaugh, *Social-Science Commentary on John*, 103.

The above characteristics and social functions of gossip imply that gossip takes place where there is agreement on the norms and values of a specific community.

> Thus, for someone to become the subject of gossip, that one must do something to draw attention to him/herself, usually something that goes against social norms, or undercuts the managed impression of the way things or individuals should be . . . In other words . . . for a gossip event to occur there must be an unexpected or unusual event that causes it, at least two persons engaged in the communicative event (gossiper and listener), a third party subject of the gossip, and some sort of social setting where . . . persons normally get together to socialize.[118]

From the above it is clear that gossip and status and honor go hand in hand. Gossip reinforced behavioral norms, and conformity to these norms became the basis of social reputation and competition for acquired honor. Gossip was, in quoting Gluckman, "one of the chief weapons which those who consider themselves higher in status use to put those whom they consider lower in their proper place."[119] Competition for honor, social ranking and higher status thus went together with gossip. As Rohrbaugh puts it, "The point, then, is that in the degree to which evaluation or moral judgment is involved, gossip becomes a way of manipulating moral status (acquired honor) or other prospects in the "interests" of some person or group." And since "competition for reputation . . . is a matter of honor, and honor is the core value in the Mediterranean world," it is clear that gossip played a pivotal role in the maintenance of one's honor in the Mediterranean world. Failure of any kind, but especially failure to defend honor, therefore always was the subject of gossip.[120]

In the reading of the parable to follow, it will be indicated that the three excuses in the parable, when interpreted through the lens of gossip as a social game in nonliterate cultures, can help the modern interpreter of the parable to avoid an ethnocentric interpretation of these excuses.

Meals as Ceremonies

In the Mediterranean world meals taken together were seen as a confirmations of shared values and structures, status and honor ratings.

118. Daniels, "Gossip's Role in Constituting Jesus," 17–18, 30.
119. Gluckman, "Gossip and Scandal," 319.
120. Rohrbaugh, "Gossip in the New Testament," 242–43.

> When people gathered for meals in first-century Mediterranean cultures, the event was laden with meaning. Meals were highly stylized occasions that carried significant social coding, identity formation, and meaning making. Participating in a meal entailed entering into a social dynamic that confirmed, challenged, and negotiated both who the group as a whole was and who the individuals within in it were.[121]

> If food is treated as a code, the message it encodes will be found in the pattern of social relations being expressed. The message is about different degrees of hierarchy, inclusion and exclusion, boundaries and transactions across the boundaries.[122]

Meals, from a social-scientific point of view, are ceremonies—events that occur regularly, are called for, and function to confirm roles and statuses within a given group. Meals-as-ceremonies bolstered the boundaries that defined specific groups, confirmed established roles and statuses, and attended to stability and continuity; meals-as-ceremonies replicated a group's basic social system, values, lines, and classifications.[123]

Because meals had to do with different degrees of hierarchy, inclusion and exclusion, and boundaries, likes only ate with likes—that is, people ate with others of the same social standing, status and honor rating. This means that members of the elite, who occupied the walled-off center of the city, only ate with (certain) other members of the elite behind the inner wall, but not with the nonelites occupying the outlying area of the city located between the inner and outer walls of the city, or with those (the impure and marginalized) who lived outside the city walls. Contact between the elite and the latter two groups was nearly nonexistent, and where contact did take place, it was mainly for economic reasons (the exchange of goods and services); socializing and eating together simply did not take place.

The "social dynamic" of meals, referred to by Taussig, also relates to what is known as reciprocity (the way goods were exchanged in first-century Palestine) and patronage.[124] Reciprocity between equals, known as balanced reciprocity (the idea of quid pro quo), meant that an invitation to a meal was to be followed up by the same kind of invitation to the one who invited a person first. An invitation to a meal, in short, increased the social

---

121. Taussig, *In the Beginning Was the Meal*, 22. See also Wright, *Jesus the Storyteller*, 114.

122. Douglas, *Implicit Meanings*, 249.

123. Neyrey, "Ceremonies in Luke-Acts," 363.

124. Malina, *Christian Origins and Cultural Anthropology*, 98–106.

indebtedness of others to the host.[125] Patronage, in this context, is a form of reciprocity. If a host distributes food, what would he want in return?[126] Attending a meal in the first-century Mediterranean world thus was serious business.

Purity and Pollution

During the Second Temple period the priestly elite and Pharisees understood God in terms of his holiness as expressed, for example, in Leviticus 19:2 ("Be holy because I, the LORD your God, am holy"). God's holiness was embedded in the way God created. The way God created was to separate, as expressed in Genesis 1. He separated day from night, the days of the week from the Sabbath; birds, animals, and fish were created different from one another and only in "pure" forms (no hybrids), land was separated from the sea (the waters), and every living creature were allocated its proper place in creation (e.g., the fish in the water and the birds in the sky). God's creation, in *nuce*, meant order in terms of place, time, living beings and status (hierarchy). There was a place for everything, and everything had its place. God's holiness meant order, and to be holy as God is holy meant that God's order—as set up at creation—had to be respected. God's creation expressed the divine order of the world; "it encoded various 'maps' of lines which God made for Israel to perceive and to follow."[127]

In the time of Jesus, the temple (as the *axis mundi*), the central religious symbol of the Jewish *ethnos*, personified God's presence and holiness (order). To replicate God's holiness purity laws were put into place. These rules inter alia determined which animals could be sacrificed (no hybrids or animals with defects), which persons were to preside over the sacrifices, who were allowed to take part in these sacrifices (only "pure" Israelites with no bodily defects), and when and where these sacrifices had to take place.

Also, the human body was seen as a replica of the social body.[128] As the social body drew lines, restricted admission, expelled undesirables and guarded its entrances and exits, boundaries and margins existed for the human body as well. The boundary of the body was seen as the skin, with orifices as gateways to the interior of the body, just as walled cities had gates. Lepers, for example, were seen as persons who had no respect for bound-

125. Scott, *Hear Then the Parable*, 169.

126. Neyrey, "Ceremonies in Luke-Acts," 374.

127. Van Eck, "Jesus and Violence," 114. See also Neyrey, "Symbolic Universe of Luke-Acts," 277; Van Eck, *Galilee and Jerusalem in Mark's Story of Jesus*, 196–206.

128. Douglas, *Purity and Danger*, 15; Douglas, *Natural Symbols*, 93.

aries because of their "leprosy" and therefore were rendered ritually and socially unclean. "Too little" and "too much" was also important; bodies that had too little, like the deaf, blind, or lame, were also rendered unclean.[129] The place for these "unclean" persons was normally outside the city walls; after all, there was a place for everything, and everybody, and everything and everybody had its place.

Reading the Parable

What will an etic reading of the parable look like when interpreted against the backdrop of the prendustrial city, and through the social-scientific lenses of meals as ceremonies, purity, gossip, status, honor, and reciprocity?

Luke 14:16b sets the scene of the parable: A certain man (ἄνθρωπός τις) prepared a great feast (δεῖπνον μέγα)—the main meal Jews usually ate in the evening[130]—and invited many (πολλοὺς) guests.[131] Although the host of the feast is simply introduced in Luke 14:16b as a certain man (ἄνθρωπός τις), in can be deducted from the parable that he was a wealthy person. The host has the means to entertain "many" (πολλοὺς) with a big feast (δεῖπνον μέγα), and has the services of a slave (Luke 14:16b, 17, 20–23). He was a "great man," referred to as "master of the house" (οἰκοδεσπότης; Luke 14:21), and addressed by his slave as "master," "lord" or "owner" (κύριος Luke 14:21, 22, 23).[132] The double invite in the parable further illustrates the man's wealth, since the double invite was a special sign of courtesy practiced

129. Neyrey, "Symbolic Universe of Luke–Acts," 284.

130. The term δεῖπνον Luke 14:16b uses to describe the feast has two possible meanings: "a meal whether simple or elaborate" (thus generic) or "the principal meal of the day, usually in the evening—'supper, main meal.'" Louw and Nida, Greek-English Lexicon, 1:252. See also Hultgren, Parables of Jesus, 336. Louw and Nida, Greek-English Lexicon, 1:252., Str-B., 207, as well as parable scholars like Stein and Linnemann, connect the second meaning to Luke 14:16b. The Jews in Palestine, unlike the Greeks, who ate three meals a day and the Romans who ate four, normally ate only two meals—the first was a late breakfast, and the second in the evening when there was no longer sufficient light to work. Stein, Introduction to the Parables, 84, 159, n. 3–5). Luke's use of δεῖπνον most probably refers to the second meal the Jews ate. Ibid., 84; Linnemann, Parables of Jesus, 88.

131. In the interpretation that follows, the parable is divided into eight scenes: (1) the preparation of the feast and a first invitation (Luke 14:16b), (2) a scene not narrated (see below), (3) a second invitation (Luke 14:17), (4) the excuses (Luke 14:18–20), (5) first report back from the slave and the reaction of the host (Luke 14:21a and 21b); 6) a third invitation (Luke 14:21c), (7) the second report back of the slave (Luke 14:22), and (8) the fourth invitation (Luke 14:23).

132. Bailey, Poet and Peasant, 94.

by the wealthy.[133] This description of the host of the feast places him among the urban elite, as "a leading member of that urban group which both sets the terms for and controls access to social interaction between itself and others in the society."[134] Finally, if those invited in Luke 14:21 and 23—the people living inside the city between the inner and outer walls in the wider streets and squares and the narrow streets and alleys (τὰς πλατείας καὶ ῥύμας τῆς πόλεως; Luke 14:21), and those in the roads and country lanes or hedges (τὰς ὁδοὺς καὶ φραγμοὺς; Luke 14:23) outside the city walls—are understood as the socially impure (expendables),[135] the host most probably was a Jew.[136] The host thus most probably was one of the elite who occupied the walled-off center of the city.

Since likes (people with the same social standing, status, and honor rating) only ate with likes in the first-century Mediterranean world, it can be supposed that the invitees of Luke 14:18–20 were also part of the elite who occupied the walled-off center of the city. The parable gives us enough information in the excuses of three of the many guests invited to the feast to make this conclusion. The first invitee has acquired a piece of land. No peasant would sell his land if it was not the final option. Because of rents, taxes (extracted by the elite) and high interest rates on loans (made available by the elite), numbers of peasants in first-century Palestine lost their land, or had to sell it. Available land normally was bought by the elite who had the means to acquire land, and much of the land outside cities in first-century Palestine indeed was owned by the elite.[137] The person behind the second excuse was also one of these landowning elite. According to Jeremias, the general size of the land of a peasant farmer was more or less 10–20 hectares, which needed 1–2 yoke of oxen to plow.[138] In Luke 14:19 the person has bought five yoke of oxen, which means that the land he owned was at least 50 hectares in size. If one also takes into consideration that normally half of a land was left fallow each year, a landowner needing five oxen was the owner

---

133. Scott, *Hear Then the Parable*, 169.

134. Rohrbaugh, "Pre-Industrial City," 140.

135. Duling, *Marginal Scribe*, 67–71. See also Wright, *Jesus the Storyteller*, 114.

136. Jeremias is very specific in his description of the host; the host is a tax gatherer who became wealthy and invited people from the highest circles to endorse his new position. There is no evidence in the parable for such a clear-cut description. Jeremias, *Parables of Jesus*, 178–179. Schottroff, who reads the parable in the context of the Jewish tradition of loving deeds and the rights of the poor in the sense of Israel's Torah, also depicts the host as a well-to-do Jewish man. Schottroff, *Parables of Jesus*, 50–53.

137. Rohrbaugh, "Pre-Industrial City," 142–143.

138. Jeremias, *Parables of Jesus*, 177.

of a very large piece of land. [139] The third guest that had recently got married (Luke 14:20) most probably also was part of the elite, although in his case only indirect inferences can be made. Marriage in the Mediterranean world always was parentally arranged, and went hand in hand with honor and status, as well as political and economic concerns.[140] Since this guest was on the list of those invited, he most probably was in the same honor, economic, and political league of the other invitees.[141] He was therefore also one of the elite, as were the rest of the "many" (Luke 14:16b) invited who also did not show up at the feast. Since likes only ate with likes, the other guests most probably were of the same status.

From an etic perspective, the scene set by Luke 14:16b is thus that of Jewish elite inviting other elite—all of whom occupied the walled-off center of the city—to the main meal of the day (supper). The parable then continues with three scenes of which only the third (the second invitation) and fourth scene (some of the guests excusing themselves) are narrated. The second scene is not narrated, namely, what happened "backstage" between the first and second invitation. This nonnarrated event (second scene) is important to understand the parable; it binds the first four scenes of the parable as a unit, and serves as stimulus for the final four scenes of the parable.

In the first four scenes of the parable, when looked at as a unit, the host follows the typical Near Eastern custom practiced by the wealthy elite, extending two invitations to his potential guests, who then all excuse themselves. To understand the social dynamics of these four scenes it is necessary to look more closely at the excuses being offered and to revisit the purpose of the double invite (the first two invitations) in the parable.

The three excuses in Luke 14:18–20 are interpreted in more or less four ways (with some scholars having more than one opinion). The first position is that the excuses have to be interpreted in terms of orality and storytelling, that is, in terms of their intended effect on the parable. According to this

139. The estimates of the size of land owned by peasants in first-century Palestine by Schottroff, Stegemann, and Oakman, as well as the size of the land owned by the person who bought five yoke of oxen, concurs with this conclusion. Rohrbaugh, "Pre-Industrial City," 143.

140. Van Eck, "Huwelik, Egbreuk, Egskeiding En Hertrou," 104–8.

141. "Marriages in antiquity were made by extended families, not individuals, and were parentally arranged; they were not agreements between a man and a woman who have been romantically involved . . . [I]ndividuals really did not get married. Families did. One family offered a male, the other a female. Their wedding stood for the wedding of the larger extended families and symbolized the fusion of honour of both families involved. It would be undertaken with a view to political and/or economic concerns—even when it may be confined to fellow ethnics, as it was in first-century Israel." Malina and Rohrbaugh, *Social-Science Commentary on the Synoptic Gospels*, 28, 240.

position, the excuses are hyperbolic,[142] exaggerated,[143] or even absurd.[144] This, however, can be explained: Although most unusual, "in a parable unusual actions such as this are frequently portrayed and would be accepted as part of the storyteller's freedom in telling the story."[145] The excuses should thus be understood in terms of the rule of good storytelling,[146] as evidence of the rule of three and the economy of the parables of Jesus.[147] Also, the use of threes in the parable (the three invitations and three excuses) helps to aid the memory, and is evidence that the parable was formulated and passed down orally.[148]

A second position sees the excuses as valid, especially when the untimeliness of the invitations is taken into consideration. Crossan, for example, opines that the excuses are valid and extremely polite,[149] as does Perkins—the excuses are "acceptable or at least probable excuses in polite form."[150] Funk interprets the excuses in the same vein; the three invitees refuse for quite legitimate reasons,[151] "in accordance with the regulations that allow those conscripted to complete essential tasks."[152]

The third and minority position is that of Linnemann. The excuses, Linnemann argues, are not weak excuses, but a notice to the host that they indeed will come, but will be late. After all, one is in the act of buying a field and another has to go and try out five yoke of oxen.[153]

142. Weder, *Die Gleichnisse Jesu als Metaphern*, 187.

143. Funk et al., *Five Gospels*, 352.

144. Jeremias, *Parables of Jesus*, 178.

145. Stein, *Introduction to the Parables*, 85.

146. Hultgren, *Parables of Jesus*, 336.

147. Snodgrass, *Stories with Intent*, 306.

148. Funk et al., *Five Gospels*, 352. The excuses thus lack verisimilitude and cannot be related to the possibility that all the invited guests, for a specific reason, indeed excused themselves.

149. Crossan, *Historical Jesus*, 261.

150. Perkins, *Hearing the Parables*, 97.

151. Funk et al. are not clear on this point. Earlier they state that the excuses are "most trifling." Funk et al., *Five Gospels*, 352, 354.

152. This position seems to be built on the premise that only one invitation was extended to the invitees.

153. Linnemann, *Parables of Jesus*, 89. This interpretation is built on the content of the rest of the parable—especially the reaction of the host and his reaction to invite other guests instead—ignores the third excuse, and lacks a close reading of the text.

The fourth and dominant interpretation is that the excuses are flimsy and spurious, even comic,[154] and do not stand the test.[155] No one buys a field before inspecting it, buys five oxen before testing them out, or accepts an invitation to a banquet and forgets that he was getting married or decides to spend time with the unimportant sex (a woman) if one can spend it with a man[156]—all tasks that could have been done on any other day.[157] The excuses are insulting,[158] or even deliberately insulting and extremely offensive; by accepting it, the first invitation it became a command that had to be honored.[159]

These four interpretations of the excuses in the parable, first of all, focus on the content of the excuses with a typically modern approach of true or false. To be fair, some interpreters do refer to spirit and essence of the excuses, namely, that it seems the invitees do not want to go.[160] The three given excuses, however, are not related to the deafening silence of the other invited guests (the many invited). The question should not be why the three invitees did not attend the feast, but why everybody turned the invitation down. Second, even when one focuses on the content of the three excuses in Luke 14:18–20, the stock interpretation given by most scholars should not simply be accepted at face value. Luke 14:1–20 does not suggest that a field was bought before any inspection, that the five yoke of oxen were not tested out earlier, or that a newlywed all of a sudden forgot that he was getting married.[161] But again, this is not the point. The point is what lies behind

154. Wright, *Jesus the Storyteller*, 115.

155. Bailey, *Poet and Peasant*, 94; Boice, *Parables of Jesus*, 89; Hultgren, *Parables of Jesus*, 336; Jeremias, *Parables of Jesus*, 179; Kilgallen, *Twenty Parables*, 84–85; Kistemaker, *Stories Jesus Told*, 163; Scott, *Hear Then the Parable*, 169; Snodgrass, *Stories with Intent*, 687; Wenham, *Parables of Jesus*, 136.

156. Bailey, *Poet and Peasant*, 99; Scott, *Hear Then the Parable*, 169; Snodgrass, *Stories with Intent*, 687.

157. Kilgallen, *Twenty Parables*, 86.

158. Bailey, *Poet and Peasant*, 94; Wenham, *The Parables of Jesus*, 136.

159. Hultgren, *Parables of Jesus*, 336; Kistemaker, *Stories Jesus Told*, 163.

160. Kistemaker, *Stories Jesus Told*, 163; Lockyer, *All the Parables*, 276–77; Morgan, *Parables and Metaphors*, 181–82; Schippers, *Gelijkenissen van Jezus*, 41; Scott, *Re-Imagine the World*, 109–17.

161. Why is it not also possible that the field already was inspected before, and now was going to be inspected for a specific reason? Maybe the new owner had some work done on the plot he recently bought, like plowing or the possibility of starting to plow because of the season, moving his sheep from one part of the plot to another to manage grazing, fencing, or progress with the erection of a dwelling or any other project? Why is not the possibility that the five yoke of oxen were going to be tried out on a different kind of terrain, with a new driver or plow, or even with changing the pairs of oxen around? And why is it not possible that the third person indeed recently got married,

these excuses, and why *all* the invited turned down the invitation. In the third place, these interpretations work with the premise that the first invitation implied a definite yes or no on the part of the invitees, since a number was needed for the preparation of the banquet. Thus, what is at play here is common courtesy towards a host, a gesture that will make it possible for a host not be shamed at a banquet where there is not enough to eat or drink. Who, in our modern society, would like to be part of such an embarrassing situation?

The "dominant interpretation" of the invitations and excuses in the parable, which can be called the "received view," exposes our uncritical lenses when interpreting ancient text that are the products of cultures vastly different from ours. In an effort to overcome this "hermeneutical deficit," the relationship between the first two invitations and the excuses in the parable should rather be understood as the result of gossip as a cultural form or social game that was engrained in the cultural world that produced the parable.

The purpose of the first invitation was not to give ample notice of an occasion that was going to take place, to get the number of guests that will attend, or an invitation that expected an answer. In essence, the first invitation was an honor challenge to the invited. [162] As Rohrbaugh puts it,

> a double invitation would have several purposes. Initially the *potential* guest would have to decide if this was a social obligation he could afford to return in kind. Reciprocity in regard to meals was expected . . . But more importantly, *the time between the invitations would allow opportunity for potential guests to find out* what the festive occasion might be, who is coming, and whether all had been done appropriately in arranging the dinner.[163] *Only then* would the discerning guest be comfortable showing up. The nearly complete social stratification of pre-industrial cities required keeping social contacts across class lines to a minimum

but the marriage feast was extended past the normal-period feast of seven days? See Ferguson, *Backgrounds of Early Christianity*, 55; Malina and Rohrbaugh, *Social-Science Commentary on the Synoptic Gospels*, 70–71. Many more reasons can be added to these listed here, just as possible or impossible. The validity or invalidity of these possibilities is just the point. It is not about the content of the excuses but about what possible social dynamics behind the excuses can be identified.

162. *Contra* Snodgrass, who argues that nothing in the parable "suggests that the host gave his banquet as a quest for honor," although he is also of the opinion that meals in the world of the parable were a means of organizing society. Snodgrass, *Stories with Intent*, 308.

163. That is, the second nonnarrated scene of the parable.

and elaborate networks of informal communication monitored
such contacts to enforce rigidly the social code.[164]

What Rohrbaugh clearly implies is that after the first invitation, the gossip network of the community kicked in (the second nonnarrated scene): the invitation extended to many is now discussed (gossiped) in the community with the view of clarification and boundary maintenance and enforcement. The host is morally assessed, and boundary maintenance is taking place.

On the day of the banquet, the second invitation goes out (third scene), not only to those who accepted the first invitation, but again to all invited. In other words, on the day of the banquet the host is inquiring about his honor rating in the community. And the answer he receives is not positive: he has not made it—peer approval is not forthcoming. This host obviously had an honor rating in the community, as all had. What this rating was is not stated. What we do know is that the man must have been part of the elite: he is wealthy enough to entertain many, and owns a slave. Since meals were occasions that carried significant social coding and identity formation, the host saw himself as their peer and equal, or hoped that by accepting, his guests—who are part of the elite—will either affirm his current honor–rating or rating he is aspiring to. But something is wrong with the feast. What parable is, the parable does not say. What is clear is that his invitation was unexpected or unusual, and went against the accepted and agreed social norms of the community. The host therefore became the subject of gossip because his, and the honor rating in the community, was at stake. This can be deducted from the excuses given to his slave, excuses that are, as a result of the gossip that took place, a riposte of the invitees and community to his challenge implied in the first invitation. Again, Rohrbaugh is on the spot:

> Their excuses, seemingly irrelevant to the Western, industrialized mind, are standard fare in the dynamics of honor-shame societies. *The point is not the excuses at hand, but social disapproval of the arrangement being made*, a point to which their seeming irrelevance contributes. Something is wrong with the supper being offered or the guests would not only appear, social opinion would demand that they do so.[165]

Thus, what is important for the understanding the parable at this point is not the content of the excuses but rather what lies behind them. A few parable scholars indeed, as referred to above, have identified this important

164. Rohrbaugh, "Pre-Industrial City," 141; italics added.
165. Ibid., 141–142. Emphasis added.

aspect of the three excuses in the parable.[166] None of these scholars, however, sees the social dynamics of gossip as a social game as the important key to understand the excuses. With gossip as the interpretative key the three excuses given in the parable are not the result of the oral transmission of the parable in its preliterary form following the rule of threes in good storytelling. Also, it does not matter if the excuses are valid or invalid, or a notice of latecomers. In the world of the parable this does not matter at all. What matters is what the excuses convey: the host is shunned.[167] He played the social game according to the rules, but did not make it—as a result of gossip.

Why can this be stated in such categorical terms? Because no one attends the feast, not only the three who excused themselves, but also not one of the many others invited. The excuses of the three guests represent the outcome of the gossip network operating in the community. Attendance was socially inappropriate. The elite guests played according to the rules, value system, and norms of the community: "their excuses conceal the real reason for the disapproval as the system demands. Nor do they break ranks. If one does not show, none do. None will risk cutting himself off from their peers."[168]

When the slave reports back to the host that not one of the invited elite was going to attend his feast, he gets angry (fifth scene). The reason for this is obvious. Boundaries were drawn, and as a result of gossip he was rejected and shamed. Those he thought or hoped would see him as a peer rejected him—his honor–challenge (invitation) did not make it. Not one of the elite invited was willing to acknowledge him as patron, or put them in a position in which they had to reciprocate. What could he do to save face?

What the host then did is the surprising element of the parable. He decides to be a different kind of patron, a patron that is not interested in honor ratings or balanced reciprocity, that is, what he can get out of inviting people to his feast. He sends his slave to invite people living in the wider streets and squares and the narrow streets and alleys (τὰς πλατείας καὶ ῥύμας τῆς

---

166. Lockyer, for example, refers to the same spirit and essence of the excuses, Scott notes that the excuses have "the appearance of a concerted effort on the part of those invited," and Plummer calls the excuses "a conspiracy." See Lockyer, *All the Parables*, 276; Scott, *Hear Then the Parable*, 171; Plummer, *St. Luke*, 54–56. Some also agree that with the excuses the host is effectively snubbed (Scott and Galstone), that the excuses indicate some hostility towards the host from those who were invited because they did not like the host, and that the invitees "boycotted the invitation, likely because of some social impropriety." See Scott, *Hear Then the Parable*, 169; Galston, *Embracing the Human Jesus*, 108; Braun, in Swartley, "Unexpected Banquet People," 186–187.

167. So Wright, *Jesus the Storyteller*, 114.

168. Rohrbaugh, "Pre-Industrial City," 143.

πόλεως; Luke 14:21), that is, those who live inside the city between the inner and outer walls (scene six). And when the slave reports back that there is still room for more (scene seven), he sends his slave to invite (compel or convince) those in the roads and country lanes or hedges (τὰς ὁδοὺς καὶ φραγμοὺς; Luke 14:23), the socially impure (expendables) living outside the city walls (scene eight).

Thus, while the urban elite first invited took significant steps to avoid contact with those living outside the inner and outer walls of the city except to obtain goods and services, the host socializes and eats with them. By this the host abandons the ever present competition for acquired honor in the first-century Mediterranean world, replaces balanced reciprocity (*quid pro quo*) with generalized reciprocity (giving without expecting anything back), and declares the purity system which deems some as socially and ritually (culturally) impure null and void. All walls have been broken down, and the world is turned upside down.[169]

Note, however, from the perspective of the kingdom of God, the point Jesus wanted to make with the parable. In the kingdom patrons are real patrons when they act like the host: giving to those who cannot give back, breaking down physical (walls) and manmade boundaries (purity and pollution), and treating everybody as family (generalized reciprocity), without being afraid of being shamed. This was the kingdom of God, a kingdom in which the pivotal value of honor that organized and stratified society had no role, a kingdom in which purity did not ostracize and marginalize the so-called unclean or expendables.[170] When patrons are real patrons, the kingdom of God is visible, and not the kingdom of Rome (honor) or the kingdom of the temple (purity).

A Parable of Jesus?

The parable, as interpreted above, has all the earmarks of a Jesus parable. Typical of Jesus' parables, the parable of the Feast cuts against the social grain, and most probably represents the earliest layer of the historical Jesus tradition It resonates with Jesus' own eating practice (Matt 9:10–13; Mark

169. "Indeed, the parable corrupts privilege by turning the gathering into a party of nobodies." Galston, *Embracing the Human Jesus*, 109. See also Wright, *Jesus the Storyteller*, 116.

170. "The story portrays an incident in which the collapse of the current social order opens the way . . . for the hungry to be fed. It has nothing to do with anyone's repentance, but a great deal to do with the inexorable and earthly coming of God's kingdom." Wright, *Jesus the Storyteller*, 118.

2:15–17, Luke 5:29–32; Matt 11:19, Luke 7:34; see also Luke 15:2; 19:5–10), with his stance on reciprocity and his attitude toward the temple purity system (inclusivity). In terms of the criteria of early, multiple, and independent attestation, and coherence, the parable displays typical values that Jesus advocated—general reciprocity, challenge to laws governing pollution and purity, and status reversal, namely, that those who are part of the kingdom are like real brothers and sisters (in the sense of fictive-kin).

Jesus' stance in the parable on general reciprocity echoes his sayings in Q 6:34–35 and Gos. Thom. 95:1–2 (lend without return), Q 6:33 (not only to do good to those who can do good to you), and Q 6:36 (be compassionate to everybody as God is compassionate toward everybody). With regard to Jesus' critique on the temple's purity system, the parable parallels Jesus' sayings in Mark 7:14–15; Matt 15:10–11; and Gos. Thom. 4:5 (it is not what goes in that defiles, but what goes out).[171] The parable, finally, iterates the kind of fictive family that makes up the kingdom. The kingdom consists of those who are like children (who had no status in the first-century Mediterranean world; Mark 10:13–16, *par.* Matt 19:13–15 and Luke 18:15–17; see also Gos. Thom. 22:2; John 3:3, 5), those who love their enemies (Q 6:27) and not only loves those who love them (Q 6:32). Like the host, the kingdom belongs to those who do the will of God (Q 8:21; *par.* Gos. Thom. 99:2).

The values in the parable are also paralleled in other Jesus parables, either in a positive or negative way. In the parables of the Mustard Seed (Q 13:18–19; *par.* Gos. Thom. 20:1–4) and the Leaven (Q 13:20–21; *par.* Gos. Thom. 96:1–2) the kingdom is respectively also described as consisting of "unclean" weed, "clean" seed and the "impure." In the parables of the Friend at Midnight (Luke 11:5–8) and the Rich Man and Lazarus (Luke 16:19–26), the neighbor and the rich man are criticized by Jesus for their lack of patronage in the form of general reciprocity; they should be like the host who invited those without status to his feast and the shepherd of the parable of the Lost Sheep who does his utmost that everybody has enough. And in the parable of the Vineyard Laborers (Matt 20:1–5) we find the same status reversal as in the parable of the Feast.

Like the host in the parable, Jesus regularly associated with the so-called impure and ate with the so-called sinners of his day. Because of this, Jesus was called a glutton and drunkard and a friend of tax collectors and sinners (Luke 7:34). In the eyes of the dominant kingdoms of his time,

---

171. "The aphorism . . . is a categorical challenge to the laws governing pollution and purity. Since the saying need not be taken entirely literally . . . it can also be made to apply to other forms of pollution . . . [I]t challenges the everyday, the inherited, the established, and erases social boundaries taken to be sacrosanct." Funk et al., *Five Gospels*, 69.

Rome and the temple, Jesus had no honor because of his eating practice and associations. He was a foolish patron who extended patronage to the wrong people and did not respect the boundaries of society—like the host in the parable.

CHAPTER 5

The Lost Sheep (Luke 15:4–6): A Surprising Shepherd

The history of the interpretation of the parable of the Lost Sheep shows that its interpretation has not significantly changed since its earliest allegorical interpretations. Almost all interpretations see the parable as either emphasizing God's forgiveness, grace, mercy, love, and compassion for the lost, or God's joy when a sinner is found. The reason for this unanimity is that almost all interpretations see the shepherd in the parable as a metaphor for God or Jesus. This is also the reason why themes like forgiveness, repentance, sinners, and salvation are identified in the parable. A straightforward literal reading of the parable, however, shows that these themes are not present in the parable.

In the reading of the parable here a different approach is followed. As is the case all the parables read in this volume, the parable will be interpreted as a parable of the historical Jesus (thus not in its synoptic context), using social-scientific criticism as approach in trying to avoid the fallacies of anachronism and ethnocentrism. In the reading of the parable special attention will be given to the economic and social registers presupposed in the parable. But first I offer a short overview of the history of the parable's interpretation.

History of Interpretation

The earliest interpretations of the parable of the Lost Sheep,[1] apart from its use by the Matthew and Luke, are the allegorical interpretations of Tertul-

1. The premise taken here is that the Lukan version of the parable represents the Q version, and therefore is most probably closest to the earliest layer of the historical Jesus-tradition (see below). The focus here is therefore on the history of the interpretation of

lian, Aquinas, and Calvin.[2] Modern scholars who read the parable in its
Lukan context—not seeing it as the original context of the parable—identify
in the parable a reference to God's grace and mercy,[3] his love for the marginalized and the lost,[4] or God's joy when a sinner is found.[5] Those who see the
shepherd as a metaphor for the activity of Jesus emphasize the evangelical
intent of the parable.[6]

Most interpreters see the setting of the parable in Luke as secondary
but argue that Luke's setting concurs with the original historical context in
which Jesus told the parable. Interestingly all these scholars without exception see the main focus of the parable as God's joy when the lost (the sinner)
is found,[7] with subthemes of God's forgiveness,[8] God's compassion and
love,[9] salvation,[10] and the importance of repentance.[11]

---

the Lukan version of the parable.

2. According to Tertullian, the parable was directed at Pharisees and is proof of
God's willingness to forgive—the lost sheep refers to the Jews, and the reference intends
to shame the Pharisees because they thought repentance was only necessary for the
Gentiles. Aquinas and Calvin both focused on the shepherd as a metaphor for God:
the shepherd typified the grace of God (Aquinas), and Calvin saw in the shepherd a
God that rejoices over the repentance of one sinner. Kissinger, *History of Interpretation*,
4–5, 40, 52. Other interpretations in the early church understood the shepherd's going
to find the sheep as a reference to Jesus' incarnation to recover lost humanity, and the
ninety-nine as angels. Bengel went as far as to see the return of the shepherd as referring
to Jesus' ascension. See Snodgrass, *Stories with Intent*, 103, 107.

3. Capon, *Parables of Grace*, 31–39; Kähler, *Jesu Gleichnisse als Poesie und Therapie*,
131; Westermann, *Parables of Jesus*, 135, 184.

4. Black, "Die Gleichnisse als Allegorien," 275; Buzy, "Auslegung der Gleichnisse,"
101; Reid, *Parables for Preachers*, 249.

5. Hendrickx, *Parables of Jesus*, 149; Jones, *Matthean Parables*, 275; Trimp, *Sprekende Beelden*, 42.

6. Wenham, *Parables of Jesus*, 89. See also Bruce and Jones, in Kissinger, *History of
Interpretation*, 69, 156. Buttrick here is an exception to the rule. He sees the parable as
a Lukan creation with as focus about partying, relating to Luke's special interest in the
Lord's Supper. Buttrick, *Speaking in Parables*, 156.

7. Bailey, *Poet and Peasant*, 142; Boice, *Parables of Jesus*, 49; Dodd, *Parables of the
Kingdom*, 230; Hultgren, *Parables of Jesus*, 54; Kilgallen, *Twenty Parables*, 100–104;
Linnemann, *Parables of Jesus*, 66; Oveja, "Neuenundneunzig Sind Nich Genug," 211;
Scott, *Hear Then the Parable*, 407; Schottroff, *Parables of Jesus*, 152; Snodgrass, *Stories
with Intent*, 93.

8. Hultgren, *Parables of Jesus*, 59; Snodgrass, *Stories with Intent*, 93.

9. Bailey, *Poet and Peasant*, 142; Boice, *Parables of Jesus*, 50; Snodgrass, *Stories with
Intent*, 93.

10. Hultgren, *Parables of Jesus*, 54; Linnemann, *Parables of Jesus*, 66.

11. Bailey, *Poet and Peasant*, 142; Hultgren, *Parables of Jesus*, 61; Kilgallen, *Twenty
Parables*, 100–104; Schottroff, *Parables of Jesus*, 152. Snodgrass' interpretation of the

Finally, those who see the Lukan version of the parable as going back to the earliest layer of the historical Jesus tradition emphasize the apologetic character of the parable: a defense by Jesus of his associating with tax collectors and sinners vis-à-vis the point of view of the Pharisees and the scribes. In the parable Jesus is vindicating the good news against his opponents and declares God's character and his delight in forgiveness as the way he himself receives sinners.[12] The themes identified by these scholars are the same as themes described directly above: repentance,[13] forgiveness,[14] God's grace, compassion and love for sinners,[15] the possibility of forgiveness and salvation,[16] God's seeking the lost,[17] and God's joy when the sinner is found.[18]

The history of interpretation of the Lost Sheep shows that the interpretation of the parable has not changed since its earliest allegorical interpretations. When the shepherd is taken as a metaphor for God, almost all interpretations come to the same conclusion: the parable emphasizes God's forgiveness, grace and mercy, love and compassion for the lost, and God's joy when a sinner is found. When the shepherd is seen as a metaphor for Jesus, the conclusions also do not differ essentially: the parable has as its focus repentance and salvation. All these interpretations are "theological-allegorical." The moment the shepherd is seen as a metaphor for God or Jesus, the interpretation can go in no other direction. This is also the reason why themes like forgiveness, repentance, sinners and salvation are identified in

---

parable can be seen as representative of almost all these interpretations. According to him, the parable deals with the themes of lost and recovery, the presence of the kingdom and the compassion of God. The parable reveals the character of God, the value God places on the least deserving, and depicts God as not being passive but the seeking God who takes initiative to bring people back. In the parable Jesus demonstrates the presence of the kingdom and that forgiveness is available to all. Snodgrass, *Stories with Intent*, 93.

12. Derrett, "Fresh Light on the Lost Sheep," 40; Donahue, *Gospel in Parable*, 148; Hunter, *Interpreting the Parables*, 56; Jeremias, *T Parables of Jesus*, 40; Stein, *Introduction to the Parables*, 62.

13. Perkins, *Hearing the Parables*, 31.

14. Jeremias, *Parables of Jesus*, 40; Perkins, *Hearing the Parables*, 31.

15. Drury, *Parables in the Gospels*, 140; Hunter, *Then and Now*, 19; Lambrecht, *Once More Astonished*, 43–44; Lockyer, *All the Parables*, 283; Perkins, *Hearing the Parables*, 31; Stein, *Introduction to the Parables*, 52.

16. Hedrick, *Many Things in Parables*, 49; Kistemaker, *Stories Jesus Told*, 173.

17. Stein, *Introduction to the Parables*, 52; Zimmermann, *Puzzling the Parables of Jesus*, 228–31.

18. Boucher, *The Parables*, 96; Groenewald, *In Gelykenisse Het Hy Geleer*, 174; Hunter, *Then and Now*, 56; Linnemann, *Parables of Jesus*, 66.

the parable. A straightforward literal reading of the parable, however, shows that these themes are not present in the parable.

The parable of the Lost Sheep is a story about a shepherd (not God or Jesus) and a sheep (not a sinner) that gets lost. A realistic and social-scientific reading of the parable, without taking the shepherd as a metaphoric reference to either God or Jesus, yields a different reading. When the parable is detached from its Lukan context, and a possible context in the life and teaching of Jesus of Nazareth is postulated, a different reading is possible. Attention given to pastoralism in first-century Palestine also has a direct bearing on the parable's possible meaning. Above all, if the shepherd is seen as a despised and unclean person (and not God or Jesus), the interpretation of the parable leads in a different direction.

Integrity and Authenticity

Three versions of the parable are documented: Matt 18:12–14, Luke 15:4–7 and Gos. Thom. 107:1–3. The version of the parable in Gos. Thom. 107[19] differs from the versions in the Synoptic tradition to such an extent that it can be argued that it has moved away from the original.[20] In Gos. Thom. 107:2 the sheep that gets lost is the "largest" in the flock, and the one that the shepherd loves more than the ninety-nine which he left behind to go and look for the lost one (Gos. Thom. 107:3). The "motif of the largest" is also found in Gos. Thom. 8:2 and 96:2; a theme in the Gospel of Thomas— seen by some interpreters as the superior status of the gnostic Christian in relation to the ordinary Christian—that prompted Thomas to change the

19. The version of the Lost Sheep in Thomas reads as follows: "The [Father's] empire is like a shepherd who had a hundred sheep. One of them, the largest, went astray. He left the ninety-nine and looked for the one until he founds it. After he had struggled, he said to the sheep: 'I love you more than the ninety-nine.'" Translation from Miller, *Complete Gospels*, 302. A reference to the parable is made in the Secret Book of James 16:15 (written in the first half of the second century), and in the Gospel of Truth 31–32 (written in the second half of the second century) where the parable is interpreted from a gnostic point of view. In the Gospel of Truth the play on numbers is important. For the gnostic the number one hundred is perfect, and ninety-nine is not. The shepherd thus has to go out and complete the perfect number. Also, the gnostic reader would understand the "left" and "right" in the Thomasine version as references to the left and right of the demiurge God or throne of Jesus. Perkins, *Gnosticism and the New Testament*, 57. This gnostic version of the parable is most probably derived from the Matthean version. Tuckett, "Gospel of Truth and the Testimony of Truth," 134.

20. Within the general theology of the Gospel of Thomas, "the 'largest' sheep is the ideal Christian celibate ascetic whom Jesus 'loves more than the ninety-nine' others. That is, to put it rather mildly, a very different interpretation of the Lost Sheep parable than those of Luke and Matthew." Crossan, *Power of Parable*, 42.

parable. The version of the parable of the Lost Sheep in Gos. Thom. 107 can thus be dismissed as representing the earliest layer of the historical Jesus tradition.[21]

Between the Matthean and Lukan versions of the parable there is little in common.[22] The two versions differ to such an extent that many scholars assign them to M and L respectively, raising the question whether these two versions are related at all.[23] In following Kloppenborg, the view taken here is that both synoptic versions stem from Q.[24]

The Matthean version of the parable has been redactionally edited by the evangelist. The parable is shaped to fit into Matt 18, a chapter that served as a manual for the community of the evangelist, focusing on its leaders.[25] Matt 18 consists of six teachings: humility (one must become like a child [= little one]; Matt 18:1–5), caring for the little ones (Matt 18:6–9), looking for the little ones who have gone astray and God's joy when the strayed are found (Matt 18:10–14), reconciliation (Matt 18:15–17), binding and losing (Matt 18:18–20), and forgiveness (Matt 18:21–35). The parable is fitted between the second and fourth teaching, running from Matt 18:10–14, and forms a well-rounded inclusio.[26] The focus of the parable, namely, to look

---

21. Funk et al., *Five Gospels*, 529. See also Snodgrass, *Stories with Intent*, 101. Petersen argues for the Gos. Thom. 107 as the earliest version of the parable, and most probably earlier than the Q version. Petersen, "Parable of the Lost Sheep," 128–47. See also Jeremias, *Parables of Jesus*, 24; Patterson, *Gospel of Thomas and Jesus*, 71. According to Petersen, the Gos. Thom. 107 reflects a Jewish (not gnostic) tradition in which God loves Israel more than the other nations. Quispel, by pointing to Ezek 34:16, follows the same line of argument. Quispel, *Gnosis and the New Sayings of Jesus*, 233. See, however Patterson, who is of the opinion that the Gospel of Thomas contains no allegorization. Patterson, *Gospel of Thomas and Jesus*, 71.

22. Snodgrass, *Stories with Intent*, 99–100.

23. Kistemaker, *Stories Jesus Told*, 171; Manson, *Teaching of Jesus*, 68; Streeter, *Four Gospels*, 265.

24. Kloppenborg, *Q Parallels*, 174–75; Kloppenborg, *Excavating Q*, 96. See also see also Davies and Allison, *Matthew,* 3:768; Buttrick, *Speaking Parables*, 155; Donahue, *Gospel in Parable*, 147; Fitzmyer, *Gospel according to Luke*, 2:1073; Hedrick, *Many Things in Parables*, 49; Hendrickx, *Parables of Jesus*, 142; Hunter, *Then and Now*, 19; Jones, *Matthean Parables*, 273; Lambrecht, *Once More Astonished*, 37–42; Lambrecht, *Out of the Treasure*, 44; Oveja, "Neuenundneunzig sind nich Genug," 205; Perkins, *Hearing the Parables*, 29; Scott, *Hear Then the Parable*, 410.

25. When read from a pre-Paschal perspective, the parable is addressed at the disciples (the leaders). According to Jeremias, the transmission of the materials of the gospels shows that a strong tendency was at work to transform parables which Jesus addressed at the crowd or his opponents into parables addressed at the disciples, a tradition that reached its conclusion in the Gospel of Thomas. This aspect of Matt 18:12–14 also indicates it secondary nature. Jeremias, *Parables of Jesus*, 42.

26. For the structure of the inclusio in Matt 18:1014, see Snodgrass, *Stories with Intent*, 100.

for those in the community (the little ones) who have gone astray, has clearly been influenced by its context. The topic of "the little ones" is a distinctive Matthean theme (Matt 10:42, 18:6, 10, 14), and the question that introduces the parable (Τί ὑμῖν δοκεῖ; Matt 18:12) is typically Matthean (it does not occur in either Mark or Luke; see Matt 17:25; 21:28; 22:17, 42; 26:66; 27:17). Matthew's application of the parable (Matt 18:14) is a Matthean addition and linked to the content of the parable. Finally, Matthew's use of ἐπὶ τὰ ὄρη (on the hills; Matt 18:12)—instead of Luke's ἐν τῇ ἐρήμῳ (in open country or in the desert/wilderness; Luke 15:4)—also shows Matthew's redactional hand (most probably referring to Jer 50:6 = LXX 27:6),[27] and Matthew's use of ἀμὴν λέγω ὑμῖν (I truly tell you; Matt 18:13) is common to Matthew when compared with the other Synoptics.[28] Finally, Matthew rounds off his "manual for the community" in chapter 18 by adding the parable of the Unforgiving Servant (Matt 18:21–35)—applying the parable with a focus on forgiving those who have gone astray (πλανηθῇ; Matt 18:12).

The Lukan version of the parable is the first of a triad of parables in Luke 15 that consists of the parable of the Lost Sheep (Luke 15:4–7), the Lost Coin (Luke 15:8–10), and the Lost (Prodigal) Son (Luke 15:11–32). Typically Lukan, this chapter is carefully constructed. Luke 15:1–3 serves as introduction to all three parables, and is most probably secondary;[29] Luke 15:3 actually should read "parables," not parable (τὴν παραβολὴν). The following formal aspects of the three parables bind them into a close and well-constructed unit: the terms "sinner" and "to sin" occur in the introduction and all three parables (Luke 15:1–2, 7, 10, 18, 21), all three parables have the same scheme of lost-found-joy, in all three there are plays on the same words[30] and numbers (one in a hundred [Luke 15:4–7], one in ten [Luke 15:8–10] and one in two [Luke 15:11–32], indicating the parable of

27. Hultgren, *Parables of Jesus*, 55.

28. In spite of this obvious redactional activity of Matthew (and its setting), there are some scholars who see the Matthean version as more original. See, for example, Bultmann, *Synoptic Tradition*, 71; Drury, *Parables in the Gospels*, 140; Fitzmyer, *The Gospel according to Luke*, 2:1074; Hedrick, *Many Things in Parables*, 16; Linnemann, *Parables of Jesus*, 67; Smith, *Parables of the Synoptic Gospels*, 189; Snodgrass, *Stories with Intent*, 103. Jeremias, however, has argued convincingly that the context of the parable in Matthew is that of the early church, and thus secondary. Jeremias, *Parables of Jesus*, 40. See also Scott, *Hear Then the Parable*, 406.

29. Contra Jeremias who considers Luke 15:1–3 as reflecting the original historical situation in which Jesus told the three parables, and thus not secondary. Jeremias, *Parables of Jesus*, 100. See, however, Luke 5:29–32, in which Luke has the exact same introduction to the narrative of the calling of Levi.

30. See ἀπόλλυμι (Luke 15:4, 6, 8–9, 24, 32), εὑρίσκω (Luke 15:4–6, 8–9, 24, 32) and χάρα, χαίρω, and συγχαρω (Luke 15:5–7, 9–10, 24, 32).

the Prodigal as the climax of the unit), and all three parables are rounded off by the theme of joy (Luke 15:7, 10, 32). By creating an introduction to the three parables (Luke 15:1–3), and linking the three with respectively Luke 15:7, 10 and 32, Luke thus created a well-structured unit.

When the integrity of Luke 15:4–7 is considered in terms of the above described unit, it seems that Luke added Luke 15:7 to Luke 15:4–6 in line with Luke 15:10 and 32.[31] Luke 15:7 is most probably secondary and links the "moral" of the parable with its introduction in Luke 15:1–3.[32] Luke 15:4–6 thus reflects the earliest form of the parable. Luke 15:4–6 represents the Q version of the parable and most probably is the closest to the earliest layer of the historical Jesus tradition.[33] The introduction to the parable (τίς ἄνθρωπος ἐξ ὑμῶν ἔχων; Luke 15:4) is widely attested in Q (Q 11:11; 12:25),[34] and several other parables in Q start with a question (e.g., Q 12:42; 15:8). In Luke's Sondergut parables the phrase τίς ἐξ ὑμῶν is commonly used (Luke 11:5; 14:28; 17:7; see however Luke 12:25), another indication that Luke's version stems most probably from Q.

---

31. The use of λέγω ὑμῖν in Luke 15:7 is a common use in Luke to introduce the application of a parable (Luke 11:9; 15:7, 10: 16:9; 18:8, 14; 19:26). The use of οὕτως in Luke 15:7, and the theme of repentance, are also typically Lukan. Luke 15:4–7 also takes the form of a three-stanza poem with a chiastic structure which shows Luke's redactional hand. Bailey, *Poet and Peasant*, 145–46. Luke 15:7 thus could be seen as a Lukan addition to the parable. Most scholars see Luke 15:7 as a secondary addition to the Q-parable or source used by Luke. Bultmann, *Synoptic Tradition*, 171; Cadoux, *Art and Use*, 231; Dodd, *Parables of the Kingdom*, 92; Fitzmyer, *The Gospel according to Luke*, 2:1073; Funk et al., *Five Gospels*, 355; Hedrick, *Many Things in Parables*, 91; Linnemann, *Parables of Jesus*, 68; Perrin, *Rediscovering the Teaching*, 99; Smith, *Parables of the Synoptic Gospels*, 191; Stein, *Introduction to the Parables*, 62; Donahue, *Gospel in Parable*, 148; Hultgren, *Parables of Jesus*, 60–61; Schottroff, "Das Gleichnis vom Verlorenen Sohn," 34. Lambrecht considers Luke 15:6–7 as secondary elements in Luke's version; the shepherd's coming home and rejoicing with friends and neighbors "does not fit into the picture of a shepherd on the hills." Lambrecht, *Out of the Treasure*, 43–44. Below it will be indicated that this understanding of Luke 15:6 lacks a realistic reading of the parable. Read from a realistic point of view (verisimilitude), Luke 15:6 is part of the parable that stems from Q.

32. "Luke has provided the conclusion in v. 7. The parable is interpreted as an allegory in which the lost sheep stands for sinners, while the ninety-nine, who do not stray, represent the virtuous Judeans. This, of course, reflects the pastoral interests of the new movement and accords with the concluding remarks Luke has provided elsewhere (cf. Luke 12:21; 14:33; 17:10)." Funk et al., *Five Gospels*, 355.

33. See also Bailey, *Poet and Peasant*, 153; Hultgren, *Parables of Jesus*, 49; Jeremias, *Parables of Jesus*, 40; Miller, *Complete Gospels*, 161; Montefiore, *Synoptic Gospels*, 987; Scott, *Hear Then the Parable*, 406. For a different construction of a possible Q version of the parable, see Robinson et al., *Critical Edition of Q*, 478–83.

34. Kloppenborg, *Excavating Q*, 95–96.

To summarize, Luke 15:4–6 is most probably the original form of the parable. The content of Luke 15:4–6 is not influenced by the context of Luke 15, as is the case with Matt 18:12–14. Without its context, Luke 15:4–6 can stand on its own, and should be interpreted on its own .

Realism (Verisimilitude)

The history of the parable's interpretation shows that questions relating to certain aspects of the parable are asked by almost all interpreters. These questions relate to the reputation of shepherds, the size of the flock, ownership, the value of one sheep, and whether the shepherd did or did not abandon the ninety-nine when he went to look for the one lost sheep. In answering these questions, Kloppenborg and Callon correctly assert that most parable scholars routinely neglect "the wealth of social and economic documentation available from documentary papyri and other sources from the late Hellenistic and early Roman periods" in trying to answer these questions.[35]

> A key problem in the interpretation of the parables is the degree to which the elements in the story are simply part of what a first-century eastern Mediterranean audience would take for granted and what it would regard as hyperbolic, unusual, striking, or counterintuitive . . .[36] The issues of what in the parable exhibits verisimilitude and what features are unusual *are of significant moment*, because interpreters normally fix upon either what they believe to be the parable's reflection of the typicalities of pastoralism in order to suggest an argument from analogy . . . ; or they focus on what they suppose to be the unusual features of

35. Kloppenborg and Callon, "Parable of the Shepherd," 4.

36. "The New Testament . . . consists of documents written in what anthropologists call a 'high context' society where the communicators presume a broadly shared acquaintance with and knowledge of the social context of matters referred to in conversation or writing. Accordingly, it is presumed in such societies that contemporary readers will be able to 'fill in the gaps' and 'read between the lines.'" Elliott, *Social-Scientific Criticism*, 11. See also Hall, "Context and Meaning," 79. The main problem for modern readers of the Bible therefore is *that we do not know what we do not know. The spare descriptions of context in the Bible often leave us without the essential ingredients for understanding the message.*" Rohrbaugh, "Hermeneutics as Cross-Cultural Encounter," 567; italics added. To know what we do not know, attention has to be given to the social and economic registers presupposed by the parable. Kloppenborg and Callon, "Parable of the Shepherd," 2.

the story and build interpretation upon these. Hence, it is crucial to determine *what was normal and what was not.*[37]

The following remark from Snodgrass serves as an example of the approach referred to above by Kloppenborg and Callon:

> Would a shepherd abandon the ninety-nine other sheep? *What relevance does a decision here have for understanding?* A number of commentators are sure the shepherd abandoned the ninety-nine sheep and interpret the parable accordingly as absurd as showing that God's mercy is a mystery or that the shepherd is irresponsible . . . *This approach violates both cultural and literary sensitivities.* Care for one sheep does not preclude care for all the sheep, and certainly some provision would be made for the ninety-nine, to leave them either in some enclosure or more likely with another shepherd. A flock this size may have had more than one shepherd anyway . . . Did the shepherd carry the lost sheep home and leave the ninety-nine in the wilderness? Should we think he took the lost sheep back to the ninety-nine? . . . Parables are marked by focus and brevity and do not care about unnecessary issues. Like all literature they often have gaps. *This parable does not care about any of these questions, for it is focused on the certainty of searching and the celebration at finding. Nothing else counts*, and to make such issues matters of interpretation is catastrophic. Interpretation based on elements not there is almost certainly wrong.[38]

The fact of the matter is that a responsible interpretation of the parable of the Lost Sheep should care about these questions. These questions count. It is the brushing away of these "unnecessary issues" that "violates both cultural and literary sensitivities"[39] that are part and parcel of the parable. If one wants to guard against an ethnocentric and anachronistic reading of the parable, one must pay attention to the social and economic registers presupposed by the parable. To these we turn now.

37. Kloppenborg and Callon, "Parable of the Shepherd," 3; italics added.
38. Snodgrass, *Stories with Intent*, 105; italics added.
39. Ibid.

Reading Scenarios

Did Shepherds Own Sheep?

Answers to this question differ somewhat among interpreters of the parable. Almost all interpreters see the shepherd as the owner of the flock.[40] Bailey and Wenham take a middle position: when the flock is small, the owner (or someone who is part of the extended family) cares for the flock, and when the flock belongs to several people who are part of an extended family (thus a larger flock), a shepherd is hired who is part of that extended family.[41] This is why, Bailey argues, a shepherd always feels responsible for every sheep that is part of the flock since the loss of one sheep is a loss to the entire family clan. Mein and Schottroff, on the other hand, opine that the shepherd normally did not own the flock.[42] Interestingly, no reasons are given for the above different points of view on ownership, except in the case of Bailey; the fact that the shepherd is part of an extended family can be seen in the whole clan rejoicing when the lost sheep is found (Luke 15:6).

In contrast to the above "received view," documented papyri and other sources indicate that it was common practice in pastoralism for owners to employ shepherds (hirelings, strangers) to take care of their sheep.[43] Tractate *Baba Qamma* 6.2, in the Mishna, for example, states that when an owner places his sheep "with a (professional) shepherd, the latter substitutes him

40. See, for example, Jeremias, *Parables of Jesus*, 133; Snodgrass, *Stories with Intent*, 102; Levine, *Short Stories by Jesus*, 35. Jeremias bases his point of view on his estimation that the owner was not a rich man, since hundred sheep constituted "a medium-size flock." Jeremias, *Parables of Jesus*, 133.

41. Bailey, *Poet and Peasant*, 148–50; Wenham, *Parables of Jesus*, 100. "This does not mean that the shepherd in this parable is a 'hireling.' The extended family owns the sheep. The shepherd is not a 'hireling' nor a 'stranger.' He is a member of the extended family and naturally feels responsible before the entire family clan; any loss is a loss to all of them." Bailey, *Poet and Peasant*, 148.

42. Mein, "Profitable and Unprofitable Shepherds," 497; Schottroff, *Parables of Jesus*, 152.

43. Kloppenborg and Callon, "Parable of the Shepherd," 6–12.

(as regards liability for damages)."[44] P.Princ. II 24 (Oxyrhynchus, 21 CE),[45] a contract between an owner and a shepherd for tax purposes, states the relationship between the owner and shepherd even more clearly: it contains the name of the owner and the shepherd, how many sheep and goats the shepherd is responsible for (109 sheep and three goats), to whom the newborn lambs will belong, where the sheep will graze, and who will pay the necessary taxes. It also takes it for granted that the shepherd will be transient.[46] *Contra* Bailey and Wenham, even in the case of small crops, owners made use of hired shepherds,[47] likely because owners had other more important duties to attend to, and identification with the role of a shepherd would have amounted to status degradation.[48] Although not the main focus of these declarations, it is clear that the normal practice was for a shepherd to be a hireling or stranger—someone who did not own the sheep.

44. "If one drive his sheep into a sheep-cot and properly bolt the gate, but still they manage to come out and do damage, he is free. If he do not properly bolt the gate, he is liable. If they break out in the night time, or robbers break in the gate, and the sheep come out and cause damage, he is free. If the robbers lead them out, they are responsible for the damage. If one exposes his cattle to the sun, or he places them in the custody of a deaf-mute, a fool, or a minor, and they break away and do damage, he is liable; if, however, *he places them with a (professional) shepherd, the latter substitutes him (as regards liability for damages).* If the cattle fall into a garden and consume something, the value of the benefit they derive is to be paid. If, however, they enter the garden in the usual way, the value of the damage is paid. How is the value of the damage to be ascertained? It is appraised how much a measure of the land required for planting a saah was worth before and how much it is worth after" (*m. B. Qam.* 6.2); italics added.

45. See Kloppenborg and Callon, "Parable of the Shepherd," 6–7.

46. Ibid., 7. Kloppenborg and Callon list several similar declarations by owners of flocks tended by a shepherd: P.Berl. Möller 7 (8–9 CE); P.Oxy. LV 3779 (20 CE); P.NYU inv. 35 (20–21 CE); P.Oxy. LV 3778 (21 CE); P.Oxy. II 350 (24–25 CE); P.Oxy. II 245 (26 CE); P.Oxy. II 356 = SB XVI 12761 (27 CE); P.Oxy. II 353 (27–28 CE); P.Ross. Georg. II 13 (54–68 CE); P.Oxy. II 357–61 (77–90 CE); P.IFAO I 21 (54–68 CE); P.Batav. 8 (1 CE); and P.Oxy. XLVII 3338 (150 CE). For the number of sheep, goats, and owners involved in these declarations, see ibid. Also note that the flocks referred to in these papyri vary between 87 and 146 sheep, excluding goats, which were almost always part of a flock.

47. See P.IFAO III 43 (20–21 CE); P.Oxy. II 245 (26 CE); P.Oxy. II 353 (27–28 CE); P.Köln II 86 (98–99 CE); P.Phil. 8 (136/7 CE); SB XII 10794 (21 CE); P.Oxy. II 245 (26 CE); P.Oxy. II 353 (27–28 CE); P.Oxy. II 351 = SB XII 10795 (28 CE); P.Oxy. II 355 = SB XVI 12763 (40–41 CE); and P.Oxy. I 74 (116 CE). See Kloppenborg and Callon, "Parable of the Shepherd," 7.

48. Ibid., 7–8.

How Big Was a Flock?

Again interpreters differ substantially in answering this question. Bailey estimates that an average family had five to fifteen animals, and a flock of hundred therefore was made up of the flocks of people belonging to the same extended family.[49] Hultgren, taking as his base Bedouin flocks in the Middle East, also sees hundred as a large number. The number of sheep in the parable should rather be seen as a round number that paints a picture on a grand scale. Schottroff, on the other hand (in following Jülicher and Derrett) sees the number one hundred as composing a small flock. Jeremias (in following Dalman) and Scott take a middle position: one hundred sheep constituted "a medium-size flock."[50] Like Bailey, Jeremias bases his estimate on what is known from contemporary Bedouin flocks, and also makes use of information available in Jewish law—Bedouin flocks vary from twenty to two hundred head of small cattle, and in Jewish law three hundred head is seen as an unusually large flock: "Hence, with 100 sheep the man possesses a medium-sized flock."[51]

By now it is clear, with the data Kloppenborg and Callon have put on the table, that a flock of one hundred "is unexceptional as a flock to be put in the care of a single shepherd."[52] It is, as Jeremias has argued, a medium-sized flock. Note, however, that the estimate of Kloppenborg and Callon is based on evidence that can be tested, and not based on anachronistic evidence.

Reputation of Shepherds

Shepherding indeed was a despised trade. Shepherds were associated with tax collectors and not to be used as witnesses (*b. Sanhedrin* 25b), were seen as robbers (because they drove their herds onto other people's land; *m. Qidd.* 4.14),[53] and were seen as finding it difficult to repent and make resti-

49. Bailey, *Poet and Peasant*, 148.

50. Hultgren, *Parables of Jesus*, 53; Schottroff, *Parables of Jesus*, 152; Jeremias, *Parables of Jesus*, 133; Scott, *Hear Then the Parable*, 412.

51. Jeremias, *Parables of Jesus*, 133.

52. Kloppenborg and Callon, "Parable of the Shepherd," 8. In terms of available papyrological evidence, Kloppenborg and Callon estimate most flocks in first-century Palestine between twenty-five and a hundred fifty animals that were tended to by a single shepherd. They also list evidence from early Roman texts that have the same numbers. Ibid., 9.

53. Derrett, *Law in the New Testament*, 60; Hultgren, *Parables of Jesus*, 58; Jeremias, *Jerusalem in the Time of Jesus*, 305; Scott, *Hear Then the Parable*, 413; Snodgrass, *Stories with Intent*, 102.

tution (*b. B. Qam.* 94b). Shepherds were rendered unclean (the ἀμαρτωλοί) because they belonged to one of the proscribed trades (with e.g., excise men, tax collectors, donkey drivers, peddlers, and tanners) and were seen as dishonest.[54] Being a herdsman was not a trade sought after (*m. Qidd.* 4.14). As was the case with tax collecting, tending sheep was avoided by Jews.[55]

Kloppenborg and Callon's study on pastoralism in the Mediterranean adds significant features to the perceived figure of the shepherd in first-century Palestine. The shepherd spent most of his time unsupervised, was transient ("moving his flock over a large range of agriculturally marginal land"),[56] and was armed with a sling and club.[57] Because of this, "shepherds in antiquity were stigmatized figures, often associated with bandits and agitators."[58] As Grünewald has indicated, it was easy for shepherds to become involved in criminality because of freedom of movement and because they were armed.[59]

In light of the above, it is interesting that Derrett and Schottroff state that it is not important for the interpretation of the parable that shepherds had a bad reputation.[60] Boucher goes as far as to state that despite the fact that shepherds were regarded as dishonest, Jesus did not hesitate to use the figure of the shepherd as a positive symbol.[61] Clearly, Jesus' reference to a shepherd is a feature of the parable that is unusual, and therefore "of significant moment" in the interpretation of Luke 15:4–6. *Contra* Snodgrass—to use his own words—it does "have relevance . . . for understanding," and

54. Jeremias, *Parables of Jesus*, 132. See also Bailey, *Poet and Peasant*, 147; Boucher, *Parables*, 98.

55. Donahue, *The Gospel in Parable*, 148.

56. Kloppenborg and Callon, "Parable of the Shepherd," 10.

57. This description of shepherds concurs with the point of view of Malina and Rohrbaugh: To meet the needs of shepherding, shepherds carried a sling, club and rod, and were usually ranked with ass drivers, tanners, sailors, butchers, and camel drivers (i.e., despised occupations). Shepherds were perceived as men with no honor (they were not home at night to protect their women), as well as thieves, since they grazed their flocks on the property of others. Malina and Rohrbaugh, *Social-Science Commentary on the Gospel of John*, 182; Malina and Rohrbaugh, *Social-Science Commentary on the Synoptic Gospels*, 232. See, however, Levine, who argues the direct opposite. Levine bases her point of view on positive comments about shepherds made by Philo, the rabbis, the Old Testament, and the Dead Sea Scrolls. In her positive assessment of shepherds she does not, however, take into consideration that the texts she refers to relates to a nomadic period during which shepherds indeed were seen as positive figures. Levine, *Short Stories by Jesus*, 38–41.

58. Kloppenborg and Callon, "Parable of the Shepherd," 11.

59. Ibid., 12.

60. Derrett, "Fresh Light on the Lost Sheep," 40; Schottroff, *Parables of Jesus*, 152.

61. Boucher, *Parables*, 96.

ignoring it can only lead to violating "both cultural and literary sensitivities" that are part of the story. The interpretation of the parable indeed "care(s) about these questions."[62]

Why Look for One Lost Sheep? Wages and Value

In the parable, when one sheep gets lost, the shepherd leaves (καταλείπει) the ninety-nine in the wilderness (ἐν τῇ ἐρήμῳ) and goes to search for the lost one. Καταλείπει, the verb used by Luke, literally means "to leave behind" (see Luke 5:28; 10:40);[63] the shepherd literally abandons the ninety-nine.[64] Interpreters of the parable explain the καταλείπει action of the shepherd quite differently. Some argue that the shepherd did not leave the ninety-nine alone: whether the shepherd left the sheep in an enclosure[65] or outdoors under another shepherd's guard,[66] the ninety-nine were cared for.[67] Those who argue that the shepherd abandoned the ninety-nine interpret this possibility in different ways. Either they see this aspect of the parable as absurd (Buttrick), or they see the action of the shepherd as irresponsible (Hedrick) or foolish (Scott), or they call the shepherd as a symbol of risk taking (Huffman, Hultgren, and Perrin).[68]

Is this aspect of the parable important for its interpretation? Some think it is not important, while others answer this question in the affirmative. According to Hultgren, the question whether the shepherd left the ninety-nine alone or not is hypercritical. Snodgrass also deems this

62. Snodgrass, *Stories with Intent*, 105.

63. See Scott, *Hear Then the Parable*, 415.

64. Καταλείπει, in certain cases, can also be translated with "leaving behind without help" or "abandon." BAGD, 414.

65. Bishop, "Lost or Wandering Sheep," 47; Hendrickx, *Parables of Jesus*, 147.

66. Bailey, *Poet and Peasant*, 149–50; Bishop, "Lost or Wandering Sheep," 45; Bussby, "Did a Shepherd Leave Sheep," 95; Jeremias, *Parables of Jesus*, 133; Levison, *Parables*, 152; Smith, *Parables of the Synoptic Gospels*, 188; Wenham, *Parables of Jesus*, 100.

67. Kilgallen, *Twenty Parables*, 98; Schottroff, *Parables of Jesus*, 152; Snodgrass, *Stories with Intent*, 105.

68. Buttrick, *Speaking Parables*, 154; Hedrick, *Many Things in Parables*, 14; Scott, *Hear Then the Parable*, 417; Huffman, "Atypical Features," 211; Hultgren, *Parables of Jesus*, 53–54; Perrin, *Rediscovering the Teaching*, 415. See also the points of view of Agnew, "Parables of Divine Compassion," 38; Perkins, *Hearing the Parables*, 31; Groenewald, *In Gelykenisse Het Hy Geleer*, 173; Capon, *Parables of Grace*, 37. According to Agnew, the shepherd's action shows that God's mercy is a mystery, or that one could be so lucky to find the others still there on one's return. Groenewald argues that the shepherd had to do it because it was his duty, and Capon is of the opinion that it will be no problem if the ninety-nine got lost since the Good Shepherd will find them also.

question unnecessary: the "parables are marked by focus and brevity and do not care about unnecessary issues"; whether the shepherd abandoned the ninety-nine is not important at all, especially because the parable "focuses on the certainty of searching and the celebrating at finding." This is also the view of Capon: the leaving behind of the ninety-nine is not important because "Jesus is parabolically thumping the tub for the saving paradox of lostness." Linnemann, on the other hand, argues that the effectiveness of the parable would be lost if this feature was not introduced; the contrast between the one and ninety-nine would lose its significance if the shepherd did not abandon the ninety-nine.[69]

A possible approach to this aspect of the parable is the question put by Hedrick: What would justify this risk? If the shepherd did abandon the sheep—and we accept here that he did—for what reason would he do it?[70] Interestingly, parable scholars who do reflect on this question are almost unanimous in their verdict: it is not because of the value of the sheep. Jeremias, for example, states that it was not the high value of the sheep that caused the shepherd to set out on his search, but the fact that it belonged to him, and without his help it could not find its way back to the flock. Boucher argues in the same vein: the shepherd does not go and look for the sheep because it is of great value, but simply because it has gone astray and cannot find its way back by itself. Scott concurs: the sheep has little intrinsic value; its value is in being found, in the joy of its recovery.[71]

Schottroff, on the other hand, argues that one sheep out of a hundred represents a value for the person affected; a shepherd, and perhaps his family as well, depends on the sheep to live.[72] When the recent study of Kloppenborg and Callon is taken into consideration, Schottroff has struck the correct key. In their realistic reading of the parable, Kloppenborg and Callon indicate that the wages typically paid to shepherds were meager, and that the intrinsic value of a sheep, relative to a shepherd's wage, was high. Due to the fact that the shepherd's work was physically demanding, the averages wage of a shepherd, "was pitifully small." *De ru rustica* 2.10.3 and P.Lond. III 1171 indicate that the wage of a shepherd was more or less sixteen drachmas per month—thus less than a farm laborer, sewage cleaner, water carrier, or mule driver, and half the wage of a carpenter, stonemason, or baker.[73]

69. Hultgren, *Parables of Jesus*, 54; Snodgrass, *Stories with Intent*, 105; Capon, *Parables of Grace*, 37; Linnemann, *Parables of Jesus*, 65.

70. Hedrick, *Many Things in Parables*, 50.

71. Jeremias, *Parables of Jesus*, 134; Boucher, *Parables*, 98; Scott, *Hear Then the Parable*, 407.

72. Schottroff, *Parables of Jesus*, 152.

73. See Kloppenborg and Callon, "Parable of the Shepherd," 13–16. That shepherds

When the wage of a shepherd is compared with the intrinsic value of one sheep, the reason why the shepherd went to look for the lost sheep becomes even clearer. SB XX 14525 indicates that the price of a male was not less than ten drachmas, and that of a female close to double the amount. In the case of the leasing of a flock, the numbers were more or less the same (eleven drachmas for a male; P.Amst. I 41). Since a shepherd was held accountable for livestock losses (see, e.g., P.Amst. I 41.8), it means that the loss of a male was close to one month's wage, and the loss of a female more than the wage for one month:[74]

> Thus, the motivation to recover one lost sheep becomes exceedingly clear: the replacement cost of a male would be about one month's wages, the loss of a female would likely amount to more than a month's wages, and if the herd were leased, the loss of an animal would not only represent a replacement cost but it would also reduce the income from the flock with which the lessee paid the rental costs.[75]

Thus, what justified the risk the shepherd took? Clearly it was economic survival—survival that led to "irresponsible" and "risky" behavior. This then, also explains the shepherd's celebration with friends and neighbors in Luke 15:6.

Reading the Parable

Almost all interpreters of the parable take as a point of departure the shepherd imagery of the Old Testament as interpretative key to unlock its meaning. Some argue that texts such as Gen 48:15 and 49:24; Ps 23; 77:20; 80:1; and 119:176; Isa 40:10; 53:6 and 60:4; Jer 23:1–4 and 50:6; Zech 11:4–17; and especially Ezek 34 provided the imagery for the parable: God or Jesus is the good shepherd who tends his sheep, and the lost sheep is the "sinner."[76]

---

engaged in theft is thus hardly surprising. Wages, no supervision, mobility and the carrying of weapons afforded them the means and opportunity for theft and the temptation for other forms of criminality. Ibid., 13–14.

74. See Kloppenborg and Callon, "Parable of the Shepherd," 14–15.

75. Ibid., 15–16.

76. Hendrickx, for example, states in this regard the following: "The image solely and unambiguously refers to God who requires his lost sheep . . . to be searched for and looked after." Hendrickx, *Parables of Jesus*, 146. The following remark of Snodgrass is also worth noting since it represents scholarly consensus with regard to the interpretative key of the parable: "At the very least the parable has been framed on the OT shepherd tradition . . . At least with respect to Luke, the analogy of the shepherd refers to both the character of God and the activity of Jesus." Snodgrass, *Stories with Intent*, 105,

Lambrecht goes as far to state that "without this . . . Christological dimension every explanation of the parable is superficial."[77]

Does the parable fit this tradition? Most probably not, when the image of the shepherd in first-century Palestine is taken into consideration. As Malina and Rohrbaugh put it, "These old traditions account for a certain idyllic quaintness in the use of the metaphor that does not square with the real view of shepherds in Jesus' day."[78] In the history of the interpretation of the parable, it is only Scott and, in a marginal sense, Buttrick who identify this anachronistic reading of the parable.[79] According to Buttrick, the parable draws on traditional biblical imagery, but that the social positions of shepherds may have skewed the parable a bit. It is argued here that the parable does not draw on the shepherd imagery of the Old Testament. The reason for this position is the fact that by the time of Jesus, Palestine was an advanced agrarian society consisting of large estates and small holdings. Scott correctly indicates that in the Old Testament Israel was nomadic, a situation in which shepherds were positively perceived. There was little or no "property" onto which shepherds could drive their herd, and it was not necessary to drive a flock over a large range of agriculturally marginal land to feed the flock. In first-century Palestine, on the other hand (a "primarily agricultural and urban economy"), shepherds sometimes had to drive a flock over the property of others, and had to look for pastures in agriculturally marginal land.[80] Did this happen in the time of Jesus? The well-attested despised image of the shepherd confirms this fact.[81] If one, like Schottroff, anachronistically assumes that the milieu described in the parable includes nomadic conditions, it is understandable that she can also state that the reputation of the shepherd is not important for the interpretation of the parable.[82] If one, however, takes seriously the first-century Palestinian social and economic registers presupposed by the parable, shepherd imagery as found in the Old Testament cannot be used as an interpretative key to the

---

107. See also Bailey, *Poet and Peasant*, 147; Buttrick, *Speaking Parables*, 153; Donahue, *Gospel in Parable*, 158; Hultgren, *Parables of Jesus*, 52–53; Perkins, *Hearing the Parables*, 32; Wenham, *Parables of Jesus*, 99.

77. Lambrecht, *Once More Astonished*, 45.

78. Malina and Rohrbaugh, *Social-Science Commentary on the Gospel of John*, 179.

79. Scott, *Hear Then the Parable*, 405; Buttrick, *Speaking Parables*, 154.

80. Scott, *Hear Then the Parable*, 413.

81. See, for example, respectively *m. Qidd.* 4.14 and *m. B. Qam.* 10.9: "A man should not teach his son to be an ass-driver or a camel-driver, or barber or a sailor, or a herdsman or a shopkeeper, for their craft is the craft of robbers," and "None may buy wool or milk from herdsmen, or wood or fruit from them that watch over fruit-trees."

82. Schottroff, *Parables of Jesus*, 152.

parable. Rather, when Jesus started to tell the parable, its hearers would have been shocked; for herdsmen, just like Samaritans (Luke 10:30–35), were not supposed to be the heroes of a story.

This presupposition leads to another. If one does see the shepherd imagery in the Old Testament as the blueprint for the parable, it would be difficult to equate a responsible and caring God or Jesus with an irresponsible despised person. A bit of maneuvering is needed to overcome this obvious obstacle when one perceives the characters in Jesus' parables as analogies to God or Jesus himself. To equate God with a despised shepherd inevitably leads to a "moral dilemma."[83] The fact of the matter is that in spite of the general tendency among parable scholars to identify the actors or characters in the parables with God or Jesus, the characters in Jesus' parables are not analogies for God or Jesus (or sinners in the case of Luke 15:4–5).[84] Jesus' parables are not stories of God; they are stories about God's kingdom.[85] Or, in the words of Herzog: "The parables were not earthly stories with heavenly meanings, but earthly stories with heavy meanings."[86] The characters in the parables do not point to God. The parables point to the kingdom of God. Put differently, "there is something about the parable as a whole that is like the kingdom of God."[87] The parable of the Lost Sheep, therefore, is not a story about God, Jesus and sinners, but a story about a despised shepherd and a lost sheep—a story that points to what the kingdom of God is like. Read this sentence literally.

The conclusions reached from the reading scenarios discussed above will guide how we read this parable. In terms of verisimilitude, the social and economic registers presupposed by the parable are that a flock of hundred sheep was a medium-sized flock that most probably belonged to more than one owner; the shepherd contracted to care for the flock was most likely not the owner of the sheep; shepherding was a despised trade, and shepherds were rendered unclean and seen as robbers, criminals, and thieves; shepherds were also unsupervised, transient, and armed, and were often associated with bandits and agitators; wages paid to shepherds were poor; and the intrinsic value of a sheep, relative to a shepherd's wage, was high.

With these presuppositions in mind, we can now read the parable. First-century Palestine, the world in which Jesus told his parables, was an

---

83. Van Eck, "Friend at Midnight," 2–7.
84. Van Eck, "Lost Sheep," 318.
85. Funk, "Jesus of Nazareth," 90.
86. Herzog, *Parables as Subversive Speech*, 3.
87. McGaughy, "Fiction of the Kingdom," 11.

advanced agrarian society[88] under the control of the Roman Empire and centered in the temple in Jerusalem (whose officials ruled indirectly). Advanced agrarian societies were divided into the haves (rulers) and the have-nots (the ruled). The haves, who despised manual labor, controlled most of the wealth (up to 65 percent) by exploiting the land and sea, its produce, and its cultivators (the peasantry and fishermen), whose labor (including the cheap labor of slaves and tenant farmers) created the produce. Local, regional, and imperial elites imposed tributes, taxes, and rents; extracting wealth from nonelites by taxing the production, distribution, and consumption. The priestly aristocracy in Judea was no different: to keep their base of power (the temple system) intact, they added to the Roman tribute their own tithes, offerings, and contributions during festivals. All this left the peasantry "on the edge of destitution, and often over the edge."[89] People lived from hand to mouth and had no provisions beyond what was needed for the day, living extremely marginalized lives.[90] Not everybody could make ends meet.[91] This was the kingdom of Rome and the kingdom of the temple.

Against this background, Jesus tells a story of a different kingdom, a kingdom in which everyone has enough. It is a story about a shepherd and a flock. The flock is medium sized, and the shepherd does not own the flock; he is a hireling. Normally a contract between the owner(s) of the flock and the shepherd would have been in place, stating the number of sheep (and goats) the shepherd would be responsible for, to whom the lambs to be born would belong, who would pay the necessary taxes, and what the shepherd would be paid. Because the sheep had to be kept away from planted crops, the contract also stated where the sheep would graze. The shepherd would therefore be a nomad, away from home for a lengthy time as predetermined

---

88. For a short summary of the salient attributes of an advanced agrarian society, see Hanson and Oakman, *Palestine in the Time of Jesus*, 14.

89. Borg, *Jesus*, 227.

90. Schottroff, *Parables of Jesus*, 189.

91. Peasants who owned and farmed land had economic obligations that severely limited their prospects for moving above the level of subsistence. Obligations were internal and external. Internal obligations were made up of produce for subsistence, seed for planting the next crop, feed for livestock, and the reservation of some produce to use as trade (for acquiring equipment, utensils, or food the family did not produce). External obligations consisted of social or religious dues (e.g., participation in weddings or local festivals), tithes, rent, and taxes. With regard to the latter, peasants in Roman Palestine paid taxes of 35 to 40 percent. With all the other obligations factored in, a peasant family most probably only had more or less 20 percent of their annual produce available for subsistence. See Malina and Rohrbaugh, *Social-Science Commentary on the Synoptic Gospels*, 390–91; Oakman, *Jesus and the Peasants*, 148–49.

by the contract. He grazed the flock in the wilderness (ἐν τῇ ἐρήμῳ), most probably far from where he made his home.[92]

Using a shepherd in a story about the kingdom of God would have shocked those who listened to the parable. In the first-century Mediterranean world, in which the pivotal social value was honor,[93] a shepherd was someone without honor. To Jesus' listeners a shepherd was someone without any shame. Several obvious reasons lead to this estimation. First of all, an honorable person was expected to protect the women in his family. Obviously, being nomadic and away from home, the shepherd was not able to do so. Consequently he had no shame, and therefore no proper concern about his honor (i.e., the "sensitivity to one's own reputation [honor] or the reputation of one's family").[94] A second reason for the negative perception of shepherds was the peasantry's understanding of limited good, an understanding reinforced by the level of subsistence they experienced.[95] This perception of limited good, according to Foster, consisted of the peasant's perception that all of the desired things in life, such as land and wealth, always existed in limited quantities and were always in short supply.[96] Because of this, peasants believed that when persons improved themselves it was always at the expense of others. An honorable man, therefore, would only be interested in what was rightfully his; any kind of acquisition, like grazing a flock on somebody else's property, was seen as stealing.[97] This is why herdsmen were seen as thieves: they drove the herds they tended to onto other people's land. Finally, shepherds were rendered unclean because they belonged to one of the proscribed trades. Therefore, hearing about a shepherd in a parable pointing to the kingdom of God was shocking.

If herding sheep, like tax collecting, was avoided by Jews, why was this man a shepherd? Why intentionally choose a trade that will stigmatize a person? Most probably because it was one of the few options left that would have enabled him to support his family. Maybe he was (like Lazarus, who ended up at the front gate of the rich [Luke 16:19–26]) the second or third son of a peasant farmer who only had enough land for the eldest son to inherit; maybe he had to leave the family plot and seek work elsewhere because there were too many mouths to feed in the household, or because

92. *Contra* Schottroff, *Parables of Jesus*, 152.

93. Malina and Rohrbaugh, *Social-Science Commentary on the Synoptic Gospels*, 369.

94. Ibid., 371.

95. Malina and Pilch, *Social-Science Commentary on the Book of Acts*, 217.

96. Foster, "Peasant Society," 304.

97. Malina and Pilch, *Social-Science Commentary on the Book of Acts*, 217.

they could hardly make ends meet; or maybe his father had lost his land because of rising indebtedness and eventual foreclosure on his mortgage by one of the exploiting urban elite.[98] Our shepherd may even have been a smallholder of inherited land who had lost his land for the same reasons.

Since the elite had contempt for manual labor and exploited cheap labor, there must have been ample opportunities for our main character to become a herdsman. The wage, obviously, was not that good. As Kloppenborg and Callon have indicated, the wage of a shepherd was more or less sixteen drachmas per month, or 192 drachmas per year. If one takes into consideration that the standard remuneration at the time of Jesus was one denarius for a day's work, and that the Greek drachma roughly equaled the value of the Roman denarius, it means that a shepherd earned more or less just over half (sixteen denarii) the normal wage for a month. Could this possibly be enough to sustain a family of four adults for a month? According to Oakman, the buying power of a denarius gives us a good indication how far this income could be stretched.[99] Two denarii represented around three weeks' worth of food for one person, and in terms of a family of four, "two denarii would stretch a week to a week and a half for a family; one denarius would supply 3–6 days for a family." A year's supply of food for a family of four thus required between sixty and 122 denarii. If the shepherd worked for a full year (which was unlikely), he and his family had more than enough for food (192 denarii). However, this was only for food. If other necessities such as buying clothes and paying taxes and religious dues are also taken into consideration, 250 denarii per annum (twenty denarii per month) was a poverty-level income.[100] Hence, a shepherd's wage of sixteen drachmae per month was well below a poverty-level income.

So, when one sheep got lost, the shepherd had no other option but to go and look for it. Remember that a shepherd was held accountable for livestock losses, and that the intrinsic value of one male sheep was less than ten drachmas, and that of a female close to double the amount. Leaving the lost sheep by itself would have meant, in the case of a male, the loss of close to one month's wages, and the loss of a female the loss of more than the one month's wages. Also remember that the wage of the shepherd was already below the poverty line. The shepherd's duties, undoubtedly, carried several risks. Was it risky to leave the ninety-nine behind? It was. Was it irresponsible? It was. But there was no other option. He and his family already

98. Herzog, *Parables as Subversive Speech*, 119. See also Van Eck, "Rich Man and Lazarus," 8.

99. Oakman, *Jesus and the Peasants*, 43–44.

100. MacMullan, in ibid., 44.

lived below the poverty line. He was in dire straits. He was already seen as a despised and unclean person—a category that the kingdom of Rome and the kingdom of the temple forced him into. In a certain sense, there was nothing left to lose, nothing except the well-being of his family. That was all that was left, and that alone made it worth his while.

Therefore, when the shepherd found the lost sheep, he rejoiced (Luke 15:5). But the real celebration had to wait for later. After finishing his contract with the owner(s), he drove the flock back, and after accounting for all the sheep he had to tend to, and receiving the contracted wage, he returned home, and then the celebration started (Luke 15:6).[101] At least his hard labor was enough to support his family, proving that risks sometimes do pay off.

What does this parable say about the kingdom? First of all, the kingdom of God is also for those who are rendered unclean by the kingdom of the temple. In fact, the kingdom of God in itself is "unclean," as depicted in the parable of the leaven (Q 13:20–21; *par.* Gos. Thom. 96). In the time of Jesus, as Bernard Scott indicates, leaven was a symbol of moral evil, corruption, and uncleanness; just as a shepherd was not the appropriate character to image God's people or God's kingdom, so also leaven was not the proper symbol for God's people or God's kingdom (see Exod 12:19; Mark 8:15 and *par.*; 1 Cor 5:7; Gal 5:9).[102] The kingdom is also available to shepherds and women. After all, in the parable of the Leven, it is by a women's doing that the kingdom of God is identified with the unclean and the impure. And, as the parable of the despised and unclean Samaritan (Luke 10:30–35), as in the parable of the father who welcomes back an unclean prodigal (Luke 15:11–31), and as in the parable about the elite host who fills up his feast with the unclean (Q 14:16–23; *par.* Gos. Thom. 64) show, it is in the action of Samaritans, nonpatriarchal fathers, and elite hosts—and shepherds—that the kingdom becomes visible. The kingdom of God is therefore not like the kingdom of Rome or the temple.

This parable also teaches that the kingdom becomes visible in the unexpected. Just as in the parable of the elite vineyard owner (patron) who pays all his workers the same wage in spite of their working different hours (Matt 20:1–15), just as in the parable of the Samaritan who stops to help

101. According to Snodgrass, this aspect of the parable is not realistic. Snodgrass, *Stories with Intent*, 102. Linnemann, who understands Luke 15:6 in the sense that the shepherd returns home directly after finding the lost sheep, thus leaving the ninety-nine in the wilderness, also sees this aspect of the parable as unrealistic. Linnemann, *Parables of Jesus*, 68. See also Hedrick, *Many Things in Parables*, 14. Bailey, on the other hand, sees this aspect of the parable as realistic; only the celebration takes place that same evening, since the shepherd returned home every evening. Bailey, *Poet and Peasant*, 150. Clearly these interpretations lack a realistic reading of the parable.

102. Scott, "Reappearance of Parables," 95–119.

someone of a different ethnicity (Luke 10:30–35), and just as in the parable of the father who throws a party for a prodigal, who should be excommunicated (Luke 15:11–32)—all types of unexpected behavior—so in the parable of the shepherd, he acts unexpectedly. There were other possibilities available to him to cut his losses. Armed with a sling and club, and unsupervised with freedom of movement, banditry was a logical option. But then the unexpected happens: the shepherd takes the risk to go and look for the one sheep that is lost. This then also shows that the kingdom is achieved by nonviolence. Just as the vineyard owner maintains honor by not answering violence with violence (Gos. Thom. 65),[103] so the shepherd becomes a symbol of the kingdom by refraining from violence to solve his problem.

Pen ultimately, the kingdom is also present there where everybody has enough. The kingdom becomes visible when a patron hires everybody who waits at the marketplace to be hired in order to feed their families, and pays everybody one denarius, enough food for three to six days (Matt 20:1–15), and when the sower shares the "leftover" yield to support those in need (Mark 4:3b–8)—just as the kingdom becomes visible in a shepherd who risks everything in order for his family to have enough.

Finally, being part of the kingdom is risky, some would even say irresponsible. Telling stories like this parable—stories that cut against the social and religious grain of the day; stories that challenge the normalcies of society; stories in direct opposition to the way "we do things here"; stories that shock and question the status quo, power, and privilege; and stories that characteristically call for a reversal of roles and so frustrate common expectations[104] are risky. Some people would say that telling stories of a different world, of the way things ought to be, of "life as ruled by God's generosity and goodness"[105]—stories that reenvision the actual world in wholly unaccustomed ways[106] and offer its hearers an alternative world to the world created by aristocratic society (Rome), by privilege and power, by tradition and custom, by religious authorities, by temple rituals and sacred texts—is irresponsible.[107] Such a storyteller can, after all, end up on a cross.

---

103. Van Eck, "Tenants," 930–36.

104. Laughlin, *Remedial Christianity*, 91; Hoover, "Incredible Creed, Credible Faith," 92, 94; Beutner, "Haunt of Parable,"; Scott, "Reappearance of Parables," 15–16, 118.

105. Hoover, "Incredible Creed, Credible Faith," 92.

106. Scott, "Reappearance of Parables," 15–16.

107. Hoover, "Incredible Creed, Credible Faith," 98; Borg, *Jesus*, 167.

CHAPTER 6

The Vineyard Laborers (Matt 20:1–15): An Unexpected Patron

THE INTERPRETATION OF THE Vineyard Laborers has in the past hinged on several decisions: Since the owner has a manager, should his face-to-face recruitment of workers in the marketplace be interpreted as normal or abnormal practice? Who are the workers being hired? Why does the owner not agree with those being recruited later in the day on a specific wage? Why does the owner recruit workers up to five o'clock? Why are the workers paid in a reverse order? Is the owner in the parable a symbol for God, and does the vineyard represent Israel? And, finally, should the actions of the owner in the parable be interpreted as negative or positive? Is he depicted as a positive or a negative figure in the parable?

While in the past interpreters have tried to answer these questions without paying much attention to *actual* agricultural practices in antiquity, and hence debate whether, for example, the owner is a figure for God or a villainous exploiter of the poor, this reading of the parable attends closely to social and economic practices in the agricultural sector of the Roman economy in order to assess both the degree of realism in specific details of the parable, and the points at which the narrator deliberately confronts audience expectations with what is normal about a narrative artifice that produces a surprising outcome. In the interpretive tradition since Dodd, this reading of the parable argues that parables trade in realistic scenarios from Palestinian life, but depict figures in those stories as acting in odd ways, in this case, as an unexpected patron of his agricultural workers.

History of Interpretation

Most of the earliest interpreters of the parable, as expected, have immediately allegorized the parable.[1] The earliest allegorization of the parable is that of Matthew: By placing the parable between Matt 19:30 and 20:16 (the last-first and first-last revision of positions), Matthew anticipates the request of the mother of the sons of Zebedee in Matt 20:20–21, and Jesus' response in Matt 20:26–28; the first are those who slave for the benefit of other. For Matthew, the parable thus has as focus discipleship: The parable is intended "to exclude arrogance, ideas of superiority over others in the kingdom, and any idea that God's assessment is to be understood by some kind of reckoning."[2]

Another popular allegorical reading of the parable is to equate the early workers with the Jews, and those who started working later with the Gentiles. With this as a cue, the grumbling of the first workers is interpreted as a judgment of the Gentiles based on salvation by works.[3]

An allegorical-theological reading of the parable is also common among many interpreters. In this reading the owner of the vineyard is seen as a symbol of God. With this as lens, the parable is interpreted as an

1. See Tevel, "Labourers in the Vineyard," 356–60. Origen's allegorical interpretation of the parable is well known. In his reading the five recruitments represent the five periods from Adam to Noah (Origen, *Comm. in Matt.* 15:33–34), while others see in the five recruitments the five senses or the five stages in life at which people experience conversion. Wailes, *Medieval Allegories*, 137–44. Some modern interpreters also read the parable allegorically: Culbertson sees the vineyard as a symbol for Israel, and for Stern the wages received represent the gift of eternal life. Culbertson, "Matthean Vineyard Parables," 261; Stern, *Rabbi Looks at Jesus' Parables*, 102–14. Linked to this interpretation, Blomberg argues that the parable shows that there are no degrees of reward in heaven; all the workers recruited are God's true people, and all are rewarded equally. Blomberg, *Interpreting the Parables*, 282, 285. Trench, finally, identifies divine election in the parable: many are called to God's vineyard, but few retain the humility which will allow them in the end to be partakers of God's salvation. Trench, *Notes on the Parables*, 151.

2. Snodgrass, *Stories with Intent*, 375. See also Davies and Allison, *Matthew,* 3:333; Elliott, "Matthew 20," 52–65; Blomberg, *Interpreting the Parables*, 222; Kistemaker, *Stories Jesus Told*, 74; Hagner, *Matthew 14-28*, 572; Cowan, *Economic Parables,* 47–59.

3. Drury, *Parables in the Gospels*, 92–95; Lambrecht, *Out of the Treasure*, 84; Hagner, *Matthew 14-28*, 574; Patte, "Two Parables," 96.

example of God's grace[4] or justice,[5] or a short narrative teaching that salvation is gained by grace alone.[6]

Scholars who are interested in the original setting in which the parable was told, in most cases, follow the interpretation of Jeremias. According to Jeremias, the original setting of the parable was the public criticism by the Pharisees (represented by the murmurers in Matt 20:11–12) because of Jesus' eating with tax collectors and sinners. The parable, he argues, was Jesus' defense against these criticisms to show how "unjustified, hateful, loveless and unmerciful" their criticism aimed at him was.[7] God is merciful and even has place for the tax collectors and sinners in the kingdom. Interestingly, in these interpretations the owner is also seen as a reference to God.[8]

Not all scholars who are interested in reading the parable in the context of the historical Jesus (27–30 CE) follow Jeremias' interpretation. Scholars like Scott, Herzog, Levine, Borg, Bailey, Crossan, Vearncombe, and Shillington read the parable against the socioeconomic realities of first-century Palestine, depicting the owner of the vineyard as either a negative or positive symbol.

According to Herzog, the parable codifies the oppression of the peasantry by wealthy landowners in the time of Jesus. Jesus told the parable to expose the contradiction between the actual situation of the hearers of the parable and God's justice. This is also the point of view of Borg and Crossan. The parable, in Borg's interpretation, raises consciousness about the domination system in Jesus' time. Crossan's reading follows a similar line: The parable focuses on the idleness of the workers, intending to raise the audience's consciousness about the distinction between personal justice and injustice (practiced by the owner), and systemic justice and injustice (present in the economy).[9] The obvious difficulty with these interpretations is that they presuppose post-Enlightenment analyses and conceptual frameworks. It is well known that the concept of economy—that is, a conception

4. Bultmann, *Synoptic Tradition*, 190; Jones, *Matthean Parables*, 42; Ball, *Radical Stories of Jesus*, 124; Young, *Parables*, 69; Hultgren, *Parables of Jesus*, 35; Stiller, *Preaching Parables*, 59; Hunter, *Then and Now*, 52; Fisher, *The Parables of Jesus*, 88.

5. Buttrick, *Parables of Jesus*, 163.

6. Jülicher, *Gleichnisreden Jesu*, 67; Oesterley, *Gospel Parables*, 109–10; Bornkamm, *Jesus of Nazareth*, 142; Via, *Parables*, 155.

7. Jeremias, *Parables of Jesus*, 38, 139.

8. See, for example, Dodd, *Parables of the Kingdom*, 95; De Ru, "Conception of Reward," 208; Perrin, *Rediscovering the Teaching*, 117; Linnemann, *Parables of Jesus*, 84–86; Stein, *Introduction to the Parables*, 127–28; Schottroff, "Human Solidarity," 145–46; Donahue, *Gospel in Parable*, 82–83.

9. Herzog, *Parables as Subversive Speech*, 97; Borg, *Jesus*, 181–83; Crossan, *Power of Parable*, 98.

of macrostructural systems of exchange—was not part of ancient thinking. *Oikonomia* was, as the name suggests, "household management." Likewise, the notion of "domination" presupposes post-Marxist analyses of modes of production, ideology, and class, none of which existed as discourses in antiquity. One does find criticism of *people* who were regarded as wealthy, arrogant, abusive, unjust and the like, but systemic critiques are absent because the conceptual frameworks to support such critiques were yet to be invented.

Shillington sees the owner as a positive symbol. By paying all the workers the same wage, he argues, the owner enables all the workers to keep the Sabbath; because all were paid the expected daily wage, all could celebrate their achievements during the week and could rest from their labor on the Sabbath to follow. Bailey also sees the owner of the vineyard as a positive symbol; the focus of the parable is the owner's amazing compassion and sensitivity for the unemployed.[10]

Scott, in employing a social-scientific approach, reads the parable through the lens of patronage and clientism. The recruitment of the laborers, in his opinion, sets up a patron-client relationship. By paying all the workers the same wage, the owner in essence makes them all equal, and by doing this, destroys the order of the world and breaks up the Roman patron-client system that dominated the world of the exploited in first-century Palestine. For Scott, the owner thus also functions as a positive symbol in the parable.[11]

Levine, finally, argues that the parable "encourages householders to support laborers, all of them."[12] Jesus speaks in the parable to some who do not recognize their responsibility to people with less,[13] and in telling the parable, Jesus "encouraged landowners" to enact the graciousness of God by "speaking of a vineyard owner who generously assisted some impoverished day laborers."[14] Understood from this perspective, the owner in the parable is a role model for the rich; the rich should "continue to call others to the field and righteously fulfill a contract whose conditions are from the beginning to pay 'what is right'—and what is right is a living wage."[15] In this reading the owner of the vineyard is thus also a positive symbol (*contra* Herzog),

10. Shillington, "Saving Life and Keeping Sabbath," 98–101; Bailey, *Jesus through Middle Eastern Eyes*, 355. See also Wright, who sees the owner as "canny," a landowner "who plans to teach his day-labourers a lesson through the granting of equal pay for different hours" as an act of true justice. Wright, *Jesus the Storyteller*, 148.

11. Scott, *Hear Then the Parable*, 289, 294; Scott, "Reappearance of Parables," 111–12.

12. Levine, *Short Stories by Jesus*, 218.

13. Ibid., 215.

14. Ibid., 217, in following Capper.

15. Ibid., 217.

and the first workers are the tyrants and exploiters who do not want the last recruited to have a living wage.[16]

In perhaps the most sophisticated analysis to date, Vearncombe, after examining the particulars of viticulture in the first century, the status of ἐργάται vis-à-vis other agricultural workers, and the expectations in an agrarian culture of balanced reciprocity, concludes that

> in a socio-economic setting characterized by extreme asymmetry and valuing self–interest, the householder creates a new social bond in the giving of a "gift," however small it may be, to the laborers. The parable may consequently be interpreted as follows: the kingdom of heaven represents a reversal of the world's values. It is like someone who acts contrary to the general concern for profit and self-interest in demonstrating a certain reciprocal solidarity with persons of a much lower social status.[17]

The common assumption that the owner in the parable is a place holder for God will be challenged below, despite the fact that this is the way Matthew wishes to construe the parable. Owners of vineyards were not typically drawn from social ranks that inspired admiration. Nevertheless, the parable does trade in some generally realistic representations of viticulture in first-century Jewish Palestine and invokes cultural scripts shared by its hearers, but at critical points it interrupts those scripts. Knowledge of the realities of ancient viticulture will enable the interpreter of the parable to identify its surprising narrative turns. Fundamental to the social world invoked by the parable is the ambivalence between two models of social and economic exchange—the strict quid pro quo exchange of the labor market, and the balanced reciprocity of the practice of patronage. In its use of narrative artifice, the parable constructs the unusual actions of the owner as a patron, someone who emulates what it means to be δίκαιος. But first I comment on the integrity of the parable.

Integrity

There is almost unanimity among scholars about the integrity of the parable; the argument runs that 20:16 is a redactional addition of Matthew.[18]

16. Ibid., 215, 218. See also Levine and Myrick, "Standard and Poor," 95–115.

17. Vearncombe, "Redistribution and Reciprocity," 235. Citing Oakman, *Jesus and the Economic Questions*, 165. "Generosity undercuts the prevailing order established on the assumption of a *quid pro quo* and a self-sufficient household economy."

18. The only exceptions here are the views of Crossan and Via. Crossan delimits the

As noted earlier, Matthew most probably added 20:16 to echo 19:30, and, linking these two verses with 20:8b, applied the parable received from the tradition to focus on discipleship. The saying in Matt 20:16 and 19:30 (in reverse order) most probably derives from Q 13:30 (οἳ ἔσονται πρῶτοι καὶ εἰσὶν πρῶτοι οἳ ἔσονται ἔσχατοι), a shorter version of which also occurs in Gos. Thom. 4:2 (see also Mark 9:35; Luke 14:9). Interestingly Chrysostom, as early as in the fourth century, sensed the tension between the parable and Matt 20:16.[19] The excision of Matt 20:16 from the parable goes part of the way toward eliminating the powerful allegorizing impulse with which interpreters of the parable have had to deal. An assessment of what is realistic in the parable, and what is not, will add additional reasons to resist an allegorizing or even moralizing interpretation.

Realism

How realistic is the parable? According to Snodgrass, "the picture the parable presents uses realistic but exaggerated features." The realistic features in the parable are the recruitment of workers from the market at a time of need, the wage paid, and the owner (who "is probably reasonably well-off, but not so wealthy that he leaves oversight of his vineyard to agents") doing the recruiting. Unrealistic are the excessive number of recruitments (why were the last recruited not seen earlier, and why could the owner not calculate his needs better?), and the equal pay of all the laborers.[20]

Recent studies[21] have shown that papyri from early Roman Egypt provide "solid ancient *comparanda* on the practices and social realities which the sayings of Jesus and the parables presuppose."[22] Documentary papyri

---

parable to Matt 20:1–13. According to him, Matt 20:2 and 13 form a chiasm; because of Matthew's emphasis on a good-evil contrast, he added Matt 20:14–16. Crossan, *In Parables*, 113–14; Crossan, "Servant Parables," 35. Via delimits the parable to Matt 20:1–14a, arguing that the parable has as focus the grumbling workers, and not the goodness of the owner. Via, *Parables*, 150; Via, "Parable and Example Story," 125.

19. See Chrysostom, *Hom. Matt.,* 64.3–4.

20. Snodgrass, *Stories with Intent*, 369. See also Funk et al., who are also of the opinion that the parable "exaggerates the actions of the vineyard owner." Funk et al., *Five Gospels*, 225.

21. See, for example, Kloppenborg, *Tenants in the Vineyard*; Kloppenborg, "Violence in Synoptic Parables," 232–51; Kloppenborg, *Synoptic Problems*, 491–511, 556–76, 577–99; Kloppenborg, "Burglar in Q," 287–306; Bazzana, "Q Concept of Kingship," 153–68; Bazzana, "*Basileia* and Debt Relief," 511–25; Bazzana, "Violence and Human Prayer," 1–8; Van Eck, "Tenants," 909–36; Van Eck, "Lost Sheep," 1–10; Van Eck, "Jesus and Violence," 101–32.

22. Kloppenborg, *Synoptic Problems*, 2. The Greco-Egyptian papyri, and a few

are important because they are nearly contemporary with Jesus' parables, and because they reflect the actual economic and social practices presupposed by the parables but often ignored by more elite writers. Moreover, the practices evidenced in early Roman Egypt cohere with practices that are later mentioned (albeit in a much more lapidary and fragmentary way) in rabbinic writings from Palestine in the third and following centuries.

The parable of the Vineyard Laborers presupposes most of the same practices as those imagined in the parable of the Tenants (Mark 12:1–12 and par.; Gos. Thom. 65). The latter parable has been the subject of an extensive study by Kloppenborg, who made use of documentary papyri dating from 258 BCE to the fourth century CE.[23] Several features of ancient viticulture are salient.

The parable, first, takes for granted a system of land tenure in which most of the productive land was held by large-scale (elite) owners.[24] As many have indicated, beginning in the First Temple period and continuing into the Second, a pronounced shift in the patterns of land tenure took place, from smallholders producing the Mediterranean triad of grain, grapes, and olives for subsistence to large estates orientated to large-scale production and export crops.[25] Documentary papyri show that the creation of large estates in Palestine was in full swing in the Hellenistic period.[26] In cases at least, these large estates were converted to viticulture and dedicated

---

papyri preserved from the 'Arava, are contemporary with first-century Palestine and reflect similar nonelite social strata and processes. With "due allowance made for legal and cultural differences between Egypt and Palestine," these papyri "can provide useful comparative data for understanding the realia which the parables presuppose." Kloppenborg, "Burglar in Q," 289.

23. Kloppenborg, *Tenants in the Vineyard*, 278–316.

24. For papyrological evidence on elite owning large states, see P.Lond. VII 1948; PSI VI 554; P.Köln III 144; P.Cair. Zen. II 59162, IV 59186; P.Fouad I 43; P.Hamb. I 23 and P.Laur. IV 166. Also see Pliny, *Natural History* 17.171 and Columella, *De ru rustica* 3.13, 5.3.

25. Oakman, *Jesus and the Peasants*, 189.

26. Apollonius, the finance minister (*dioikētēs*) of Ptolemy II Philadelphos, for example, owned several estates, including one somewhere in the Galilee (see PSI VI 554; P.Lond. VII 1948). For evidence of his Egyptian estates, see, for example, PSI V 518, VI 554, and P.Cair. Zen. II 59173, and Rostovtzeff, *Large Estate in Egypt*. See also Fiensy, *Land Is Mine*, 21–22.

to export crops.[27] Literary sources also indicate the existence of substantial Herodian estates in the early Roman period.[28]

The shift from subsistence farming (polycropping) to monoculture, especially viticulture, had a profound effect on the structure and nature of labor. Viticulture was the most labor-intensive of agricultural pursuits, requiring more permanent workers than cereal and other agricultural production: Cato (*De agricultura* 11.1–13) recommends 16 permanent workers to care for a 100 *iugera* (25.3 ha.) vineyard.

Vineyards, however, required large temporary labor inputs during the agricultural cycle for clearing brushwood, weeding, burning weeds, hoeing, and pruning.[29] The most demanding period for extra workers was the vintage period when pickers and treaders were needed in large numbers. Once ripe, grapes had to be picked quickly and could not be stored for long without rotting; extra workers thus were needed to tread and press the picked grapes within a few days after harvest. The vintage period thus created an exceptional labor demand and, as documented papyri attest, it was normal to make use of day laborers to fill this seasonal large demand for labor.[30] Rathbone estimates that for Cato's 100 *iugera* vineyard an additional forty pickers would be needed, and in addition, workers to transport, sort, and press the vintage.[31] This temporary labor recruited in the marketplace

27. Owners of large estates increased their tenure "through foreclosures on loans, leading to hostile takeovers of peasant farms. When possible the land so annexed was converted into vineyards so it could produce a product with a higher return than the mixed grains grown by subsistence peasant farmers." Herzog, *Parables as Subversive Speech*, 85. There is plenty of evidence in documentary papyri of the conversion of land into vineyards; see, for example, P.Lond. II 483, VII 1948; BGU IV 1122, XII 2177; P.Mich. 9229; P.Mil. Vogl. II 69, VII 308; P.Cair. Masp. I 67097; P.Col. Zen. II 79; P.Flor. II 134; P.Oxy. IV 707; P.Ryl. II 427; PSI VI 554; P.Cair. Zen. II 59162; IV 59816, and P.Köln III 144. As to Herzog's claim about the mechanism by which land was acquired, there is very little direct evidence, so Herzog's claims must remain suppositions.

28. Josephus, *Jewish Antiquities* 15.264; 17.305–307; Josephus, *The Life* 33; 47; 115; 422; 429; Josephus, *Jewish War* 1.403–5; 3.36. See also Fiensy, *Land Is Mine*, 55–57.

29. For special and seasonal tasks related to viticulture, see P.Heid. III 326; P.Oxy. XIV 1631, 1692; P.Col. Zen. I 59103. II 79; IV 59176, 59548, 59549 and P.Zen. Pestm. 64. Also see a detailed list of specialized and seasonal tasks needed in vineyards in Kloppenborg, *Tenants in the Vineyard*, 578.

30. For evidence from documented papyri on the use of day laborers, see P.Lond. VII 1957; P.Cair. Zen. IV 59748, 59827 and P.Mich. II 1 27, and I 200. Documented papyri also abundantly attest to the payment of daily wages for workers. See list of papyrological evidence in ibid., 579–80. On the use of day laborers in viticulture, see Fiensy, *Land Is Mine*, 85–90; Malina and Rohrbaugh, *Social-Science Commentary on the Synoptic Gospels*, 100–101.

31. Rathbone concludes: "It would probably be an underestimate to assume the employment by the villa during the vintage of casual labourers to the value of 1,000

comprised probably smallholders who needed to supplement their farm incomes, and unlanded laborers, perhaps displaced peasant farmers.

A second important aspect of viticulture in the first century attested by documented papyri is its association with wealth and the wealthy. Viticulture not only demanded high labor costs but also required substantial capital input.[32] A newly planted vineyard took four to five years to come into full production, which means that an owner had to rely on other sources of income during the initial growth period. Owners also had to cope with bad weather that damaged crops, with neglect, with theft, with the degradation of soil conditions, and with falling prices. Only the wealthy thus could afford to engage in medium- and large-scale intensive, export-orientated viticulture. Yet vineyard owners prior to the second century CE were not typically the old patricians who regarded viticulture as too expensive and risky, despite Columella's attempts to persuade his peers of the value of vines. On the contrary, vineyard owners in the first century were the nouveau riche, imperial freedmen with disposable cash.[33] Although we have no direct evidence from Jewish Palestine of the wealth of vineyard owners, the basic needs for high capitalization and wage inputs, and the instability of yields and markets, imply that also only the middling wealthy were able to engage in intensive viticulture. In addition, the distribution and location of large winepresses along trunk roads leading to the coast indicates a strong orientation to export rather than purely local consumption.[34]

A final aspect of viticulture evoked by the parable is that of absenteeism. Owner absenteeism was the norm in viticulture.[35] Vineyards were not only capital intensive, requiring investment from those with sufficient capital to sustain up to five years of care for a nonproducing vineyard, but they required specialized agricultural expertise from vinedressers. Owners

---

man-days." Rathbone, "Development of Agriculture," 12–13. See also Murray, "Viticulture and Wine Production," 585–90; Kloppenborg, *Tenants in the Vineyard*, 288–90.

32. Capital investment was needed inter alia for outlays for vine supports, for the installation of irrigation, for the erection of fences, for the construction of a stone-built field tower for the storing of tools, and for facilities for pressing and storage, for the construction of waterwheels, catch basins, storage tanks and a press, for the excavation of a treading floor, and for the purchase of iron tools and draft animals. Van Eck, "Tenants," 924. See also Cato, *Agriculture* 11.2—13.2. For a detailed list of an owner or lessor's expenses documented in papyri, see Kloppenborg, *Tenants in the Vineyard*, 560–61, 570.

33. Kloppenborg, *Tenants in the Vineyard*, 299–302.

34. Frankel, *Wine and Oil Production in Antiquity*, 141; Kloppenborg, *Tenants in the Vineyard*, 302–3.

35. Kloppenborg, *Tenants in the Vineyard*, 314–16.

were typically wealthy subelites, and vinedressers were agricultural workers who may have doubled as managers.[36]

Owners were seldom involved in the day-to-day management of the vineyard and still less in the recruitment and payment of temporary help.[37] If an owner were to visit his or her vineyard, it would be either a surprise inspection to ensure that the manager was protecting the owner's interests, or at harvest, not to direct or manage the details of the harvest but to ensure that there was no pilferage and that the full extent of the harvest was realized to the owner's account. For other matters, the operation of the vineyard was left in the hands of slave labor[38] supervised by a *vilicus*,[39] or day laborers supervised by a manager. Another option available to vineyard owners was to lease their vineyards to tenants[40] who could properly care for their vineyards.

A papyrus letter from the Zenon archive illustrates this well (P.Cair. Zen. III 59317):[41]

1 Ζήνωνι χαίρειν Ὧρος. ἀπὸ μηνὸς Χοίαχ ἕως
Μεσορὴ μηνῶν θ'. δεῖ ἐμὲ ἐγμετρῆσ‹α›ι
τὰ ἔργα καὶ πολλά εἰσιν τὰ ἔργα· ἀνηλώσω δὲ
εἰς ταῦτα χάρτας δ' (ὧν) εἰς τὸν οἰκοδομικὸν

5 λόγον γ' καὶ εἰς τὰ ἔργα τῶν ἀμπελουργῶν
ἀκαλῶς ἂν οὖν ποιήσαι‹ς› συντάξας ἐμοὶ
δοῦναι, ὅπως ἐγμετρήσω τὰ ἔργα ἐν τάχ‹ε›ι.
εὐτύχει.
καὶ περὶ τοῦ ὀψωνίου, ἀπὸ μηνὸς Παχὼν{ο}ς

---

36. Purcell, "Wine and Wealth in Ancient Italy," 3; Kloppenborg, *Tenants in the Vineyard*, 295–303.

37. On estate management, see Carlsen, *Vilici and Roman Estate Managers*, 58–63. Choi remarks that direct "management [of estates] was infrequently employed in the case of large landholders. Instead, large landholders typically resided in urban centers, from whence instructions were issued concerning the management of their rural property. This is particularly true in the case of vineyard owners, for viticulture was not only labour-intensive, but also required specialized labour." Choi, "Urban-Rural Relations," 107.

38. See, for example, P.Col. Zen. II 90, and P.Mich. I 49.

39. Carlsen, *Vilici and Roman Estate Managers*, 57.

40. See, for example, P.Col. Zen. II 79; P.Ryl. IV 583; P.Köln III 144; BGU IV 1119, 1122; P.Lond. II 163; P.Harr. I 137; P.Oxy. IV 729; P.Flor. III 369; P.Ross. Georg. II 19; P.Oxy. XIV 1631, 1692, and P.Oxy. XLVII 3354.

41. Cited from Kloppenborg, *Tenants in the Vineyard*, 400–401.

10 ἕως μεσορὴ μηνῶν δ᾽ (γίνονται) (δρ.) μ᾽. εἰς τοῦτο
ἔχω παρὰ Κάλλωνος (δρ.) ι᾽, λο(ιπὸν) (δρ.) λ᾽ (ὧν) ὑπολόγη–
σ‹ό›ν μ‹οι› εἰς ὃ προσοφείλω (δρ.) ιε᾽, λο(ιπὸν) (δρ.) ιε᾽. καλῶς
ἂν ποιήσαις καὶ τοῦτο ἐμοὶ δού‹ς›,
ἵνα μᾶλλον πρὸς τοῖς ἔργοις εὐτακτήσω.

15 L λς᾽, Θῶθ λ᾽. Ὧρος χαρτῶν,
ὀψωνίου.[42]

Zenon was the manager (οἰκονόμος) of the many estates of Apollonios, the *dioikētēs* of Ptolemy II Philadelphos (285–246 BCE), but was not involved in the daily management of any of those estates. Horos, whose title is not given, but who functioned like Matthew's ἐπίτροπος, was responsible for managing the vineyard, including assigning work to the vinedressers and keeping accounts that would be audited by the owner or his agents. Ἐργάται are not mentioned, probably because of the date of the papyrus (Thoth 30 = November 23), well after the conclusion of the vintage period. Nevertheless, it would have been the manager, not the owner or his agents, responsible for directing the work of pruning and weeding from Choiak (late January) onward, and especially for the harvest (in Mesore = September).[43] Each of these tasks required the labor inputs not only from the vinedressers, who were often salaried employees or slaves, but also from recruited day laborers (ἐργάται).

How realistic is the parable of the Vineyard Laborers? From the above evidence from documented inscriptions and papyri, it is clear that the story

42. (1) Horos to Zenon, greetings. From the month of Choiak until Mesore is nine months. I must apportion the work, and there are many things to be done. Now I will use four papyrus rolls on these things, three for the construction (5) account and one for the work of the vinedressers. Therefore please arrange to give me (more) so that I can apportion the work quickly. Farewell. Now in regard to my monthly salary: from the months of Pachons (10) to Mesore is four months, making 40 dr. In payment I have received from Kallon 10 dr., leaving 30 dr. From this you should deduct the 15 dr. that I still owe (you). This leaves 15 dr. It would be good if you could give this to me so that I will be conscientious in regard to my job. <verso> (15) Year 36, Thoth 30. Horos, regarding papyrus scrolls (and) (his monthly) salary.

43. *Contra* Schottroff: "It is an everyday occurrence for the owner of a vineyard to hire workers in the marketplace." Schottroff, "Human Solidarity," 129. Rightly Donahue and Carter: The householder's act of going out early in the morning to hire day laborers for his vineyard is unusual, since this usually was the manager's task. Donahue, *Gospel in Parable*, 79–80; Carter, *Matthew and the Margins*, 395–96. See also Herzog: "If the householder does belong to the urban elite, why does he, not his steward, go to the agora to hire day laborers? Ordinarily, elites remained invisible, preferring to let their retainers do the visible work, such as recruiting day laborers for the lowest wage possible." Herzog, *Parables as Subversive Speech*, 86–87.

begins in an entirely recognizable vein: the harvest is approaching and a large (temporary) labor force is needed to bring in the vintage, which must be picked and processed quickly in order to prevent spoilage and theft.

The scenario in the parable involves two management figures: the owner (called an οἰκοδεσπότης in Matt 20:1, and ὁ κύριος τοῦ ἀμπελῶνος in Matt 20:8) and his manager (ἐπίτροπος, Matt 20:8). Matthew's term οἰκοδεσπότης is perhaps a Mattheanism: It is redactional in Matt 10:25 and 21:33, the phrase ἄνθρωπος οἰκοδεσπότης occurs only in Matthean parables (Matt 13:52; 20:1; 21:33), and in the latter two instances identifies the protagonist of the parable with God.[44] Whether the οἰκοδεσπότης is editorial or not, there are two odd features in the story: The active nature of the owner during the harvest, and the scenario of multiple recruitments.

A propos to the first point, Choi remarks:

> When the manager is introduced half-way through the parable (v. 8) . . . , the owner's membership in the urban and not the rural population becomes clear. As a member of the urban population, both the owner's presence at and his participation in the activities of the vineyard would have struck the original audience as peculiar.[45]

She concludes:

> The parable's portrait of the vineyard owner, then, would have struck the original audience as peculiar in at least three ways. First, since landholders were typically absent, the mere presence of the owner was peculiar. Second, since the purpose of these visits was one of inspection, all of the owner's participation in the affairs of the vineyard was peculiar: his participation in the recruitment of day laborers, the multiple trips to the *agora*, and his presence when the wages were paid, for these were the responsibilities of the manager. Third, since urban-rural interaction typically occurred in the urban domain, the presence of the owner in the parable is peculiar not only with respect to his status as the owner, but also as a member of the urban population who had travelled against the normal direction of movements and had engaged in urban-rural interaction in the rural domain.[46]

44. Matt 10:25R; 13:27S, 52S; 20:1S, 11S; 21:33R; 24:43 (= Q). Three times Matthew uses the phrase ἄνθρωπος οἰκοδεσπότης: Matt 13:52; 20:1; and 21:33. ('R' = Matthean redaction; 'S' = Matthew's *Sondergut*).

45. Choi, "Urban-Rural Relations," 116.

46. Ibid., 118.

The second odd feature of the story is the scenario of multiple recruitments. It seems pointless to argue whether this is a realistic detail or not. Presumably competent and experienced managers (and even owners) knew the size of the labor force required to bring in the vintage. Evidently the story does not imagine a labor shortage, since those recruited later report οὐδεὶς ἡμᾶς ἐμισθώσατο (Matt 20:7). The multistage recruitment scenario, though rather artificial, is essential to the telling of the parable. Without it there would be no story.

Although the presence of the owner, especially his involvement in recruiting, is unusual, it is also essential to the story. One could imagine a story in which a local ἐπίτροπος acted in the unusual way in which Matthew's owner acted and even replied to the full-day worker, ἑταῖρε, οὐκ ἀδικῶ σε·οὐχὶ δηναρίου συνεφώνησάς μοι; (Matt 20:13). But he would not have been able to say οὐκ ἔξεστίν μοι ὃ θέλω ποιῆσαι ἐν τοῖς ἐμοῖς; (Matt 20:15), since the ἐπίτροπος had a fiduciary responsibility to act in the interests of his employer (or owner).

The parable, then, is a combination of verisimilitude and unusual features. This is quite typical of many of the parables ascribed to Jesus, which proceed by telling a story that is realistic, if somewhat unusual, and deliberately invoke certain cultural scripts or beliefs about the world. Then it challenges or problematizes those scripts and beliefs through an unexpected narrative turn. Narrative realism is essential, for it is only by means of a realistic idiom that hearers can be induced to identify with characters in the story before the "trap" is sprung.[47]

Reading the Parable

In the Vineyard Laborers the kingdom is compared with the actions of an owner, someone who owns a vineyard (Matt 20:1). The owner is not obviously, as many assume, a stand-in for God; he is the owner of a vineyard (ὁ

---

47. Kloppenborg, *Tenants in the Vineyard*, 287. See also Hedrick: Interpreting "the parables requires knowledge of first-century Palestinian society, economics, politics, religion, and farming practices if they are to be understood in that context. Such knowledge of first-century practices evokes awareness of subtleties in the narrative missed by the heavy-handed searcher for theological ideas . . . Knowledge of the social world acts as a brake to the overeager imaginations of all who mine the parables for theological insights . . . Readers unaware of such almost subliminal social values are easily led astray in their readings." Hedrick, *Many Things in Parables*, 43. Herzog shares this sentiment: "To understand the parable, it is necessary to know who appears in its social script." Herzog, *Parables as Subversive Speech*, 84.

κύριος τοῦ ἀμπελῶνος) as stated in Matt 20:8.[48] For the hearers, the parable starts with a shock. First, as in the parables of the Lost Sheep, the Great Feast, and the Merchant, the kingdom is likened to a negatively marked character, someone not normally associated with the kingdom.[49] The owner, when identified in the context of available contemporary evidence, most probably was one of the wealthy subelites who owned large estates and converted the land to viticulture dedicated to the production of export crops. The owner was undoubtedly well-off, since only the wealthy could afford to engage in medium- and large-scale intensive, export-orientated viticulture, as has been pointed out. Yet there is a social taint to such persons, who were not the *optimi* and *honestiores* of ancient society, but the second tier of the newly wealthy.[50] It is no doubt an exaggeration to suppose that the original audience of the parable would think that the owner was evil and a thief;[51] but the owner was not obviously a positive figure either. We are not told how such persons acquired their land—perhaps through expropriation or default on loans, or through receiving gift estates from conquered lands, or through making a purchase from failing farmers. Whichever the case, the new focus on monoculture, and viticulture in particular, had a significant and not altogether positive impact on the daily lives of the peasantry. Monoculture

48. In Hultgren's view, the landowner "is surely a metaphor for God (cf. the designation of him as ὁ κύριος ["the lord/Lord"] at 20:8). Jesus' parables typically speak of kings, fathers, and masters as the major figures, and in each case the hearer or reader makes the metaphorical connection. To do so is not to allegorize. To fail to do so, or to refuse to do so, is to tear the parables from their *symbolic universe.*" Hultgren, *Parables of Jesus*, 36; italics added. See also Snodgrass, *Stories with Intent*, 373. Shillington, on the other hand, opines that Jesus would have presumed that when he told a parable about an owner and a vineyard, the *cultural repertoire* of his audience (social universe, in Berger's terms) would have made the association between the vineyard and Israel and the owner and God. Shillington, "Saving Life and Keeping Sabbath," 87–101. Both Hultgren and Shillington allegorize the parable, interestingly using direct opposite bases for their interpretations. Both seem to presume that κύριος and "vineyard" were ineluctably tethered to theological ideas and that one could not speak of either without invoking God and Israel. This view is based on Matthew's interpretation of the parable, which is already an allegorization of the parable received in the tradition.

49. Van Eck, "Lost Sheep"; Van Eck, "Feast"; Van Eck, "Merchant."

50. See also Klausner: The owner is a "man of property" and has a manager, indicating his wealth, because a manager "supervised the numerous servants of a great property while the wealthy owner lived in the city or was absent travelling in pursuit of business." Klausner, *Jesus of Nazareth*, 180. Scott places the owner among the class of patrons, and Herzog describes him as wealthy; he has a vineyard, and "vineyards were most likely owned by elites because they produce a crop that can be converted into luxury items (wine), monetized and exported." Scott, *Hear Then the Parable*, 289; Herzog, *Parables as Subversive Speech*, 85.

51. See Malina, *New Testament World*, 84.

meant increased pressure on smallholders, an increasingly monetized form of exchange,[52] and the vagaries of labor demand. For several reasons, therefore, the parable starts with a shock: How can the kingdom be likened to a dubious character such as an owner of a vineyard?

In hearing the parable, the hearer's initial shock most probably quickly turned into puzzlement. As documented papyri indicate, it was normal for landowners to function as absentees, leaving the operation of their vineyards in the hands of agents or managers. The owner in the parable, however, is not only present, but directly involved; he sets off to the marketplace (ἀγορά) early in the morning (at six o'clock) to recruit laborers.[53] This was not normal practice, contrary to their normal experience, and must have puzzled hearers, especially since the owner had the services of a manager.[54]

52. Linked to the concept of limited good was the peasants' perception of production and the mode of exchange. Peasant production was primarily for use rather than exchange (e.g., export), and evaluated the world of persons and things in terms of *use*, and not exchange. For peasants it was unacceptable to sell commodities at a profit; it was considered as "unnatural." Profitmaking was seen as evil and socially destructive, since it was perceived as "a threat to the community and community balance." Rohrbaugh, "Text of Terror," 33; Malina, *New Testament World*, 97. See also Van Eck, "Minas," 5.

53. Day laborers, though free, were among the most disadvantaged of ancient workers. While slaves represented a capital investment to be protected against loss and peril, ἐργάται were more "disposable." Varro counsels using free labor rather than slaves for especially heavy work (*opera rustica maiora*) and in areas where the land was unhealthy (*Rust.* 1.17.2–3). Nevertheless, it is an exaggeration to treat all of these as belonging to a single class of "expendables," as some have argued. See, for example Herzog, *Parables as Subversive Speech*, 88. Since the parable is set at harvest time, some of those recruited were likely the landless, "otherwise they would have harvested their own crops." Malina and Rohrbaugh, *Social-Science Commentary on the Synoptic Gospels*, 101. Some may have been smallholders hungry for cash, deferring their own harvests. Kloppenborg, *Tenants in the Vineyard*, 289. Buttrick is thus not correct in arguing that laborers were available simply because they were the undesirables of society. Buttrick, *Speaking in Parables*, 114.

54. Interpreters of the parable differ on the question whether the action of the owner should be seen as normal or abnormal. Schottroff, Linnemann, Levine and Myrick, and Wright argue for the first position. Schottroff, *Parables of Jesus*, 212; Linnemann, *Parables of Jesus*, 82; Levine and Myrick, "Standard and Poor," 101; Wright, *Jesus the Storyteller*, 144–45. According to Schottroff, the owner does the recruiting himself because he appears not to be one of the great landowners who live in the cities, but, as in the case of the Prodigal (Luke 15:11b–32), lives on the farm. For Linnemann, the recruiting by the owner is normal; what is abnormal are the several times he goes out. Levine and Myrick believe it is normal because the owner is a Jew, basing their argument on later rabbinical sources such as *m. Middot* 7.1. This Mishnaic text, however, does not state that the recruiting is done by the owner himself. Most scholars who see the recruiting by the owner as abnormal base their opinion on the conviction that the owner should be seen as a symbol for God, and that the recruiting is an act of grace. See, for example, Oesterley, *Gospel Parables*, 107, 109; Kistemaker, *Stories Jesus Told*, 73.

Why hadn't the manager, who later pays the workers on the instruction of the owner, recruited the laborers?

While recruiting by the owner was unusual, the recruiting itself takes place in the normal manner. In deciding on the wage, the workers and the owner agree on a daily wage of one denarius[55] (see συμφωνήσας in Matt 20:2, and συνεφώνησάς in Matt 20:13), whereafter the workers are sent to work in the vineyard. Scott suggests that the agreement to pay the workers establishes a patron-client relationship between the owner and the workers.[56] One of the essential features of a patron-client relationship, however, was that it entailed a *long-term* social-interpersonal obligation, and moral obligations on both sides.[57] This is not the case in the parable, at least at the beginning: The workers are recruited for a day's work, and their obligation to the owner and his to them ceases at the end of the day.

For Herzog, the recruiting is abnormal, with the motive of the owner being a later face-to-face exploitation (shaming) of the recruited workers. Herzog, *Parables as Subversive Speech*, 83. Scott also sees the action as abnormal, with the intention of the owner to set up patron-client relationships. Scott, *Hear Then the Parable*, 289, 294. Bailey sees it as "odd," motivated by the owner's compassion for the unemployed. Bailey, *Jesus through Middle Eastern Eyes*, 357–58.

55. It is claimed *ad nauseam* that one denarius was the usual daily wage and exegetes frequently debate whether 1 denarius/day is "a fair but not exorbitant payment," or "subsistence pay at the best," or a "subsistence or lower–than–subsistence wage." See respectively Levine and Myrick, "Standard and Poor," 102; Linnemann, *Parables of Jesus*, 82; Herzog, *Parables as Subversive Speech*, 90. We have, however, little direct information on the wage structure from first-century Palestine. Evidence from Egypt ranges from 0.5 obols/day (i.e., 1/12 drachma; mid 300 BCE) to 3–4 obols/day (1/2–2/3 drachma; 78 CE), 1 drachma/day (200 CE), with the majority of wages being less than 1 denarius/drachma. Moreover, what is needed is evidence of wage structures *and* contemporary prices of wheat in order to estimate the real value of wages. Such a combination is lacking for most locales (including Palestine), and for most periods, except early Roman Egypt. Harris estimates HS 1.0–1.5 for an "unskilled" laborer in Egypt in the first century. "Let us say HS 1 [0.25 den.] in the first century. To meet expenses of HS 210 a year . . . seems therefore to be just beyond the capacity of such a man . . . Many inhabitants of Roman Egypt probably suffered to varying degrees from destitution, and a whole social class would have disappeared if it had not been for the casual labor of women and children." Harris, *Rome's Imperial Economy*, 44–45. The most important factor to consider is that ancient authors are prone both to exaggerate and to give sums in round numbers. This means that audiences were likely to take such numbers as symbolic rather than as actual figures. Scheidel, "Finances, Figures and Fiction," 224.

56. Scott, *Hear Then the Parable*, 289, 294.

57. Saller, *Personal Patronage*, 41–78. For the salient features of patronage and clientism, see Eisenstadt and Roniger, "Patron-Client Relations," 42–77; Eisenstadt and Roniger, *Patrons, Clients and Friends*, 48–49; Moxnes, "Patron-Client Relations," 241–68; Wallace-Hadrill, "Patronage in Roman Society," 63–87; Malina, *Social World of Jesus*, 143–47; Malina and Rohrbaugh, *Social-Science Commentary on the Synoptic Gospels*, 388; Neyrey, "God, Benefactor and Patron," 465–92.

At nine o'clock the owner again sets off to the marketplace, and finds workers standing around, not working (ἑστῶτας ἐν τῇ ἀγορᾷ ἀργούς). Seeing this, he also offers them work, promising to pay them what is fair (ὃ ἐὰν ᾖ δίκαιον δώσω ὑμῖν; Matt 20:4). The same happens at twelve and three o'clock, and again workers are recruited with the same agreement. With the owner acting in the same way (ἐποίησεν ὡσαύτως; Matt 20:5), it can be assumed that these workers are also promised to be paid what is fair (ὃ δίκαιον). Finally, at five o'clock the owner again goes to the marketplace and finds workers, as was the case at nine o'clock, standing around (ἑστῶτας; Matt 20:6). The owner asks them why they are still at the marketplace (ἑστήκατε), and their answer is, because nobody has recruited them (ὅτι οὐδεὶς ἡμᾶς ἐμισθώσατο; Matt 20:7), after which these workers are also sent to work in the vineyard.

Before we move on to the final part of the parable, a few remarks are necessary. First, although the recruitments at twelve, three, and five o'clock are described in a condensed manner, it can be assumed that the workers recruited first, after six in the morning were all promised the same wage, that is, what is fair (ὃ ἐὰν ᾖ δίκαιον δώσω ὑμῖν; Matt 20:4). This can be deduced from the expression ἐποίησεν ὡσαύτως in Matt 20:5. Important for the understanding of the parable is that the early workers agreed to be paid one denarius, and those who started later agreed to be paid what was fair (ὃ ἐὰν ᾖ δίκαιον).

Second, some interpreters pejoratively interpret the standing (ἑστῶτας) of the workers at the marketplace as "idling" or "loitering" (being lazy), an attitude, they argue, that is confirmed by the owner's question directed at the "five o'clock workers:" τί ὧδε ἑστήκατε ὅλην τὴν ἡμέραν ἀργοί.[58] This reads too much into the parable, and is an interpretation based on a basic mistranslation of the meaning of ἑστῶτας ἐν τῇ ἀγορᾷ ἀργούς (Matt 20:3), ἑστῶτας (Matt 20:6), and ἑστήκατε ὅλην τὴν ἡμέραν ἀργοί (Matt 20:6). The basic meaning of ἀργός is "not working" or "without work," and lacks the pejorative sense of "idling" or "loitering." The view of Borg and Crossan anachronistically assumes an economy in which full employment is normal, whereas in fact the structure of the ancient agricultural economy inevitably resulted in chronic *underemployment*.[59] The meaning "not working" is

---

58. Borg, *Jesus*, 182; Crossan, *Power of Parable*, 96.

59. Erdkamp, "Agriculture," 556–72; Pleket, "Labor and Unemployment," 267–76. See also P.Lond. III 1170v.45, 129 (259 CE), a monthly farm account which lists various workers under the heading λόγος ἐργατῶν ἀργησάντων, which include workers who are in town, or ill, and who nonetheless are allowed wine. These workers appear to be attached to the farm but for various reasons are not available for agricultural work, and so are ἀργός.

also confirmed by the answer of the "five o'clock workers:" ὅτι οὐδεὶς ἡμᾶς ἐμισθώσατο (Matt 20:7). The workers recruited after the initial morning hire were not loitering or lazy; they were looking for work, hoping that someone would recruit them. Moreover, it cannot be assumed with confidence that at the different hours the owner recruited all the workers waiting in the marketplace who were hoping to find work, or that those recruited later only showed up later.[60] The parable does not provide enough information to make these conclusions. The parable, however, does state that those who were recruited at five waited at the marketplace the whole day (ὅλην τὴν ἡμέραν; Matt 20:6), hoping to be recruited, which probably implies that the owner had a choice about whom to recruit at nine, twelve, three, and five o'clock. As will be indicated below, this possibility is an important aspect in trying to get to a possible meaning of the parable.

The third remark, linked to the above, relates to the question of real-ism: Is the action of the owner—recruiting extra workers at nine, twelve, three and five o'clock—realistic? What motivated him to recruit workers up to as late as five o'clock? For Hultgren, the answer to these questions lies in the fact that the parable does not describe a real event; for Crossan, it is because the owner was a cheapskate (trying to have as few workers as possible to pay); and the well-known opinion of Herzog is that the owner deliberately wanted to exploit the workers by taking advantage of those who were looking for work to meet his harvesting needs by offering them work without a wage agreement.[61] Jeremias, on the other hand, has made the sug-gestion that the parable should be read against the backdrop of harvest time (near the onset of the rainy season), which would make the many recruit-ments understandable.[62]

If we take the papyrological evidence into consideration, Jeremias' suggestion is most probably correct. As I indicated earlier, in the vintage

---

60. Beare, *Gospel according to Matthew*, 402.

61. Hultgren, *Parables of Jesus*, 37; Crossan, *Power of Parable*, 97; Herzog, *Parables as Subversive Speech*, 85–86.

62. "The vintage and the pressing had to be finished before the onset of the rainy season." Jeremias, *Parables of Jesus*, 136. See also Breech, *Silence of Jesus*, 145. Bailey follows the suggestion of Jeremias, adding the possibility that the urgent recruiting of the owner also could be because of the need to prune the vines in time. Bailey, *Jesus through Middle Eastern Eyes*, 357. Derrett also sees the recruitments taking place at harvest time, adding that the next day was the Sabbath, and therefore the urgency of the recruitments. Derrett, "Workers in the Vineyard," 72. Linnemann (also following Bultmann), on the other hand, is of the opinion that if the parable is placed within the harvest it ruins the parable: it mitigates the generosity of the owner because he then shows gratitude to only those who came last, who "did not leave him in the lurch in a crucial situation." Linnemann, *Parables of Jesus*, 82.

period ripe grapes had to be picked and treaded quickly before rotting, a process that needed a large number of extra workers. Because of this need for seasonal workers, day laborers flocked to the farms at harvest time.[63] Interpreting the many (urgent) recruitments of the owner against this scenario not only explains why the owner goes out to the marketplace to recruit workers up to as late as five o'clock, but also why some were willing to wait all day in the hope to be recruited.[64] This scenario may even suggest that the owner had a large vineyard, affirming his wealth. Above all, this scenario affirms the realism of this aspect of the parable, *contra* Snodgrass, who argues, not only that the number of recruitments is excessive, but that the workers recruited in the middle of the day are not really necessary for the plot of the parable.[65]

The workers recruited in the middle of the day are not only an essential part of the plot of the parable, but are also the key to understanding the payment of the workers by the manager. This becomes clear when the owner instructs his manager to call the workers and pay them in reverse order; a sequence that Hultgren sees as "surprising."[66] Interpreters of the parable have speculated as to the reason of this sequence: According to Buttrick, for example, it shows that the owner is both unjust and arrogant,[67] while Herzog is of the opinion that the owner deliberately insults and shames the first workers by paying them last.[68] These readings of the parable contradict the description of the owner in Matt 20:15, namely, that he is good (ὅτι ἐγὼ ἀγαθός εἰμι). How can the owner be good and "bad" at the same time, especially since he recruited workers up to as late as five o'clock?

The key to understanding why the owner pays the workers in a reverse order lies in his recruitment of those who started working later, not setting a fixed wage and promising them a wage that is fair or just (δίκαιος). Malina and Rohrbaugh make the following remark in this regard:

> The good householder pays all by agreement. However, anything given over and above the agreed-for wage requires a previous patron-client relationship. The patron shows patronage

63. Schottroff, "Human Solidarity," 30.

64. *Contra* Levine and Myrick, who argue that the parable makes no mention of the need for more labor, and that the owner brings as many as possible workers into his vineyard because he wants to help those without work. Levine and Myrick, "Standard and Poor," 107.

65. Snodgrass, *Stories with Intent*, 369.

66. Hultgren, *Parables of Jesus*, 38.

67. Buttrick, *Speaking in Parables*, 114.

68. Herzog, *Parables as Subversive Speech*, 91. See also Jeremias, *Parables of Jesus*, 137; Ford, *Parables of Jesus*, 117.

by "giving to this last the same as I give to you" (v. 14). This is favor as one expects from a patron. Non-clients get merely what is their due, and for this they cast an evil eye (of envy) on the patron. The evil eye does not work, because the patron is good.[69]

This remark of Malina and Rohrbaugh explains why the workers are paid in reverse order, and why the owner, when he recruits those who started working later, does not set a fixed wage. He is recruiting clients, workers with whom he has a long-standing patron-client relationship. As I mentioned earlier, one of the salient features of patron-client relationships was that it entailed a long-range social-interpersonal obligation, which included a strong element of solidarity that was sealed by exchange, couched in terms of interpersonal loyalty and attachment between patrons and clients.[70] The owner, as patron of some of the workers, therefore has to pay his clients first. He needs them at a crucial time of the harvest, and they respond positively. They also trust his patronage when he recruits them without setting an agreed wage.[71] This is clearly a relationship that includes a strong element of solidarity, yet again sealed by exchange based on interpersonal loyalty and attachment between patron and client. When this parable is read in terms of the cultural script behind the parable, there is not "something . . . incongruous about all of this, since Jesus does not offer any practical reasons for the householder's behaviour," as Breech has argued.[72] Given that the parable is a high-context text, the "practical reasons" are not given in the parable. To miss this point is to read the text from an anachronistic perspective.

The owner of the vineyard thus is not just a good employer, as Jeremias would have it, paying the agreed wage to some, but also a patron, offering benefits beyond the strict norms of economic exchange. The owner's assertion, "οὐκ ἔξεστίν μοι ὃ θέλω ποιῆσαι ἐν τοῖς ἐμοῖς;" underscores the fact that he has stepped out of the role of the owner, who thinks only in terms of a strict balance sheet, and into the role of a patron/benefactor, whose

---

69. Malina and Rohrbaugh, *Social-Science Commentary on the Synoptic Gospels*, 101.

70. Sahlins, *Stone Age Economics*, 220; Wallace-Hadrill, "Patronage in Roman Society," 72.

71. Herzog is thus not correct in stating that the owner does not bargain with the later workers because of his unilateral power and authority to decide "what is right." Herzog, *Parables as Subversive Speech*, 86. This also holds for the point of view of Schottroff, namely, that the workers who started later are in such a weak position that they go off to work without any clear agreement on wages, running the risk of getting paid less than the hoped for. Schottroff, "Human Solidarity," 131.

72. Breech, *The Silence of Jesus*, 146.

actions create enduring and effective bonds with his clients, and who is en-titled to benefit persons differentially.

In the description of the owner as being δίκαιος, the parable stands in the prophetic tradition of Isaiah and Jeremiah, and Jesus himself. In the prophetic tradition, being δίκαιος has the meaning of looking out for the orphan and the widow—that is, for those who are the most vulnerable in so-ciety.[73] In Matt 5:6 and 10, being δίκαιος carries the same meaning, namely, that everyone has enough. Crossan describes δίκαιον as distributive justice, namely, that everyone should have enough.[74] It is in this sense that Levine and Myrick are correct in stating that Jesus speaks in the parable to some who do not recognize their responsibility to people with less.[75] The owner, like the sower in the parable of the Sower, the shepherd in the Lost Sheep, and the elite host in the parable of the Feast, is a role model for those who have more than enough; the first workers are the tyrants and exploiters, who do not want the last recruited to have a living wage.[76]

A Parable of Jesus?

The parable of the Vineyard Laborers has several markings of a Jesus par-able. Just as in the parables of the Lost Sheep (Luke 15:4–6), the Merchant (Matt 13:45–46), the Feast (Luke 14:16b–23), and the Samaritan (Luke 10:30–35), so in this parable the kingdom is compared to the actions of a dubious character. The grumbling of those who started working first is echoed in the actions of the older brother in the Prodigal (Luke 15:11–32) and the shameless neighbor in the parable of the Friend at Midnight (Luke 11:5–8). Finally, the parable concurs with the meaning of the parables of the Lost Sheep and the Sower, namely, that the actions of someone (dubious) result in everybody's having enough.

73. See, for example, Isa 61:17; and Jer 67:6 and 22:3.
74. Crossan, *Greatest Prayer*, 14.
75. Levine and Myrick, "Standard and Poor," 99.
76. Ibid., 110.

CHAPTER 7

The Unmerciful Servant (Matt 18:23–33): Honor Redefined

THE HISTORY OF THE interpretation of the Unmerciful Servant indicates that—in spite of different exegetical approaches, different points of view on the integrity of the parable, and differences of opinion regarding the reference to the king in Matt 18:23 as metaphorically referring to God or not—almost all interpretations of the parable echo Origen's third-century allegorical-theological interpretation of the parable. According to these readings, the debt referred to in the parable is a sin against either God or fellow human beings, and because God (the king) forgives abundantly, the same forgiveness should be extended to other human beings.

To avoid this anachronistic reading of the parable, cultural awareness of the "other," and cultural and theological self-awareness is needed. For such a reading, we have to assemble solid ancient *comparanda* on the practices and social realities that the parable presupposes. Several recent studies on Christian ancient texts (like the parables) have indicated that papyri from early Roman Egypt, sometimes as our only source, can provide some of this needed information on the social realities and practices assumed in the parables.

Here the Unmerciful Servant is read against the background of attested royal ideology on debt release in documented papyri. The reading I offer is a social-scientific reading that focuses on patronage and clientism, and honor and shame. In the parable, Jesus advocates that in the *basileia* of God debt should be forgiven according to the norms of general reciprocity, the way patrons cancel debt for the sake of honor.

History of Interpretation

The earliest interpretations of the parable of the Unmerciful Servant are the allegorical interpretations of Matthew, the church fathers, and later interpretations from the medieval period.[1] Not all the church fathers, though, interpreted the parable from an allegorical perspective. Origen (182–254) combined allegorical and theological interpretation of the parable; interpreting the debt of the two servants as sin against God and fellow humans, he read the parable as a moral teaching of Jesus on forgiveness, namely, on the teaching that forgiveness received from God should lead to forgiveness extended to fellow humans.[2]

When one looks at the history of the interpretation of the parable, Origen's allegorical-theological interpretation has become the standard interpretation of the Unmerciful Servant; the essence of his interpretation can be traced in interpretations of the parable through the medieval period and up to the most current interpretations being offered. In Thomas Aquinas' (1225–1274) and John Maldonatus' (1533–1583) interpretations, for example, Origen's influence is clear. In Aquinas' view, the focus of the parable is the mercy of God, the nature of ingratitude, and the judgment of the ungrateful,[3] whilst Maldonatus drew from the parable the "theological truth" that God will not forgive us unless we forgive one another.[4]

As Aquinas' and Maldonatus' readings do, so almost all modern interpretations of the parable concur with Origen's allegorical-theological interpretation, either confirming his interpretation or highlighting aspects

1. In Augustine's interpretation of the parable, the debt of the two servants is seen as sins against the law, the debtor's wife and his children represent excessive desire and works of the law, and the greater and lesser debtors represent the Jews and Gentiles. Wailes, *Medieval Allegories*, 132–37. The forgiveness of the king, in his reading, refers to baptism, which gives every sinner a new beginning (*Sermon XXXII*). According to Chrysostom (*Hom. Matt. LXII*), the contrast between the ten thousand talents and hundred denarii refers to sins against God and sins against man. In Bede's (673–735 CE) interpretation, the Unmerciful Servant represents the Jews, who, although they were subject to the Decalogue, were guilty of many transgressions. Some modern scholars also tend to read the parable allegorically. Drury, for example, interprets the king as a reference to God, the servants as referring to two kinds of sinners, and the debt as sin. Drury, *Parables in the Gospels*, 92. Keach, as a final example, understands the vast debt of the Unmerciful Servant as a reference to the great evil that resides in humaniry when compared to God's holiness. Keach, *Exposition of the Parables*, 451.

2. Origen ends his interpretation of the parable with the following summary: "All of us who have obtained the forgiveness of our own sins, and have not forgiven our brethren, are taught at once that we shall suffer the lot of him who was forgiven but did not forgive his fellow-servant." See Origin, *Commentary on Matthew* XIV, 13.

3. Kissinger, *History of Interpretation*, 43.

4. Maldonatus, *Commentary on the Holy Gospels*, 103.

thereof. Almost all scholars who interpret the parable in its Matthean context link the king (Matt 18:23) with Matt 18:35 ("So also my heavenly Father will do to every one of you, if you do not forgive your brother from your heart"), and as a result see behind the king a metaphor for God.[5] This "obvious" link between Matt 18:23 and 18:35 is then used as key to interpret the parable as a description of God's forgiveness, mercy, compassion, or judgment, and/ or as a moral teaching on the effect these attributes of God should have on the one who has received forgiveness. Interestingly, scholars who read the parable in its Matthean context with the premise that Matt 18:35 is a Matthean addition also see in the king a metaphoric reference to God, and read the parable in the same way.[6] Moreover, scholars who explicitly read the parable as a parable of Jesus—thus not in its Matthean context—also come to the same conclusion as Origen. The fact that some scholars argue Matt 18:35 was part of the original parable[7] and others argue that it is not,[8] does not make any difference to their respective interpretations. This is also the case whether these scholars equate the king in the parable with God or not.[9] In a nutshell, despite these different interpretive approaches, despite

5. See, for example, Boucher, *Parables*, 116–18; Inrig, *Parables*, 63–78; Brouwer, *De Gelijkenissen*, 51–79; Stiller, *Preaching Parables*, 44–55; Kistemaker, *Stories Jesus Told*, 65–70; Manson, *Sayings of Jesus*, 213–15; Reid, *Parables for Preachers*, 131–42; Groenewald, *In Gelykenisse Het Hy Geleer*, 125–33; Capon, *Parables of Grace*, 43; Hultgren, *Parables of Jesus*, 20–33; Hunter, *Then and Now*, 70–72; Kendall, *The Complete Guide to the Parables*, 158–67; Morgan, *Parables and Metaphors*, 89–93; Borg, *Jesus*, 177; Weder, *Die Gleichnisse Jesu als Metaphern*, 177–84; Oesterley, *Gospel Parables*, 95; Donahue, *Gospel in Parable*, 72–79. Only two scholars who read the parable in its Matthean context, Schippers and Ford, do not consider the king as a metaphoric reference to God. Schippers, *Gelijkenissen van Jezus*, 133–38; Ford, *Parables of Jesus*, 47–64.

6. Scholars who argue that Matt 18:35 is a Matthean addition but still see the king in the parable (Matt 18:23) as a metaphor for God, are Via, Oesterley, Donahue, and Weder. Via, *Parables*, 137–44; Oesterley, *Gospel Parables*, 95; Donahue, *Gospel in Parable*, 72–79; Weder, *Die Gleichnisse Jesu als Metaphern*, 177–84.

7. See inter alia Jeremias, *Parables of Jesus*, 210–12; Boice, *Parables of Jesus*, 179–83; Blomberg, *Preaching the Parables*, 71–82; Blomberg, *Interpreting the Parables*, 314–32; Wenham, *Parables of Jesus*, 151–55; Lockyer, *All the Parables*, 217–19; Pentecost, *Parables of Jesus*, 61–63; Snodgrass, *Stories with Intent*, 61–76; Barclay, *Parables of Jesus*, 86–91.

8. See Lambrecht, *Out of the Treasure*, 53–68; Perrin, *Rediscovering the Teaching*, 125; Funk et al., *Five Gospels*, 218–19; Crossan, *In Parables*, 101–9; Linnemann, *Parables of Jesus*, 105–13.

9. Scholars who interpret the parable as stemming from Jesus, and argue that Jesus intended the king to be a metaphoric reference to God are Jeremias, *Parables of Jesus*, 210–12; Boice, *Parables of Jesus*, 179–87; Blomberg, *Preaching the Parables*, 71–82; Blomberg, *Interpreting the Parables*, 314–32; Snodgrass, *Stories with Intent*, 61–76; Wenham, *Parables of Jesus*, 151–55; Lockyer, *All the Parables*, 217–19; Lambrecht, *Out of the Treasure*, 53–68; Pentecost, *Parables of Jesus*, 61–63; Linnemann, *Parables of Jesus*,

competing opinions on the inclusion or exclusion of Matt 18:35, and despite differing opinions about whether the king refers to God or not—almost all interpretations point in the same direction, echoing that of Origen.

An overview of interpretations of the Unmerciful Servant offered by parable scholars substantiates this conclusion. The following examples will suffice: The parable teaches that God's forgiveness is a gift that must be shared,[10] and that forgiving must take place on numerous occasions;[11] the parable focuses on the quality of forgiveness[12] and teaches that God's forgiveness can only be received if forgiveness is shown to others;[13] or the parable teaches that forgiveness must be given without measure.[14] Other themes identified are the coming judgement of God when one does not forgive,[15] the compassion[16] or the mercy of God,[17] the limitless nature of divine forgiveness,[18] that one will lose authentic life if one does not forgive as God does,[19] or that forgiveness among humans is a sign of God's presence.[20] Finally, the most common interpretation offered is that forgiveness received must turn into forgiveness given.[21]

105–113; Barclay, *The Parables of Jesus*, 86–91. For scholars who read the parable from the same perspective, but do not see the king as a metaphorical reference to God, see Perrin, *Rediscovering the Teaching*, 125; Funk et al., *Five Gospels*, 218–19; Crossan, *In Parables*, 101–9.

10. Via, *The Parables*, 139, 142–43; Boucher, *The Parables*, 114–15.

11. Inrig, *The Parables*, 46.

12. Brouwer, *De Gelijkenissen*, 162.

13. Barclay, *The Parables of Jesus*, 88.

14. Capon, *The Parables of Grace*, 43.

15. Jeremias, *The Parables of Jesus*, 213; Boice, *Parables of Jesus*, 186; Blomberg, *Preaching the Parables*, 72–73; Blomberg, *Interpreting the Parables*, 319; Kendall, *The Complete Guide to the Parables*, 159.

16. Morgan, *Parables and Metaphors*, 92; Borg, *Jesus*, 177.

17. Weder, *Die Gleichnisse Jesu als Metaphern*, 180.

18. Oesterley, *The Gospel Parables*, 95; Schippers, *Gelijkenissen van Jezus*, 138; Linnemann, *Parables of Jesus*, 111–13.

19. Dietzfelbinger, "Das Gleichnis von der Erlassenen Schuld," 437–51.

20. Schottroff, *Parables of Jesus*, 201.

21. Stiller, *Preaching Parables*, 49; Kistemaker, *Stories Jesus Told*, 67; Manson, *Sayings of Jesus*, 213; Reid, *Parables for Preachers*, 140; Groenewald, *In Gelykenisse Het Hy Geleer*, 217; Hultgren, *Parables of Jesus*, 23; Hunter, *Interpreting the Parables*, 71; Hunter, *Then and Now*, 71; Lockyer, *All the Parables*, 217; Snodgrass, *Stories with Intent*, 61; Wenham, *Parables of Jesus*, 153; Pentecost, *Parables of Jesus*, 63; Lambrecht, *Out of the Treasure*, 63; Donahue, *The Gospel in Parable*, 76–77; Ford, *Parables of Jesus*, 47; Crossan, *In Parables*, 104. Linked to this interpretation are the interpretations of Perrin and Funk. According to Perrin, the parable challenges its hearers to forgive because the new reality of God's reign has arrived in Jesus, whilst for Funk Jesus told the parable to invite

All these interpretations echo that of Origen. The debt of the Unmerciful Servant is seen as sin against God, and the debt of the fellow slave as sin against a fellow human being. Because the merciful and compassionate God forgives, those who have received forgiveness should also forgive, otherwise judgment awaits. These interpretations are not only allegorical-theological but also anachronistic. As stated earlier, an anachronistic interpretation of the parables entails an interpretation that reads into the text information or theological perspectives from some present social context, rather than comprehending the text in accord with its own contemporary social and cultural scripts.[22] Because sin, from a theological perspective, is seen by many as a debt to God or fellow humans, this understanding of debt is projected onto the parable; the king is seen as God, and the interpretation can only go in one direction—as the history of the interpretation of the Unmerciful Servant described above illustrates. To read the parable from this perspective is to depict a Jesus that made theological statements. Jesus, on the contrary, had no doctrine of God, made no theological statements, and never used abstract language.[23] In an effort to avoid anachronistic interpretations of identified social and cultural scripts in the parable, I will attempt a culturally sensitive reading (social-scientific criticism) below. Social-scientific criticism approaches texts from the premise that texts always are the products of specific social systems; therefore, to understand a text, attention must first be given to the social system that produced the text. Social-scientific criticism has developed several reading scenarios (models) to interpret specific identified social realia in biblical texts. Two of these models, namely patronage and clientism, and honor and shame, will be employed in the reading of the parable below.

----

the listener to choose the appropriate mode of behavior. The interpretation of Perrin and Funk thus only differs from the "standard" reading in the sense that forgiveness received must turn into forgiveness given because in Jesus the kingdom has arrived as a new reality. Perrin, *Rediscovering the Teaching*, 125; Funk et al., *The Five Gospels*, 219.

22. See, again, Elliott, *Social-scientific Criticism*, 11.

23. See in this regard Funk, who states that the parables of Jesus "are not stories of God—they are stories about God's estate." Funk, "Jesus of Nazareth," 2007, 90. Or, as put by Herzog: "The parables were not earthly stories with heavenly meanings, but earthly stories with heavy meanings." Herzog, *Parables as Subversive Speech*, 3. See also the following quote from Kloppenborg: "Few nowadays would defend the preposition that Jesus was an allegorist, speaking in one discursive realm but in fact intending to evoke other discursive realms, for example, salvation history or the care of the soul." Kloppenborg, *Synoptic Problems: Collected Essays*, 490.

Integrity

Matthew 18:23–35 is the only extant version of the parable of the Unmerciful Servant. There is a general consensus among Matthean scholars that Matthew has structured his narrative of Jesus around five discourses (Matt 5:1—7:27; 10:1–42; 13:1–52; 18:1–35; 24:1–25). All these discourses conclude with an eschatological warning (Matt 7:15–27; 10:32–42; 13:49–50; 18:35; 25:31–46), whereafter Matthew uses a familiar (similar) formula to link the discourses to the next section of his narrative (Matt 7:28; 11:1; 13:53; 19:1; 26:1). Matthew has placed the Unmerciful Servant parable at the end of his fourth discourse, ending the parable and discourse with an eschatological warning in Matt 18:35. This already gives an indication that Matt 18:35 most probably is anaddition to an earlier version of the parable.

Matt 18 is Matthew's so-called narrative on church order and consists of five shorter narratives. Matt 18:1–10 deals with the question of who is the greatest in the kingdom: Jesus' answer is that the greatest ones in the kingdom are those who are as humble as a child (Matt 18:4), who do not cause the little ones (ἕνα τῶν μικρῶν τού τωντῶν; Matt 18:6) to sin, and who do not despise the little ones (ἑνὸς τῶν μικρῶν τούτων; Matt 18:10) in the believing community. The second micronarrative of the discourse is the parable of the Lost Sheep (Matt 18:12–14), which Matthew allegorizes to fit as an example of how believers in the community should take care of the little ones. This Matthew has done with the use of ἓν τῶν μικρῶν τούτων in 18:14, linking the parable with 18:6 and 18:10. The third micronarrative (Matt 18:15–20) has as its focus how the transgression of a community member should be dealt with. The fourth micronarrative (Matt 18:21–22) consists of Peter's question and Jesus' answer on the limits of forgiveness, and then follows the parable of the Unmerciful Servant (Matt 18:23–35).

Although some scholars argue that Matt 18:21–22 should be seen as part of the parable,[24] the parable makes no reference to unlimited forgiveness mentioned in Matt 18:22, and the king in the parable surely does not live up to Jesus' saying on repeated and unlimited forgiveness.[25] Moreover, when the king in the parable is seen as a metaphor for God (based on Matt 18:35), the picture of God painted in the parable becomes quite unflattering in that God is pictured as "a vindictive person whose mercies are dependent on human behavior."[26] The parable clearly does not fit its Matthean context

24. See, for example, Lambrecht, *Out of the Treasure*, 54; Oesterley, *Gospel Parables*, 93–94; Brouwer, *De Gelijkenissen*, 162.

25. This, of course, only being the case when Matt 18:24–35 is seen as part of the parable.

26. Funk et al., *Five Gospels*, 218.

(following Matt 18:21–22), which means that Matthew attached the parable of the Unmerciful Servant (stemming from M) to the end of his discourse in Matt 18 to further elaborate on forgiveness in the community.[27]

Matthew has redacted 8:23 (Διὰ τοῦτο ὡμοιώθη ἡ βασιλεία τῶν οὐρανῶν ἀνθρώπῳ βασιλεῖ, ὃς ἠθέλησεν συνᾶραι λόγον μετὰ τῶν δούλων αὐτοῦ) in several ways to join it with 18:21–22. This connection enables him to incorporate the version of the parable received from M into his discourse in chapter 18 for his own (allegorical) purposes.[28] Διὰ τοῦτο, first, is from Matthew's hand. Matthew uses διὰ τοῦτο ten times in his gospel as an introductory formula: twice as an introduction to a parable (Matt 13:52; 18:23) and eight times to introduce a conclusion made by the Matthean Jesus (Matt 6:25; 12:27; 12:31; 13:13; 14:2; 21:43; 23:34; 24:24). Of these occurrences of διὰ τοῦτο in Matthew, only two are taken over from Mark (Mark 6:14; 11:49; *par.* resp. Matt 14:2 and 23:34), and one is paralleled in Luke (Luke 11:19; *par.* Matt 12:27).

Second, the expression ἡ βασιλεία τῶν οὐρανῶν is typically Matthean. Only Matthew uses this expression, occurring twenty-five times in the gospel.[29] Of these twenty-five occurrences, Matthew uses ἡ βασιλεία τῶν οὐρανῶν eleven times in combination with either ὡμοιώθη (Matt 13:24; 18:23; 22:2), ὁμοία (Matt 13:13, 33, 44, 45, 47; 20:1), ὅμοιός (Matt 13:52), or ὁμοιωθήσεται (Matt 25:1) to introduce a parable.[30] This introductory

27. Some interpreters see no clash between Matt 18:21–22 and the parable, arguing that Matt 18:21–22 deals with the quantity of forgiveness, while the parable deals with its quality. Lambrecht, *Out of the Treasure*, 56; Donahue, *Gospel in Parable*, 73. Schottroff also sees no clash between Matt 18:21–22 and the parable, arguing that the readers of the parable would not have equated the king in the parable with God since it would have been seen as blasphemy in the eyes of the Jewish tradition. Schottroff, *Parables of Jesus*, 200–201. For a history of the interpretation of this aspect of Matt 18, see Luz, *Mt 18–25*, 3:346–48. For a discussion of the possible clash between Matt 18:21–22 and 23–35, see Dodd, *Parables of the Kingdom*, 33; Hultgren, *Parables of Jesus*, 30; Snodgrass, *Stories with Intent*, 67, 71; Herzog, *Parables as Subversive Speech*, 132; Crossan, *In Parables*, 103, 105–6; Davies and Allison, *Matthew*, 3:791–94.

28. Herzog, *Parables as Subversive Speech*, 132–34; Linnemann, *Parables of Jesus*, 105–6; Via, *The Parables*, 138; Boucher, *Parables*, 117; Blomberg, *Interpreting the Parables*, 315; Manson, *Sayings of Jesus*, 215; Jeremias, *Parables of Jesus*, 210; Crossan, *In Parables*, 205.

29. *Contra* Scott, *Hear Then the Parable*, 269, n. 6.

30. Matthew also uses ὁμοιωθήσεται in Matt 7:24 and ὁμοιώσω in Matt 11:16 without ἡ βασιλεία τῶν οὐρανῶν to introduce the parables of the Wise and Foolish Builders (Matt 7:24–27; *par.* Luke 6:47–49), and the parable of the Children at the Marketplace (Matt 11:16–19; *par.* Luke 7:3–35). Luke, in both these cases, follows Q (ὅμοιός ἐστιν in Q 6:48 and ὁμοιώσω in Q 7:31). Matthew 11:16 follows Q 7:31, and Matt 7:24 renders Q 6:48 as ὁμοιωθήσεται. Since in the case of Q 6:48 both the readings of Matt 7:24 and Luke 6:48 are possible renderings of Q 6:48, it seems that Matthew, when not adding ἡ

formula from Matthew is only paralleled in Luke 13:18 (before the parable of the Mustard Seed; *par.* Matt 13:24) and Luke 13:20 (before the parable of the Leaven; *par.* Matt 13:33). In both cases Luke replaces Matthew's introductory formulae with ὁμοιώσω ἡ βασιλεία τοῦ θεοῦ. From this it is clear that Matthew's use of ἡ βασιλεία τῶν οὐρανῶν, in combination with either ὡμοιώθη, ὁμοία or ὁμοιωθήσεται, is a typical Matthean addition used to introduce the parables. Therefore, ὡμοιώθη ἡ βασιλεία τῶν οὐρανῶν in Matt 18:23 most probably was not part of the version of the Unmerciful Servant used by Matthew, and should be considered as a Matthean addition.

Third, Matthew also most probably added ἄνθρωπός in 18:23. Part of the Matthean style is to describe persons with the use of two nouns ("double designation"): ἄνθρωπον κωφὸν (Matt 9:32), ἐχθρὸς ἄνθρωπος (Matt 13:28), ἀνθρώπῳ ἐμπόρῳ (Matt 13:45), ἀνθρώπῳ οἰκοδεσπότῃ (Matt 13:52; 20:1), and ἀνθρώπῳ βασιλεῖ (Matt 22:2). That it is Matthew's tendency to make use of this double designation is clear from Q 11:14 (which reads κωφόν) and Q 14:16 (which reads ἄνθρωπος). While Luke 11:14 and 14:16 respectively read κωφόν and ἄνθρωπος (thus following Q), Matthew changes these two descriptions from Q into ἄνθρωπον κωφὸν (Matt 9:32) and ἀνθρώπῳ βασιλεῖ (Matt 22:2), adding ἄνθρωπον in 9:32 and βασιλεῖ in 22:2. Because of Matthew's consistent use of this "double designation," based on his redactional changes to Q 11:14 and 14:16, there is a reasonable possibility that Matthew changed βασιλεῖ in M to ἀνθρώπῳ βασιλεῖ. In light of the above, Matthew thus most probably changed an earlier version that read "βασιλεῖ ὃς ἠθέλησεν συνᾶραι λόγον μετὰ τῶν δούλων αὐτοῦ" into "Διὰ τοῦτο ὡμοιώθη ἡ βασιλεία τῶν οὐρανῶν ἀνθρώπῳ βασιλεῖ, ὃς ἠθέλησεν συνᾶραι λόγον μετὰ τῶν δούλων αὐτοῦ."

A further Matthean redaction of the Unmerciful Servant parable is the use of μυρίων ταλάντων in 18:24. Matthew's use of μυρίων ταλάντων is interpreted differently, depending on the interpreter. Perkins and Linnemann, for example, argue that the sum is not exceptional, since it would have reminded the Jewish audience of the parable of the riches of Egyptian and Persians kings that they had heard about from distant times and lands.[31] Snodgrass sees the sum as pseudorealistic, but "not unthinkable."[32] Almost

---

βασιλεία τῶν οὐρανῶν, follows Q. Robinson et al., *Critical Edition of Q*, 98–99.

31. Perkins, *Hearing the Parables*, 124; Linnemann, *Parables of Jesus*, 108.

32. Snodgrass, *Stories with Intent*, 68. As evidence he sites Esth 3:9 (Haman's promise to pay ten thousand talents into the treasury), Josephus (*Ant.* 14.78; Pompey exacting ten thousand talents from the Jews after his siege of Jerusalem in 63 BCE), and Josephus (*Ant.* 12.175–176; Joseph, a tax farmer, offering Ptolemy to collect sixteen thousand talents). For further examples to substantiate his point of view, see ibid., 604, n. 26.

all other interpreters of the parable see the number as unrealistic,[33] in most cases referring to Josephus, who indicates that Herod the Great's annual income at the time of his death in 4 BCE amounted only to nine hundred talents (Josephus, *Ant.* 17.318–320). (Some commentators add that Josephus was known for inflating numbers.[34]) To address the unrealistic number of Matthew, several scholars have suggested a correction to Matthew's use of μυρίων ταλάντων. De Boer's suggestion is that the version used by Matthew most probably read "denarii" and was changed by Matthew into "talents."[35] Matthew's purpose for making this change was to align the high number with βασιλεῖ in 18:23, impelling the hearer of the parable to interpret the parable allegorically and to understand the king as a figure for God. In Lambrecht's view, de Boer's suggestion is most probably correct for two reasons. First, the Unmerciful Servant states in Matt 18:26 that if the master has patience with him, he would be able to pay back everything he owes. If the sum owed by the servant was ten thousand denarii—called a loan (τὸ δάνειον; Matt 18:27)—it indeed was repayable. Second, in the parable of the Talents (Matt 25:14–30)—as in the Unmerciful Servant—Matthew changed the original ἡμνᾶ (Luke 19:16, 18, 20) of the Q parable into τάλαντα (Matt 25:15, 16, 20, 22, 28).[36]

Finally, 18:35 was also most probably added to the version of the parable known by Matthew. The expression ὁ πατήρ μου ὁ οὐράνιος in 18:35 is a key Matthean phrase (Matt 5:48; 6:14, 26, 32; 15:13; 18:35; 23:9). As indicated above, Matt 18:35 is the conclusion of the entire discourse in Matthew 18, and thus the possibility exists that it was not intended by Matthew to be part of the parable.[37] However, if it was part of the parable, Matthew

---

33. Jeremias has argued that ten thousand (as a number) and talent (as a currency unit) were the highest magnitudes in use in the whole of the Near East. Jesus inflated the figure in the parable to a magnitude of debt beyond conception to heighten the impression made on the audience by its contrast with the trifling debt of one hundred denarii of the second slave. Jeremias, *Parables of Jesus*, 210. Most scholars have followed Jeremias in this interpretation. See Boucher, *Parables*, 117; Blomberg, *Interpreting the Parables*, 318; Malina and Rohrbaugh, *Social-Science Commentary on the Synoptic Gospels*, 95; Barclay, *Parables of Jesus*, 87; Boice, *Parables of Jesus*, 183. In Hertzog's view, the figure is an exaggeration that contributes to the purpose of the codification of the parable as a type of political cartoon, and for Scott the figure conjures up the high finance of the empire. Herzog, *Parables as Subversive Speech*, 135; Scott, *Hear Then the Parable*, 271.

34. Herzog, *Parables as Subversive Speech*, 143.

35. De Boer, "Ten Thousand Talents," 228. For a discussion of other suggestions, see Hultgren, *Parables of Jesus*, 24 n. 10.

36. Lambrecht, *Out of the Treasure*, 59–60.

37. Crossan, *In Parables*, 103; Herzog, *Parables as Subversive Speech*, 133; Via, *Parables*, 139.

most probably added it to the M version as a moral attachment to give the parable an explicit meaning.[38] Finally, the addition of verse 35 also enables Matthew to turn the parable into a warning.[39]

Matt 18:34 was most probably also added by Matthew. As Perrin has indicated, Matt 18:34 and 35 are required to convert the original challenge of the parable into a warning. The parable, he argues, without the redaction of Matt 18:23, "stand[s] pretty much as Jesus told it."[40] Oesterley also argues for 18:34 as a later addition reflecting the apocalyptic interests of Matthew.[41] Below it will be argued that the parable, when read through comparative social realia and through the lenses of patronage and clientism, honor and shame, and reciprocity, forms a unitary narrative running from Matt 18:23 to 33 and excluding the Matthean additions to Matt 18:23 (i.e., διὰ τοῦτο, ὡμοιώθη ἡ βασιλεία τῶν οὐρανῶν, and ἄνθρωπος).[42]

Realistic and Social-Scientific Readings of the Parable

Apart from the dominant allegorical-theological interpretations of the parable discussed above, a few scholars have attempted a realistic reading of the parable against the backdrop of its social realia.

38. Crossan, *In Parables*, 203; Buttrick, *Speaking in Parables*, 108, 112–13; Herzog, *Parables as Subversive Speech*, 135; Blomberg, *Interpreting the Parables*, 315; Deidun, "Parable of the Unmerciful Servant," 219, 222; Bultmann, *Synoptic Tradition*, 177; Scott, *Hear Then the Parable*, 269.

39. Reid, *Parables for Preachers*, 139, n. 22; Donahue, *Gospel in Parable*, 74.

40. Perrin, *Rediscovering the Teaching*, 125.

41. Oesterley, *Gospel Parables*, 99–100. See also Harnisch, *Die Gleichniserzählungen Jesu*, 259–62.

42. Interpreters of the parable also suggest other possibilities in demarcating the parable used by Matthew. Weder, for example, argues that the parable ends with Matt 18:30 since the latter part of the parable relativizes the focus on the mercy of God. Weder, *Die Gleichnisse Jesu als Metaphern*, 211–18. Fuchs argues for the parable to end at Matt 18:31, arguing that verses 32–35 overstep the limits of the image of the king. Fuchs, *Frage nach dem Historischen Jesus*, 32–34. Finally, some scholars argue for Matt 18:23–35 as the parable used by Matthew. According to Snodgrass, the parallel structure of the three acts in the parable demonstrates that Matt 18:34 should be considered as part of the parable, while Matt 18:35 is a typical Jewish *nimshal* and therefore should not be excluded. Snodgrass, *Stories with Intent*, 69. In the view of Boucher and Smith, Matt 18:35 completes the intention of the parable, and therefore should be included. Boucher, *Parables*, 118; Smith, *Parables of the Synoptic Gospels*, 217, 219. Hultgren makes a similar point: Matt 18:35 is the application of the story, and makes the point of comparison in the parable as explicit as possible. Hultgren, *Parables of Jesus*, 35. Finally, Capon argues that Matt 18:35 should be seen as ironic, indicating that within the story there is a sense of covenant; one's relationship with God is not a one-way affair. Capon, *The Parables of Grace*, 43.

Herzog, as first example, reads the parable against the backdrop of the extracting of tribute by rulers in agrarian (aristocratic) societies.[43] The primary conflict in the parable is between a ruler and an important retainer at his court, and for the sake of contrast, between this highly placed retainer and other midlevel retainers. The king's initial decision to punish the servant, his subsequent decision to forgive the servant's debt, and his final withdrawal of mercy express the ruler's absolute power and total command. The servant's failure to produce the expected tribute is part of the ongoing battle in bureaucracies to exert control; he has grown too confident in his power as retainer of the king. The king immediately recognizes this and asserts his control with his decision to punish the servant. When the servant reacts with desperation, as the king desired, the king reverses his previous decision. The servant again knows his proper place on the power scale, recognizes the ultimate power of the king, and is therefore forgiven. "He has been a good client and may be so again. Perhaps what is needed is an unexpected act of patronage generosity. So the king reverses himself, even forgiving the debt."[44] Because of what happened between the servant and the king, spread by gossip through the bureaucracy, the retainer now has to find ways to reassert his control. This he does by acting as a patron towards a midlevel bureaucrat, treating him as a client by demanding payment to show that he is as strong as ever. By this action the servant shames the king and violates his honor, making him look like a weak fool. "Backed into a corner, the king reverts with a vengeance to business as usual, delivering the courtier to the torturer."[45] What, according to Herzog, is the overarching message of the parable? The parable is about the fulfilment of sabbatical and messianic hopes. The act of the king to cancel the largest debt imaginable depicts a messianic moment; the messianic king has arrived and the messianic age has begun. What follows in the rest of the parable, however, shows the inadequacy of messianic hope and of kingship and the role of retainers. People will have to look elsewhere to reshape their world.[46]

In a second realistic reading of the parable, Scott sees in the parable a Gentile situation and tax farming.[47] The parable itself is a tale that describes an accounting story in which a Gentile king will sit in judgment on those who must give account. An accounting story, Scott argues, invokes in a

43. Herzog, *Parables as Subversive Speech*, 138–49.

44. Ibid., 142. See also where Herzog describes the king's remission of the servant's debt as "an extraordinary act, quite uncharacteristic of any agrarian ruler." Ibid., 146.

45. Ibid., 147.

46. Ibid., 148.

47. Scott, *Hear Then the Parable*, 273–78.

patron-client culture "the hierarchical structure through which the patron sets things in order."[48] The enormous amount owed by the servant functions to distance the servant from the king. When the servant cannot pay up, the punishment dished out accentuates Gentile cruelty, an action forbidden by Jewish law. The master's decision to have pity on the servant, and his unexpected remission, calls Jewish superiority into question. The injustice of the first servant's action towards his fellow servant, however, reaffirms the stereotyped expectations of the Jewish hearers, confirming their stereotyped propaganda against Gentiles. When fellow servants of the king are outraged by the first servant's injustice, the hearer is drawn into the story, and identifies with the fellow servants. By doing this, they become like the Gentiles and forfeit their superiority. From this perspective argues, the parable is intended to reject Jewish notions of superiority, and indicates that the standards of this world are totally inadequate for the kingdom.

In a subsequent reading of the parable,[49] Scott again emphasizes the unexpected compassion of the secular ruler, and the relationship between the first and second slave is again described as a patron-client relationship between two unequals. He also adds that what provokes the king is not economics or justice but that the slave has violated the king's honor and shamed him by not following his example. Hence the king has no other option than to protect his honor and thus wipe out the shame the slave has brought upon him. The king's initial forgiveness signals the fulfilment of jubilee hopes, but the slave's lack of forgiveness brings this jubilee hope to an end, and the king's final action brings it crashing down. Therefore, the parable represents a fundamental challenge to popular notions of messianic kingship and indicates that the system of patron-client power distribution cannot distribute forgiveness or the blessing of jubilee. Because of this, the parable implies that a wholly other system is needed, a system outside honor and shame, outside patron-client relations and royal power. Therefore, the parable points to the corruption and irredeemable character of a world organized by imperial rule.

A third realistic reading of the parable is that of Derrett.[50] Like Scott, Derrett sees the backdrop of the parable as tax farming, with the servant failing to honor his contract with the king. The king's release of the servant's debt occurs for two reasons: First, the king needs the servant's specialized skill and his vast network of clients to extract tribute from the provinces. Second, the king, on a point of honor, sees his forgiveness of the servant's

---

48. Ibid., 273.

49. Scott, *Re-Imagine the World*, 97–107.

50. Derrett, *Law in the New Testament*, 32–47.

debt as the first in a series of actions to lighten the burdens of his provinces and to break the cycle of ruthless exploitation and extraction. The servant's release from debt thus is provisional; he now has to follow the example set by the king. When the servant does not release the debt of a fellow servant, he does not act on the king's example, and continues the cycle of extraction and exploitation. Thus, what was meant to initiate acts of debt remission has come to a halt with the servant's action. This leaves the king with no other option but to defend his honor and release the first servant from his position.[51]

Below it will be indicated that Scott's and Herzog's interpretations of the parable through the lens of patronage and clientism are most probably the correct approach, and helpful in reading the parable in terms of its social *realia*. It will, however, be indicated that both these scholars do not apply the salient features of patronage and clientism in a consistent manner. Also, they do not take comparative social realia into consideration when interpreting the parable. As a result, they misinterpret the patron's motive for canceling the first servant's debt (excluding Scott's second reading on this point) as well as the parable's second scene (the interaction between the first and second servants). Moreover, their understanding that canceling the first servant's debt is an unexpected act of patronage generosity is incorrect, as evidenced by documented papyri. It will also be indicated that all three scholars' inclusion of Matt 18:34 as part of the parable seriously flaws their interpretations. The parable is not about the exertion of control by patrons, or about retainers challenging the power of patrons (Herzog); it is not about the inadequacy of messianic hope and kingship (Herzog and Scott); it is not about Jewish superiority (Scott) or the ending of the cycle of ruthless exploitation and extraction by the elite (Derrett)—which, by the way, is unthinkable in any agrarian society. Above all, *contra* Herzog and Scott, the parable does not suggest that hearers should look elsewhere, outside honor and shame, patron-client relations, royal power, and empire to reshape their world. On the contrary, the kingdom is to be found in the parable, especially where debt release is driven by ascribed honor.

---

51. Another realistic interpretation of the parable is that of Beutner, which is only mentioned here in brief. According to Beutner, the parable is about the adversarial, crooked, alien and dangerous world of the first-century patronage system under which peasants lived. When Jesus tells a parable about a despised elite king who uses his authority to release debt, Jesus is indicating how authority should be exercised in the kingdom of God. Beutner, "Mercy Unextended," 35–37.

Reading Scenarios

Patronage, Debt Release, and Honor as Backdrop of the Parable

Bazzana, in a study on the forgiveness of debts in the Lord's Prayer (Q 11:2b–4), has indicated the important contribution documentary papyri can make to the historical and exegetical study of ancient Christian texts like the parables.[52] By comparing the wording of Q 11:4 (καὶ ἄφες ἡμῖν τὰς ἁμαρτίας ἡμῶν, καὶ γὰρ αὐτοὶ ἀφίομεν παντὶ ὀφείλοντι ἡμῖν·καὶ μὴ εἰσενέγκῃς ἡμᾶς εἰς πειρασμόν) in the Lord's Prayer with documented Ptolemaic amnesty decrees, he shows that key ideas in the prayer (the cancelation of debts and the euergetic characterization of God's kingdom) "may have reminded readers and hearers of Hellenistic royal ideology."[53] In reading the prayer, Bazzana suggests, the readers "imagined the awaited divine sovereignty by reversing and reinscribing certain cultural symbols spread in the eastern regions of the Mediterranean by Hellenistic royal propaganda."[54]

In the Lord's Prayer the request for release of personal debts and the debt of others are described as "ἄφες . . . ὀφειλήματα" and "ἀφήκαμεν . . . ὀφειλέταις," terms connected to the lexical sphere of ὀφείλ–, and the verb ἀφίημι. In his study of available documented papyri, Bazzana identifies five documents (P.Hib. 1.41; P.Köln 7.313; SB 20.14106; P.Oxy. 2.237 8.7–1; W.Chr. 29) in which this word pair occurs, showing a significant connection.[55] In P.Hib. 1.41 (Hibeh, 261 BCE), the phrase "allow him to collect the arrears," is rendered as "ἄφες αυτόν εἰσαγαγεῖν τα ὀφείληματα." In P.Köln 7.313 (Oxyrhynchus second century BCE; a royal decree promulgated in 186 BCE to celebrate, with an amnesty for crimes and debts, King Ptolemy V's victory over a rebellion in southern Egypt), the release of debt on leases and dikes is respectively described as "Ἀφίησιν . . . ὀφείληματων" and "Ἀφίησιν . . . ὀφειλόμενα," and the release of payments from proprietors on vineyards and orchards and baths as "Ἀφίησιν." In the third papyrus, SB 20.14106 (provenance unknown, 18 BCE), the release of debts is described with "ἀφιάσι . . . πάντας τών ὀφείλομένω." Important to note is that this document, as in the case of P.Köln 7.313, is a decree wherein Ptolemy and Cleopatra proclaim inter alia a release of debt in respect to the farming of the grain tax and the money taxes in the fiftieth year of the reign of King Ptolemy. In P.Oxy. 2.237 8.7–13 (Oxyrhynchus, 186 CE) debtors and debt

52. Bazzana, *"Basileia* and Debt Relief," 511–525.

53. Ibid., 511.

54. Bazzana, "Q Concept of Kingship," 511.

55. For a detailed description of the background, context and content of these papyri, see Bazzana, *"Basileia* and Debt Relief," 514–17.

are described as ἀφέντες and ὀφείλουσι, and in the final document, Chr. Wilck. 29 (Antinoopolis, 196 CE), ἀφείθημεν is used for the exemption from any kind of liturgies, and ὀφειλημάτων for the payment of public expenses (taxes).

In his analysis of the above papyri, Bazzana makes three important observations: First, the enforcement of these Ptolemaic ordinances was usually not restricted only to debt due to the royal treasury; the cancelation of debt was extended to what each subject in the kingdom owed one another (P.Köln 7.313, 24–25; P.Tebt. 1.5.221–47).[56] As Bazzana indicates,

> In royal decrees . . . the remittance granted by the sovereign was extended to the private sphere of economic relationships. Hence, the subjects were forced to assimilate their own behavior to the king's and, through this act of obedience, to reinscribe the image of the king as the ideal broker of divine providence to the world.[57]

Second, the royal habit of conceding debt remittances was not a practice restricted only to the Ptolemaic kingdom in Egypt. Available evidence indicates that the debt forgiveness was also part of an ideology present in other areas of the eastern Mediterranean and in the land of Israel.[58] Herodotus *(Hist.* 6.59), for example, refers to the tradition of Spartan and Persian kings, when taking office, to release all their subjects from debt, and both Arrian *(Anab. 7.5)* and Diodorus Siculus *(Bibl. hist.* 17.109.1–2) mention Alexander's liquidation of all his soldiers' debts after his return to Babylon from India. According to Bazzana, this precedential act by Alexander became a standard feature of Hellenistic royalty.[59] Finally, 1 Macc 13:36–39 cites an official letter of Demetrius II (the new Seleucid king) addressed to Simon the high priest, the elders, and the Jewish people, which shows that the habit of releasing debt at the inception of a new reign was also practiced in the land of Israel. In this apocryphal text, Demetrius undertakes to remit (ἀφίεμεν) inter alia the crown tax that is owed (ὤφείλετε) by the temple, as well as any other tax that may have been collected in Jerusalem (1 Macc 13:39).

56. See also similar provisions in BGU 4.1156.24 (Alexandria, 15 BCE) and BGU 1053.2, 7 (Alexandria, 13 BCE). As Bazzana explains, "In both of these deeds of loan it is stated that the debtor will have to repay the money, even though the political authorities will proclaim a πρόσταγμα φιλάνθρωπων." Ibid., 517. The term πρόσταγμα φιλάνθρωπων is normally used to describe decrees such as P.Köln 7.313, and SB 20.14106, described above.

57. Ibid., 523–24.

58. Ibid., 517.

59. Ibid., 518.

Third, a few documentary papyri (see P.Münch. 3/1.45.2; UPZ 1.113.6; P.Tor. Choach. 12.7.14, and BGU 8.1764.1, 5 connect the royal decrees on debt remittance to the concept of *basileia*, indicating that it was of paramount importance for Hellenistic sovereigns to care for the welfare and prosperity of their subjects.[60] Bazzana's conclusion is that these texts "make it easy to see how the first hearers and readers of the Lord's Prayer may have connected the Christian text with their everyday experience."[61]

Taking Bazzana's analysis of these texts into consideration, the same case can be made with regard to the Unmerciful Servant parable because of the obvious correspondences between these papyri and the parable. First, in the parable the terms used for "debt" and "debtor"[62] in the release of the first servant's debt[63] show close similarities with the lexical sphere of ὀφείλ– and with the verb ἀφίημι. In both the documented papyri Bazzana discusses and in the parable, the word pair ὀφείλ– and the verb ἀφίημι show a significant connection. Second, the king's canceling the first servant's debt is reminiscent of debt release in especially P.Köln 7.313, SB 20.14106, and 1 Macc 13:39. Based on these three correspondences, and the fact that the royal habit of releasing debt was also part of an ideology present in the land of Israel (1 Macc 13:39),[64] it is not difficult to see that the first hearers of the Unmerciful Servant may have connected the social realia in the parable with their everyday experience.

Below I will show that when the Unmerciful Servant is read against the background of attested royal ideology on debt release in especially P.Köln 7.313, SB 20.14106, and 1 Macc 13:39, the parable suggests that in the *basileia* of God, debt should be released in terms of general reciprocity, the way patrons cancel debt for the sake of honor.

Reading the Parable

Matt 18:23–25 sets the scene of the parable. A king wishes to settle his accounts, a servant who cannot pay is brought before him, and the king

60. Ibid., 520–21.

61. Ibid., 517.

62. See ὀφειλέτης (Matt 18:24), ὤφειλεν and ὀφείλεις (Matt 18:28), ὀφειλόμενον (Matt 18:30) and ὀφειλὴν (Matt 18:32).

63. See ἀφῆκεν (Matt 18:27) and ἀφῆκά (Matt 18:32).

64. See also *Midrash Tanḥumah Emor* 8.30 (on Lev 23:39–40), that has a parable in which a king forgives the taxes owed by one of his provinces. Although this text is part of the later Jewish writings, and employs the parable as an example of how God forgives, the text gives evidence of knowledge of the royal ideology of releasing debt.

orders the servant to be sold with his family and his belongings to cover the outstanding debt. This introductory scene evokes two sets of political and social realia. First, the king's decision to sell the servant indicates that the king is non-Jewish since the sale of a wife was absolutely forbidden under Jewish law.[65] The parable thus depicts a non-Jewish (i.e., Gentile) situation.[66]

The second set of social realia implied by the introductory scene is that of patronage and clientism. Patronage and clientism were part and parcel of aristocratic (advanced agrarian) societies like the first-century Mediterranean world.[67] In aristocratic societies political power was obtained and exercised inter alia through patronage.[68] Those in the upper echelons of political power, like kings (rulers), could not rule without developing patron-client relationships. These patron-client relationships were socially fixed and based on a strong element of inequality between the parties (already implicit in the term *cliens*). The patron-client relationship was voluntary and reciprocal, focused on honor and respect, and was held together by loyalty (a strong, binding, long-range, social and interpersonal obligation from both sides). The basic structure of these relationships was an exchange of different and very unequal resources. A patron had social, economic, and political resources that a client needed. Once the client had been granted favor, the client promised to pay the patron back whenever and however the patron determined.

When looking through this lens at the relationship between the king and the servant in the parable, it is clear that the interaction in the parable has all the markings of a patron-client relationship. First, the relationship is based on a strong element of inequality and a stark difference in power. The servant most probably is an official serving the king,[69] indicating the

---

65. Jeremias, *Parables of Jesus*, 211.

66. Under Roman law this was normal practice. See, for example, Diogenes Laertius, *Life of Bion* 4.46–47. For the prohibition in Jewish law to sell a debtor's wife, see *m. Soṭa* 3.8, *m. Giṭṭen* 4.9, *t. Soṭa* 2.9, and *Sifre Deut.* 26. Snodgrass, on the basis that *Sifre Deut.* 26 does not explicitly mention a Gentile king, argues that the parable "do not necessarily indicate a Gentile context." Snodgrass, *Stories with Intent*, 69. This is an *argumentum ex silentio* that can simply be reversed, since the text neither explicitly mentions a Jewish king.

67. Seneca (*Ben.* 1.2.1) goes so far as to call it "a practice that constitutes the chief bond of human society."

68. Saller, *Personal Patronage*, 41–78, 119–43.

69. According to Jeremias, in the East the term "servants of the king" was normally used for higher officials. Jeremias, *Parables of Jesus*, 210. Linnemann, Boucher, and Wenham argue that the servant was a provincial governor. Snodgrass, Hultgren, and Scott depict him as a tax farmer, Herzog pictures the slave as a retainer, and Glancy and Beavis are of the opinion that the servant was a slave. Linnemann, *Parables of Jesus*, 108; Boucher, *Parables*, 117; Wenham, *Parables of Jesus*, 152; Snodgrass, *Stories with*

unequal status between the king and the servant, an inequality confirmed
in the parable by the expressions προσεκύνει (Matt 18:26),[70] ὁ κύριος τοῦ
δούλου (Matt 18:27), and ὁ κύριος αὐτοῦ (Matt 18:32). Second, by granting
the servant a loan (τὸ δάνειον; Matt 8:27),[71] the king favored the servant
by giving him access to economic and political resources otherwise not
available. Finally, by accepting the loan, the servant promised to pay back
the loan as and when determined by the king. In the parable, this moment
had now arrived. The client (servant) now has the opportunity to show his
loyalty to his patron.

When the servant cannot pay his debt, the king's first decision is to
sell the servant to make up for his loss (Matt 18:25). The servant, however,
desperately begs (προσεκύνει) the king to have patience until he is able to
pay his debt (Matt 18:26). The king then, because of this request and out
of compassion (σπλαγχνισθεὶς) decides to overturn his initial decision and
cancels the servant's debt. To avoid an anachronistic reading of the parable,
we must stress the importance of interpreting the king's decision against the
background of the social realia of the parable.

In patron-client relationships the client was to behave in specific ways.
Because patron-client relationships involved a strong element of personal
obligation, patrons were expected to show generosity.[72] As Malina and
Rohrbaugh put it,

Intent, 68; Hultgren, *Parables of Jesus*, 24; Scott, *Hear Then the Parable*, 72; Herzog, *Parables as Subversive Speech*, 137; Glancy, "Slaves and Slavery," 67–90; Beavis, "Ancient Slavery," 37–54. Pinpointing the exact position of the servant makes no difference in the interpretation of the parable. What matters, and this is clear from the parable, is that the king (patron) and the servant (client) are of unequal status.

70. The word προσεκύνει is "often used of obeisance by an inferior to a superior." Snodgrass, *Stories with Intent*, 69.

71. Again, it does not matter for the interpretation of the parable whether the debt of the servant was incurred as a result of the undercollecting of taxes from his province, that the servant did not honor his contract with the king as a tax farmer, that the servant was in arrears paying back a loan, or that the debt of a tax farmer was turned into a loan. Jeremias, *Parables of Jesus*, 210; Malina and Rohrbaugh, *Social-Science Commentary on the Synoptic Gospels*, 95; Via, *Parables*, 138; Schippers, *Gelijkenissen van Jezus*, 136; Linnemann, *Parables of Jesus*, 108; Boucher, *Parables*, 107; Herzog, *Parables as Subversive Speech*, 140; Reid, *Parables for Preachers*, 135; Schottroff, *Parables of Jesus*, 197; Snodgrass, *Stories with Intent*, 68; Hultgren, *Parables of Jesus*, 24; Scott, *Hear Then the Parable*, 270; Lambrecht, *Out of the Treasure*, 152; Manson, *The Sayings of Jesus*, 213; De Boer, "Ten Thousand Talents," 47; Morgan, *Parables and Metaphors*, 92; Derrett, *Law in the New Testament*, 36–37. Important for the interpretation of the parable on this point is that a patron granted him a favor (loan) and now is calling that favor (debt) in. Also see Josephus (*Ant.* 3.282), and 4 Macc 2:8 that uses τὸ δάνειον in reference to debt incurred.

72. Neyrey, "Ceremonies in Luke-Acts," 370; Moxnes, "Patron-Client Relations,"

The king decides to act in terms of "mercy," that is, an appeal to his royal honor to pay his debts of interpersonal obligation to a "household member." On the basis of such "mercy" the king forgives the debt.[73]

That the king's mercy is indeed part of his motivation to forgive the slave's debt is attested in Matt 18:33, when the king affirms that he forgave the servant out of mercy (κἀγὼ σὲ ἠλέησα). The second reason why the king cancels the frist servant's debt is linked to the element of personal obligation and seems to be the king's desire for repute and honor. Patron-client relationships featured a strong element of solidarity, which was sealed by exchange and often couched in terms of interpersonal loyalty and attachment between patrons and clients.[74] This solidarity, as Eisenstadt and Roniger indicate, was "often closely related to conceptions of personal identity, especially of personal honour."[75] Thus, what the patron loses in material wealth is more than compensated for with an honorable reputation. The motive behind the seeking of public honor was *philotīmiā* ("love of honor"). and, as Dover notes, "the advantage sought by *philotīmiā* was inter alia the reputation which was brought about by the discharge of financial obligations."[76] Thus, because the king expected he servant to enhance his royal reputation (with repeated public praise of his "merciful patron"), the king forgave his debt.[77] That praise was expected from the (unequal) client in patron-client relationships is clear from P.Merton 1.12.6–9 (dated 26 April 58). In this personal letter, most probably between two physicians, the writer states that since he and the addressee (Dionysius) are friends (equals), he "may dispense with writing to you with a great show of thanks; for it is for those who are not friends that we must give thanks in words" (γὰρ τοῖς μὴ φίλοις οὖσι διὰ λόγων εὐχαριστεῖν; P.Mert. 1.12.8–9).

Modern readers may find incredible the suggestion that the patron-king forgives the servant's debt in order to increase his own honor and to

---

249.

73. Malina and Rohrbaugh, *Social-Science Commentary on the Synoptic Gospels*, 95–96. See also: "Those toward whom one has such a debt are equally obliged to maintain the relationship by further favors . . . [T]he mercy involved is not simply feelings of compassion for one who suffers unjustly, but paying one's debt of interpersonal obligation by forgiving . . . debt." Malina, "Hospitality," 86.

74. Sahlins, *Stone Age Economics*, 270; Wallace-Hadrill, "Patronage in Roman Society," 72.

75. Eisenstadt and Roniger, "Patron-Client Relations," 50.

76. Dover, *Greek Popular Morality*, 230.

77. Pilch, *Cultural Dictionary of the Bible*, 62. See also Malina, "Hospitality," 87; Moxnes, "Patron-Client Relations," 250; Hobbs, "Reflections on Honor," 502–503.

establish a relationship of obligation with the servant. The reason for our incredulity rests in the fact that we as moderns bring to the text our own political and social bias toward a Western-style democracy with a central government and bureaucracy wherein everybody expects to have equal access to goods and services provided by the state.[78] To understand the social realia in ancient texts, cultural awareness of the "other" and cultural self-awareness are needed. Added to this, as Kloppenborg has insisted, we need "to assemble solid ancient *comparanda* on the practices and social realities which the sayings of Jesus and the parables presuppose."[79]

In the case of the Unmerciful Servant, this *comparanda* is provided by the practice of patronage (as described above) and in the social realities depicted in P.Köln 7.313, SB 20.14106 and 1 Macc 13:39. These documented papyri mirror the parable of the Unmerciful Servant—not only with regard to the words that appear in the story (those belonging to the lexical sphere of ὀφείλ- and the verb ἀφίημι) but also with regard to social reality. In these three documents kings (Ptolemy V, Ptolemy and Demetrius II) forgive the debts of their subjects. This was political power at play between rulers (patrons) and subjects (clients), relationships based on a strong element of inequality and differences in power. And since political power in these aristocratic societies was exercised by developing patron-client relationships, it is not difficult to see that the first hearers of the Unmerciful Servant would have connected the social realia in the parable with these releases from debt. Also, the hearers of the parable would have taken it for granted that these releases from debt as acts of royal care for subjects were aimed at acquiring honor.

Based on the correspondences between these texts and the parable, the parable's hearers did not interpret the king's forgiveness of the servant's debt as unexpected compassion,[80] an "unexpected act of patronage generosity,"[81] or an act "quite uncharacteristic of any agrarian ruler."[82] For the hearers of the parable the servant's release from debt was quite ordinary. For them this was no surprise. This is how rulers acted; in their constant quest for honor (*philotīmiā*) they turned their subjects with acts of "mercy" into clients who then had to reciprocate by publicly recognizing the generosity they had received.

78. See Moxnes, "Patron-Client Relations," 243.
79. Kloppenborg, *Synoptic Problems*, 2.
80. Scott, *Re-Imagine the World*, 104.
81. Herzog, *Parables as Subversive Speech*, 142.
82. Ibid., 146.

The scene between the two servants (Matt 18:28–30), and the first servant's decision not to forgive a much smaller debt (Matt 18:31) can also be understood against the social realia evoked by the documented papyri that Bazzana discusses. As Bazzana has shown, the enforcement of the Ptolemaic ordinances was usually not restricted only to debt due to the royal treasury but extended to what each subject in the kingdom owed to other subjects (P.Köln 7.313, 24–25; P.Tebt. 1.5.221–47). Thus, when the second servant asks the servant whose debt has been forgiven to have patience until he can pay his debt, the expectation of the other servants looking on would have been twofold: First, the servant will honor the king by proclaiming openly his forgiveness of the debt; and second, as act of obedience, out of personal obligation to his patron, the king, the first servant will emulate his patron by forgiving the debt of his fellow servant, most probably someone of equal status (see ὁ σύνδουλος αὐτοῦ; Matt 18:29).[83] This does not happen, and by his decision the first servant instead shames the king. The other servants, most probably also clients of the king acting inter alia as his informers,[84] report to the king (gossip about) what happened, whereafter the first servant is summoned.

Then comes the surprise in the parable. Thus far the parable has developed as expected in terms of its known social realia and the everyday experiences of its hearers. Kings forgive debts in search of honor, and clients reciprocated accordingly. Patron-client relationships between unequal persons entailed balanced reciprocity (the serving of mutual interests).[85] These relationships were based on personal obligation, solidarity, and loyalty—not on altruistic motives in the sense of extreme solidarity (generalized reciprocity). Thus, although the patronage system had a kinship glaze over it (see Dionysius of Halicarnassus, *Ant. rom.*2.9), it was "a system dominated by the elite (patrons) and their values; a system that was set up in order to ensure the preservation of their privileged positions and power."[86] Therefore,

83. Several scholars have argued that the second servant should be positioned at a lower end of the social hierarchy, and thus of unequal status to the first servant. Jeremias identifies the second servant as a minor official, and Linnemann and Herzog see him as a middle-class bureaucrat. Jeremias, *Parables of Jesus*, 212; Linnemann, *Parables of Jesus*, 109; Herzog, *Parables as Subversive Speech*, 137. That the two servants are of equal status is clear from the description of the second servant in Matt 18:28 as τῶν συνδούλων αὐτοῦ. See also the description of the other servants as οἱ σύνδουλοι (Matt 18:31).

84. Herzog, *Parables as Subversive Speech*, 142.

85. Malina, *Christian Origins and Cultural Anthropology*, 98–106; Neyrey, *Render to God*, 253; Neyrey, "God, Benefactor and Patron," 469–70.

86. Van Eck, "Friend at Midnight," 10. See also Moxnes, "Patron-Client Relations," 244.

the purpose of patron-client relationships—while masking "the fundamentally unbalanced and exploitative nature of the exchange"[87]—was to exercise power over others, a core value of advanced agrarian societies.[88]

Therefore, when the first servant does not reciprocate as expected, the king has to defend his honor, power, and privilege. In a world where honor and power were core values, it was considered shameful not to defend one's honor and power. But this is exactly what the king does. Totally unexpectedly, he does not react by defending his honor, or in the first servant's typical and socially accepted ruthless way. This is clear from his words in Matt 18:33: When someone asks to be forgiven a debt, you show mercy, no matter what the socially prescribed response should be. Honor comes not from doing what everyone expects should be done (from playing expected roles) but from doing a good deed. Forgiving a debt should be done altruistically—that is, not in terms of balanced reciprocity but in terms of general reciprocity. When this happens, the *basileia* of God is visible. To act differently, makes one wicked (πονηρέ; Matt 18:33).

From this perspective, Jesus uses the parable to question first-century Mediterranean social relations based on balanced reciprocity and the pivotal value of honor. A world based on the value of honor is dominated by the powerful and ensures the preservation of privileged positions and power, and, because it is fundamentally unbalanced, leads to exploitation and debt. This world is not the *basileia*. On the contrary, the *basileia* of God is present when debt forgiveness—when the act itself rather than the socially prescribed role—becomes honorable. At the end of the parable, this option is left open before the hearers, implied by the rhetorical question in 18:33.

A Parable of Jesus?

Most scholars see the Unmerciful Servant as going back to an earlier parable of Jesus.[89] The above interpretation concurs with this point of view. The parable has all the hallmarks of a Jesus parable, typically cutting against

87. Kloppenborg, *Synoptic Problems*, 492.

88. Herzog, *Prophet and Teacher*, 55; Hanson and Oakman, *Palestine in the Time of Jesus*, 72; Oakman, *Jesus and the Peasants*, 138–42. Also Elliott. "The codes of patronage effectively masked the deeply exploitative nature of the tribute- and slave-based economy by simultaneously concealing the rapacity of the ruling class and naturalizing fundamentally unequal relationships through routines of theatrical reciprocity." Elliott, *Arrogance of Nations*, 29.

89. See, for example, Crossan, *In Parables*, 103; Funk et al., *Five Gospels*, 208; Hultgren, *Parables of Jesus*, 29; Jeremias, *Parables of Jesus*, 212; Davies and Allison, *Matthew*, 3:794; Linnemann, *Parables of Jesus*, 106.

the grain of several practices and values dominating his social world. The king's stance on honor, for example, is paralleled in Gos. Thom. 65, where the owner refrains from violence and does not try to defend his honor and status. This also the case, as we have seen, in the parable of the Lost Sheep (Luke 15:4–6), where the shepherd refrains from violence in order to feed his family; and in the parable of the Feast (Luke 14:16b–23), where the host, after being shunned by his elite invitees, fills up his banquet hall with those without any honor. Jesus' stance on general reciprocity in the parable also parallels his sayings in Q 6:27–28, 29, 30, 33, 11:33,[90] and Q 12:42–46.[91]

90. Howes, "Placed in a Hidden Place," 311–15.
91. Howes, "Food for Thought," 6.

CHAPTER 8

The Tenants (Gos. Thom. 65):
A Surprising Nonviolent Patron

FOR THE SHEPHERD IN the Lost Sheep (Luke 15:4–6), when one of the flock he attended to strayed, stealing and using violence was maybe the easiest solution to make up his loss. Armed with a sling and club, and unsupervised, with freedom of movement, banditry was a logical option. But then the unexpected happens: the shepherd takes the risk to go and look for the one that is lost, trying to make sure that everybody has enough. Therefore, the kingdom in the Lost Sheep is made visible through nonviolence. This was also the case in the Unmerciful Servant (Matt 18:23–33); the patron-king refrains from violence and does not try to defend his honor and status when one of his servants does not want to forgive the small debt of a fellow servant after the patron-king has forgiven his much larger debt. In the kingdom, honor lies in nonviolence.

In the Tenants, as will be indicated below, Jesus' stance on the relationship between violence and the kingdom is the same. When read through the lens of patronage, and honor and shame, the Tenants parable indicates that honor lies in nonviolence, especially in not exercising the "right" to defend possessions by force. In the kingdom status and honor are not retained or gained by the use of violence. On the contrary, in the kingdom honor lies in refraining from violence.

History of Interpretation

Just as the synoptic versions of the Tenants parable are theological-allegorical, so the earliest interpretations, those of the church fathers, are also.[1] The

---

1. Chrysostom (349–407 CE), in his *Hom. on Matt.* 69.1–3, argued that the parable portrays God's long-suffering, his providential care, and the ingratitude of the Jews,

most common interpretation of the Tenants, which overlaps with certain aspects of these earliest theological-allegorical interpretations of the parable, is a reading that understands the parable as an allegorical story of Jesus' confrontation with Israel's leaders. In this reading, the vineyard is seen as a symbol for Israel, the tenants are the Jewish religious leaders, the owner of the vineyard is God, the servants sent to collect the owner's part of the harvest are the prophets, the beloved son is Christ, the tenants' punishment symbolizes the ruin of Israel, and the "others" who will receive the vineyard are the non-Jews.[2] Scholars who read the parable in this way, in almost all cases, believe that the narrative setting of the extant versions of the parable in the Synoptics represent the original situation in which Jesus told the parable; Jesus told the parable in Jerusalem when the chief priests, scribes, and elders questioned his authority (Mark 11:27–33 and *par.*). Also common among these readings is an emphasis on judgment[3] and the belief that the parable has christological significance[4] and that the quotation from Ps 118:22–23 was part of the parable spoken by Jesus.

---

and the "others" in the parable to whom the vineyard will be given the non-Jews (Gentiles). Irenaeus 130–202 CE), as Chrysostom, interpreted the "others" in the parable as the non-Jews. Irenaeus, *Haer.* IV.xxxvi.2. In Aquinas' (1225–1274 CE) reading, the vineyard is also equated with the Jewish people, and the tower is the wine of God's love pressed out through the depths of the Scriptures. See Kissinger, *History of Interpretation*, 43. Calvin (1509–1564 CE), in his interpretation, theologically linked the parable to the offices in the church: the tenants of the vineyard (church) refer to the appointed pastors in the church, and the owner is a reference to God who acts as proprietor, expecting the pastors to cultivate the vineyard (church) and annually deliver the proceeds. Calvin, *Harmony of the Gospels*, 3:16–23. For more examples of the allegorical interpretation of the parable up to the medieval period, see Wailes, *Medieval Allegories*, 147–153.

2. See, for example, Snodgrass, *Stories with Intent*, 276–92; Wright, *Victory of God*, 597–601; Evans, *Mark 8:27—16:20*, 210–40; Hultgren, *Parables of Jesus*, 361–67; Blomberg, *Interpreting the Parables*, 331–33; Groenewald, *In Gelykenisse Het Hy Geleer*, 89; Brouwer, *De Gelijkenissen*, 28–29; Stein, *Introduction to the Parables*, 151; Morgan, *Parables and Metaphors*, 111–12; Barclay, *Parables of Jesus*, 140–45; Pentecost, *Parables of Jesus*, 131–34; Boice, *Parables of Jesus*, 190; Kistemaker, *Stories Jesus Told*, 84, 87; Hunter, *Then and Now*, 105–7; Lockyer, *All the Parables*, 225–27; Boucher, *Parables*, 146–52; Bailey, *Jesus through Middle Eastern Eyes*, 410–24; Kilgallen, *Twenty Parables*, 166–67; Voris, *Preaching Parables*, 121. See also Thuren for a similar reading, arguing that the parable challenges the religious authorities to accept that John and Jesus indeed are God's ultimate messengers. Thuren, *Parables Unplugged*, 176.

3. See, for example, Hultgren, *Parables of Jesus*, 369–70; Stein, *Introduction to the Parables*, 151; Morgan, *Parables and Metaphors*, 111–12; Barclay, *Parables of Jesus*, 140–45; Kistemaker, *Stories Jesus Told*, 87; Boucher, *Parables*, 146.

4. See, for example, Groenewald, *In Gelykenisse Het Hy Geleer*, 89; Bailey, *Jesus through Middle Eastern Eyes*, 425; Snodgrass, *Stories with Intent*, 276.

Snodgrass' reading is representative of this interpretation. According to him, the Tenants is one of the few parables that is "historically rooted in a particular time of Jesus' life," namely, the questioning of Jesus' authority after the temple cleansing. "If it is taken out of the sphere of Jesus' confrontation with Israel's leaders, the interpretations are odd, especially for first-century Palestine, and are unconvincing." For Snodgrass, the parable has "direct and major christological significance," which is clear from the quotation of Ps 118:22–23 in Mark 12:10–11 and *par.*: "the religious leaders have rejected the son, the climatic envoy of God, but this rejection will be reversed by God and the leaders will lose their role in God's purposes." Therefore, the parable is an (allegorical) "metaphorical narrative about God, his people, and God's judgment.[5]

Those who read the parable as a realistic story focus either on the owner, the tenants, or the relationship between the owner and the tenants. The readings of Dodd, Cadoux, Smith, Jeremias, Derrett, and Hengel fall in the first category. Dodd first de-allegorized the parable by removing Mark 12:5 (the sending of the third slave and the mistreatment of many servants), Mark 12:9b (the owner destroying the tenants), and Mark 12:10–11 (the allusion to Ps 118:22–23). Without these later additions, Dodd argued, the parable is a realistic story that reflects the revolutionary ferment that prevailed in Palestine since the time of Judas the Galilean in 6 CE; agrarian discontent, tensions between foreign absentee landlords, and Zealot-inspired tenants are the telltale of the parable.[6] Cadoux, preferring Luke's version (which lacks the allusions to Isa 5:2 and 5:5), argues that in this parable Jesus did not intend to claim messiahship but rather meant to challenge the attitudes and behavior of his opponents. These are the same that tried to kill Jesus to preserve their own authority.[7] Smith, like Cadoux, is troubled by the self-referential nature of Mark's version, and sees agrarian

5. Snodgrass, *Stories with Intent*, 276, 290, 292. See also, for example, Hultgren and Boucher. According to Hultgren, the parable is about "divine care, human treachery, resurrection and responsibility," and speaks of judgement. Hultgren, *Parables of Jesus*, 369, 370. So Boucher: the parable is Jesus' final warning to the religious leaders; it tells "how God has made his final and definite appeal through him, how it is rejected, and how despite this and even because of it God's reign will be opened to all believers." Boucher, *Parables*, 146.

6. Dodd, *Parables of the Kingdom*, 98–102. Despite his removing what he considers as later (allegorical) additions to the parable, Dodd's reading is still allegorical. By reading the parable through the double lens of Isa 5:1–17 and Mark 12:12, Dodd has the tenants as the rulers of Israel who refused their landlord (God) his due and therefore will be punished. Dodd thus, in trying to avoid allegorization, fell back into allegory. See Kloppenborg, *Tenants in the Vineyard*, 109–10.

7. Cadoux, *Art and Use*, 40–42.

social unrest in Galilee as the social situation presupposed by the parable. From this perspective, the parable (which Smith delimits to Mark 12:1–5, 9a) emphasizes the escalating violence against the owner's envoys, and most probably implies a threat of judgment (Mark 12:9a).[8]

According to Jeremias, the parable in Mark (and even more in Matthew) is "evidently pure allegory."[9] The version of the parable in *Gos. Thom.* 65, however, is an authentic story by Jesus about an owner. In following Dodd, Jeremias argues that the Tenants is a "realistic description of the revolutionary attitude of the Galilean peasants towards the foreign landlords, an attitude which had been aroused by the Zealot movement which had it headquarters in Galilee." In the time of Jesus, most of Galilee was parceled out to foreign landlords in the form of *latifundia*. On the basis of καὶ ἀπεδήμησεν in Mark 12:1, the owner of the vineyard is clearly a foreigner, and the appearance of the son made the tenants believe that the landlord was dead and that the son had come to take up his inheritance. The tenants—by killing the heir and making the vineyard ownerless—believed that they could claim the vineyard because they were "first on the spot." Jeremias, especially on the grounds of "the others" in Mark 12:9, concludes that the point of the parable is that of the vindication of the offer of the gospel to the poor.[10]

Derrett, in his reading, focuses on the peculiar features of a vineyard (not merely a wheat field or vegetable patch). Viticulture was a speculative undertaking that required substantial capital investment with an ever persistent possibility of failure. Moreover, newly planted vineyards normally only came into full production after four years. Therefore it was normal for a landowner to plant a vineyard, rent it to expert vinedressers, and then depart until it matured.[11] The tenants in the parable were cultivators who

8. Smith, *Parables of the Synoptic Gospels*, 224. Clearly, as Kloppenborg has indicated, this reading is also allegorical, since it offers "a reading of salvation history in allegorical dress." Kloppenborg, *Tenants in the Vineyard*, 111.

9. Jeremias, *Parables of Jesus*, 70.

10. Ibid., 74–76. Kloppenborg rightly asserts that the law of adverse possession or *usucaptio* (an existing law according to which the estate of an interstate proselyte could be appropriated by a claimant who was already occupying it) is only a footnote to Mishnaic law, and there is no reason to believe that this law was in force two centuries prior to the codification of the Mishnah. Kloppenborg, *Tenants in the Vineyard*, 112, 113. Also, since "the others" (ἄλλοις; Mark 12:9) are not described in the parable, it is very difficult to identify "the others" with the poor. Jeremias' translation the verb ἀπεδήμησεν, as "going abroad" and thus referring to a foreign landlord, is also questioned by Kloppenborg. The verb simply means "to depart," a meaning also supported by papyrological usage. Ibid., 113.

11. Derrett, "Wicked Vinedressers," 15.

were paid a fixed percentage of the harvest (in contrast to waged labor), and most probably, at least during the first four years, supported their income by living on vegetables that were intercultivated among the vines.[12] The reason for the hostile reception of the first servant, and the second and third slave in successive years, was due to outstanding payment by the owner to the tenants for capital expenditures in preparing the vineyard for production.[13] To make sense of the tenants' actions with respect to the son, Derrett employs the principle of adverse possession: that is, an assertion of possession through undisputed usufruct for three years. By killing the son, the tenants believe they can claim possession of the vineyard.[14] Hengel's contribution to the understanding of the Tenants was to show that its scenario of a tenant revolt is documented in the Zenon papyri. The main character in the parable is the owner, and the point of the parable is polemical, anticipating Jesus' death and warning of its consequences; just as the murder of the son by the tenants will bring a direct consequence the intervention of the owner, the murder of Jesus will lead to the judgment of those who are responsible.[15]

Via, Newell and Newell, and Crossan also read the parable as a realistic story with as focus the actions of the tenants. Via, after stripping the Markan version of its allegorical features (the reference to Isa 5, the summary in Mark 12:5b, the murder of the third servant, and the use of ἀγαπητός in Mark 12:6), sees the focus of the parable as the depravity of the tenants' actions and their blindness to see that their actions would bring about their own destruction.[16] In the Newells' reading of the parable the tenants are depicted in a positive light. The owner symbolizes foreign domination and expropriation of land that once belonged to the people of Israel, and by telling the parable, Jesus sympathized with the goal of the recovery of ancestral lands taken over by foreigners.[17] As a story addressed to a peasant audience sympathetic to the cause of the Zealots, Jesus does not attack the

12. Ibid., 21.

13. Ibid., 26.

14. In Kloppenborg's view, the assaults of the servants as a means of protest over missing wages seems fanciful, and Derrett's appealing to the principle of adverse possession (an assertion of possession through undisputed usufruct for three years)—which means that the tenants could claim the vineyard in the fourth year—is without foundation since it lacks textual support. Also, what we know of standard viticultural procedures in the first-century makes Derrett's reading implausible. Kloppenborg, *Tenants in the Vineyard*, 115–18.

15. Hengel, "Den Bösen Weingärtnern," 15–38.

16. Via, *Parables*, 133–34.

17. Newell and Newell, "Wicked Tenants," 236.

goals of the tenants, only their methods.[18] What is at stake is the question whether a resort to violence is wise, given the untouchable power of the foreign occupiers.

Crossan's reading of the parable also focus on the tenants, arguing that their actions are pictured positively. The parable is a shocking story of a successful murder. The tenants "recognized their situation, saw their opportunity, and acted resolutely upon it."[19] By killing the only heir, they accomplished their purpose to take possession of the vineyard. Therefore, the parable illustrates the "prudent grasping of one's immoral choice";[20] the tenants are antiheroes whose decisive action in a situation of crisis leads to unexpected gain.[21]

Finally, Malina and Rohrbaugh, Hester, Herzog, and Schottroff read the parable as a realistic story about an owner and tenants. These readings have three features in common: the owner is depicted as a villain, the tenants are seen as the heroes in the story, and the reader or interpreter takes as the ideological narrative point of view the values and actions of the owner.[22] Malina and Rohrbaugh were first to view the owner as the villain rather than the hero in the story. According to them, the historical Jesus told the parable as a warning to landowners who were expropriating and exporting the produce of the land from their tenants.[23] Hester's reading builds on three assumptions. First, the key characters of the Tenants, the landowner (likely an aristocrat), and the tenants (representing those who have lost their patrimonial land due to the growth of large estates through debt) evoke the contrast between the two socioeconomic groups in conflict over the possession of land. Second, ownership of land is seen not a matter of economy, but as a matter of one's own identity. Losing land meant losing one's Israelite identity, and normally lead to working as a day laborer or becoming a beggar. Third, the parable focuses on the motif of inheritance, the question of true heirship of the land. From this point of view, Hester opines that that the

18. The Newells' assumption, and that of Dodd and Jeremias, that the Zealots as a political faction was active in the time of Jesus has been contested by Horsley and Hanson. According to them, the Zealots as a movement only came into being in 66–67 CE during the Jewish War. Before the Jewish War social banditry (as a prepolitical form of rebellion), however, was common. Horsley and Hanson, *Bandits, Prophets, and Messiahs*, xiv–xvi, 48–51. See also Van Eck, *Galilee and Jerusalem*, 63.

19. Crossan, *In Parables*, 94.

20. Crossan, "Wicked Husbandmen," 465.

21. Kloppenborg, *Tenants in the Vineyard*, 128.

22. Ibid., 139.

23. Malina and Rohrbaugh, *Social-Science Commentary on the Synoptic Gospels*, 199–200.

heart of the parable is a conflict over basic values of Israelite identity, peasant attachment of the land, and the imperative of subsistence, all of which being put in danger by elite expropriation and control of lands.[24] *Contra* Crossan, the tenants are not rouges, but rather people that are contesting an elite ideology of land control.[25]

Herzog also reads the parable against the background of a revolt by peasant farmers, whose subsistence is endangered by land expropriation by the foreign elite, trying to reassert its laims to land in virtue of the belief that the land was God's inheritance and as such belonged to Israel. The owner in Mark's parable is one of the local elite of Galilee or Judea (not a foreigner), and (in following Derrett) the sending of the slaves were spaced in one–year intervals. The motive behind the tenants' action is to incite violence as a protest agaunst converting their farmland into a vineyard (turning smallholders into tenants), a move that threatens their (and others') subsistence. Therefore, the parable serves as a warning to tenants that the use of violence in trying to reassert their honorable status as heirs of God's land is futile and destined to failure.[26]

According to Schottroff, the point of the Tenants is to paint (in a realistic fashion) the picture of conflict in Jewish Palestine and tenants (suffering from social dislocation) seizing an opportunity to usurp land by means of self-help as a way out of economic misery.[27] In his reading, the parable is a critique of the elite and its exploitation and expropriation of peasants and land.[28] Finally, in the most extensive study of the Tenants thus far, Kloppenborg reads the parable against the background of viticulture in inter alia first-century Palestine. He comes to the conclusion that the Tenants (in its Thomasine version) falls in the category of those parables of Jesus that depict wealthy persons (with ascribed status and honor) finding themselves "unexpectedly in circumstances that challenge their values or the values of the hearers of the parables."[29]

24. For a similar reading, see Schottroff, *Parables of Jesus*, 21.

25. Hester, "Parable of the Tenants," 34–54.

26. Herzog, *Parables as Subversive Speech*, 101–13. See also Wright, *Jesus the Storyteller*, 162.

27. Schottroff, "Den Bösen Weingärtnern," 21.

28. Ibid., 29–31. The positive aspect Schottroff's interpretation is that he indicates that, from an emic point of view, many facts are stated in the parable that are not so self-evident for the modern reader: vineyard owners tended to come from the middling rich, absenteeism was a normal pattern of elite exploitation of the land, indebtedness was systemic, and violence and conflict was more the norm than the exception. See Kloppenborg, *Tenants in the Vineyard*, 140.

29. Kloppenborg, *Tenants in the Vineyard*, 352.

In the reading of the parable to follow, the following will serve as points of departure: The parable is a realistic narrative that depicts several aspects of viticulture in first-century Palestine (Kloppenborg). Some of these aspects are discontent, tension, and conflict between foreign absentee landlords and tenants (Dodd). As a matter of fact, "conflict was a common feature of tenancy relationships."[30] These conflicts, at times, led to violence, as depicted in the parable. Was this violence acceptable or not? More specifically, was violence in general an acceptable way to resolve conflict? The answer to this question is what Jesus is addressing in the parable. In this regard, Perkins is correct when she argues that the focus of the parable is "Jesus' policy of non-violence and love of enemy."[31] Given Jesus' stance on violence, the actions of tenants are not pictured positive in the parable (*contra* Crossan); they are indeed the rouges in the story (*contra* Hester). Also, the owner, when the Thomasine version of the parable is seen as the version closest to the rhetoric of the earliest layer of the Jesus tradition, is not the villain in the story but rather the hero (*contra* Malina and Rohrbaugh). The parable is not a story about blindness that prevents one from seeing that violence will bring about destruction (Via); it is not a story asking if resorting to violence is wise or not (Newell and Newell); finally, the parable is not judging that the use of violence is futile and destined to fail (Herzog). The Tenants rather is a story that challenges the values of both the elite (with ascribed status and honor) and the hearers of the parable; should one resolve conflict through violence, and when honor is at stake, is violence the option to regain lost honor? Or does honor lie in refraining from violence, no matter what the circumstances are?

Authenticity and Integrity

We have four extant versions of the Tenants, namely, Mark 12:1–12; Matt 21:33–46; Luke 20:9–19; and Gos. Thom. 65. Some scholars see the parable in Mark as a creation of the early church.[32] Others attempt, by bracketing

30. Ibid., 316. Several factors accounted for this conflict: the normal level of rents, the increased demand for wine, the intrinsic value of the grape harvest, absenteeism, export demands, and the late payment or nonpayment of wages. For a discussion of these factors, see ibid., 316–22.

31. Perkins, *Hearing the Parables*, 194. *Contra* Snodgrass, who states that the "concern of the parable is *not* about raising questions about violence." Snodgrass, *Stories with Intent*, 289; italics original.

32. Mark 12:1–12, according to Jülicher, resisted a realistic reading at every turn; it cannot be regarded as an authentic parable of Jesus: "its message is completely wedded

possible later insertions in the Tenants, to make a case for the authenticity of Mark 12:1–11,[33] while some, like Snodgrass, include virtually all of Mark

---

to a second-level narrative of the conflict between Jesus and the priestly elite," serving christological ends and seeking a justification for the death of Jesus. Jülicher, *Gleichnisreden Jesu*, 406. Kümmel concurred with Jülicher: the beloved son in the parable would not have had a messianic meaning in pre-Christian Judaism; it was only the early church who would have no difficulty in understanding the reference to the beloved son as a reference to Jesus as the Son of God. Kümmel, "Den Bösen Weingärtner," 129. Carlston and Blank came to the same conclusion: the specifically Christian beliefs that are encoded in the parable are only intelligible when the Tenants is seen as an allegorical post-Easter product about the death of Jesus and its consequences. Carlston, *The Parables of the Triple Tradition*, 178–90; Blank, "Die Sendung des Sohne," 21. See also Schweizer, *Das Evangelium nach Markus*, 131; Gnilka, *Das Evangelium nach Markus*, 2:148–49; Bultmann, *Synoptic Tradition*, 177; Klostermann, *Das Markusevangelium*, 135; Montefiore, *The Synoptic Gospels*, 273–75; Luz, *Mt 18–25*, 3:218–20; Loisy, *Les évangiles Synoptiques*, 312; Beare, *Gospel according to Matthew*, 428; Grant, *Letter and the Spirit*, 44; Drury, *Parables in the Gospels*, 64–65; Crossan, "Wicked Husbandmen," 461–65; Lambrecht, *Out of the Treasure*, 127–32; Smith, *Parables of the Synoptic Gospels*, 19–26; Jones, *Art and Truth*, 80–109, 135; Linnemann, *Parables of Jesus*, 21–23. Building on especially the work of Kümmel, Steck identified the Hellenistic Christian community as creators of the Tenants: the tenants of the parable stand for Israel as a whole and should be understood as an instance of Deuteronomistic theology. Steck, *Israel und das Gewaltsame Geschick der Propheten*, 269–73. The recent work of Mell draws in principle the same conclusion: Mark 12:1–11 is an allegory from its beginning rather than a nonallegorical story that was secondarily allegorized, and cannot be traced back to Jesus. Mell, *Die Anderen Winzer*, 114–15. For a detailed discussion of the contributions of Jülicher, Kümmel, Carlson, Black, and Steck, see Kloppenborg, *Tenants in the Vineyard*, 53–66. *Contra* this point of view are Jeremias and Snodgrass. According to Jeremias, the parable's complete silence about the resurrection makes it unlikely that the early church invented the parable. Jeremias, *Parables of Jesus*, 72–73. Snodgrass suggests that "while 'son of God' is not specifically a messianic title, the claim that 'son of God' had no messianic significance in pre-Christian Judaism has been proven erroneous, especially by the Qumran scrolls." Snodgrass, *Stories with Intent*, 294. See also De Moore, who argues that all of the allegorical details in the parable can be attested as current in Jewish exegetical traditions prior to 70 CE. De Moor, "Targumic Background of Mark 12," 63–80.

33. See, for example, Hubaut, Klauck, and Weder, who argue that the allusion to Isa 5:1–7 (LXX) was not part of the original parable. Hubaut, *La Parabole des Vignerons Homicides*, 127; Klauck, *Allegorie und Allegorese*, 286–316; Weder, *Die Gleichnisse Jesu als Metaphern*, 147–62. Weder (and Dodd) also removes Mark 12:5b (the sending of the third slave and the mistreatment of many servants) from the Markan version of the parable, while Smith brackets Mark 12:6–8 (the sending and killing of the beloved son). Weder, *Die Gleichnisse Jesu als Metaphern*, 158; Dodd, *Parables of the Kingdom*, 98–102; Smith, *Parables of the Synoptic Gospels*, 224. Several scholars believe that the reference to Ps 118:22–23 in Mark 12:10–11 should be considered a later addition to the parable. Jülicher, *Gleichnisreden Jesu*, 405; Bultmann, *Synoptic Tradition*, 177; Hultgren, *Parables of Jesus*, 363, 366; Dodd, *Parables of the Kingdom*, 99; Jeremias, *Parables of Jesus*, 73–74; Carlston, *Parables of the Triple Tradition*, 180–81; Donahue, *Gospel in Parable*, 53; Taylor, *Gospel according to St. Mark*, 473; Lambrecht, *Out of the Treasure*,

12:1b–11 in the original parable, and assume that Mark 12:1a–12 reflects the original setting of the Tenants.[34]

Mark clearly reworked the version of the parable he received in the tradition to fit into his plot and theology;[35] thus this parable displays features that are typical neither of Mark's other parables nor of Jesus' parables in general.[36] In Mark the Tenants is an allegory of salvation history that features Jesus' death as the climactic moment of God's relationship with

---

110. *Contra* Perkins, *Hearing the Parables*, 181; Gundry, *Mark*, 687; Snodgrass, *Stories with Intent*, 287. Depending on what is seen in the parable as later additions or not, the parable is either delimited to Mark 12:1–8, thus ending with the killing of the son (Jeremias, Carlston, and Scott), Mark 12:1–9a (Bultmann, Dodd, Smith, and Taylor), or Mark 12:1b–9b (Hultgren, Donahue, and Lambrecht). Jeremias, *Parables of Jesus*, 74; Carlston, *Parables of the Triple Tradition*, 180; Scott, *Hear Then the Parable*, 248; Bultmann, *Synoptic Tradition*, 177; Dodd, *Parables of the Kingdom*, 97; Smith, *Parables of the Synoptic Gospels*, 224; Taylor, *Gospel according to St. Mark*, 476; Hultgren, *Parables of Jesus*, 364; Donahue, *The Gospel in Parable*, 53–56; Lambrecht, *Out of the Treasure*, 111–12. Efforts to preserve the Tenants in its Markan form for the historical Jesus encounter substantial difficulties, even in the case when one eliminates from the parable those detail that most critics find problematic (Kloppenborg, *Tenants in the Vineyard*, 103–5). Hubaut, Weder, and Klauck's interpretation of the Tenants, for example, is informed exactly by what they eliminate—despite that they eliminate the Isaiah intertext, it remains an allegory of salvation history and one that features Jesus' death as the climactic moment of God's relationship with Israel, "a motive that is otherwise completely absent from the Jesus tradition." Ibid., 78. To add to this irony is the fact that these critics reconstruct an original parable that are almost identical with Gos. Thom. 65, in which the owner is not God, the slaves not (the) prophets, the vineyard not the covenant, and the son not Jesus. This suggests that for these scholars the Isaian intertext remains the dominant interpretative key in understanding the Tenants. Ibid., 104.

34. Snodgrass, *Parable of the Wicked Tenants*, 47–58.

35. Three features stand out in Mark's version of the Tenants. First is the intimate connection between the parable, Mark's plot, and Mark's passion narrative. Kloppenborg, *Tenants in the Vineyard*, 219–20. See also Van Eck and Van Aarde, "Narratological Analysis of Mark 12:1–12," 778–99. Mark's framing of the Tenants by Mark 12:1a, 6a, 7c, and 12, integrates the parable into his plot, highlighting the hostility of Jesus' opponents that started in Mark 3:6 and is ever present in the narrative (e.g., Mark 7:1–5; 8:11–13; 12:13–17; 12:18–27; 12:35–37). Of special importance is υἱὸν ἀγαπητόν in Mark 12:6a, a Markan addition to the original parable that integrates the parable into Mark's Christology (see, e.g., Mark 1:1, 1:9–11; 8:31–32; 9:7; 9:31; 10:33–34; 15:39). The second distinguishing feature of the parable is Mark's close relationship to texts of the Tanak (Isa 5:2, 5; Gen 37:20, 24). The third distinguishing feature is the allusion to the Deuteronomistic pattern of God's repeated sending of the prophets to Israel and their repeated and violent rejection (Mark 12:5b), the only trace of the Deuteronomistic schema in Mark. Moreover, Mark's use of the Isaian intertext (Isa 5:1–7) makes almost inevitable an allegorical reading of the parable: the owner is God, the vineyard is Israel and the fruit is some behavior or response God expects from Israel. Kloppenborg, *Tenants in the Vineyard*, 221–48.

36. Kloppenborg, *Tenants in the Vineyard*, 223–41.

Israel. Mark's Tenants is a piece of theology, "a reading of salvation history in allegorical dress."[37] In the Matthean version the emphasis is on Jesus' conflict with the Jerusalem temple elite; it is apologetically employed to provide an explanation for the destruction of the temple by Titus, and didactically aims to exhort Matthew's readers to produce good works. Luke, on the other hand, uses the Tenants to illustrate the contrast between the people and their leaders, and to introduce a principle of judgement that one's reaction to Jesus as the Christ will define one's fate.[38] In all three cases, the parable is only intelligible when read from a postpaschal perspective.

Another clear indication that the synoptic versions of the parable do not go back to the layer of the historical Jesus tradition is the way in Jesus' stance towards violence is depicted. Mark 12:1–12 and *par.* suggest that Jesus condoned, even instigated, violent behavior. In the Markan version Jesus, after describing the violent behavior of the tenants, asks a rhetorical question about what the owner of the vineyard will do with his violent tenants. His answer is simple: violence will be answered with violence—the owner will kill the tenants and give the vineyard to others. In the Matthean version the question asked by Jesus is not rhetorical, and it is answered by those present in the temple (Matt 21:23) in more or less the same way, but with one exception: the tenants will be killed (as in Mark), *so that* the vineyard can be given to others who will render the owner his "rightful" part of the crop; Jesus receives this answer in a positive way. Simply stated, these instances can be understood as Jesus condoning not only violence but also the expropriation of peasant land by the aristocratic elite with the view of accumulating wealth and status. This, however, is not the end of the story, since the Lukan Jesus goes even further. After Jesus tells the parable and puts the same rhetorical question forward as the Markan version does, those present vehemently oppose Jesus' answer to fight fire with fire. Jesus, however, dismisses their reaction by quoting Ps 118:22 and adding a Midrash-like interpretation with an overt violent implication (Luke 20:18). This depiction of Jesus' attitude toward violence does not concur with what we have seen in the parables of the Lost Sheep and the Unmerciful Servant; Jesus propagated nonviolence, as will be indicated in more detail below.

This brings us to Thomas' version of the Tenants in Gos. Thom. 65. Kloppenborg has convincingly argued that the Thomasine version of the parable represents an independent tradition that most probably brings us the closest we can get to the rhetoric of the earliest Jesus movement, and

37. Ibid., 111.
38. Ibid., 173–218.

perhaps to the discourse of the historical Jesus.[39] In his realistic analysis of the Thomasine version of the Tenants, using extensive papyrological evidence on viticulture in inter alia first-century Palestine from 300 BCE to 300 CE, Kloppenborg shows that Gos. Thom. 65 has a ring of verisimilitude in terms of describing large-scale landholding and tenancy, absenteeism, conflict, and the sending of a son as a status marker.[40] Also, Gos. Thom. 65 lacks precisely those features of the Tenants in the Synoptic Gospels that identifies the version of the Tenants in Mark as an originally realistic narrative secondarily allegorized.[41]

Realism

By using a selection of fifty-eight papyri[42] (dating from 300 BCE to 300 CE) that illustrates various features of ancient viticulture, Kloppenborg has shown that the parable's reference to large-scale landholding and tenancy,[43]

39. Ibid., 352. See also Jeremias, *Parables of Jesus*, 70–72; Quispel, "Thomas and the New Testament," 205–6; Montefiore, "Parables of Thomas and the Synoptic Gospels," 62–63; Koester, "Three Thomas Parables," 199–200; Morrice, "Parable of the Tenants," 104–107; Perkins, *Hearing the Parables*, 181; Crossan, *In Parables*, 84–94.

40. Kloppenborg, *Tenants in the Vineyard*, 284–349.

41. Three details in Mark (but missing in Thomas), namely the planting of a new vineyard (Mark 12:1), the committing of murder with a view of inheritance (Mark 12:7), and the principle of self-help (Mark 12:8) are not susceptible to a realistic reading of the Tenants. Ibid., 281–84, 326–47. See also Crossan, who argues that the synoptic versions of the parable are "strained" allegories. Gospel of Thomas 65, on the other hand, does not include the allusions to Isa 5:1–7 at the start and end of the parable. Also, only two single servants are sent, and nobody is killed before the murder of the son. In Gos. Thom. 65 there is also no reference to the son being thrown "outside the vineyard," and there is no concluding question and answer. "From all this it is clear that there is no overt allegory *within* the story in this version." Crossan, *In Parables*, 86; italics original. These differences, Crossan argues, makes it clear that "this story is quite independent from the version found in the synoptic tradition." Ibid., 92. See also Hedrick, *Many Things in Parables*, 15.

42. See Appendix I, and Index to Appendix I in Kloppenborg, *Tenants in the Vineyard*, 355–583.

43. Literary and archeological evidence (beginning in the First Temple period and continuing through the Hellenistic and Roman periods) indicates a general tendency toward the creation of large estates. Free smallholders farming with grain, olives and grapes aimed at local consumption were displaced by larger estates concentrating on monoculture dedicated to the production export crops. The effect of this tendency was severe on the structure and nature of labor, especially in the case of viticulture which was the most labor-intensive of ancient agricultural pursuits. It created and exploited a class of underemployed nonslave laborers, forced smallholders off their productive land to marginal land, and drew on the labor inputs from underemployed nonslave labor

absenteeism,[44] conflict,[45] and the sending of a son[46] reflects a realistic picture

---

and smallholders at certain key periods (e.g., cropping). Viticulture needed substantial capitalization, was uncertain and risky (a vineyard took four to five years to come into full production), and was normally associated with wealth and the wealthy. Textual evidence indicates that vineyard owners normally came from the population sector just below the class of civic and political elite (the upper-class cavalry, soldiers, officers and administrators). Although risky and uncertain, viticulture was highly profitable, part of which had to do with the increasing demand for wine, especially in the early imperial period. The tenants of vineyards normally were either villagers working the property of an absentee landlord or smallholders who could not live off their own land and had to assume a tenancy in order to support their families. Tenants of vineyards mostly were skilled vinedressers. Ibid., 284–309.

44. Absenteeism went hand in hand with the shift from freehold polycropping or small-scale viticulture to larger-scale viticulture, thus from peasant farmers to wealthier entrepreneurs. The latter class of landowners despised hand labor, had neither the inclination nor the expertise to work their land, and therefore turned to either slave-run estates or tenancies to skilled vinedressers. Given the nature of viticulture, it was more the rule than the exception for an owner not to be present on his property. Ibid., 314–16.

45. Conflict was part of ancient viticulture, more than in other agricultural sectors, since the stakes were high. Literature evidence indicates that several factors, some peculiar to viticulture, accounted for this conflict; the level of rents, poor harvests, rental structures typical of viticulture (where the tenant normally retained one-third of the harvest), the substantial cost of occasional labor, the cost of repairs to iron tools and vineyard equipment, care for traction animals, fertilizer, guards and cartage—all this led to chronic indebtedness and tenants hovering at the level of subsistence. Potential for conflict was especially high during harvest time because the interests of landlords and tenants with regard to the crop sometimes clashed. The owner, for example, driven by the high profitability of viticulture and export demands for quality wine might have the interest to harvest the grapes early in order to maximize the quality of the wine, while the tenants' interests were to harvest the grapes later in order to secure a larger volume of wine, although with less quality. It was therefore in the landlord's interest to be present during harvest time, and the tenants' interest not to have the landlord or his agents present. From the landlord's point of view, harvest time was when tenants concealed some of the harvest. From the tenants' perspective, harvest time was when the crop could be pilfered by thieves or seized outright by the landowner (in the case of indebted tenants); further, neighbors or enemies of the landowner might prevent the tenants from entering the vineyard (wanting to seize the vineyard with a chance to appropriate the revenue of the harvest). A present landowner could also underestimate the crop, thus curtailing the tenants' revenue in terms of crop sharing. The structures of leasing in principle made way for conflicting interests: owners wished to maximize their profit and maintain stable production with minimum input of expense; and tenants required a stable income, security for the crop, and freedom from various forms of interference. Ibid., 316–22.

46. Literature evidence indicates that conflict between landlords and tenants normally was handled by correspondence or agents, since landlords tried to avoid direct intervention. In cases where a dispute was protracted and where tenants ignored the owner's deputies, the strategy was to send representatives of increasing social status. The sending of a son, from a landlord's point of view, was seen as a social trump card, a

of economic, social, and legal aspects of the Mediterranean during the early Roman period and especially of viticultural practices in Jewish Palestine.

> The wealth of the landowner is completely in keeping with Mediterranean economic patterns during the early Roman period; absenteeism seems to have been the norm rather the exception when it came to viticulture; conflicts between tenants and landlords was usual and, in the case of viticulture, fuelled by the high stakes for both landlord and tenants; and conflict resolution typically involved a graduated scale in which forms of social power were applied.[47]

Read from this perspective, the Tenants is a realistic story that "invoke certain 'normal' aspects of life in Jewish Palestine," "the middling rich and their pursuit of wealth, the prevalence of absenteeism, and ubiquitous resorts to status displays," and then that "challenge[s] the values underlying these 'normalcies' by means of the clever turn of its narrative."[48]

What are the "normal" sociocultural aspects and social values evoked by the parable that Jesus challenges? To this we now turn.

Reading Scenarios

An etic reading of the parable in Gos. Thom. 65 (from an outsider's point of view) gives us a story about a vineyard owner, tenants, and the owner's collection of his share of the crop. In an effort to collect his share of the crop, the owner first sends one of his slaves, and after he is beaten by the tenants, a second slave. When the second slave is also beaten, he decides to send his son, thinking that the tenants will show him some respect at least. This decision by the owner does not have a happy result; no respect is shown, and his son is killed.

An emic reading of the parable (from a native's point of view) evokes several cultural norms (social values) of the first-century Mediterranean world that are implicitly embedded in the parable. As Kloppenborg has indicated, the parable assumes large-scale landholding and tenancy, absenteeism, conflict, and the sending of a son as a form of social power and appeal to the differences in social status between tenants and owner. Therefore, the parable assumes a patron-client relationship between owner and tenants, as

form of social power—the owner's appeal to the differences in social status between the tenants and the owner. Ibid., 322–25.

47. Ibid., 325–26.

48. Ibid., 349.

well as the pivotal value of honor. Patron-client relations in the first-century Mediterranean world were closely linked with the pivotal value of honor. The actions of the tenants, the beating the first two slaves and killing the owner's son, thus represent a challenge to the owner's honor and status.

The social-scientific model of patronage and clientism is used to understand and explain a range of apparent different social relationships such as owner-slave or landlord-tenant.[49] Moxnes describes patron-client relationships as follows:

> Patron-client relations are social relationships between individuals based on a strong element of inequality and difference in power. The basic structure of the relationship is an exchange of different and very unequal resources. A patron has social, economic and political resources that are needed by a client. In return, a client can give expression of loyalty and honor that are useful for the patron.[50]

As I mentioned earlier, the aspects salient to the characteristics of patron-client relationships are the simultaneous exchange of different types of resources, a strong element of solidarity linked to obligations, a binding and long-range relationship, and a strong element of inequality and difference in status.[51]

When these characteristics are applied to the parable of the Tenants in Gos. Thom. 65, it is clear that the parable has all the makings of the story of a patron-client relationship. In terms of *a strong element of inequality and difference in power and status*, the wealth and status of the landowner is implied by his designation as usurer,[52] a designation that locates the owner

49. Blok, "Variations in Patronage," 366.

50. Moxnes, "Patron-Client Relations," 242.

51. Eisenstadt and Roniger, *Patrons, Clients and Friends*, 48–49.

52. In following Dehandschutter, Patterson, and Sevrin, Kloppenborg restores the lacuna in the Coptic text with "usurer" or "creditor," and not with "good man," as proposed by Guillaumont and Layton, Valantasis, and Schoedel. See Kloppenborg, *Tenants in the Vineyard*, 250–57. Kloppenborg's choice is inter alia informed by his reading of Gos. Thom. 65 (and 66) in its Thomasine context. Gospel of Thomas 65 is part of a triad of parables in Thomas, consisting of Gos. Thom. 63–65. Gospel of Thomas 63 is a parable about a rich man's decision to invest in agriculture and his desire to achieve a secure life. His premature death, however, lampoons the confidence that he placed in his investments. In the second parable, Gos. Thom. 64 (Thomas' version of the parable of the Feast; Q 14:16–24), the interest of Thomas resides in its potential as a critique of commerce: commercial activities are an impediment to accepting a divine intervention. Ibid., 251. The context of Gos. Thom. 63–64 thus suggests strongly "usurer" rather than "good man." Usurers belonged to the social class of merchants and entrepreneurs situated just below the old aristocracy (civic and political elite). Ibid., 299, 303.

above the class of day laborers, vinedressers, and smallholders. He is part of a class who owns productive and large-scale land[53] and has sufficient capital to make loans and agricultural investments. Viticulture in the first century was associated with wealth and the wealthy, and required substantial capitalization.[54] Only the wealthy could afford to engage in medium- or large-scale viticulture.[55] The fact that the owner in Gos. Thom. 65 also owns (multiple) slaves reiterates this conclusion. Above all, more clients meant more honor. The tenants in Gos. Thom. 65, on the other hand, are most probably smallholders producing the Mediterranean triad of grain, grapes, and olives for subsistence.[56] Some of the tenants maybe had vineyards of their own, most probably occupying more marginal land as indicated earlier in the reading of the Sower. However, since most smallholders could not live off their own land, they assumed tenancy to support their families. The possibility also exists that the tenants in Gos. Thom. 65 were landless, having lost their land through debt, usurpation or by the occupation of a more powerful party.[57] A strong element of inequality and difference in power and status between landowner and tenants can therefore be assumed in Gos. Thom. 65: the landowner is a usurer, is wealthy, and is of high social status. The tenants, on the other hand, are poor, living at the level of subsistence. If they are landless, they would have had no social status at all.

In terms of describing the *simultaneous exchange of different types of (unequal) resources*, Gos. Thom. 65 also assumes a patron-client relationship. The benefits of tenancy for the owner lie first and foremost in the elite's contempt for productive and manual labor;[58] as an absentee landlord, he contributed no productive or manual labor; at the most his role was one of indirect supervision of the vineyard. By leasing his vineyard to vinedressers (whose skills an owner probably did not possess), the landlord could obtain from one-half to two-thirds of the crop. If the rent was paid in cropshare, the landowner was also reasonably assured of a constant income. Skilled

53. Regarding land, wealth and the elite, Carter, in following Lenski and Lenski, makes the following comment: "The Roman Empire was . . . an agrarian empire. Its wealth and power was based in land. The elite did not rule by democratic elections. In part they ruled by hereditary control of the empire's primary resources of land and labor. They owned its land and consumed some 65 percent of its production." Carter, *Roman Empire*, 3.

54. Kloppenborg, *Tenants in the Vineyard*, 295.

55. Ibid., 287–88.

56. Ibid., 284.

57. See Ibid., 39; Horsley, *Jesus and Empire*, 93–95; Carter, *Roman Empire*, 8–14; Herzog, *Prophet and Teacher*, 43–56.

58. Carter, *Roman Empire*, 9.

vinedressers as tenants therefore had a lot of resources to offer that the owner needed for successful viticulture. Moreover, when tenants found themselves in arrears with regard to the payment of rent, their indebtedness created a situation of social obligation that landlords could exploit. The tenants, on the other hand, also benefited in various ways as the lessees. Given that peasnat farmers were unable to provide for their families or to own small holdings, tenancy provided a way out of living at the level of subsistence. Tenancy also offered potential access to the landlord's network of contacts and influence; the protection from other creditors; access to the official elite who controlled resources such as irrigation, draft animals, woodlots, and reed beds for vine stakes or fertilizer; and access to other inputs such as loans.[59]

Finally, in terms of *a patron-client connection resting on a binding and long-range relationship*, Gos. Thom. 65:1 explicitly states that the usurer rented his vineyard to farmers. The owner of a producing vineyard most probably would have looked at a long-term lease, thereby ensuring a steady relationship with his tenants as well as a consistent and quality crop. It is thus reasonable to assume that a lease of tenancy existed between owner and farmers, including a strong element of solidarity linked to obligations— all characteristic of a patron-client relationship.

Gospel of Thomas 65 is a product of a high-context society,[60] a society wherein "people have been socialized into widely shared ways of perceiving and acting."[61] In high-context societies few things are spelled out, because few things have to be spelled out. Because of this, the fact that Gos. Thom. 65 assumes a patron-client relationship is "mystified."[62] When the parable, however, is "demystified" by means of the above social-scientific model of patronage and clientism, readers become aware of the intense inequality and difference in social status and power between usurer and tenant, the potential conflict embedded in this relationship, as well as honor, the pivotal value in the first-century Mediterranean world, that is at stake.

As I indicated earlier, in the first-century Mediterranean world patron-client relations were closely linked with the pivotal value of honor.[63]

---

59. See Kloppenborg, *Tenants in the Vineyard*, 307.

60. Malina, "Social-Scientific Models," 5.

61. Malina, "Reading Theory Perspective," 20.

62. "High context societies produce sketchy and impressionistic documents, leaving much to the reader's or hearer's imagination and common knowledge. Since people living in these societies believe that few things have to be spelled out, few things in fact are spelled out . . . [T]he typical communication problem in high context societies is not giving people enough information, thus '*mystifying*' them." Ibid.; italics added.

63. For a description of the social-scientific model of honor and shame (and more

Honor is the positive value of a person in his own eyes as well as the positive appreciation of that person in the eyes of others (i.e., claim and acknowledgement). Honor is thus linked to "saving face" and "respect" and indicates a person's social standing and status.[64] Honor can either be ascribed or acquired. Ascribed honor happens passively through kinship or endowment by notable persons of power (e.g., a client king, a procurator, or aristocrat). Acquired honor, on the other hand, is the socially recognized claim to worth obtained by someone through achievements.[65]

Honor, as a limited good in the first-century Mediterranean world, was particularly acquired by means of the social interaction of challenge and riposte. Challenge and riposte, as social interaction within the context of honor, has at least three or four phases: (1) a challenge (in word, deed, or both) from the challenger, (2) a perception of the challenge by the challenged one and by the public as a challenge to honor, (3) a response to the challenge by the one challenged, and (4) a public evaluation of this response.[66]

In a reading of the Tenants in Gos. Thom. 65, below, from the perspective of the above social-scientific model of honor and shame (and the social

specific aspects thereof), see inter alia Bechtel, "Shame as Sanction of Control," 47–76; Douglas, *Purity and Danger*; Malina, "Limited Good," 162–67; Malina, "Individual and the Community," 62–76; Malina, *New Testament World*; Malina, *Christian Origins and Cultural Anthropology*; Malina, "Conflict Approach to Mark 7," 3–30; Malina, *Social World of Jesus*; Malina and Neyrey, "Honor and Shame in Luke-Acts," 25–65; Malina and Neyrey, *Portraits of Paul*; Malina and Rohrbaugh, *Social-Science Commentary on the Synoptic Gospels*, 369–72; Moxnes, "Honor and Righteousness in Romans," 61–77; Moxnes, "Patron-Client Relations"; Moxnes, "Quest for Honor," 202–30; Moxnes, "Honor and Shame," 19–40; Neyrey, *Honor and Shame*; Neyrey, *Render to God*; Pitt-Rivers, *Fate of Shechem*; Van Eck, *Galilee and Jerusalem in Mark's Story of Jesus*, 165–69.

64. In the first-century Mediterranean world family and citizenship determined a person's status, that is, whether someone belonged to the upper class or not. Moreover, wealth did not automatically mean status. Status, however, could help one accumulate wealth and power. Status and power thus were more important than wealth. Wealth and power were unequally distributed and mostly in the hands of the elite, and social classes were organized in strict hierarchical order. Because of this strict hierarchical order, honor and status were considered limited goods. In the first-century Mediterranean world things of value were available on limited scale, especially honor, as a pivotal value of this world. Since the elite made up only a small percentage of first-century Mediterranean society, few people had the privilege of enough status, either being born into nobility or acquiring honor. Honor therefore was a *limited good*. People therefore competed fiercely against one another for honor, giving expression to the first-century Mediterranean world as an agonistic (strongly competitive) society. Malina, "Limited Good," 162–67.

65. Malina and Neyrey, "Honor and Shame in Luke-Acts," 25–46; Malina and Rohrbaugh, *Social-Science Commentary on the Synoptic Gospels*, 369–72; Neyrey, *Render to God*, 261.

66. Malina and Neyrey, "Honor and Shame in Luke-Acts," 29–30.

interaction of challenge and riposte) at least three assumptions are made. First, the honor (and status) of the vineyard owner is most probably both ascribed and acquired. Ascribed honor, as I indicated above, happens passively through kinship or by endowment from notable persons of power.[67] Papyri used by Kloppenborg in his study of the Tenants confirm that many landowners acquired large portions of land by virtue of kinship or endowment from powerful people.[68] In terms of acquired status, the acquiring of land led not only to wealth but also to the possibility of the more land acquisition, which in turn led to the possibility of more patron-client relationships. Thus, by acquiring more (and more) land, more (and more) clients became indebted to the landowner, receiving accumulating expressions of loyalty and honor. One can therefore assume that the owner in the Tenants was an honorable man, that he had honor that had to be protected. Sending his son to the vineyard as status marker (Gos Thom. 65:6) underlines this social standing.[69]

Reading the Parable

The Tenants in Gos. Thom. 65 is a realistic narrative that depicts several aspects of viticulture life in first-century Palestine, including the middling rich and their pursuit of wealth; the prevalence of absenteeism; ubiquitous resorts to status displays; and discontent, tension, and conflict between absentee landlords and tenants. The Tenants in Gos. Thom. 65 challenges these normalcies through a clever turn of its narrative.[70]

67. First-century personality was perceived in a stereotyped way: individuals from a certain kinship group (e.g., Herodian), region (e.g., Alexandria) or craft or trade (Roman soldier, Roman appointees or leading men of the cities like councilors or administrators) received an automatic and specific honor rating. Malina and Neyrey, *Portraits of Paul*, 85–90.

68. For example, Apollonios (administrator of Ptolemy II Philadephos), Eirēnē (a Macedonian resident who received an estate as a beneficiary gift), and Aurelia Apollonides (an Alexandrian councilor named Gaius). Kloppenborg, *Tenants in the Vineyard*, 297–303. Fiensy, focusing on large estates in Palestine in the Herodian period, also indicates that that Herod and his retainers (soldiers, administrators and officers), as well as various individuals belonging to the Jewish aristocracy (including people from influential priestly families) owned large portions of land in Judea and Galilee. Fiensy, *Land Is Mine*, 21–60. Both Kloppenborg's and Fiensy's descriptions of large-estate landowners illustrate that the Roman Empire's elite ruled by *hereditary* control of the empire's primary resource—land—as well as through benefaction and endowment; therefore these landowners maintained high levels of social status and honor in society. See Carter, *Roman Empire*, 3.

69. Kloppenborg, *Tenants in the Vineyard*, 322–26.

70. Ibid., 325–26.

The owner of the vineyard is a usurer, most probably one of the nouveau riche or imperial freedmen with disposable cash.[71] By owning a vineyard and leasing it to farmers (Gos. Thom. 65:1), most probably in the form of a cropshare lease, the landowner puts his honor at stake in two ways: if his whole enterprise of acquiring and equipping a vineyard in the end turns out to be a failure, he would at least lose face within his peer group (e.g., the elite)[72]. Second, by leasing his vineyard to farmers, the landowner brings into existence a patron-client relationship, thereby risking the possibility that the farmer clients could become disloyal by not honoring their part of the rental agreement.

As I discussed earlier, one of the characteristics of patron-client relationships is a strong element of solidarity linked to obligations. If one assumes that in Gos. Thom. 65 a cropshare lease is operational, a realistic reading of the parable brings the following obligations of the tenants and the owner (in honoring the lease and the patron-client relationship) to the fore: The tenants, most probably including skilled vinedressers, had to look after the vineyard, ensuring, as far as possible, a successful crop. The tenants had to pay for guards, cartage, fertilizer, and the maintenance of iron tools; they had to pay for the press and waterwheel. The owner, on the other hand, had to carry the cost of irrigation and a waterwheel, reeds, vine shoots, stakes, taxes, and a reservoir. He also had to pay wages to the tenants in the case of a vineyard not fully developed yet (sometimes a token amount of wine was given in exchange for labor).[73]

The landlord's failure to pay wages or to advance payments for laborers and to meet other expenses meant, from the tenants' point of view, that the owner was not honoring his part of the contract, and that they were being exploited. Tenants also felt exploited when landowners underestimated the crop (thus curtailing their revenue from crop sharing), when landowners tried to maximize their profit, or when landowners tried to maintain stable production while incurring only minimal expenses. All these possible scenarios, especially in cases where the tenants—from their side—fulfilled all their obligations, meant conflict.

71. Ibid., 299–302. Given that starting up intensive viticulture required substantial capital and had to offer high wages to be successful, only the middling wealthy were able to pursue the business as vineyard owners. See Frankel, *Wine and Oil Production in Antiquity*, 141; Kloppenborg, *The Tenants in the Vineyard*, 302–303.

72. See Kloppenborg, quoting Nicholas Purcell: "[Viticulture is] an extremely uncertain and risky, almost marginal agricultural activity." Kloppenborg, *Tenants in the Vineyard*, 297.

73. Ibid., 560.

When the owner, most probably after four years into the leasing agreement, sends a slave to collect his part of the crop (Gos. Thom. 65:2), conflict arises. The slave is grabbed, beaten, and almost killed (Gos. Thom. 65:3a). No reason is given why the tenants act in this manner. Maybe it is because of the late payment or nonpayment of wages, or the nonreimbursement for needed occasional labor. Maybe the owner did not supply a sufficient irrigation system, did not erect a waterwheel or reservoir in time, or did not supply an efficient irrigation system. Or maybe the owner did not supply enough reeds, vine shoots, and stakes. It could even have been the case that the owner, driven by the high profitability of viticulture and export demands for quality wine, expected the tenants to harvest the grapes early in order to maximize the quality of the wine, while the tenants wanted to harvest the grapes later in order to secure a larger volume of wine. Or maybe the landowner underestimated the crop, and therefore wanted to collect more than his share.

Although it is impossible to know why the tenants violently grabbed and beat the slave, in an honor-shame culture, the actions of the tenants (riposte) was a challenge to the owner's honor. The landowner, in one way or another, did not keep his part of the deal, and so challenged the honor of the tenants. The tenants therefore, had to reciprocate. Their riposte is to grab the slave, beating him nearly to death, and so to challenge the honor of the owner. When the slave returns to the owner telling him what happened (Gos. Thom. 65:3b), the owner indeed perceives the actions of the tenants as a challenge of his honor, since "the agent of a person is like the person himself."[74]

How does the owner react to this challenge of his honor? First he tries to save face with his messenger-slave (and most probably with his other subordinates) by opining that if the tenants knew that the slave sent indeed was his, they would have reacted differently (Gos. Thom. 65:4).[75] By reacting this way to the treatment of his slave, the landlord likely recuperated his standing with the slave and his other subordinates. In trying to regain his honor with regard to his tenants, his riposte to their challenge is to send a second slave, most probably one who is well known to them (Gos. Thom. 65:5). Since the owner's honor was now seriously at stake, one can assume that he meticulously selected the second slave, making sure that this time no misunderstanding was possible—if there indeed had been a misunderstanding when the first slave arrived at his vineyard.

74. Ibid., 323.
75. "Perhaps he didn't know them." Translation from Funk et al., *Five Gospels*, 510.

This riposte of the owner, however, is answered by a second challenge by the farmers. What happened to the first slave is also the fate of the second (Gos. Thom. 65:5). Although the events are not narrated as they had been with the first slave, one can assume that the second slave also reported to the owner what happened. The owner's honor now really is at stake. Not only have the tenants again challenged the collection of the landlord's share, but the landlord also has he lost face with his slave (and his other subordinates)—especially after the owner's interpretation that there had actually been no problem except for the farmers' not recognizing the first slave as his legal representative.

The owner, now realizing what is at stake, decides to pull out all the stops. His riposte to the second challenge of the farmers is to send his son (Gos. Thom. 65:6). Why his son? Kloppenborg's realistic reading of the Tenants helps to answer this question. In cases where tenants ignored the owner's deputies (slaves), the normal strategy was to send agents of increasing social status.[76] In a sense, this had already happened when the vineyard owner sent his second slave—that is, a slave who other people (including the tenants) knew belong to him. However, since his first riposte does not work, the owner now decides to play his social trump card: by sending his son, the owner appeals to the difference between his social status and that of the tenants. Since it was customary for persons from the upper class to dress and speak in a way that exhibited social status and power, the owner's decision to send his son is not surprising: the vineyard owner's personal presence and personal power are now at play. Important to note is the owner's remark before sending his son (Gos. Thom. 65:6),[77] namely, that he actually acknowledges not only that his honor is at stake, but that he already has lost some honor since no respect was shown towards his first two slaves.

When the son arrives at his father's farm to collect the crop, the story takes an unexpected turn. What happens is exactly what the owner does not expect: the tenants kill his son (Gos. Thom. 65:7). From an honor-and-shame point of view, the story thus takes an ironic turn: exactly what the owner thought would solve his problem (a display of his social status) leads to his demise and the loss of status. By pulling out all the stops, he has lost everything—his vineyard, his status (land being one of the principal

76. In cases where tenants ignored the landlord's deputies, the normal strategy was to send agents (slaves in Gos. Thom. 65) of increasing status. Kloppenborg, *Tenants in the Vineyard*, 324–26. The strategy of sending representatives with increasing social status is well attested in papyri dating from 300 BCE to 300 CE (see, e.g., P.Cair. Zen. I 59015, P.Cair. Zen. I 59018 and P.Oxy. III 645). Ibid., 323–26.

77. "Perhaps they'll show my son some respect." Translation from Funk et al., *Five Gospels*, 510.

markers of status), his honor in the eyes of his subordinates, and now also his son (therefore also his ability to carry on his name).

How does the owner react when his son is killed? This is the twist or surprise in the Thomasine version of the parable. The owner does nothing! Lintott has indicated that in the Roman Empire possession normally was a function "of the ability to take, hold, and exploit land. Possession involved force." The possession of land, by force was seen by the aristocracy as a right. Moreover, "possessions which were originally acquired by force will therefore in the end have to be defended by force."[78] The owner of the vineyard, in Gos. Thom. 65, does not exercise this "right"; he does not use force (violence) to defend the ownership of the vineyard. And in doing so, he is the honorable person in the parable! Honor is gained by acting in precisely the opposite way that was regarded as normal. Status and honor are not retained or gained by using violence. The honorable person is the one who refrains from using violence; as was the case with the patron-king in the Unmerciful Servant parable. This is how patrons act who emulate the kingdom.

What happens to the farmers? The parable is silent on their fate. Can we conclude that they won the social game of challenge and riposte? Did they gain ownership of the vineyard by killing the son? Did their violent reaction to the owner's challenge protect their honor? In the end, they may have gained a vineyard, but was it in an honorable way? The parable is clearly open-ended. It is the hearers of the parable who have to decide who acted in a way that aligns with the values of the kingdom. In the kingdom, the use of status or violence to protect honor leads to nothing; refraining from violence, on the other hand, leads to honor. Anyone who have ears had better listen (Gos. Thom. 65:8).

A Parable of Jesus?

Jesus' stance on violence in the Tenants clearly concurs with Jesus' denouncement of violence in the parables of the Lost Sheep and the Unmerciful Servant. Violence does not lead to honor. On the contrary, what does bring honor is answering violence with mildness (Q 6:29). This is the shock and surprise of the Tenants, and of the Unmerciful Servant. That this most probably was Jesus' stance on violence (and honor) is attested by several other sayings of Jesus, such as Q 6:27 (love your enemies),[79] Q 6:29 (turn the

78. Lintott, *Violence in Republican Rome*, 30.

79. Mediterraneans were in-group persons, constantly counting their enemies (those not part of the in-group). This led to a situation of constant conflict that had

other cheek, and offer the shirt as well when asked for your cloak), and Q 6:30 (give to those who beg from you and do not ask anything back).

---

the ability to erupt into all kinds of violence. Theissen has argued convincingly that Jesus' reference to enemies in Matt 5:44, since it is formulated in the plural (ἀγαπᾶτε τοὺς ἐχθροὺς), did not refer to an enemy in village life but to an out-group. Theissen, "Political Dimension of Jesus' Activities," 233. Understood from this perspective, Q 6:27 (answering violence with prayer) concurs with Jesus' saying in Q 6:29 (answering violence with mildness). This differs markedly from Mark 12:1–12 and *par.* where Jesus condones the answering of violence with violence.

CHAPTER 9

The Merchant (Matt 13:45–46): An Outsider Becomes an Insider

THE HISTORY OF THE interpretation of the Merchant indicates that interpreters focus on the pearl in an effort to unravel the meaning of the parable. Here it is argued that when the parable is read against the social realia (cultural scripts) evoked by this short narrative, the focus of interpretation should be on the merchant and his actions, and not on the pearl. Literary evidence indicates a general trend of negative perception toward merchants and mercantilism in the Mediterranean world, spanning an era from the fourth century BCE up to the third century CE. When interpreting the parable, this perception of merchants, as well as the perception of limited good in first-century Palestine, should be taken into consideration. Read from this perspective, the parable is a surprising story about a dubious outsider who becomes an insider, someone who epitomizes the values of the kingdom.

History of Interpretation

The earliest interpretations of the parable of the Merchant[1] are the allegorical interpretations of the church fathers.[2] The more recent interpretations of the

1. The parable in Matt 13:45–46 is normally referred to as the parable of the Pearl. See, for example, Funk et al., *Red Letter Edition*, 46–47. Since the focus of the parable is not the pearl but rather the actions merchant, the parable will be referred to as the parable of the Merchant.

2. According to Origen, the valuable pearls refer to good humans, and the most valuable pearl to Jesus Christ. In Jerome's interpretation, the good pearls are people who do business with the Law and the Prophets, and the most valuable pearl found is a symbolic reference to Christianity (*Hom. Matth.* 10.8–10). Jerome also equates the pearl found by the merchant with the word of God (*Epist. X.3*) or spiritual food (*Epist.*

parable are almost unanimous, identifying discipleship and commitment to the kingdom as the core meaning of the parable. In these interpretations the valuable pearl found by the merchant is seen as a metaphoric reference to the kingdom, the merchant is metaphorically interpreted as referring to the disciples (or hearers of the parable), and the selling of everything is understood as the willingness to give up everything to participate in the kingdom.[3] A few scholars, reading the parable in sequence with its "twin," the parable of the Treasure (Matt 13:44), see the joy of attaining the kingdom as its main point.[4]

The only real point of contention in the interpretation of the parable is the investment made by the merchant to obtain the pearl (πέπρακεν πάντα ὅσα; Matt 13:46), which leaves him owning nothing but the pearl. Most scholars see the merchant's act as hyperbolic and not relevant to the meaning of the parable. Snodgrass, for example, argues that the hyperbole underscores "that the kingdom cannot be fitted into some previously existing system"; for Hultgren the purpose of the hyperbole is to highlight the

---

XV.1). Irenaeus (*Haer.* 4.26.1) sees the pearl as referring to Christ, and for Chrysostom (*Hom. Matt.* XLVII.20) the pearl is a reference to the gospel. In Cyprian's reading the pearl stands for heaven (*Treatise* 8.7), and the selling of everything as giving to the poor (*Treatise* 12.3.1). In other readings by the church fathers, the pearl is identified as love or the church, the merchant is seen as a reference to Christ, while the idea of selling it all is seen as abandoning old sinful practice. See Wailes, *Medieval Allegories*, 120–24. An allegorical reading of the parable is also present in more recent interpretations of the parable. Trench sees Christ in the merchant, and for Glombitza the merchant represents God who seeks people, and who has given all for them. Trench, *Notes on the Parables*, 137; Glombitza, "Der Perlenkaufmann," 158–59. Pentecost also identifies the merchant with Christ and sees in the pearl the Gentiles. Pentecost, *Parables of Jesus*, 60–61. Capon, finally, sees in the merchant the unevangelized world, and the owner of the valuable pearl as the church who must be willing to sell the pearl to the world. Capon, *Parables of the Kingdom*, 143–44.

3. See, for example, Snodgrass, *Stories with Intent*, 252; Hultgren, *Parables of Jesus*, 419; Fiensy, *Jesus the Galilean*, 118; Blomberg, *Interpreting the Parables*, 381; Ball, *Radical Stories of Jesus*, 32; Cowan, *Economic Parables*, 136; Young, *Parables*, 199; Smith, *Parables of the Synoptic Gospels*, 146; Linnemann, *Parables of Jesus*, 199–200; Dodd, *Parables of the Kingdom*, 85–86; Jones, *Matthean Parables*, 352; Donahue, *Gospel in Parable*, 68; Hunter, *Interpreting the Parables*, 65; Hagner, *Matthew 14–28*, 117; Buttrick, *Parables of Jesus*, 27; Oesterley, *Gospel Parables*, 84; Stern, *Rabbi Looks at Jesus' Parables*, 61; Stein, *Introduction to the Parables*, 81. Although these scholars are almost unanimous with regard to the overall meaning of the parable, different aspects of the parable are emphasized: Some, such as Donahue, Snodgrass, Hultgren, Fiensy, Blomberg, Young, Oesterley, Stern, Stein, Smith, Dodd, Jones, and Hagner, highlight the radical obedience that is required to participate in the kingdom. Ball, Linnemann, and Buttrick emphasize the availability, surpassing worth and presence of the kingdom, while Cowan emphasizes the invitation of Jesus to search for the kingdom.

4. Jeremias, *Parables of Jesus*, 200; Fisher, *Parables of Jesus*, 71; Armstrong, *Gospel Parables*, 156.

way the merchant searches; Hagner interprets the hyperbole as a reference to commitment.[5]

For some scholars, however, the action of the merchant is not hyperbolic and is relevant to the meaning of the parable. According to Scott's interpretation, the total investment required to acquire the pearl relativizes its value. The merchant will have to sell the pearl, or else he will be broke. The pearl only generates value in being sold. "The thing of value, the pearl, has no ultimate value." This, Scott argues, indicates that the kingdom "cannot be possessed as a value in itself." The merchant will have to sell the pearl. "And that is the kingdom's corrupting power—the desire to possess it."[6]

For Miller, the parable begins where it ends. The parable ends with the merchant left owning nothing but the pearl; he has nothing left with which to make a living or support his family. What seems to be a happy ending is actually a no-win situation.[7] Therefore the parable characterizes the merchant as a fool "in the sense that the term 'fool' has in the Jewish wisdom tradition."[8] In this tradition the essence of wisdom is living with the long run in mind; a fool is someone "whose short-sightedness and immature judgement makes him vulnerable to disasters that the wise know how to avoid. Fools are a danger to themselves and to others, not because they are malicious, but because they are foolish."[9] From this perspective, Miller argues, the parable is autobiographical. Jesus sees himself (and his followers) as the merchant. Like the merchant, Jesus was single-minded in his campaign on behalf of the kingdom, driven by his passion. He campaigned for the kingdom as if there was no tomorrow. This made him and his followers vulnerable; it made them foolish. But not in the kingdom. The kingdom blinds people by its beauty and goodness. It is because of the kingdom that they are willing to be foolish and "unwilling to envision a future for themselves in which they are not committed to it. They cannot respond otherwise."[10] The parable, Miller thus argues, is counterwisdom.

---

5. Snodgrass, *Stories with Intent*, 252; Hultgren, *Parables of Jesus*, 421; Hagner, *Matthew 14–28*, 117. To interpret the act of the merchant as hyperbolic, seems to be the dominant interpretation. See Montefiore, *Synoptic Gospels*, 644; Smith, *Parables of the Synoptic Gospels*, 146; Oesterley, *Gospel Parables*, 84; Dodd, *Parables of the Kingdom*, 86; Linnemann, *Parables of Jesus*, 101; Stein, *Introduction to the Parables*, 103; Gundry, *Matthew*, 173.

6. Scott, *Hear Then the Parable*, 319.

7. Miller, "Pearl," 65–82.

8. Ibid., 67.

9. Ibid., 69.

10. Ibid., 82.

According to Levine, commentators cannot conclude what the pearl represents because perhaps they are looking in the wrong place. The parable, she argues, challenges us to determine our own pearl of great price, our ultimate concern, which sometimes is just as absurd and unfulfilling as selling everything and in the end being left with only a pearl. If we know what this is, we would be less acquisitive, and "better able to love our neighbours, because we will know what is most important to them."[11] Therefore, the parable tells us what we already know to be true but do not want to acknowledge.

Levine is correct in her opinion that interpreters cannot conclude what the parable represents because they are looking in the wrong place. In all the interpretations of the parable, as the history of its interpretation shows, the focus is the pearl. The focus of the parable, as we will see below, when read against the social realia (cultural scripts) evoked by this short narrative, should rather be the merchant and his actions. The role the pearl plays in the parable should not be overemphasized. The pearl is not a metaphorical reference to the kingdom. Its value, however, is important. Read from this perspective, the parable is indeed about corruption, but not in the sense understood by Scott. As in the case of the shepherd in the Lost Sheep, the host in the Feast, the owner in the Vineyard Laborers, and the patron-king in the Unmerciful Servant, the parable is an surprising story about outsiders who unexpectedly act in a way conformant with the kingdom and its values. Using a merchant in a story about the kingdom of God would have shocked those who listened to the parable.

Integrity and Authenticity

Two versions of the parable are documented, namely, Matt 13:45–46 and the Gos. Thom. 76.1–3.[12] Scholars in most cases see the Thomasine version as secondary because of its gnostic tendencies. Snodgrass, for example, sees the pearl in the Thomasine version as referring to "the inner self,"[13] Hultgren is of the opinion that the pearl refers to "the divine spark within the self,"[14]

---

11. Levine, "Teachings from Jesus."

12. The Father's imperial rule is like a merchant who had a supply of merchandise and then found a pearl. The merchant was prudent; he sold the merchandise and bought the single pearl for himself. "So also with you, seek his treasure that is unfailing, that is enduring, where no moth comes to eat and no worm destroys" (Gos. Thom. 67:1–3). Translation from Funk et al., *Five Gospels*, 515.

13. Snodgrass, *Stories with Intent*, 250.

14. Hultgren, *Parables of Jesus*, 418.

and Scott sees the pearl as "a symbol for Christ or the soul," linking *Gos. Thom.* 76 to the hymn of the pearl in the *Acts of Thomas* 113:104–5.[15]

Recently Patterson, Bethge, and Robinson have argued convincingly that the Gospel of Thomas is not gnostic.[16] They date the Gospel of Thomas in the last decades of the first century and place the sayings collection in the Gospel of Thomas within the well-used genre of ancient literature known as *logoi sophon* (sayings of the wise).[17] Rather than being gnostic, the Gospel of Thomas is one of the earlier attempts to read the Jesus tradition through the lens of Middle Platonism.[18] The editing of the Merchant parable in the Gospel of Thomas therefore is not a gnosticizing of the parable but rather an editorial reworking of the parable to accommodate a disapproval of mercantilism, as is the case in the *Gos. Thom.* 64:2.[19] This the Gospel of Thomas has done in several ways: The merchant is described as being prudent (*Gos. Thom.* 76:6). Because he is prudent, he does not sell all his belongings as in Matt 13:46. The merchant in the Gospel of Thomas also does not find a pearl of great value (πολύτιμον μαργαρίτην; Matt 13:46), but simply a pearl.[20] Finally, the Gospel of Thomas adds 76:3 to highlight disapproval of mercantilism. Rather than looking for something that is failing (like a pearl), the hearers/readers of the saying in *Gos. Thom.* 76 are called upon to look for something unfailing.[21]

15. Scott, *Hear Then the Parable*, 317. See also Young, *Parables*, 203; Jones, *Matthean Parables*, 353.

16. Patterson et al., *Fifth Gospel*, 33–38.

17. Ibid., 41.

18. Ibid., 47.

19. Funk et al., *Five Gospels*, 515.

20. Scott notes that Matthew's description of the pearl as πολύτιμον μαργαρίτην (Matt 13:46) is peculiar since it fits "a gnostic ideology at least as well as and probably better than Thomas' pearl." Scott, *Hear Then the Parable*, 317, n. 62. When the parable is read with the perspective that the Gospel of Thomas is not gnostic, and given that in the *Gos. Thom.* 76 the author disapproves of mercantilism, this difference between the wording in Thomas and Matthew is not puzzling.

21. Contra Snodgrass, who interprets *Gos. Thom.* 76:3 as a Thomasine addition, linking its version of the Merchant to the parable of the Treasure. Snodgrass, *Stories with Intent*, 250. Snodgrass, like several other parable scholars, reads the parable of the Merchant in light of the Treasure (or vice versa), because Matthew transmitted them together. Since the Gospel of Thomas has transmitted these two parables separately—the Treasure is transmitted by the Gospel of Thomas as saying 109—these two parables should not necessarily be read in light of being "twins." Here the two parables are treated as independent from one another. See also Bultmann and Jeremias, who are of the opinion that the two parables were transmitted to Matthew independent of one another. Bultmann, *Synoptic Tradition*, 173; Jeremias, *Parables of Jesus*, 90–91.

The question of whether the two extant versions of the parable stem from the same tradition[22] or from different traditions[23] is difficult to answer. While some scholars are of the opinion that the Thomasine version represents the original parable,[24] others argue that the Thomasine version is derived from Matthew.[25] Others, again, see the parable as stemming from Jesus,[26] while some argue that the parable is a Matthean creation.[27]

Although it is impossible to reconstruct with certainty the originating story Matthew and Thomas used for their respective versions, Hedrick and Breech have made interesting and useful suggestions in this regard. According to Hedrick, the structure of the parable in the two extant versions, excluding the redactional additions in both, is virtually identical. This identical structure, Hedrick argues, most probably consisted of the following sequence: The kingdom is like a merchant who found a pearl, who then went and sold and bought.[28]

Breech's suggestion for the possible originating structure of the parable concurs with that of Hedrick.[29] According to Breech, Matthew wanted to compare the kingdom with a treasure and a pearl, and so redacted the versions of the two parables received from the tradition to fit his purpose. Matthew, however, in the case of the Merchant, was not thorough enough in his editorial work. The original wording of the parable can be discerned behind his version in the expression "the kingdom is like a merchant who . . ." That the Treasure and the Merchant originally were worded in this way is confirmed when the Matthean versions are compared with the Gospel

22. See, for example, Scott, Jeremias, Breech, Montefiore, and Funk, who argue that both versions stem from the same tradition and that both versions are a modification of an original version. Scott, *Re-Imagine the World*, 318; Jeremias, *Parables of Jesus*, 24; Breech, *Silence of Jesus*, 75; Montefiore, "Comparison of the Parables of Thomas and the Synoptic Gospels," 66–67; Funk et al., *Red Letter Edition*, 46.

23. Stein, *Introduction to the Parables*, 99.

24. Scott, *Re-Imagine the World*, 318; Hedrick, *Many Things in Parables*, 129.

25. For this point of view, see Snodgrass, *Parable of the Wicked Tenants*, 250; Davies and Allison, *Matthew*, 3:440; Luz, *Mt 8–17*, 2:275; Weder, *Die Gleichnisse Jesu Als Metaphern*, 139; Hultgren, *Parables of Jesus*, 417–18.

26. See Jeremias, *Parables of Jesus*, 198; Bultmann, *Synoptic Tradition*, 173; Hultgren, *Parables of Jesus*, 421; Jones, *Matthean Parables*, 352; Luz, *Mt 8–17*, 2:350; Dodd, *Parables of the Kingdom*, 85–87; Funk et al., *Five Gospels*, 196. These scholars also argue that the Matthean version is the closest to the original. Scott and Hedrick are also of the opinion that the parable goes back to Jesus, but they argue for the Thomasine version as closest to the original parable. See Scott, *Hear Then the Parable*, 318; Hedrick, *Many Things in Parables*, 117.

27. See Gundry, *Matthew*, 275–77.

28. Hedrick, *Many Things in Parables*, 127–29.

29. Breech, *Silence of Jesus*, 74–76.

of Thomas versions, which respectively read "the kingdom is like a man" and "the kingdom is like a merchant."[30] In short, Breech argues that the two parables initially were not about a treasure and a pearl, but about a man and a merchant; "originally these parables were *about specific men,* not about what they found, which is, in the view of the early Christian teacher, the kingdom."[31]

Although Hedrick's and Breech's reconstructions of the 'original' parable are hypothetical, they do make an important point. The parable in Matt 13:45–46 initially was not a parable about a pearl but a parable about a merchant; a story that challenged its hearers, who because of a feeling of superiority "regularize the everyday by imposing their normalizing patterns on reality."[32] Put differently, the parable depicts the kingdom as a new and different reality.

Reading Scenarios

Merchants and Limited Good

Because most scholars focus on the pearl in their interpretations of this parable, it is not surprising that the merchant, the main character in the parable, has not received much attention. The little attention the merchant has received are a few remarks about the kind of merchant depicted in the parable, as well as about the merchant's social status. Jeremias describes the merchant as a "wholesale trader, a big businessman" (ἔμπορος) in contrast with a shopkeeper (κάπηλος).[33] For Jeremias, however, it is more important that the merchant is a dealer in pearls, which makes the merchant "a secondary feature" in the parable. Hultgren makes the same distinction between merchants and shopkeepers, quoting Plato's *Republic* 2.371D as evidence.[34] With regards to the merchant's social status, Scott depicts the merchant as

---

30. Ibid., 75.

31. Ibid.; italics original.

32. Ibid.

33. Jeremias, *Parables of Jesus,* 199.

34. "Or is not shopkeepers (οὐ καπήλους) the name we give to those who, planted in the agora, serve us in buying and selling, while we call those who roam from city to city merchants (ἐμπόρους)." Hultgren, *Parables of Jesus,* 419. Evidence from documented papyri supports Plato's distinction between merchant and shopkeeper. See, for example, P.Oxy. 1 36; P.Oxy. 10 1253. See also Philo in *De opificio mundi* 147.6 and *De Iosepho* 15.1.

an upper-class character, and Miller describes the merchant as belonging to a class higher than the hearers of the parable.[35]

The above description of the merchant identifies what can be termed as "'that' or 'what' information," but gives us "less insight into the questions concerning 'how,' 'why,' and 'what for.'"[36] Elliott continues:

> In addition to details about specific individuals . . . what might be known about how ancient societies was organized and operated? How were attitudes, expectations, values, and beliefs shaped by the . . . social environment? How did *shared social and cultural knowledge provide the basis for shared meaning and communication?*[37]

What Elliott argues is that it is not enough to identify the merchant as a wholesale trader and someone belonging to a class higher than the hearers of the parable. More important to ask is what the hearers' beliefs (perceptions shaped by their cultural environment) were when it came to merchants, and how these beliefs influenced their attitude towards merchants. Put differently: What were the hearers' beliefs about and attitudes toward merchants drawn from their common experience? And in what way did this common experience influence their reception of the parable? Using such experience as the source of the scenario in the parable, Malina and Rohrbaugh note, "is significant since authors in high-context societies . . . presumed common knowledge between themselves and their audiences. Jesus seems able to depend on that since explanations are not provided."[38] Or, as Miller phrased it, "The parables clearly require some context. For Jesus and the audience

35. Scott, *Hear Then the Parable*, 316; Miller, "Pearl," 66.

36. Elliott, *Social-Scientific Criticism*, 12.

37. Ibid., 12–13. Emphasis added.

38. Malina and Rohrbaugh, *Social-Science Commentary on the Synoptic Gospels*, 78. The importance of this aspect for the interpretation of ancient texts deserves the following lengthy quote from Malina and Rohrbaugh: "The New Testament was written in what anthropologists call a 'high-context' society. People who communicate with each other in high-context societies presume a broadly shared, well-understood knowledge of the context of anything referred to in conversation or in writing . . . Thus writers in such societies usually produce sketchy and impressionistic writings, leaving much to the reader's or hearer's imagination . . . In this way, they require the reader to fill in large gaps in the unwritten portion of the writing. All readers are expected to know the context and therefore to understand the references in question. In this way, the Bible, like most documents written in the high-context Mediterranean world, presumes readers to have broad and adequate knowledge of its social context. It offers little by way of explanation." Ibid., 11.

to which he pitched the parables, the context was their lived situation: what they brought to the telling and hearing of these oral stories."[39]

What were the beliefs about merchants in the social context in which Jesus told the parable? And what was the common attitude toward someone that was a merchant (wholesale trader)? In other words, what was the shared social and cultural knowledge of the hearers of the parable that provided the basis for shared meaning and communication that Jesus depended on when he told the parable?

Snodgrass, when discussing the merchant as one looking for pearls, in a passing comment that some "in the world had little respect for merchants," citing Sir 26:29 as evidence.[40] The only other reading of the parable that remarks on the perception people may have had of merchants is that of Hultgren; he states that although "some Roman writers looked down upon them as a class, merchants were generally held in high regard among Jews. Yet even in Jewish tradition it could be said that a 'merchant [LXX, ἔμπορος] can hardly keep from wrongdoing'" (also citing Sir 26:29).[41]

Sirach (c. 190–170 BCE) in fact, makes several negative remarks about merchants. In Sir 37:7–11, where he gives advice regarding those who cannot be trusted to give fair advice, he mentions merchants along with persons who only counsel for their own benefit and are envious, cowards, buyers and sellers, the unmerciful and lazy, and idle persons. Also, in Sir 41:17—42:5, in a list of things one should be ashamed of, he lists the indifferent selling of merchants (Sir 42:5) along with whoring, unjust dealings, gazing at someone else's wife, upbraiding speeches before friends, and theft.

Sirach's negative perception of merchants is especially echoed in the writings of Philo (25 BCE—50 CE). Philo, a Jewish Hellenistic writer and contemporary of Jesus, describes merchants, and those who do business, as impure and foolish, equating them with Balaam, the symbol of a vain people, a runaway and a deserter.[42] The life of a merchant, or commerce,

---

39. Miller, "Pearl," 75.

40. Snodgrass, *Stories with Intent*, 251.

41. Hultgren, *Parables of Jesus*, 419. As evidence, Hultgren refers to Jeremias, *Jerusalem in the Time of Jesus*, 31, 49. The evidence cited by Jeremias are references to traders in *t. Terumot* X.9 and y. *Peah* I.6, and y. *Peah* 16c.53, where mention is made of a priest's shop. He also cites *t. Betzah* III.8 and 205, which refers to two scholars who were merchants in Jerusalem all their life. Finally, Deutero-Zechariah 14.21 is cited as evidence for traders in the temple's sanctuary. Clearly, these references do not refer to roaming wholesale traders but to localized shopkeepers or localized places of trading/selling. It is most probably because of this "positive" evidence that Hultgren sees the merchant in the parable as a metaphorical reference for the disciples. See Hultgren, *Parables of Jesus*, 420.

42. Philo, *De cherubim* X.32–33.

Philo continues, only leads to distress.[43] In *De migratione Abrahami* 216–17, Philo describes the search for wisdom as the mind "travelling through the land," but not in the absurd way merchants and dealers cross the seas for the sake of gain, without consideration for important things in life such as "the society of friends, or the unspeakable pleasures arising from wife, or children, or one's other relations, or love of one's country, or the enjoyment of political connections."[44] Merchants, in Philo's view, lack wisdom, the "most beautiful and desirable of all possessions."[45] They also lack reason devoted to contemplation[46] and a vehement love for knowledge,[47] and they never take part in discussions on virtue;[48] for instead of attending to these important matters, they turn their minds to mercantile affairs, the gains to be derived from their profession, and the enjoyments that derive from the indulgence of an amorous appetite.[49] In a metaphoric reference to mercantilism, Philo advises that when setting out on a difficult journey (referring to Moses), what will be helpful are "instruction, improvement, study, desire, admiration, enthusiasm, prophecy, and the love of doing good actions,"[50] and not "silver, nor any gold, nor any other of those things which consist of perishable materials."[51] Merchants are also barbaric slave dealers,[52] and at times ignorantly confess to gain.[53] At the markets they are so wicked that they have to be put in subjection to the superintendents of the market, who have to make sure that they do not practice any wicked maneuvers to the injury of those who purchase from them.[54] Even when discussing the Essenes, Philo compares the Essenes' positive traits—keeping their own minds in a state of holiness and purity and refraining from any kind of violence[55]—with mercantilism, one of the perverted occupations with wicked purposes.[56]

43. Ibid., X.34.4.

44. Philo, *De migratione Abrahami* 217.

45. Ibid., 218.1–2.

46. Philo, *De congressueru ditionis gratia* 63.

47. Ibid., 64.

48. Ibid., 64.

49. Ibid., 65.

50. Ibid., 112.

51. Ibid., 112.1–2.

52. Philo, *De Iosepho* 1.18–19. See also Josephus, *Ant.* 12.209 and 299, where a direct connection is made between mercantilism and slave trading, including the trading of young boys and girls.

53. Philo, *De Iosepho* 1.39.

54. Philo, *De specialibus legibus* IV.193–94.

55. Philo, *Quod omnis probus liber sit* 75.

56. Ibid., 78.

Several other Greek, Roman, and Jewish writings also depict merchants in a negative light. Herodotus of Halicarnassus (484–425 BCE), when discussing different classes in Egypt, places merchants below the swineherds.[57] The orations of Demosthenes (382–322 BCE) contain several negative references to merchants. From *Contra Dionysodorum* 1–4 it can be inferred that Dionysodorus, a merchant, took a loan from Demosthenes but acted in a fraudulent manner and robbed the money he took as a loan. In his *In Theocrinem* 1–12, Demosthenes argues in court that Theocrines has laid baseless charges against merchants, believing his charge would succeed because of the general perception that all merchants are dishonest. And in *In Aristocratem* 146–147 merchants, with farmers, silver miners and those who make speeches and move resolutions for hire, are named amongst the unprincipled breed of citizens. *The Testament of the Twelve Patriarchs* 4.6 describes merchants as sly and evasive. Cicero (106–43 BCE) lists wholesale merchants (with tax-gatherers and usurers) as vulgar, describing them as businessmen who make no profit "without a great deal of downright lying; and verily, there is no action that is meaner than misrepresentation."[58] Herodianus (c. 170–240 CE), in his *Ab excessu divi Marci* 4.10.4, depicts merchants as smugglers, and Diogenes Laertius (c. 300 CE) laments the negative perception of commerce (traders), since the professions of medicine and farming, like trading, all are injurious to one man but beneficial to another.[59] Diogenes most probably would not have made this remark if there was not a general negative perception of merchants.

Turning to biblical writings, James and Revelation also depict a negative image of merchants (and commerce). In James 4:13–16 merchants are described as being godless and evil. The only thing merchants (ἐμπορευσόμεθα; Jas 4:13) are interested in is gain (κερδήσομεν; Jas 4:13). They believe they can plan their future without asking what the will of God is, and therefore their plans will vanish like mist. They boast in their arrogance, and "all such boasting is evil" (Jas 4:15). Rev 18:3, 15 and 23 describe merchants that "have grown rich with the wealth of her wantonness" (οἱ ἔμποροι τῆς γῆς ἐκ τῆς δυνάμεως τοῦ στρήνους αὐτῆς ἐπλούτησαν; Rev 18:3), people who gained wealth from the earth (οἱ πλουτήσαντες ἀπ᾽ αὐτῆς; Rev 18:15), great men of the earth, who deceived all nations by their sorcery (ὅτι οἱ ἔμποροί σου ἦσαν οἱ μεγιστᾶνες τῆς γῆς, ὅτι ἐν τῇ φαρμακείᾳ σου ἐπλανήθησαν πάντα τὰ ἔθνη; Rev 18:23).

---

57. Herodotus, *Historiae* 2.164.

58. Cicero, *De Officiis* 1.150.42.

59. Diogenes Laertius, *Lives, Pyrrho* IX.81.

Finally, the Gospel of Thomas also paints a negative picture of merchants. In Gos. Thom. 64 the excuses in the parable of the Feast (buying a farm, buying five pair of oxen and just getting married; Q 14:18–20) are changed (and expanded) to recovering debt from merchants (Gos. Thom. 64:3), buying a house (Gos. Thom. 64:4), arranging a wedding banquet (Gos. Thom. 64:7) and buying an estate (Gos. Thom. 64:9). The parable in Gospel of Thomas also ends with an added general remark that buyers and merchants would not enter the places of my father (Gos. Thom. 64:12).[60] Gospel of Thomas 76 also was edited to accommodate its disapproval of mercantilism by adding Gos. Thom. 76:3 to highlight his disapproval of mercantilism.

The above evidence indicates a general trend of negative perception regarding merchants and mercantilism in the Mediterranean world, spanning an era from the fourth century BCE up to the third century CE, which should therefore be taken into consideration in the interpretation of the Merchant.

Why this negative perception of merchants and mercantilism? Persons living in the first-century (Mediterranean) world saw their existence as determined and limited by the natural and social resources of their immediate area and their world, a perception and belief that lead to the idea that all goods available to a person were limited; the so-called concept of limited good.[61] The concept of limited good meant that a larger share for any individual or group means a smaller share for someone else; in short, the pie was limited. Linked to the concept of limited good, as Rohrbaugh has indicated, were the peasants' perceptions of production and the mode of exchange.[62] Peasant production was primarily for use rather than exchange. Living a subsistence economy, peasantas saw the purpose of labor as maintaining the well-being of their family and the village; the purpose of labor was not

60. See Kloppenborg, *Tenants in the Vineyard*, 251.

61 Malina, *New Testament World*, 89; Malina, "Wealth and Poverty," 354–67. The concept of limited good was first developed by Foster, who defined the concept as follows: "Broad areas of peasant behavior are patterned in such fashion as to suggest that peasants view their social, economic, and natural universes—their total environment—as one in which all of the desired things in life such as land, wealth, health, friendship and love, manliness and honor, respect and status, power and influence, security and safety, exist infinite quantity and *are always in short supply as far as the peasant is concerned*. Not only do these and all other 'good things' exist in finite and limited quantity, but in addition there is no way directly within peasant power to increase the available quantities." Foster, "Image of Limited Good," 296; italics added. See also Aristotle, *Politica* 1.1256b: "For the amount of such property sufficient in itself for a good life is not unlimited."

62. Rohrbaugh, "Text of Terror," 33.

to create wealth. Peasants thus evaluated the world of persons and things in terms of *use*, and not exchange. For peasants it was therefore acceptable to sell commodities in order to get money to buy other needed commodities; to use money to buy commodities that one then sold again at a profit, however, was "unnatural." Profitmaking was seen as evil and socially destructive, since it would have been perceived as "a threat to the community and community balance."[63] Malina continues: "Since all goods are limited, one who seeks to accumulate capital is necessarily dishonorable . . . A person could not accumulate wealth except through the loss and injury suffered by another."[64]

Because of this perception, rich people were seen as inherently evil and as thieves.[65] To gain more than one has was to steal from others. Traders (intercity import-export merchants), who were often freedmen or urban nonelite persons secretly subsidized by wealthy Roman citizens or other elites,[66] fitted this category. Merchants bought needed commodities in one place and sold them in another at monopoly prices, getting as much as they could regardless of their own costs. All forms of capital accumulation, Malina emphasizes, were perceived to be forms of usury (i.e., making money in using money), and "profit and gain normally refer to something that accrue to a person by fraud or extortion, that is, something other than wages, custom-

63. Malina, *New Testament World*, 97.

64. Ibid.

65. In agrarian societies, including the first-century Mediterranean world, a widespread notion existed that rich people were inherently evil. "Rich people are associated with thievery because to have gained, to have accumulated more than one started with in a limited-good world, is to have taken the share of someone else." Rohrbaugh, *Cross-Cultural Perspective*, 114. Plutarch, for example, stereotypes the wealthy as invariably greedy, and compares the quest for wealth to madness. The rich, Rohrbaugh, argues, always wanted more. In this regard he quotes from Plutarch's *De cupiditate divitiarum* VII.525.15 a rich man saying "I've put everything under lock and seal or lay it out with moneylenders and agents and yet, I go on amassing and pursuing new wealth, wrangling with my servants, my farmers, my debtors." Rohrbaugh also refers to Jerome, who believed that every rich person "is either a thief or the heir of a thief." Jerome, *In Hieremiam* II.V.2. See Ibid., 114–15.

66. Since the trafficking of wares (commerce) carried a stigma, Roman writers, many of whom were aristocrats, looked down on merchants and traders. D'Arms, *Commerce and Social Standing*, 3–5. Keen to increase their wealth (with concomitant power and prestige), many aristocrats took part in commerce and trading. To avoid the stigma that was attached to merchants involved in trading and commerce, many in the aristocracy engaged in trade and commerce through "agents" (trusted slaves or freedmen), acting as their patrons and in most cases supplying the capital. Ibid., 39–40. See also Sidebotham, "Trade and Commerce," 63. See also Demosthenes (*Zenoth.* 1–2; *Lacr.* 1–2; *Pro Phorm.* 1–4), from which the practice of patrons supplying capital (mostly in the form of loans) to merchants is clear.

ary rent, reciprocal lending, or direct sale from producer to customer."[67] The trader, like the moneylender and the tax collector, was therefore considered dishonorable, immoral, and basically godless.[68] The fact that merchants had to make use of ships for their import-export trade, and that most shipowners were non-Jewish,[69] added to the negative perception the peasantry had of merchants.

The book of Revelation, especially Rev 18, gives expression to the general attitude towards merchants in the first-century. In a social-scientific reading of Revelation, Oakman approaches the text of Revelation as a response to a specific socioeconomic system (context).[70] The context of the text, Oakman argues, is the political ancient economy of the first-century Roman Empire.[71] This economy was based on the forced extraction of goods (taxes), cash crops and commercial farming that constantly drained agricultural resources out of the provinces to supply the elite and the city of Rome; an economy that encouraged trade and the movement of goods (commerce). Long-distance trade needed merchants and shippers, which was organized by Rome by way of organized associations who did the bidding on their behalf.[72] As a result of this political economy, a major transformation of the countryside took place; subsistence farming was replaced by a focus on commerce. This new approach did enormous harm to inland peasant farmers. Through taxes, rents and loans, the elite (and merchants)[73] appropriated more and more land, and the switch to commercial crops (livestock and wine)[74] resulted in peasants becoming more dependent on the largesse of their patrons.[75] Revelation, Oakman argues, "speaks specifically

67. Malina, *New Testament World*, 98.

68. Ibid.

69. Applebaum, "Economic Life in Palestine," 688.

70. Oakman, *Jesus and the Peasants*, 70–83.

71. Ibid., 74.

72. Ibid., 78.

73. There is some evidence that merchants also owned large estates in first-century Palestine. Three Jewish merchants (Nakdimon ben Gorion, Kalba Sabbua, and Ben Zizet Hakaset), according to *Midrash Lamentations* I, were able to provide Jerusalem with the necessary provisions for ten years. Applebaum, "Economic Life in Palestine," 659. Applebaum remarks that this most probably means that they were not simply merchants, since "they would have derived at least part of their produce from their own lands." Ibid., 687. Another merchant, Eleazer ben Harsum, whose family and large estates go back to the pre-70 period, owned several ships in the Hadrianic period. Ibid., 689.

74. Evidence from documented papyri supports this trend with several references to wine merchants. See, for example, P.Oxy. 7 1055; P.Oxy. 22 2342; P.Oxy. 31 2576.

75. Oakman, *Jesus and the Peasants*, 80.

against . . . [this] . . . political arrangements of Roman commerce," which God will overthrow and destroy, especially the merchants (Rev 18:11, 15) and shipmasters (Rev 18:17): The merchants will weep and mourn, since no one will buy their cargo any more (Rev 18:11), and they will stand far off, in fear of torment, weeping and mourning (Rev 18:15).[76]

Reading the Parable

In the parable of the Merchant, the kingdom is likened to the actions of a merchant. As I suggested earlier, the focus of the parable is the merchant, and not what he found. The pearl only plays a secondary role in the meaning of the parable. For the first hearers of the parable, most probably peasants in Galilee, this depiction of the kingdom must have been shocking. Because of the perception of limited good in advanced agrarian societies, and the conviction that production was primarily for use rather than exchange (i.e., supporting immediate families and the village), the profits made by merchants were perceived as a form of usury and as unnatural. Their trade was socially destructive and a threat to the community. In the eyes of the peasantry, merchants were evil and considered thieves. The fact that merchants had to make use of ships for their import-export trade, and that most shipowners were non-Jewish, added to this negative perception. Merchants owned large parts of land, and were part of the apparatus of the political ancient economy of the first-century Roman Empire. They assisted the movement of goods accumulated through forced extraction of goods, cash crops, and commercial farming. Therefore, merchants played a major role in the transforming the peasantry's daily lives that focused on subsistence, and not commercial trade.

The peasantry's negative perception of mercantilism is echoed by several Jewish, Greek, and Roman writers; mercantilism was generally seen as a perverted occupation with wicked purposes. Sirach links merchants with unjust dealings, and Philo depicts merchants as foolish, only focusing on gain (see also Jas 4:13); they are slave traders and practice wicked maneuvers to injure those who purchase from them. According to Demosthenes, merchants are part of the unprincipled breed of citizens, and in *The Testament of the Twelve Patriarchs* they are described as sly and evasive. Cicero lists them among the vulgar tradespeople because of their dishonesty, and Herodianus depicts merchants as smugglers. In nuce, merchants personified the godless, symbolizing everything that was unacceptable.

76. Ibid., 81.

Thus here is the shock in the parable: the kingdom is like the actions of a merchant. Likening the kingdom with the unacceptable and the "outsider," however, is typical of Jesus' parables. In the parable of the Lost Sheep (Luke 15:4–6), the main character is a shepherd, someone who also practiced a despised trade not to be followed.[77] Shepherds were associated with tax collectors, were not to be used as witnesses, were perceived as robbers, and were typified as dishonest people finding it difficult to repent and make restitution.[78] They were also associated with bandits and agitators,[79] and, in a world dominated by honor and shame, considered shameless persons: Being nomadic, shepherds were seen as thieves (grazing flocks on somebody else's property) and were rendered unclean because they belonged to one of the proscribed trades (i.e., ass drivers, tanners, sailors, butchers, and camel drivers). In the parables of the Unmerciful Servant (Matt 18:23–33) and the Vineyard Laborers (Matt 20:1–15), as we have seen, the kingdom is also likened to negatively–marked (dubious) characters (a patron–king and vineyard owner), persons not normally associated with the kingdom. Also, in the parable of the Samaritan (Luke 10:30–35), the actions of the figure of a despised and unclean Samaritan—probably also a merchant[80]—is also used as a symbol for the kingdom.

Jesus also depicted the kingdom itself as "unclean," as can be seen from the parable of the Leaven (Q 13:20–21). Leaven, in the time of Jesus, was a symbol for moral evil, corruption, and the unclean.[81] And in the parable of the Mustard Seed (Q 13:14–18), the kingdom is likened to a man that plants a mustard seed in his garden, violating the law of diverse kinds, and polluting a garden.[82] The garden is unclean, a symbol of chaos. If a garden is a metaphor for the kingdom, the kingdom of God is thus polluted and unclean.[83] In the parable of the Feast (Luke 14:16b–23) Jesus again uses the actions of an unacceptable figure to depict what the kingdom is like: A patron, part of the wealthy city elite (thus a "thief") competing for honor and being shunned by his peers, invites the unclean to his feast. By doing this, he

---

77. See, for example, *m. Qiddušin* 4.14 ("A man should not teach his son to be an ass-driver or a camel-driver, or barber or a sailor, or a herdsman or a shopkeeper, for their craft is the craft of robbers"), and *m. Baba Qamma* 10.9 ("None may buy wool or milk from herdsmen, or wood or fruit from them that watch over fruit-trees").

78. Van Eck, "Lost Sheep," 1–10.

79. Kloppenborg and Callon, "Parable of the Shepherd," 11.

80. The fact that the Samaritan, travelling for Jerusalem, had oil (ἔλαιον) and wine (οἶνον) with him (Luke10:34), indicates that he most probably was a merchant.

81. Scott, "Reappearance of Parables," 95–119.

82. Scott, *Hear Then the Parable*, 381.

83. Van Eck, "Mustard Seed," 226–54.

nullifies the role the pivotal value of honor played in organizing a stratified society, as well as the purity system which deemed some socially and ritually (culturally) impure and unacceptable.[84]

Jesus therefore does not hesitate to use unacceptable or "impure" figures or symbols (leaven and the mustard seed) as positive symbols for the kingdom. But how can the merchant in the parable be a positive symbol for the kingdom? In what he does. In his travels, he finds a pearl. In the world of the hearers of the parable, pearls occupied "the very highest position among all valuables,"[85] and thus were expensive. The merchant in the parable, however, does not find just another pearl; he finds a pearl of great value (εὑρὼν δὲ ἕνα πολύτιμον μαργαρίτην; Matt 13:46). The value of the pearl is so high that he has to sell everything he owns to buy it. This act of the merchant is not hyperbolic, and indeed relevant to the meaning of the parable.[86] His act of selling everything he owns, when not read hyperbolically, does not indicate that the parable should be seen as an autobiographical reference to Jesus (and his disciples),[87] or, as Scott argues, that the merchant now will have to sell the pearl, or else he will be broke.[88] If this were implied by the parable, not only the merchant but also Jesus would have been judged by the hearers as a fool.[89]

The merchant's selling everything thus must refer to something else. This reading of the parable suggests that it means that the merchant stopped being a merchant. He sold all he owned (most probably his merchandise; see Gos. Thom. 76.2) and took leave of the trade he had practiced. This is the focus of the parable, not the pearl. The role played by the pearl in the parable is secondary; only its value is important. Because the pearl is of "great value" (πολύτιμον; Matt 13:46), the merchant has to sell all his merchandise to acquire it. Given that the hearers of the parable perceived a pearl as the most valuable item that exists, Jesus could not have used a better example of preciousness than the pearl. Because he found a pearl, and in this case a very special pearl, the merchant must sell all he has.

---

84. Van Eck, "Feast," 1–14.

85. Pliny the Elder, *Naturalis historia* 9.54.

86. *Contra* Linnemann, *Parables of Jesus*, 101; Snodgrass, *Stories with Intent*, 252.

87. Miller, "Pearl," 76–81.

88. Scott, *Hear Then the Parable*, 319.

89. In the Jewish wisdom tradition, the "essence of wisdom is living with the long-run in mind . . . The wise take the end into account and choose their path accordingly. Those without wisdom are fools, that is, those who are attracted by what is immediate and act without knowledge or regard for long-term consequences." Miller, "Pearl," 67–68.

Taking leave of the despised trade he practiced, the merchant now is part of the kingdom. No more trading, especially not usury, will take place. In the kingdom there is no place for usury,[90] a destructive practice that threatens community. Further, in the kingdom neither is there a place for being part of the exploitative economic and political apparatus of the first-century Roman Empire. Being part of the kingdom, one also cannot support the forced extraction of goods, cash crops, and commercial farming, which worked to the detriment of those who already lived close to or below a level of subsistence.

In short, in the parable a merchant stopped being a merchant. An outsider has become an insider, and insiders act according to kingdom principles. Read from this perspective, this short parable criticizes the exploitative political economy of Jesus' day. The merchant in the parable exercised his options and left the despised profession.

What will the once merchant do with the pearl? This question is left open to the hearers of the parable. Maybe he will sell the pearl and, like the shepherd in the Lost Sheep, do everything in his power to assist everybody in having enough;[91] he may, like the elite patron in the parable of the Feast, invite the "polluted" and "unclean" to his table;[92] or, like the Samaritan, me may come to the aid of those in need. This question, however, is not really important for the understanding of the parable. The parable already makes its point: a despised outsider has become an insider to the benefit of those previously exploited by his actions.

Finally, the parable also challenged those who already were part of the kingdom. As Hultgren has argued, two implied themes in the parable are discipleship and commitment.[93] If one wants to be part of the kingdom, one must be willing, like the merchant, to give up "everything." The parable, for example, also echoes Jesus' "hard saying" in Luke 14:26.[94] The kingdom is based on a new kind of (fictive) kinship. The one who is not willing to let go the values that ruled the most important relationship of that time, namely, kinship (e.g., patriarchy, status, honor), cannot be part of the kingdom.

---

90. Van Eck, "Minas," 1–12.

91. Van Eck, "Lost Sheep," 1–10.

92. Van Eck, "Feast," 1–14.

93. Hultgren, *Parables of Jesus*, 421.

94. "If any one comes to me and does not hate his own father and mother and wife and children and brothers and sisters, yes, and even his own life, he cannot be my disciple" (Luke 14:26, RSV).

A Parable of Jesus?

The Merchant has all the markings of a Jesus parable. As in the case of Unmerciful Servant (Matt 18:23–33), the Vineyard Laborers (Matt 20:1–15), the Lost Sheep (Luke 15:4–6), the Samaritan (Luke 10:30–35), and the Feast (Luke 14:16b–23), in the Merchant the kingdom is likened to the actions of a negatively marked (dubious) character, a person not normally associated with the kingdom. The Merchant parable also resonates with aspects the parables of the Leaven (Q 13:20–21), the Mustard Seed (Luke 13:14–18), and Feast (Luke 14:16b–23); the kingdom also includes the "impure" and "polluted"—even someone like a merchant. Moreover, the condensed meaning of the parable, namely, that the merchant stopped being a merchant, is consistent with the kind of discipleship and commitment that makes one part of the kingdom. When Jesus called tax collectors to follow him, they left their profession and followed him (e.g., Mark 2:13–14). As a disciple, the tax collector ceased to be a tax collector, and in the parable the merchant ceased to be a merchant as he disciples himself to the kingdom.

CHAPTER 10

The Friend at Midnight (Luke 11:5–8): A Shameless and Exploiting Neighbor

THE HISTORY OF THE interpretation of the Friend at Midnight (Luke 11:5–8) shows that most scholars read the parable in terms of its literary context in Luke 11:1–13, concluding that the parable should be understood as a teaching of Jesus on prayer. When one reads the parable in its literary context, one can hardly come to a different conclusion. However, this is also the case with many interpreters who consider the literary context of the parable secondary and interpret it as an independent tradition. This clearly shows to what extent the literary context of the parable has influenced its interpretation. Another common feature of most interpretations is that the neighbor is seen as a metaphor for God. This reading has led to many interpreters' assertion that the difficult ἀναίδειαν in Luke 11:8 refers to the shamelessness of the host. This reading argues that the parable, when read within the cultural and historical context of the historical Jesus (first-century Palestine), has nothing to do with prayer, that the neighbor in the parable does not serve as a reference to God, and that ἀναίδειαν in Luke 11:8 refers in a negative manner to the neighbor of the parable (and not the host). The parable tells the story of an alternative world, a world wherein neighbors are kin and practice general reciprocity. The gist of the parable is that when neighbors do not act as neighbors, God's kingdom is not visible.

History of Interpretation

The earliest interpretations of the Friend at Midnight (Luke 11:5–8), except for Luke's theological-allegorical application of the tradition he received, are allegorical interpretations[1] that are typical of parable interpretation up to

1. Most of the earlier interpretations understood the parable in terms of prayer.

227

the famous work of Jülicher at the turn of the twentieth century. Bruce, one of the earliest parable scholars to break with the allegorical interpretation, understood the parable as being didactic in character, teaching perseverance in prayer.[2] Bruce's interpretation opened the way for most scholars to interpret the parable in terms of its literary context in Luke 11:1–13. Sandwiched between Luke's version of the Lord's Prayer (Luke 11:1–4) and three short "ask/receive" sayings that relate to prayer (Luke 11:9–13), the parable focuses on the result of persistent asking (praying). Also, since the same topic is present in the parable of the Unjust Judge (Luke 18:6b–8), these two parables have often been seen as parallel parables (or "twins")[3] in Luke, and have therefore been read together.[4] The interpretation of the parable in terms of its micro- and macrocontext has thus clearly influenced its interpretation.[5]

This becomes evident when one looks at the history of the parable's interpretation; the majority of interpreters understand the parable as a teaching of Jesus on prayer.[6] A few examples will suffice: The parable

---

Also, for some, "the bread represents some form of spiritual benefit, the friend represents Christ, and the petitioner represents a believer." See Snodgrass, *Stories with Intent*, 441. Augustine interpreted the parable in terms of the difference between man and God; man gives because he sometimes has to, while God gives because he wants to. In the patristic period most interpreters saw the three loaves as referring to the Father, the Son, and the Holy Spirit. Luther suggested that the parable teaches that all believers are beggars before God, and Bede saw in the parable a teaching on the evil of money—there is nothing wrong when man makes use of the fruit of the earth, but he is to be reprimanded when putting trust in money. See Kissinger, *History of Interpretation*, 40.

2. Bruce, *Parabolic Teaching*, 55.

3. See especially the parallel between μοι κόπους πάρεχε· (Luke 11:7), and διά γε τὸ παρέχειν μοι κόπον (Luke 18:5).

4. See, for example, Boice, *Parables of Jesus*, 157–66; Buttrick, *Speaking Parables*, 185–87; Donahue, *Gospel in Parable*, 187; Fitzmyer, *Gospel according to Luke*, 2:910; Hendrickx, *Parables of Jesus*, 215–33; Jeremias, *Parables of Jesus*, 159; Schottroff, *Parables of Jesus*, 188–94; Snodgrass, *Stories with Intent*, 440. Jeremias also links Luke 11:5–8 and 18:1–8 to Q 11:10 (Luke 11:10 and *par.*) Jeremias, *Parables of Jesus*, 159–60. Levison is one of the few that explicitly denies any relationship between Luke 11:5–8 and Luke 18:1–8. See Levison, "Importunity?," 460.

5. Snodgrass goes as far as to suggest that in an effort to understand the troublesome ἀναίδειαν in Luke 11:8, "one must reach outside vv. 5–8 for the solution." Snodgrass, *Stories with Intent*, 444.

6. See, for example, Blomberg, *Interpreting the Parables*, 276; Boice, *Parables of Jesus*, 157–65; Boucher, *Parables*, 112–14; Buttrick, *Speaking Parables*, 185–87; Donahue, *Gospel in Parable*, 185; Fitzmyer, *The Gospel according to Luke*, 2:910; Forbes, *God of Old*, 72–79; Groenewald, *In Gelykenisse Het Hy Geleer*, 104–10; Hendrickx, *Parables of Jesus*, 218; Hultgren, *Parables of Jesus*, 232–33; Kistemaker, *Stories Jesus Told*, 148–50; Levison, "Importunity?" 456–60; Lockyer, *All the Parables*, 264–66; Manson, *Sayings of Jesus*, 267; Mertz, "Freundschaft Verplichtet," 556–63; Oesterley, *Gospel Parables*, 225;

teaches that one can speak freely with God, who, as a perfect friend, will always supply in all our needs;[7] "the believer can pray with confidence and assurance";[8] persistent inconvenience is sometimes necessary to motivate a neighbor but is not needed when something is asked of God;[9] the shameless boldness of the man at the door is an example of how Christians can ask God for the Holy Spirit;[10] God responds to persistent prayers, and his children should therefore be encouraged to pray unrelentingly and persistently—even though it may seem impertinent—as God will respond;[11] God wants us to be unrelentingly persistent in our prayers;[12] the parable encourages perseverance and boldness in praying because God, who is not like the sleeper, hears prayers and responds;[13] the parable teaches that one should practice bold and unabashed forthrightness in prayer;[14] and God, as the householder, is more willing to give when we pray perseveringly.[15] Schottroff, who reads the parable from an eschatological perspective, also comes to the same conclusion: the subject of the parable is prayer, and the gift of God is the gift of the Holy Spirit; for if a friend and neighbor (who is quite annoyed by a midnight visit) will give bread, how much more will God hear your prayers.[16]

A minority of scholars, who also focus on the parable in its literary setting, have come to different conclusions regarding the meaning of the parable. For Capon, parable is a parable of grace that allegorically refers to Jesus' death and resurrection. The neighbor (Jesus) will get up (ἀναστὰς from ἀνίστημι; Luke 11:7)—a reference to Jesus' resurrection—because of

Perkins, *Hearing the Parables*, 194; Smith, *Parables of the Synoptic Gospels*, 148; Stiller, *Preaching Parables*, 92; Snodgrass, *Stories with Intent*, 437.

7. Buttrick, *Speaking in Parables*, 187; Manson, *Teaching of Jesus*, 267; Mertz, "Freundschaft Verplichtet," 561–62.

8. Forbes, *God of Old*, 79.

9. Hendrickx, *Parables of Jesus*, 218; Perkins, *Hearing the Parables*, 215.

10. Donahue, *Gospel in Parable*, 185.

11. Hultgren, *Parables of Jesus*, 232–33; Boucher, *Parables*, 114.

12. Kistemaker, *Stories Jesus Told*, 148–50; Stiller, *Preaching Parables*, 92.

13. See Snodgrass, *Stories with Intent*, 437, 447–48. Snodgrass states, "If among humans a request is granted even when or because the request is rude, how much more will your heavenly Father respond to your requests?" Snodgrass, "Anaideia and the Friend at Midnight," 513. See also Boice, *Parables of Jesus*, 157–65; Groenewald, *In Gelykenisse Het Hy Geleer*, 104–110.

14. Blomberg, *Interpreting the Parables*, 276.

15. Lockyer, *All the Parables*, 266.

16. "This is the very strength of the parable: that through its depiction of persistence in a situation of solidarity it invites us to persistence toward God." Schottroff, *Parables of Jesus*, 190.

the ἀναίδειαν (shamelessness, referring to death) of the host.[17] Fleddermann suggests that the parable should be read as a parallel to the parable of
the Good Samaritan (Luke 10:25–37); both parables teach that one is always
obliged to respond to human need, as the host does, even if it means violating all social norms.[18] In Hunter's reading, the parable teaches us to count
the cost and to sacrifice everything for God's cause; the parable is not only
about the willingness to hear Jesus' teaching but also about the willingness
to practice it.[19] Jüngel, as a last example, reads the parable as a challenge to
its hearers to discern the nature of the kingdom of God by participating in
its reality (as the neighbor did).[20]

Scholars who read the parable as independent from its Lukan context
have come to diverse conclusions regarding the meaning of the parable.
For Bultmann the original meaning of the parable is irrecoverable. The
parable's original intent, however, most probably was as an exhortation to
pray for the coming of God's reign.[21] Dodd, in line with his eschatological
reading of the parables, sees the parable as one of crisis that depicts the
correct response to a sudden crisis of need: thus Dodd clearly relates it to
the parousia.[22] Cadoux reads the parable against the background of the
charges leveled against Jesus, namely, that he was dividing the nation by
incorporating the Gentiles into the kingdom of God. From this perspective,
the parable should be understood in relation to Jesus' efforts to restore the
correct use of the court of the Gentiles, and therefore is related to Jesus'
cleansing the temple.[23] Jeremias, who also sees the context of the parable
in Luke 11:1–13 as secondary, links the original meaning of the parable to
the customs of hospitality in first-century Palestine. Just as unthinkable as
it is that a Palestinian peasant, who knows exactly what accepted hospitality
in a village entails, would not help his neighbor who is in dire straits, even
more so with God. The disciples can therefore know that in the tribulation
to come, God will not ignore their needs. The parable is not concerned with
the shamelessness of the host but "with the certainty that the petition will

---

17. Capon, *Parables of Grace*, 68–83.

18. Fleddermann, "Three Friends at Midnight," 281.

19. Hunter, *Interpreting the Parables*, 128.

20. Jüngel, *Paulus und Jesus*, 169–72. See also Via, who read the parable as a language
event and comes to more or less the same conclusion; the parable calls for a decision to
act in the same way as the neighbor. Via, "Parable and Example Story," 53.

21. Bultmann, *Synoptic Tradition*, 174–75.

22. Dodd, *Parables of the Kingdom*, 19.

23. Cadoux, *Art and Use*, 155.

be granted."[24] Crossan, finally, sees the parable as a parable of action;[25] the advent of the kingdom demands an adequate and definitive response, even if this means also accepting the bothersome inevitability of what must done. However, the "what must be done," is not spelled out by Crossan.[26]

Only a few scholars thus far have attempted a reading of the parable using a social-scientific approach. These scholars place the parable in the context of rural village life and focus in their interpretations on the cultural codes of honor and shame, hospitality, and friendship in the first-century Mediterranean world.

Scott sees the parable as a story of reversal—ἀναίδειαν in Luke 11:8 refers to the neighbor, meaning "shamelessness." The neighbor does not act out of friendship (honor) but out of shamelessness. Because he has a proper sense of shame, he acts in a way that will not bring shame on him and his family. Therefore, the parable serves as a model for envisioning the kingdom of God.[27] Herzog, following Scott, interprets the parable as an example of "the moral economy of the peasant," which "Jesus identified as one place where the values of the reign of God could be found."[28] Jesus, as pedagogue of the oppressed, used parables (subversive speech) to undermine the social structures that exploited and oppressed the peasantry. In this parable ἀναίδειαν is the element that subverts the first-century Palestinian cultural value of friendship. Friendship in the time of Jesus had become entangled in the web of patron-client relationships. The peasants in the villages, in defiance of the values of the elite, embraced ἀναίδειαν by extending hospitality even to strangers, because it was the honorable thing to do. The sleeping neighbor is not motivated by the social value of friendship but by his ἀναίδειαν. He acts honorably because he does not want to shame himself, his family, and his village. In doing this the sleeping neighbor engages in a limited act that challenges the efforts of their oppressors to dehumanize them and to reduce them to creatures (who were obsessed by the desire to survive). Therefore, the peasants "participated in a 'shameless' social order where their small, but continual, redistributions of wealth and food foreshadowed a different order for human relations—one molded by

24. Jeremias, *Parables of Jesus*, 159.

25. Crossan, *In Parables*, 83–84.

26. When one reflects on the interpretations of Cadoux, Dodd and Jeremias, Herzog is correct in his remark that these scholars' interpretations, although they see the Lukan context of the parable in Luke 11:5–8 as secondary, still are "subtly anchored to Lukan moorings." Herzog, *Parables as Subversive Speech*, 197–98.

27. Scott, *Hear Then the Parable*, 89–91. See also Malina and Rohrbaugh, *Social-Science Commentary on the Synoptic Gospels*, 273.

28. Herzog, *Parables as Subversive Speech*, 194.

justice and mutual reciprocity."[29] Bailey reads the parable in terms of the honor-shame culture of the first-century Mediterranean world. Just as the sleeper will respond to avoid shame (or escape disgrace), so much more will God respond.[30] The sleeper is a man of integrity and therefore gives the petitioner more than he needs. The parable, in sum, teaches "that God is a God of honor and that man can have complete assurance that his prayers will be answered."[31]

From the above it is clear that the majority of parable scholars see the parable as a teaching of Jesus on prayer. When one reads the parable in its literary context, one can hardly come to a different conclusion. This conclusion, however, is also found among those scholars who consider the literary context of the parable as secondary, and interpret it as an independent tradition. Even the some social-scientific reading of Bailey comes to this conclusion. This shows, since the interpretation of Bugge, how the literary context of the parable has influenced its interpretation. Another common feature of most interpretations is that the neighbor is seen as a metaphor for God. This reading, as will be indicated below, has led to many interpreters' asserting that the difficult ἀναίδειαν in Luke 11:8 refers to the shamelessness of the host, who knocks, and not to the neighbor inside.

Integrity and Authenticity

In terms of the narrative framework of Luke, the Friend at Midnight is part of Luke's travel narrative (Luke 9:51—19:27)—a Lukan creation—in which Jesus instructs his disciples on a variety of topics. Its more immediate context is Luke 11:1–13, which is also a Lukan redactional construct. Luke has sandwiched the parable between his version of the Lord's Prayer (Luke 11:1–4), and three short "ask-receive" sayings (Luke 11:9–13) that have persistent prayer as topic, a typical Lukan theme.[32] The parable in Luke 11:5–8 is linked to the Lord's Prayer (Luke 11:1–4) by the request for bread present in both the Lord's Prayer and the parable. The three sayings in Luke 11:9–13 that follow directly after the parable are linked to (and elaborate on) Luke 11:5–11: the first saying (Luke 11:9–10) elaborates on the theme of persistence in prayer; the second saying (Luke 11:11–12) repeats the form

29. Ibid., 214.

30. Bailey, *Poet and Peasant*, 128–33. See also Nolland, *Luke 9:21—18:34*, 624–27.

31. Bailey, *Jesus through Middle Eastern Eyes*, 119.

32. Luke's emphasis on prayer can be seen most vividly in his redactional activity where Jesus and prayer is the topic. Luke has seven references to the prayer life of Jesus that are not present in Matthew and Mark (Luke 3:21; 5:16; 6:12; 9:18; 9:28; 11:1; 23:24).

of the parable; and the third saying draws the conclusion implied by the two sayings preceding it.[33] The three sayings in Luke 11:9–3 (taken from Q) stress the need for "asking" and "knocking," a recollection of the action of the host in the parable in Luke 11:5–8.[34]

That Luke 11:1–13 is a Lukan creation is also clear when it is compared to Matthew. In Luke the Lord's Prayer (Luke 11:2–4) follows a request directed at Jesus by one of the disciples to teach them how to pray. In Matthew the Lord's Prayer (Matt 6:9–13) is part of Jesus' teaching of the Sermon of the Mount, and is not introduced by a request to teach the disciples to pray. Luke 11:9–13, as Herzog has indicated, is linked to the parable, elaborating on it. In Matthew, the saying in Luke 11:9–13 is found in Matt 7:7–12 (close to the end of the Sermon on the Mount), where Jesus teaches on a variety of topics, including on judging others (Matt 7:1–6), the narrow and wide gates (Matt 7:13–14), and a tree and its fruit (Matt 7:15–23). In Luke 11:9–13 the emphasis is on asking for the Spirit; in Matt 7:7–12 the saying cluster ends with the call of Jesus relating to the greatest commandment. Evidently, as is often the case, Matthew and Luke have used Q (in this case Q 11:9–13) in a way that suits their respective narrative strategies and theology. Moreover, since Q 11:9–13 as well as the Lord's Prayer (Q 11:2–4) are both attested to as individual sayings, it is clear that Luke 11:1–13 is a Lukan redactional construct and that the parable in Luke 11:5–8 is either a Lukan construct or an independent tradition stemming from Jesus and taken up by Luke and incorporated into 11:1–13 (as part of a teaching on prayer).

Scholars differ with regards to the integrity of the parable. Some scholars treat Luke 11:5–13 as a unit, with Luke 11:9–13 as the application of the parable.[35] The majority of scholars interpret the parable as consisting of Luke 11:5–8; some treat it in its literary context[36] and others as a separate tradition.[37] Interestingly, the majority of the latter group of scholars—who

33. See Herzog, *Parables as Subversive Speech*, 196–97.

34. Donahue, *Gospel in Parable*, 186.

35. Scholars who see the purpose of the parable in Luke 11:5–8 as being unfolded in Luke 11:9–13 are, for example, Buttrick, *Speaking in Parables*, 185–87; Groenewald, *In Gelykenisse Het Hy Geleer*, 104–10; Lockyer, *All the Parables*, 264–66; Schottroff, *Parables of Jesus*, 188; Stiller, *Preaching Parables*, 92.

36. See, for example, Boice, *Parables of Jesus*, 157–65; Boucher, *Parables*, 112–14; Donahue, *Gospel in Parable*, 185–87; Hultgren, *Parables of Jesus*, 225–26; Kistemaker, *Stories Jesus Told*, 148–50; Mertz, "Freundschaft Verplichtet," 556–63; Waetjen, "Subversion of World," 706.

37. See, for example, Bailey, *Poet and Peasant*, 119; Bultmann, *Synoptic Tradition*, 175; Herzog, *Parables as Subversive Speech*, 194–214; Jeremias, *Parables of Jesus*, 158; Scott, *Hear Then the Parable*, 86–93.

see the context of the parable in Luke 11:1–13 as secondary—also links the meaning of the parable to some or other aspect of prayer.

The parable most probably should be delimited to 11:5–8. But does Luke 11:5–8 go back to Jesus, or is it a creation of Luke, or is it from Q? No scholar sees the parable as a Lukan creation, and only Fleddermann argues that the parable stems from Q. Most scholars interpret the parable in its Lukan context as a parable of Jesus, accepting with it (subconsciously perhaps) the fact that the contextual fit of the parable in Luke 11:1–13 predetermines its meaning. Only a few scholars consciously interpret the parable as an authentic Jesus tradition apart from its secondary context in Luke.[38] These scholars agree that the parable most probably originated with Jesus, and some are of the opinion that the parable's meaning has been obscured by Luke's contextualization.

Since the parable is only attested to in Luke the criteria of early, multiple, and independent attestation cannot be used to identify the parable as stemming from Jesus or not. The criterion of coherence therefore will have to play a major role in the decision-making process. To apply this criterion in a responsible way, the first task will be to read the parable in the cultural and historical context of the historical Jesus. The meaning of the parable that evolves from this reading will then have to be compared with the values of Jesus apparent in sayings that do pass the criteria of early, multiple, and independent attestation.

Reading Scenarios

From an emic point of view, the parable is a story about a peasant villager who, in the middle of the night (μεσονυκτίου; Luke 11:5), receives a visitor (φίλος; Luke 11:6) traveling through the village. Because he has nothing to offer his visitor to eat (Luke 11:6), he goes to one of his neighbors (φίλον; Luke 11:5) and asks him for bread in order to be able to serve his guest a meal. The neighbor, who is in bed with his children, at first does not want to be bothered (μοι κόπους πάρεχε; Luke 11:7) and makes excuses as to why he cannot get up and help the man (φίλον; Luke 11:8) at his door. Eventually, however, he gets up and gives the petitioner/host whatever (as much as) he needs (ὅσων χρῄζει; Luke 11:8). The story ends by stating the reason for the

38. See Bultmann, *Synoptic Tradition*, 175; Cadoux, *Art and Use*, 155; Dodd, *Parables of the Kingdom*, 19; Funk et al., *Five Gospels*, 327–28; Herzog, *Parables as Subversive Speech*, 194–214; Jeremias, *Parables of Jesus*, 158–59; Scott, *Hear Then the Parable*, 88–91.

neighbor's change of mind; he gives the host what he needs, not because he is his friend (φίλον; Luke 11:5), but because of his ἀναίδειαν (Luke 11:8).

The story is short and clear, except for one aspect. To whose attitude does ἀναίδειαν refer? To the host's or the neighbor's? Also, precisely what is the attitude being described with ἀναίδειαν?

From an etical perspective the parable—as a high-context text—evokes several cultural values that were part of the first-century Mediterranean world; honor and shame, hospitality, friendship, reciprocity, patronage and clientism, limited good, and first-century village life (or the relationship between city and village). As the reading scenarios (social values or scripts) of honor and shame, patronage and clientism, and limited good already have been discussed, these will not be repeated here. A discussion of hospitality, friendship, first-century village life, and the meaning of ἀναίδειαν, however, need our attention. Also, although reciprocity has been discussed earlier, a few extra remarks will be made on reciprocity as it relates to family and friends.

Hospitality

In first-century Palestine, where there was no system of inns and hotels as in our modern world, hospitality played an important role.[39] Hospitality in the first-century Mediterranean world in essence was the process of receiving outsiders and changing them from strangers to guests.[40] Where friends were involved, hospitality was extended as a normalcy; "it is part of friendship to offer hospitality."[41] "Hospitality was considered a sacred duty throughout the Mediterranean world of antiquity, even when the visitor was

39. In the New Testament only two references are made to "inns"; Luke 2:7 (κατάλυμα), and Luke 10:34 (πανδοχεῖον). The former was not an inn in the strict sense of the word. A κατάλυμα was more of a large furnished room attached to a peasant house, and is best translated as "guest room." Malina and Rohrbaugh, *Social-Science Commentary on the Synoptic Gospels*, 376. A πανδοχεῖον, on the other hand, was a commercial inn. These places had a dubious character. Everybody was welcome, monies had to be paid for lodging, and the female workers at the inn offered sexual favors to guests as a rule. See Leonhardt-Balzer, "Wie Kommt ein Reicher in der Abrahams Schoß," 545.

40. Malina, "Hospitality," 86–87. See also Malina and Pilch, *Social-Science Commentary on Acts*, 213–15.

41. Schottroff, *Parables of Jesus*, 189. See also Bailey, *Poet and Peasant*, 122; Kreuzer and Schottroff, "Freundschaft," 169–70; Scott, *Hear Then the Parable*, 87; Snodgrass, *Stories with Intent*, 441; Waetjen, "Subversion of World," 7.

a stranger,"[42] and was part of "the virulent shame and honor system of the ancient world."[43]

Thus, a stranger (or friend) arriving in a community (village) served as a challenge to the community—the host had to protect the honor of his guest, and had to show concern for the guest's needs. The guest, in turn, was embedded in the honor of his host, and in the honor of the host's group (e.g., the village).[44] An unexpected guest thus was considered a guest of the entire village, which meant that the entire village was responsible for lodging.[45] Everyone in the village, therefore, was bound to help the host to serve his guest a meal.[46] Because of this responsibility, a host could call on others in the village to help him. When treated in an honorable way, the guest would afterward spread the praises of the host and the community he stayed with.[47]

Friendship

In the first-century Mediterranean world friends were defined as persons who treated each other as if they were family. Friendship was voluntary, and what bound friends together "was their mutual concern for each other's honor, and because honor was the highest value, a friend would supply whatever was needed to uphold the honor of a friend."[48] Friendship meant that friends could rely on each other; it implied true commitment. "Without batting an eyelash, people would help each other for friendship's sake and even go out of their way for each other."[49] "Friendship carried many obligations, but first and foremost the moral obligation to help a friend when he was in need. In order to be an honorable man one must fulfill one's obligation to one's friends"[50] With all of the above taken into consideration, Malina and Rohrbaugh give the following ample definition of friendship:

42. Hultgren, *Parables of Jesus*, 229.

43. Snodgrass, *Stories with Intent*, 441.

44. Malina et al., *Time Travel to the World of Jesus*, 34.

45. Bailey, *Poet and Peasant*, 122. See also Buttrick, *Speaking in Parables*, 185–87; Waetjen, "Subversion of World," 705.

46. Bailey, *Poet and Peasant*, 123.

47. Malina, "Hospitality," 106.

48. Herzog, *Parables as Subversive Speech*, 208.

49. Malina et al., *Time Travel to the World of Jesus*, 32. See also Kreuzer and Schottroff, "Freundschaft," 167.

50. Moxnes, "Honor and Righteousness in Romans," 62.

The chief characteristic of a friend is that he . . . seeks the well-being of his friend. And a "good" friend is one who has a recognized honor rating, that is, one who is "worthy." Of course, friendship is a reciprocal affair, with friends mutually seeking the well-being of each other.[51]

Also, if two people that did not know each other (person A and B) had a mutual friend (person C), it meant that person A and B were also friends.[52] In Jewish Palestinian society friendship and being good neighbors were also seen as one and the same thing; neighbors were friends.[53] *Sirach* 6:17, for example, states that whoever "fears the Lord directs his friendship aright, for so he is, so is his neighbor also." This is also the gist of Proverbs 3:28–29: "Do not say to your neighbor, 'Go, and come again, tomorrow I will give it'—when you have it with you. Do not plan harm against your neighbor who lives trustingly beside you."[54] Friendship in first-century Palestine thus consisted of an interlocking web, or network, of relationships, meaning that one could have friends you did not even know.

Reciprocity

In first-century Palestine the exchange of goods took place in the form of reciprocity. As discussed earlier, three types of reciprocity existed in the first-century Mediterranean world: generalized, balanced, and negative. *Generalized reciprocity* (to give without the expectation for return) took place within the sphere of the family or household (family, kin, or clan) in the form of child rearing, hospitality, gifts, and brotherly love. It was altruistic and showed extreme solidarity to one's kin–group. *Balanced reciprocity* (the idea of *quid pro quo*) either took place between persons with the same (equal) status, or between persons of unequal status. In the case of the former (neighbors, fellow villagers, friends) it served mutual interests and took the form of, for example, bartering, assistance, and hospitality. The latter was typical of patron–client relationships in first-century Palestine—socially fixed relations between social unequals. *Negative reciprocity* (exploitation, the unsocial extreme) served self–interest at the expense of the "other."

51. Malina and Rohrbaugh, *Social-Science Commentary on the Synoptic Gospels*, 364.

52. Malina et al., *Time Travel to the World of Jesus*, 30.

53. Scott, *Hear Then the Parable*, 90.

54. For examples of friendship in the Old Testament (e.g., Pss 41:10; 55:14; Prov 17:17; 18:24; 27:5, 9, 10), see Kreuzer and Schottroff, "Freundschaft," 169.

The first-century Mediterranean world was an aristocratic society, which means that patronage and clientism was part of its social fabric. The rich (e.g., the Herodians and Jerusalem elite) competed for clients in order to increase their honor. In Judea and Galilee the rich ("haves") were mostly from the urban areas and controlled the economic and political resources of society, so becoming patrons for the urban poor and the village peasants (the "have–nots") seeking for favors from these elite. The elite, in their turn, seeking to aggrandize their family's position and honor and status, competed to add dependent clients (as having few clients was seen as shameful). In this way formal and mutual obligations "degenerated into petty favor seeking and manipulation—clients competed for patrons, just as patrons competed for clients, in an often desperate struggle to gain economic or political advantage."[55] This situation led to extensive and extractive relationships between patrons and clients (elites and peasants). The elite were concerned with plundering rather than developing. Taxation existed for the benefit of the elite. They exploited resources for their own benefit; the focus was primarily on trade, and the elite were always looking for control over land (mostly by expropriation and the creation of debt).[56] So, for many peasants in first-century Palestine, it was a case of subsistence, leading inter alia to loans (esp. because of taxes), and the consequent expropriation of ancestral plots. Patronage and clientism in first-century Palestine at the best of times—although it may have had a "kinship glaze" over it–[57]thus was a system dominated by the elite (patrons) and their values; a system that was set up in order to ensure the preservation of their privileged positions by the exploitation of the poor.[58] The purpose of patron–client relationships was to exercise power over others, a core value of advanced agrarian societies.[59]

First-century Galilean Village Life

The backdrop of the parable is Jewish–Palestinian rural village life in the third decade of first-century CE. Villages in first-century Galilee were what one might call nucleated villages; located in the midst of fields (that included the smallholdings of individual peasants and the common land

55. Malina and Rohrbaugh, *Social-Science Commentary on the Synoptic Gospels*, 389.

56. See Eisenstadt and Roniger, *Patrons, Clients and Friends*, 208.

57. Neyrey, *Render to God*, 250.

58. Moxnes, "Patron-Client Relations," 244.

59. See Herzog, *Prophet and Teacher*, 55; Hanson and Oakman, *Palestine in the Time of Jesus*, 72.

that belonged to the village), sometimes adjacent to the ever growing large estates in Galilee.[60] Villages were organized along kinship, or quasi–kinship lines, comprising of members of one (or more) extended families.[61] Though some of the villagers were not kin, they were still considered to be neighbors or friends,[62] and mutual help between neighbors was expected in the form of general reciprocity. Economic exchange thus took place within the familial or quasi–familial context (generalized reciprocity).[63] This also meant that hospitality was extended towards friends and people known to villagers (see Luke 8:3; 10:38; 11:5; 24:28–29).

In Palestine it was customary to travel during the day because of the sea breeze from the Mediterranean, and breezes on elevated terrain like Upper Galilee. A person arriving in the middle of the night in a Galilean village was therefore somewhat unexpected.[64]

Another aspect of village life alluded to in the parable is the baking of bread. The women in the villages baked bread for a week (not for the day), using a community oven with some kind of rotating schedule. Because of this schedule everyone in the village knew who had freshly baked bread.[65]

60. Applebaum, "Economic Life in Palestine," 363; Herzog, *Parables as Subversive Speech*, 203–4.

61. Oakman, *Jesus and the Peasants*, 149.

62. See Luke 1:58 (οἱ περίοικοι καὶ οἱ συγγενεῖς), Luke 15:6 (τοὺς φίλους καὶ τοὺς γείτονας), and Luke 15:9 (τὰς φίλας καὶ γείτονας).

63. Oakman, *Jesus and the Peasants*, 149.

64. Bailey, *Poet and Peasant*, 121. See also Hultgren, *Parables of Jesus*, 228; Schottroff, *Parables of Jesus*, 188–89. *Contra* some Buttrick, Kistemaker, Lockyer, and Oesterley, who argue that it was rather customary in first-century Palestine to travel at night in order to avoid the intense heat of the day. See Buttrick, *Speaking in Parables*, 185–87; Kistemaker, *Stories Jesus Told*, 148–50; Lockyer, *All the Parables*, 264–66; Oesterley, *Gospel Parables*, 221. Bailey, however, states that night travel was only customary in the desert areas of Syria, Jordan and Egypt. Schottroff is also of the opinion that the visit was unexpected ("unusual"), but for different reasons than Bailey. The reason for the unexpected visit, according to her, is that the traveler most probably did not find room in a lodging place, and therefore was forced to go farther. Schottroff, *Parables of Jesus*, 188–89.

65. See Bailey, *Poet and Peasant*, 122; Huffard, "Parable of the Friend at Midnight," 157; Scott, *Hear Then the Parable*, 87. Levison differs, arguing that that each peasant family baked bread every Friday before Sabbath, and then as often as needed during the week. Because peasant families could not afford to bake new bread until the old bread ran out, they would not bake bread on a regular schedule. Levison, *Parables*, 457. So Oesterley, adding that the supply of bread was kept in a basket until the supply ran low; only then was it time to bake another batch. Oesterley, *Gospel Parables*, 221. Jeremias believes that each day's supply of bread was baked before sunrise, and that it was generally known in the village who still had bread left. Jeremias, *Parables of Jesus*, 157. See also Boucher, *Parables*, 113; Lockyer, *All the Parables*, 264–66.

The kind of bread baked was in the form of small rolls (three of which were considered adequate for a meal).[66]

Ἀναίδειαν

Almost all interpreters of the parable agree that the interpretation of the parable hinges on the meaning of the word ἀναίδειαν in Luke 11:8. Linked to the question of its meaning is the question of whom it refers to in the parable. To the host or the neighbor?

One group of scholars argues that ἀναίδειαν in Luke 11:8 refers to the host, in which case the meaning of ἀναίδειαν is negatively rendered as "importunity," "persistence," "shamelessness," or "unselfconsciouslessness";[67] "disgraceful conduct," "insensitivity," or "rudeness";[68]); and "troublesome or determined persistence," "raw nerve," or "brazen tenacity" (from the Hebrew *chutzpah*).[69] This meaning of ἀναίδειαν normally goes hand in hand with the parable being read in its Lukan context, with the added conviction that the neighbor is a symbol of God. Because of this, ἀναίδειαν cannot refer to the attitude of the neighbor; such an interpretation does not pay much of a compliment to God and leads to a "theological morass" as it pictures God as a reluctant grouch who only answers prayers out of divine shame.[70] This understanding presupposes that, although the host acts in an importune and shameless (negative) way, it is exactly because of this attitude that his request is adhered to. As such, his actions in the end should be understood as positive.[71]

66. Jeremias, *Parables of Jesus*, 157; Huffard, "Parable of the Friend at Midnight," 158. Bailey is of the opinion that larger loaves were baked, one of which would be more than enough for a guest. Bailey, *Poet and Peasant*, 122. See also Hultgren, *Parables of Jesus*, 229. The kind of bread that was baked does not really matter for the interpretation of the parable. What is important is that the host, as a sign of honor and hospitality, had to put in front of his guest more than he could eat.

67. Funk et al., *Five Gospels*, 327; Donahue, *Gospel in Parable*, 185; Kistemaker, *Stories Jesus Told*, 150; Lockyer, *All the Parables*, 264.

68. Snodgrass, "Anaideia and the Friend at Midnight," 510; Snodgrass, *Stories with Intent*, 443.

69. Hultgren, *Parables of Jesus*, 227. See also Cadoux, *Art and Use*, 34–35; Crossan, *In Parables*, 84; Fitzmyer, *Gospel according to Luke*, 2:912; Jülicher, *Gleichnisreden Jesu*, 273; Liefeld, "Parables on Prayer," 51; Manson, *Teaching of Jesus*, 268; Oesterley, *Gospel Parables*, 221; Perkins, *Hearing the Parables*, 195; Schottroff, *Parables of Jesus*, 190; Smith, *Parables of the Synoptic Gospels*, 147; Snodgrass, *Stories with Intent*, 442, 732; Wenham, *The Parables of Jesus*, 181.

70. Buttrick, *Speaking in Parables*, 186.

71. See, for example, Waetjen's interpretation of ἀναίδειαν. Waetjen, "The

Another interpretation of ἀναίδειαν suggested by some scholars is also "shamelessness," but referring to the attitude of the neighbor, who knocks, not the host inside.[72] According to Jeremias, it would have been inconceivable to Palestinian peasants (rooted in the values of village life) that a neighbor, even if he was woken up in the middle of the night, would not be willing to fulfill his obligation of hospitality but would instead make excuses. A neighbor who acts like this would be shamed, and as a result he and his family would lose face in the village.[73] This is also Bailey's understanding of ἀναίδειαν; it refers to the attitude of the neighbor as shamelessness.[74] Bailey argues that the understanding of ἀναίδειαν as "persistence" is not supported by the parable, as the parable gives no evidence to repetitive calling. The parable, because of its origin in the Palestinian context, included Aramaic words and phrases, which, when they were translated into Greek, were changed. The word for "shame" in Aramaic, namely, *kissuf*, was translated as αἰδώς, adding to it the alpha privative. The word αἰδώς itself does refer to "shame" in a negative sense, but by adding the alpha privative, the translator rendered it as ἀναίδειαν in the sense of "avoidance of shame."[75] Thus, by means of the parable's translation, the negative ἀναίδειαν (shamelessness)

Subversion of World," 703–721. According to Waetjen, Jesus' use of ἀναίδειαν in Luke 11:8 is the first positive use of this term, meaning "good shamelessness." He continues: "Imprudence, effrontery, and dishonorable conduct are divinely legitimated in the pursuit of justice in all the arenas of social life." Ibid., 717. God does not respond on the basis of reciprocity or friendship. The ideology of reciprocity based on friendship, and the world of honor-shame culture, is being undermined as the petitioner resorts to shameless conduct in order to obtain bread. Therefore, the parable subverts our view of the world.

72. Bailey, *Poet and Peasant*, 132; Jeremias, *Parables*, 158; Herzog, *Parables as Subversive Speech*, 209; Funk et al., *Five Gospels*, 273; Scott, *Hear Then the Parable*, 89–91; Culpepper, *Luke*, 236; Derrett, "Friend at Midnight," 840; Fridrichsen, "Exegetisches zum Neuen Testament," 40–43; Johnson, "Lukan Kingship Parable," 123–31; Jüngel, *Paulus und Jesus*, 156; Marshall, *Gospel of Luke*, 465; Nolland, *Luke 9:21—18:34*, 622; Paulsen, "Die Witwe und der Richter," 27; Perrin, *Rediscovering the Teaching*, 128–29; Huffard, "Parable of the Friend at Midnight," 156.

73. Jeremias, *Parables of Jesus*, 158. Levison follows Jeremias' interpretation; ἀναίδειαν refers to the sleeping neighbor. If ἀναίδειαν refers to the host seeking help, it pictures God (who is represented by the sleeping neighbor) as someone that can be badgered into submission. To solve this problem, Levison suggests that ἀναίδειαν should be translated with "strengthen," picturing God as one that would come to the aid of the believer in his or her time of need by strengthening the believer. Levison, "Importunity?" 460. Herzog's critique of Levison's reading is on the mark: "Although this sleight of hand solved his theological problem, it did not solve the more basic lexical issue." Herzog, *Parables as Subversive Speech*, 203.

74. Bailey, *Poet and Peasant*, 128–132.

75. Ibid., 132.

changed into a positive quality "appropriate to a parable teaching something about prayer."[76] Herzog also believes that ἀναίδειαν refers to the attitude of the neighbor, meaning shamelessness. The neighbor's adherence to the code of honor and his desire to avoid shaming himself, his family, and his village motivates him to "get up and give him whatever he needs."[77] Malina and Rohrbaugh also argue for this meaning of ἀναίδειαν:

> Western commentaries notwithstanding, there is no evidence that the Greek word rendered "importunity" (RSV) or "persistence" (NRSV) ever had those meanings in antiquity. The fact is that the word means "shamelessness," the negative quality of lacking sensitivity (as sense of shame) to one's public honor status . . . Thus the petitioner threatens to expose the potential shamelessness of the sleeper. By morning the entire village would know of his refusal to provide hospitality. He thus gives in to avoid public exposure as a shameless person.[78]

Both these interpretations of ἀναίδειαν are problematic. First, identifying ἀναίδειαν with the host, when taking the cultural scripts of hospitality and friendship in first-century Palestine into consideration, is an ethnocentric reading of the parable. In terms of these cultural scripts the action of the host cannot be interpreted as negative. How can what is considered normal be interpreted as negative? It is only because of the Lukan context of the parable—when Luke 11:5–8 is interpreted in terms of Luke 11:1–13—that the action (ἀναίδειαν) of the host is linked to prayer (and to his attitude when "praying"). This begs the question of whether one can get to the meaning of ἀναίδειαν if the parable is read in its Lukan context. Did the parable in its original context, for example, have prayer as its topic? Moreover, there are good grounds to argue that the characters in the parables of Jesus did not point to God but rather to the kingdom of God.

But identifying ἀναίδειαν with the neighbor also has it problems. Scholars that opt for this possibility see ἀναίδειαν as negative—translating it as "shamelessness" (the negative quality of lacking sensitivity to one's public honor status)—but then still interpret the actions of the neighbor in a positive way by arguing that the neighbor's desire to avoid shaming himself, his family, and his village, is what motivates him to adhere to the request of the host. He thus acted according to the expectations of his group (the village), even if he did not want to; meaning that he actually had shame, that

---

76. Ibid., 130.

77. Herzog, *Parables as Subversive Speech*, 209.

78. Malina and Rohrbaugh, *Social-Science Commentary on the Synoptic Gospels*, 273. See also Hultgren, *Parables of Jesus*, 231; Scott, *Hear Then the Parable*, 91.

is, the proper concern for his honor. In short, he acted positively because of his sensitivity to the opinion of others, a highly desirable quality in the first-century Mediterranean world. Scholars who opt for this interpretation thus set out to interpret ἀναίδειαν from a negative point of view ("shamelessness") but end up interpreting ἀναίδειαν in a positive way (as "having shame").

The dilemma with both of these interpretations is that ἀναίδειαν, in all its occurrences from the eighth century BCE up to the period of the church fathers, is always and without exception used in a negative and pejorative manner. In the early Jewish writings,[79] and in the LXX,[80] ἀναίδειαν is used negatively. This is also the case in Graeco-Roman writings,[81] in early

79. See Sirach 23:6 (The north wind raises clouds; so an impudent [ἀναιδεῖ] face provokes the tongue), Sirach 25:22 (A woman, if she maintain her husband, is full of anger, impudence [ἀναίδεια], and much reproach), Sirach 26:11 (Watch over an impudent [ἀναιδοῦ] eye: and marvel not if she trespass against thee), and Sirach 40:30 (Begging is sweet in the mouth of the shameless [ἀναιδοῦς]: but in his belly there shall burn a fire). Josephus also always uses the word in a negative sense. See *Jewish War* 1.84 (O you most impudent [ἀναιδέστατον] body), *Jewish War* 6.199 (But why do I describe the shameless impudence [ἀναίδειαν] that the famine brought on men in their eating inanimate things, while I am going to relate a matter of fact, the like to which no history relates, either among the Greeks or Barbarians? It is horrible to speak of it, and incredible when heard), and *Jewish Antiquities* 13.317 (And now, O you most impudent [ἀναιδέστατον] body of mine, how long will you retain a soul that ought to die, in order to appease the ghosts of my brother and my mother? Why do you not give it all up at once?) and *Jewish Antiquities* 17.119 (Nay, such is that impudence [ἀναιδείᾳ] of yours on which you confided, that you desire to be put to the torture yourself).

80. See Deut 28:50, 1 Samuel 2:29, Prov 7:13, 25:23, Qoheleth 8:1, Isa 56:11, and Dan 8:23. Prov 25:23, for example, reads "The north wind raises clouds; so an impudent (ἀναιδὲς) face provokes the tongue."

81. See Homer (*Od.* 22.424)]; Archilochus (*Archil.* 78), Sibylline Oracles (*Sib. Or.* 4.36), Sophocles (*El.* 607), Herodotus (*Hist.* 6.129; 7.210), Aristophanes (*Fr.* 226), Plato (*Phaed.* 254d; *Leg.* 647a), Herodianus (*Hdn. Gr.* 2.453), Aristotle (*Top.* 150b), Demosthenes (*Mid.* 62, *Oratio* 21; *Theocr.* 6, *Oratio* 24), Menander Comicus (*Frag.*1090.1–2), Plutarch (*Mor.* 31.2; *Is. Os.* 363F–364A), and Dio Cassius (*Rom. Hist.* 45.16.1). A few examples here will suffice. Plato (*Leg.* 647a) says "Does not, then, the lawgiver, and every man who is worth anything hold this kind of fear in the highest honor and name it 'modesty' (ἀναίδειαν); and to the confidence which is opposed to it does he not give the name 'immodesty' (ἀναίδειαν), and pronounce it to be for all, both publicly and privately, a very great evil?" Demosthenes, *In Midiam* 62, *Oratio* 21, writes "No one has ever been so lost to shame (ἀναίδεια) as to venture on such conduct as this," and in his *In Theocrinem* 6, *Oratio* 4 writes "It seems to me that, so far as effrontery (ἀναίδεια) goes, such a man is ready to do anything." Plutarch also uses the word in a negative way. In *Moralia* 31.2 he writes that this "is the extremity of evil. For when shamelessness (ἀναίδεια) and jealousy rule men, shame (αἰδώς) and indignation leave our race altogether, since shamelessness (ἀναίδεια) and jealousy are the negation of these things whereas shamelessness (ἀναίδεια) is not a counterfeit of shame, but its extreme opposite, masquerading as frankness of speech." And in *Isis and Osiris* 363F–364A he says

244 The Parables of Jesus the Galilean

Christian writings such as those of Hermas (*Vis.* 3.3.2; 3.7.5; *Mand.* 11.12) and Basil (*On the renunciation of the world* 31.648.21),[82] and in later Jewish writings (*b. Berakot* 31b; *Midr. Pss* 28.6). The negative use of ἀναίδειαν is also well attested in the writings of the church fathers, with specific references to ἀναίδειαν in Luke 11:8. Without exception, the attitude of the host is negatively described with the words "shamelessness" or "importunity."[83]

Available Egyptian papyri also attest to the negative meaning of ἀναίδειαν. In P.Lond. II 342 (185 CE) the adjective is used for someone who proves himself ἀναιδὴς ἐν τῇ κώμῃ by levying contributions on the inhabitants, and in P.Ryl. II 421 (37 CE) some shamelessly refuse to pay (ἀναιδευόμενοι μὴ ἀποδῶναι) what they owe. In P.Cair. Isid. 75.16 (316 CE, a petition submitted by Isidorus, son of Ptolemeaus, to Aurelius Gerontius, praepositus of the fifth pagus of the Arsinoite nome) Isidorus complains that six of his fellow villagers broke into his house and smashed his furniture, because they were drunk and shamelessly (ἀναιδίας) felt secure from punishment by reason of their wealth. A final example: In SB 6.9421.13 (a petition submitted by Aurelius to Aurelius Alexander, a police magistrate) Aurelius complains that Didyme, the wife of Agathos Daimon, the cook, treated his family with insolence, using speakable and unspeakable expressions—a woman abundantly furnished with the utmost shamelessness (ἀναιδείᾳ) and effrontery.

A final example of the negative connotation of ἀναίδειαν is an inscription on the stone in the Areopagus on which an accuser stood demanding the full penalty of the law against one accused of homicide; this stone is called the λίθος ἀναιδείας, a clear negative use of ἀναίδειαν.[84]

"God hates ἀναίδεια." Translations from Snodgrass, *Stories with Intent*, 439.

82. "Humility is the imitation of Christ, but high-mindedness, boldness, and shamelessness (ἀναίδεια) are the imitation of the devil." Translation from ibid.

83. See, for example, Tertullian, (*Marc.*), Tatian (*Diat.*), Origen (*Comm. Matt.*), Augustine (*Anic. Fal. Prob.*, letter to the widow of Sextus Petronius Probus, 412 CE), Chrysostom (*On the epistle of St. Paul the apostle to the Ephesians*; *Homily XXVII, Hebrews xi. 28–31*, written at Rome in 384 CE; *Homily XXII, Matt. VI. 28, 29*); John Cassian (*The Conferences of John Cassian, The first conference of Abbot Isaac, on Prayer, Chapter XXXIV*); Ambrose (*Off. I. XXX*)). Chrysostom, in *On the epistle of St. Paul the apostle to the Ephesians*, writes "Limit it not, I say, to certain times of the day, for hear what he is saying; approach at all times; 'pray,' said he, 'without ceasing.' (1 Thess. v. 17.) Hast thou never heard of that widow, how by her importunity she prevailed? (Luke xviii. 1–7.) Hast thou never heard of that friend, who at midnight shamed his friend into yielding by his perseverance? (Luke xi. 5–8.) Hast thou not heard of the Syrophoenician woman (Mark vii. 25–30.), how by the constancy of her entreaty she called forth the Lord's compassion? These all of them gained their object by their importunity."

84. See Liddel and Scott, *A Greek-English Lexicon*, 105.

In all the above examples ἀναίδειαν, and its cognates (e.g., ἀναιδεῖ, ἀναίδεια, ἀναιδοῦ, ἀναιδοῦς, ἀναιδέστατον, αἰδώς, ἀναιδίας, ἀναιδὴς, and ἀναιδευόμενοι) are translated with either "shamelessness," "impudence," "immodesty," or "effrontery," as "someone who acts with insolence," as *unverschämtheit* or *dreistigkeit*.[85] It thus becomes clear "that the meaning of *anaideian* remained consistently censorious from the classical through the Hellenistic and early church periods."[86]

Taking this negative meaning of ἀναίδειαν seriously, Herzog argues that the meaning of ἀναίδειαν (and its related forms) fit into two major categories: greed (e.g., 1 Sam 2:29, LXX; Sir 23:6; Isa 56:11) and attitudes that challenge and break socially constructed boundaries or behaviors (e.g., Deut 28:50, LXX; 1 Bar. 4:15; Sir 25.22; 26:10–11; 40:30; Josephus, *Ant.* 17.118–119; Prov 7:10–27; 21:29; Jer 8:4).[87] With regard to the latter category, Herzog states: "In every case, the words refer to attitudes that disregard boundaries and social conventions or to behavior that violates socially and religiously sanctioned boundaries.[88]" Herzog's remark, as well as the consistent negative use of ἀναίδειαν in available literature and papyri, should be taken seriously when interpreting the parable.[89]

85. Bauer, *Griechisch-Deutsches Wörterbuch*, 99; Herzog, *Parables as Subversive Speech*, 202; Liddel and Scott, *A Greek-English Lexicon*, 105; Snodgrass, *Stories with Intent*, 438–40.

86. Herzog, *Parables as Subversive Speech*, 202. *Contra* Snodgrass, *Stories with Intent*, 443. Snodgrass writes: "No positive use of this word—referring to a good sense of what is shameful and a desire to avoid it—occurs except where Christians have adapted it after the beginning of the second century in dependence on Luke 11:8." So also Derrett, who tries to solve the pejorative meaning of ἀναίδειαν in Luke 11:8 by arguing that the word's meaning had shifted from an invariably pejorative to a more neutral meaning of "boldly" or "unselfconsciously." Derrett, "Friend at Midnight," 84. As the parable indicates, the word has not been "adapted" by Christians in a positive sense, since the word is used in the parable with a negative connotation. A positive meaning of ἀναίδειαν does not fit into a reading of the parable in its Lukan context. To solve this problem, Herzog argues, the early church interpreted ἀναίδειαν in terms of Luke 18:1–8 and either rendered it as "importunity" or "tried to retain the scent of its scandalous past by translating it as 'shameless boldness.'" Herzog, *Parables as Subversive Speech*, 202. Herzog is also correct in his evaluation of Derrett's point of view: "the preponderance of the evidence suggests otherwise." Ibid.

87. Herzog, *Parables as Subversive Speech*, 212–13.

88. Ibid.

89. This meaning of ἀναίδειαν does not fit easily into a reading of the parable in its Lukan context. To solve this problem, the early church interpreted ἀναίδειαν in terms of Luke 18:1–8, rendering it either as "importunity," or "tried to retain the scent of its scandalous past by translating it as 'shameless boldness.'" Ibid., 202. See also Derrett, who tries to solve the pejorative meaning of ἀναίδειαν in Luke 11:8 by arguing that the word's meaning had shifted from an invariably pejorative, to a more neutral meaning of "boldly" or "unselfconsciously." Herzog is correct in his evaluation of Derrett's point

Reading the Parable

In first-century Jewish Palestine, as I discussed earlier, the elite lived at the expense of the nonelite and shaped the social experience of the peasantry, determining their quality of life, exercising power, controlling wealth, and enjoying high status in the process. Social control was built on fear, and the relationship between the ruling elite and the ruled peasantry was one of power and exploitation. Because of this the peasantry was suspicious and hostile toward city elites and the temple hierarchy. Over and above, the peasantry also had to cope with drought, famine, floods, overgrazing, overpopulation, and scarce land. All this left the peasantry on the edge of destitution, and often over the edge.[90]

This situation had a negative impact on traditional village life and traditional village values. Village families were hard-pressed to provide their own families with something to eat because of the pressure of debt and taxation. Villagers were under tremendous stress to survive, which impacted heavily on the relationships between families.[91] Some villagers, who previously felt responsible to help their neighbors in times of shortage, were no longer willing to do so. "Local feuds, which could have been easily resolved in normal time, now often erupted into insults, fistfights, and family feuds . . . Villagers . . . were at each other's throats."[92] In an effort to survive, some peasants began to cultivate ties with powerful patrons.[93] The elite were obviously more than willing to enter into patron-client relationships with the poor. Although these relationships had a "kinship glaze" over them, these relationships rested on negative reciprocity: the elite exploited the peasantry by serving its self-interest at the expense of the "other." These relationships enabled the elite to enhance honor and status, to display their wealth and power, to secure loyalty, and, above all, to build dependency. For

---

of view; "the preponderance of the evidence suggests otherwise." Ibid. It is exactly this evidence that should be taken seriously when the parable is interpreted.

90. "The peasant village in Palestine during the early decades of the first century was under increasing stress. The cumulative effects of Herodian rule, combined with the rigors of Roman colonialism and the demands of the Temple hierarchy, had taken their toll. The monetization and commercialization of the local economy had led to increasingly predatory relationships between elites and peasants . . . [T]here is evidence for rising debt and defaults on loans; accompanied by the hostile takeover of peasant small-holdings and the reduction of peasants to more dependent economic statuses. These practices can be traced back to the fact that elites made loans to peasants and held their land as collateral." Herzog, *Parables as Subversive Speech*, 206.

91. Ibid., 207.

92. Horsley and Silberman, *Message and the Kingdom*, 55.

93. Herzog, *Parables as Subversive Speech*, 207.

the peasantry, these patron-client relationships, in spite of exploitative features, at least enabled them to secure something more than just subsistence living. Some peasants also started to mimic their Roman overlords and the Jerusalem temple elite by setting up patron-client relationships with other peasants and villagers. The Roman overlords and the temple elites used patronage to their benefit. From their point of view, the hospitality shown by the peasantry (in terms of generalized reciprocity) gained nothing in return. The little the peasantry had would have been put to better use were it saved for hard times or used to gain some sort of benefit.[94] This became the viewpoint of some villagers. Because of hard times, some peasants saw the way forward in the principle of balanced reciprocity, even if it meant the exploitation of fellow villagers and the building of dependency. Some of the exploited thus became exploiters themselves. Self-interest turned one's own into the "other."

The scarcity of goods also started to challenge the traditional value of hospitality. Showing hospitality became more and more difficult in a situation where, even in the best of times, there simply was not enough for one's own survival. Some villagers reacted in a positive way to their situation. They reduced their food consumption or ate foods of lesser quality and sought to strengthen kinship ties and village friendships.[95] To survive, some villages developed a system that spread the risk as widely as possible; the problems of one family became the problem of all the families in the village.[96] Balanced reciprocity between villagers (e.g., barter, assistance, and hospitality), which normally took place on a quid pro quo basis, was replaced by generalized reciprocity. Villagers gave without expecting something in return, as in many instances there simply was nothing to return. In this way, the reciprocity that (normally) took place within the sphere of the family or household (family, kin, or clan) became the norm for village life. Villagers regarded their neighbors and friends as they did their family and kin. Some villagers, however, were not willing to subscribe to the sacred duty and village value of hospitality, and were not willing to share what they had in terms of generalized reciprocity. The Friend at Midnight mirrors the socioeconomic conditions of "people who live from hand to mouth and have no provisions beyond those for today."[97] The parable also exemplifies both the positive and negative reactions to this situation described above.

94. Ibid., 213–14.
95. Ibid., 207.
96. Scott, *Hear Then the Parable*, 86.
97. Schottroff, *Parables of Jesus*, 189.

A peasant villager, in the middle of the night (μεσονυκτίου; Luke 11:5), has an unexpected visitor that is his friend (φίλος; Luke 11:6). Because he is his friend, the host considers him as family. The visitor knew he could count on his host, since both of them (being friends), are concerned for each other's honor. His friend would supply whatever was needed to uphold his honor. Friendship after all meant that friends could rely on one another; it implied true commitment, especially when a friend was in need. Moreover, hospitality was extended to friends as a normalcy; it was part of friendship to offer hospitality.

The host, however, has nothing to offer his friend to eat (Luke 11:6). But this was not a problem, as, in his village an unexpected guest was considered a guest of the entire village. Thus, with his friend's arrival, not only was the host's honor at stake, but so also was the honor of the whole village. The entire village was responsible to put a meal on the table for the host's friend, and because of this he could call on others in the village to help him. But on whom should he call? He would go to his neighbor, whose wife, according to the rotating schedule of their village, had baked bread in the community oven the previous morning. This family would have freshly baked bread that he could offer, thus honoring his friend. After all, in his village friendship and being good neighbors were seen as one and the same thing: neighbors were friends. The host had a friend to call on who was as much responsible to help him as a friend as he, as host, had the responsibility to look after his friend. Moreover, his guest was also the friend of the one he was going to call upon, even if they did not know one another. Because the host was friends with both, they were friends too.

After identifying the neighbor and friend who could help him, the host goes to that neighbor's house. He knows the door is already locked, and that his neighbor is most probably already in bed with his family, but this does not matter. What matters was that both of them, as friends, have to help a friend. When the host arrives, he calls out to his sleeping friend: "Friend (φίλε), lend me three loaves of bread; for a friend (φίλος) of mine has arrived, and I have nothing to set before him" (Luke 11:5). This calling out to his sleeping neighbor was done according to the custom of village life so that the sleeping neighbor could recognize his neighbor's voice. No villager knocked on his neighbors' doors, only strangers did.[98] Also, by calling him friend and by telling him that he had a friend as unexpected visitor, he made it clear that his request was based on their friendship, and that their honor was at stake. Even more important, because a guest was the guest of the whole village, the honor of the entire village was at stake.

98. Huffard, "Parable of the Friend at Midnight," 156.

In terms of the social values of friendship and hospitality in village life, the request of the host was "scarcely riveting or revolutionary."[99] It was a normal request that simply had to be met. This explains the abrupt request of the host: "Lend me three loaves." The directness of the request implies closeness, not rudeness.[100] Also, in terms of friendship, the host's use of χρῆσόν (lend; Luke 11:5) does not mean that the will "pay him back" with three loaves as soon as his wife bakes her next batch of bread; it rather acknowledged the mutuality involved in their friendship.[101]

The neighbor's reaction, however, is negative: "Do not bother me (μή μοι κόπους πάρεχε); the door has already been locked, and my children are with me in bed; I cannot get up and give you anything" (Luke 11:7). The way we as modern readers understand this excuse of the neighbor is important for the eventual interpretation of the parable. The host's request was literarily an invitation to a friend (φίλε and φίλον; Luke 11:5) to help him honor another friend (φίλος; Luke 11:6). Also, as Derrett indicates, the host's request (to ask as if the thing requested were the property of the asker) was a proof of friendship between the host and his neighbor.[102] In essence, therefore, the host is not asking for three loaves of bread; he is asking a friend to honor a friendship; "the sleeping neighbor is not being irritated by his neighbor but is being honored by being asked to contribute to the meal."[103] And, in terms of friendship, "jolted doors and sleeping children were minor obstacles easily overcome."[104]

The neighbor, therefore, is not making excuses. He is actually, in a veiled way, saying that he does not consider himself a friend of the host. Therefore he is not willing to get out of bed to do what is normal where friendship is involved. Some in the village, in the face of their difficult situation to provide something for their own families to eat (because of the pressure of debt and taxation), might have opted for a system that spread

99. Catchpole, "Q and the Friend at Midnight," 413.

100. Derrett, "Friend at Midnight," 83–84.

101. See Herzog, *Parables as Subversive Speech*, 208. Herzog continues: A host always asked directly for what was needed, since no social distance existed between villagers; "the assumption that the host is simply borrowing bread that he will readily return is questionable. The contributions to the meal are not loans but direct gifts, provided to fulfill the ritual obligations of the village and maintain its reputation." Ibid., 201. See also Levison, "Importunity," 457. *Contra* Buttrick, Jeremias, and Kistemaker, who are of the opinion that the host intended to borrow the bread and "return it at once." Buttrick, *Speaking in Parables*, 185–87; Jeremias, *Parables of Jesus*, 157; Kistemaker, *Stories Jesus Told*, 149.

102. Derrett, "Friend at Midnight," 83–84.

103. Herzog, *Parables as Subversive Speech*, 201.

104. Ibid., 202.

the risk as widely as possible. It is their choice. He is also aware that, in an effort to survive, some in the village—including the host at his door—have decided to practice generalized reciprocity (to give without expecting a return), and by implication to consider neighbors and friends as kin.[105] The host has decided not to make that choice. The little he has can better be used in looking after his own family, and the extra he (may) have, he will rather keep to be able to ensure the well-being of his own family. He is therefore not interested in friendship and being hospitable; and because of this, he is not willing to get out of bed.

But this is not the end of the parable. The neighbor is not finished. He is not willing to help as a friend, but he has an offer to make. He thus continues from behind the bolted door: "What I am willing do, not as your friend, but because of my ἀναίδειαν, is to get up out of bed and open the door and give you as much as you need (δώσει αὐτῷ ὅσων χρήζει" (Luke 11:8). Just as in the case of the neighbor's first reply, his second reply must be read carefully. The neighbor has no shame; he is shameless in every way possible, making his attitude that of ἀναίδειαν. He knows that his conversation with the host is not private, as by this time some of the other villagers are listening to the conversation between him and the host. And he knows that many of those listening have the same attitude as the host. But he does not care. After all, these are times of survival.

Therefore, what the neighbor is willing to do is to make the host a client. Mimicking the Roman overlords and the Jerusalem temple elite, he is setting up a patron-sclient relationship with the host. We have seen that the Roman overlords and the temple elite used patronage to their benefit, and indeed they did benefit! Hospitality shown (in terms of generalized reciprocity) will benefit nobody; the neighbor will get nothing in return. He is, however, willing to go for balanced reciprocity. The neighbor also wants to benefit from the transaction, as other patrons do. These are his rules, and the host can take it or leave it. And, yes, he has ἀναίδειαν: something with which he is quite comfortable that the rest of the village is also taking note of. This will, at least, inform them of what to expect when they come calling at his door in future. They know what the rules will be. And of course they are welcome; the more clients, the more the benefit will be. One of the exploited has become an exploiter himself; self–interest has turned the "own" into the "other."

This reading of the parable takes serious cognizance of the fact that the meaning of ἀναίδειαν has been read only in a negative sense from the eighth

---

105. Village people made decisions on important topics after long discussions with their friends. Families, communities and villages are tightly knit together. See Bailey, *Jesus through Middle Eastern Eyes*, 303.

century BCE to the period of church fathers, and that in every case its usage refers to "attitudes that disregard boundaries and social conventions, or to behavior that violates socially and religiously sanctioned boundaries."[106] This interpretation of the neighbor's actions concurs with this use of ἀναίδειαν. Support for this reading comes from Oakman, the only other scholar who interprets ἀναίδειαν in the way described above:

> The neighbor's importunity is often seen as the point of the similitude, but I take the second *autou* of 11:8 to refer to the man in bed, not the man at the door. Besides, a truly shameless man would not be at the door at midnight out of sight of everyone. The meaning of the parable does hinge upon the word *anaidein*. Egyptian papyri strongly urge the meaning "shameless desire for personal gain." The point then is: The man in bed may not get up at midnight to provide for an embarrassed neighbor, but to keep the other in debt he certainly will. The "friend" will make a loan at midnight on this basis.[107]

So, what was Jesus' intention with the parable? While in the other parables discussed so far Jesus uses the actions of negative figures such as patrons, shepherds, and merchants as examples of kingdom behavior, here Jesus criticizes nonkingdom behavior. A just village, and just neighbors, "would resist the moral corruption of Roman occupation by refusing to treat one another as the Romans had hoped they would."[108] But this is exactly what the neighbor does not do. Instead of being part of a kingdom village, he shamelessly turns a neighbor into a client. And this is playing the game of Rome, the exploiter and oppressor. Therefore, "the parable makes in painfully clear what is needed for peasant and village to act with integrity."[109]

Two final remarks will suffice. This reading also takes seriously the fact that the contextual fit of (at least some) of Jesus' parables in the Synoptics predetermine their "meaning," as is indeed the case with Luke 11:5–8. Because of its context in Luke (Luke 11:1–13), as the parable's history of the interpretation has shown, the meaning of the parable is linked to some or other aspect of prayer. This was not the intention with which Jesus told the parable. It is Luke's application of this parable of Jesus, in order for it to fit into his theological intent. Removed from their original sociocultural settings retold in new contexts, the parables of Jesus lose something of their

---

106. Herzog, *Parables as Subversive Speech*, 213.

107. Oakman, *Jesus and the Peasants*, 94; italics original.

108. Bessler-Northcutt, "Learning to See God," 58.

109. Ibid., 60.

radical nature and power.[110] In the case of Luke 11:5–8, its new context has changed its initial meaning quite extensively. It is therefore necessary—if we at least want to come close to what Jesus intended with his parables–to read his parables against the sociocultural, political, and economic situation in which Jesus' public ministry took place.

This reading, finally, takes seriously the viewpoint that the characters used by Jesus in his parables do not point to God; the characters point rather to the kingdom of God. When God is seen as the metaphoric equivalent of the neighbor in Luke 11:5–8, the parable gives expression to the vertical relationship between God and man. However, if the parable is taken out of the secondary context of Luke, and the neighbor is not equated with God, the possibility opens up to read the parable as focusing on horizontal relationships between man and man. And, specifically, on what honorable actions are, as well as on the principle of generalized reciprocity between two peasants vis-à-vis the principles of balanced or negative reciprocity.

A Parable of Jesus?

Although the parable does not pass the criteria of early, multiple, and independent attestation (it is only attested in Luke), it does most probably go back to Jesus. In terms of the criterion of coherence, the parable displays typical values that Jesus supported, which can be identified by using the criteria of early, multiple, and independent attestation.

Jesus did *not* advocate balanced reciprocity but generalized reciprocity, an aspect of Jesus' teaching that has been illuminated convincingly by Oakman.[111] Q 6:27–28, 29, 30, 6:31 (cf. Gos. Thom. 6:3), and Q 6:34–35 (cf. Gos. Thom. 95:1–2) attest to the fact that Jesus advocated general reciprocity. Jesus, second, redefined kinship. Jesus thus advocated a "kinship economy" (operating in the realm of generalized reciprocity) between people that were not kin in the normal sense of the word, but kin in terms of fictive kinship.[112] Like fathers who know how to give their children good gifts (Q 11:11–13; Gos. Thom. 2:1–4, 92:1, 94:1–3), his followers had to give without expecting something in return (Luke 6:30–38; 10:33–36; 12:33; 14:13–14; Matt 18:23–34).

These aspects of Jesus' teaching are clearly detectable in the parable. For some villagers reciprocity that (usually) took place within the sphere of the family or household (family, kin, or clan) became the norm for village

110. Waetjen, "Subversion of World," 716.

111. See Oakman, *Jesus and the Peasants*, 66, 94, 97, 103–105, 157–60.

112. See Stansell, "Gifts, Tributes, and Offerings," 359.

life. Villagers regarded their friends and neighbors in the same way as they did their family—as kin. When neighbors are neighbors, in this sense, the kingdom becomes visible. However, when neighbors do not act like neighbors, nothing of God's kingdom is visible.

The parable thus tells the story of a different world, of the way things ought to be, of "life as ruled by God's generosity and goodness."[113] The parable offered its hearers an alternative world to the world created by aristocratic society (the Roman and religious elite). For Jesus, this alternative world was the kingdom; a world wherein neighbors are kin and practice general reciprocity. Therefore, the parable questions the ἀναίδειαν of the neighbor, his participation in a world created by the oppressing elite, and his enforcement of the elite's oppressive mores in acting against his friend and neighbor.[114] When neighbors exploit neighbors, they are not part of the kingdom. This was not the way to act.

113. Hoover, "Gaining and Losing," 92.
114. Bessler–Northcutt, "Learning to See God," 56.

CHAPTER 11

The Rich Man and Lazarus (Luke 16:19–26): An Unwilling Patron

THE PARABLE OF THE Rich man and Lazarus is an illustration of the great class disparity that existed between the urban elite and the exploited rural peasantry in first-century Palestine. In the parable the rich man symbolizes the elite and Lazarus the exploited poor. That the poor man is given a name, Lazarus, is not accidental—it typifies the way in which Jesus sided with the poor, the expendables, and the socially impure of his day. The gist of the parable is that when patrons, who have in abundance, do not cross the gate to the poor, a society is created wherein the chasm between rich (elite) and poor (peasantry) cannot be crossed. When this happens, when patrons do not fulfill their role as patrons, no one becomes part of the kingdom—neither Lazarus nor the rich man. Therefore, the parable identifies Jesus' historical activity essentially as politics (the restructuring of society), and not as religion or theology.

History of Interpretation

The earliest interpretations of the parable of the Rich Man and Lazarus, except for Luke's application of the parable, are the allegorical interpretations of Augustine, Gregory the Great, and Ambrose.[1] In an attempt to break

1. According to Augustine, the rich man refers to the Jews, Lazarus to the Gentiles, the five brothers to the five books of the Law, and Lazarus' sores to confession. In Augustine's view, Lazarus typifies the Christ figure, while Ambrose sees Lazarus as Paul. In Gregory the Great's (540–604 CE) interpretation, the rich man represents the Jews, who used the law for vain motives, while Lazarus symbolizes the Gentiles, who were not ashamed to confess their sins (Lazarus' many wounds and sores). The crumbs that fall from the rich man's (from the Jews') table represent the Jewish law, and the licking of Lazarus' sores signifies healing, the confessing of sins to the holy doctors (papacy).

away from these allegorical interpretations, Luther and Calvin employed a historical and literal approach to the parable (that can be characterized as theological). They did not, however, succeed in avoiding the perils of allegorization.[2]

The first historical-critical reading of the parable was that of Jülicher, in which he identified two (loosely connected) parts in the parable: Luke 16:19–26 (the opposing and very different lives of the rich man and poor Lazarus in this world) and Luke 16:27–31 (the complete and permanent reversal of the fortunes of the rich man and Lazarus in the afterlife).[3] Jülicher's interpretation of the parable has, in a certain sense, dominated the interpre-

---

Because the Gentiles' sins are forgiven, they will go to heaven, and the Jews will receive eternal torment upon their lips as a result of the law that was on their lips, but which they chose not to fulfill. Morally speaking, the parable cautions against ostentation, exalts the virtue of poverty, and admonishes the believer to lose no opportunity for doing good works of mercy. See Wailes, *Medieval Allegories*, 255–56; Kissinger, *History of Interpretation*, 38.

  2. Luther's historical-Christological interpretation of the parables focused of the Scriptures in their "plain sense" (a plain and literal reading of the text without considering, if possible, hidden or symbolic meanings in the text). Each text has as reference point (center of meaning), namely, Jesus Christ (Luther's so-called Christum treibet). Luther identified at least three meanings in the parable: First, the parable teaches that it is not sufficient merely to do no evil and to do no harm, but rather that one must be helpful and good. Second, the parable shows that God does not desire the dead to teach us, but that one should cling to the Scriptures. And third, it is an abominable and pagan practice, before the eyes of God, to consult the spirits and practice necromancy. In this theological interpretation the Reformation's *sola Scriptura* principle is clearly visible, which also speaks for Luther's interpretation of "Abraham's bosom" as referring to the faith (*sola fidei*) that is promised in the gospel. In his interpretation of the parables, Calvin tried to avoid any kind of allegorization, and looked for the central theme of each parable. The central point of the Rich Man and Lazarus is to show the final state of those who neglect the poor while reveling in pleasures and indulging themselves. See Kissinger, *History of Interpretation*, 44–48. Calvin also commented on the meaning of "Abraham's bosom"; it is a metaphor which points to the fact that God's children are strangers and pilgrims in the world, but if they follow the faith of their father Abraham, they will inherit the blessed rest when they die. Calvin, *Harmony of the Gospels*, 3:116–22. Just as Luther's interpretation of this parable showed his *sola Scriptura* principle, so Calvin's theological interpretation of the parable shows traces of the *sola fidei* principle of the Reformation; his is an allegorical reading in a theological dress. See also Rauschenbusch, who replaces the *sola fidei* principle of Luther and Calvin with the concept of economic injustice. Jesus regarded a life of sumptuous living and indifference to the want and misery of a fellow human at the doorstep as deeply sinful and immoral. This is clear from the parable, as the rich man is not accused of any crimes or vices, and yet he is sent to hell. Wealth is characterized as a dividing power, since it creates semihuman relations between social classes. Jesus thus told the parable to warn the rich that they must show generosity before it is too late and they are also cast into hell as Dives (the rich man) was. Rauschenbusch, *Gospel for the Social Awakening*, 73–75.

  3. Jülicher, *Gleichnisreden Jesu*, 634.

tation of the parable up to the present in three ways:[4] First, most scholars divide the parable into two parts,[5] "an opinion that has been a staple of the scholarly literature ever since."[6] Second, most scholars look for the main point of the parable in its second part.[7] A minority of scholars, however, find the main point of the parable in its first part,[8] and some identify a distinctive message expressed in each part.[9] Third, scholars have proposed an array of extrabiblical stories that the first part of the parable has supposedly borrowed from.[10] Hock aptly describes this direction the interpretation of the parable has taken:

4. According to Herzog, most interpretations of the parable have been deeply indebted to Bultmann's insight that the parable could be divided into two parts. Herzog, *Parables as Subversive Speech*, 115. Hock, however, is correct indicating that this division of the parable already formed part of Jülicher's analysis in 1910. Hock, "Lazarus and Micyllus," 449.

5. See Hock for a list of scholars who interpret the parable by dividing it into the two parts identified by Jülicher. Hock, "Lazarus and Micyllus," 449, n. 5. To Hock's list can be added the interpretations of Cadoux, *Art and Use*; Gressmann, *Von Reichen Mann und Armen Lazarus*; Oesterley, *Gospel Parables*; Smith, *Parables of the Synoptic Gospels*.

6. Hock, "Lazarus and Micyllus," 449.

7. See, for example, Jeremias, *Parables of Jesus*, 182–86. The thrust of the parable (that should be named the parable of the Six Brothers) is that of "the challenge of the hour" in which evasion is impossible. The emphasis of the parable is to be found in its added "epilogue"; the rich man's five brothers—like their rich brother—live careless lives in selfish luxury, deaf to God's word in the belief that death ends all. Jesus tells the parable to warn men who resemble the brothers of the rich man of this impeding danger. The parable is not commentary on a social problem or a teaching on the afterlife; it is a warning to those for whom everything is at stake to make the right decision. See also Jones, *Studying the Parables of Jesus*, 163.

8. See, for example, Crossan, *In Parables*, 66–68; Scott, *Hear Then the Parable*, 146–50.

9. Bultmann divides the parable in two distinct parts, each of which expresses a distinctive message. Luke 16:19–26 is a story based on a folkloric account of the reversal of fortunes in the afterlife, and Luke 16:27–31 constitutes a polemic against the need for signs to augment the Torah and Prophets for revealing the will of God. In following Bultmann, Smith argues that Jesus shifted the meaning of the traditional materials about the afterlife (Luke 16:19–26) to focus on the adequacy of the Torah (Luke 19:27–31). Oesterley is of the opinion that Luke 16:19–25 was addressed to the Pharisees, while Luke 16:27–31 was spoken to correct Sadducean beliefs. Cadoux sees Luke 16:19–26 as an authentic parable of Jesus that was used in his debate with the Pharisees over the importance of signs (Luke 16:27–31). Bultmann, *Synoptic Tradition*, 210; Smith, *Parables of the Synoptic Gospels*, 135–41; Oesterley, *Gospel Parables*, 208–10; Cadoux, *Art and Use*, 124–28.

10. This idea was first championed by Gressmann, who identified the Egyptian folktale of the journey of Si-Osiris, the son of Setme Chamoïs, to the underworld as parallel for Luke 16:19–26. Gressmann, *Von Reichen Mann und Armen Lazarus*, 115–21. Jeremias and Bultmann, on the other hand, see a Jewish legend (a folktale about a rich and

For decades, we have seen, scholars have been investigating the
parable within the framework that goes back to the first part of
century. Since Jülicher, scholars have virtually accepted as a giv-
en the division of the parable into two parts. Since Gressmann
scholars have looked to an Egyptian folktale for the background
of at least the first part of the parable and for the interpretation

---

godless married couple) as parallel for Luke 16:19–26. According to Jeremias, following
the work of Salm, Jesus used a Jewish version of the story of Gressmann's Egyptian story
of Setme. Alexandrian Jews brought this story to Palestine where it became popular as
the story of the rich tax collector Bar Ma☒jan and a poor scholar; a story that found its
way into the (Aramaic) Palestinian Talmud (*y. Sanh.* 6.23c; *y. Hag.* 2.77). This folktale
ends where Bar Ma☒jan stands at the bank of a stream, unable to reach the water (cf.
Luke 16:26). Bultmann sees Luke 16:19–26 as a Jewish legend, a variation of the Egyptian and Jewish folkloric story based on a folkloric account of the reversal of fortunes in
the afterlife. Jeremias, *Parables of Jesus*, 182–83; Bultmann, *Synoptic Tradition*, 103–5.
See also Smith, *Parables of the Synoptic Gospels*, 54. According to Hock, the first part
of the parable points to a Graeco-Roman parallel. In the Cynic writings of Lucian (e.g.,
Gall.) we find two stories of the shoemaker Micyllus, a poor man, which parallel the
Rich man and Lazarus with comparisons and characterization through dialogue. The
two stories tell how and why Megapenthes (a rich man in Cataplus) is sent to hell; his
use of his wealth, his licentiousness, his sexual offenses, his murders, his confiscations,
his arrogance, and his moneylending (hedonism). In the end it is a question of self-
control (Micyllus) and no self-control (Megapenthes) that seals their fate. According
to Hock, all this is paralleled in the parable: in the parable, the rich man is compared
with Lazarus in terms of his hedonism. The parable thus has a Cynic coloring. Lazarus
is the good one because his life of poverty excludes him from the damning life of the
rich man. In the parable Jesus the Cynic is thus speaking. Hock, "Lazarus and Micyllus," 457–62. Aalen and Nickelsburg have noted parallels in 1 Enoch. Aalen, "St. Luke's
Gospel and 1 Enoch," 1–13; Nickelsburg, "Riches, the Rich, and God's Judgment,"
324–44. See also Snodgrass for other possible parallels. Snodgrass, *Stories with Intent*,
420–23. Almost all scholars who identify an extrabiblical parallel for the first part of
the parable are of the opinion that Jesus used an extrabiblical tale and reinterpreted
it by adding a conclusion that is the key to understand the parable. Hock, "Lazarus
and Micyllus," 449. Jeremias goes as far to argue that the folktale is "essential" for understanding the parable. Jeremias, *Parables of Jesus*, 183. Pax, on the contrary, argues
that the Oriental social experience itself is sufficient to explain the similarities between
the parable and the folktale. Pax, "Der Reiche und Arme Lazarus," 254–68. Hultgren
holds the same view. Although stories about the fate of the rich and the poor in the
afterlife are abundant, the parable is not an exact replica of any of these stories. While
it is related to common folklore, it is a creation in its own right. Hultgren, *Parables of
Jesus*, 111. Snodgrass also argues that any specific extrabiblical parallel for the parable
is unlikely. There are dozens of stories in various cultures over thousands of years that
tell of trips to the realm of the dead, often castigating the rich (e.g., the *Gilgamesh Epic*,
the *Odyssey*, and 1 Enoch). Moreover, the Gospel story is different from the Egyptian
and Jewish accounts. "The Gospel story uses common folkloric motifs shared by several
cultures: descent to the underworld, reversal of circumstances, and denunciation of
the rich for their neglect of the poor." Snodgrass, *Stories with Intent*, 427. Lucian's use
of these themes in a variety of works also shows that even an indirect dependence on a
specific account is not likely.

of details in the parable. And since Bultmann, scholars have increasingly had to decide whether Jesus or the church is the origin of the parts of the parable.[11]

Jülicher's interpretation of the parable has influenced almost all subsequent interpretations of the parable in yet another way. According to Jülicher, the main point in the Rich Man and Lazarus is that it shows the ultimate consequences of a life of wealth and pleasure.[12] Almost all subsequent interpretations of the parable have come to more or less the same conclusion. The parable's moral point is the dangers that arise from the love of wealth, a command to take care of the poor, a warning to the rich to take heed of this command, and a condemnation of the rich that ignore this warning.[13] When one looks at most modern critical studies of the parable, this indeed seems to be the case. Moreover, it also seems that whatever the approach, the result of the interpretation is more or less the same. Differences are that of emphasis. The following examples substantiate this point.

Most scholars who see the parable as a Lukan composition or interpret it in terms of its narrative context in Luke find some moral lesson about the rich (the dangers that arise from the love of wealth) and the poor (or poverty) in the parable; a well-established motif in Luke (and Acts).[14] According to Bultmann, the parable (Luke 16:19–26) intended to tell the poor to be contented with their lot, and Talbert sees the parable as a command to take care of the poor (cf. Deut 15:7–11) and as a condemnation of the rich.[15] Hultgren reads the parable in the same vein. The parable serves to warn the rich about the perils of neglecting the needs of the poor, even and especially those whom it would have been socially acceptable to be indifferent to.[16] This is also the opinion of Schottroff. The parable forms part of Luke 16,

11. Hock, "Lazarus and Micyllus," 451.

12. Jülicher, *Gleichnisreden Jesu*, 317.

13. "From the earliest days interpreters have focused on the parable's moral impact with its denunciation of the wealthy who neglect the poor. Other options are minority opinions. In modern critical studies most interpreters still see the parable as denouncing the misuse of resources and the neglect of the poor." Snodgrass, *Stories with Intent*, 426.

14. Hughes' interpretation is an exception. In the parable Luke gives the reason why the early followers of Jesus failed so miserably in their attempt to evangelize the Jews. Hughes, "Rich Man and Lazarus," 29–41.

15. See Bultmann, *Synoptic Tradition*, 203; Talbert, *Reading Luke*, 156–59.

16. Hultgren sees the parable, in its Lukan form, as a Christian allegorization that goes back to a nucleus that can be attributed to Jesus. This "nucleus" had the same meaning as its present Lukan form, namely, the teachings of God concerning care for the poor that are clear in the Law and the Prophets. Hultgren, *Parables of Jesus*, 115. See also Perkins, *Hearing the Parables*, 21; Donahue, *Gospel in Parable*, 171.

which is "a chapter of halakah on the subject of money, from the perspective of the Lukan communities," and in its context communicates that a good life based on the misery of the poor is not part of the kingdom. In the kingdom money should rather be used for the universal liberation of the people to become a reality.[17] Snodgrass, who defines the parables as expanded analogies used to convince and persuade (stories with intent), and who interprets the parables in terms of their respective narrative contexts in the canonical gospels, comes to the same conclusion.[18] The parable has two equally important themes: judgment for the use of wealth, and the sufficiency of the Scriptures. The parable expresses God's identification with the poor. The error of the rich man (who is a child of Abraham) is the neglect of the poor and those in need, including Lazarus (who is also a child of Abraham). The children of Abraham are those who obey Moses and the prophets and share their wealth with the poor.[19] This is also the result of Leonhardt-Balzer's reading. The main focus of the parable is the rich man, and the name Lazarus is a symbol for all poor people. The Torah and the prophets emphasize the social responsibility of the rich to care for the poor, and the hearer of the parable is called to either identify, or not, with the rich man.[20]

Scholars like Smith, Stein, Herzog, and Hock, who like Jülicher (and Jeremias), attribute both parts of the parable to Jesus,[21] formulate the main point of the parable in a similar vein to Jülicher. According to Smith, Jesus

17. Schottroff, *Parables of Jesus*, 160.

18. Snodgrass sees the contexts of the parables given by the evangelists as the proper framework for interpreting the parables, since the parables express "the general context of the ministry of Jesus in first century Palestine." He continues: "Jesus' parables may not legitimately be torn from that context and placed elsewhere. To do so will not allow interpretation of Jesus' parables, nor allow hearing him, but *will make one a creator of a new parable with absconded materials.*" Snodgrass, *Stories with Intent*, 20; italics original. The implication of Snodgrass' point of view is that there is no difference in meaning between the parables as spoken by the historical Jesus, and the versions in the gospels, even if the contexts of the respective gospels are not that of Jesus' first-century (Galilean) Palestine.

19. Ibid., 428–33.

20. Leonhardt-Balzer, "Wie Kommt ein Reicher in der Abrahams Schoß," 647–660.

21. The process of parabolic transmission, Smith argues, makes it possible that the majority of the parables in the Synoptic Gospels represent authentic parables of Jesus. Also, since Jesus' teaching on poverty and wealth was a fundamental part of his eschatological gospel, the Rich man and Lazarus most probably goes back to Jesus himself. Smith, *Parables of the Synoptic Gospels*, 113. Stein bases his contention that most of the synoptic parables go back to Jesus on two arguments: First, the parables meet the criterion of dissimilarity or distinctiveness (the parables of Jesus did not derive from the Judaism of Jesus' day or from the early church). Second, the content and language of the parables agree with what is found in other sayings of Jesus. Stein, *Introduction to the Parables*, 38–39. See also Schweizer, *Good News according to Luke*, 262.

equates poverty with piety in the parable, and wealth with ungodliness, and states that the measure of a person's fitness to enter the kingdom is his readiness to do without the things of this world. Stein defines the parable as a story parable (a parable that refers to a singular event), an example of those teachings of Jesus that involve the generous use of possessions. More specifically, the parable says that love is manifested by the wise use of one's possessions to perform acts of love. Although the rich man did not actively harm Lazarus, his sin was that he did not do any positive good to him.[22] Herzog sees the central contrast of the parable as the great class disparity between the urban elites (epitomized by the rich man) and the desperate expendables (epitomized by Lazarus). The parable codifies the relationship between rich and poor in first-century Palestine, and is representative of Jesus' pastoral attitude toward the poor. The parable is good news for Lazarus but bad news for the rich; in the afterlife the situation of this life will be reversed. Lazarus will take part in the eschatological banquet simply because he was poor.[23] Hock, who suggests that Graeco-Roman intellectual traditions (esp. Cynic views on wealth and property) should be seen as the cultural bedrock of the parable, understands the parable as a harsh charge against the rich (esp. hedonism), while Lazarus is judged innocent because of his poverty.[24]

Scholars who attribute only the first part of the parable to Jesus also link the meaning of the parable to the dangers that arise from the love of wealth and the responsibility of the rich towards the poor.[25] Scott's interpre-

22. Stein, *Introduction to the Parables*, 79, 111, 135.

23. Herzog, *Parables as Subversive Speech*, 128–29. See also Segundo, *Historical Jesus*, 114.

24. Hock, "Lazarus and Micyllus," 462. The opinions of Cave, Wright, Cadoux, Hunter, Oesterley, and Regalado can be noted here as exceptions. In the readings of Cave and Wright the parable describes how Jesus, during his ministry, welcomed the sinners (Lazarus as symbol of the poor in Abraham's bosom—a sign that the return from exile, or resurrection, has started. From this perspective, the parable is a warning directed at the Pharisees (or at Israel in general) to repent. Cave, "Lazarus," 319–25; Wright, *Victory of God*, 255–56. Cadoux argues that the parables of Jesus must be understood within the context of Jesus' relationship with the Jews. Jesus only used parables in situations where controversy reigned. Therefore, Jesus' parables had a polemical and apologetic intent. Jesus told the parable as a response to the Pharisees' request for a sign from heaven (Mark 8:11–12). Cadoux, *Art and Use*, 80–115. Hunter argues that the parable was directed at the Sadducees, who did not believe in a future life, and Regalado sees the main point of the parable as the importance of living by the Word of God (Moses and the prophets). Hunter, *Interpreting the Parables*, 113; Regalado, "Jewish Background of the Rich Man," 346. In Oesterley's reading, the first part of the parable is addressed to the Pharisees, while the second part is addressed to the Sadducees to correct their belief on the afterlife. Oesterley, *Gospel Parables*, 208–10.

25. One exception in this regard is the interpretation of Crossan. Crossan identifies

tation can here serve as example. In his interpretation of the parables, Scott focuses on the social dynamics of first-century peasant culture, as well as on the linguistic, mythical, and wisdom traditions in which the parables of Jesus operated. This parable is one of boundaries and oppositional parallels. The most important oppositional parallel in the parable is that of space; the rich man is inside, and Lazarus is outside. These oppositions reflect the limited-goods society of the first-century Mediterranean world, where the social status of the poor and the rich were fixed. The hinge that binds the oppositional parallel of space together is the gate—it can let in or keep out. The rich man's fault is that he does not pass through the gate to help Lazarus. The kingdom, however, provides a gate to the neighbor. This gate means grace and is a metaphor for the kingdom. The parable attacks the blindness that does not see the gate's purpose, and "subverts the complacency that categorizes reality into rich and poor or any other division. The standard is not moral behavior as individual, isolated act, but the ability to go through the gate, metaphorically, to the other side; solidarity." In *nuce*, the parable states that "the kingdom of God is the manifestation of God's righteousness in the face of injustice."[26]

Finally, Via's interpretation of the parable can be mentioned. Via, who reads the parables as aesthetic objects and employs a structuralist reading, defines this parable as an example story, an illustrative example of what one is to do or not to do. From this point of view, the parable simply states that one should look after the poor.[27]

---

three basic categories of parables that Jesus told: parables of advent, reversal, and action. The Rich man and Lazarus (Luke 16:19–26) falls under the category of reversal. In the parable the rich man becomes "poor" and the poor Lazarus becomes "rich." The kingdom shatters and reverses everything that seems certain and firm. Jesus was not interested in moral instruction about riches. The parable is about the reversal that comes with the kingdom's advent. Crossan, *In Parables*, 33–35. In his most recent reading of the parable, Crossan typifies the parable as a parable of challenge. From an economic point of view, the parable challenges "any world's standard presumptions about the fortunate rich and the unfortunate poor." Crossan, *Power of Parable*, 93–94.

26. Scott, *Hear Then the Parable*, 141–159.

27. Via, *Parables*, 114–19. In his structuralist reading of the parables, Via distinguishes between the story and the discourse of a parable (the identified story in the text that is to be interpreted), then analyzes the parable from an actantial point of view (which enables the reader to understand the identified story), and finally translates the vehicle of the parable (that which is well known) into the tenor, which makes the parable a parable of the kingdom of God.

Integrity and Authenticity

Although there is a "scholarly consensus" on the main point of the parable, the parable's history of interpretation indicates that scholarly opinion is divided on the authenticity and integrity of the parable. Some scholars argue that the parable cannot be attributed to Jesus. For some the parable is a unit, with the first part paralleled in extrabiblical literature, and the second part added by Luke or the early church. Some see the whole parable as a Lukan composition, while others argue that the parable consists of two parts, with the first part paralleled in extrabiblical literature, and the second part added by Luke or the early church. For some both parts of the parable stem from the early church.[28]

Scholars who argue for the authenticity of the parable also either defend the integrity of the parable (with both parts stemming from Jesus to form a unit) or argue that the parable consists of two separate narratives (with the first part paralleled in extrabiblical literature used by Jesus, and the second part stemming from Jesus himself). Some see only the first part as stemming from Jesus and the second part added by Luke, while others view only parts of both narratives as authentic sayings of Jesus.[29]

---

28. See Van Eck, "Rich Man and Lazarus," 3.

29. Talbert argues that the parable is part of a carefully constructed unit (Luke 16) and functions as Luke's answer to Luke 16:14–18. The first part of the parable (Luke 16:19–26) refers to Luke 16:14–15, demonstrates the ambiguity of wealth as a sign of God's blessing, and fulfills Luke 16:15b. The second part of the parable (Luke 16:27–31) exemplifies Luke 16:16–18. The law is still in force (as the witness of Moses and the prophets indicate; Luke 16:29), and therefore also in force iss the command to take care of the poor (Deut 15:7–11). Talbert, *Reading Luke*, 156–59. Hock bases the unity of the parable on the following arguments: First, the Egyptian folktale is not a close literary parallel for the parable and thus is not essential for understanding the parable. Second, the opening verses of the parable (Luke 16:19–21) depict the contrast between the rich man and Lazarus, which sets up the principal action of the parable (their deaths in Luke 16:22 and their reversal of fortunes in Luke 16:23) with the following dialogue between Abraham and the rich man (Luke 16:24–31), underscoring the permanence of this reversal and the negative characterization of the rich man. If one breaks the parable at Luke 16:26, the dialogue between Abraham and the rich man becomes divided in the middle. Hock, "Lazarus and Micyllus," 454, 462. For Herzog, the unity of the parable lies "in the way the description of social classes in the first part sets up the exhortation to read Moses and the Prophets in the second part." The parable is not a story about two abstract social types, but a story about representatives of two social classes, the urban elite and the desperate expendables, and serves as a codifying legitimization of these two social classes in first-century Palestine. Herzog, *Parables as Subversive Speech*, 129. If one looks closely at Herzog's interpretation of the parable, the question can be asked if his interpretation really needs the second part of the parable. For Snodgrass, when one compares the parable with other descent stories that have as their theme the revelation of the fate of the dead to the living (Luke 16:27–31; see the story of Setme and its Jewish

Where does the parable end? When Luke 16:19–31 is seen as a Lukan composition, being part of the well-knit literary composition Luke 16, the parable's integrity is obviously above suspicion. What if, however, the parable is taken from its Lukan context, and a possible historical Jesus setting for the parable is proposed? Does the literary unity of Luke 16 not suggest that the parable was appended or reworked to fit into its literary context? And do the two parts of the parable as opposite poles really need one another, as some have argued? Do all the opposites in the parable not already occur in the first part of the parable? And does the second part of the parable not introduce a new theme (the validity of the prophets and the Torah) that is not necessary for the first part to function as a cohesive unit on its own?

The strongest arguments against the integrity of the parable have come from Funk, Crossan, and Scott. Funk argues that Luke 16:27–31 has as content the early Christian theme of the Judean lack of belief in the resurrection of Jesus (cf. Luke 16:31; a clear reference to Jesus). Moreover, the testimony of Moses and the prophets, appealed to in Luke 16:29 and 31, resonates with the resurrection stories in Luke 24:13–35 and 24:36–49 (esp. Luke 24:27 and 44). The ending of the parable is therefore most probably a Lukan creation.[30]

Crossan and Scott also doubt the possibility of Luke 16:27–31 being part of the parable, viewing it as an added piece of tradition from the early church, reworked by Luke to fit his interests. For Crossan, the conclusion of the parable fits the style and program of Luke-Acts, and a clear parallel between Luke 16:27–31 and Luke's resurrection account in 24:44–47 can be indicated. Crossan notes the following parallels: the theme of disbelief (Luke 16:29, 31 and Luke 24: 12, 25, 41); the use of Moses and the prophets (Luke 16:29, 31 and Luke 24:27, 44); the use of ἀνίστημι in Luke 16:31 and

---

counterpart, Jannes and Jambres, and several Greek accounts), one would expect such a continuation of the story as we have it in Luke 16:19–31. If the narrative ended at Luke 16:26 the story would be left incomplete. Moreover, Snodgrass argues, recent literary analyses do not divide the story merely into two sections separated at Luke 16:26, the middle of the dialogue between the rich man and Abraham. The parable should be divided into three parts, not two: Luke 16:19–21, 22–23, and 24–31. With this division, the parable provides two snapshots (before and after) and a dialogue. This structure preserves the unity of the dialogue, a unity evidenced by the parallels between Luke 16:24 and Luke 16:27. Snodgrass, *Stories with Intent*, 427–28.

30. Funk et al., *Five Gospels*, 362. The implication of Funk's argument is that if the parable goes back to Jesus, the second part cannot come from Jesus; otherwise one has to assume that Jesus is "foretelling" his resurrection. One must also bear in mind that both the resurrection stories Funk refer to are Lukan-Sondergut, which makes the appeal to Moses and the prophets in Luke 16:29, 31, and Luke 24:27 and 44, most probably a Lukan creation. Even in the light of this evidence, Snodgrass calls the similarities between Luke 16:27–31 and the resurrection story in Luke 24 "superficial." Snodgrass, *Stories with Intent*, 428.

24:46 (the verb "to rise up" is used with "from the death" only in these two occurrences in Luke); and the use of the theme of repentance (Luke 16:30 and Acts 2:38; 3:19; 8:22; 17:30; 26:20).[31]

In support of Crossan, Scott has also noted the parallel between διαμαρτύρηται (διαμαρτύρομαι; Luke 16:28) and πεισθήσονται (πείθω; Luke 16:31) in the parable's conclusion, words that are frequently used in Acts (see Acts 18:4–5; 28:23).[32] These parallels, according to Crossan and Scott, indicate a Lukan hand in the conclusion of the parable in order for the parable to fit his apologetic needs. The conclusion most probably was not part of the original parable and was appended to relate the parable to either Judean disbelief in Jesus' messiahship[33] or Judean lack of belief in the resurrection of Jesus.[34] The arguments of Funk, Crossan, and Scott are compelling enough to conclude that the parable most probably ends at Luke 16:26: "Once Abraham pronounces the chasm, the great dividing line, the story has reached its conclusion."[35]

Most scholars who question the authenticity of Luke 16:19–21 base their arguments on the possibility of the parable's being paralleled in folkloric stories or legends of the reversal of fortunes in the afterlife. Some argue for a parallel in the Enoch literature, while others see the whole parable as a Lukan composition or as a creation from in the early church.[36]

The Jesus Seminar is divided on whether the story is traceable to Jesus and voted the parable grey. The fellows of the Jesus Seminar who question the authenticity of the parable support the argument that folktales about the reversal of fate in the afterlife were widespread in the ancient Near East. They also note the following features of the parable that most probably make it a Lukan composition: the parable is the only parable that gives characters

---

31. Crossan, *In Parables*, 67. For a detailed discussion of Crossan's arguments, see Scott, *Hear Then the Parable*, 142–43. With regard to Crossan's last parallel, Luke's use of the theme of repentance in Luke 16:30 and the kerygmatic speeches in Acts, Scott notes that Crossan might have added Acts 5:31, 11:18 and 20:21. Scott is also of the opinion that Crossan could have made his case even stronger if he had also noted the parallels between the theme of repentance in Luke16:30 and the Gospel itself (e.g., Luke 3:8; 11:32; 13:3, 5; 15:7, 10; 17:3–4).

32. "*Diamartyromai* occurs nine times in Luke–Acts, and only in this parable in the Synoptics. *Peitho*[set macron over o] is used twenty–one times in Luke–Acts, thirty–two times in the New Testament." Scott, *Hear Then the Parable*, 145 n. 13.

33. Scott, *Re-Imagine the World*, 146.

34. Funk et al., *The Five Gospels*, 362.

35. Scott, *Hear Then the Parable*, 146.

36. For these points of view, see the discussion in Van Eck, "Rich Man and Lazarus," 5.

proper names; attention to the poor is a special characteristic of Luke;[37] and the bosom of Abraham (Luke 16:22) is most probably an allusion to Luke 3:8.[38] Scott also doubts the authenticity of the parable, since it is the only parable that depicts a scene from the afterlife.[39]

Scholars who argue the opposite note that there were "dozens of stories in various cultures over thousands of years that tell of trips to the realm of the dead, often castigating the rich," and note that "the use of preexisting materials is evident in other parables and would not be surprising."[40] The parable does differ in many respects from its Egyptian and Jewish counterparts. The folktales in the ancient Near East normally include a judgment scene, which the parable does not have,[41] and in the parable the fates of the rich man and Lazarus are simply reversed, reminiscent of Jesus' technique of storytelling.[42] Moreover, known folktales about rich and poor understand rich and poor mostly in economic terms. This is not the case in Luke. The parallels between the parable and available folktales are in any case only indirect, and "neither as compelling nor as explanatory as these claims suggest."[43] Also, if a popular tale does in fact lie behind the parable, this does not automatically mean that the parable could not have been told by Jesus.[44] Thus, while the parable can be related to common folklore, it is also possible that it is a creation in its own right.[45]

Regarding the proper names in the parable, the name Lazarus is not accidental but essential to the meaning of the parable. The same holds true for Abraham. The reason for the introduction of Abraham in Luke 16:22 is not Luke 3:8 but rather the theme of hospitality in the parable. Abraham is a suitable figure for heavenly reward, as he was not only rich, but also well known for his hospitality. The rich man is not pictured negatively for being rich but rather because of his indifference and lack of hospitality.[46] The contrast between rich and poor in the parable is therefore most probably

37. Luke, for example, contrasts the blessedness of the poor with the condemnation of the rich in his first beatitude and woe (Luke 6:20). Funk et al., *Red Letter Edition*, 64.

38. Ibid.; Funk et al., *Five Gospels*, 361.

39. Scott, *Hear Then the Parable*, 141.

40. Snodgrass, *Stories with Intent*, 426, 427.

41. Funk et al., *The Five Gospels*, 361.

42. Funk et al., *Red Letter Edition*, 64. See, for example, Matt 20:1–15; Q 14:16–24; Gos. Thom. 64:1–11; and Luke 15:11–31.

43. Hock, "Lazarus and Micyllus," 452; Bauckham, *The Fate of the Dead*, 97–118.

44. Hultgren, *Parables of Jesus*, 111; Hock, "Lazarus and Micyllus," 452; Snodgrass, *Stories with Intent*, 427.

45. Hultgren, *Parables of Jesus*, 111.

46. Funk et al., *Red Letter Edition*, 64.

not a creation of Luke; Luke would have condemned the rich man simply because he was rich. The parable also parallels the Friend at Midnight (Luke 11:5–13), another parable of Jesus that has hospitality as theme, together with the crossing of accepted cultural boundaries—an obvious theme in Luke 16:19–26). The Rich Man and Lazarus also parallels Matt 18:23–55, which also describes the indifference of a rich man (one that has) toward a poor man (one that does not have) in a wrenchingly pathetic situation.[47] Finally, the reversal of fortunes in the parable echoes Q 6:20 and Gos. Thom. 54, a saying that most probably goes back to Jesus.

Can the parable be traced back to the historical Jesus, or is it a pre-Lukan or Lukan composition? The arguments for and against its authenticity do not seem to outweigh one another. Or can one argue that the parable at least goes back to a nucleus of Jesus' teaching on topics such as patronage, power and privilege, class, status, and the economic exploitation of the peasantry by the elite? Moreover, can a social-scientific interpretation of the parable help in answering these questions?[48] To these questions we now turn.

47. Funk et al., *Five Gospels*, 361.

48. The interpretation history of the parable of the Rich Man and Lazarus indicates that not much has been done in terms of a social-scientific analysis of the parable, except for the interpretations of Scott, Hultgren, and Herzog. In his analysis of the parable, Scott typifies the parable as a story of boundaries and opposite parallels and understands the different locations of the rich man (inside the gate) and Lazarus (outside the gate) as reflecting the limited-goods society of the first-century Mediterranean world where the social statuses of the poor and the rich are fixed. The relationship between the rich man and Lazarus implies a relationship of patron and client. In his analysis of the parable he does not, however, explore this possibility any further except for putting forward the question, "Will the rich man use the gate to come to Lazarus' aid?" See Scott, *Hear Then the Parable*, 146–51. For Hultgren "the parable presupposes an ancient agrarian economy in which a person like Lazarus is more than just poor." Hultgren, *Parables of Jesus*, 115–16. Hultgren does not explore the implications of this statement, namely, that being poor in first-century Palestine was not simply a case of being economically poor but also referred to persons who could not maintain their inherited statuses due to debt, the exploitative practices of the elite (like the rich man), and sickness. In Herzog's reading, the parable assumes the social structure of an advanced agrarian society, and in the rich man and Lazarus it brings together the two extremes of that social structure: class disparity, the difference between city and countryside, and the oppressive system it incorporates. Lazarus is depicted as either the second or third son of a peasant farmer who has lost his land because of the wealth accumulated by the systemic exploitation of the poor—through taxes, through oppressive foreclosure of mortgages by the urban elite, and through the twisting of the Torah—who then becomes a day laborer and finally drifts to the city to become a beggar. During his descent from a former landowner or an excess child of a peasant household to a day laborer, and finally a beggar, Lazarus most probably sought patronage but failed to find it. He probably did not find work, became malnourished, and could no longer compete for jobs. He became vulnerable to disease, which later made even begging

Reading Scenarios

Social-scientific criticism, as an exegetical approach, analyzes texts in terms of their *strategy* and *situation*. The situation of a text refers to the social circumstances in which the text was produced, and the text's strategy refers to "its pragmatic and rhetorical dimension, the manner in which the text in its totality of form and content (syntactic and semantic dimensions) is designed to have a specific effect upon . . . receiver(s)."[49]

Almost all interpretations that focus on the structure of the parable focus on opposites within the parable.[50] Luke 16:19–21 introduces the first two characters of the parable: one inside the gate[51] (the one who the gate belongs to), and one outside the gate. The man inside the gate has no name,[52] is described as rich, puts on purple and fine linen,[53] and feasts sumptuously

---

impossible. Herzog, *Parables as Subversive Speech*, 117–30. Herzog's reading of the parable shows much potential, especially his conviction that the parable stems from the historical Jesus. Herzog, however, does not consider the possibility that with the parable Jesus may be addressing the barriers erected by class and privilege and is criticizing the principle of patronage, and wealth accumulated by the systemic exploitation of the poor in first-century Palestine.

49. Elliott, *Social-Scientific Criticism*, 55.

50. These oppositions have been described in detail. See especially the analysis by of Scott, *Hear Then the Parable*, 146–55.

51. The gate most probably was "a large ornamental gateway to a city or a mansion," or indicated "a nobly built mansion." See, respectively, Marshall, *Gospel of Luke*, 653; Oesterley, *Gospel Parables*, 205. If this indeed is the case, even the gate to the rich man's house exemplified his wealth.

52. In trying to remedy this seeming anomaly in the parable, various names have been attached to the rich man. P[75] (third century, Alexandrian) gives a reading ὀνόματι νευης ("named Neves"), and the ancient writer Priscillian named him Finees. The Vulgate (fourth century, Western) opens with the words "homo quidam erat dives," ("a certain man was rich"). This phrase became popularly to be understood as "there was a certain man, Dives." This is why the parable is sometimes named the parable of Dives and Lazarus. See Leonhardt-Balzer, "Wie Kommt ein Reicher in der Abrahams Schoß," 651.

53. The man's richness is exemplified by the clothing he wears and his eating habits. Purple clothing and fine linen were rare and very expensive because of the difficult process of obtaining the best dye from marine snails. Smith, *Parables of the Synoptic Gospels*, 135. Twelve thousand purple snails produced only one gram of purple dye. Leonhardt-Balzer, "Wie Kommt ein Reicher in der Abrahams Schoß," 651–52. Purple was a mark of luxurious living, the color of kings (Judg 8:26; Esth 8:15; 2 Sam 1:24; Ezek 23:6; Dan 5:7; Acts 16:14; Rev 18:12). See also *Midrash Rabbah* on Exod 38:8, in Hadas, "Rabbinic Parallels," 46. Purple normally was worn by those that were proud of their wealth (e.g., 1 Macc 8:14; 1 Esd 3:6; Mark 15:17). See Hultgren, *Parables of Jesus*, 112. Purple was also a sign of official power and honor. Scott, *Hear Then the Parable*, 148. Generals often honored brave soldiers with purple-bordered robes (Seneca, *Ben.* 1.5.3). The purple the rich man wore thus insinuates that he lived like a king, was wealthy and

every day (εὐφραινόμενος καθ᾽ ἡμέραν λαμπρῶς).[54] The person outside the gate does have a name, Lazarus,[55] is described as poor, is dressed in sores, and does not feast at all. The rich man has food and friends in abundance, while Lazarus is hungry (longing to be fed with what falls from the rich man's table),[56] and only has dogs for companionship.[57] The rich man has the ability to give; Lazarus can only beg, if he is indeed still able to do so.[58] Moreover, since the gate belongs to the rich man, he is able to cross it, while Lazarus is not. This situational difference between the rich man and Lazarus is summarized in Luke 16:25: the rich man receives good things and experiences comfort, while Lazarus receives evil things and experiences anguish.

In Luke 16:22 both the rich man and Lazarus die; and a reversal of their previous respective fortunes takes place. Lazarus is carried away by the

---

honorable, and occupied a position of privilege and power. Fitzmyer, *Gospel according to Luke*, 2:1130. The fine linen he wore most probably was from Egypt; it was the most luxurious fabric of the ancient world. Manson, *Sayings of Jesus*, 295. This kind of fine linen is referred to in 1 Chr 2:13, and Ezek 27:16 as a luxury articles. Leonhardt-Balzer, "Wie Kommt ein Reicher in der Abrahams Schoß," 651.

54. The expression "to make merry" (εὐφραίνω) is also used in the parables of the Rich Farmer (Luke 12:19), and the Prodigal (Luke 15:23, 24 and 32), meaning "to make a feast." "It entails a feast well beyond those occasional celebrations that enlivened the otherwise boring and monotonous existence of Mediterranean peasants." Scott, *Hear Then the Parable*, 149. See also Louw and Nida, who translate εὐφραίνω as "to make glad, to cheer up, to cause to be happy." Louw and Nida, *Greek-English Lexicon*, 1:303.

55. Lazarus, which means "God helps," is a shortened form of the name Eliezer (or Eleazar), the name of Abraham's servant in Gen 15:2.

56. The food that fell from the rich man's table are not crumbs or food that fell accidentally but pieces of bread the guests at the rich man's table used to wipe their hands before throwing them under the table. See Montefiore, *Synoptic Gospels*, 538. Contra Hultgren, *Parables of Jesus*, 112. Rabbinic traditions cite reasons of purity and hygiene for adhering to this practice, and also command the gleaning of the leftovers for sharing with the poor. Jeremias, *Parables of Jesus*, 184. This obviously does not take place in the parable—another indication of the conspicuous consumption of the rich man. Herzog, *Parables as Subversive Speech*, 118.

57. The dogs that licked Lazarus most probably were wild street dogs, a plague in the ancient world. The dogs referred to in the parable thus were not household pets helping him, but scavengers (street dogs) seeking nourishment. Scott, *Hear Then the Parable*, 151. Derrett, to the contrary, sees the dogs to be the rich man's guard dogs, allowed into the dining hall after the guests have departed in order to clean the table droppings (cf. Mark 6:28). Derrett, *Law in the New Testament*, 89–91.

58. Lazarus, because of his situation, most probably, was vulnerable to disease, which later made begging impossible. Herzog, *Parables as Subversive Speech*, 118–19. His condition is described with the indicative passive of βάλλω (ἐβέβλητο; thrown down or cast down), which means he was probably bedridden or crippled, thus unable to beg. Fitzmyer, *Gospel according to Luke*, 2:205.

angels to Abraham,[59] where he is comforted at Abraham's bosom.[60] The rich man is buried and finds himself in a place of torment and anguish. Lazarus now has in abundance (water) and is able to give, while the rich man longs for a mere drop of water,[61] just as Lazarus had desired the crumbs that fell from the table of the rich man. The situations of the rich man and Lazarus thus have drastically changed. Lazarus is now "inside," and the rich man "outside," and between them is a chasm that cannot be crossed.

The strategy of the parable, however, is not only about opposites. One similarity in the parable can be indicated: a similarity surrounded and highlighted by all the oppositions in the parable. Both the rich man and Abraham are unwilling to help the one that needs help. In terms of the strategy of the parable, this is its main point. All the oppositions in the parable drive at highlighting this one aspect of its strategy. The parable offers many opposites but only one similarity. The fortunes of the rich man and Lazarus have changed drastically, but one thing has stayed the same: those who have the ability to help do not help. This similarity has not received much attention. This similarity is not only the key to unlocking the meaning of the parable but may also be key to answering the question of the parable's authenticity.

From an etic perspective, the above emic reading implies several social and cultural conventions (native concepts and perceptions) that construed reality in the first-century Mediterranean world.[62] Herzog, Scott, and Hultgren, in their respective analyses of the parable, have correctly identified some of the salient cultural scripts of the world implied in the parable. The parable assumes the social structure of an advanced agrarian society, with the rich man and Lazarus exemplifying the class disparity inherent in that social structure. Also part of the cultural script of the parable is the difference that existed between city and countryside, and the oppressive system that accentuated this difference.[63] Another of the cultural scripts for this parable is the system of patronage and clientism. Yet another was the notion that the first-century Mediterranean world was a limited–goods society where the social statuses of the poor and the rich were fixed.[64] To this can be

59. See Gen 5:24 and 2 Kgs 2:11.

60. The metaphor "at Abraham's bosom" suggests a child at a mother's bosom (place of protection), a place of honor at a banquet, or the place of the patriarchs (Gen 15:15). See Scott, *Hear Then the Parable*, 152. It also suggests a place of hospitality or honor. Respectively Ibid., 153; Herzog, *Parables as Subversive Speech*, 141.

61. This request of rich man equates him with the dogs that licked Lazarus' sores. Jensen, "Diesseits und Jenseits des Raumes eines Textes," 55.

62. Elliott, *Social-Scientific Criticism*, 29.

63. Herzog, *Parables as Subversive Speech*, 117–30.

64. Scott, *Hear Then the Parable*, 151–52; Hultgren, *Parables of Jesus*, 115–16.

added the lavish meals of the rich man, which functioned as ceremonies to confirm the values and structures of that society as well as the pivotal values of honor and shame. Very important, also, is the figure of Abraham, which evokes the important principle of hospitality. Finally, the physical state of Lazarus relates to the important principle of being socially (and ritually) pure or impure. All of these cultural scripts (reading scenarios) have been described earlier and will be employed in the reading of the parable, to which we now turn.

Reading the Parable

The parable of the Rich Man and Lazarus is a story about the great class disparity in first-century Palestine, about the divide between the urban elite, who controlled all the wealth, power, and privilege, and the exploited rural peasantry, who lived in the narrow margin between subsistence and famine.[65]

In the parable the elite are represented by the rich man, most probably one of the Jewish aristocracy with official power. (He knows Abraham, and he wears purple.) To show his status he flaunts his wealth through conspicuous consumption stemming from lavish spending.[66] The clothes he wears (rare and expensive Egyptian linen underwear and purple clothing) are also a status marker, since purple was the color of kings and honorable men, a mark of luxurious living and a sign of official power worn by those that were proud of their wealth. Since he was able to maintain his wealth, he was a man of honor. To enhance his honor and status, he "made merry" (feasted) every day, most probably with other elites who stood with him in patron-client relationships. As part of the elite, he also competed for clients among the poor and the peasantry. These patron-client relationships put him in a position to control more and more land, produce, and labor.

At his gate one of the products of his exploitation, Lazarus, spends his days. Lazarus had become one of the expendables of the society the rich man and other members of the elite class had created. Lazarus was no longer of any use to the rich man. Since he was at the rich man's gate every day,[67] he could not really beg or take part in the daily salutation of the patron. Lazarus' presence gave the rich man no occasion for almsgiving or for enhancing his own honor. Nothing could be gained by making Lazarus

65. Malina and Rohrbaugh, *Social-Science Commentary on the Synoptic Gospels*, 295. See also Wright, *Jesus the Storyteller*, 129.

66. Fiensy, *Jesus the Galilean*, 91.

67. Fitzmyer, *Gospel according to Luke*, 2:1131.

a client, even in terms of negative reciprocity, and to show *hospitium* to him (e.g., by tending to his sores) would have made Lazarus his equal. This, of course, would have meant a loss of honor. To the rich man, Lazarus was expendable in every sense of the word.

Lazarus, on the other hand, represents the exploited peasantry, the poor and the destitute. The reason Lazarus ended up at the gate of the rich man can only be speculated on. Maybe he was the second or third son of a peasant farmer who only had enough land for the eldest son to inherit. Maybe he had to leave the family plot and seek work elsewhere because there were too many mouths to feed in a household living below, or just at, the level of subsistence. Or maybe his father had lost his land because of rising indebtedness and eventual foreclosure on his mortgage by one of the exploiting urban elite.[68] He may even have been a smallholder of inherited land who, because of inter alia the excessive tax burden imposed by the ruling elite, lost his land. Whatever the case may have been, the road that led to the gate of the rich man was a one-way street. First Lazarus might have been a tenant, then a day laborer; next he drifted to the city where work was scarce. Most probably he did not find work, and finally he ended up a beggar. The parable describes the final stretch of the road he traveled. He became malnourished and covered with sores, not even able to beg anymore. Lazarus had no honor left,[69] was economically poor, and he was poor in the sense that he could not maintain his status as a peasant smallholder.[70] He had no family ties left, and, above all, he was labeled socially and ritually impure. The meaning of his name said it all: only God can help.

In the parable the name Lazarus is not accidental. Given that the name Lazarus means "God is my help," Jesus' use of the name in the parable illustrates the way Jesus sided with the poor, the expendables, and the socially impure. In a situation where Jesus very well knew that the exploiting rich were only becoming richer and the poor poorer (Mark 4:25; Q 19:26; Gos. Thom. 41:1–2), Jesus' concern for the poor is not surprising.[71] He congratulated

68. Herzog, *Parables as Subversive Speech*, 119.

69. Maybe the only honor Lazarus has left is that he did not beg, as can be deducted from Sir 40:18–30: "Child, do not lead the life of a beggar; it is better to die than to beg. When one looks to the table of another, one's way of life cannot be considered a life. One loses self-respect with another person's food, but one who is intelligent and well instructed guards against that. In the mouth of the shameless begging is sweet, but it kindles a fire inside him." See Scott, *Re-Imagine the World*, 90.

70. Hollenbach, "Defining Rich and Poor," 58; Malina, "Wealth and Poverty," 355.

71. Jesus' concern for the poor can be inferred from several sayings in the New Testament that most probably—in terms of the criteria of independent, early, and multiple attestation, and the criteria of coherence—can be traced back to the historical Jesus. For a definition and discussion of these criteria, see Funk et al., *Five Gospels*, 19–33;

the poor and the hungry (Q 6:20, 21; Gos. Thom. 54, 69:2), damned the rich
and those who were well-fed at the cost of the poor,[72] and exhorted the rich
to sell their possessions and give to the poor.[73] He also criticized patronage
and clientism, based on the principle of negative reciprocity, by modeling all
personal relations on those of close kin (generalized reciprocity).[74] He encouraged hosts to invite the poor, crippled, lame, and blind, who could not
repay them, and called on his listeners to love their enemies (Q 6:27), to do
good for and pray for their abusers (Q 6:28), and to lend to others expecting
nothing in return (Q 6:30; Gos. Thom. 95:1–2; Did. 1:4b, 5a—a sequence of
sayings confirmed by the summary statement in Luke 6:35).[75] He called on
hearers to treat people in the same way they wanted to be treated (Q 6:31;
Gos. Thom. 6:3) and to forgive the debts of others (Q 6:37; Mark 11:25;
Matt 18:23–35). Jesus even tried to turn the hearts of the powerful to the
powerless and dishonored poor,[76] and criticized those patrons who were
constantly looking for new ways to enhance their honor by means of saluta-
tions from their clients (Mark 12:38–40 and par.; Q 11:43). Moreover, he ate
indiscriminatingly with the so-called sinners[77] and healed the sick.[78] From
this it becomes clear that Jesus' sympathies indeed lay with the poor.[79] There
was help, after all, for Lazarus—especially in a kingdom where God was

Wallace, "Rule of Love," 68–69; Tatum, In Quest of Jesus, 102–107.

72. Although this saying is only attested in Luke 6:24–25, it most probably, in terms
of the criterion of coherence, goes back to Jesus.

73. All the call stories in the gospels (e.g., Mark 1:16–18, 19–20; 2:14; 10:17–22,
and par.) indicate that discipleship and the renunciation of possessions went hand in
hand. Fiensy, Jesus the Galilean, 115–18. This is also the case in the parables of the
Treasure (Matt 13:44; Gos. Thom. 109:1–3) and the Merchant (Matt 13:45–46; Gos.
Thom. 76:1–2), where everything is sold to gain the kingdom.

74. Oakman, Jesus and the Peasants, 103–107.

75. See Funk et al., Five Gospels, 291.

76. This can be inferred from Luke in his discriminating use of the radical Jesus
tradition (Luke 12:48; 19:8–9; 22:26). Oakman, Jesus and the Peasants, 161. The fact
that Luke 22:26 finds support in Mark 10:31; Q 13:30; and Gos. Thom. 4:2–3 makes
this a plausible argument.

77. P.Oxy. 1224 2.5, Mark 2:13–17a and par., Gospel of the Ebionites 1c, and Luke
15:1–2. See Crossan, Historical Jesus, 440.

78. Almost all historical Jesus scholars agree that Jesus practiced an open table and
healed the sick (and performed exorcisms).

79. Jesus' concern for the poor thus stands clearly in line with the priestly, Deuteronomic, wisdom, and prophetic traditions in the Old Testament, which call to protect
the poor from the exploitative practices and systemic violence by the rich (e.g., Exod
22:25; Lev 19:10; Deut 15:4–11; Prov 14:31; 22:9, 22; Isa 3:14–15; Amos 2:6–7). See
Fiensy, Jesus the Galilean, 96, 132.

the patron, and not a member of the ruling aristocratic elite.[80] Where God is patron, the gate is open and the threshold is crossed. This, however, was neither the kind of patron the rich man was, nor the way he acted. Nothing prevented him from doing otherwise. The gate was there, it even belonged to him. But he did not cross it, simply because there was nothing in it for him. And, if he did, he could only lose some honor.

When the rich man dies, he has the opportunity of viewing the way things are from the other side of the gate. He is confronted with the kind of patronage towards, and solidarity with, the poor and destitute that Jesus advocated. Abraham, the example par excellence of hospitality in the Old

---

80. Many Graeco-Roman philosophers also criticized the many patron-client relationships of their day. They saw virtue (moral goodness and propriety) as more important than benefaction, and the ideal was generalized reciprocity. According to Seneca, the bestowal of a benefit "is a mark of virtue, and to bestow it for any other reason other than merely the bestowing of it is a most shameful act" (*Ben.* 4.2.4). Seneca also stated that one should give "to the one who, though poor, is good; for he will be grateful in the midst of extreme poverty, and, when he lacks all else, this heart he will still have. It is not gain that I try to get from a benefit; nor pleasure; nor glory; content with giving pleasure to one human being, I shall give with the single purpose of doing what I ought" (*Ben.* 4.11.3). Benefits were seen as goodwill—more important than the benefit itself was the spirit in which a gift was given: Seneca also makes interesting remarks on the way in which benefits should be given. Benefits should be given "willingly, promptly and without hesitation" (*Ben.* 2.1.1), and one must always try to anticipate one's own desire, and indulge in giving that to someone else, even before someone had to beg (*Ben.* 2.2.1). "Therefore we ought to divine each man's desire, and, when we have discovered it, he ought to be freed from the grievous necessity of making a request; the benefit that takes the initiative, you may be sure, will be the one that is agreeable and destined to live in the heart" (*Ben.* 2.1.2). Also, "just as in the case of the sick suitability of food aids recovery, and plain water given at the right time serves as a remedy, so a benefit, no matter how trivial and commonplace it may be, if it has been given promptly, if not an hour has been wasted, gains much in value and wins more gratitude than a gift that, though costly, has been lagged and long resisted" (*Ben.* 2.2.2). Benefits should also be given quietly so that they will be known only to those who receive the benefit (*Ben.* 2.9.2). Pleasure should not come from being seen doing a favor, but from doing the favor itself (*Ben.* 2.10.3). And: "The gifts that please are those that are bestowed by one who wears the countenance of a human being, all gentle and kindly; by one who, though he was my superior when he gave them, did not exalt himself above me, but, with all the generosity in his power, descended to my own level, and banished all display from his giving; who thus watched for the suitable moment for the purpose of coming to my rescue with timely, rather than with necessary, aid" (*Ben.* 2.13.3). And finally: "The more need a man has of a benefit, the greater is the benefit he receives" (*Ben.*3.35.3). When these opinions of Seneca (a coeval of Jesus) are related to the relationship between the rich man and Lazarus, they are indeed interesting. See also Virgil (*Aen.* 6.600) on the punishments for "bad" patrons.

Testament,[81] clearly embodies Jesus' attitude toward the poor.[82] Lazarus is sitting at the table (bosom) of Abraham. *Hospitium* has been extended to him. But the rich man, although being in torment and thirsty, is not worried. Abraham is his father too, and given what is known of Abraham's hospitality, he believes it will be extended to him as well. Now he is the one who is in need. And those who are in need are looked upon favorably by Abraham, just as Lazarus has been. The rich man just has to ask.

But then comes the surprise in Jesus' parable! Abraham is not willing to help. Abraham doesn't even offer one drop of water to be licked from Lazarus' finger. Even the dogs that licked Lazarus' sores were better off than the rich man is now. This is indeed an oxymoron—Abraham not being hospitable! How is this possible? This simply cannot happen where Abraham is involved. But it does happen. The unthinkable happens: Abraham does not show hospitality. And then comes the parable's final shock; the gate cannot be opened. The threshold cannot be crossed. The gate has been closed forever.

This is the gist of the parable. When patrons, that have in abundance, do not open the gate and cross the threshold to the poor, a society is created wherein the chasm between rich (elite) and poor (peasantry) becomes so wide it cannot be crossed. The worlds of the urban elite and the peasantry drift so far apart that the gap between them eventually cannot be closed. Go through the gate while you can. As unthinkable as it is for Abraham not to show hospitality, so unthinkable should it be for people who can help not to show hospitality. Abraham, being the example of hospitality, had no reason to turn his back on the rich man. The same held for the rich man during his life—nothing stood in the way of his helping Lazarus. It was not impossible to help Lazarus. The protection of his status and honor, however, made it impossible. And when this happens, nobody becomes part of the kingdom—neither Lazarus nor the rich man. This is the result when patrons (unlike the host in Jesus' parable of the Feast) protect their so-called honor and status. Real patrons are children of Abraham; they look out for the poor (Luke 19:8–9).

81. For a description of Abraham's hospitality, see Scott, *Hear Then the Parable*, 87, 153; Herzog, *Parables as Subversive Speech*, 130.

82. *Contra* Leonhardt-Balzer, who views Abraham not as a character in the parable, but the voice of God. Leonhardt-Balzer, "Wie Kommt ein Reicher in der Abrahams Schoß," 654.

A Parable of Jesus?

The question of the authenticity of this parable can now be answered. In the Rich man and Lazarus, Abraham's hospitality embodies Jesus' attitude toward the poor. The parable embodies the nucleus of Jesus' teaching on topics like patronage, power and privilege, class, status, generalized reciprocity, and the economic exploitation of the peasantry by the ruling elite. The ideas contained in the parable are his and are paralleled in some of his parables that can be traced back to the earliest layer of the Jesus tradition (e.g., Luke 10:30–35; 11:5–8; 14:16–24). The way the kingdom is described in this parable (including those with so-called impurities) is parallel to the parables of the Mustard Seed (Q 13:18–19; Gos. Thom. 20:1–4) and the Leaven (Q 13:20–21; Gos. Thom. 6:1–2). The parable is also paralleled in the Gospel of the Nazoreans in its commentary on Matt 19:16–30.[83] In its commentary on Matt 19:16–30, the Gospel of the Nazoreans has as content a parallel of the situation pictured in Luke 16:19–26; the poor, called "sons of Abraham," are being mistreated by the rich ("thy house is full of many good things and nothing at all comes forth from it to them"). Finally, the parable also highlights what can be called the main focus of the historical Jesus' main activity, aptly described by Oakman: "Jesus' historical activity was essentially about politics and the restructuring of society, and not about religion or theology."[84]

---

83. "This gospel has as content "material . . . which . . . in some instances reflects early traditions of Jesus." Cameron, *Other Gospels*, 98.

84. Oakman, *Jesus and the Peasants*, 296.

CHAPTER 12

The Minas (Luke 19:12b–24, 27):
Protesting for the Sake of the Kingdom

F ROM THE HISTORY OF interpretation of the Minas (or Talents) it is clear that one specific interpretation has dominated. Almost without exception, the nobleman in the parable is seen as a positive figure, the actions of the first two slaves are praised, and the third slave is vilified. Interestingly, this stock interpretation again and again surfaces, independent of what interpretational approach is taken. This dominant approach can be seen in the allegorical interpretations of the parable, those interpretation that read the parable in its literary context in Matthew or Luke, and even in the interpretations that intend to read the parable in a 30 CE, historical Jesus context.

Rohrbaugh's groundbreaking social-scientific interpretation of the parable, in which the third slave is not the villain but the hero of the story,[1] has shown that this dominant interpretation is most probably the best example of the fallacy of ethnocentrism (and anachronism) in previous and current parable interpretation. Ethnocentrism and anachronism, as already indicated, involve reading "into the text information from some present social context rather than comprehending the text in accord with its own contemporary social and cultural scripts."[2] Rohrbaugh's reading of the parable shows an understanding of the cultural values and social dynamics of the social world of Jesus and his hearers is an absolute necessity if the interpreter wants to avoid this fallacy in so far as avoidance is possible.

Taking Rohrbaugh's interpretation of the parable as starting point, this reading gives attention to an aspect much neglected in the interpretation of the parable, namely, that the third slave in the parable is not condemned, an aspect of the parable that is important for understanding the parable's

---

1. See Rohrbaugh, Text of Terror," 32–39.
2. Elliott, *Social-Scientific Criticism*, 11.

strategy and gist. The parable does not only show how, in the time of Jesus, the elite exploited the nonelite; it also shows how to protest such exploitation in a situation where the peasantry (the exploited) had no legitimate way of protesting against the exploitative practices of the elite.

History of Interpretation

The earliest interpretations of the parable, including Matthew's (Matt 25:14–30), and in a sense, Luke's (Luke 19:12b–27) theological-allegorical application of this parable of Jesus, are the allegorical interpretations typical of early (and sometimes later) parable interpretation. Some of these interpretations focused on the minas received by the slaves as gifts, either spiritual (Bede and Maldonatus) or worldly (Aquinas and Chrysostom). The correct use of these gifts would result in receiving additional similar gifts, while those who do not use their gifts would lose them.[3] Others saw the received minas as the reception of the gospel, with the first slave representing the conversion of the Jews, the second slave representing the conversion of the Gentiles, and the third representing the unconverted.[4] Another focus was the slaves as referring to teachers: the first was sent to the Jews, the second to the Gentiles, and the third slave represented those teachers who did not proclaim the gospel as they should have.[5] In these early allegorical interpretations we also find an interpretation—still popular among some modern parable scholars—that the man who departs refers to Jesus' ascension, that his return refers to Jesus' parousia, and that the reckoning refers to the Final Judgment. A good example of this interpretation is that of Calvin: in the parable Jesus teaches the disciples that they will face troubles and hardships for an extended time before they finally inherit the kingdom; it would be wrong for them to be idle during this interim, for each person is entrusted a certain office in which he may engage. At Jesus' return, all will be judged according to what they did with the offices they received.[6]

The latter interpretation of the parable is still abundantly popular in modern parable scholarship, especially in those readings that interpret the parable in its literary context. These readings, generally speaking, see the parable in Luke as a parable of the historical Jesus, and interpret the parable as a reference to Jesus' second coming. Consequently, the parable is

3. See Kissinger, *History of Interpretation*, 33, 40, 43, 60.

4. See Snodgrass, *Stories with Intent*, 528.

5. See Ibid., 529.

6. See Kissinger, *History of Interpretation*, 55.

understood as an eschatological warning.[7] To mention a few examples, a person is prepared for the coming of the Lord when he acts responsibly with the gifts God has bestowed on him;[8] the parable warns against an attitude that will bring about future exclusion from God's kingdom;[9] the conduct of all servants and citizens of the kingdom of God will be made known when Christ comes to reward and punish;[10] "in the end, all the disciples of Jesus are accountable to him";[11] and the master (God) expects profit (good deeds) that will be rewarded at the day of judgement.[12]

Another popular interpretation in modern parable scholarship is to focus less on the eschatological theme and more on stewardship. Themes that are subsequently identified in the parable that relate to positive stewardship are faithfulness,[13] watchfulness,[14] responsibility,[15] the proper use of money,[16] the proper use of grace,[17] trust,[18] accountability,[19] and preaching.[20] A few scholars, on the contrary, have focused on some negative traits of stewardship, namely, fear of failure,[21] playing it safe,[22] or making excuses.[23] Schottroff rightly notes that it is difficult to understand how in these interpretations and the allegorical interpretations mentioned earlier Jesus can be equated with the nobleman leaving and returning when the description of

7. "The parable depicts the time from Jesus' death and resurrection to the parousia and is directed towards the disciples to encourage kingdom living. This is the traditional and most obvious understanding of the present form of the parable." Snodgrass, *Stories with Intent*, 529.

8. Groenewald, *In Gelykenisse Het Hy Geleer*, 223–31.

9. Donahue, *The Gospel in Parable*, 109; Münch, "Gewinnen Oder Verlieren," 240–54.

10. Lockyer, *All the Parables*, 305–309.

11. Hultgren, *Parables of Jesus*, 289.

12. Kilgallen, *Twenty Parables*, 157–64.

13. Bailey, *Jesus through Middle Eastern Eyes*, 398–409; Jülicher, *Gleichnisreden Jesu*, 317; Snodgrass, *Stories with Intent*, 539–40; Stein, *Introduction to the Parables*, 64–65.

14. Keach, *Exposition of the Parables*, 701–736; Kistemaker, *Stories Jesus Told*, 123.

15. Capon, *The Parables of Judgment*, 86; Manson, *The Sayings of Jesus*, 249; Via, "Parable and Example Story," 119–120.

16. Reid, *Parables for Preachers*, 203.

17. Oesterley, *The Gospel Parables*, 149.

18. Dodd, *Parables of the Kingdom*, 61–62.

19. Stiller, *Preaching Parables*, 66–75; Wenham, *Parables of Jesus*, 88.

20. Drury, *Parables in the Gospels*, 155–57.

21. Donahue, *Gospel in Parable*, 106–8.

22. Voris, *Preaching Parables*, 101–103.

23. Boice, *Parables of Jesus*, 202–7.

the nobleman in the parable is taken into consideration.[24] The problem with these interpretations, however, is much deeper; the general tendency among parable scholars to identify the characters in the parables with God or Jesus himself. To read the parables from this perspective is to depict a Jesus that made theological statements and told stories about heaven. Jesus had no doctrine of God, made no theological statements, and never used abstract language. The parables were not "earthly stories with heavenly meanings, but earthly stories with heavy meanings."[25] The characters in the parables do not point to God. The parables point to the kingdom of God.[26]

Most scholars who read the parable independent of its literary context in Luke (i.e., as a parable of the historical Jesus in a 27–30 CE context), interestingly, have come to more or less the same conclusion regarding Jesus' intention with the parable. When Jesus told the parable, he had the religious leaders in mind. God's revelation had been entrusted to them, but these religious leaders, whose emphasis was on the law and the tradition, excluded certain groups from salvation and made religion sterile. The parable repeats Jesus' concern for the Gentiles, sinners, and tax collectors, and should be understood as a rebuke of those religious leaders who avoided the unclean to keep the Torah pure. In these readings the actions of the third slave refer to the religious leaders in general,[27] the Pharisees,[28] those pious Jews who practice exclusiveness,[29] or the scribes.[30] Perkins, on the other hand, argues that the parable is directed at the disciples; Jesus told the parable to address the issue of paralyzing fear in the face of their mission to follow, with the only road to success being risk taking of the first two servants. This is the

24. Schottroff, *Parables of Jesus*, 185.

25. Herzog, *Parables as Subversive Speech*, 3.

26. According to Crossan's reading of the parable, the intention of Jesus was to create a debate "between the Roman pro-interest tradition within the empire and the Jewish anti-interest tradition within the Torah." Crossan, *Power of Parable*, 105. Crossan continues: "The parable is not simply about interest, but about world." Ibid., 106. Even if one disagrees with Crossan's reading, he makes an important point. The parable is not about God, but God's kingdom. If the nobleman is a symbol for God, it would make God admit to being harsh, and God supporting exploitation. If the parable focuses on the kingdom of God, then the parable asks a different question: how should the earth fairly be distributed as a world for all God's people? See ibid., 99–106.

27. Boucher, *Parables*, 142; Hunter, *Interpreting the Parables*, 106–9; McGaughy, "Fear of Yahweh," 235–45.

28. Cadoux, *Art and Use*, 106.

29. Dodd, *Parables of the Kingdom*, 61–62.

30. Jeremias, *Parables of Jesus*, 58–63. According to Jeremias, the parable in its Lukan setting has a christological meaning. This is the result of the kerygma of the primitive church, interpreting the original parable of Jesus as a warning to the community not to become slack because of the delay of Christ's return. Ibid., 63.

only attitude that a disciple can take. There is no "safe" position.[31] Scott, also reading the parable in its 30 CE context, takes a somewhat different approach. In the parable it emerges how one goes about claiming the future. Is it claimed by preserving the precious gift or in freedom of action? The parable demands that the servant act boldly. Thus, the parable is about how one goes about claiming the future.[32] Some scholars, finally, read the parable not as pointing to the delay of the parousia, but in light of God's in-breaking kingdom.[33] Important to note is that all the above interpretations, without exception, interpret the nobleman in the parable as a positive figure, praise the actions of the first two slaves, and vilify the third slave.

Rohrbaugh's groundbreaking social-scientific reading of the parable seriously questions the "alleged capitalist motif" or ethnocentric readings of the parable "that has been particularly dear to exegetes of our own time."[34] In his reading, the focus is on the salient features of peasant economics, especially the notion of limited good, the mode of production, the pattern of exchange relations among agrarian peasants, and how the story might

31. Perkins, *Hearing the Parables*, 146–53.

32. Scott, *Hear Then the Parable*, 234.

33. Crossan, *In Parables*, 119; Buttrick, *Speaking in Parables*, 174; Johnson, "The Lukan Kingship Parable," 139–59; Lambrecht, *Out of the Treasure*, 184–87; Weder, *Die Gleichnisse Jesu Als Metaphern*, 206–7; Wohlgemut, "Entrusted Money," 119; Wright, *Victory of God*, 631–39.

34. Rohrbaugh, "Text of Terror," 33. Regarding the abundant capitalist readings of the parable, Rohrbaugh makes the following remark: "It should not take a great deal of thought to recognize a striking similarity between the parable's fundamental ideas . . . and the basic tenets of modern capitalism—or, at least, so it seems to minds conditioned by the capitalist societies of the West. Indeed, commentators of the nineteenth and twentieth centuries have genuinely reveled in the parable's seeming exhortation to venturous investment and diligent labor. It appears to be nothing less than praise for a homespun capitalism on the lips of Jesus." Ibid. Bailey holds the same opinion: "[E]ach of us perceives reality through the lenses of our language, culture, history, politics, economic theories, religion and military. As Westerners, one of our lenses is capitalism . . . [T]he parable of the pounds need to be liberated from the presuppositions of capitalism that perhaps have unconsciously influenced our translations and interpretations of this story." Bailey, *Jesus through Middle Eastern Eyes*, 307. The same critique on the capitalist reading of the parable is voiced by Ford: "This parable suffers from a pervasive misconception, the consequence of an unfortunate collusion between modern Western values, and the altogether different motives of the Gospel editors of Matthew and Luke. Taken together, however, these perspectives imbue the story's exacting master both with integrity and with the consequent authority accurately to evaluate his well-positioned slaves. In the judgment of nearly every contemporary First World commentator, this dominant parable protagonist is someone to be believed. Only Western readers, steeped in the mores of modern capitalism, could so thoroughly miss what was the obvious to Jesus' original peasant audiences, namely, that this master's mode of operation is criminal." Ford, *Parables of Jesus*, 35.

have been heard by a peasant in first-century Palestine. Limited good, according to Rohrbaugh means that the pie is limited. First-century peasants
viewed all desired things (e.g., land and wealth) as in short supply (limited)
as far as the peasant is concerned: there was no way directly within peasant's
reach or power to increase available quantities. A larger share for one thus
automatically meant a smaller share for someone else. Linked to this aspect
of advanced agrarian societies was the peasants' perception of production
and the mode of exchange relations among agrarian peasants. Peasant production was primarily for use rather than exchange. As part of subsistence
economies, peasants did not see the purpose of labor as creating wealth, but
simply as maintaining the family and the well-being of the village. As a result, peasants evaluated the world of persons and things in terms of use and
not exchange. For peasants it was therefore acceptable to sell commodities
in order to get money to buy other needed commodities; but to use money
to buy commodities that one then sold again at a profit was "unnatural."
Profitmaking was therefore seen as evil and socially destructive (e.g., usury
and the trade in money), and rich people were seen as evil and as thieves. To
gain more than one had was to steal from others. Read from this perspective, the actions of the nobleman—laying out his money to agents, with the
first two slaves pursuing and amassing new wealth—may have been good
news from the perspective of the elite or rich, but from a peasant's perspective, it was bad news. The good news in the parable, for the peasants, would
rather have been the actions of the third slave: by tying his entrusted money
in a cloth he did the honorable thing, namely, protecting the money of his
nobleman. And by doing this, he also refrained from participating in the
nobleman's scheme to exploit (steal) from others. The third slave (and not
the first two thieves) is the hero, and the point of the parable is to warn those
who exploit or mistreat the poor.[35]

Taking Rohrbaugh's reading of the parable as starting point, Herzog
also views the actions of the third slave as positive, characterizing him as
a "whistle-blower." According to Herzog, the setting of the parable focuses
on the household of an urban aristocrat. These aristocratic households normally controlled several estates and villages. The wealth created by these
estates and villages was harvested, stored, redistributed or monetized, and
exported. Because the head of the household could not always stay home to

---

35. Rohrbaugh, "Text of Terror," 33–35. See also Cardenal, *Gospel in Solentiname*,
39–40; Fortna, "Talents through Underclass Eyes," 214; Kähler, *Jesu Gleichnisse als Poesie und Therapie*, 171–79. According to Cardenal, the parable is "a very ugly example . . .
of exploitation," Fortna describes the master as engaged in an exploitative enterprise,
while Kähler describes the master as inhumanly hard, a bloodsucker, an oppressor, a
thief, a usurer, and a loan shark.

protect his interests—if he intended to expand his influence (e.g., by travel-ing abroad to increase investments, initiate new investments, or build new patron-client networks)—he had to make use of retainers. These retainers were not household slaves (*oiketeia*), although they may have been called *douloi* to emphasize their dependence on their patron-master. In the par-able two of the three retainers (slaves) most probably made loans to peasant farmers (with interest rates that could range between 60 and 200 percent) to make it possible for these farmers to plant their crops. In essence, how-ever, the purpose of these loans was not to help the farmers but to get their land as collateral and threaten possible foreclosure if the peasant farmers could not cover their incurred indebtedness. To increase the wealth of their patron, the retainers honored him by exploiting the peasantry, setting the rules of the economic game played by an oppressive elite and an oppressed rural population. The third retainer, however, describes the aristocrat for what he is: an exploiter who lives off the productive labor of others. This depiction of the aristocrat by the third slave exposes the codification of the retainer's world in the households of powerful elites, and to cover himself, the third slave returns to the aristocrat what is duly his. This makes the third slave the hero of the story.[36]

The difference between Rohrbaugh's and Herzog's readings and all the other readings of the parable discussed above is clear: While the stock read-ing of the parable sees the nobleman as a positive figure, praises the actions of the first two slaves, and vilifies the third slave, these two social-scientific readings interpret the parable in a directly opposite way—the actions of the nobleman and the first two slaves are seen as negative, and that of the third slave as positive.

Integrity and Authenticity

The parable of the talents or minas is found in Matt 25:14–30, Luke 19:12b–27, and in the Gospel of the Nazoreans 18 as recorded by Eusebius in his *Theophania* 4.22 (on Matt 25:14–15).[37] Which of these versions of the par-able most probably goes back to the earliest layer of the Jesus tradition?

36. Herzog, *Parables as Subversive Speech*, 155–68.

37. "(18) But since the Gospel (written) in Hebrew characters which has come into our hands enters the threat not against the man who hid (the talent), but against him who had lived dissolutely—*for he (the master) had three servants: one who squandered his master's substance with harlots and flute-girls, one who multiplied the grain, and one who hid the talent; and accordingly one was accepted (with joy), another merely rebuked, and another cast in prison*—I wonder whether in Matthew the threat which is uttered after the word against the man who did nothing may refer not to him, but by epanalepsis

Most scholars view the Nazorean version of the parable as a later rein-terpretation of Matthew's version of the parable. According to the Nazorean version, the first servant squanders the money on prostitutes, the second multiplies the grain of the master, and the third hides the master's money in the ground. These actions result in three outcomes: the first servant is accepted, the second is rebuked, and the third is thrown into prison.[38] Jer-emias, for example, calls it a "moralistic perversion which the parable has undergone in the Jewish-Christian church"; the early church most probably took offense at the judgment passed on the third servant (Matt 25:30) and on the basis of texts like Luke 12:45 and 15:30 substituted extravagance for unfaithfulness. The early church thus "corrected" (moralized) this point of Matthew's parable.[39] The Nazorean version of the parable can therefore be dismissed as a possible starting point if one is interested in the version of the parable that most probably goes back to the earliest layer of the Jesus tradition.

Turning to the Matthean and Lukan versions of the parable, Herzog correctly states that the differences between these two versions are signifi-cant enough "to raise the question . . . whether they are different versions of a common source or distinctive variations on a common theme."[40] This question has been answered in different ways by scholars. Some scholars argue that both versions stem from Q,[41] while others are of the opinion that the differences between the two versions indicate that they stem from the special *Sondergut* traditions used by Matthew (M) and Luke (L).[42] Other possibilities suggested are that the two parables stem from a presynoptic eschatological discourse concluding with several parables, one of which was the parable of the talents/minas,[43] that both versions are original and

---

(reversed parallel sequence) to the first who had feasted and drunk with the drunken." Translation from Funk et al., *Red Letter Edition*, 55; italics original.

38. See Rohrbaugh and Herzog below for a different interpretation of this version of the parable. Rohrbaugh, "Text of Terror," 32–39; Herzog, *Parables as Subversive Speech*, 152.

39. Jeremias, *Parables of Jesus*, 58. See also Dodd, *Parables of the Kingdom*, 120; Lambrecht, *Out of the Treasure*, 183; Wohlgemut, "Entrusted Money," 111.

40. Herzog, *Parables as Subversive Speech*, 15.

41. Buttrick, *Speaking in Parables*, 171–77; Donahue, *Gospel in Parable*, 105; Funk et al., *Five Gospels*, 255; Lambrecht, *Out of the Treasure*, 67; Münch, "Gewinnen oder Verlieren," 240–54; Weder, *Die Gleichnisse Jesu als Metaphern*, 193.

42. Boucher, *Parables*, 139; Crossan, *In Parables*, 98; Dodd, *Parables of the Kingdom*, 114; Jeremias, *Parables of Jesus*, 59–60; Manson, *Sayings of Jesus*, 245; Snodgrass, *Stories with Intent*, 525, 529–531; Weiser, *Die Knechtgleichnisse*, 256; Wohlgemut, "Entrusted Money," 105.

43. Wenham, *Jesus' Eschatological Discourse*, 52, 101.

were told by Jesus on two different occasions,[44] and that the Matthean and Lukan versions go back to the same original parable (not Q).[45] In an effort to unravel the tradition history of the parable, some scholars have tried to construct an "original parable,"[46] while others have suggested that the different versions in Matthew and Luke should at least—at the very least—be attributed to some "original" form.[47] The similarity between the vocabulary, and other elements of the Matthean and Lukan versions of the parable, which will be discussed below, proves adequate to argue that both these versions stem from Q.[48]

The majority of scholars render the Matthean version as the one closest to the original but at the same time are of the opinion that it contains secondary features that makes Matt 25:14–30 an apocalyptic eschatological version of the original Jesus parable.[49] The following eschatological features

44. Blomberg, *Interpreting the Parables*, 220; Capon, *Parables of Judgment*, 78; Groenewald, *In Gelykenisse Het Hy Geleer*, 224; Kistemaker, *Stories Jesus Told*, 12; Oesterley, *The Gospel Parables*, 143–144.

45. Boucher, *Parables*, 43. See Kloppenborg for a detailed discussion (and bibliography) of the different possibilities regarding the origin and relationship between the Matthean and Lukan versions of the parable. Kloppenborg, *Q Parallels*, 200.

46. Crossan, *In Parables*, 100; Herzog, *Parables as Subversive Speech*, 155; Lambrecht, *Out of the Treasure*, 165–95; Scott, *Hear Then the Parable*, 215–18; Weder, *Die Gleichnisse Jesu als Metaphern*, 202–3; Weiser, *Die Knechtgleichnisse*, 230–31, 237, 247; Wohlgemut, "Entrusted Money," 103–120.

47. Dodd, *Parables of the Kingdom*, 117; Jeremias, *Parables of Jesus*, 61–62; Jülicher, *Gleichnisreden Jesu*, 482; Manson, *Sayings of Jesus*, 245; Smith, *Parables of the Synoptic Gospels*, 168; Via, "Parable and Example Story," 115.

48. McGaughy, "Fear of Yahweh," 235; Scott, *Hear Then the Parable*, 229.

49. Buttrick, *Speaking in Parables*, 173; Funk et al., *Red Letter Edition*, 55; Herzog, *Parables as Subversive Speech*, 155; Hultgren, *Parables of Jesus*, 279; Jeremias, *Parables of Jesus*, 60; Scott, *Hear Then the Parable*, 223; Smith, *Parables of the Synoptic Gospels*; Wohlgemut, "Entrusted Money," 106; Young, *Jesus and His Jewish Parables*, 168. According to Jeremias, Matthew has preserved the earliest version of the parable, "although even here secondary features are to be observed." In Herzog's view, Matt 25:14b–28 should be seen as "the working version of the parable attributed to Jesus." There is an anomaly in Herzog's argument. In taking Matt 25:14b–28 as the working version of the parable that can be attributed to Jesus, Herzog includes Matt 25:15b, 19, 21 and 23— aspects of the parable that have clear eschatological overtones—as part of the parable attributed to Jesus. In essence Herzog, in this decision, denies his own understanding of the stages of the tradition of the parable, namely that the eschatological application of the parable should be seen as the final stage of its transitional development. Interesting also is that Herzog makes use of certain aspects of Luke's version of the parable εὐγενὴς (Luke 19:12b) and συναγαγὼν and διεσκόρπισεν in Luke 15:13 (the parable of the Prodigal) to read the Matthean version of the parable against the background of an urban aristocratic household, and to argue that the first two retainers monetized the wheat that the peasant farmers winnowed on behalf of their patron. Herzog, *Parables as Subversive Speech*, 158, 194. If the eschatological application of the parable presents the

of Matt 25:14–30 can be indicated: First, the parable is part of Matthew's apocalyptic discourse of judgement (Matt 24–25) that emphasizes the need for faithful activity while the second coming is delayed,[50]and is the conclusion to a triad of eschatological parables in Matt 24–25: the Wise and Faithful Slave (Matt 24:45–51), the Closed Door (Matt 25:1–13), and the Talents (Matt 25:14–30).[51] The introductory formula (Ὥσπερ γὰρ; Matt 25:14), second, links the parable to the parable of the Closed Door (Matt 25:1–13) which is evidently apocalyptic and eschatological in content.[52] Matt 25:30, third, turns the κύριος into an eschatological judge,[53] the *kurios* of the Christian community.[54] The parable, furthermore, has as basic topic the delay and the certainty of the parousia, as well as the responsibility (proper action) in the face of absent masters.[55] The parable, finally, is congenial to Matthew's view that some in the Matthean community are not suitable for the final joy at the end of time.[56]

When compared to Luke's version, Matthews' apocalyptic, eschatological application of the parable can also be detected in his redactional activity: the κύριος only returns Μετὰ δὲ πολὺν χρόνον (now after a long time; Matt 25:19), a reference to the delay of the parousia.[57] Second, the first two slaves are rewarded for what they achieved by the invitation εἴσελθε εἰς τὴν χαρὰν τοῦ κυρίου σου (enter into the joy of your master; Matt 25:21, 23), which refers to the messianic eschatological banquet.[58] Third, the addition of Matt

---

final stage of its transitional development, the eschatological overtones in Matt 25:15b, 19, 21 and 23 simply cannot be part of a "working version" of the parable attributed to Jesus.

50. Scott, *Hear Then the Parable*, 219; Donahue, *The Gospel in Parable*, 108; Hultgren, *Parables of Jesus*, 274; Lambrecht, *Out of the Treasure*, 212–13; Perkins, *Gnosticism and the New Testament*, 146.

51. Reid, *Parables for Preachers*, 202.

52. Herzog, *Parables as Subversive Speech*, 151; Hultgren, *Parables of Jesus*, 274; Oesterley, *Gospel Parables*, 143; Snodgrass, *Stories with Intent*, 526; Weder, *Die Gleichnisse Jesu als Metaphern*, 194.

53. Via, *Parables*, 114.

54. Hultgren, *Parables of Jesus*, 278; Snodgrass, *Stories with Intent*, 526.

55. Hultgren, *Parables of Jesus*, 108–9; ibid., 274; Buttrick, *Speaking in Parables*, 172.

56. Funk et al., *Red Letter Edition*, 67. See also Matt 13:24b–43a (the Planted Weeds), Matt 13:47–50 (the Dragnet), and Matt 22:2–14 (the Wedding Banquet), that have the same theme, namely the separation of the good and the bad.

57. Buttrick, *Speaking in Parables*, 172; Hultgren, *Parables of Jesus*, 278; McGaughy, "Fear of Yahweh," 237; Wohlgemut, "Entrusted Money," 108.

58. Buttrick, *Speaking in Parables*, 172; Hultgren, *Parables of Jesus*, 277–78; Jeremias, *Parables of Jesus*, 60; Lambrecht, *Out of the Treasure*, 178; McGaughy, "Fear of Yahweh," 237; Via, *The Parables*, 114; Wohlgemut, "Entrusted Money," 108.

25:30 (the judgement of the third slave) is typical of Matthew's apocalyptic discourse of judgement (see also Matt 8:12; 13:42, 50; 22:13; 24:51).[59]

Certain other features in Matthew's version of the parable are also typically Matthean: the description of events on a grand scale (the use of τάλαντα instead of μνᾶ), the repetition of key phrases and the parallelism in Matt 25:19–24 are reminiscent of the same techniques in Matt 18:23–30 and 20:1–13; and the description of the first two slaves as being faithful over a little (ἐπὶ ὀλίγα ἧς πιστός)—which is hardly accurate, since a talent is hardly a little—concurs with the description of the disciples in Matthew as having little faith (ὀλιγόπιστοι; see e.g., Matt 6:30; 8:26; 14:31; 16:8).[60] Finally, it is typical of Matthew to link ethics with eschatology; each slave therefore receives their talent ἑκάστῳ κατὰ τὴν ἰδίαν δύναμιν (Matt 25:15b).[61]

Luke's version lacks Matthew's eschatological coloring. The only eschatological aspect of the parable is its introduction (Luke 19:11) that links the parable to the Zacchaeus narrative in Luke 19:1–10, which resulted in some presuming that the long-awaited parousia was approaching. Luke 19:11 is part of Luke's redactional framing of the parable. Luke 19:11 should therefore not be considered part of the version Luke received in the tradition, which most probably starts at Luke 19:12b.[62] An important facet of Luke's version is that it is more realistic than Matthew's version. First of all, Luke's use of μνᾶ (Luke 19:13, 16, 18, 20, 24), instead of Matthew's τάλαντα (Matt 25:15, 16, 20, 22, 24, 25, 28), is more realistic and does not create the problem of Matt 25:21 and 23 (ἐπὶ ὀλίγα ἧς πιστός = you have been faithful over a little). A talent was not a little.[63] Second (and importantly, Luke's version contains some features that mirror the historical, political,

59. Hultgren, *Parables of Jesus*, 278; Wohlgemut, "Entrusted Money," 106; Buttrick, *Speaking in Parables*, 172; McGaughy, "Fear of Yahweh," 237.

60. See Donahue, *Gospel in Parable*, 108–109.

61. Scott, *Hear Then the Parable*, 226.

62. See Bultmann, *Synoptic Tradition*, 113; Kilgallen, *Twenty Parables*, 157. Scott's argument, that the inclusion of Luke 19:12b and 14 in Luke's version of the parable also indicates an eschatological tendency, can be interpreted in a different way, namely, that it refers to a historical event known by the hearers of the parable. Scott, *Hear Then the Parable*, 222. This possibility will be explored below.

63. A talent was a silver coinage, weighted between fifty–seven and seventy–four pounds, equaling six thousand denarii. One denarius was the average subsistence wage for a day laborer. A mina equaled one hundred denarii or drachmas (sixty minas equaled one talent). One talent thus represented the wage of a day laborer for fifteen to twenty years, and one mina the wage of a day laborer for two to three months. See Bailey, *Jesus through Middle Eastern Eyes*, 398; Boucher, *Parables*, 139; Donahue, *Gospel in Parable*, 107; Hultgren, *Parables of Jesus*, 274; Jeremias, *Parables of Jesus*, 60; Schottroff, *Parables of Jesus*, 184; Scott, *Hear Then the Parable*, 224; Snodgrass, *Stories with Intent*, 528.

and socioeconomic background of 30-CE Jewish Palestine. These features include the story of a well–born man who goes to receive a kingdom, has his leadership contested by his subjects, and proceeds to slaughter his opponents on his return (the so-called Throne Claimant parable; Luke 19:12b, 14 and 27), the first two slaves being appointed over respectively ten and five cities (Luke 19:17, 19), and the description of the nobleman as being a harsh man (ἄνθρωπος αὐστηρὸς), taking where he did not deposit and reaping where he did not sow (Luke 19:21, 22).[64] A final important aspect of Luke's version is that the third slave is not judged, but only labeled a πονηρὲ δοῦλε, a bad or evil slave (Luke 19:22). This feature of the parable thus far has been emphasized only by Scott;[65] an important aspect of Luke's version of the parable that has not thus far received its due attention in the interpretation of the parable.

Luke's version is thus most likely the closest we can get to the Jesus tradition, with Matthew reworking Q to fit his eschatological focus in Matthew 24–25. Luke's version of the parable also fits well into what has been indicated as typical of Jesus the Galilean's message.[66] The parable is evidence of the social stratification, patron-client relationships, the exploitative relationship between elite and nonelite, conflict, and peasant resistance that were part of first-century Jewish Palestine as an advanced agrarian society under the control of the Roman Empire—issues, as we have seen, that are addressed in almost all of Jesus' parables. The parable, especially, fits well in the central theme of Jesus' parables, namely, the nonapocalyptic kingdom of God; it is a story about God's kingdom, and not a story about God.[67]

But what about the integrity of the Lukan version? The version Luke received in the tradition most probably consisted of Luke 19:12b–24 and 27 (excluding Luke 19:25–26). Luke 19:11–12b, as indicated above, is the result of Luke's redactional activity, linking the parable to the Zacchaeus narrative in Luke 19:1–10. Luke 19:25 is also considered by most interpreters a secondary addition.[68] From a textual-critical perspective, Luke 19:25 is missing

---

64. Crossan remarks in this regard: "It is . . . obvious from the master in the parable . . . that Jesus was interested in realistic rather than idealistic masters." Crossan, *In Parables*, 101.

65. Scott, *Hear Then the Parable*, 222.

66. See Van Eck, "Interpreting the Parables," 310–21.

67. Matthew's version of the parable is clearly "a story about God." The setting of the parable in Matthew, as well as its (redactional) eschatological features, links Matthew's version to the time between Jesus' resurrection and Parousia, instructing its hearers on a specific way of acting in this intervening time. This setting of the parable makes no other reading possible than that of equating the man that goes on a journey and comes back to judge with Jesus.

68. See Crossan, *In Parables*, 99; Hultgren, *Parables of Jesus*, 278; Jeremias, *Parables*

in two important Greek witnesses, namely, Codices Bezae and Washington, as well as in some old Latin, Syriac and Coptic versions (69, pc, b, e, ff², sy^{s.c}, and bo^{ms}). In terms of the strategy of the parable, the third slave is reckoned with in Luke 11:24, and those who opposed the nobleman's being appointed as king (Luke 19:14), in Luke 19:27; hence repeating the pattern of Luke 19:13 (that focuses on the slaves) and Luke 19:14 (that focuses on the opposers). If Luke 19:25 (and Luke 19:26) is dismissed as Lukan, the speech of the nobleman is not interrupted. The parable ends with the nobleman deciding on the action to be taken with his two "opposers" in the parable: the third slave and those who did not want him to be king.

Luke 19:26 is seen by most interpreters as a "free-floating proverb," since it occurs elsewhere in the gospels (Mark 4:25; Matt 13:12; Luke 18:18; 19:26) and in Gos. Thom. 41.[69] Luke 19:26 can therefore also be omitted from the "original" parable.

Luke 19:12, 14 and 27—the description of a well–born man who goes to receive a kingdom, has his leadership challenged by his subjects, and proceeds to slaughter his opponents (the so–called Throne Claimant parable)— is seen by several scholars as a separate and original parable of Jesus about a claimant for a throne, reflecting the historical situation in 4 BCE when Archelaus journeyed to Rome to get his kingship over Judea confirmed. At the same time a Jewish embassy of fifty persons went to Rome in order to resist Archelaus' appointment. Archelaus was appointed, and when he returned to Judea, took revenge on those that had opposed him (see Josephus, *War* 2.80–100, 111; *Ant.* 17.208–249, 299–314).[70] This independent parable was fused with the parable of the talents in either the pre–Lukan tradition or by Luke himself, and with the provided setting in Luke 19:11, used by Luke allegorically to allude to the ascension of Jesus and his Parousia.[71] This

---

of Jesus, 62; Weiser, *Die Knechtgleichnisse*, 251–52.

69. Bultmann, *Synoptic Tradition*, 176; Crossan, *In Parables*, 99; Davies and Allison, *Matthew*, 3:410; Dodd, *Parables of the Kingdom*, 116–18; Donahue, *Gospel in Parable*; Herzog, *Parables as Subversive Speech*, 151; Jeremias, *Parables of Jesus*, 60; Jülicher, *Gleichnisreden Jesu*, 478; Lambrecht, *Out of the Treasure*, 230–32; Manson, *Sayings of Jesus*, 248; Smith, *Parables of the Synoptic Gospels*, 167; Via, *Parables*, 114; Weiser, *Die Knechtgleichnisse*, 253; Wohlgemut, "Entrusted Money," 106.

70. According to Perkins, the insertion in the parable does not refer to Archelaus but to the events that took place when Herod the Great came to the throne. Perkins, *Hearing the Parables*, 147. Scott also dismisses the possibility that Luke 19:12, 14, and 27 refer to the events surrounding Archelaus' journey to Rome in an effort to be confirmed as ruler over Judea; the theme of a throne claimant was common enough to render historical connections unnecessary. Scott, *Hear Then the Parable*, 222.

71. Blomberg, *Interpreting the Parables*, 218–21; Boucher, *Parables*, 140; Crossan, *In Parables*, 99; Herzog, *Parables as Subversive Speech*, 154–55; Hultgren, *Parables of Jesus*, 284–85; Jeremias, *Parables of Jesus*, 59; Lambrecht, *Out of the Treasure*, 176; Smith,

interpretation builds on the premise that the parable is determined by Luke 19:11, giving it an eschatological flavor. When Luke 19:11 is seen as Luke's redactional activity, Luke's version of the parable has no eschatological coloring and mirrors the historical, political, and socioeconomic background of 30 CE, with the Throne Claimant parable in all probability part of the version of the parable as told by Jesus. Moreover, this interpretation can only work if the actions of the two slaves in the parable are interpreted positively. This, as will be indicated below, is not necessarily the case.

If one includes the Archelaus narrative, the parable is no longer about a man leaving, returning, and reckoning (alluding to the ascension of Jesus, his parousia, and judgment), and two good slaves and one bad slave. Rather, it is a story about a normalcy that was part of the first-century world of Jesus: elite looking for power, power that exploits, and the exploited who resist.[72] Seen from this perspective, the parable is about a well-born man looking for more power, two groups of the exploited protesting in different ways, two ways of adhering to the well-born man's instruction to "do business" with entrusted money, and two reckonings. The inclusion of the Archelaus story rounds of the parable nicely, linking Luke 19:12b with Luke 19:27.

Support for this reading comes from Schottroff:

> Luke 19:11–27 . . . does not combine two independent parables about slaves and a claimant to a throne; it tells a story that is coherent in itself, about the beginning of the reign of a vassal king, his management of the administration of his kingdom, and the establishment of his power.[73]

Parables of the Synoptic Gospels, 537; Weder, *Die Gleichnisse Jesu als Metaphern*, 195; Weiser, *Die Knechtgleichnisse*, 262–72; Wenham, *Jesus' Eschatological Discourse*, 73; Wright, *Victory of God*, 2:633.

72. The parable of the talents, in Rohrbaugh's view, is "indeed a parable and not an allegorical story. It draws upon events familiar from the real world to create an imaginary and open-ended situation . . . which hearers are invited to ponder." Rohrbaugh, "Text of Terror," 33. Jesus told parables that give evidence to those elements that were common of advanced agrarian (aristocratic) societies like debt, patrons, elite using their status to coerce tenants, the existence of large estates, tenants working these estates, elite that amass wealth by putting money out on loan at very high rates, and the poor being neglected. These stories not only assume knowledge of the Palestinian countryside under the early Roman Empire, but also reveal the ugly face of the exploitation of the peasantry by the elite so common to advanced agrarian (aristocratic) societies. By telling these parables, Jesus most probably acknowledged the needs and frustrations of the peasants in his first-century rural context. Oakman, *Jesus and the Peasants*, 118.

73. Schottroff, *Parables of Jesus*, 187. *Contra* Snodgrass and Buttrick, who respectively argue that the "throne claimant elements shift the focus of the parable and weave a second plot that causes some loss," and that the "added material, an overdrawn theological allegory, does not fit the structure of the parable terribly well." Snodgrass, *Stories*

Realism

The parable is realistic in its description of slaves being entrusted with money with which they had to trade; it is realistic in its description of slaves who made extensive profits, slaves who were appointed over cities.[74] Finally, it is realistic in its depiction of a nobleman who takes from what he did not deposit, and reaps where he did not sow. These aspects of the parable, that were normalcies in first-century Jewish Palestine, require further explanation if one wants to read the parable against the background of Jewish Palestine in 30 CE.

In Luke 19:21 the third slave describes the nobleman who entrusts money to his slaves to do business with (πραγματεύσασθε; Luke 19:13)[75] as someone who takes what he did not put down and reaps what he did not sow (αἴρεις ὃ οὐκ ἔθηκας καὶ θερίζεις ὃ οὐκ ἔσπειρας). To what aspects of first-century Palestinian life does this description refer? Palestine in the first century was part of the Roman Empire. Rome claimed sovereignty over land and sea and their yield, the distribution of this yield and its cultivators (the peasantry). This was done through an exploitative tax system. Rome ruled Palestine through native collaborators from the elite who had the responsibility of paying the annual tribute, extracted from the peasantry, to Rome (Herod Antipas in Galilee and Archelaus in Judea). These client kings had lavish and consumptious lifestyles, and the wealth that was required to support this type of lifestyle came from the peasantry by means of a second level of tribute and taxes: the ruling elite claimed the so-called surplus of the harvest and added tribute and taxes. This left the peasantry living at barely a subsistence level. The only way to survive was to borrow from the elite, and the elite were always willing to invest in loans with interest rates of up to 20 percent.[76]

The elite class was so excessively wealthy that they were not able to spend all they had through consumption and the erection of large buildings. The elite were always looking for opportunities to invest, and extending

---

with Intent, 536; Buttrick, Speaking in Parables, 173.

74. Contra Hultgren, who is of the opinion that the first and second slave s being appointed over respectively ten and five cities is a secondary addition to the parable. Hultgren, Parables of Jesus, 287.

75. See also διεπραγματεύσαντο in Luke 19:15, which can be translated as "how many business have been transacted." See Bailey, Jesus through Middle Eastern Eyes, 402.

76. Goodman, "First Jewish Revolt," 402–29. Interest rates up to 48 percent are attested (Brutus' loan to Salamis; see Cicero, Att. 5.21.10–12). In general, however, interest was limited to 12 percent by edict, although rates of 20 percent are also attested (see P.Mur. 114; P.Mur. 18). Kloppenborg, The Tenants in the Vineyard, 4.

credit to small farmers became an enormous source of profit. The aim of these investments was to acquire land when debt repayments failed. Indebted farmers were frequently enslaved and became the property of their new masters. To borrow from elite meant that the borrower became a client of a patron; that is, the peasant farmer became part of a patron-client relationship.[77] Patronage took on many forms, one of which was brokerage. In brokerage a broker functioned as a mediator who gave a client access to the resources of a patron. In the parable, in fact, the slaves function as brokers. The nobleman, as part of the ruling elite, "reaps what he did not sow" by taxing the peasantry and claiming the so-called land surplus. He "takes what he did not put down," and his slaves are acting as his brokers in giving loans ("doing business") to make profit for their master.

What does it mean that the nobleman appoints the first and second slaves over ten and five cities respectively? According to Llewelyn, early republican Rome made use of tax farmers to collect state revenue. These *publicani* inter alia collected all direct taxes on crops and pasture dues. With the demise of the Republican order, direct taxation was entrusted to the cities and local communities. This was the case in Roman Egypt and Roman Judea.[78] Direct taxes were the responsibility of a government agent, and indirect taxes (e.g., custom duties, tolls, market taxes and trade taxes) were the responsibility of the *publicani*. The government agent, for example the procurator in Judea or Herod Antipas in Galilee, made use of officials (*conductores*) in gathering the taxes,[79] but the use of slaves was forbidden.[80]

This, however, is exactly what Archelaus did. One of the accusations laid before Augustus by the embassy that protested his appointment as king was that he imposed on his subjects that "they were to make liberal presents to himself, to his domestics and friends, and to *such of his slaves as were vouchsafed the favour on being his tax gatherers*" (Josephus, *Ant.* 17.299–314).[81] And this is again what Archelaus did after his appointment as *etnarch* (leader of the nation) on his return: the two slaves that did so well

77. Goodman, "First Jewish Revolt," 426.

78. Llewelyn, "Taxation," 47–76. See also Rostovtzeff, *Geschichte Der Staatpracht*, 101.

79. If Scott is correct that αὐστηρὸς in Luke 19:21 and 22 is also used to refer to government officials that are strict in their examination of accounts, it clearly links Archelaus in the parable with the gathering of taxes. Scott, *Hear Then the Parable*, 230. See also BAGD, 121, which gives "government finance inspector" as one of the possible meanings of αὐστηρὸς.

80. Llewelyn, "Taxation," 53.

81. Italics added.

in "doing business" with his money, are appointed over ten and five cities to gather taxes. As Schottroff puts it:

> In the parable the slaves make large profits with very little money: ten and five times the original sum (19:16, 18). In doing so, they have proved to the satisfaction of the new king that they can form the backbone of his administration . . . Now the slaves can relate in grand style what they so successfully accomplished on a small scale: exploiting people and the land to increase the wealth of their master.[82]

Reading the Parable

The structure (or strategy)[83] of the parable is made up of five sets of "twos." In an effort to enhance his power, privilege, and wealth, the nobleman does two things. He sets off with the hope of being proclaimed king (Luke 19:12b), and before he leaves he entrusts money to ten of his slaves to "do business" (πραγματεύσασθε) with one mina each (Luke 19:13). These two actions of the nobleman lead to two sets of reactions in the parable; one of adhering and one of protesting. Two slaves in the parable do business with their minas, and they receive compensation they expect from the nobleman (Luke 19:16, 18). Two characters in the parable protest against the actions of the nobleman. An embassy (as a character group) sets off to ask that the nobleman not be installed as king (Luke 19:14), and one slave protests against the instruction of the nobleman by not doing business with the mina he was entrusted with (Luke 19:20–21).

When the nobleman returns, two different sets of actions again take place. First, the two slaves who are able to show good profits are praised and awarded for their efforts. In two scenes in the parable (Luke 19:17, 19) the first slave is awarded ten cities, and the second slave five. Up to this point in the parable, there is a consistency in its strategy: two actions, two protests, two compliances and two awards. In the last set of twos, when the nobleman reckons with his two protestors, the consistency in the parable is broken down. The enemies of the nobleman are judged and killed (Luke 19:27), but the third slave is not condemned (Luke 19:22–23). He is only labeled as

82. Schottroff, *Parables of Jesus*, 185.

83. Social-scientific criticism, as exegetical method, analyses texts in terms of their *strategy* and *situation*. The situation of a text refers to the social circumstances in which the text was produced, and the text's strategy, as defined by Elliott, refers to "its pragmatic and rhetorical dimension, the manner in which the text in its totality of form and content (syntactic and semantic dimensions) is designed to have a specific effect upon . . . [its] . . . receiver(s)." Elliott, *Social-Scientific Criticism*, 54–55.

a bad or evil slave (πονηρὲ δοῦλε). In terms of the structure of the parable thus far, the hearers of the parable would have expected that both the third slave and the embassy who protested would be judged and condemned. But then comes the inconsistency and surprise: the ruthless and hard man who takes what he did not put down and reaps what he did not sow, who exploits and does not stand for any opposition in what he wants to achieve, lets the third slave go only by labeling him as bad or evil. It is in this surprise in the parable that we have to look for its meaning.[84]

When the parable is read in a 30-CE context as a parable of Jesus the Galilean, with the help of the insights of social-scientific criticism, and when the strategy of the parable is taken seriously, the parable of the Minas is not about a man who leaves and then returns to judge those who were entrusted with the "gifts" he bestowed on them before he left (alluding to the ascension of Jesus, his parousia, and his judgment). It is not a parable about two good slaves and one bad slave. The parable is about the exploitative normalcies that were part and parcel of first-century Palestine: it is about elite constantly seeking more honor, power, and privilege; it is about members of the elite using their power to exploit; it is also an example of the way the exploited could resist. "The narrative is absolute clear. It describes the economic and political structure of an exploitative kingship."[85]

One is tempted, as Jeremias was, to make a strong case for the probability that the parable is a copycat of the incident in 4 BCE when Archelaus went to Rome to have his kingship confirmed by Augustus. In this incident the embassy that went to Rome contested his appointment. Archelaus was eventually appointed etnarch and subsequently returned to exact revenge on those who had contested his kingship.[86] The parallels between the two stories are obvious. In the parable, as in the Archelaus story, a nobleman (Archelaus) travels to a far country (Rome) to receive a kingdom (to be installed by Augustus as a vassal king). An embassy of fifty citizens went to Rome to ask that the nobleman should not reign over them (the plea of the Jewish embassy before Augustus), the nobleman received the kingdom (Archelaus was installed as *etnarch*), returned and appointed two of his slaves over some of the cities placed under his governance (e.g., Stratos

84. From this description of the strategy of the parable, it is clear that the parable cannot do without the throne claimant story, whether it refers to Archelaus or not. Therefore the throne claimant story cannot be seen as a later addition that is unnecessary for the structure of the parable. *Contra* Hultgren, *Parables of Jesus*, 285.

85. Schottroff, *Parables of Jesus*, 185.

86. Jeremias, *Parables of Jesus*, 59. See also Wright, *Jesus the Storyteller*, 138–40.

Tower, Sebaste, Joppe and Jerusalem; Josephus, *Ant.* 17.315–323), and finally killed those who did not want him to reign over them.[87]

As I argued earlier, in terms of its strategy, the parable cannot portray its core purpose without the throne-claimant story to make its point. One can argue that it is unnecessary to see the parable as a direct reference to the Archelaus story. The reason is that what is "described (in the parable) is not a particular, individual historical event, but a structure."[88] Therefore, Jesus may or may not have made use of the Archelaus story to make this point—notwithstanding the obvious parallels. In other words, the parable does not merely want to focus on the events that occurred in 4 BCE, but rather on the normalcy of first-century Palestinian life; the economic and political structure of exploitative kingship. Put differently: one of the points the parable wants to make is about the way the elite exploited nonelite. The point of departure taken here is that Jesus, to make his point, most probably made use of the Archelaus story as an example of the exploitation by the elite.

The iniquities of which the embassy accused Archelaus before Augustus, after all, were exactly the same as those the nonelite (peasantry) were experiencing: exploitative and excessive taxation and tributes (including the taking of the so-called surplus of the harvest) to fund inter alia the lavish and consumptious lifestyles of the elite, and loans at high rates with the aim of acquiring land when repayment of debts failed, thus creating large estates which in turn lead to a commercialized economy.[89] According to Josephus (*Ant.* 17.299–314), this is exactly what Archelaus did after the death of Herod the Great: he destroyed the Jews, as Herod did when many perished under his rule because of his adorning of certain cities. He filled the nation with the utmost degree of poverty and confiscated estates. Besides laying annual impositions on everyone, he demanded liberal presents for himself and for his domestics and friends, and he treated many inhumanely.

87. Josephus has no direct reference to this aspect of the parable. He, however, states that "Archelaus took possession of his ethnarchy, and used not the Jews only, but the Samaritans also, barbarously; *and this out of his resentment of their old quarrels with him*" (Josephus, *War* 2.311); italics added.

88. Schottroff, *Parables of Jesus*, 185.

89. This situation of the peasantry in first-century Palestine is aptly described by Herzog: "The peasant village in Palestine during the early decades of the first century was under increasing stress. The cumulative effects of Herodian rule, combined with the rigors of Roman colonialism and the demands of the Temple hierarchy, had taken their toll. The monetization and commercialization of the local economy had led to increasingly predatory relationships between elites and peasants . . . [T]here is evidence for rising debt and defaults on loans; accompanied by the hostile takeover of peasant small-holdings and the reduction of peasants to more dependent economic statuses. These practices can be traced back to the fact that elites made loans to peasants and held their land as collateral." Herzog, *Parables as Subversive Speech*, 206.

This, then, is the first point the parable wants to make: the elite are exploiting the nonelite. The elite are like the nobleman and his two slaves.[90] This is what the kingdom of Caesar looks like.

The second and main point of the parable lies in its surprise: both the embassy and the third slave oppose the nobleman, but only those who do not want the nobleman to be king are condemned. Why? Because in a situation such as first-century Palestine, where the relation between empire and subjected people was one of power, where all matters of importance were in the hands of the elite with the peasantry having no legitimate channel for political participation,[91] there were only two ways to protest: the wrong way and the correct way.

In Luke 19:12b the man who journeys to a far country is described as ἄνθρωπός τις εὐγενής; he is well-born, most probably noble from birth. He is thus a person with ascribed honor. In the first-century Mediterranean world ascribed honor was obtained passively through birth (e.g., Archelaus was the son of Herod the Great, and thus had ascribed honor). When honor is ascribed, "it is bestowed on someone by a notable person of power, such as a king or governor."[92] More important, "the powerful one ascribing the honor has the sanction of power to make the grant of honor stick,"[93] and, of course, the power to annul the honor status. If one sees the nobleman in the parable as Archelaus, this means that Archelaus went to Rome to have his ascribed honor sanctioned by Augustus. He also, however, sought acquired honor[94] in his bid to receive the kingship over the territories that belonged to his father Herod the Great, and not his brothers Antipas or Philip.

Important to remember is that in the first-century Mediterranean world ascribed honor was equal to wealth (it resembled inherited wealth), and acquired honor was wealth obtained through one's efforts.[95] Moreover, in first-century Palestine "'rich' or 'wealthy' as a rule meant 'avaricious, greedy,' while 'poor' referred to persons scarcely able to maintain their honor or dignity."[96] Traditional peasant societies (like the first-century Mediterranean) perceived all resources in terms of "limited good," and therefore saw wealthy persons as "thieves" who had benefited at the expense of the

90. Rohrbaugh, "Text of Terror," 32–39.

91. Horsley, *Spiral of Violence*, 5, 11; Fiensy, *Jesus the Galilean*, 34.

92. Malina, *Christian Origins and Cultural Anthropology*, 82.

93. Ibid., 83.

94. Acquired honor "is honor actively sought and achieved, most often at the expense of one's equals in the social context of challenge and riposte." Malina and Neyrey, "Honor and Shame in Luke-Acts," 28.

95. Ibid.

96. Malina, "Wealth and Poverty," 355. See also Rohrbaugh, "Text of Terror," 34–35.

poor.[97] A poor person, therefore, was someone who could not maintain his inherited status due to circumstances that befell him and his family (like debt). At the same time, the rich person was one who was able to maintain his status.[98] The terms "rich" and "poor" in first-century Palestine, therefore, were political before they were economic.[99] To be rich was to have the power to maintain what one had or even to increase it.[100]

When the embassy contested Archelaus' appointment as king, they in fact thus contested his honor, the most pivotal value in the first-century eastern Mediterranean world. Discursively, they contested his power to maintain and increase his wealth and status. In essence, they played a political game in a world in which they had no legitimate channel for political participation, ultimately receiving the customary penalty dished out by the elite in cases like this.[101] This clearly, according to the parable, was evidently not the way to protest.

But what would be the appropriate way to protest? How could nonelites negotiate a world of material domination that appropriate their agricultural production and labor by excessive taxation? One approach is to proceed like the first two slaves; do not protests and thereby legitimate the domination of the elite. Alternatively one can, like the embassy, try to play the political game without any legitimation and subsequently carry the consequences. Or one can act like the third slave—a way of protest that Scott calls the "hidden transcript" or "the weapons of the weak."[102]

97. Malina, New Testament World, 71–93; Malina, "Wealth and Poverty," 363.

98. According to Hollenbach, this does not mean that the terms poor and rich in the first-century Mediterranean world did not also have some economic content. In oppressive aristocratic-peasant societies, in which peasants are dominated and exploited by aristocrats, peasants in principle are the poor, and the aristocrats the rich. The poor and the rich, therefore, are also permanent groups within society, at least in economic-political terms. Hollenbach, "Defining Rich and Poor," 58.

99. Rohrbaugh, "Text of Terror," 35.

100. Malina, "Wealth and Poverty," 356–61.

101. See, for example, the messianic movements of Judas son of Hezekiah (4 BCE), Simon (4 BCE) and Athronges (4–2 BCE; Josephus, War 2.55–65). The participants in these messianic movements were primarily peasants with the goal to overthrow Herodian and Roman domination and to restore the traditional ideals for a free and egalitarian society. Horsley and Hanson, Bandits, Prophets, and Messiahs, 111–27. These movements were all subdued in a violent way. The parallel between what we know of these movements and the embassy in the parable, is clear. The embassy also consisted of peasants (nonelite), hoped to attain dissolution of kingly government, and wanted to live by their own laws. Their fate is also the same; they are violently killed. See κατασφάξατε in Luke 19:27), which means "to be slaughtered or cut in pieces."

102. Scott, Weapons of the Weak, xvi.

The peasantry in the time of Jesus, although they had no legitimate way for protest, could, and did, resist. The forms of their resistance were called the "hidden transcript" (vis-à-vis the public transcript of events controlled by the rulers).[103] This hidden transcript was a discourse that took place "offstage," and captured "what the oppressed say to each other and distills what they really think about their rulers but are too intimidated to express openly."[104] This, however, does not mean that the hidden transcript was never expressed in public. It was, as "weapons of the weak" in the form of inter alia encoded forms of speech,[105] "a disguised, ambiguous, and coded form of speech dedicated to maintaining the hidden transcript of resistance while leaving a public transcript that is in no way actionable."[106]

This is also Carter's point of view:

> More often, since direct confrontations that are violent or defiant provoke harsh retaliation (like what happened to the embassy in the parable), protests among dominated groups are hidden or "offstage." Apparent compliant behavior can be ambiguous. Often protest is disguised, calculated and self-protective. It may comprise of telling stories that offer an alternative or counter-ideology to negate the elite's dominant ideology and to assert the dignity or equality of nonelites. It may employ coded talk . . . or "double talk" that seems to submit to elites . . . but contains, for those with ears to hear, a subversive message.[107]

This is how the excuse of the third slave can be understood. As correctly interpreted by Rohrbaugh, the nobleman is a thief in the eyes of the third slave. He does not want any part in the exploitation of the peasantry. So what does he do? First he ties the mina in a cloth to protect the existing share of the owner, "exactly what in the peasant view an honorable person should do."[108] Second, when confronted by his master, he does not characterize his master as a hard man to justify his fear and consequent inactivity with the mina. He rather employs the "weapons of the weak": "I knew I had to be careful, and I have been."[109] How would the nobleman have heard this? Most probably in the sense of "Master, I have so much respect for you (I am honoring you) that I did not want to take a chance with your money.

103. Scott, "Protest and Profanation," 12–16.
104. Scott, *Domination and the Arts of Resistance*, 18.
105. Ibid., 19.
106. Herzog, *Prophet and Teacher*, 189.
107. Carter, *Roman Empire*, 11–12.
108. Rohrbaugh, "Text of Terror," 37.
109. Ibid.

I did what I thought was the honorable thing to do, that is, to protect what belongs to you." But what did the peasants, who most probably were part of the audience when Jesus told the parable, hear? Most probably they wanted to hear, "You are a thief, and I am not willing to be part of what you are do-ing!" And what did the nobleman do? Since he knew that the social control and power he enjoyed was built on fear, and that this led to the action of the third slave, the slave's action in a sense was a result of his (the master's) own doing. Nonetheless the slave acted responsibly. He was a "bad slave," com-pared to the other two. But yet he respected (honored) his master, although he made no profit. Consequently, the master let him go with only a label around his neck.

When read from this perspective, the parable of Jesus in itself is a "hidden transcript." Perceived from the elite's point of view, it tells a story of honor, power, and legitimated judgement. This is how the elite would have interpret it. But for the peasants it had a different meaning. This is the way to protest. "Honor" those that exploit you, without taking part in their exploitation. To confront those that exploit directly, will not work. Rather be "as sly as a snake and as simple as a dove." (Matt 10:16b; Gos. Thom. 39:3).

A Parable of Jesus?

In the parable Jesus condemns the master's viewpoint,[110] and by doing this, he criticizes the use of honor to enhance power and privilege, class, status, and wealth. He also criticizes the economic exploitation of the peasantry by the ruling elite. These ideas contained in the parable are incontestably those of Jesus and are paralleled in other parables that can be traced back to the earliest layer of the historical Jesus (e.g., Luke 12:16–20; Gos. Thom. 63:1–3; Luke 16:19–26; Matt 20:1–16). Jesus' condemnation of the rich, his siding with the poor, and his critique of honor and status are also attested in several sayings of Jesus that pass the criteria of early, multiple, and inde-pendent attestation. (see, e.g., Q 6:20; Gos. Thom. 54; Q 6:21; Gos. Thom. 69:2; Mark 12:38–39 and *par.*) Several sayings of Jesus that pass the criteria of early, multiple, and independent attestation concur with the viewpoint of the third slave, who did not partake in the exploitation of others by loan-ing money and taking interest (i.e., generalized reciprocity; see e.g. Q 6:30; Gos. Thom. 95:1–2; Luke 6:35; Q 6:35b; Gos. Thom. 95:1–2). Generalized reciprocity, according to the opinion of several historical Jesus scholars, was one of the core values of Jesus' teaching.[111] Several of Jesus' parables also

110. Ibid., 38.

111. For Jesus, God's rule was a power opposed to the social order established in

advocate general reciprocity (see, e.g., Luke 10:30–35; 11:5–8; Q 14:16–24; Gos. Thom. 64:1–12). The gist of the parable is clearly connected to these values.

Rome. Jesus made use of kinship religion and kinship economy to address the exploitative political economy and political religion of Rome. In Jesus' parables he favored a fictive family in which relations were modeled on those of close kin, with exchanges taking place through arrangements of generalized reciprocity and taking no account of exchanges or debt. Oakman, *Jesus and the Peasants*, 105.

CHAPTER 13

The Social Prophet from Galilee

W HO WAS JESUS, THE Galilean from Nazareth? Since Reimarus' (1694–1768) answer to this question in 1778, scholars interested in the historical Jesus have answered it in different ways.[1] Schweitzer's Jesus was the direct opposite of Reimarus' Jesus: for Schweitzer, Jesus was a typical Jewish apocalyptic that proclaimed a futuristic (heavenly) kingdom.[2] Vermes pictured Jesus as a Galilean Hasid (a holy man or rabbi in the charismatic tradition of Galilee), Brandon understood him as a zealot-like Jewish revolutionary who had political aims, while Smith described him as a miracle worker (magician).[3] Since 1985, an abundance of divergent profiles of Jesus have been suggested by scholars.[4] In these varied profiles a Jesus emerges who is anything from an itinerant Cynic-like philosopher[5] to a Jewish Mediterranean peasant[6] to a Spirit-filled person or charismatic holy man[7] to an eschatological prophet who announced the restoration of

---

1. In his *Fragments*, published after his death by Lessing (1729–1781), Reimarus argued that Jesus saw himself as a (political) kingly messiah who wanted to establish an earthly kingdom during his lifetime by delivering his people from the bondage of Rome. Jesus was not the "spiritual" messiah that died for the sins of humankind, was resurrected, and will return in glory. This picture of Jesus, Reimarus argued, was an invention of his disciples after his death.

2. Schweitzer, *Quest of the Historical Jesus*. See also Bornkamm, *Jesus of Nazareth*.

3. Vermes, *Jesus the Jew*; Brandon, *Jesus and the Zealots*; Smith, *Jesus the Magician*.

4. Nineteen eighty-five is seen as the year in which the so-called Third Quest or Renewed New Quest (depending on the approach taken) to the historical Jesus started. This renewed interest in who the historical Jesus was gave rise to many (and varied) profiles of Jesus.

5. Mack, *Myth of Innocence*; Downing, *Christ and the Cynics*.

6. Crossan, *Historical Jesus*.

7. Borg, *New Vision*; Borg, *Jesus*; Twelftree, *Jesus the Exorcist*.

Israel in terms of a nonapocalyptical kingdom within space-time history[8] to a prophet of social change[9] to a prophet and child of Sophia[10] to a marginal Jew[11] to a Jewish Messiah of sorts[12] to a fatherless Jew[13] to a Galilean shamanic figure.[14]

The readings of the parables presented in this work make a serious claim that the understanding of Jesus as an ethical-eschatological social prophet should be taken seriously, at least when it comes to Jesus' parables.[15]

First, it is clear that some of Jesus' contemporaries saw him as one of the "ancient prophets" (Luke 9:19) like John the Baptist, Elijah, or Jeremiah (Mark 8:28 and *par.*). Simon the Pharisee clearly assumed that Jesus was popularly held to be a prophet (Luke 7:39). When Jesus entered Jerusalem he was greeted as the "prophet from Nazareth of Galilee" (Matt 21:11), and while Jesus was in Jerusalem, the religious leaders cautiously plotted his arrest because they feared the crowd who held Jesus to be a prophet (Matt 21:46). Even members of Antipas' court thought that Jesus was one of the prophets of old (Mark 6:15 and *par.*). In the Emmaus narrative also, Jesus is referred to as a "prophet mighty in word and deed" (Luke 24:19).[16]

Second, the parables in the Synoptic Gospels, and the Gospel of Thomas paint a picture of Jesus as a prophet of old. Many of the issues and themes addressed by Old Testament prophets such as Isaiah, Jeremiah, Micah, Amos, and Hosea, can be found in Jesus' parables; the two most prominent themes are most probably inclusivism and a critique of social injustice.

8. Sanders, *Historical Figure of Jesus*; Casey, *From Jewish Prophet to Gentile God*; Wright, *New Testament and the People of God*; Wright, *Victory of God*; Allison, *Jesus of Nazareth*.

9. Theissen, *Shadow of the Galilean*; Horsley and Hanson, *Bandits, Prophets, and Messiahs*; Kaylor, *Jesus the Prophet*; Horsley, *Spiral of Violence*.

10. Schüssler Fiorenza, *Jesus: Miriam's Child*.

11. Meier, *Marginal Jew*.

12. Stuhlmacher, *Jesus of Nazareth*; Dunn, "Messianic Ideas and Their Influence"; De Jonge, *Jesus, the Servant-Messiah*; Bockmuehl, *This Jesus*.

13. Van Aarde, *Fatherless in Galilee*.

14. Craffert, *Life of a Galilean Shaman*.

15. This statement does not imply that Jesus was also, for example, a healer and an exorcist. The argument put forward is that one of the attributes of Jesus, in terms of the sample of the parables discussed in this volume, at least should be that of also being a social prophet.

16. These references take it for granted "that Jesus was popularly acclaimed as a prophet or called a prophet by his opponents," thus making it quite likely that Jesus was called a prophet during his lifetime. Herzog, *Prophet and Teacher*, 99. It is unlikely the early church invented the many sayings that call Jesus a prophet. The reason for this is that it is theologically risky to do so, since it might have appeared "that he was simply being put on a level with all the other prophets." Wright, *Victory of God*, 162.

Prophetic Traditions in the Old Testament:
Inclusivism and Social Injustice

Second Isaiah lived in the period of the Second Temple and had an openness to the Gentile world.[17] Second Isaiah gives evidence of Israel already being a confessional community that accepts proselytes. In Isa 44:3–5, for example, the Abraham tradition (Gen 12:1–3) is interpreted so that the blessing of the nations is understood as adherence to the religion of Abraham's descendants. Moreover, adherence to this religious community comes about by personal decision, excluding circumcision. Isaiah 45:20–25 carries the same message: Gentiles are invited to turn to Yahweh to accept salvation from him, salvation that implies a confession of faith in Yahweh (Isa 45:23; see also Isa 45:14; Exod 18:8–12; Josh 2:9–11; 2 Kgs 5:15).[18] This universalistic approach of Second Isaiah is also present in Third Isaiah.[19] In Isa 56:1–8, Yahweh gives the assurance of salvation, not only to foreigners, but even to eunuchs (the socially impure). Clearly here incorporation and membership "are determined not on ethnic or national considerations but on a profession of faith."[20] Israel, in future, will also include Gentiles.

Gelston finds, like Blenkinsopp, the same perspective in Second Isaiah.[21] Isa 43:8–13; 44:3–5; and 44:6–8; and to a lesser extent Isa 43:21 affirm Second Isaiah's universalistic tendencies. These passages speak of the Gentiles who will recognize that Yahweh is the only God and supreme power of the world—"surely a form of universalism."[22] Like Blenkinsopp, Gelston sees Isa 44:3–5 as an indication of Second Isaiah's universalistic tendency; "individuals who are not Israelites by birth will become adherents of YHWH."[23] Isa 45:22 carries the same message: the Gentiles are also invited to experience the salvation offered by God—the same salvation (inclusion

---

17. See, for example, Blenkinsopp, "Prophet of Universalism," 83–103; Gelston, "Universalism in Second Isaiah," 377–398. Blenkinsopp goes so far as to argue that Second Isaiah provided the model for Jesus' and early Christianity's openness to the Gentile world vis-à-vis the religious particularism of the Second Temple. Blenkinsopp, "Prophet of Universalism," 99.

18. Blenkinsopp, "Prophet of Universalism," 86. See also Lohfink and Zenger, *God of Israel and the Nations*, 47–49.

19. Blenkinsopp, "Prophet of Universalism," 93. See also Lohfink and Zenger, *God of Israel and the Nations*, 53–57.

20. Blenkinsopp, "Prophet of Universalism," 95.

21. Gelston, "Universalism in Second Isaiah," 377–97.

22. Ibid., 385.

23. Ibid., 386.

in the kingdom) Jesus spoke about when he told stories about the kingdom of God.[24]

Apart from this emphasis on inclusivity, the priestly,[25] Deuteronomic,[26] wisdom,[27] and prophetic traditions (see, e.g., Isa 3:14–15) in the Old Testament strongly voice the protection of the poor from the exploitative practices and systemic violence of the rich.[28] The Old Testament prophets vehemently opposed the exploitative practices of the elite at the expense of the common peasants, of which Amos and Hosea are maybe the best examples. Amos and Hosea's prophetic activity took place in the eighth century BCE, when Jeroboam II reigned in Israel (the north), and Uzziah in Judah (the south).[29] This period of history has striking similarities to first-century occupied Palestine. Under the leadership of Jeroboam II and Uzziah, Israel and Judah experienced unprecedented economic growth and political stability.[30] Jeroboam II and Uzziah colonized vast amounts of territory to the east, west, and south (2 Chr 26:6–8). As is almost always the case, this colonization resulted in economic gains that almost exclusively favored the rich (the elite ruling class), at the expense of the majority of the population— the peasantry.[31] Using the urban centers (growth of which can be shown during this period) as political and administrative hubs, the elite set up a system of taxation that effectively extracted the surplus from rural areas. Agricultural activities were commercialized, which in turn made it possible for the elite to import horses and chariots for local specialty items like wine and oil. This procurement of military items gave the elite the military power and political control to dominate the peasantry. To support their lifestyle of leisure and luxury (conspicuous consumption, the use of luxury items such as fine linen, expensive ornaments and perfume), the elite sought as many trade relations as possible, which in turn meant extracting the biggest economic surplus possible. To gain maximum economic advantage, more and more land was used for the production of commercial crops, leaving only the staples for the peasantry. In order to survive, the peasantry had to turn to the local markets to buy food they produced themselves, where the merchants took advantage of the peasantry. The peasantry was thus in debt

24. Ibid., 391.
25. See, for example Exod 22:25, and Lev 19:10.
26. See, for example Deut 15:4–11.
27. See, for example, Prov 14:31, 22:9 and 22.
28. Fiensy, *Jesus the Galilean*, 96, 132.
29. Mays, *Hosea*, 4.
30. Premnath, "Amos and Hosea," 126.
31. Ibid., 127; Escobar, "Social Justice in the Book of Amos," 170.

and in dire straits, and in times of drought had to borrow money to survive. Peasants' failure to repay loans meant the foreclosure of land; this servedthe aim of the elite to create large estates and to commercialize agricultural activity. Turning to the courts did not help the peasantry; controlled by the elite, the courts were biased and used as an instrument by the elite to subvert justice.[32]

Amos and Hosea criticized this situation in sharp terms. Amos called the elite—who hoarded, plundered, and looted in their palaces (Amos 3:10)—to come and see the oppression in Samaria (Amos 3:9). He further warned the elite that their strongholds and fortresses would be plundered (Amos 3:11). Hosea also criticized the exploitative urban centers; Israel had forgotten its Maker and had built palaces, and Judah had multiplied fortified cities that would be devoured by Yahweh (Hos 8:14; cf. Hos 6:1–3). Hosea condemned the elite's trust in military power (Hos 10:13–14) as well as their treaties with Assyria and Egypt that enabled them to procure military equipment (Hos 12:1). Amos had stern words regarding the excessive extraction of surplus. The elite exploited the poor by taking taxes on wheat (Amos 5:11), trampled the head of the poor into the dust (Amos 2:7), oppressed the poor, and crushed the needy (Amos 4:1). In Hos 7:5 the excessive lifestyle of the elite is criticized (they drink so much wine that they become sick), and in Amos 8:5–6 the corrupt practices of the market merchants are condemned. To this can be added Amos' critique on the interest on loans (Amos 2:6), of taking collateral for loans (Amos 2:8), of exacting payment in kind (Amos 2:8), and of subverting justice (Amos 5:7, 10). Hosea also critiqued the sociopolitical and economic policies of the elite (Hos 1:2–9, 7:7; 8:4).[33] The same message came from Micah, who prophesized in the same century as Amos and Hosea. He criticized the elite for their ruthless acquisition of peasant land (Mic 2:2) and for their failure to serve the cause of justice (Mic 3:1–2); he condemned the cities in which the elite lived (Mic 1:5).

Jesus as Social Prophet in His Parables

As Amos and Hosea condemned the exploitative "kingdoms" of Jeroboam II and Uzziah, Jesus spoke against the "kingdoms" of Rome and the temple elite. The exploitative practices of these kingdoms were the same, as were the social critiques of Amos, Hosea, and the social prophet Jesus.

32. Premnath, "Amos and Hosea," 129–31.
33. See ibid., 129–32; Mays, *Hosea*, 12–13.

In his parables Jesus frequently addressed the "social illnesses" of his day: religious exclusivism (as advocated by the Jerusalem temple elite in their understanding of God in terms of holiness), and social injustice—as practiced by the Roman and Jewish elite. Jesus' parables, as we have seen, cut against the grain of the exploitative cultural symbols of first-century Palestine. Jesus redefined the role of patronage, criticized the pivotal role of honor and social status, condemned violence, criticized the exploitative political economy of his day, and advocated general reciprocity in place of exploitative balanced reciprocity. His kingdom was a kingdom in which everyone had enough.

Contrary to the Jerusalem temple elite's "politics of holiness," Jesus advocated a "politics of compassion," a kingdom that also included the socially impure (e.g., the lame, the blind, cripples, lepers, and women).[34] Two of the parables discussed have the inclusion of the impure as their topic, even depicting the kingdom as impure. In the Mustard Seed (Q 13:18–19), the kingdom is likened to a mustard seed that reseeds itself and grows very rapidly and aggressively; it spreads like a weed or invasive shrub. Because of its tendency to take over, the mustard plant needs persistent control. In the parable, the kingdom of God is not only like a mustard seed, but like a mustard seed planted in a garden. This makes the garden impure. If the kingdom of God is like a garden with an invasive mustard plant, then the kingdom of God is polluted and unclean. The ordered kingdom of the temple has been replaced by a chaotic and polluted kingdom. But it has not only replaced; it has been taken over by a unclean "mixed kind" that grows wild, that is invasive and difficult—almost impossible—to control. As such, the kingdom of God is dangerous and deadly. In time it will take over the ordered and unpolluted garden (ordered society) centered in the temple. Order is turned into chaos; the kingdom of God is taking over the kingdom of the temple. The mustard seed, however, is also taking over the kingdom of Rome. The mustard seed turns into a tree with branches strong enough for wild birds to roost and nest in. As pesky intruders of cultivated lands, the natural enemies of the sown, they feed off the land by plundering the cultivated fields. From their safe haven they take from the kingdom of Rome by plundering its base of taxation. And this means only one thing: the smaller the harvest and the "surplus of the land," the less tax went into the coffers of the kingdom of Rome. The parable thus tells of a kingdom where God is associated with uncleanness, where boundaries are porous, and where separation cannot and should not be maintained.

34. Borg, *Meeting Jesus Again*, 46–68.

The parable of the Feast (Luke 14:16b–23) also has the inclusion of the impure in the kingdom as topic. In the Feast a member of the wealthy elite invites other urban elites who live in the walled-off city center to a feast. Only a few of the many invited guests made excuses, and nobody shows up. Clearly the community gossip network has come to a decision. The host's honor rating does not make it. Boundaries had been drawn, and as a result of gossip, the host is rejected and shamed. How does he save face? The host decides to be a different kind of patron, a patron who is not interested in honor ratings or balanced reciprocity (that is, in what he can get out of inviting people to his feast). The host sends his slave to invite people living in the wider streets and squares and in the narrow streets and alleys, and when there is still room for more guests, he sends his slave to invite those who live in the roads and country lanes—the socially impure (expendables) living outside the city walls. With these invitations, the host declares null and void the purity system that deemed some as socially and ritually (culturally) impure. All walls have been broken down, and the world is turned upside down. The kingdom is visible.[35]

The host in the Feast, by including the socially and ritually impure at his feast (the kingdom), also redefines patronage: he abandons the role status plays, as well as the ever-present competition for acquired honor in the first-century Mediterranean world. He also replaces balanced reciprocity with generalized reciprocity. In the kingdom, patrons are real patrons when they act like the host, giving to those who cannot give back, breaking down physical walls and manmade boundaries (purity and pollution codes), and treating everybody as family (practicing generalized reciprocity) without being afraid of being shamed or losing his so-called status.

These themes, as I have indicated, are present of several of the parables discussed. In the Vineyard Laborers (Matt 20:1–15), the kingdom is compared with the actions of a vineyard owner, a negatively marked character and someone not normally associated with the kingdom. The owner most

---

35. In the parable of the Leaven (Q 13:20–21; Gos. Thom. 96:1–3), the kingdom of God is also typified as unclean and inclusive. The parable is only a short "one-liner," but it's explosive. The kingdom is like a woman who leavens flour until it is all leavened. Why is this explosive? Because the kingdom is blasphemously juxtaposed with leaven—a symbol for moral evil and corruption, and the unclean—that is impure. Above all, this is described as the doing of a woman. Thus, just as it is in the parable of the Mustard Seed and the Feast, the divine is identified with the unclean and the impure, present in the activity of a peasant in a rural area, not in the activities of the temple elite in Jerusalem. See Scott, *Re-Imagine the World*, 25; Scott, "Reappearance," 99–101; Boucher, *Parables*, 75. In the Leaven, the kingdom is at the "wrong place," and includes the "wrong people." God's active location is shifted from "purity" to "impurity," a "scandalous relocation of the divine presence." Bessler-Northcutt, "Learning to See God," 59.

probably was one of the wealthy subelites who owned large estates, perhaps through expropriation, or default on loans, or as gift estates from conquered lands. These lands normally were converted to viticulture dedicated to the production of export crops. This new focus on monoculture, and on viticulture in particular, had a significant and not altogether positive impact on the daily lives of the peasantry. The large estates increased pressure on smallholders, who faced an increasingly monetized form of exchange and the vagaries of labor demand. In the parable, this vineyard owner, typically a negative character, becomes an exemplary patron, acting in unexpected ways. Instead of being absent, he hires workers at six o'clock, agreeing on a daily wage of one denarius. This happens again at nine, twelve, and three o'clock, and even as late as five o'clock. During each hiring spree, the owner promises the recruited workers a wage that is fair. At the end of the working day, all recruited are paid the same wage. Unexpectedly, the owner is not someone who exploits the vulnerable, but a patron who offers benefits beyond the strict norms of economic exchange. He does not think only in terms of a strict balance sheet but steps into the role of a patron whose actions create enduring and effective bonds with his workers. He is a patron who is δίκαιος, making sure that everyone has enough.

In the Unmerciful Servant (Matt 18:23–33), Jesus again subverted the traditional practice of patronage, the role of status, balanced reciprocity, and the pivotal role of honor in the first-century Mediterranean world. A king settles his accounts, and instead of selling a servant, his family, and his belongings to cover the servant's unpayable outstanding debt, the king forgives the servant the outstanding debt. This the king, as patron, does out of mercy, but also because of his desire and love for honor (*philotīmiā*). There is nothing new here. The servant, however, does not reciprocate (as the king would have expected) by acknwoeldging in public the generosity he received. Rather, when the servant meets another servant who owes him a much smaller debt, he demands payment. And then comes the surprise in the parable. When the first servant flouts social expectations and does not reciprocate his patron's generosity, the king—totally unexpectedly—does not defend his own honor, power, and privilege. When the first servant is brought before him, he reprimands his servant as only a kingdom patron would do. When someone asks to be forgiven his debt, you show mercy without expecting a socially prescribed response. Honor does not lie in the eye of the beholder, but in the act itself. The forgiveness of debt should be offered altruistically—not in terms of balanced reciprocity, but in terms of general reciprocity. When this happens, the *basileia* of God is visible. To act differently, makes one wicked.

Jesus also criticized the exploitative political economy of his day. In the parable of the Merchant (Matt 13:45–46), the kingdom again is likened to the actions of a negatively marked (dubious) character, a person not normally associated with the kingdom of God. For the first hearers of the parable, Jesus' equating the kingdom of God with the actions of a merchant must have come as a shock. Because of the perception of limited good in advanced agrarian societies, and the conviction that production was primarily for use rather than exchange (i.e., for supporting immediate families and the village), profits made by merchants were perceived as a form of usury and as unnatural. In the New Testament world, the commerce of merchants was socially destructive and a threat to the community. In the eyes of the peasantry, merchants were evil and considered thieves. The fact that merchants had to make use of ships for their import-export trade, given that most shipowners were not Jewish, added to this negative perception of merchants. Merchants owned large parcels of land and were part of the political and economic apparatus of the Roman Empire in the first century. They assisted the movement of goods accumulated through forced extraction, cash crops, and commercial farming. Merchants thus played a major role in transforming the daily lives of peasants, which focused on subsistence and not commercial trade. For the peasantry, merchants personified the godless, symbolizing everything that was unacceptable.

But then comes the surprise in the parable. On his travels, the merchant finds a pearl of great value. The value of the pearl is so high that he has to sell everything he owns to buy it. By doing this, the merchant stops being a merchant. Taking leave of the despised trade he has practiced, the merchant now becomes part of the kingdom. No more trading, no more usury, will take place. In the kingdom there is no place for usury, no place for destructive actions that threaten the community. Living in the kingdom of God means one must leave behind a life as part of the apparatus of the exploitative Roman Empire. Being part of the kingdom, one could not support the forced extraction of goods, the growth of cash crops, or commercial farming—all of which were detrimental to those who lived close to or below subsistence. In the parable of the Merchant, an outsider becomes an insider, and insiders act according to kingdom principles.

How was one to protest the exploitative political economy of first-century Jewish Palestine? This question Jesus addressed in the parable of the Minas (Luke 19:12b–24, 27). In an effort to enhance his power, honor, privilege, and wealth, a nobleman sets off with the hope of being proclaimed king, and before he leaves entrusts money to ten of his slaves to "do business" with, one mina each. When the nobleman returns, two slaves are able to show good profits and are praised and rewarded for their efforts. This was not the way to protest. By doing what the nobleman expected, these two slaves only legitimated the domination of the elite. The way to protest was to act like the third slave, the "hero" of the story. In the eyes of the third slave, the nobleman was a thief who exploited the peasantry, and the third slave he did not want to participate in such exploitation. So what does he do? First he ties the mina in a cloth to protect the existing share for the owner: this is exactly what an honorable person should do, from a peasant's point of view. Second, when confronted by his master, the third slave does not characterize his master as a hard man in order to justify his fear and consequent inactivity with the mina. He rather employs the "weapons of the weak" by honoring and praising the nobleman for his status and achievements. At least this is how his remarks would have been heard by the nobleman. But what did the peasants, who most probably were part of the audience when Jesus told the parable, hear? Most probably the peasants heard the third slave both praise the nobleman but also call him out as a thief. In response, what does the nobleman do? Because he thinks the slave has honored and praised him, the nobleman lets the third slave go. This is the way to protest, says Jesus. "Honor" those who exploit you, without taking part in their exploitation.

In some of his parables, Jesus specifically criticized the role patronage played in his world. In the Friend at Midnight (Luke 11:5–8), a peasant neighbor is criticized for mimicking the exploitative patronage the elite normally extended to the vulnerable to turn the poor into dependents. The neighbor, instead of practicing hospitality and generalized reciprocity in his village, because of his ἀναίδειαν, becomes an exploiter of the exploited. The door between him and his neighbor will open only if the neighbor at the door is willing to become his client. The awakened neighbor is willing to practice only balanced reciprocity. But this is not, according to Jesus, kingdom behavior. This is the game of Rome, the exploiter and oppressor. In the kingdom, on the contrary, one should give without expecting something in return. Being part of the kingdom, one does not participate in a world created by the oppressive elite; when neighbors exploit neighbors, they are not part of the kingdom.

The Rich Man and Lazarus (Luke 16:19–26) is another parable in which Jesus criticized the traditional way patronage was practiced by the exploiting elite, as well as honor and status. In the parable the elite are represented by the rich man, and the poor are represented by Lazarus. Lazarus had become one of the expendables of the society that the rich man and other elite had created. Lazarus was no longer of any use to the rich man. Since he was stationed outside the rich man's gate every day, he could not really beg or take part in the daily salutation of the patron. For the rich man, coming upon Lazarus offered no occasion for almsgiving or enhancing his own honor. The rich man could gain nothing by making Lazarus a client, even in terms of negative reciprocity. Further, to show hospitium to him would have made Lazarus his equal. This, of course, would have meant a loss of honor for the rich man. To him, Lazarus was expendable in every sense of the word. Therefore, for Lazarus, the rich man's gate stayed closed. When the rich man and Lazarus die, the rich man has the opportunity to see how things are from the other side of the gate. Lazarus is sitting at the table of Abraham, and the rich man is now the one in need. But Abraham is not willing to help. The unthinkable happens—Abraham does not show hospitality. The gate cannot be opened. The threshold cannot be crossed. The chasm has been closed forever. When patrons, who have in abundance, do not cross the threshold past their gate, to the poor, a society is created wherein the chasm between rich (elite) and poor (peasantry) becomes so wide it cannot be crossed. The worlds of the urban elite and the peasantry drift so far apart that the gap between them eventually cannot be closed. Go through the gate while you can. As unthinkable as it is for Abraham not to show hospitality, so unthinkable should it be for people who can help not to show hospitality. Abraham, the examplar of hospitality, has no reason to turn his back on the rich man. The same holds for the rich man—during his earthly life, nothing stood in the way of his helping Lazarus. It was not impossible to help Lazarus. The protection of his status and honor, however, made it impossible. And when this happens, nobody becomes part of the kingdom—neither Lazarus nor the rich man. This is what happens when patrons protect their so-called honor and status. Real patrons are children of Abraham; they look out for the poor.

Two parables discussed in this volume, have as topic Jesus' stance on violence. The parable of the Tenants (Gos. Thom. 65) is a realistic narrative that depicts several aspects of viticulture in first-century Palestine, including the middling rich and their pursuit of wealth; their ubiquitous status displays; and discontent, tension, and conflict between absentee landlords and tenants. The Tenants, in Gos. Thom. 65, challenges these normalcies by means of the clever turn of its narrative. The vineyard owner leases his vineyard to farmers, most probably in the form of a cropshare lease. When the owner, most probably after four years into the leasing agreement, sends a slave to collect his part of the crop, conflict arises. The slave is grabbed, beaten, and almost killed. The owner reacts to this challenge of his honor by sending another slave, one known to the tenants. The fate of the second slave, however, is the same as the fate of the first. As a last resort, the owner sends his son. By sending his son, the owner appeals to the difference between his social status and that of the tenants. When the son arrives at his father's farm to collect the crop, the story takes an unexpected turn. What happens is exactly what the owner did not expect; the violence of the tenants escalates, and the son is killed. How does the owner react when his son is killed? This is the surprise in the parable: The owner does nothing! The owner of the vineyard does not exercise his right to forcefully or violently defend his ownership of the vineyard. And in doing nothing, he is the honorable person in the parable. Status and honor are not retained or gained by the use of violence; the honorable person is the one who refrains from using violence. This is also the case with the patron-king in the Unmerciful Servant parable. This is how patrons act who live according to the kingdom of God.

In the Lost Sheep (Luke 15:4–6), nonviolence again is pictured as a kingdom value. Shepherds in the first-century Mediterranean world were persons with no honor. They were seen as thieves, and armed with a sling and club, were frequently associated with banditry. When one of the herd gets lost, what does the shepherd do? Because of the low wage shepherds earned, the shepherd had no other option but to go and look for the lost sheep. The shepherd, after all, was to be held accountable for livestock losses. Also, he and his family already lived below the poverty line. He therefore took the risk of leaving the other sheep behind, and went looking for the lost sheep. When he found the lost sheep, he rejoiced. After his contract with the owner expired, he drove the flock back, and after accounting for all the sheep he had to tend to, he received the contracted wage, returned home, and celebrated with his family. Because of the risk he took, everybody had enough to eat, at least for a while. The gist of the parable, however, lies in something else beside the success of finding the lost sheep. There were other possible ways for the shepherd to recuperate his losses. Armed with a sling and club, and unsupervised, with freedom of movement, the shepherd could have resroted to banditry (violence) . But this is not what the shepherd does. He goes and look for the one sheep that is lost. The kingdom is achieved by nonviolence. Just as the owner of a vineyard maintains his honor by not answering violence with violence, so the shepherd becomes a symbol of the kingdom by refraining from violence to solve his problem.

Jesus' parables, finally, speak of a world in which everyone have enough. This we have seen in the Lost Sheep, the Merchant, and the Vineyard Laborers. This is specifically the case in the Sower (Mark 4:3b–8). In spite of what happens to the harvest (the parts that go to the Roman and temple elites), what can happen to the harvest is more important. Many seeds fall on good soil, grow, and produce a crop that yields a harvest of thirty-, sixty- and one hundredfold; this part of the harvest belongs to the peasant farmer. When this part is shared with those who barely live above subsistence, the kingdom is visible. What is left can be used to support others in need by sharing, by giving to everyone who begs from you (Q 6:30), by not asking for goods taken from you (Q 6:30), by doing to others as you would have them do to you (Q 6:31), and by lending expecting nothing in return (Q 6:35)—in short, by being merciful, just as the Father is merciful (Q 6:36). Therefore, the kingdom is good news to the poor (Luke 4:18): the place where the hungry will have a feast (Q 6:21), where those who weep will laugh (Q 6:21), where bread is provided day by day (Q 11:3), where everyone who asks receives (Q 11:10); the kingdom is a place where one does not have to worry about what one is going to eat (Q 12:22). Those who have left house or brothers or sisters or mother or father or children or lands for the sake of the kingdom will receive a hundredfold now, houses and brothers and sisters and mothers and children and lands (Mark 10:29–30).

Final Remarks

In the exploitative world of first-century Jewish Palestine created by the "kingdom of Rome" and the "kingdom of the temple," the central message of Jesus was the kingdom of God. This kingdom was not a futuristic, apocalyptic reality but ethical-eschatological in content. It was a kingdom here and now, a transformed world, a kingdom "that challenged the kingdoms of this world." This kingdom was "the immediate reign of God that is now present in the potential of the human imagination to see the world differently and to act accordingly." It was ethical and this-worldly, and involved "committing oneself ethically to life and to one's neighbour here and now, in this world, and in the present." The kingdom of God was a kingdom "for the earth." It was "political and religious and involved a transformed world." It was a kingdom of this world. [36]

Jesus' parables are not to be read for a view on the future or the end of time,[37] but rather should be interpreted for a view of an imagined "kingdom" (reality), where different social relations and power structures operate. Jesus' parables were "dangerous speech." In a society where politics and kinship were the only exclusive arenas of life, any "religious" statement was, in essence, political.[38] The aristocratic kingdom of Rome dealt with the

36. Funk, "Jesus of Nazareth," 90.

37. Mediterranean people were rather markedly present orientated, with the past second and the future third. See, for example, Matt 6:34. Malina, "Christ and Time," 1–31. See also Kloppenborg: "For peasants, the future is tomorrow or the next harvest, not some distant *parousía*." Kloppenborg, *Tenants in the Vineyard*, 5. Italics original.

38. Malina, *Social Gospel of Jesus*, 15–16. All societies might be viewed as consisting of at least four social institutions: kinship, politics, economics and religion. While

nonelite through social institutions characterized by power and resource inequities (political economy). Jesus' parables, conversely, "were underwritten by culturally informed values that envisioned alternate institutions."[39] The alternative institution Jesus envisioned was the kingdom of God.

When Jesus spoke in his parables about the presence of a new kingdom, other than the aristocratic kingdom of the Roman Empire and the kingdom of the temple elite, he was making a political statement. When Jesus urged his hearers to be a community where God's presence, and not Rome's or the temple's presence, was fully established, a community where there was justice for everyone (including one's enemy), a community that welcomed strangers and the impure, he was making a political statement. When Jesus spoke of God's rule as a power opposed to the social order established in Rome, he was making a political statement. When Jesus told stories that applauded members of the elite who practiced generalized reciprocity, he was making a political statement. And when Jesus told stories that transgressed the purity rules of the temple, making impure leaven and mustard seed positive symbols for God's presence, he was making a political statement. Any talk about values that envisioned an alternative to the power and privilege of Rome and the temple was political. Jesus' parables, therefore, were political. They were stories of social critique against the first century's oppressive political, religious, and social context. They did not describe "a specific historical event, but a political structure."[40] Jesus' parables, as we have seen, did not only grind against the temple and Roman elites. Criticism was also leveled at peasant interests.

Herzog is therefore correct when he describes Jesus' parables as "a form of social analysis."[41] From this perspective, the parables picture Jesus

---

modern societies generally attend to these four institutions as separate spheres of life, first-century Mediterranean people treated politics and kinship as the only exclusive arenas of life. In the political sphere, there was political religion and political economy, but no separate religion and economy. And in the kinship sphere, there was domestic (kinship) religion and domestic (kinship) economy, but no separate religion and economy. See Malina, "Religion in the World of Paul," 92–101; Malina, "Religion in the Imagined New Testament World," 1–26.

39. Oakman, *Jesus and the Peasants*, 253. "For Jesus God's rule was a power opposed to the social order established in Rome." Jesus made use of kinship religion and kinship economy to address the exploitative political economy and political religion of Rome. In Jesus' parables, he favored a fictive family in which relations were modelled on those of close kin, with exchanges taking place through arrangements of generalized reciprocity, taking no account of exchanges or debt. Jesus' parables, urging an alternative kinship economy that could be called the kingdom of God, therefore were political. Ibid., 97, 105.

40. Schottroff, *Parables of Jesus*, 103.

41. Herzog, *Parables as Subversive Speech*, 3. So Oakman: "The kingdom represents

as a social prophet. In a colonial situation, such as existed in the times of Amos, Hosea, and Jesus, the elite always had a substantial stake in maintaining the status quo. Interests had to be protected. Even the "middle strata" (e.g., scribes and scholar-teachers like the Pharisees and Sadducees in the time of Jesus) made adjustments to find themselves a role in the colonial system.[42] There were, however, also those from the "ordinary" section of life who took up the role of prophetic spokespersons for God and leaders of the people.[43] Jesus took up this role and, following in the footsteps of those before him (like Isaiah, Jeremiah, Amos, and Hosea), proclaimed an inclusive God who condemns exploitation and structural violence against the "small ones" of society. Just as Isaiah, Amos, and Hosea did, Jesus decided to walk the dangerous path of justice and righteousness. It is thus understandable that some of his contemporaries saw him as "one of the prophets of old."

In first-century Palestine (27–30 CE) the elite (Roman and Jewish) shaped the social experience of the peasantry, social control was built on fear, and the relationship between the ruling elite and the ruled nonelite was one of power and exploitation. Because of this, the peasantry lived at the edge of destitution. In this exploitative situation Jesus spoke in his parables of a new and different world—the kingdom of God. His parables were political stories about God's kingdom, "not earthly stories with heavenly meanings, but earthly stories with heavy meanings,"[44] exploring how human beings could respond to an exploitative and oppressive society created by the power and privilege of the elite. The parables of Jesus the social prophet were the kingdom, a "society" that posed a real threat to Rome's and the temple's rule. Eventually, this led to conflict with the religious authorities and the powers of Jesus' day.

---

social challenge and transformation. Jesus' historical activity was essentially about politics and the restructuring of society, and not about religion or theology." Oakman, *Jesus and the Peasants*, 296. See also Carter: "In the . . . first-century world, religion and politics did mix. Imperial politics, economics, societal structures, and religion were interwoven, each playing an interconnected part in the societal fabric and maintaining of elite control. Thus, to engage the gospels as religious texts concerned only with religious issues is a-historical and anachronistic. Our world is shaped by our western attempts to separate religion from the rest of life, and therefore we, when reading the gospels, arbitrarily select, detach, isolate, and elevate a religious aspect of the . . . first-century world, while ignoring political, economic, and cultural factors and their interconnectedness." Carter, "Matthew's Gospel," 199.

42. Horsley, *Spiral of Violence*, 16.

43. Horsley, *Jesus and Empire*, 103.

44. Herzog, *Parables as Subversive Speech*, 3.

Bibliography

Aalen, Sverre. "St. Luke's Gospel and the Last Chapters of 1 Enoch." *NTS* 13 (1967) 1–13.

Abrahams, Roger D. "A Performance-Centered Approach to Gossip." *Man: Journal of the Royal Anthropological Institute* 5 (1970) 290–301.

Agnew, Francis H. "The Parables of Divine Compassion." *The Bible Today* 27 (1989) 35–40.

Allison, Dale C. *Jesus of Nazareth: Millenarian Prophet.* Minneapolis: Fortress, 1998.

Andreassen, Randi. "Gossip in Henningsvær." *Etnofoor* 11 (1998) 41–56.

Applebaum, Shimon. "Economic Life in Palestine." In *The Jewish People in the First Century: Historical Geography, Political History, Social, Cultural and Religious Life and Institutions*, edited by Shmuel Safrai, M. Stern, and David Flusser, 2:631–700. Compendia Rerum Iudaicarum Ad Novum Testamentum, Section 1. Assen: Van Gorcum, 1976.

———. "Judaea as a Roman Province: The Countryside as a Political and Economic Factor." *Aufstieg und Niedergang der Römischen Welt* II.8 (1977) 355–96.

Arens, Edmund. "Ein Tischgespräch über Essen und (Ex)Kommunikation: Das Gleichnis Vom Festmahl (Lk. 14, 16–24)." *Kategetische Blätter* 111 (1986) 449–52.

Aristotle. *Nicomachean Ethics.* LCL. Cambridge: Harvard University Press, 1947.

Aristotle. *Politics.* Translation by H. Rockham. Cambridge: Harvard University Press, 1950.

Armstrong, Edward A. *The Gospel Parables.* New York: Sheed & Ward, 1967.

Arndt, William F., and Wilbur F. Gingrich, Frederick W. Danker, eds. *A Greek–English Lexicon of the New Testament and Other Early Christian Literature.* 3rd ed. Chicago: University of Chicago Press, 2000.

Arno, Andrew. "Fijian Gossip as Adjudication: A Communication Model of Informal Social Control." *Journal of Anthropological Research* 36 (1980) 343–60.

Aviam, Mordechai. "The Book of Enoch and the Galilean Archeology and Landscape." In *Parables of Enoch: A Paradigm Shift*, edited by James H. Charlesworth and Darrell Bock, 159–69. Jewish and Christian Texts Series 11. London: Bloomsbury, 2013.

Baarslag, Derk J. *Gelijkenissen des Heeren.* 2 vols. Baarn: Bosch & Keuning, 1940.

Bailey, Kenneth E. *Jesus through Middle Eastern Eyes: Cultural Studies in the Gospels.* Downers Grove, IL: IVP Academic, 2008.

———. *Poet and Peasant: A Literary-Cultural Approach to the Parables in Luke.* Grand Rapids: Eerdmans, 1983.

Ball, Michael. *The Radical Stories of Jesus: Interpreting the Parables Today.* Regent's Study Guides 8. Oxford: Regent's Park College, 2000.

Barclay, William. *And Jesus Said: A Handbook to the Parables of Jesus.* Philadelphia: Westminster, 1970.

Bauckham, Richard. *The Fate of the Dead: Studies on the Jewish and Christian Apocalypses.* Novum Testamentum Supplements 93. Leiden: Brill, 1998.

Bauer, Walter. *Griechisch-Deutsches Wörterbuch zu den Schriften Des Neuen Testaments und der übrigen Urchristlichen Literatur.* Berlin: Töpelmann, 1952.

Bazzana, Giovanni V. "*Basileia* and Debt Relief: The Forgiveness of Debts in the Lord's Prayer in the Light of Documentary Papyri." *CBQ* 73 (2011) 511–25.

———. "BASILEIA—The Q Concept of Kingship in Light of Documented Papyri." In *Light from the East: Papyrologische Kommentare zum Neuen Testament. Akten des Internationalen Symposions Vom 3.-4. Dezember 2009 am Fachbereich Bibelwissenschaft und Kierchengeschichte der Universität Salzburg,* edited by Peter Arzt-Grabner and Christina M. Kreinecker, 153–68. Philippika—Marburger Alterumskundlische Abhandlungen 39. Wiesbaden: Harrassowitz, 2010.

———. "Violence and Human Prayer to God in Q 11." *HvTSt* 70 (2014) 1–8.

Beare, Francis W. *The Earliest Records of Jesus: A Companion to the Synopsis of the First Three Gospels.* New York: Abingdon, 1962.

———. *The Gospel according to Matthew.* San Francisco: Harper & Row, 1981.

Beasley-Murray, George R. *Jesus and the Kingdom of God.* Grand Rapids: Eerdmans, 1986.

Beavis, Mary Ann. "Ancient Slavery as an Interpretive Context for the New Testament Servant Parables with Special Reference to the Unjust Steward (Luke 16:1–8)." *JBL* 111 (1992) 37–54.

Bechtel, Lyn M. "Shame as Sanction of Control in Biblical Israel: Judicial, Political, and Social Shaming." *JSOT* 49 (1991) 47–76.

Bessler-Northcutt, Joe. "Learning to See God: Prayer and Practice in the Wake of the Jesus Seminar." In *The Historical Jesus Goes to Church,* edited Roy W. Hoover et al., 51–63. Santa Rosa, CA: Polebridge, 2004.

Beutner, Edward F. "Comedy with a Tragic Turn: The Dishonest Manager." In *Listening to the Parables of Jesus,* edited by Edward F. Beutner, 59–63. Jesus Seminar Guides 2. Santa Rosa, CA: Polebridge, 2007.

———. "The Haunt of Parable." In *Listening to the Parables of Jesus,* edited by Edward F. Beutner, 1–6. Jesus Seminar Guides 2. Santa Rosa, CA: Polebridge, 2007.

———. "How Jesus Took the Gist from the Liturgist: Luke 18:10–14." In *Listening to the Parables of Jesus,* edited by Edward F. Beutner, 15–20. Jesus Seminar Guides 2. Santa Rosa, CA: Polebridge, 2007.

———, ed. *Listening to the Parables of Jesus.* Jesus Seminar Guides 2. Santa Rosa, CA: Polebridge, 2007.

———. "A Mercy Unextended: Matthew." In *Listening to the Parables of Jesus,* edited by Edward F. Beutner, 33–39. Jesus Seminar Guides 2. Santa Rosa, CA: Polebridge, 2007.

Bidnell, David R. "A Cultural-Literal Reading of Luke's Parables." PhD diss., University of Birmingham, 2012.

Bishop, E. F. F. "The Parable of the Lost or Wandering Sheep: Matthew 18.10–14; Luke 15.3–7." *Anglican Theological Review* 44 (1962) 44–57.

Black, M. "Die Gleichnisse Als Allegorien." In *Gleichnisse Jesu: Positionen der Auslegung von Adolf Jülicher bis zur Formgeschichte*, edited by Wolfgang Harnisch, 262–80. Wege der Forschung 366. Darmstadt: Wissenschaftliche Buchgesellschaft, 1982.

Blank, Josef. "Die Sendung des Sohnes: Zur Christologischen Bedeutung des Gleichnisses von den Bösen Winzen Mk 12,1–12." In *Neues Testament und Kirche: Für Rudolf Schnackenburg zum 60. Geburtstag*, edited by Joachim Gnilka, 11–41. Freiburg: Herder, 1974.

Blenkinsopp, Joseph. "Second Isaiah—Prophet of Universalism." *JSOT* 42 (1988) 83–103.

Blok, Anton. "Variations in Patronage." *Sociologische Gids* 16 (1969) 365–78.

Blomberg, Craig L. *Interpreting the Parables*. Downers Grove, IL: InterVarsity, 2012.

———. *Preaching the Parables: From Responsible Interpretation to Powerful Proclamation*. Grand Rapids: Baker Academic, 2004.

Charlesworth, James H, and Darrell Bock, eds. *Parables of Enoch: A Paradigm Shift*. Jewish and Christian Texts Series 11. London: Bloomsbury, 2013.

Bockmuehl, Markus. *This Jesus: Martyr, Lord, Messiah*. Edinburgh: T. & T. Clark, 1994.

Boer, Martinus C. de. "Ten Thousand Talents? Matthew's Interpretation and Redaction of the Parable of the Unforgiving Servant (Matt. 18:23–35)." *CBQ* 50 (1988) 214–32.

Boice, James Montgomery. *The Parables of Jesus*. Chicago: Moody, 1983.

Borg, Marcus J. *Jesus, a New Vision: Spirit, Culture, and the Life of Discipleship*. San Francisco: Harper & Row, 1987.

———. *Jesus: Uncovering the Life, Teachings, and Relevance of a Religious Revolutionary*. New York: HarperCollins, 2006.

———. *Meeting Jesus Again for the First Time: The Historical Jesus & the Heart of Contemporary Faith*. San Francisco: HarperOne, 1994.

Borg, Marcus J. et al. "Con: Jesus Was not an Apocalyptic Prophet." In *The Apocalyptic Jesus: A Debate*, edited by Robert J. Miller, 31–82. Santa Rosa, CA: Polebridge, 2001.

Borg, Marcus J., and N. T. Wright. *The Meaning of Jesus: Two Visions*. New York: HarperSanFrancisco, 2007.

Bornkamm, Günther. *Jesus of Nazareth*. Translated by Irene and Fraser McLuskey with James M. Robinson. 1960. Reprinted, Minneapolis: Fortress, 1995.

Boucher, Madeleine I. *The Parables*. New Testament Message 7. Wilmington, DE: Glazier, 1981.

Bowker, John. "Mystery and Parable: Mark 4:1–20." *JTS* 25 (1974) 300–317.

Brandon, S. G. F. *Jesus and the Zealots: A Study of the Political Factor in Primitive Christianity*. Manchester: Manchester University Press, 1967.

Braun, Willi. *Feasting and Social Rhetoric in Luke 14*. Society for New Testament Studies Monograph Series 85. Cambridge: Cambridge University Press, 1995.

Breech, James. *The Silence of Jesus: The Authentic Voice of the Historical Man*. Philadelphia: Fortress, 1983.

Brouwer, A. M. *De Gelijkenissen*. Leiden: Sijthoff, 1946.

Bruce, Alexander B. *The Parabolic Teaching of Christ: A Systematic and Critical Study of the Parables of Our Lord*. New York: Hodder & Stoughton, 1886.

Brueggemann, Walter. *Hopeful Imagination: Prophetic Voices in Exile*. Philadelphia: Fortress, 1986.

————. *The Land: Place as Gift, Promise, and Challenge in Biblical Faith*. Overtures to Biblical Theology 1. Philadelphia: Fortress, 1977.

Bugge, Christian A. *Die Haupt Parabeln Jesu: Mit einer Einleitung über die Methode der Parabel-Auslegung*. 2 vols. 1903. Reprinted, Whitefish, MT: Kessinger, 2013.

Bultmann, Rudolf. *History of the Synoptic Tradition*. Translated by John Marshall. Oxford: Blackwell, 1963.

Bussby, F. "Did a Shepherd Leave Sheep upon the Mountains or in the Desert?" *Anglican Theological Review* 45 (1963) 93–94.

Buttrick, David A. *Speaking Parables: A Homiletic Guide*. Louisville: Westminster John Knox, 2000.

Buttrick, George A. *The Parables of Jesus*. New York: Harper & Row, 1928.

Buzy, D. "Zur Auslegung der Gleichnisse in den Evangelien." In *Gleichnisse Jesu: Positionen der Auslegung von Adolf Jülicher bis zur Formgeschichte*, edited by Wolfgang Harnisch, 83–101. Wege der Forschung 366. Darmstadt: Wissenschaftliche Buchgesellschaft, 1982.

Cadoux, Arthur T. *The Parables of Jesus: Their Art and Use*. London: James Clarke, 1930.

Calvin, John. *A Harmony of the Gospels Matthew, Mark, and Luke*. Edited by David W. Torrance and Thomas F. Torrance. Translated by A. W. Morrison. Calvin's New Testament Commentaries—A New Translation 3. Grand Rapids: Eerdmans, 1972.

Cameron, Ron, ed. *The Other Gospels: Non-Canonical Gospel Texts*. Philadelphia: Westminster, 1982.

Capon, Robert F. *The Parables of Grace*. Grand Rapids: Eerdmans, 1989.

————. *The Parables of Judgment*. Grand Rapids: Eerdmans, 1989.

————. *The Parables of the Kingdom*. Grand Rapids: Eerdmans, 1991.

Cardenal, Ernesto. *The Gospel in Solentiname*. 4 vols. Translated by Donald D. Walsh. Mary-knoll, NY: Orbis, 1982.

Carlsen, Jesper. *Vilici and Roman Estate Managers until AD 284*. Analecta Romana Instituti Danici Supplementum 24. Rome: L'Erma di Bretschneider, 1995.

Carlston, Charles E. *The Parables of the Triple Tradition*. Philadelphia: Fortress, 1975.

Carney, Thomas F. *The Shape of the Past: Models and Antiquity*. Lawrence, KS: Coronado, 1975.

Carter, Warren. *Matthew and the Margins: A Sociopolitical and Religious Reading*. Maryknoll, NY: Orbis, 2000.

————. "Matthew's Gospel, Rome's Empire, and the Parable of the Mustard Seed (Matt 13:31–32)." In *Hermeneutik der Gleichnisse Jesus: Methodische Neuansätze zum Verstehen urchristlicher Parabeltexte*, edited by Ruben Zimmerman and Gabi Kern, 181–201. WUNT 231. Tübingen: Mohr/Siebeck, 2008.

————. *The Roman Empire and the New Testament: An Essential Guide*. Abingdon Essential Guides. Nashville: Abingdon, 2006.

Casey, Maurice. *From Jewish Prophet to Gentile God: The Origins and Development of New Testament Christology*. Edward Cadbury Lectures. Louisville: Westminster John Knox, 1991.

Catchpole, David R. "Q and 'The Friend at Midnight' (Luke xi.5–8/9)." *JTS* 34 (1983) 407–24.

Cave, C. H. "Lazarus and the Lukan Deuteronomy." *NTS* 15 (1969) 319–25.

Chancey, Martin A. "Disputed Issues in the Study of Cities, Villages, and the Economy in Jesus' Galilee." Paper presented at Society of Biblical Literature Annual Meeting, Boston, 2008. Published in *The World of Jesus and the Early Church: Identity and*

Interpretation in Communities of Faith, edited by Mark Evans, 53–68. Peabody, MA: Hendrickson, 2011.

Charlesworth, James H. "The Date and Provenience of the Parables of Enoch." In *Parables of Enoch: A Paradigm Shift*, edited by James H. Charlesworth and Darrell Bock, 37–57. Jewish and Christian Texts Series 11. London: Bloomsbury, 2013.

———. "Jesus Research and Archeology: A New Perspective." In *Jesus and Archaeology*, edited by James H. Charlesworth, 11–63. Grand Rapids: Eerdmans, 2006.

Choi, Agnes. "Urban-Rural Relations and the Economy of Lower Galilee." PhD diss., Toronto School of Theology, 2010.

Conzelmann, Hans. *The Theology of St. Luke*. Translated by Geoffrey Buswell. New York: Harper & Brothers, 1960.

Cottor, Wendy J. "The Parables of the Mustard Seed and Leaven: Their Function in the Earliest Stratum of Q." *Toronto Journal of Theology* 8 (1992) 37–51.

Cowan, David. *Economic Parables: The Monetary Teachings of Jesus Christ*. Colorado Springs: Paternoster, 2007.

Craffert, Pieter F. *The Life of a Galilean Shaman: Jesus of Nazareth in Anthropological-Historical Perspective*. Matrix: The Bible in Mediterranean Context 3. Eugene, OR: Cascade Books, 2008.

Crossan, John Dominic. *The Birth of Christianity: Discovering What Happened in the Years Immediately after the Execution of Jesus*. San Francisco: HarperCollins, 1999.

———. *The Greatest Prayer: Rediscovering the Revolutionary Message of the Lord's Prayer*. New York: HarperOne, 2010.

———. *The Historical Jesus: The Life of a Mediterranean Jewish Peasant*. San Francisco: HarperCollins, 1991.

———. *In Parables: The Challenge of the Historical Jesus*. 1973. Reprinted, Sonoma, CA: Polebridge, 1992.

———. "The Parable of the Wicked Husbandmen." *JBL* 90 (1971) 451–65.

———. *The Power of Parable: How Fiction by Jesus Became Fiction about Jesus*. New York: HarperOne, 2012.

———. "The Servant Parables of Jesus." *Semeia* 1 (1974) 17–62.

Culbertson, Philip L. "Reclaiming the Matthean Vineyard Parables." *Encounter* 49 (1988) 257–83.

Culpepper, R. Alan. *Luke*. New Interpreter's Bible 9. Nashville: Abingdon, 1997.

Cupitt, Don. "Reforming Christianity." In *The Once & Future Faith*, edited by Karen Armstrong and Robert W. Funk, 51–64. Santa Rosa, CA: Polebridge, 2001.

Dahl, Nils Ahlstrop. "The Parables of Growth." 1953. Reprinted in *Jesus in the Memory of the Early Church*, 141–66. Minneapolis: Augsburg, 1976.

Danby, Herbert. *The Mishnah: Translated from the Hebrew with Introduction and Brief Explanatory Notes*. Peabody, MA: Hendrickson, 2011.

Daniels, John W. "Gossip's Role in Constituting Jesus as a Shamanic Figure in John's Gospel." PhD diss., Department of New Testament, University of South Africa, 2008.

D'Arms, John H. *Commerce and Social Standing in Ancient Rome*. Cambridge: Harvard University Press, 1981.

Davie, G. J., trans. *A Commentary on the Holy Gospels: St. Matthew's Gospel*, by John Maldonatus. London: Hodges, 1888.

Davies, William D., and Dale C. Allison. *A Critical and Exegetical Commentary on the Gospel according to Saint Matthew.* Vol. 3. International Critical Commentary. Edinburgh: T. & T. Clark, 1997.

Deidun, Thomas. "The Parable of the Unmerciful Servant (Mt. 18:23–35)." *BTB* 6 (1976) 203–24.

Derrett, John D. M. "Fresh Light on the Lost Sheep and the Lost Coin." *NTS* 26 (1980) 36–60.

———. "Fresh Light on the Parable of the Wicked Vinedressers." *Revue Internationale des Droits de l'antiquité* 10 (1963) 11–41.

———. "The Friend at Midnight: Asian Ideas in the Gospel of St. Luke." In *Donum Gentilicium: New Testament Studies in Honour of David Daube*, edited by Ernst Bammel et al., 78–87. Oxford: Oxford University Press, 1978.

———. *Law in the New Testament.* 1974. Reprinted, Eugene, OR: Wipf & Stock, 2005.

———. "Workers in the Vineyard: A Parable of Jesus." *Journal of Jewish Studies* 25 (1974) 64–91.

De Ru, G. "The Conception of Reward in the Teaching of Jesus." *NovT* 8 (1966) 202–22.

de Ste Croix, G. E. M. *The Class Struggle in the Ancient Greek World: From the Archaic Age to the Arab Conquests.* Ithaca, NY: Cornell University Press, 1981.

Dewey, Johanna. *Markan Public Debate: Literary Technique, Concentric Structure, and Theology in Mark 2.1—3.6.* Society of Biblical Literature Dissertation Series 48. Chico, CA: Scholars, 1980.

Dibelius, Martin. *From Tradition to Gospel.* Translated by B. L. Woolf. The Library of Theological Translations. London: James Clarke, 1971.

Dietzfelbinger, Christian. "Das Gleichnis von Der Erlassenen Schuld: Eine Theologische Untersuchung von Matthäus 18, 23–35." *Evangelische Theologie* 32 (1972) 437–51.

Dillon, Richard J. "Towards a Tradition-History of the Parables of the True Israel (Matthew 21, 33–22, 14)." *Biblica* 47 (1966) 1–42.

Dodd, Charles H. *The Parables of the Kingdom.* New York: Scribner, 1961.

Dommelen, Peter Alexander René van. "Roman Peasants and Rural Organisation in Central Italy: An Archaeological Perspective." In *Theoretical Roman Archaeology: First Conference Proceedings*, edited by Eleanor Scott, 167–86. Worldwide Archaeology Series 4. Aldershot, UK: Avebury, 1993.

Donahue, John R. *The Gospel in Parable: Metaphor, Narrative, and Theology in the Synoptic Gospels.* Philadelphia: Fortress, 1988.

Douglas, Mary. *Implicit Meanings: Selected Essays in Anthropology.* London: Routledge & Kegan Paul, 1975.

———. *Natural Symbols: Explorations in Cosmology.* New York: Vintage, 1973.

———. *Purity and Danger: An Analysis of Concepts of Pollution and Taboo.* London: Routledge & Kegan Paul, 1966.

Dover, Kenneth J. *Greek Popular Morality: In the Time of Plato and Aristotle.* Oxford: Blackwell, 1974.

Downing, Francis G. *Christ and the Cynics: Jesus and Other Radical Preachers in First-Century Tradition.* JSOT Manuals 4. Sheffield: Sheffield Academic, 1988.

Dronsch, Kristina. "Vom Fruchtbringen (Sämann Mit Deutung)—Mk 4,3–9(10–12.)13–20, (Mt 13,3–9.18–23 / Lk 8,5–8.11–15 / EvThom 9 / Agr 220)." In *Kompendium der Gleichnisse Jesu*, edited by Ruben Zimmermann et al., 297–316. Munich: Gütersloher, 2007.

Drury, John. *The Parables in the Gospels: History and Allegory.* New York: Crossroad, 1985.

Duling, Dennis C. *A Marginal Scribe: Studies in the Gospel of Matthew in a Social-Scientific Perspective.* Matrix: The Bible in Mediterranean Context 7. Eugene: Cascade Books, 2012.

Dunn, James D. G. "Did Jesus Attend the Synagogue?" In *Jesus and Archaeology*, edited by James H. Charlesworth, 206–22. Grand Rapids: Eerdmans, 2006.

———. "Messianic Ideas and Their Influence on the Jesus of History." In *The Messiah: Developments in Earliest Judaism and Christianity*, edited by James H. Charlesworth, 365–81. Minneapolis: Fortress, 1992.

Dupont, Jacques. "Le Couple Parabolique Du Sénevé et Du Levain, Mt 13,31–33; Lc 13,18–21." In *Jesus Christus in Historie und Theologie: Neutestamentliche Festschrift für Hans Conzelmann zum 60. Geburtstag*, edited by Georg Strecker, 331–45. Tübingen: Mohr/Siebeck, 1975.

Edwards, James R. *The Gospel according to Mark.* Grand Rapids: Eerdmans, 2002.

Eisenstadt, Shmuel N., and Luis Roniger. "Patron-Client Relations as a Model of Structuring Social Exchange." *Comparative Studies in Society and History* 22 (1980) 42–77.

———. *Patrons, Clients and Friends: Interpersonal Relations and the Structure of Trust in Society.* Themes in the Social Sciences. Cambridge: Cambridge University Press, 1984.

Elliott, John H. *A Home for the Homeless: A Social-Scientific Criticism of 1 Peter, Its Situation and Strategy.* 2nd ed. 1990. Reprinted, Eugene, OR: Wipf & Stock, 2005.

———. "Matthew 20:1–15: A Parable of Invidious Comparison and Evil Eye Accusation." *BTB* 22 (1992) 52–65.

———. "Patronage and Clientism in Early Christian Society: A Short Reading Guide." *Foundations and Facets Forum* 3 (1987) 39–48.

———. *What Is Social-Scientific Criticsm?* Guides to Biblical Scholarship. Minneapolis: Fortress, 1993.

Elliott, Neil. *The Arrogance of Nations: Reading Romans in the Shadow of Empire.* Paul in Critical Contexts. Minneapolis: Fortress, 2008.

Erdkamp, Paul. "Agriculture, Underemployment, and the Cost of Rural Labour in the Roman World." *Classical Quarterly* 49 (1999) 556–72.

Escobar, Donoso S. "Social Justice in the Book of Amos." *Review and Expositor* 92 (1995) 169–74.

Evans, Craig A. *Mark 8:27—16:20.* WBC 34B. Nashville: Thomas Nelson, 2001.

———. *To See and Not Perceive: Isaiah 6.9–10 in Early Jewish and Christian Interpretation.* JSOT Supplements 64. Sheffield: Sheffield Academic, 1989.

Ferguson, Everett. *Backgrounds of Early Christianity.* Grand Rapids: Eerdmans, 1987.

Fiebig, Paul. *Altjüdische Gleichnisse und die Gleichnisse Jesu.* Tübingen: Mohr/Siebeck, 1904.

Fiensy, David A. *Jesus the Galilean: Soundings in a First Century Life.* Piscataway, NJ: Gorgias, 2007.

———. *The Social History of Palestine in the Herodian Period: The Land Is Mine.* Studies in the Bible and Early Christianity 20. Lewiston, NY: Mellen, 1991.

Finley, Moses I. *The Ancient Economy.* Sather Classical Lectures 43. Berkeley: University of California Press, 1973.

Fisher, Neal F. *The Parables of Jesus: Glimpses of God's Reign.* Rev. ed. New York: Crossroad, 1990.

Fitzmyer, Joseph A. *The Gospel according to Luke X–XXIV: Introduction, Translation, and Notes.* Anchor Bible 28A. New York: Doubleday, 1985.

Fleddermann, Harry T. "The Mustard Seed and the Leaven in Q, the Synoptics, and Thomas." In *Society of Biblical Literature 1989 Seminar Papers,* edited by David J. Lull, 216–36. Atlanta: Scholars, 1989.

———. "Three Friends at Midnight (Lk 11,5–8)." In *Luke and His Readers: Festschrift A. Denaux,* edited by R. Bieringer et al., 265–82. Bibliotheca Ephemeridum theologicarum Lovaniensium 182. Leuven: Leuven University Press, 2005.

Flusser, David. *Die Rabbinischen Gleichnisse und der Gleichniserzähler Jesus,* Vol. 1, *Das Wesen der Gleichnisse.* Judaica et Christiana 4. Bern: Lang, 1981.

Forbes, Greg W. *The God of Old: The Role of the Lukan Parables in the Purpose of Luke's Gospel.* Journal for the Study of the New Testament Supplement Series 198. Sheffield: Sheffield Academic, 2000.

Ford, Richard Q. *The Parables of Jesus: Recovering the Art of Listening.* Minneapolis: Fortress, 1997.

Fortna, Robert F. "Reading Jesus' Parable of the Talents through Underclass Eyes: Matt. 25:14–30." *Foundations and Facets Forum* 8 (1995) 221–28.

Foster, George M. "Peasant Society and the Image of Limited Good." *American Anthropologist* 67 (1965) 293–315.

———. "Peasant Society and the Image of Limited Good." In *Peasant Society: A Reader,* edited by Jack M. Potter et al., 300–323. Boston: Little, Brown, 1967.

Foxhall, Lin. "The Dependent Tenant: Land Leasing and Labour in Italy and Greece." *JRS* 80 (1990) 97–114.

France, R. T. *The Gospel of Mark: A Commentary on the Greek Text.* New International Greek Testament Commentary. Grand Rapids: Eerdmans, 2002.

Frankel, Rafael. *Wine and Oil Production in Antiquity in Israel and Other Mediterranean Countries.* JSOT/ASOR Monographs 10. Sheffield: Sheffield Academic, 1999.

Freyne, Seán. *Galilee from Alexander the Great to Hadrian 323 B.C.E. to 135 C.E.: A Study of Second Temple Judaism.* Wilmington, DE: Glazier, 1980.

———. *Jesus, a Jewish Galilean: A New Reading of the Jesus-Story.* London: T. & T. Clark, 2004.

———. "Urban-Rural Relations in First-Century Galilee: Some Suggestions from the Literary Sources." In *The Galilee in Late Antiquity,* edited by Lee. I. Levine, 75–91. New York: Jewish Theological Seminary of America, 1992.

Fridrichsen, Anton. "Exegetisches zum Neuen Testament." *Symbolae Osloenses* 13 (1934) 40–43.

Fuchs, Ernst. *Zum Hermeneutischen Problem in der Theologie: Die Existentiale Interpretation.* Tübingen: Mohr/Siebeck, 1959.

———. *Die Frage nach dem Historischen Jesus.* Gesammelte Aufsätze Ernst Fuchs 2. Tübingen: Mohr/Siebeck, 1960.

Funk, Robert W. *Funk on Parables: Collected Essays.* Edited by Bernard B. Scott. Santa Rosa, CA: Polebridge, 2006.

———. *Honest to Jesus: Jesus for a New Millennium.* San Francisco: Harper, 1996.

———. "Jesus of Nazareth: A Glimpse." In *Listening to the Parables of Jesus,* edited by Edward F. Beutner, 89–93. Jesus Seminar Guides 2. Santa Rosa, CA: Polebridge, 2007.

———. *Language, Hermeneutic, and Word of God.* New York: Harper & Row, 1966.

———. "The Looking-Glass Tree Is for the Birds." *Interpretation* 27 (1973) 3–9.

Funk, Robert W., et al. *The Five Gospels: What Did Jesus Really Say? The Search for the Authentic Words of Jesus: New Translation and Commentary.* New York: Macmillan, 1993.

Funk, Robert W., et al. *The Parables of Jesus: Red Letter Edition.* Sonoma, CA: Polebridge, 1988.

Galston, David. *Embracing the Human Jesus: A Wisdom Path for Contemporary Christianity.* Salem, OR: Polebridge, 2012.

Garland, David E. *Reading Matthew: A Literary and Theological Commentary.* Reading the New Testament 1. New York: Crossroad, 1993.

Garnet, Paul. "The Parable of the Sower: How the Multitudes Understood It." In *Spirit within Structure: Essays in Honor of George Johnston on the Occasion of His Seventieth Birthday*, edited by Edward J. Furcha, 39–45. Pittsburgh Theological Monographs 3. Allison Park, PA: Pickwick Publications, 1983.

Garnsey, Peter, and Greg Woolf. "Patronage of the Rural Poor in the Roman World." In *Patronage in Ancient Society*, edited by Andrew Wallace-Hadrill, 153–70. London: Routledge, 1989.

Gelston, Anthony. "Universalism in Second Isaiah." *JTS* 43 (1992) 377–98.

Gilmore, David. "Varieties of Gossip in a Spanish Rural Community." *Ethnology* 17 (1978) 89–99.

Gladden, Washington. *Things New and Old in Discourses of Christian Truth and Life.* Columbus: A. H. Smythe, 1883.

Glancy, Jennifer A. "Slaves and Slavery in the Matthean Parables." *JBL* 119 (2000) 67–90.

Glombitza, Otto. "Der Perlenkaufmann: Eine Exegetische Studie zur Matth. XIII.45–46." *NTS* 7 (1961) 153–61.

Gluckman, Max. "Gossip and Scandal." *Current Anthropology* 4 (1963) 307–16.

Gnilka, Joachim. *Das Evangelium Nach Markus.* Vol. 2. Evangelisch–Katholischer Kommentar Zum Neuen Testament, II. Zürich: Benziger, 1978.

———. *Das Matthäusevangelium.* Vol. 2. Freiburg: Herder, 1993.

Gonzales, Justo L. *Faith and Wealth: A History of Early Christian Ideas on the Origin, Significance, and Use of Money.* 1990. Reprinted, Eugene, OR: Wipf & Stock, 2002.

Goodman, Martin. "The First Jewish Revolt: Social Conflict and the Problem of Debt." *Journal of Jewish Studies* 33 (1982) 402–29.

———. *The Ruling Class of Judaea: The Origins of the Jewish Revolt against Rome, A.D. 66–70.* Cambridge: Cambridge University Press, 1987.

Gottwald, Norman K. *The Tribes of Yahweh: A Sociology of the Religion of Liberated Israel, 1250–1050 BCE.* Maryknoll, NY: Orbis, 1979.

Goulder, M. D. *Midrash and Lection in Matthew.* London: SPCK, 1974.

Gräbel, Georg. "Mehr Hoffnung Wagen (Vom Senfkorn)—Mk 4,30–32." In *Kompendium der Gleichnisse Jesu*, edited by Ruben Zimmermann et al., 327–36. Munich: Gütersloher, 2007.

Grant, Robert M. *The Letter and the Spirit.* 1957. Reprint, Eugene: Wipf & Stock, 2009.

Grässer, Erich. *Das Problem der Parusieverzögerung in den Synoptischen Evangelien und in der Apostelgeschichte.* Beihefte zur Zeitschrift für die Neutestamentliche Wissenschaft 22. Berlin: Töpelmann, 1960.

Gressmann, Hugo. *Von Reichen Mann und Armen Lazarus.* Abhandlungen der König-lich preussischen akademie der wissenschaften. Philosophische-historische klasse 7. Berlin: Verlag der Königliche Akademie der Wissenschaften, 1918.

Groenewald, Evert P. *In Gelykenisse Het Hy Geleer.* Kaapstad: Kerk–Uitgewers, 1973.

Guelich, Robert A. *Mark 1—8:26.* WBC 34A. Waco, TX: Nelson, 1989.

Gundry, Robert H. *Mark: A Commentary on His Apology for the Cross.* Grand Rapids: Eerdmans, 2000.

———. *Matthew: A Commentary on His Literary and Theological Art.* Grand Rapids: Eerdmans, 1982.

Gutiérrez, Gustavo. *A Theology of Liberation: History, Politics, and Salvation.* Translated and edited by Sister Caridad Inda and John Eagleson. Maryknoll, NY: Orbis, 1973.

Hadas, Moses. "Rabbinic Parallels to Scriptores Historae Augustae." In *Essays in Greco-Roman and Related Talmudic Literature,* edited by Henry A. Fischel, 43–47. New York: Ktav, 1977.

Hagner, Donald A. *Matthew 14–28.* WBC 33A. Nashville: Nelson, 1995.

Hall, Edward T. "Context and Meaning." In *Intercultural Communication: A Reader,* edited by Larry A. Samovar and Richard E. Porter, 60–90. Belmont, CA: Wadsworth, 1994.

Handelman, Don. "Gossip in Encounters: The Transmission of Information in a Bounded Social Setting." *Man: Journal of the Royal Anthropological Institute* 8 (1973) 210–27.

Hanson, K. C., and Douglas E. Oakman. *Palestine in the Time of Jesus: Social Structures and Social Conflicts.* 2nd ed. Minneapolis: Fortress, 2008.

Harnack, Adolf von. *What Is Christianity?* Translated by Thomas Bailey Saunders. Fortress Texts in Modern Theology. Philadelphia: Fortress, 1986.

Harnisch, Wolfgang. *Die Gleichniserzählungen Jesu: Eine Hermeneutische Einführung.* Uni-Taschenbücher 1343. Göttingen: Vandenhoeck & Ruprecht, 1985.

Harris, W. V. *Rome's Imperial Economy: Twelve Essays.* Oxford: Oxford University Press, 2011.

Haviland, John Beard. *Gossip, Reputation, and Knowledge in Zinacantan.* Chicago: University of Chicago Press, 1977.

Hedrick, Charles W. "The 'Good News' about the Historical Jesus." In *The Historical Jesus Goes to Church,* edited by Roy W. Hoover et al., 91–103. Santa Rosa, CA: Polebridge, 2004.

———. *Many Things in Parables: Jesus and His Modern Critics.* Louisville: Westminster John Knox, 2004.

———. *Parables as Poetic Fictions: The Creative Voice of Jesus.* 1994. Reprinted, Eugene, OR: Wipf & Stock, 2005.

Heil, John P. "Reader-Response and the Narrative Context of the Parables about Growing Seed in Mark 4:1–34." *CBQ* 54 (1993) 278–86.

Henaut, Barry W. *Oral Traditions and the Gospels: The Problem of Mark 4.* Journal for the Study of the New Testament Supplement Series 82. Sheffield: JSOT Press, 1993.

Hendrickx, Herman. *The Parables of Jesus.* Rev. ed. Studies in the Synoptic Gospels. London: Chapman, 1986.

Hengel, Martin. "Das Gleichnis von den Bösen Weingärtnern, Mc 12:1–12 im Lichte der Zenonpapyri und der Rabbinischen Gleichnisse." *Zeitschrift für die neutestamentliche Wissenschaft* 59 (1968) 1–39.

Herzog, William R., II. *Parables as Subversive Speech: Jesus as Pedagogue of the Oppressed*. Louisville: Westminster John Knox, 1994.

———. *Prophet and Teacher: An Introduction to the Historical Jesus*. Louisville: Westminster John Knox, 2005.

Hester, James D. "Socio-Rhetorical Criticism and the Parable of the Tenants." *JSNT* 45 (1992) 27–57.

Hill, David. *The Gospel of Matthew*. New Century Bible Commentary. London: Oliphants, 1972.

Hobbs, T. Raymond. "Reflections on Honor, Shame, and Covenant Relations." *JBL* 116 (1997) 501–3.

Hock, Ronald F. "Lazarus and Micyllus: Greco-Roman Backgrounds to Luke 16:19–31." *JBL* 106 (1987) 447–63.

Hollenbach, Paul. "Defining Rich and Poor Using the Social Sciences." In *SBL 1987 Seminar Papers*, edited by Kent H. Richards, 50–63. Atlanta: Scholars, 1987.

Hoover, Roy W. "The Art of Gaining and Losing Everything." In *The Historical Jesus Goes to Church*, edited by Roy W. Hoover et al., 11–30. Santa Rosa, CA: Polebridge, 2004.

———. "Incredible Creed, Credible Faith: Problem and Promise." In *The Once & Future Faith*, edited by Karen Armstrong and Robert W. Funk, 81–100. Santa Rosa, CA: Polebridge, 2001.

Hopkins, Keith. "Rents, Taxes, Trade and the City of Rome." In *The Ancient Economy*, edited by Walter Scheidel and Sitta Von Reden, 190–230. Edinburgh Readings on the Ancient World. Edinburgh: Edinburgh University Press, 2002.

Horn, Friedrich W. *Glaube und Handeln in der Theologie des Lukas*. Göttinger theologische Arbeiten 26. Göttingen: Vandenhoeck & Ruprecht, 1983.

Horsley, Richard A. *Archeology, History, and Society in Galilee: The Social Context of Jesus and the Rabbis*. Valley Forge, PA: Trinity, 1996.

———. *Covenant Economics: A Biblical Vision of Justice for All*. Louisville: Westminster John Knox, 2009.

———. *Jesus and Empire: The Kingdom of God and the New World Disorder*. Minneapolis: Fortress, 2003.

———. *Jesus and the Spiral of Violence: Popular Jewish Resistance in Roman Palestine*. 1987. Reprint, Minneapolis: Fortress, 1993.

Horsley, Richard A., and John S. Hanson. *Bandits, Prophets, and Messiahs: Popular Movements at the Time of Jesus*. Minneapolis: Winston, 1985.

Horsley, Richard A., and Neil A. Silberman. *The Message and the Kingdom: How Jesus and Paul Ignited a Revolution and Transformed the Ancient World*. 1997. Reprinted, Minneapolis: Fortress, 2002.

Howes, Llewellyn. "Food for Thought: Interpreting the Parable of the Loyal and Wise Slave in Q 12:42–46." Paper presented at University of Bloemfontein, 2014.

———. "Placed in a Hidden Place: Illuminating the Displacement of Q 11:33, 34–35." *Neotestamentica* 47 (2013) 303–22.

Hubaut, Michel. *La Parabole des Vignerons Homicides*. Cahiers de la Revue Biblique 16. Paris: Gabalda, 1976.

Huffard, Evertt W. "The Parable of the Friend at Midnight: God's Honor or Man's Persistence?" *Restoration Quarterly* 21 (1978) 154–60.

Huffman, Norman A. "Atypical Features in the Parables of Jesus." *JBL* 97 (1978) 207–20.

Hughes, Frank W. "The Parable of the Rich Man and Lazarus (Luke 16:19–31) and Graeco-Roman Rhetoric." In *Rhetoric and the New Testament: Essays from the 1992 Heidelberg Conference*, edited by Stanley E. Porter and Thomas H. Olbricht, 29–41. Journal for the Study of the New Testament Supplement Series 90. Sheffield: JSOT Press, 1993.

Hultgren, Arland J. *The Parables of Jesus: A Commentary*. The Bible in Its World. Grand Rapids: Eerdmans, 2000.

Hunter, Archibald M. *Interpreting the Parables*. Philadelphia: Westminster, 1961.

———. *The Parables: Then and Now*. Philadelphia: Westminster, 1971.

Hunter, Virginia. "Gossip and the Politics of Reputation in Classical Athens." *Phoenix* 44 (1990) 299–325.

Inrig, Gary. *The Parables: Understanding What Jesus Meant*. Grand Rapids: Discovery House, 1991.

Jameson, Fredric. *The Political Unconscious: Narrative as a Socially Symbolic Act*. Ithaca, NY: Cornell University Press, 1981.

Jensen, Hans J. L. "Diesseits und Jenseits des Raumes eines Textes: Textsemiotische Bemerkungen zur Erzählung: Von Reichen Mann und Armen Lazarus (Lk 16,19–31)." *Linguistica Biblica* 47 (1980) 39–60.

Jeremias, Joachim. *Jerusalem in the Time of Jesus: An Investigation into Economic and Social Conditions during the New Testament Period*. Translated by F. H. Cave and C. H. Cave. Philadelphia: Fortress, 1969.

———. "Palästinakundliches zum Gleichnis vom Saemann." *NTS* 13 (1966) 8–53.

———. *The Parables of Jesus*. 2nd ed. Translated by S. H. Hooke. London: SCM, 1972.

Johnson, Luke T. "The Lukan Kingship Parable (Lk. 19:11–27)." *NovT* 24 (1982) 139–59.

Jones, Geraint V. *The Art and Truth of the Parables: A Study in Their Literary Form and Modern Interpretation*. London: SPCK, 1964.

Jones, Ivor H. *The Matthean Parables: A Literary and Historical Commentary*. Novum Testamentum Supplements 80. Leiden: Brill, 1995.

Jones, Peter R. *Studying the Parables of Jesus*. Macon, GA: Smyth & Helwys, 1999.

Jonge, Marinus de. *Jesus, the Servant-Messiah*. New Haven: Yale University Press, 1991.

Josephus. *The Complete Works of Josephus: Flavius Josephus*. Translated by William Whiston. Grand Rapids: Kregel, 1987.

Jülicher, Adolf. *Die Gleichnisreden Jesu*. Tübingen: Mohr/Siebeck, 1888.

Jüngel, Erberhard. *Paulus und Jesus: Eine Untersuchung zur Präziserung der Frage Nach dem Ursprung der Christologie*. Hermeneutishe Untersuchungen zur Theologie 2. Tübingen: Mohr/Siebeck, 1962.

Kähler, Christoph. *Jesu Gleichnisse als Poesie und Therapie: Versuch eines Integrativen Zugangs zum Kommunikativen Aspekt von Gleichnissen Jesu*. WUNT 78. Tübingen: Mohr/Siebeck, 1995.

Kaylor, R. David. *Jesus the Prophet: His Vision of the Kingdom on Earth*. Louisville: Westminster John Knox, 1994.

Keach, Benjamin. *Exposition of the Parables in the Bible*. Grand Rapids: Kregel, 1978.

Kendall, R. T. *The Parables of Jesus: A Guide to Understanding and Applying the Stories Jesus Told*. Grand Rapids: Chosen, 2006.

Kilgallen, John J. *Twenty Parables of Jesus in the Gospel of Luke*. Subsidia Biblica 32. Rome: Pontificio Instituto Biblico, 2008.

Kim, Chan–Hie. "The Papyrus Invitation." *JBL* 94 (1975) 391–402.

Kissinger, Warren S. *The Parables of Jesus: A History of Interpretation and Bibliography.* ATLA Bibliography Series 4. London: Scarecrow, 1979.

Kistemaker, Simon J. *The Parables: Understanding the Stories Jesus Told.* Grand Rapids: Baker, 1980.

Klauck, Hans-Josef. *Allegorie und Allegorese in Synoptischen Gleichnistexten.* Neutestamentliche Abhandlungen 13. Münster: Aschendorff, 1978.

Klausner, Joseph. *Jesus of Nazareth: His Life, Times and Teaching.* Translated by H. Danby. New York: Macmillan, 1925.

Klein, Hans. "Botschaft für Viele—Nachfolge von Wenigen: Überlegungen zu Lk 14,15–35." *EvT* 57 (1997) 427–37.

Kloppenborg, John S. "Ernest van Eck on the Unmerciful Servant." Presented at the PhD seminar of the Department of Religion, University of Toronto, October 22, 2014.

———. *Excavating Q: The History and Setting of the Sayings Gospel.* Minneapolis: Fortress, 2000.

———. *The Formation of Q: Trajectories in Ancient Wisdom Collections.* Studies in Antiquity and Christianity. Philadelphia: Fortress, 1987.

———. "The Parable of the Burglar in Q: Insights from Papyrology." In *Metaphor, Narrative, and Parables in Q,* edited by Dieter T. Roth et al., 287–306. WUNT 315. Tübingen: Mohr/Siebeck, 2014.

———. *Q Parallels: Synopsis, Critical Notes & Concordance.* FF: Reference Series. Sonoma, CA: Polebridge, 1988.

———. "The Representation of Violence in Synoptic Parables." In *Mark and Matthew I: Comparative Readings; Understanding the Earliest Gospels in Their First-Century Settings,* edited by Eve-Marie Becker and Anders Runesson, 232–351. WUNT 271. Tübingen: Mohr/Siebeck, 2011.

———. *Synoptic Problems: Collected Essays.* WUNT 329. Tübingen: Mohr/Siebeck, 2014.

———. *The Tenants in the Vineyard: Ideology, Economics, and Agrarian Conflict in Jewish Palestine.* WUNT 195. Tübingen: Mohr/Siebeck, 2006.

Kloppenborg, John S., and Callie Callon. "The Parable of the Shepherd and the Transformation of Pastoral Discourse." *Early Christianity* 1 (2010) 1–43.

Kloppenborg, John S. et al. *Q-Thomas Reader.* Santa Rosa, CA: Polebridge, 1990.

Klostermann, Erich. *Das Markusevangelium.* Handbuch zum Neuen Testament. Tübingen: Mohr/Siebeck, 1926.

Knapp, J. J. *Gelijkenissen des Heeren.* Nijkerk: Callenbach, 1920.

Knibb, Michael A. *The Ethiopic Book of Enoch.* 2 vols. Oxford: Clarendon, 1978.

Koester, Helmut. *Ancient Christian Gospels: Their History and Development.* Philadelphia: Trinity, 1990.

———. "Three Thomas Parables." In *The New Testament and Gnosis: Essays in Honor of Robert McL. Wilson,* edited by Alastair H. B. Logan and Alexander J. M. Wedderburn, 195–203. Edinburgh: T. & T. Clark, 1983.

Kreuzer, Siegfried, and Luise Schottroff. "Freundschaft." In *Sozialgeschichtliches Wörterbuch zur Bibel,* edited by Frank Crüsemann et al., 166–70. Gütersloh: Gütersloher, 2009.

Kümmel, Werner G. "Das Gleichnis von den Bösen Weingärtner (Mark 12,1–9)." In *Aux Sources de la Tradition Chrétienne: Mélanges Offerts à M. Maurice Goguel à l'Occasion de son Soixante-Dixième Anniversaire*, edited by Werner G. Kümmel, 120–31. Bibliothèque théologique. Paris: Delachaux & Niestlé, 1950.

———. *Promise and Fulfilment: The Eschatological Message of Jesus.* Translated by Dorothea M. Barton. Studies in Biblical Theology 23. Naperville, IL: Allenson, 1957.

Küng, Hans. *Global Responsibility: In Search of a New World Ethic.* Translated by John Bowden. London: SCM, 1990.

Pliny, the Elder. *Natural History.* Translated by H. Rockham. LCL 529. Cambridge: Harvard University Press, 1961.

Lambrecht, Jan. *Once More Astonished: The Parables of Jesus.* New York: Crossroad, 1981.

———. *Out of the Treasure: The Parables in the Gospel of Matthew.* Louvain Theological & Pastoral Monographs 10. Louvain: Peeters, 1992.

———. "The Parousia Discourse." In *L'Évangile selon Mattieu*, edited by M. Didier, 309–42. Louvain: Louvain University Press, 1970.

Landé, Carl H. "The Dyadic Basis of Clientelism." In *Friends, Followers, and Factions: A Reader in Political Clientelism*, edited by Steffen W. Schmidt, 13–37. Berkeley: University of California Press, 1977.

Lang, G. H. *Pictures and Parables.* London: Paternoster, 1955.

Laughlin, Paul A. *Remedial Christianity: What Every Believer Should Know about the Faith, but Probably Doesn't.* Santa Rosa, CA: Polebridge, 1999.

Lenski, Gerhard E. *Power and Privilege: A Theory of Social Stratification.* New York: McGraw-Hill, 1966.

Leonhardt-Balzer, Jutta. "Wie Kommt Ein Reicher in Der Abrahams Schoß? (Vom Reichen Mann Und Armen Lazarus)." In *Kompendium der Gleichnisse Jesu*, edited by Ruben Zimmermann et al., 647–60. Munich: Gütersloher Verlagshaus, 2007.

Levine, Amy-Jill. "4 Teachings from Jesus That Everybody Gets Wrong." *Belief Blog*, September 21, 2014. http://religion.blogs.cnn.com/2014/09 /21/four-teachings-from-jesus-that-everybody-gets-wrong/.

———. *Short Stories by Jesus: The Enigmatic Parables of a Controversial Rabbi.* San Francisco: HarperOne, 2014.

Levine, Amy-Jill, and C. Shinall Myrick. "Standard and Poor: The Economic Index of the Parables." In *The Message of Jesus: John Dominic Crossan and Ben Witherington III in Dialogue*, edited by Robert B. Stewart, 95–115. Minneapolis: Fortress, 2013.

Levison, M. "Importunity? A Study of Luke XI. 8." *Expositor* Series 9 (1925) 456–60.

Levison, Nahum. *The Parables: Their Background and Local Setting.* Edinburgh: T. & T. Clark, 1926.

Liddel, Henry G., and Robert Scott. *A Greek-English Lexicon.* Oxford: Clarendon, 1968.

Liebenberg, Jacobus. *The Language of the Kingdom and Jesus: Parable, Aphorism, and Metaphor in the Sayings Material Common to the Synoptic Tradition and the Gospel of Thomas.* Beihefte zur Zeitschrift für die Neutestamentliche Wissenschaft 102. Berlin: de Gruyter, 2001.

Liefeld, Walter L. "Parables on Prayer (Luke 11:5–13; 18:1–14." In *The Challenge of Jesus' Parables*, edited by Richard N. Longenecker, 240–62. Grand Rapids: Eerdmans, 2000.

Linnemann, Eta. *Parables of Jesus: Introduction and Exposition.* Translated by John Sturdy. 3rd ed. London: SPCK, 1964.

Lintott, Andrew W. *Violence in Republican Rome*. Oxford: Oxford University Press, 1999.

Llewelyn, Stephen R. "Taxation." In *New Documents Illustrating Early Christianity, 8: A Review of the Greek Inscription and Papyri (Published 1984–85)*, edited by Stephen R. Llewelyn, 47–105. Grand Rapids: Eerdmans, 1988.

Loader, William. *Sexuality and the Jesus Tradition*. Grand Rapids: Eerdmans, 2005.

Lockyer, Herbert. *All the Parables of the Bible*. Grand Rapids: Zondervan, 1963.

Lohfink, Gerhard. *Jesus of Nazareth: What He Wanted, Who He Was*. Translated by Linda M. Maloney. Collegeville, MN: Liturgical, 2012.

Lohfink, Norbert, and Erich Zenger. *The God of Israel and the Nations: Studies in Isaiah and the Psalms*. Translated by Everett R. Kalin. Collegeville, MN: Liturgical, 2000.

Loisy, Alfred F. *Les évangiles Synoptiques*. Ceffonds, Près Montier-en-Der: Chez l'auteur, 1908.

Louw, Johannes, and Eugene A. Nida, eds. *Greek-English Lexicon of the New Testament Based on Semantic Domains*. Vol. 1. Goodwood: National Book Printers, 1988.

Luther, Martin. *Luther's Works*. Edited by Jaroslav Pelikan et al. Vol. 54. Philadelphia: Fortress, 1957.

Luz, Ulrich. *Das Evangelium Nach Matthäus (Mt 8–17)*. Evangelisch-Katholischer Kommentar zum Neuen Testament 1. Zurich: Benziger, 1990.

———. *Das Evangelium Nach Matthäus (Mt 18–25)*. Evangelisch-Katholischer Kommentar zum Neuen Testament 1. Zurich: Neukirchener, 1985.

Mack, Burton L. *The Myth of Innocence: Mark and Christian Origins*. Philadelphia: Fortress, 1988.

Maldonatus, John. *A Commentary on the Holy Gospels*. Translated by John Davies. London: Hodges, 1888.

Malina, Bruce J. "Christ and Time: Swiss or Mediterranean?" *CBQ* 51 (1989) 1–31.

———. *Christian Origins and Cultural Anthropology: Practical Models for Biblical Interpretation*. 1986. Reprinted, Eugene, OR: Wipf & Stock, 2010.

———. "A Conflict Approach to Mark 7." *Foundations and Facets Forum* 4 (1988) 3–30.

———. "Hospitality." In *Handbook of Biblical Social Values*, edited by Bruce J. Malina and John J. Pilch, 115–18. Peabody: Hendrickson, 1998.

———. "The Individual and the Community: Personality in the Social World of Early Christianity." *BTB* 9 (1979) 62–76.

———. "Limited Good and the Social World of Early Christianity." *BTB* 8 (1978) 162–67.

———. *The New Testament World: Insights from Cultural Anthropology*. 1st ed. Philadelphia: Westminster, 1981.

———. *The New Testament World: Insights from Cultural Anthropology*. 3rd ed. Louisville: Westminster John Knox, 2001.

———. "Reading Theory Perspective: Reading Luke-Acts." In *The Social World of Luke-Acts: Models for Interpretation*, edited by Jerome H. Neyrey, 3–23. Peabody: Hendrickson, 1991.

———. "Religion in the Imagined New Testament World: More Social Science Lenses." *Scriptura: International Journal of Bible, Religion and Theology in Southern Africa* 51 (1994) 1–26.

———. "'Religion' in the World of Paul." *BTB* 16 (1986) 92–101.

———. *The Social Gospel of Jesus: The Kingdom of God in Mediterranean Perspective*. Minneapolis: Fortress, 2001.

———. "Social-Scientific Models on Historical Jesus Research." In *The Social Setting of Jesus and the Gospels*, edited by Wolfgang Stegemann et al., 3–26. Minneapolis: Fortress, 2002.

———. *The Social World of Jesus and the Gospels*. London: Routledge, 1996.

———. "Wealth and Poverty in the New Testament and Its World." *Interpretation* 41 (1987) 354–67.

Malina, Bruce J., and Jerome H. Neyrey. "Honor and Shame in Luke–Acts: Pivotal Values of the Mediterranean World." In *The Social World of Luke–Acts: Models for Interpretation*, edited by Jerome H. Neyrey, 25–65. Peabody, MA: Hendrickson, 1991.

———. *Portraits of Paul: An Archeology of Ancient Personality*. Louisville: Westminster John Knox, 1996.

Malina, Bruce J., and John J. Pilch. *Social-Science Commentary on the Book of Acts*. Minneapolis: Fortress, 2008.

Malina, Bruce J., and Richard L. Rohrbaugh. *Social-Science Commentary on the Gospel of John*. Minneapolis: Fortress, 1998.

———. *Social-Science Commentary on the Synoptic Gospels*. 2nd ed. Minneapolis: Fortress, 2003.

Malina, Bruce et al. *A Time Travel to the World of Jesus: A Modern Reflection of Ancient Judea*. Johannesburg: Orion, 1996.

Manson, T. W. *The Sayings of Jesus*. Cambridge: Cambridge University Press, 1951.

———. *The Teaching of Jesus: Studies of Its Form and Content*. 2nd ed. Cambridge: Cambridge University Press, 1945.

Marcus, Joel. *Mark 1–8: A New Translation with Introduction and Commentary*. Anchor Yale Bible Commentaries 27. New York: Doubleday, 2000.

———. *The Mystery of the Kingdom of God*. Society of Biblical Literature Dissertation Series 90. Atlanta: Scholars, 1986.

Marshall, I. Howard. *Eschatology and the Parables*. London: Tyndale, 1963.

———. *The Gospel of Luke*. New International Greek Testament Commentary. Exeter, UK: Paternoster, 1978.

Mays, James L. *Hosea: A Commentary*. Old Testament Library. Philadelphia: Westminster, 1969.

McGaughy, Lane C. "Fear of Yahweh and the Mission of Judaism: A Postexilic Maxim and Its Early Christian Expansion in the Parable of the Talents." *JBL* 94 (1975) 235–45.

———. "Jesus' Parables and the Fiction of the Kingdom." In *Listening to the Parables of Jesus*, edited by Edward F. Beutner, 7–13. Jesus Seminar Guides 2. Santa Rosa, CA: Polebridge, 2007.

McIver, Robert K. "One-Hundred-Fold Yield—Miraculous or Mundane? Matthew 13.8, 23; Mark 4.8, 20; Luke 8.8." *NTS* 40 (1994) 606–8.

Mealand, David L. *Poverty and Expectation in the Gospels*. London: SPCK, 1980.

Meier, John P. *A Marginal Jew—Rethinking the Historical Jesus*. Vol. 1, *The Roots of the Problem and the Person*. Anchor Bible Reference Library. New York: Doubleday, 1991.

Mein, Andrew. "Profitable and Unprofitable Shepherds: Economic and Theological Perspectives on Ezekiel 34." *JSOT* 31 (2007) 493–504.

Mell, Ulrich. *Die "Anderen" Winzer: Eine Exegetische Studie zur Vollmacht Jesu Christi nach Markus 11,27—12,34*. WUNT 77. Tübingen: Mohr/Siebeck, 1994.

Merz, Annette. "Freundschaft Verplichtet (vom Bitttenden Freund)—Lk 11,5–8." In *Kompendium der Gleichnisse Jesu*, edited by Ruben Zimmermann et al., 556–63. Munich: Gütersloher, 2007.

Miller, Robert J., ed. *The Apocalyptic Jesus: A Debate*. Santa Rosa, CA: Polebridge, 2001.

———, ed. *The Complete Gospels*. Salem, OR: Polebridge, 2010.

———. "Introduction." In *The Apocalyptic Jesus: A Debate*, edited by Robert J. Miller, 1–13. Santa Rosa, CA: Polebridge, 2001.

———. "Is the Apocalyptic Jesus History?" In *The Once & Future Faith*, edited by Karen Armstrong and Robert W. Funk, 101–16. Santa Rosa, CA: Polebridge, 2001.

———. "The Pearl, the Treasure, the Fool, and the Cross." In *Listening to the Parables of Jesus*, edited by Edward F. Beutner, 65–82. Jesus Seminar Guides 2. Santa Rosa, CA: Polebridge, 2007.

Montefiore, Claude G. *The Synoptic Gospels*. London: Macmillan, 1909.

Montefiore, Hugh. "A Comparison of the Parables of the Gospel according to Thomas and of the Synoptic Gospels." In *Thomas and the Evangelists*, edited by Hugh Montefiore and Henry E. W. Turner, 220–48. Studies in Biblical Theology 35. Naperville, IL: Allenson, 1962.

Moor, Johannes C. de. "The Targumic Background of Mark 12:1–12: The Parable of the Wicked Tenants." *Journal for the Study of Judaism* 29 (1998) 63–80.

Morgan, G. Campbell. *The Parables and Metaphors of Our Lord*. London: Marshall, Morgan & Scott, 1953.

Morrice, William G. "The Parable of the Tenants and the Gospel of Thomas." *Expository Times* 98 (1987) 104–7.

Moxnes, Halvor. *The Economy of the Kingdom: Social Conflict and Economic Relations in Luke's Gospel*, 1988. Reprinted, Eugene, OR: Wipf & Stock, 2004.

———. "Honor and Righteousness in Romans." *JSNT* 32 (1988) 61–77.

———. "Honor and Shame." In *The Social Sciences and New Testament Interpretation*, edited by Richard L. Rohrbaugh, 19–40. Peabody, MA: Hendrickson, 1996.

———. "Patron-Client Relations and the New Community in Luke-Acts." In *The Social World of Luke-Acts: Models for Interpretation*, edited by Jerome H. Neyrey, 241–68. Peabody, MA: Hendrickson, 1991.

———. *Putting Jesus in His Place: A Radical Vision of Household and Kingdom*. Louisville: Westminster John Knox, 2003.

———. "The Quest for Honor and the Unity of the Community in Romans 12 and in the Orations of Dio Chrysostom." In *Paul in His Hellenistic Context*, edited by Troels Engberg-Pedersen, 202–30. Minneapolis: Fortress, 1995.

Münch, Christian. "Gewinnen oder Verlieren (Von den Anvertrauten Geldern)." In *Kompendium der Gleichnisse Jesu*, edited by Ruben Zimmermann et al., 240–54. Munich: Gütersloher, 2007.

Murray, Mary A. "Viticulture and Wine Production." In *Ancient Egyptian Materials and Technology*, edited by Paul T. Nicholson and Ian Shaw, 577–608. Cambridge: Cambridge University Press, 2000.

Mussner, Franz. "1Q Hodajoth und das Gleichnis vom Senfkorn (Mk 4:30–32 Par.)." *Biblische Zeitschrift* 4 (1960) 128–30.

Newell, Jane E., and Raymond R. Newell. "The Parable of the Wicked Tenants." *NovT* 14 (1972) 226–37.

Neyrey, Jerome H. "Ceremonies in Luke-Acts." In *The Social World of Luke–Acts: Models for Interpretation*, edited by Jerome H. Neyrey, 361–87. Peabody, MA: Hendrickson, 1991.

———. "God, Benefactor and Patron: The Major Cultural Model for Interpreting the Deity in Greco-Roman Antiquity." *JSNT* 27 (2005) 465–92.

———. *Honor and Shame in the Gospel of Matthew*. Louisville: Westminster John Knox, 1998.

———. "John 18–19: Honor and Shame in the Passion Narrative." *Semeia* 68 (1996) 113–37.

———. *Render to God: New Testament Understandings of the Divine*. Minneapolis: Fortress, 2004.

———, ed. *The Social World of Luke–Acts: Models for Interpretation*. Peabody, MA: Hendrickson, 1991.

———. "The Symbolic Universe of Luke–Acts: 'They Turn the World Upside Down.'" In *The Social World of Luke–Acts: Models for Interpretation*, edited by Jerome H. Neyrey, 271–304. Peabody: Hendrickson, 1991.

Nickelsburg, George W. E. "Riches, the Rich, and God's Judgment in 1 Enoch 95–105 and the Gospel according to Luke." *NTS* 25 (1979) 324–44.

Nolland, John. *Luke 1—9:20*. WBC 35A. Waco, TX: Nelson, 1989.

———. *Luke 9:21—18:34*. WBC 35B. Waco, TX: Nelson, 1993.

Oakman, Douglas E. *Jesus and the Economic Questions of His Day*. Studies in the Bible and Early Christianity 8. Lewiston, NY: Mellen, 1986.

———. *Jesus and the Peasants*. Matrix: The Bible in Mediterranean Context 4. Eugene, OR: Cascade Books, 2008.

———. *The Political Aims of Jesus*. Minneapolis: Fortress, 2012.

Oesterley, William O. E. *The Gospel Parables in the Light of Their Jewish Background*. New York: Macmillan, 1936.

Osborne, Grant R. *The Hermeneutical Spiral: A Comprehensive Introduction to Biblical Interpretation*. Downers Grove, IL: InterVarsity, 1991.

Oveja, Animosa. "Neunundneunzig Sind Nicht Genug! Q 15,4–5a.7." In *Kompendium der Gleichnisse Jesu*, edited by Ruben Zimmermann et al., 240–54. Munich: Gütersloher, 2007.

Paine, Robert. "Gossip and Transaction." *Man: Journal of the Royal Anthropological Institute* 3 (1968) 305–8.

———. "What Is Gossip About? An Alternative Hypothesis." *Man: Journal of the Royal Anthropological Institute* 2 (1967) 278–85.

Painter, John. *Mark's Gospel: Worlds in Conflict*. New Testament Readings. London: Routledge, 1997.

Parenti, Michael. *The Assassination of Julius Caesar: A People's History of Ancient Rome*. New Press People's History. New York: New Press, 2003.

Parsons, Talcott. *Structure and Process in Modern Societies*. New York: Free Press, 1960.

Patte, Daniel. "Bringing Out of the Gospel-Treasure What Is New and What Is Old: Two Parables in Matthew 18–23." *Quarterly Review* 10 (1990) 79–108.

Patterson, Stephen J. *The Gospel of Thomas and Jesus*. FF: Reference Series. Sonoma, CA: Polebridge, 1993.

Patterson, Stephen J. et al. *The Fifth Gospel: The Gospel of Thomas Comes of Age*. London: T. & T. Clark, 2011.

Paulsen, Henning. "Die Witwe und der Richter (Lk 18,1–8)." *Theologie und Glaube* 74 (1984) 13–38.

Pax, Elpidius W. "Der Reiche und Arme Lazarus: Eine Milieustudie." *Studii Biblici Franciscani Liber Annuus* 25 (1975) 254–68.

Payne, P. B. "The Order of Sowing and Ploughing in the Parable of the Sower." *NTS* 25 (1978) 123–29.

Pentecost, J. Dwight. *The Parables of Jesus: Lessons in Life from the Master Teacher.* Grand Rapids: Kregel, 1982.

Peppard, Michael. "The Eagle and the Dove: Roman Imperial Sonship and the Baptism of Jesus (Mark 1.9–11)." *NTS* 56 (2010) 431–51.

Perkins, Pheme. *Gnosticism and the New Testament.* Minneapolis: Fortress, 1993.

———. *Hearing the Parables of Jesus.* New York: Paulist, 1981.

Perrin, Norman. "The Christology of Mark: A Study in Methodology." *Journal of Religion* 51 (1971) 173–87. Reprinted in Perrin, *Parable and Gospel*, edited by K. C. Hanson, 73–84. Fortress Classics in Biblical Studies. Minneapolis: Fortress, 2003.

———. *The Kingdom of God in the Teaching of Jesus.* Philadelphia: Westminster, 1963.

———. *Rediscovering the Teaching of Jesus.* New York: Harper & Row, 1967.

Peters, Donald. "Vulnerable Promise from the Land." In *Jesus and His Parables: Interpreting the Parables of Jesus Today*, edited by V. George Shillington, 91–110. Edinburgh: T. & T. Clark, 1997.

Petersen, William L. "The Parable of the Lost Sheep in the Gospel of Thomas and the Synoptics." *NovT* 23 (1981) 128–47.

Pilch, John J. *The Cultural Dictionary of the Bible.* Collegeville, MN: Liturgical, 1999.

Pitt-Rivers, Julian. *The Fate of Shechem: Or, the Politics of Sex; Essays in the Anthropology of the Mediterranean.* Cambridge Studies in Social Anthropology 19. Cambridge: Cambridge University Press, 1977.

Pleket, H. W. "Labor and Unemployment in the Roman Empire: Some Preliminary Remarks." In *Soziale Randgruppen und Aussenseiter im Altertum: Referate vom Symposion Soziale Randgruppen und Antike Sozialpolitik*, edited by Ingomar Weiler, 267–76. Gräz: Leykam, 1987.

Pliny, the Elder. *Natural History*, with an English translation by H. Rockham. LCL. Cambridge: Harvard University Press, 1961.

Plummer, Alfred. *A Critical and Exegetical Commentary on the Gospel according to St. Luke.* International Critical Commentary. Edinburgh: T. & T. Clark, 1922.

Polag, Athanasius. *Fragmenta Q: Textheft zur Logienquelle.* Neukirchen-Vluyn: Neukirchener, 1979.

Polanyi, Karl. *The Great Transformation: The Political and Economic Origins of Our Time.* 1944. Reprinted, Boston: Beacon, 1957.

Premnath, D. N. "Amos and Hosea: Sociohistorical Background and Prophetic Critique." *Word & World* 28 (2008) 125–32.

Purcell, N. "Wine and Wealth in Ancient Italy." *JRS* 75 (1985) 1–19.

Quispel, Gilles. *Gnosis and the New Sayings of Jesus.* Gnostic Studies 2. Düsseldorf: Rhein, 1971.

———. "The Gospel of Thomas and the New Testament." *Vigiliae Christianae* 11 (1957) 189–207.

Rathbone, D. W. "The Development of Agriculture in the 'Ager Cosanus' during the Roman Republic: Problems of Evidence and Interpretation." *JRS* 71 (1981) 14–23.

Rauschenbusch, Walter. *A Gospel for the Social Awakening: Selections from the Writings of Walter Rauschenbusch.* Edited by Benjamin E. Mays. 1950. Reprinted, Eugene, OR: Wipf & Stock, 2008.

Reed, Jonathan L. *Archaeology and the Galilean Jesus: A Re-Examination of the Evidence.* Harrisburg, PA: Trinity, 2002.

Regalado, Ferdinand O. "The Jewish Background of the Rich Man and Lazarus." *Asia Journal of Theology* 16 (2002) 341–48.

Reid, Barbara E. *Parables for Preachers.* Vol. 1, *Year A: The Gospel of Matthew.* Collegeville, MN: Liturgical, 2001.

Robinson, James M. et al., eds. *The Critical Edition of Q: A Synopsis Including the Gospels of Matthew and Luke, Mark and Thomas with English, German and French Translations of Q and Thomas.* Hermeneia Supplements. Minneapolis: Fortress, 2000.

Rohrbaugh, Richard L. "Agrarian Society." In *Biblical Social Values and Their Meaning: A Handbook,* edited by John J. Pilch and Bruce J. Malina, 5–8. 2nd ed. Peabody, MA: Hendrickson, 1998.

———. "Gossip in the New Testament." In *Social Scientific Models for Interpreting the Bible: Essays by the Context Group in Honor of Bruce J. Malina,* edited by John J. Pilch, 239–59. Biblical Interpretation Series 53. Leiden: Brill, 2001.

———. "Hermeneutics as Cross-Cultural Encounter: Obstacles to Understanding." *HvTSt* 62 (2006) 559–76.

———. *The New Testament in Cross-Cultural Perspective.* Matrix: The Bible in Mediterranean Context 1. Eugene: Cascade Books, 2007.

———. "A Peasant Reading of the Talents/Pounds: A Text of Terror." *BTB* 23 (1993) 32–39.

———. "The Pre-Industrial City in Luke-Acts: Urban Social Relations." In *The Social World of Luke-Acts: Models for Interpretation,* edited by Jerome H. Neyrey, 125–49. Peabody: Hendrickson, 1991.

Rostovtzeff, Michael I. *Geschichte der Staatpracht in der Römischen Kaizerzeit bis Diokletian.* Philologus, Supplementumband 9. Leipzig: Dieterichsche Verlagsbuchhandlung, 1904.

———. *A Large Estate in Egypt in the Third Century B.C.: A Study in Economic History.* University of Wisconsin Studies in the Social Sciences and History 6. Madison: University of Wisconsin Press, 1922.

Rowlandson, Jane. *Landowners and Tenants in Roman Egypt: The Social Relations of Agriculture in the Oxyrhynchite Nome.* Oxford Classical Monographs. Oxford: Clarendon, 1996.

Sahlins, Marshall. *Stone Age Economics.* New York: Aldine, 1972.

Saller, Richard P. *Personal Patronage under the Early Empire.* Cambridge: Cambridge University Press, 1982.

Sanders, E. P. *The Historical Figure of Jesus.* New York: Penguin, 1993.

Sanders, Jack T. "The Ethic of Election in Luke's Great Banquet Parable." In *Essays in Old Testament Ethics,* edited by James L. Crenshaw and John T. Willis, 245–71. New York: Ktav, 1974.

Sawicki, Marianne. *Crossing Galilee: Architectures of Contact in the Occupied Land of Jesus.* Harrisburg, PA: Trinity, 2000.

Schaff, Philip. *Nicene and Post-Nicene Fathers.* Vol. 2. Christian Classics Ethereal Library 1. Grand Rapids: Eerdmans, 2009.

Scharlemann, Martin H. "The Parables of the Leaven and the Mustard Seed: A Suggested Methodological Model." In *Studies in Lutheran Hermeneutics*, edited by John Reumann, 335–54. Philadelphia: Fortress, 1979.

Scheidel, Walter. "Finances, Figures and Fiction." *Classical Quarterly* 46 (1996) 222–38.

Schippers, R. *Gelijkenissen van Jezus.* Kampen: Kok, 1962.

Schnider, Franz, and Werner Stenger. "Die Offene Tür und die Unüberschreitbare Kluft." *NTS* 25 (1979) 273–83.

Schottroff, Luise. "Das Gleichnis vom Grossen Gastmahl in der Logionquelle." *EvT* 47 (1987) 192–211.

———. "Das Gleichnis vom Verlorenen Sohn." *Zeitschrift für Theologie und Kirche* 68 (1971) 27–52.

———. *The Parables of Jesus.* Translated by Linda M. Maloney. Minneapolis: Augsburg, 2006.

———. "Von der Schwierigkeit zu Teilen (Das Große Abendmahl)—Lk 14,12–24." In *Kompendium der Gleichnisse Jesu*, edited by Ruben Zimmermann et al., 593–603. Munich: Gütersloher, 2007.

Schottroff, Luise, and Wolfgang Stegemann. *Jesus von Nazareth: Hoffnung der Armen.* Uni-Taschenbücher 639. Stuttgart: Kohlhammer, 1978.

———. *Jesus and the Hope of the Poor.* Translated by Matthew J. O'Connell. Maryknoll, NY: Orbis, 1986.

Schottroff, Willy. "Das Gleichnis von den Bösen Weingärtnern (Mk 12,1–9 Parr.): Ein Beitrag zur Geschichte der Bodenpacht in Palästina." *Zeitschrift des Deutschen Palästina-Vereins* 112 (1996) 18–48.

———. "Human Solidarity and the Goodness of God: The Parable of the Workers in the Vineyard." In *God of the Lowly: Socio-Historical Interpretations of the Bible*, edited by Willy Schottroff and Wolfgang Stegemann, 129–47. Translated by Matthew J. O'Connell. Maryknoll, NY: Orbis, 1984.

Schulz, Siegfried. *Q—Die Spruchquelle Der Evangelisten.* Zürich: Zürich Theologischer, 1972.

Schüssler Fiorenza, Elisabeth. *Jesus: Miriam's Child, Sophia's Prophet—Critical Issues in Feminist Theology.* New York: Continuum, 1994.

Schweitzer, Albert. *The Kingdom of God in the Teaching of Jesus.* Philadelphia: Westminster, 1963.

———. *The Quest of the Historical Jesus: A Critical Study of Its Progress from Reimarus to Wrede.* Translated by William Montgomery. London: Black, 1910.

Schweizer, Eduard. *Das Evangelium nach Markus.* 11 Aufl. Das Neue Testament Deutsch 1. Göttingen: Vandenhoeck & Ruprecht, 1967.

———. *The Good News according to Luke.* Translated by David Green. Atlanta: John Knox, 1984.

Scott, Bernard B. "From Parable to Ethics." In *The Once & Future Faith*, edited by Karen Armstrong and Robert W. Funk, 117–34. Santa Rosa, CA: Polebridge, 2001.

———. *Hear Then the Parable: A Commentary on the Parables of Jesus.* Minneapolis: Fortress, 1989.

———. "The Reappearance of Parables." In *Listening to the Parables of Jesus*, edited by Edward F. Beutner, 95–119. Jesus Seminar Guides 2. Santa Rosa, CA: Polebridge, 2007.

———. *Re-Imagine the World: An Introduction to the Parables of Jesus.* Santa Rosa, CA: Polebridge, 2001.

Scott, James C. *Domination and the Arts of Resistance: Hidden Transcripts.* New Haven: Yale University Press, 1990.
———. "Protest and Profanation, Part 1." *Theory and Society* 4 (1977) 1–38.
———. *Weapons of the Weak: Everyday Forms of Peasant Resistance.* New Haven: Yale University Press, 1985.
Segovia, Fernando F. "Biblical Criticism and Postcolonial Studies: Towards a Postcolonial Optic." In *The Postcolonial Biblical Reader,* edited by R. S. Sugirtharajah, 33–44. Malden, MA: Blackwell, 2006.
Segundo, Juan L. *The Historical Jesus of the Synoptics.* Translated by John Drury. Maryknoll. Orbis, 1985.
Shillington, V. George. "Saving Life and Keeping Sabbath (Matthew 20:1b–15)." In *Jesus and His Parables: Interpreting the Parables of Jesus Today,* edited by V. George Shillington, 87–101. Edinburgh: T. & T. Clark, 1997.
Sidebotham, Steven E. "Trade and Commerce (Roman)." In *Anchor Bible Dictionary,* edited by David Noel Freedman, 5:63. 6 vols. New York: Doubleday, 1992.
Smith, B. T. D. *The Parables of the Synoptic Gospels: A Critical Study.* Cambridge: Cambridge University Press, 1937.
Smith, Morton. *Jesus the Magician: Charlatan or Son of God?* New York: Harper & Row, 1978.
Snodgrass, Klyne R. "Anaideia and the Friend at Midnight (Lk 11:8)." *JBL* 116 (1997) 505–13.
———. *The Parable of the Wicked Tenants: An Inquiry into Parable Interpretation.* WUNT 7. Tübingen: Mohr/Siebeck, 1983.
———. *Stories with Intent: A Comprehensive Guide to the Parables of Jesus.* Grand Rapids: Eerdmans, 2008.
Spacks, Patricia Meyer. *Gossip.* New York: Knopf, 1985.
Stansell, Gary. "Gifts, Tributes, and Offerings." In *The Social Setting of Jesus and the Gospels,* edited by Wolfgang Stegemann et al., 349–64. Minneapolis: Fortress, 2002.
Steck, Odil H. *Israel und das Gewaltsame Geschick der Propheten: Untersuchungen zur Überlieferung des Deuteronomistischen Geschichtsbildes im Alten Testament, Spätjudentum und Urchristentum.* Wissenschaftliche Monographien zum Alten und Neuen Testament 23. Neukirchen-Vluyn: Neukirchener, 1967.
Stegemann, Ekkehard W., and Wolfgang Stegemann. *The Jesus Movement: A Social History of Its First Century.* Translated by O. C. Dean Jr. . Minneapolis: Fortress, 1999.
Stegemann, Wolfgang. "The Contextual Ethics of Jesus." In *The Social Setting of Jesus and the Gospels,* edited by Wolfgang Stegemann et al., 46–60. Minneapolis: Fortress, 2002.
Stein, Robert H. *An Introduction to the Parables of Jesus.* Philadelphia: Westminster, 1981.
Stern, Frank. *A Rabbi Looks at Jesus' Parables.* Lanham, MD: Rowman & Littlefield, 2006.
Stiller, Brian C. *Preaching Parables to Postmoderns.* Fortress Resources for Preaching. Minneapolis: Fortress, 2005.
Strack, Hermann L., and Paul Billerbeck. *Kommentar zum Neuen Testament aus Talmud und Midrasch: Das Evangelium nach Markus, Lukas und Johannes und die Apostelgeschichte.* 9th ed. Vol. 2/6. Munich: Beck, 1974.

Strange, James Riley. "The Galilean Road System." In *Life, Culture, and Society*, edited by David A. Fiensy and James Riley Strange, 263–71. Galilee in the Late Second Temple and Mishnaic Periods 1. Minneapolis: Fortress, 2014.

Streeter, Burnett Hillman. *The Four Gospels: A Study of Origins, Treating of the Manuscript Tradition, Sources, Authorship, and Dates*. New York: St. Martin's, 1930.

Stuhlmacher, Peter. *Jesus of Nazareth, Christ of Faith*. Peabody: Hendrickson, 1993.

Swartley, Willard M. "Unexpected Banquet People." In *Jesus and His Parables: Interpreting the Parables of Jesus Today*, edited by V. George Shillington, 177–90. Edinburgh: T. & T. Clark, 2000.

Talbert, Charles H. *Reading Luke: A Literary and Theological Commentary on the Third Gospel*. Reading the New Testament 3. New York: Crossroad, 1982.

Tatum, W. Barnes. *In Quest of Jesus*. Rev. ed. Nashville: Abingdon, 1999.

Taussig, Hal. *In the Beginning Was the Meal: Social Experimentation and Early Christian Identity*. Minneapolis: Fortress, 2009.

Taylor, Vincent. *The Gospel according to St. Mark: The Greek Text with Introductions, Notes and Indexes*. London: Macmillan, 1957.

Tevel, J. M. "The Labourers in the Vineyard: The Exegesis of Matthew 20,1–7 in the Early Church." *Vigiliae Christianae* 46 (1992) 356–80.

Theissen, Gerd. "The Political Dimension of Jesus' Activities." In *The Social Setting of Jesus and the Gospels*, edited by Wolfgang Stegemann et al., 225–50. Minneapolis: Fortress, 2002.

———. *The Shadow of the Galilean: The Quest of the Historical Jesus in Narrative Form*. Minneapolis: Fortress, 1987.

Theissen, Gerd, and Annette Merz. *The Historical Jesus: A Comprehensive Guide*. Translated by John Bowden. Minneapolis: Fortress, 1998.

Thuren, Lauri. *Parables Unplugged: Reading the Lukan Parables in Their Rhetorical Context*. Minneapolis: Fortress, 2014.

Timmer, John. *The Kingdom Equation: A Fresh Look at the Parables of Jesus*. Grand Rapids: Faith Alive Christian Resources, 1990.

Tolbert, Mary Ann. *Perspectives on the Parables: An Approach to Multiple Interpretations*. Philadelphia: Fortress, 1967.

———. *Sowing the Gospel: Mark's World in Literary-Historical Perspective*. Minneapolis: Fortress, 1989.

Trench, Richard C. *Notes on the Parables of Our Lord*. London: Macmillan, 1840.

Trimp, P .J. *Sprekende Beelden: Bijbelstudie over Gelijkenissen van Jezus*. Barneveld: De Vuurbraak, 1990.

Tuckett, Christopher M. "Synoptic Tradition in the Gospel of Truth and the Testimony of Truth." *JTS* 35 (1984) 131–45.

Twelftree, Graham H. *Jesus the Exorcist: A Contribution to the Study of the Historical Jesus*. WUNT 2/54. Tübingen: Mohr/Siebeck, 1993.

Van Aarde, Andries G. *Fatherless in Galilee: Jesus as Child of God*. Harrisburg, PA: Trinity, 2001.

Van Eck, Ernest. "Do Not Question My Honour: A Social–Scientific Reading of the Parable of the Minas (Lk 19:12b–24, 27)." *HvTSt* 67 (2011) 1–11.

———. *Galilee and Jerusalem in Mark's Story of Jesus: A Narratological and Social Scientific Reading*. Hervormde Teologiese Studies Supplementum 7. Pretoria: Kital, 1995.

———. "The Harvest and the Kingdom: An Interpretation of the Sower (Mk 4:3b–8) as a Parable of Jesus the Galilean." *HvTSt* 70 (2014) 1–10.

———. "Honour and Debt Release in the Parable of the Unmerciful Servant (Mt 18:23–33): A Social-Scientific and Realistic Reading." *HvTSt* 71 (2015) 1–11.

———. "Die Huwelik in die Eerste-Eeuse Mediterreense Wêreld (II): Huwelik, Egbreuk, Egskeiding En Hertrou." *HvTSt* 63 (2007) 103–28.

———. "Interpreting the Parables of the Galilean Jesus: A Social-Scientific Approach." *HvTSt* 65 (2009) 1–12.

———. "In the Kingdom Everybody Has Enough—A Social-Scientific and Realistic Reading of the Parable of the Lost Sheep (Lk 15:4–6)." *HvTSt* 67 (2011) 1–10.

———. "Invitations and Excuses That Are not Invitations and Excuses: Gossip in Luke 14:18–20." *HvTSt* 86 (2012) 1–10.

———. "Jesus and Violence: An Ideological-Critical Reading of the Tenants in Mark 12:1–12 and Thomas 65." In *Coping with Violence in the New Testament*, edited by Pieter G. R. de Villiers and Jan Willem van Henten, 101–32. Studies in Theology and Religion 16. Leiden: Brill, 2012.

———. "A Prophet of Old: Jesus the 'Public Theologian.'" In *Prophetic Witness: An Appropriate Contemporary Mode of Public Discourse?*, edited by Heinrich Bedford-Strohm and Etienne de Villiers, 47–74. Theology in the Public Square/Theologie in der Öffentlichkeit 1. Zürich: Lit, 2011.

———. "The Tenants in the Vineyard (GThom 65/Mark 12:1–12): A Realistic and Social-Scientific Reading." *HvTSt* 63 (2007) 909–36.

———. "When an Outsider Becomes an Insider: A Social-Scientific and Realistic Reading of the Merchant (Mt 13:45–46)." *HvTSt* 71 (2015) 1–8.

———. "When Kingdoms Are Kingdoms no More: A Social-Scientific Reading of the Mustard Seed (Lk 13:18–19)." *Acta Theologica* 33 (2013) 226–54.

———. "When Neighbours Are not Neighbours: A Social-Scientific Reading of the Parable of the Friend at Midnight (Lk 11:5–8)." *HvTSt* 67 (2011) 1–14.

———. "When Patrons Are not Patrons: A Social-Scientific Reading of the Rich Man and Lazarus (Lk 16:19–26)." *HvTSt* 65 (2009) 1–11.

———. "When Patrons Are Patrons: A Social-Scientific and Realistic Reading of the Parable of the Feast (Lk 14:16b–23)." *HvTSt* 69 (2013) 1–14.

Van Eck, Ernest, and John S. Kloppenborg. "The Unexpected Patron: A Social-Scientific and Realistic Reading of the Parable of the Vineyard Laborers (Mt 20:1–15)." *HvTSt* 71 (2015) 1–11.

Van Eck, Ernest, and Andries G. van Aarde. "A Narratological Analysis of Mark 12:1–12: The Plot of the Gospel of Mark in a Nutshell.'" *HvTSt* 45 (1989) 778–800.

Vearncombe, Erin K. "Redistribution and Reciprocity: A Socio-Economic Interpretation of the Parable of the Labourers in the Vineyard (Matthew 20.1–15)." *Journal for the Study of the Historical Jesus* 8 (2010) 199–236.

Verhoefen, Paul. "The First Will Be First: The Labourers in the Vineyard." In *Listening to the Parables of Jesus*, edited by Edward F. Beutner, 41–50. Jesus Seminar Guides 2. Santa Rosa, CA: Polebridge, 2007.

Vermes, Géza. *Jesus the Jew: A Historian's Reading of the Gospel*. New York: Macmillan, 1973.

Via, Dan O. "Parable and Example Story: A Literary-Structural Approach." *Semeia* 1 (1974) 105–33.

———. *The Parables: Their Literary and Existential Dimension.* 1967. Reprint, Eugene, OR: Wipf & Stock, 2007.

Vögtle, Anton. *Gott und Seine Gäste: Das Schicksal des Gleichnisses Jesu vom Grossen Gastmahl (Lukas 14,16b–24; Matthäus 22,2–14).* Biblisch-Theologische Studien 29. Neukirchen-Vluyn: Neukirchener, 1966.

Voris, Steven J. *Preaching Parables: A Metaphorical Interfaith Approach.* New York: Paulist, 2008.

Waetjen, Herman C. "The Subversion of 'World' by the Parable of the Friend at Midnight." *JBL* 120 (2001) 703–21.

Wailes, Stephen L. *Medieval Allegories of Jesus' Parables.* Publications of the UCLA Center for Medieval and Renaissance Studies 23. Berkeley: University of California Press, 1987.

Wallace-Hadrill, Andrew. "Patronage in Roman Society: From Republic to Empire." In *Patronage in Ancient Society,* edited by Andrew Wallace-Hadrill, 63–87. London: Routledge, 1989.

Wallace, Mark I. "The Rule of Love and the Testimony of the Spirit in Contemporary Biblical Hermeneutics." In *But Is It All True? The Bible and the Question of Truth,* edited by Alan G. Padgett and Patrick R. Keifert, 66–85. Grand Rapids: Eerdmans, 2006.

Weder, Hans. *Die Gleichnisse Jesu als Metaphern: Traditions- und Redaktionsgeschichtliche Analysen und Interpretatonien.* Forschungen zur Religion und Literatur des Alten und Neuen Testaments 120. Göttingen: Vandenhoeck & Ruprecht, 1984.

Weiser, Alfons. *Die Knechtgleichnisse der Synoptischen Evangelien.* Studien zum Alten und Neuen Testament 29. Munich: Kösel, 1971.

Weissenrieder, Annette. "Didaktik der Bilder: Allegorie und Allegorese am Beispiel von Mk 4,3–20." In *Hermeneutik der Gleichnisse Jesu: Methodische Neuansätze Zum Verstehen Urchristlicher Parabeltexte,* edited by Ruben Zimmerman and Gabi Kern, 494–520. WUNT 231. Tübingen: Mohr/Siebeck, 2008.

Weiss, Johannes. *Die Predicht Jesu vom Reiche Gottes.* Göttingen: Vandenhoeck & Ruprecht, 1900.

Wenham, David. "The Interpretation of the Parable of the Sower." *NTS* 20 (1974) 299–319.

———. *The Parables of Jesus: Pictures of a Revolution.* Jesus Library. London: Hodder & Stoughton, 1989.

———. *The Rediscovery of Jesus' Eschatological Discourse.* Gospel Perspectives 4. Sheffield: Sheffield, 1984.

Westermann, Claus. *The Parables of Jesus in the Light of the Old Testament.* Translated by Friedmann Golka and Alastair Logan. Edinburgh: T. & T. Clark, 1990.

White, K. D. "The Parable of the Sower." *JTS* 15 (1964) 300–307.

Wierzbicka, Anna. *What Did Jesus Mean? Explaining the Sermon on the Mount and the Parables in Simple and Human Concepts.* Oxford: Oxford University Press, 2001.

Wilder, Amos N. *Early Christian Rhetoric: The Language of the Gospel.* 1964. Reprint, Eugene, OR: Wipf & Stock, 2014.

———. "The Parable of the Sower: Naiveté and Method in Interpretation." *Semeia* 2 (1974) 134–51.

Wills, Lawrence M. "The Gospel according to Mark." In *The Jewish Annotated New Testament: New Revised Standard Version Bible Translation,* edited by Amy–Jill Levine and Marc Z. Brettler, 55–95. New York: Oxford University Press, 2011.

Wink, Walter. *When the Powers Fall: Reconciliation in the Healing of Nations.* Minneapolis: Fortress, 1998.

Wohlgemut, Joel R. "Entrusted Money (Matt. 25:14–28)." In *Jesus and His Parables: Interpreting the Parables of Jesus Today,* edited by V. George Shillington, 103–20. Edinburgh: T. & T. Clark, 1997.

Wright, N. T. *Jesus and the Victory of God.* Christian Origins and the Question of God 2. Minneapolis: Fortress, 1996.

———. *The New Testament and the People of God.* Christian Origins and the Question of God 1. Minneapolis: Fortress, 1992.

———. *Simply Jesus: A New Vision of Who He Was, What He Did, and Why He Matters.* New York: HarperOne, 2011.

Wright, Stephen I. *Jesus the Storyteller.* Louisville: Westminster John Knox, 2015.

Yerkovich, Sally. "Gossiping as a Way of Speaking." *Journal of Communication* 27 (1977) 192–96.

Young, Brad H. *Jesus and His Jewish Parables: Rediscovering the Roots of Jesus' Teaching.* Theological Inquiries: Studies in Contemporary Biblical and Theological Perspectives. New York: Paulist, 1989.

———. *The Parables: Jewish Tradition and Christian Interpretation.* Peabody, MA: Hendrickson, 1998.

Zimmermann, Ruben. "Berührende Liebe (Der Marnherzige Samariter) Lk 10,30–35." In *Kompendium der Gleichnisse Jesu,* edited by Ruben Zimmermann et al., 538–55. Munich: Gütersloher, 2007.

———. "Die Gleichnisse Jesu: Eine Leseanleitung Zum Kompendium." In *Kompendium der Gleichnisse Jesu,* edited by Ruben Zimmermann et al., 3–45. Munich: Gütersloher, 2007.

———. *Puzzling the Parables of Jesus: Methods and Interpretation.* Minneapolis: Fortress, 2015.

Zimmermann, Ruben et al., eds. *Kompendium der Gleichnisse Jesu.* Munich: Gütersloher, 2007.

Zohary, Michael. *Plants of the Bible.* Cambridge: Cambridge University Press, 1982.

www.ingramcontent.com/pod-product-compliance
Lightning Source LLC
Chambersburg PA
CBHW030811100426
42814CB00002B/76